CHILTON BOOK COMPANY

REPAIR & TUNE-UP GUIDE

AMERICAN MOTORS 1975-86

All U.S. and Canadian models of AMX • Concord • Eagle •
Gremlin • Hornet • Kammback • Matador • Pacer • Spirit • SX-4

President GARY R. INGERSOLL
Senior Vice President, Book Publishing and Research RONALD A. HOXTER
Publisher KERRY A. FREEMAN, S.A.E.
Editor-in-Chief DEAN F. MORGANTINI, S.A.E.
Senior Editor RICHARD J. RIVELE, S.A.E.

CHILTON BOOK COMPANY
Radnor, Pennsylvania
19089

SAFETY NOTICE

Proper service and repair procedures are vital to the safe, reliable operation of all motor vehicles, as well as the personal safety of those performing repairs. This book outlines procedures for servicing and repairing vehicles using safe, effective methods. The procedures contain many NOTES, CAUTIONS and WARNINGS which should be followed along with standard safety procedures to eliminate the possibility of personal injury or improper service which could damage the vehicle or compromise its safety.

It is important to note that repair procedures and techniques, tools and parts for servicing motor vehicles, as well as the skill and experience of the individual performing the work vary widely. It is not possible to anticipate all of the conceivable ways or conditions under which vehicles may be serviced, or to provide cautions as to all of the possible hazards that may result. Standard and accepted safety precautions and equipment should be used during cutting, grinding, chiseling, prying, or any other process that can cause material removal or projectiles.

Some precedures require the use of tools specially designed for a specific purpose. Before substituting another tool or procedure, you must be completely satisfied that neither your personal safety, nor the performance of the vehicle will be endangered.

Although the information in this guide is based on industry sources and is as complete as possible at the time of publication, the possibility exists that the manufacturer made later changes which could not be included here. While striving for total accuracy, Chilton Book Company cannot assume responsibility for any errors, changes, or omissions that may occur in the compilation of this data.

PART NUMBERS

Part numbers listed in this reference are not recommendations by Chilton for any product by brand name. They are references that can be used with interchange manuals and aftermarket supplier catalogs to locate each brand supplier's discrete part number.

SPECIAL TOOLS

Special tools are recommended by the vehicle manufacturer to perform their specific job. Use has been kept to a minimum, but where absolutely necessary, they are referred to in the text by the part number of the tool manufacturer. These tools can be purchased under the appropriate part number, from the tool manufacturer or an equivalent tool can be purchased locally from a tool supplier or parts outlet. Before substituting any tool for the one recommended, read the SAFETY NOTICE at the top of this page.

ACKNOWLEDGMENTS

The Chilton Book Company expresses its appreciation to the American Motors Corporation, Detroit, Michigan, for their generous assistance in the preparation of this book.

Copyright © 1987 by Chilton Book Company
All Rights Reserved
Published in Radnor, Pennsylvania 19089 by Chilton Book Company

Manufactured in the United States of America
7890   654321

Chilton's Repair & Tune-Up Guide: American Motors 1975–86
ISBN 0-8019-7746-0 pbk
Library of Congress Catalog Card No. 86-47768

CONTENTS

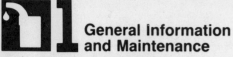

Quick Reference Specifications For Your Vehicle

Fill in this chart with the most commonly used specifications for your vehicle. Specifications can be found in Chapters 1 through 3 or on the tune-up decal under the hood of the vehicle.

Tune-Up

Firing Order _____

Spark Plugs:

    Type _____

    Gap (in.) _____

Torque (ft. lbs.) _____

Idle Speed (rpm) _____

Ignition Timing (°) _____

    Vacuum or Electronic Advance (Connected/Disconnected) _____

Valve Clearance (in.)

    Intake _____   **Exhaust** _____

Capacities

Engine Oil Type (API Rating) _____

    With Filter Change (qts) _____

    Without Filter Change (qts) _____

Cooling System (qts) _____

Manual Transmission (pts) _____

    Type _____

Automatic Transmission (pts) _____

    Type _____

Front Differential (pts) _____

    Type _____

Rear Differential (pts) _____

    Type _____

Transfer Case (pts) _____

    Type _____

FREQUENTLY REPLACED PARTS

Use these spaces to record the part numbers of frequently replaced parts.

PCV VALVE	OIL FILTER	AIR FILTER	FUEL FILTER
Type_____	Type_____	Type_____	Type_____
Part No._____	Part No._____	Part No._____	Part No._____

General Information and Maintenance

HOW TO USE THIS BOOK

Chilton's Repair & Tune-Up Guide for American Motors Cars is intended to help you learn more about the inner workings of your vehicle and save you money on its upkeep and operation.

The first two chapters will be the most used, since they contain maintenance and tune-up information and procedures. Studies have shown that a properly tuned and maintained car can get at least 10% better gas mileage (which translates into lower operating costs) and periodic maintenance will catch minor problems before they turn into major repair bills. The other chapters deal with the more complex systems of your car. Operating systems from engine through brakes are covered to the extent that the average do-it-yourselfer becomes mechanically involved. This book will not explain such things as rebuilding the differential for the simple reason that the expertise required and the investment in special tools make this task impractical and uneconomical. It will give you the detailed instructions to help you change your own brake pads and shoes, tune-up the engine, replace spark plugs and filters, and do many more jobs that will save you money, give you personal satisfaction and help you avoid expensive problems.

A secondary purpose of this book is a reference guide for owners who want to understand their car and/or their mechanics better. In this case, no tools at all are required. Knowing just what a particular repair job requires in parts and labor time will allow you to evaluate whether or not you're getting a fair price quote and help decipher itemized bills from a repair shop.

Before attempting any repairs or service on your car, read through the entire procedure outlined in the appropriate chapter. This will give you the overall view of what tools and supplies will be required. There is nothing more frustrating than having to walk to the bus stop on Monday morning because you were short one gasket on Sunday afternoon. So read ahead and plan ahead. Each operation should be approached logically and all procedures thoroughly understood before attempting any work. Some special tools that may be required can often be rented from local automotive jobbers or places specializing in renting tools and equipment. Check the yellow pages of your phone book.

All chapters contain adjustments, maintenance, removal and installation procedures, and overhaul procedures. When overhaul is not considered practical, we tell you how to remove the failed part and then how to install the new or rebuilt replacement. In this way, you at least save the labor costs. Backyard overhaul of some components (such as the alternator or water pump) is just not practical, but the removal and installation procedure is often simple and well within the capabilities of the average car owner.

Two basic mechanic's rules should be mentioned here. First, whenever the LEFT side of the car or engine is referred to, it is meant to specify the DRIVER'S side of the car. Conversely, the RIGHT side of the car means the PASSENGER'S side. Second, all screws and bolts are removed by turning counterclockwise, and tightened by turning clockwise.

Safety is always the most important rule. Constantly be aware of the dangers involved in working on or around an automobile and take proper precautions to avoid the risk of personal injury or damage to the vehicle. See the section in this chapter, Servicing Your Vehicle Safely, and the SAFETY NOTICE on the acknowledgment page before attempting any service procedures and pay attention to the instructions provided. There are 3 common mistakes in mechanical work:

1. Incorrect order of assembly, disassembly or adjustment. When taking something apart or putting it together, doing things in the wrong order usually just costs you extra time; however it CAN break something. Read the entire procedure before beginning disassembly. Do everything in the order in which the instructions say you should do it, even if you can't immediately see a reason for it. When you're taking apart something that is very intricate (for example a carburetor), you might want to draw a picture of how it looks when assembled at one point in order to make sure you get everything back in its proper position. We will supply exploded views whenever possible, but sometimes the job requires more attention to detail than an illustration provides. When making adjustments (especially tune-up adjustments), do them in order. One adjustment often affects another and you cannot expect satisfactory results unless each adjustment is made only when it cannot be changed by any other.

2. Overtorquing (or undertorquing) nuts and bolts. While it is more common for overtorquing to cause damage, undertorquing can cause a fastener to vibrate loose and cause serious damage, especially when dealing with aluminum parts. Pay attention to torque specifications and utilize a torque wrench in assembly. If a torque figure is not available remember that, if you are using the right tool to do the job, you will probably not have to strain yourself to get a fastener tight enough. The pitch of most threads is so slight that the tension you put on the wrench will be multiplied many times in actual force on what you are tightening. A good example of how critical torque is can be seen in the case of spark plug installation, especially where you are putting the plug into an aluminum cylinder head. Too little torque can fail to crush the gasket, causing leakage of combustion gases and consequent overheating of the plug and engine parts. Too much torque can damage the threads or distort the plug, which changes the spark gap at the electrode. Since more and more manufacturers are using aluminum in their engine and chassis parts to save weight, a torque wrench should be in any serious do-it-yourselfer's tool box.

There are many commercial chemical products available for ensuring that fasteners won't come loose, even if they are not torqued just right (a very common brand is Loctite℗). If you're worried about getting something together tight enough to hold, but loose enough to avoid mechanical damage during assembly, one of these products might offer substantial insurance. Read the label on the package and make sure the product is compatible with the materials, fluids, etc. involved before choosing one.

3. Crossthreading. This occurs when a part such as a bolt is screwed into a nut or casting at the wrong angle and forced, causing the threads to become damaged. Crossthreading is more likely to occur if access is difficult. It helps to clean and lubricate fasteners, and to start threading with the part to be installed going straight in, using your fingers. If you encounter resistance, unscrew the part and start over again at a different angle until it can be inserted and turned several times without much effort. Keep in mind that many parts, especially spark plugs, use tapered threads so that gentle turning will automatically bring the part you're threading to the proper angle if you don't force it or resist a change in angle. Don't put a wrench on the part until it's been turned in a couple of times by hand. If you suddenly encounter resistance and the part has not seated fully, don't force it. Pull it back out and make sure it's clean and threading properly.

Always take your time and be patient; once you have some experience, working on your car will become an enjoyable hobby.

TOOLS AND EQUIPMENT

Naturally, without the proper tools and equipment it is impossible to properly service your vehicle. It would be impossible to catalog each tool that you would need to perform each or every operation in this book. It would also be unwise for the amateur to rush out and buy an expensive set of tools an the theory that he may need one or more of them at sometime.

The best approach is to proceed slowly, gathering together a good quality set of those tools that are used most frequently. Don't be misled by the low cost of bargain tools. It is far better to spend a little more for better quality. Forged wrenches, 10 or 12 point sockets and fine tooth ratchets are by far preferable to their less expensive counterparts. As any good mechanic can tell you, there are few worse experiences than trying to work on a car with bad tools. Your monetary savings will be far outweighed by frustration and mangled knuckles.

Certain tools, plus a basic ability to handle tools, are required to get started. A basic mechanics tool set, a torque wrench, and, for 1976 and later models, a Torx bits set. Torx bits are hexlobular drivers which fit both inside and outside on special Torx head fasteners used in various places on these cars.

A special wheel bearing nut socket would be

helpful when removing the front wheel bearings on 4x4 models.

Begin accumulating those tools that are used most frequently; those associated with routine maintenance and tune-up.

In addition to the normal assortment of screwdrivers and pliers you should have the following tools for routine maintenance jobs (your car, depending on the model year, uses both SAE and metric fasteners):

1. SAE/Metric wrenches, sockets and combination open end/box end wrenches in sizes from ⅛" (3mm) to ¾" (19mm), and a spark plug socket ($^{13}/_{16}$" or ⅝"). If possible, buy various length socket drive extensions. One break in this department is that the metric sockets available in the U.S. will all fit the ratchet handles and extensions you may already have (¼, ⅜, and ½" drive).

2. Jackstands for support
3. Oil filter wrench
4. Oil filter spout for pouring oil
5. Grease gun for chassis lubrication
6. Hydrometer for checking the battery
7. A container for draining oil
8. Many rags for wiping up the inevitable mess.

In addition to the above items there are several others that are not absolutely necessary, but handy to have around. These include oil-dry, a transmission funnel and the usual supply of lubricants, antifreeze and fluids, although these can be purchased as needed. This is a basic list for routine maintenance, but only your personal needs and desires can accurately determine your list of necessary tools.

The second list of tools is for tune-ups. While the tools involved here are slightly more sophisticated, they need not be outrageously expensive. There are several inexpensive tach/dwell meters on the market that are every bit as good for the average mechanic as a $100.00 professional model. Just be sure that it goes to at least 1,200–1,500 rpm on the tach scale and that it works on 4, 6 and 8 cylinder engines. A basic list of tune-up equipment could include:

1. Tach-dwell meter
2. Spark plug wrench
3. Timing light (a DC light that works from the car's battery is best, although an AC light that plugs into 110V house current will suffice at some sacrifice in brightness)
4. Wire spark plug gauge/adjusting tools
5. Set of feeler blades.

Here again, be guided by your own needs. A feeler blade will set the point gap as easily as dwell meter will read dwell, but slightly less accurately. And since you will need a tachometer anyway ... well, make your own decision.

In addition to these basic tools, there are several other tools and gauges you may find useful. These include:

1. A compression gauge. The screw-in type is slower to use, but eliminates the possibility of a faulty reading due to escaping pressure
2. A manifold vacuum gauge
3. A test light
4. An induction meter. This is used for determining whether or not there is current in a wire. These are handy for use if a wire is broken somewhere in a wiring harness.

As a final note, you will probably find a torque wrench necessary for all but the most basic work. The beam type models are perfectly adequate, although the newer click (breakaway) type are more precise, and you don't have to crane your neck to see a torque reading in awkward situations. The breakaway torque wrenches are more expensive and should be recalibrated periodically.

Torque specification for each fastener will be given in the procedure in any case that a specific torque value is required. If no torque specifications are given, use the following values as a guide, based upon fastener size:

Bolts marked 6T
> 6mm bolt/nut — 5–7 ft.lb.
> 8mm bolt/nut — 12–17 ft.lb.
> 10mm bolt/nut — 23–34 ft.lb.
> 12mm bolt/nut — 41–59 ft.lb.
> 14mm bolt/nut — 56–76 ft.lb.

Bolts marked 8T
> 6mm bolt/nut — 6–9 ft.lb.
> 8mm bolt/nut — 13–20 ft.lb.
> 10mm bolt/nut — 27–40 ft.lb.
> 12mm bolt/nut — 46–69 ft.lb.
> 14mm bolt/nut — 75–101 ft.lb.

Special Tools

Normally, the use of special factory tools is avoided for repair procedures, since these are not readily available for the do-it-yourself mechanic. When it is possible to perform the job with more commonly available tools, it will be pointed out, but occasionally, a special tool was designed to perform a specific function and should be used. Before substituting another tool, you should be convinced that neither your safety nor the performance of the vehicle will be compromised.

Some special tools are available through your car dealer or major tool manufacturers, such as:

Service Tool Division
Kent-Moore
29784 Little Mack
Roseville, MI 48066-2298

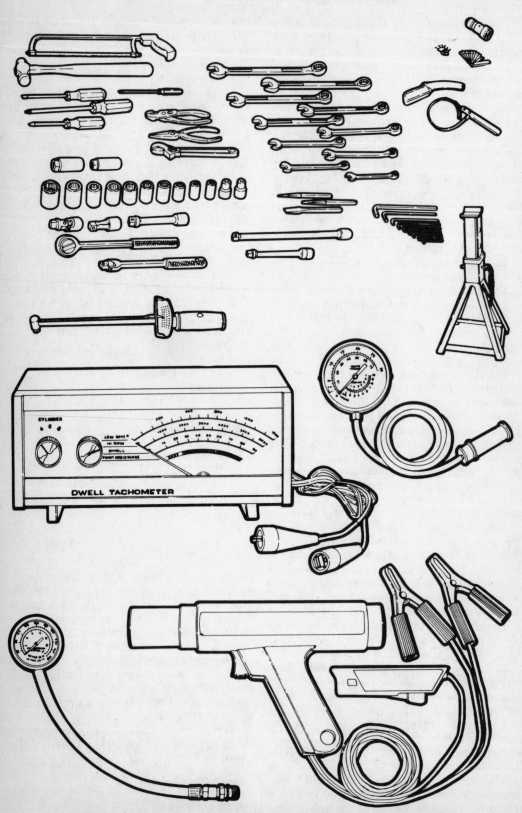

This basic collection of hand tools will handle most of your automotive needs

Miller Special Tools
Utica Tool Co.
32615 Park La.
Garden City, MI 48135

Owatonna Tool Co
Owatonna, MN 55060

Robert Bosch Corp.
2800 S.25th St.
Broadview, IL 60153

Equivalent tools may be purchased at most independent tool dealers or auto parts stores.

SERVICING YOUR VEHICLE SAFELY

It is virtually impossible to anticipate all of the hazards involved with automotive maintenance and service, but care and common sense will prevent most accidents.

The rules of safety for mechanics range from "don't smoke around gasoline," to "use the proper tool for the job." The trick to avoiding injuries is to develop safe work habits and take every possible precaution.

Dos

• Do keep a fire extinguisher and first aid kit within easy reach.

• Do wear safety glasses or goggles when cutting, drilling or prying, even if you have 20–20 vision. If you wear glasses for the sake of vision, they should be made of hardened glass that can also serve as safety glasses, or wear safety goggles over your regular glasses.

• Do shield your eyes whenever you work around the battery. Batteries contain sulphuric acid. In case of contact with the eyes or skin, flush the area with water or a mixture of water and baking soda and get medical attention immediately.

• Do use safety stands for any under-car service. Jacks are for raising vehicles; safety stands are for making sure the vehicle stays raised until you want it to come down. Whenever the vehicle is raised, block the wheels remaining on the ground and set the parking brake.

• Do use adequate ventilation when working with any chemicals. Like carbon monoxide, the asbestos dust resulting from brake lining wear can be poisonous in sufficient quantities.

• Do disconnect the negative battery cable when working on the electrical system. The primary ignition system can contain up to 40,000 volts.

• Do follow manufacturer's directions whenever working with potentially hazardous materials. Both brake fluid and antifreeze are poisonous if taken internally.

• Do properly maintain your tools. Loose hammerheads, mushroomed punches and chisels, frayed or poorly grounded electrical cords, excessively worn screwdrivers, spread wrenches (open end), cracked sockets, slipping ratchets, or faulty droplight sockets can cause accidents.

• Do use the proper size and type of tool for the job being done.

• Do when possible, pull on a wrench handle rather than push on it, and adjust your stance to prevent a fall.

• Do be sure that adjustable wrenches are tightly adjusted on the nut or bolt and pulled so that the face is on the side of the fixed jaw.

• Do select a wrench or socket that fits the

TWO-WIRE CONDUCTOR THIRD WIRE GROUNDING THE CASE

THREE-WIRE CONDUCTOR GROUNDING THRU A CIRCUIT

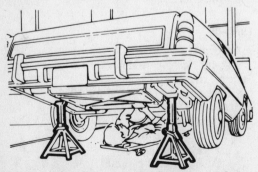
Always use jackstands when working under the car

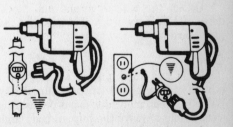
THREE-WIRE CONDUCTOR ONE WIRE TO A GROUND

THREE-WIRE CONDUCTOR GROUNDING THRU AN ADAPTER PLUG

When using electric tools make sure they are properly grounded

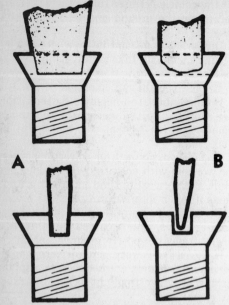

Keep screwdriver tips in good shape. They should fit the slot as shown in "A". If they look like those in "B", they need grinding or replacing

If you're using an open end wrench, use the correct size, and position it properly on the nut or bolt

nut or bolt. The wrench or socket should sit straight, not cocked.

• Do strike squarely with a hammer — avoid glancing blows.

• Do set the parking brake and block the drive wheels if the work requires that the engine be running.

Don'ts

• Don't run an engine in a garage or anywhere else without proper ventilation — EVER! Carbon monoxide is poisonous. It takes a long time to leave the human body and you can build up a deadly supply of it in your system by simply breathing in a little every day. You may not realize you are slowly poisoning yourself. Always use power vents, windows, fans or open the garage doors.

• Don't work around moving parts while wearing a necktie or other loose clothing. Short sleeves are much safer than long, loose sleeves and hard-toed shoes with neoprene soles protect your toes and give a better grip on slippery surfaces. Jewelry such as watches, fancy belt buckles, beads or body adornment of any kind is not safe working around a car. Long hair should be hidden under a hat or cap.

• Don't use pockets for toolboxes. A fall or bump can drive a screwdriver deep into you body. Even a wiping cloth hanging from the back pocket can wrap around a spinning shaft or fan.

• Don't smoke when working around gasoline, cleaning solvent or other flammable material.

• Don't smoke when working around the battery. When the battery is being charged, it gives off explosive hydrogen gas.

• Don't use gasoline to wash your hands! There are excellent soaps available. Gasoline may contain lead, and lead can enter the body through a cut, accumulating in the body until you are very ill. Gasoline also removes all the natural oils from the skin so that bone dry hands will suck up oil and grease.

• Don't service the air conditioning system unless you are equipped with the necessary tools and training. The refrigerant, R-12, is extremely cold and when exposed to the air, will instantly freeze any surface it comes in contact with, including your eyes. Although the refrigerant is normally non-toxic, R-12 becomes a deadly poisonous gas in the presence of an open flame. One good whiff of the vapors from burning refrigerant can be fatal.

SERIAL NUMBER IDENTIFICATION

Vehicle

The 13-digit vehicle identification number (VIN) is attached to the left topside of the instrument panel, so that it is visible through the windshield.

1975–80

First digit:
   A, for American Motors
Second digit:
   Last number of year, 5 for 1975
Third digit:
   Transmission type
     S: 3-Speed column
     F: 3-Speed floor
     A: Automatic-column
     C: Automatic-floor
     M: 4-Speed floor

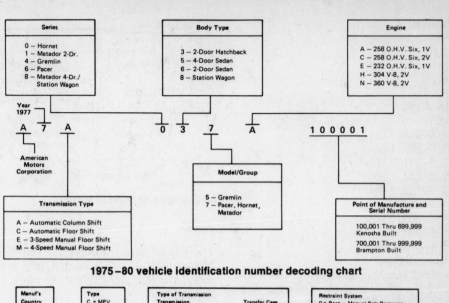

1975–80 vehicle identification number decoding chart

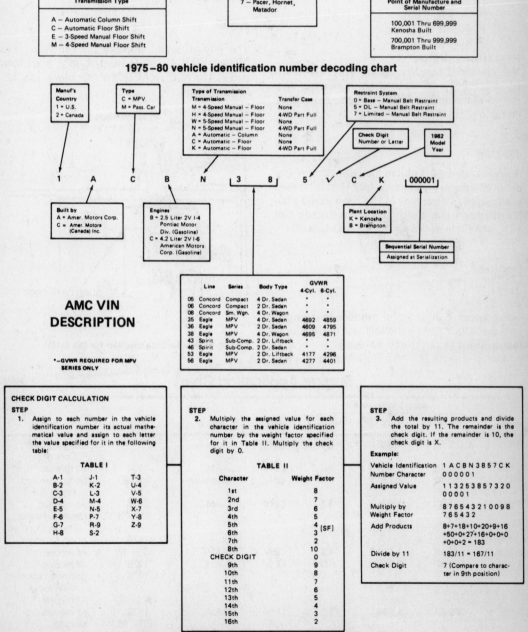

AMC VIN DESCRIPTION

*–GVWR REQUIRED FOR MPV SERIES ONLY

1981–86 vehicle identification number decoding chart

Fourth digit:
Series
Fifth digit:
Body type
Sixth digit:
Trim class
Seventh digit:
Engine:
A, 6–258, 1 bbl.
B, 6–232, 1 bbl.
C, 6–232, 2 bbl.
E, 6–232, 1 bbl.
G, 6–232, 2 bbl.
H, 8–304, 2 bbl.
N, 8–360, 2 bbl.
P, 8–360, 4 bbl.
Z, 8–401, 4 bbl.
Remaining digits:
Vehicle serial number. Numbering was started at 100,001 each year at the Kenosha, Wisconsin plant and at 700,001 at the Brampton, Ontario plant.

1981–86

A seventeen digit Vehicle Identification Number is embossed on a metal plate that is riveted to the upper left corner of the dash panel visible through the windshield. To decode the VIN, see the accompanying illustration

Engine

4–121

The 2-letter, 6-digit serial number is stamped on a machined pad on the left side of the block, just in front of the clutch housing.

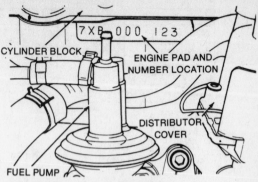

4-121 engine ID number location

4–150

The engine serial number for the American Motors built 4–150 is located on a machined pad at the rear right side of the block, just below the head.

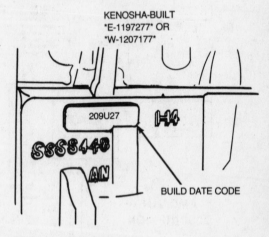

Engine serial number location for the 4-150

Engine Application Chart

| Engine | Actual Displacement | | | Type | Mfg. by | Years | Models |
	Cu. In.	CC	Liters				
4-121	120.96	1,982.2	2.0	OHC	Porsche	1977–79	Gremlin, Spirit, Concord
4-150	150.45	2,465.4	2.5	OHV	AMC	1984	All models
4-151	150.78	2,470.8	2.5	OHV	Chevrolet	1980–83	Spirit, Concord, Eagle, SX-4
6-232	231.91	3,800.3	3.8	OHV	AMC	1975	All models
						1976–78	Gremlin, Hornet, Pacer, Concord
						1979	Spirit, Concord
6-258	258.08	4,229.2	4.2	OHV	AMC	1975–87	All models
8-304	303.92	4,980.3	5.0	OHV	AMC	1975	All models
						1976	Gremlin, Hornet, Matador
						1977–79	All models
8-360	359.80	5,896.1	5.9	OHV	AMC	1975	All models
						1976–78	Matador
8-401	401.11	6,572.9	6.6	OHV	AMC	1975–76	Matador

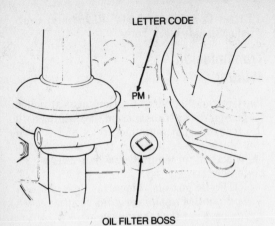

OIL FILTER BOSS

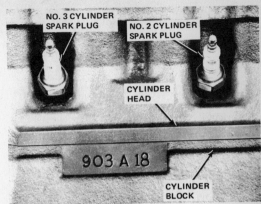

6 cylinder engine build date code location

4-150 oversized/undersized component code location

Also on the block, just above the oil filter, is the oversized/undersized component code. The codes are explained as follows:

B: cylinder bores 0.010″ (0.254mm) over

C: camshaft bearing bores 0.010″ (0.254mm)over

M: main bearing journals 0.010″ (0.254mm)under

P: connecting rod journals 0.010″ (0.254mm) under

4-151

A three character code is stamped into the left rear top corner of the block on these GM built engines. Additionally, engines built for sale in Georgia and Tennessee have a non-repeating number stamped into the left rear block flange.

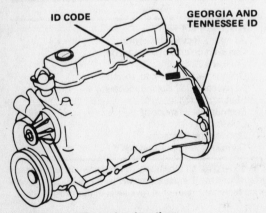

4-151 engine ID number locations

6-232 and 6-258

The American Motors engine code is, of course, found in the identification plate on the firewall. The second location is on a machined surface of the block between number 2 and 3 spark plugs. For further identification, the displacement is cast into the side of the block. The letter in the code identifies the engine by displacement (cu. in.), carburetor type and compression ratio.

On vehicles equipped with the 6-232 made prior to 1971, the engine code number is located on a machined surface, adjacent to the distributor. The letter contained in the code number denotes the cu. in. displacement of the engine. The letter, L, denotes 232 cu in. 8.5:1 compression ratio. The engine code letter is located on a boss directly above the oil filter.

On 6-232 engines built before 1971, the size code is stamped on a tag located on the left front side of the baffle above the intake manifold below the build date, and on the boss above the oil filter. The following chart explains just what the letters indicate on the 232 sixes made prior to 1971:

First Digit—Size of the bore: A, B, or C

Second Digit—Size of the main bearings: A, B, or C

Third Digit—Size of the connecting rod bearings: A, B, or C

A - Standard; B - 0.010″ (0.254mm) undersized; C - 0.010″ (0.254mm) oversized

All of the engines made after 1971 have the same undersize/oversize letter codes, located on the boss directly above the oil filter. The parts size code is as follows:

Letter B indicates 0.010″ (0.254mm) oversized cylinder bore.

Letter M indicates 0.010″ (0.254mm) undersized main bearings.

Letter P indicates 0.010″ (0.254mm) undersized connecting rod bearings.

Letter C indicates 0.010″ (0.254mm) oversized camshaft block bores.

8-304, 360, 401

On American Motors built V8 engines, the number is located on a tag attached to the

8 cylinder engine build date code location

right valve cover. For further identification, the displacement is cast into the side of the block. The letter in the code identifies the engine by displacement (cu. in.), carburetor type and compression ratio.

All of the engines made after 1971 have the same undersize/oversize letter codes, located on a tag next to the engine number. The parts size code is as follows:

Letter B indicates 0.010″ (0.254mm) oversized cylinder bore.

Letter M indicates 0.010″ (0.254mm) undersized main bearings.

Letter P indicates 0.010″ (0.254mm) undersized connecting rod bearings.

Letters PM indicate a combination of the above specifications for P and M.

Letter C indicates 0.010″ (0.254mm) oversized camshaft block bores.

Transmission

MANUAL

The transmission identification tag is attached to the rear of the transmission. It contains both the transmission manufacturer's and American Motor's part number. It is necessary to know both of these numbers when ordering replacement parts.

NOTE: *Be sure to attach the transmission identification tag it is original location when reassembling the transmission.*

AUTOMATIC

Torque-Command

A 7-digit part number is stamped on the left hand side of the transmission case, above the oil pan. A 4-digit number, indicating the date of manufacture, follows the part number.

NOTE: *If the date number is above 3500, add one for each day after 26 February 1971 to determine the date of manufacture. Hence, 3501 would be 27 February 1971, and 3809 would be 1 January 1972, etc. The final*

Front Drive Axle Application Chart

Axle Type	Years	Models
Dana 30	1970–87	All models

Manual Transmission Application Chart

Transmission Types	Years	Models
HR-1	1978–79	All models w/4-121
Tremec T-150 3-sp	1975–76	All except 6-cylinder Gremlin
	1977–78	Standard on all 6-cylinder models
	1979	Spirit w/6-232
Warner SR-4 4-sp	1977–78	Optional on all 6-cylinder models
	1979	All except 6-232 Spirit & models w/4-121
	1980–82	Standard on all models*
Warner T-4 4-sp	1982–86	Standard on all models*
Warner T-5 5-sp	1982–86	Optional on all models
	1987	Standard on all models
Warner T-14 3-sp	1975–76	Gremlin w/ 6-cylinder engine

*1982 models may come equipped with either the SR-4 or T-4, depending on availability. Make sure you know which one you have, in as much as the SR-4 uses GL-5 85W-90 gear oil and the T-4 uses Dexron® II ATF fluid. The easiest way to tell is by shift pattern: The SR-4 reverse position is to the extreme left; the T-4 reverse is to the extreme right.

Transfer Case Application Chart

Transfer Case Type	Years	Fluid Used	Models
New Process NP-119	1980–81	Dexron® II ATF	All models
New Process NP-129	1982–85	Dexron® II ATF	All models
New Process NP-128	1986–87	Dexron® II ATF	All models

Automatic Transmission Application Chart

Transmission	Years	Models
Chrysler 727	1975–76	All w/8-360, 8-401
	1977	Optional on 8-304 HD
		All 8-360
	1978	Optional on 6-258 HD and Fleet uses
		All 8-360
Chrysler 904	1975–77	All w/6-cylinder
	1978–79	All 4- and 6-cylinder engines
	1980	All except Eagle
	1981	All 4-cylinder use a wide ratio version
		6-cylinder, except Eagle, use a standard ratio
	1982	All 4-cylinder models
		6-cylinder, except Eagle, use a lock-up torque converter
	1983	All 4-cylinder models
		6-cylinder, except Eagle and Concords built for fleet sales, use a lock-up torque converter
Chyrsler 998	1975–79	All w/8-304
	1980	All Eagle
	1981–82	6-cylinder Eagle
	1983	6-cylinder Eagle
		Concord sedan and wagon built for fleet sales use a lock-up torque converter
	1984	4-cylinder models use a wide ratio version
		6-cylinder models use a lock-up torque converter
	1985–87	All models use a lock-up torque converter

Rear Axle Application Chart

Models	Years	Code	Ring Gear Dia. (in.)	Ratio	Application
AMX	1978	K(V)	7⁹⁄₁₆	2.53	w/ 4-sp and AT, exc Cal and H.A.
		H(U)	7⁹⁄₁₆	2.73	Cal 4-sp
		F(T)	7⁹⁄₁₆	3.08	Cal At and H.A. 4-sp and AT
	1979	G(S)	7⁹⁄₁₆	3.31	All w/4-121, exc Cal
		E(R)	7⁹⁄₁₆	3.58	All Cal w/4-121
		K(V)	7⁹⁄₁₆	2.53	6-258 4-sp, exc Cal 6-258 AT, exc Cal and H.A. 8-304 AT, exc Cal and H.A.
		H(U)	7⁹⁄₁₆	2.73	6-258 Cal w/4-sp 6-258 & 8-304 Cal and H.A. w/AT
		C(O)	8⁷⁄₈	2.87	8-304 w/4-sp
	1980	F(T)	7⁹⁄₁₆	3.08	All w/4-151
		K(V)	7⁹⁄₁₆	2.53	6-258 w/4-sp, exc Cal 6-258 w/AT, exc Cal and H.A.
		H(U)	7⁹⁄₁₆	2.73	Cal 6-258 w/4-sp 6-258 Cal and H.A. w/AT

Rear Axle Application Chart

Models	Years	Code	Ring Gear Dia. (in.)	Ratio	Application
Concord	1978	H(U)	7⁹⁄₁₆	2.73	All 6-232 3-sp 6-258 Wagon w/AT exc Cal. & H.A. 6-258 Calif. w/4-sp
		K(V)	7⁹⁄₁₆	2.53	All 6-232 4-sp and AT 6-258 4-sp exc Cal. & H.A. 6-258 Sedan & Hatchback w/AT
		F(T)	7⁹⁄₁₆	3.08	6-258 H.A. w/4-sp 6-258 Cal. & H.A. w/4-sp
		X(Y)	8⅞	2.56	8-304 Sdn & Wagon exc Cal and H.A.
		C(O)		2.87	8-304 Cal Sedan and Wagon 8-304 Hatchback exc Cal. & H.A.
		B(P)	8⅞		8-304 Sedan & Wagon H.A. 8-304 Hatchback Cal and H.A.
	1979	G(S)	7⁹⁄₁₆	3.31	All w/4-121, exc Cal
		E(R)	7⁹⁄₁₆	3.58	All Cal w/4-121
		K(V)	7⁹⁄₁₆	2.53	All w/6-232, exc Wagon All 6-258 w/4-sp, exc Cal All 6-258 w/AT, exc Cal and H.A. All 8-304, exc Cal and H.A.
		H(U)	7⁹⁄₁₆	2.73	Wagon w/6-232 Cal 6-258 w/4-sp Cal and H.A. 6-258 w/AT Cal and H.A. 8-304
	1980	F(T)	7⁹⁄₁₆	3.08	All w/4-151
		K(V)	7⁹⁄₁₆	2.53	6-258 w/4-sp, exc Cal 6-258 w/AT, exc Cal and H.A.
		H(U)	7⁹⁄₁₆	2.73	Cal 6-258 w/4-sp 6-258 Cal and H.A. w/AT
	1981	F(T)	7⁹⁄₁₆	3.08	All w/4-151
		J	7⁹⁄₁₆	2.37	6-258 w/4-sp, exc H.A.
		K(V)	7⁹⁄₁₆	2.53	6-258 H.A. w/4-sp 6-258 w/AT, exc H.A.
		H(U)	7⁹⁄₁₆	2.73	6-258 H.A. w/AT
	1982	F(FF)	7⁹⁄₁₆	3.08	All w/4-151
		L(LL)	7⁹⁄₁₆	2.35	6-258 w/4- or 5-sp Std on 6-258 Cal w/AT
		M(MM)	7⁹⁄₁₆	2.21	Std on 6-258, exc Cal and H.A. Opt on Cal 6-258
		J(JJ)	7⁹⁄₁₆	2.73	6-258 H.A. w/AT 6-258 Trailer Towing option
	1983	L(LL)	7⁹⁄₁₆	2.35	Std. w/4- or 5-sp, exc Cal Opt w/AT, exc Cal and H.A.
		K(V)	7⁹⁄₁₆	2.53	Std on Cal w/4- or 5-sp or AT
		M(MM)	7⁹⁄₁₆	2.21	Std w/AT, exc Cal and H.A. Opt on Cal w/AT
		J(JJ)	7⁹⁄₁₆	2.73	Std on H.A. w/AT Trailer Towing Option
Eagle	1980	F(T)	7⁹⁄₁₆	3.08	Std, exc H.A.
		A(N)	7⁹⁄₁₆	3.54	Std w/H.A.; Opt, exc H.A.

Models	Years	Code	Ring Gear Dia. (in.)	Ratio	Application
Eagle (cont.)	1981	EE(FF)	7⁹⁄₁₆	3.54	All w/4-151
		H(U)	7⁹⁄₁₆	2.73	All 6-258, exc H.A.
		F(T)	7⁹⁄₁₆	3.08	6-258 H.A. w/4-sp
		G(S)	7⁹⁄₁₆	3.31	6-258 H.A. w/AT
	1982	J(JJ)	7⁹⁄₁₆	2.73	4-151 w/4- or 5-sp, exc Cal & H.A. Std on 6-258 w/4- or 5-sp Std on 6-258 H.A. w/AT
		L(LL)	7⁹⁄₁₆	2.35	Std on 6-258 w/AT, exc H.A. Opt on 6-258 w/4- or 5-sp, exc H.A.
		G(S)	7⁹⁄₁₆	3.31	Opt on H.A. w/AT
		F(FF)	7⁹⁄₁₆	3.08	Trailer Towing option w/6-258
		E(EE)	7⁹⁄₁₆	3.54	4-151 w/AT & all Cal and H.A.
	1983	E(EE)	7⁹⁄₁₆	3.54	All w/4-151
		J(JJ)	7⁹⁄₁₆	2.73	Std on all 6-258, exc Cal w/AT
		L(LL)	7⁹⁄₁₆	2.35	Opt on 6-258 w/4- or 5-sp, exc H.A. Opt on 6-258 w/AT, exc Cal & H.A. Std on Cal 6-258 w/AT
		F(FF)	7⁹⁄₁₆	3.08	Opt on 6-258 H.A. w/AT Trailer Towing Option w/4-dr
	1984	E(EE)	7⁹⁄₁₆	3.54	All w/4-150
		J(JJ)	7⁹⁄₁₆	2.73	6-258 w/4- or 5-sp Opt on 6-258 w/AT
		L(LL)	7⁹⁄₁₆	2.35	Std on 6-258 w/AT
		F(FF)	7⁹⁄₁₆	3.08	Trailer Towing Opt on 6-258 w/AT
	1985–87	J(JJ)	7⁹⁄₁₆	2.73	All models
Gremlin	1975–76	H	7⁹⁄₁₆	2.73	Std on 6-cylinder, exc Cal
		F	7⁹⁄₁₆	3.08	Std on Cal 6-cylinder Opt on 6-cylinder, exc Cal
		K	7⁹⁄₁₆	2.53	Opt on 6-cyl w/AT, exc Cal
		B	8⁷⁄₈	3.15	Std on 8-304 w/MT Opt on 8-304 w/AT
		C	8⁷⁄₈	2.87	Opt on 8-304 w/MT Std on 8-304 w/AT
	1977	H(U)	7⁹⁄₁₆	2.73	Std, exc. 4-sp & H.A.
		F(T)	7⁹⁄₁₆	3.08	Std on H.A. Opt, exc H.A.
		K	7⁹⁄₁₆	2.53	Std w/4-sp, exc H.A. Opt w/AT, exc H.A.
	1978	G(S)	7⁹⁄₁₆	3.31	Std w/4-121, exc Cal MT
		F(T)	7⁹⁄₁₆	3.08	Std w/4-121 Cal MT Std w/Cal 6-258 AT Std w/6-258 H.A.
		H(U)	7⁹⁄₁₆	2.73	Std w/6-232 3-sp Std w/Cal 6-258 4-sp
		K(V)	7⁹⁄₁₆	2.53	Std w/6-232 4-sp and AT Std w/6-258 exc Cal & H.A.
Hornet	1975–76	H	7⁹⁄₁₆	2.73	Std on 6-cylinder, exc Cal
		F	7⁹⁄₁₆	3.08	Std on Cal 6-cylinder Opt on 6-cylinder, exc Cal

Rear Axle Application Chart (cont.)

Models	Years	Code	Ring Gear Dia. (in.)	Ratio	Application
Hornet (cont.)		K	7⁹⁄₁₆	2.53	Opt on 6-cyl w/AT, exc Cal
		B	8⁷⁄₈	3.15	Std on 8-304 w/MT Opt on 8-304 w/AT
		C	8⁷⁄₈	2.87	Opt on 8-304 w/MT Std on 8-304 w/AT
	1977	H(U)	7⁹⁄₁₆	2.73	Std on 6-cyl exc 4-sp & H.A.
		F(T)	7⁹⁄₁₆	3.08	Std on H.A. Opt on 6-cyl exc H.A.
		K(V)	7⁹⁄₁₆	2.53	Std w/4-sp, exc H.A. Opt on 6-cyl w/AT, exc H.A.
		C(O)	8⁷⁄₈	2.87	Std w/8-304
		B(P)	8⁷⁄₈	3.15	Opt w/8-304
Matador	1975–76	A	8⁷⁄₈	3.54	Std on 6-cyl Coupe w/MT Opt on 6-cyl Coupe w/AT Opt on 8-304 Coupe Opt on 8-360 Coupe Opt on 8-304 4-dr Opt on 8-360 4-dr
		B	8⁷⁄₈	3.15	Opt on 6-cyl Coupe w/MT Std on 6-cyl Coupe w/AT Opt on 8-304 Coupe Opt on 8-360 Coupe Std on 8-304 Cal 4-dr Opt on 8-304 4-dr, exc Cal Std on 8-360 Cal 4-dr Opt on 8-360 4-dr, exc Cal
		C	8⁷⁄₈	2.87	Std on 8-304 Coupe Std on 8-360 Coupe Std on 8-304 4-dr, exc Cal Std on 8-360 4-dr, exc Cal
	1977	B(P)	8⁷⁄₈	3.15	Std w/6-258 Opt w/8-304 Opt w/8-360, exc. H.A. Std w/8-360 H.A.
		A(N)	8⁷⁄₈	3.54	Opt w/6-258 Opt w/8-304 Opt w/8-360
		C(O)	8⁷⁄₈	2.87	Std w/8-304 and 8-360, exc Cal
	1978	B(P)	8⁷⁄₈	3.15	All 6-258 All Cal and H.A. V8
		C(O)	8⁷⁄₈	2.87	All V8 exc Cal and H.A.
Pacer	1975–76	H	7⁹⁄₁₆	2.73	Std, except Cal
		F	7⁹⁄₁₆	3.08	Std on Cal models Opt, exc Cal
		K	7⁹⁄₁₆	2.53	Opt, exc Cal
	1977	H(U)	7⁹⁄₁₆	2.73	Std, exc 4-sp & exc H.A.
		F(T)	7⁹⁄₁₆	3.08	Std on H.A. Opt, exc H.A.
		K(V)	7⁹⁄₁₆	2.53	Std w/4-sp, exc H.A. Opt w/AT, exc H.A.
	1978	H(U)	7⁹⁄₁₆	2.73	All 6-232 3-sp 6-258 w/AT, exc Cal and H.A. 6-258 Cal 4-sp

Models	Years	Code	Ring Gear Dia. (in.)	Ratio	Application
Pacer (cont.)		K(V)	7⁹⁄₁₆	2.53	All 6-232 4-sp and AT 6-258 4-sp, exc Cal and H.A.
		F(T)	7⁹⁄₁₆	3.08	6-258 all H.A. and Cal AT
	1979	K(V)	7⁹⁄₁₆	2.53	6-258 w/4-sp, exc Cal 6-258 w/AT, exc Cal and H.A. 8-304, exc Cal and H.A.
		H(U)	7⁹⁄₁₆	2.73	Cal 6-258 w/4-sp 6-258 Cal and H.A. w/AT 8-304 Cal and H.A.
	1980	K(V)	7⁹⁄₁₆	2.53	6-258 w/4-sp, exc Cal 6-258 w/AT, exc Cal and H.A.
		H(U)	7⁹⁄₁₆	2.73	Cal 6-258 w/4-sp 6-258 Cal and H.A. w/AT
Spirit	1979	F(T)	7⁹⁄₁₆	3.08	4-121 w/4-sp, exc H.A.
		G(S)	7⁹⁄₁₆	3.31	4-121 H.A. & all 4-121 w/AT
		H(U)	7⁹⁄₁₆	2.73	6-232 w/3-sp 6-258 Cal w/4-sp Cal and H.A. 6-258 w/AT 8-304 Cal and H.A.
		K(V)	7⁹⁄₁₆	2.53	6-232 w/4-sp or AT 6-258 w/4-sp, exc Cal 6-258 w/AT, exc Cal & H.A. 8-304, exc Cal and H.A.
	1980	F(T)	7⁹⁄₁₆	3.08	All w/4-151
		K(V)	7⁹⁄₁₆	2.53	6-258 w/4-sp, exc Cal 6-258 w/AT, exc Cal and H.A.
		H(U)	7⁹⁄₁₆	2.73	Cal 6-258 w/4-sp 6-258 Cal and H.A. w/AT
	1981	F(T)	7⁹⁄₁₆	3.08	All w/4-151
		J	7⁹⁄₁₆	2.37	6-258 w/4-sp, exc H.A.
		K(V)	7⁹⁄₁₆	2.53	6-258 H.A. w/4-sp 6-258 w/AT, exc H.A.
		H(U)	7⁹⁄₁₆	2.73	6-258 H.A. w/AT
	1982	F(FF)	7⁹⁄₁₆	3.08	All w/4-151
		L(LL)	7⁹⁄₁₆	2.35	6-258 w/4- or 5-sp Std on 6-258 Cal w/AT
		M(MM)	7⁹⁄₁₆	2.21	Std on 6-258, exc Cal and H.A. Opt on Cal 6-258
		J(JJ)	7⁹⁄₁₆	2.73	6-258 H.A. w/AT
	1983	L(LL)	7⁹⁄₁₆	2.35	Std w/4- or 5-sp, exc Cal Opt w/AT, exc Cal and H.A.
		K(V)	7⁹⁄₁₆	2.53	Std on Cal w/4- or 5-sp or AT
		M(MM)	7⁹⁄₁₆	2.21	Std w/AT, exc Cal and H.A. Opt on Cal w/AT
		J(JJ)	7⁹⁄₁₆	2.73	Std on H.A. w/AT

Letters in parenthesis indicate the code for the locking axle version, called Twin-Grip®
NOTE: a small number of 1982 axles were coded with 1981 codes, as follows:
    F as T
    E as EE and FF
    J as H and U

group of numbers is the transmission serial number.

ROUTINE MAINTENANCE

Refer to the Service Interval Chart in this Chapter for the recommended intervals for the operations in the Section.

Air Cleaner

The air cleaner has a disposable element which should be replaced at the intervals shown in the 'Service Intervals' chart. It should be checked at every oil change. To check or replace the element:

1. Remove the wing nut at the top.

2. On a 4–151 or V8, lift off the large disc under the wing nut. Remove the element.

3. On a six, detach the PCV hose at the valve cover. Don't pull the hose our of the air cleaner or you will damage it. Remove the whole top of the air cleaner and remove the element.

4. There are a couple of ways to clean the element. How well either works depends on the type of dirt trapped in the paper element. Dust and dirt can be removed by rapping the ele-

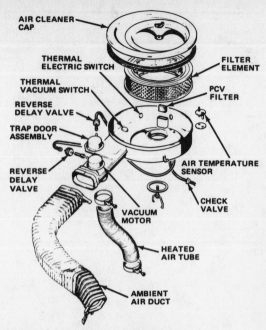

6-232, 258 air cleaner assembly

ment on a flat surface or by blowing from the inside with an air hose. If the element still appears black or clogged, replace it. A clogged filter causes a rich fuel/air mixture and low gas mileage.

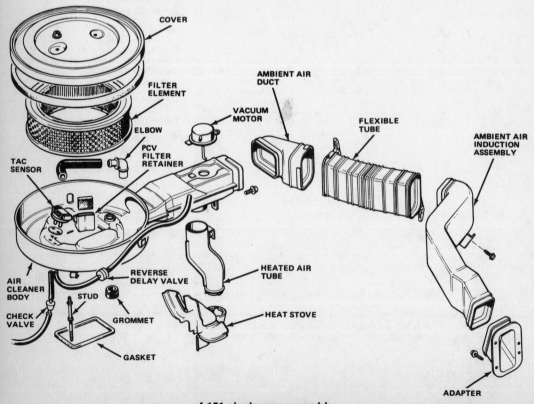

4-151 air cleaner assembly

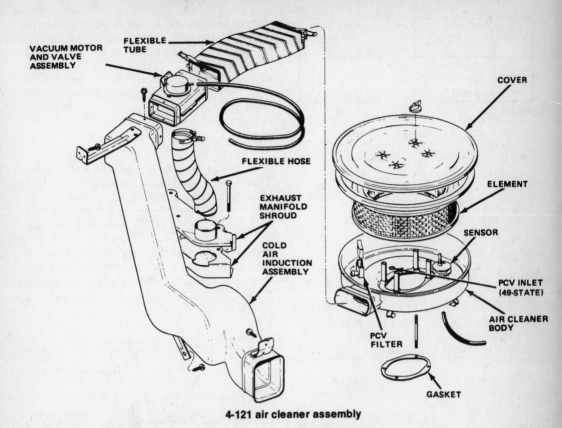

4-121 air cleaner assembly

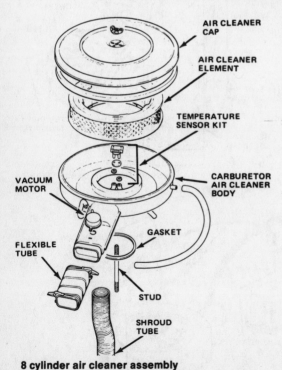

8 cylinder air cleaner assembly

5. Wipe out the housing and install the new or rejuvenated element.

6. Reinstall the top of the unit and the wing nut.

Fuel Filter
REPLACEMENT

4–121, 4–150, 6–232, 6–258, 8–304, 360 and 401

All these engines have a throwaway cartridge filter in the line between the fuel pump and the carburetor. To replace it:

1. Remove the air cleaner as necessary.

2. Put an absorbent rag under the filter to catch spillage.

3. Remove the hose clamps.

4. Remove the filter and short attaching hoses.

5. Remove the hoses if they are to be reused.

6. Assemble the new filter and hoses.

NOTE: *The original equipment wire hose*

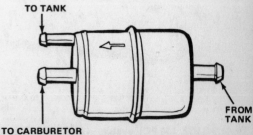

Correct fuel filter installation, except 4-151

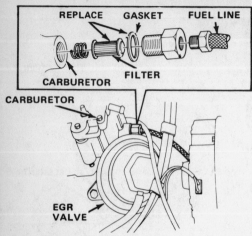

4-151 fuel filter installation

clamps should be replaced with screw type band clamps for the best results.

7. 1975 V8 and all 1976 and later filters have two outlets. The extra one is to return fuel vapors and bubbles to the tank so as to prevent vapor lock. The tank line outlet must be up.

8. Install the filter, tighten the clamps, start the engine, and check for leaks. Discard the rag and old filter safely.

4–151

The filter is located behind the large inlet nut in the carburetor. It is a small, paper, throw-away type.

CAUTION: *DO NOT perform a filter change on a hot engine!*

1. Place an absorbent rag under the carburetor inlet nut.

2. Hold the inlet nut with one wrench, while loosening the fuel line fitting with another. Remove the fuel line.

3. Unscrew the inlet nut and remove the nut, washer, spring and filter.

4. Installation is the reverse of removal. It's always best to use a new washer. Coat the threads of the inlet nut with a non-hardening, fuel-proof gasket cement. DO NOT OVERTIGHTEN THE INLET NUT! The threads are easily stripped in the carburetor. Hold the inlet nut with a wrench while tightening the fuel line fitting.

PCV System

PCV means Positive Crankcase Ventilation. This is a simple emission control system which routes crankcase fumes into the intake manifold or carburetor to be burned. A clogged PCV system will cause poor idle and rough running. There are two points of maintenance in this system: A valve and a filter. Maintenance intervals are shown in the 'Service Intervals' chart, but remember that this system can clog pretty quickly on an older engine that is using a little oil.

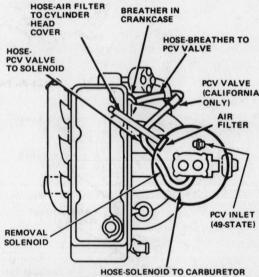

4-121 PCV system

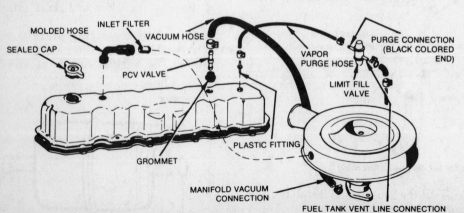

Typical 6-232, 258 PCV system; 1980–82 models don't have the purge hose. The 4-151 system is similar

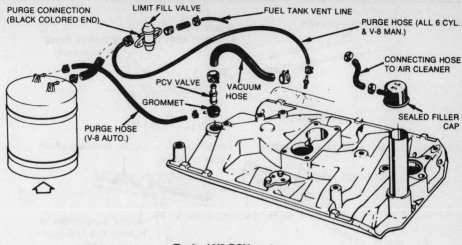

Typical V8 PCV system

On a six, the PCV valve is at the cover end of a hose leading from just below the carburetor to the valve cover. On a 4–151 or V8, it is at the intake manifold end of a hose leading from the carburetor to the intake manifold. To replace the PCV valve:

1. Pull the valve from its grommet in the intake manifold (V8) or valve cover (six).

2. Loosen the hose clamp and pull the valve from the hose. The valve can be washed in kerosene, but the best plan is to replace it. If the valve seems really sludged up, check the hose, too.

3. Push the new or cleaned valve into its hose. Push the valve into its grommet. The condition of this grommet is important. If it leaks air, the engine will idle too fast because of a lean fuel/air mixture.

To clean the system filter:

1. On a six, remove the top of the air cleaner as explained previously under 'Air Cleaner.' Turn the top upside down and pull the filter out of the hose, inside the top. Don't pull the hose off first, or you'll damage it. Wash the filter in kerosene and replace it when dry. Replace the top of the air cleaner.

2. On a 4–151 or V8, remove the oil filter cap and wash it with kerosene. The cap contains the filter element. Replace it when dry.

Fuel Vapor Canister

The canister stores carburetor and fuel tank vapors while the engine is off, holding them to be drawn into the engine and burned when it starts. This system is on some models beginning 1971, and all models beginning 1973. Look for a black container about the size and shape of a coffee tin can with some hoses attached in the engine compartment. The air filter in this canister should be changed at the in-

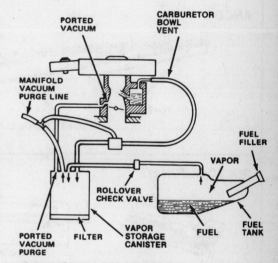

Typical fuel vapor control system

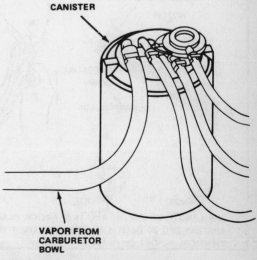

Fuel vapor storage canister and hoses

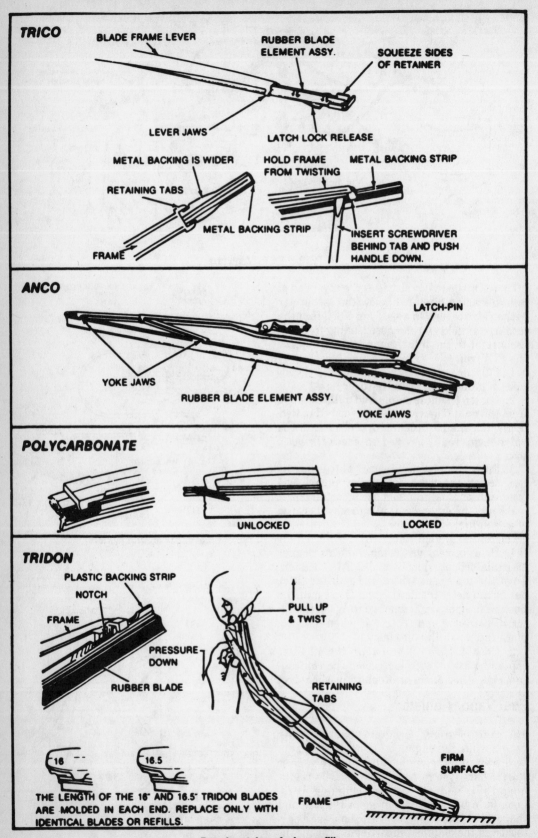

TRICO

BLADE FRAME LEVER

RUBBER BLADE ELEMENT ASSY.

SQUEEZE SIDES OF RETAINER

LEVER JAWS

LATCH LOCK RELEASE

METAL BACKING IS WIDER

HOLD FRAME FROM TWISTING

METAL BACKING STRIP

RETAINING TABS

METAL BACKING STRIP

FRAME

INSERT SCREWDRIVER BEHIND TAB AND PUSH HANDLE DOWN.

ANCO

LATCH-PIN

YOKE JAWS

RUBBER BLADE ELEMENT ASSY.

YOKE JAWS

POLYCARBONATE

UNLOCKED

LOCKED

TRIDON

PLASTIC BACKING STRIP

NOTCH

FRAME

PULL UP & TWIST

PRESSURE DOWN

RUBBER BLADE

RETAINING TABS

16

16.5

FIRM SURFACE

THE LENGTH OF THE 16" AND 16.5" TRIDON BLADES ARE MOLDED IN EACH END. REPLACE ONLY WITH IDENTICAL BLADES OR REFILLS.

FRAME

Popular styles of wiper refills

tervals shown in the 'Service Intervals' chart. To change the filter:

1. Loosen the canister clamp screw and raise the canister enough that you can work under it. Remove it as necessary.

2. Pull out the old filter from the bottom of the canister.

3. Install a new filter, making sure that it covers the whole opening.

4. Replace the canister and tighten the clamp screws.

Windshield Wipers

For maximum effectiveness and longest element life, the windshield and wiper blades should be kept clean. Dirt, tree sap, road tar and so on will cause streaking, smearing and blade deterioration if left on the windshield. It is advisable to wash the windshield carefully with a commercial glass cleaner at least once a month. Wipe off the rubber blades with a wet rag afterwards. Do not attempt to move the wipers back and forth by hand! Damage to the motor and drive mechanism will result.

If the blades are found to be cracked, broken or torn they should be replaced immediately. Replacement intervals will vary with usage, although ozone deterioration usually limits blade lift to about one year. If the wiper pattern is smeared or streaked, or if the blade chatters across the glass, the blades should be replaced. It is easiest and most sensible to replace them in pairs.

There are basically three different types of wiper blade refills, which differ in their method of replacement. One type has two release buttons, approximately ⅓ of the way up from the ends of the blade frame. Pushing the buttons down releases a lock and allows the rubber blade to be removed from the frame. The new blade slides back into the frame and locks in place.

The second type of refill has two metal tabs which are unlocked by squeezing them together. The rubber blade can then be withdrawn from the frame jaws. A new one is installed by inserting it into the front frame jaws and sliding it rearward to engage the remaining frame jaws. There are usually four jaws. Be certain when installing that the refill is engaged in all of them. At the end of its travel, the tabs will lock into place on the front jaws of the wiper blade frame.

The third type is a refill made from polycarbonate. The refill has a simple locking device at one end which flexes downward out of the groove into which the jaws of the holder fit, allowing easy release. By sliding the new refill through all the jaws and pushing through the

slight resistance when it reaches the end of its travel, the refill will lock into position.

Regardless of the type of refill used, make sure that all of the frame jaws are engaged as the refill is pushed into place and locked. The metal blade holder and frame will scratch the glass if allowed to touch it.

Belts

INSPECTION

The belts which drive the engine accessories such as the alternator or generator, the air pump, power steering pump, air conditioning compressor and water pump are of either the V-belt design or flat, serpentine design. Older belts show wear and damage readily, since their basic design was a belt with a rubber casing. As the casing wore, cracks and fibers were readily apparent. Newer design, caseless belts do not show wear as readily, and many untrained people cannot distinguish between a good, serviceable belt and one that is worn to the point of failure.

To adjust belt tension or to replace belts, first loosen the component's mounting and adjusting bolts slightly

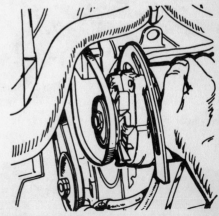

Push the component toward the engine and slip off the belt

HOW TO SPOT WORN V-BELTS

V-Belts are vital to efficient engine operation—they drive the fan, water pump and other accessories. They require little maintenance (occasional tightening) but they will not last forever. Slipping or failure of the V-belt will lead to overheating. If your V-belt looks like any of these, it should be replaced.

Cracking or weathering

This belt has deep cracks, which cause it to flex. Too much flexing leads to heat build-up and premature failure. These cracks can be caused by using the belt on a pulley that is too small. Notched belts are available for small diameter pulleys.

Softening (grease and oil)

Oil and grease on a belt can cause the belt's rubber compounds to soften and separate from the reinforcing cords that hold the belt together. The belt will first slip, then finally fail altogether.

Glazing

Glazing is caused by a belt that is slipping. A slipping belt can cause a run-down battery, erratic power steering, overheating or poor accessory performance. The more the belt slips, the more glazing will be built up on the surface of the belt. The more the belt is glazed, the more it will slip. If the glazing is light, tighten the belt.

Worn cover

The cover of this belt is worn off and is peeling away. The reinforcing cords will begin to wear and the belt will shortly break. When the belt cover wears in spots or has a rough jagged appearance, check the pulley grooves for roughness.

Separation

This belt is on the verge of breaking and leaving you stranded. The layers of the belt are separating and the reinforcing cords are exposed. It's just a matter of time before it breaks completely.

It is a good idea, therefore, to visually inspect the belts regularly and replace them, routinely, every two to three years.

ADJUSTING

Belts are normally adjusted by loosening the bolts of the accessory being driven and moving that accessory on its pivot points until the

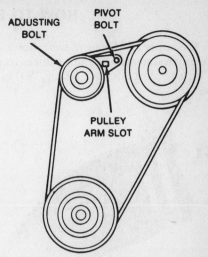

Some pulleys have a rectangular slot to aid in moving the accessories to be tightened

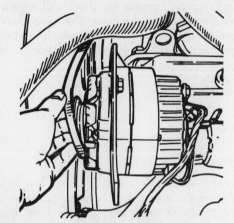

Slip the new belt over the pulley

proper tension is applied to the belt. The accessory is held in this position while the bolts are tightened. To determine proper belt tension, you can purchase a belt tension gauge or simply use the deflection method. To determine deflection, press inward on the belt at the midpoint of its longest straight run. The belt should deflect (move inward) ⅜ to ½″ (9.525–12.7mm). Some long V-belts and most serpentine belts have idler pulleys which are used for adjusting purposes. Just loosen the idler pulley and move it to take up tension on the belt.

REMOVAL AND INSTALLATION

To remove a drive belt, simply loosen the accessory being driven and move it on its pivot point to free the belt. Then, remove the belt. If an idler pulley is used, it is often necessary, only, to loosen the idler pulley to provide enough slack the remove the belt.

It is important to note, however, that on engines with many driven accessories, several or all of the belts may have to be removed to get at the one to be replaced.

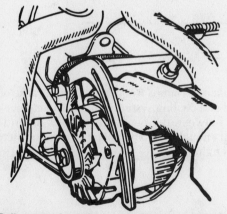

Pull outward on the component and tighten the mounting bolts

Hoses

REMOVAL AND INSTALLATION

Radiator hoses are generally of two constructions, the preformed (molded) type, which is custom made for a particular application, and the spring loaded type, which is made to fit several different applications. Heater hoses are all of the same general construction.

Hoses are retained by clamps. To replace a hose, loosen the clamp and slide it down the hose, away from the attaching point. Twist the

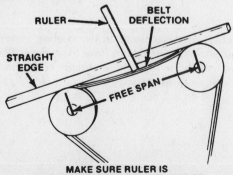

MAKE SURE RULER IS PERPENDICULAR TO STRAIGHT EDGE

Measuring belt deflection

HOW TO SPOT BAD HOSES

Both the upper and lower radiator hoses are called upon to perform difficult jobs in an inhospitable environment. They are subject to nearly 18 psi at under hood temperatures often over 280°F., and must circulate nearly 7500 gallons of coolant an hour—3 good reasons to have good hoses.

A good test for any hose is to feel it for soft or spongy spots. Frequently these will appear as swollen areas of the hose. The most likely cause is oil soaking. This hose could burst at any time, when hot or under pressure.

Swollen hose

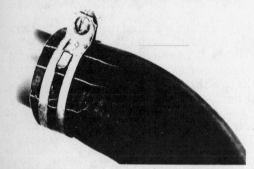

Cracked hoses can usually be seen but feel the hoses to be sure they have not hardened; a prime cause of cracking. This hose has cracked down to the reinforcing cords and could split at any of the cracks.

Cracked hose

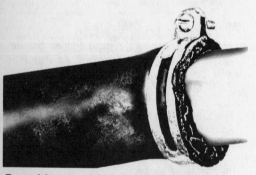

Weakened clamps frequently are the cause of hose and cooling system failure. The connection between the pipe and hose has deteriorated enough to allow coolant to escape when the engine is hot.

Frayed hose end (due to weak clamp)

Debris, rust and scale in the cooling system can cause the inside of a hose to weaken. This can usually be felt on the outside of the hose as soft or thinner areas.

Debris in cooling system

hose from side to side until it is free, then pull it off. Before installing the new hose, make sure that the outlet fitting is as clean as possible. Coat the fitting with non-hardening sealer and slip the hose into place. Install the clamp and tighten it.

Air Conditioning System

The compressor used on all models, except the 4–151 through 1980 was the 2-cylinder Tecumseh model.

The 4–151 used the GM rotary compressor.

For the 1981 model year, all vehicles built for sale in California, and equipped with the 6–258 engine, utilized a Japanese made Sankyo, 5-cylinder axial compressor. All non-California 6–258 engines utilized the Tecumseh compressor. All 4–151 engines retained the rotary GM compressor.

In 1982, the Sankyo became the compressor used on all engines except the 4–151.

All systems utilize a sight glass for system inspection.

NOTE: *This book contains simple testing and charging procedures for your car's air conditioning system. More comprehensive testing, diagnosis and service procedures may be found in CHILTON'S GUIDE TO AIR CONDITIONING SERVICE AND REPAIR, book part number 7580, available at your local retailer.*

GENERAL SERVICING PROCEDURES

The most important aspect of air conditioning service is the maintenance of pure and adequate charge of refrigerant in the system. A refrigeration system cannot function properly if a significant percentage of the charge is lost. Leaks are common because the severe vibration encountered in an automobile can easily cause a sufficient cracking or loosening of the air conditioning fittings. As a result, the extreme operating pressures of the system force refrigerant out.

The problem can be understood by considering what happens to the system as it is operated with a continuous leak. Because the expansion valve regulates the flow of refrigerant to the evaporator, the level of refrigerant there is fairly constant. The receiver/drier stores any excess of refrigerant, and so a loss will first appear there as a reduction in the level of liquid. As this level nears the bottom of the vessel, some refrigerant vapor bubbles will begin to appear in the stream of liquid supplied to the expansion valve. This vapor decreases the capacity of the expansion valve very little as the valve opens to compensate for its presence. As the quantity of liquid in the condenser decreases, the operating pressure will drop there and throughout the high side of the system. As the R-12 continues to be expelled, the pressure available to force the liquid through the expansion valve will continue to decrease, and,

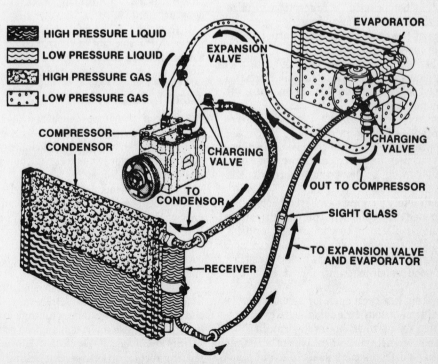

HIGH PRESSURE LIQUID
LOW PRESSURE LIQUID
HIGH PRESSURE GAS
LOW PRESSURE GAS

EVAPORATOR
EXPANSION VALVE
COMPRESSOR CONDENSOR
CHARGING VALVE
CHARGING VALVE
TO CONDENSOR
OUT TO COMPRESSOR
SIGHT GLASS
TO EXPANSION VALVE AND EVAPORATOR
RECEIVER

Basic components of an air conditioning system and the flow of refrigerant.

eventually, the valve's orifice will prove to be too much of a restriction for adequate flow even with the needle fully withdrawn.

At this point, low side pressure will start to drop, and severe reduction in cooling capacity, marked by freeze-up of the evaporator coil, will result. Eventually, the operating pressure of the evaporator will be lower than the pressure of the atmosphere surrounding it, and air will be drawn into the system wherever there are leaks in the low side.

Because all atmospheric air contains at least some moisture, water will enter the system and mix with the R-12 and the oil. Trace amounts of moisture will cause sludging of the oil, and corrosion of the system. Saturation and clogging of the filter drier, and freezing of the expansion valve orifice will eventually result. As air fills the system to a greater and greater extend, it will interfere more and more with the normal flows of refrigerant and heat.

A list of general precautions that should be observed while doing this follows:

1. Keep all tools as clean and dry as possible.

2. Thoroughly purge the service gauges and hoses of air and moisture before connecting them to the system. Keep them capped when not in use.

3. Thoroughly clean any refrigerant fitting before disconnecting it, in order to minimize the entrance of dirt into the system.

4. Plan any operation that requires opening the system beforehand in order to minimize the length of time it will be exposed to open air. Cap or seal the open ends to minimize the entrance of foreign material.

5. When adding oil, pour it through an extremely clean and dry tube or funnel. Keep the oil capped whenever possible. Do not use oil that has not been kept tightly sealed.

6. Use only refrigerant 12. Purchase refrigerant intended for use in only automotive air conditioning system. Avoid the use of refrigerant 12 that may be packaged for another use, such as cleaning, or powering a horn, as it is impure.

7. Completely evacuate any system that has been opened to replace a component, other than when isolating the compressor, or that has leaked sufficiently to draw in moisture and air. This requires evacuating air and moisture with a good vacuum pump for at least one hour.

If a system has been open for a considerable length of time it may be advisable to evacuate the system for up to 12 hours (overnight).

8. Use a wrench on both halves of a fitting that is to be disconnected, so as to avoid placing torque on any of the refrigerant lines.

ADDITIONAL PREVENTIVE MAINTENANCE CHECKS

Antifreeze

In order to prevent heater core freeze-up during A/C operation, it is necessary to maintain permanent type antifreeze protection of +15°F. or lower. A reading of –15°F. is ideal since this protection also supplies sufficient corrosion inhibitors for the protection of the engine cooling system.

NOTE: *The same antifreeze should not be used longer than the manufacturer specified.*

Radiator Cap

For efficient operation of an air conditioned car's cooling system, the radiator cap should have a holding pressure which meets manufacturer's specifications. A cap which fails to hold these pressure should be replaced.

Condenser

Any obstruction of or damage to the condenser configuration will restrict the air flow which is essential to its efficient operation. It is therefore, a good rule to keep this unit clean and in proper physical shape.

NOTE: *Bug screens are regarded as obstructions.*

Condensation Drain Tube

This single molded drain tube expels the condensation, which accumulates on the bottom of the evaporator housing, into the engine compartment.

If this tube is obstructed, the air conditioning performance can be restricted and condensation buildup can spill over onto the vehicle's floor.

SAFETY PRECAUTIONS

Because of the importance of the necessary safety precautions that must be exercised when working with air conditioning systems and R-12 refrigerant, a recap of the safety precautions are outlined.

1. Avoid contact with a charged refrigeration system, even when working on another part of the air conditioning system or vehicle. If a heavy tool comes into contact with a section of copper tubing or a heat exchanger, it can easily cause the relatively soft material to rupture.

2. When it is necessary to apply force to a fitting which contains refrigerant, as when checking that all system couplings are securely tightened, use a wrench on both parts of the fitting involved, if possible. This will **avoid** putting torque on refrigerant tubing. (It is advisable, when possible, to use tube or line

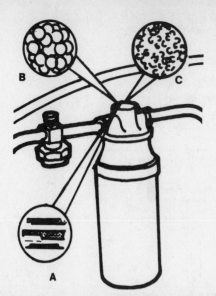

Oil streaks (A), constant bubbles (B), or foam (C) indicate there is not enough refrigerant in the system. Occasional bubbles during initial operation is normal. A clear sightglass indicates a proper charge or no charge at all. This can be determined by the presence of cold air at the outlets in the car. If the glass is clouded with a milky substance, have the receiver/drier checked professionally.

wrenches when tightening these flare nut fittings.)

3. Do not attempt to discharge the system by merely loosening a fitting, or removing the service valve caps and cracking these valves. Precise control is possibly only when using the service gauges. Place a rag under the open end of the center charging hose while discharging the system to catch any drops of liquid that might escape. Wear protective gloves when connecting or disconnecting service gauge hoses.

4. Discharge the system only in a well ventilated area, as high concentrations of the gas can exclude oxygen and act as an anesthesia. When leak testing or soldering, this is particularly important, as toxic gas is formed when R-12 contacts any flame.

5. Never start a system without first verifying that both service valves are backseated, if equipped, and that all fittings are throughout the system are snugly connected.

6. Avoid applying heat to any refrigerant line or storage vessel. Charging may be aided by using water heated to less than 125°F to warm the refrigerant container. Never allow a refrigerant storage container to sit out in the sun, or near any other source of heat, such as a radiator.

7. Always wear goggles when working on a system to protect the eyes. If refrigerant contacts the eye, it is advisable in all cases to see a physician as soon as possible.

8. Frostbite from liquid refrigerant should be treated by first gradually warming the area with cool water, and then gently applying petroleum jelly. A physician should be consulted.

9. Always keep refrigerant can fittings capped when not in use. Avoid sudden shock to the can which might occur from dropping it, or from banging a heavy tool against it. Never carry a can in the passenger compartment of a car.

10. Always completely discharge the system before painting the vehicle (if the paint is to be baked on), or before welding anywhere near the refrigerant lines.

TEST GAUGES

Most of the service work performed in air conditioning requires the use of a set of two gauges, one for the high (head) pressure side of the system, the other for the low (suction) side.

The low side gauge records both pressure and vacuum. Vacuum readings are calibrated from 0 to 30 inches and the pressure graduations read from 0 to no less than 60 psi.

The high side gauge measures pressure from 0 to at last 600 psi.

Both gauges are threaded into a manifold that contains two hand shut-off valves. Proper manipulation of these valves and the use of the attached test hoses allow the user to perform the following services:

1. Test high and low side pressures.
2. Remove air, moisture, and contaminated refrigerant.
3. Purge the system (of refrigerant).
4. Charge the system (with refrigerant).

The manifold valves are designed so that they have no direct effect on gauge readings, but serve only to provide for, or cut off, flow of refrigerant through the manifold. During all testing and hook-up operations, the valves are

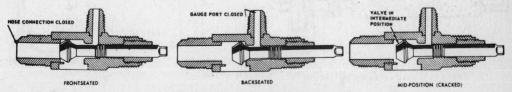

Manual service valve positions

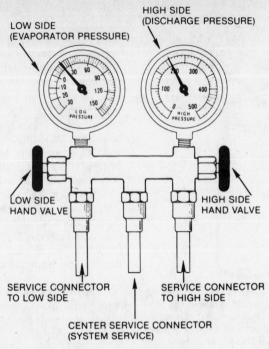

Typical manifold gauge set

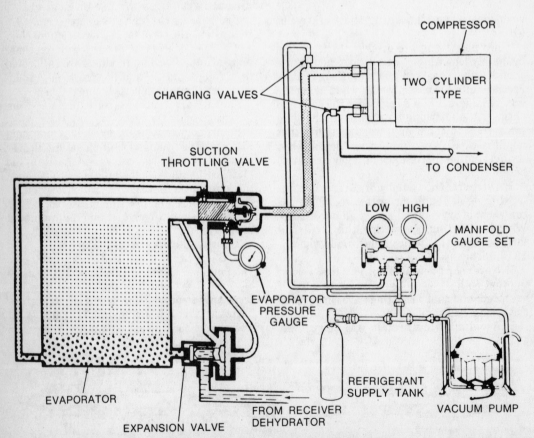

Gauge connections on the Tecumseh compressor

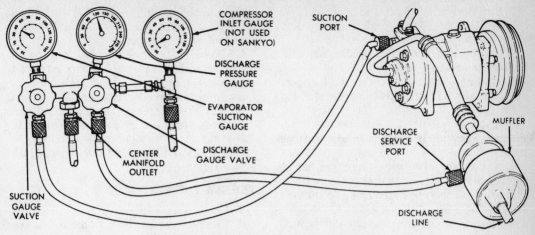

Gauge connections on the Sankyo compressor

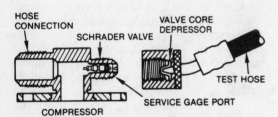

Schrader valve

kept in a close position to avoid disturbing the refrigeration system. The valves are opened only to purge the system or refrigerant or to charge it.

INSPECTION

CAUTION: *The compressed refrigerant used in the air conditioning system expands into the atmosphere at a temperature of* −21.7°F (−29.833°C) *or lower. This will freeze any surface, including your eyes, that it contacts. In addition, the refrigerant decomposes into a poisonous gas in the presence of a flame. Do not open or disconnect any part of the air conditioning system.*

Sight Glass Check

You can safely make a few simple checks to determine if your air conditioning system needs service. The tests work best if the temperature is warm (about 70°F [21.1°C]).

NOTE: *If your vehicle is equipped with an aftermarket air conditioner, the following system check may not apply. You should contact the manufacturer of the unit for instructions on systems checks.*

1. Place the automatic transmission in Park or the manual transmission in Neutral. Set the parking brake.

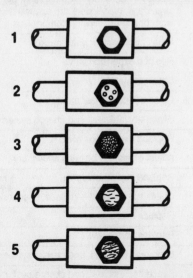

1 Clear sight glass — system correctly charged or overcharged

2 Occasional bubbles — refrigerant charge slightly low

3 Oil streaks on sight glass — total lack of refrigerant

4 Heavy stream of bubbles — serious shortage of refrigerant

5 Dark or clouded sight glass — contaminent present

Sight glass inspection

2. Run the engine at a fast idle (about 1,500 rpm) either with the help of a friend or by temporarily readjusting the idle speed screw.

3. Set the controls for maximum cold with the blower on High.

4. Locate the sight glass in one of the system lines. Usually it is on the left alongside the top of the radiator.

5. If you see bubbles, the system must be recharged. Very likely there is a leak at some point.

6. If there are no bubbles, there is either no refrigerant at all or the system is fully charged. Feel the two hoses going to the belt driven compressor. If they are both at the same temperature, the system is empty and must be recharged.

7. If one hose (high pressure) is warm and the other (low pressure) is cold, the system may be all right. However, you are probably making these tests because you think there is something wrong, so proceed to the next step.

8. Have an assistant in the car turn the fan control on and off to operate the compressor clutch. Watch the sight glass.

9. If bubbles appear when the clutch is disengaged and disappear when it is engaged, the system is properly charged.

10. If the refrigerant takes more than 45 seconds to bubble when the clutch is disengaged, the system is overcharged. This usually causes poor cooling at low speeds.

CAUTION: *If it is determined that the system has a leak, it should be corrected as soon as possible. Leaks may allow moisture to enter and cause a very expensive rust problem.*

NOTE: *Exercise the air conditioner for a few minutes, every two weeks or so, during the cold months. This avoids the possibility of the compressor seals drying out from lack of lubrication.*

TESTING THE SYSTEM

1. Connect a gauge set.
2. Close (clockwise) both gauge set valves.
3. Mid-position both service valves.
4. Park the car in the shade. Start the engine, set the parking brake, place the transmission in NEUTRAL and establish an idle of 1,500 rpm.
5. Run the air conditioning system for full cooling, but NOT in the MAX or COLD mode.
6. Insert a thermometer into the center air outlet.
7. Use the accompanying performance chart for a specifications reference. If pressures are abnormal, refer to the accompanying Pressure Diagnosis Chart.

Pressure Diagnosis

Condition	Possible Cause	Correction
Low side low—High side low	System refrigerant low	Evacuate, leak test, and charge system
Low side high—High side low	Internal leak in compressor—worn	Remove compressor cylinder head and inspect compressor. Replace valve plate assembly if necessary. If compressor pistons, rings, or cylinders are excessively worn or scored, replace compressor.
	Head gasket leaking	Install new cylinder head gasket
	Expansion valve	Replace expansion valve
	Drive belt slipping	Set belt tension
Low side high—High side high	Clogged condenser fins	Clean out condenser fins
	Air in system	Evacuate, leak test, and charge system
	Expansion valve	Replace expansion valve
	Loose or worn fan belts	Adjust or replace belts as necessary
Low side low—High side high	Expansion valve	Replace expansion valve
	Restriction in liquid line	Check line for kinks—replace if necessary
	Restriction in receiver	Replace receiver
	Restriction in condenser	Replace condenser
Low side and high side normal (inadequate cooling)	Air in system	Evacuate, leak test, and charge system
	Moisture in system	Evacuate, leak test, and charge system.

Normal Operating Temperature and Pressures*

Relative Humidity (percent)	Surrounding Air Temperature (°F)	Maximum Desirable Center Register Discharge Air Temp. (°F)	Suction Pressure PSI (REF)	Head Pressure PSI (+25 PSI)
20	70	40	11	177
	80	41	15	208
	90	42	20	226
	100	43	23	255
30	70	40	12	181
	80	41	16	214
	90	42	22	234
	100	44	26	267
40	70	40	13	185
	80	42	18	220
	90	43	23	243
	100	44	26	278
50	70	40	14	189
	80	42	19	226
	90	44	25	251
	100	46	27	289
60	70	41	15	193
	80	43	21	233
	90	45	25	259
	100	46	28	300
70	70	41	16	198
	80	43	22	238
	90	45	26	267
	100	46	29	312
80	70	42	18	202
	80	44	23	244
	90	47	27	277
	100	—	—	—
90	70	42	19	206
	80	47	24	250
	90	48	28	284
	100	—	—	—

*Operate engine with transmission in neutral. Keep vehicle out of direct sunlight.

ISOLATING THE COMPRESSOR

It is not necessary to discharge the system for compressor removal. The compressor can be isolated from the rest of the system, eliminating the need for recharging.

1. Connect a manifold gauge set.
2. Close both gauge hand valves and mid-position (crack) both compressor service valves.
3. Start the engine and turn on the air conditioning.

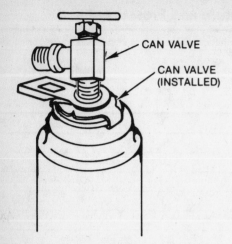

CAN VALVE

CAN VALVE
(INSTALLED)

One pound R-12 can with opener valve connected

4. Turn the compressor suction valve slowly clockwise towards the front seated position. When the suction pressure drops to zero, stop the engine and turn off the air conditioning. Quickly front seat the valve completely.

5. Front seat the discharge service valve.

6. Loosen the oil level check plug to remove any internal pressure.

The compressor is now isolated and the service valves can now be removed.

DISCHARGING THE SYSTEM

1. Connect the manifold gauge set.

2. Turn both manifold gauge set hand valves to the full open (counterclockwise) position.

3. Open both service valve slightly, from the backseated position, and allow the refrigerant to discharge **slowly**.

NOTE: *If you allow the refrigerant to rush out, it will take some refrigerant oil with it!*

EVACUATING THE SYSTEM

NOTE: *This procedure requires the use of a vacuum pump.*

1. Connect the manifold gauge set.

2. Discharge the system.

3. Connect the center service hose to the inlet fitting of the vacuum pump.

4. Turn both gauge set valves to the wide open position.

5. Start the pump and note the low side gauge reading.

6. Operate the pump for a minimum of 30 minutes after the lowest observed gauge reading.

7. Leak test the system. Close both gauge set valves. Turn off the pump and note the low side gauge reading. The needle should remain stationary at the point at which the pump was

turned off. If the needle drops to zero rapidly, there is a leak in the system which must be repaired.

8. If the needle remains stationary for 3 to 5 minutes, open the gauge set valves and run the pump for at least 30 minutes more.

9. Close both gauge set valves, stop the pump and disconnect the gauge set. The system is now ready for charging.

LEAK TESTING

Some leak tests can be performed with a soapy water solution. There must be at least a ½lb charge in the system for a leak to be detected. The most extensive leak tests are performed with either a Halide flame type leak tester or the more preferable electronic leak tester.

In either case, the equipment is expensive, and, the use of a Halide detector can be **extremely** hazardous!

CHARGING THE SYSTEM

1. Connect the gauge set.

2. Close (clockwise) both gauge set valves.

3. Mid-position the service valves.

4. Connect the center hose to the refrigerant can opener valve.

5. Make sure the can opener valve is closed, that is, the needle is raised, and connect the valve to the can. Open the valve, puncturing the can with the needle.

6. Loosen the center hose fitting at the pressure gauge, allowing refrigerant to purge the hose of air.

7. Open the low side gauge set valve and the can valve.

8. Start the engine and turn the air conditioner to the maximum cooling mode. The compressor will operate and pull refrigerant gas into the system.

NOTE: *To help speed the process, the can may be placed, upright, in a pan of warm water, not exceeding +125°F (+51.6°C).*

9. If more than one can of refrigerant is needed, close the can valve and gauge set low side valve when the can is empty and connect a new can to the opener. Repeat the charging process until the sight glass indicates a full charge. The frost line on the outside of the can will indicate what portion of the can has been used.

10. When the charging process has been completed, close the gauge set valve and can valve. Run the system for at least five minutes to allow it to normalize.

11. Back seat (turn fully counterclockwise) both service valves.

12. Loosen both service hoses at the gauges to allow any refrigerant to escape. Remove the

Troubleshooting Basic Air Conditioning Problems

Problem	Cause	Solution
There's little or no air coming from the vents (and you're sure it's on)	• The A/C fuse is blown • Broken or loose wires or connections • The on/off switch is defective	• Check and/or replace fuse • Check and/or repair connections • Replace switch
The air coming from the vents is not cool enough	• Windows and air vent wings open • The compressor belt is slipping • Heater is on • Condenser is clogged with debris • Refrigerant has escaped through a leak in the system • Receiver/drier is plugged	• Close windows and vent wings • Tighten or replace compressor belt • Shut heater off • Clean the condenser • Check system • Service system
The air has an odor	• Vacuum system is disrupted • Odor producing substances on the evaporator case • Condensation has collected in the bottom of the evaporator housing	• Have the system checked/repaired • Clean the evaporator case • Clean the evaporator housing drains
System is noisy or vibrating	• Compressor belt or mountings loose • Air in the system	• Tighten or replace belt; tighten mounting bolts • Have the system serviced

Sight glass condition
  Constant bubbles, foam or oil streaks
  Clear sight glass, but no cold air
  Clear sight glass, but air is cold
  Clouded with milky fluid
	
	• Undercharged system
	
	• No refrigerant at all
	• System is OK
	• Receiver drier is leaking dessicant
		
		• Charge the system
		
		• Check and charge the system
		
		• Have system checked

Large difference in temperature of lines	• System undercharged	• Charge and leak test the system
Compressor noise	• Broken valves • Overcharged • Incorrect oil level • Piston slap • Broken rings • Drive belt pulley bolts are loose	• Replace the valve plate • Discharge, evacuate and install the correct charge • Isolate the compressor and check the oil level. Correct as necessary. • Replace the compressor • Replace the compressor • Tighten with the correct torque specification
Excessive vibration	• Incorrect belt tension • Clutch loose • Overcharged • Pulley is misaligned	• Adjust the belt tension • Tighten the clutch • Discharge, evacuate and install the correct charge • Align the pulley
Condensation dripping in the passenger compartment	• Drain hose plugged or improperly positioned • Insulation removed or improperly installed	• Clean the drain hose and check for proper installation • Replace the insulation on the expansion valve and hoses
Frozen evaporator coil	• Faulty thermostat • Thermostat capillary tube improperly installed • Thermostat not adjusted properly	• Replace the thermostat • Install the capillary tube correctly • Adjust the thermostat
Low side low—high side low	• System refrigerant is low • Expansion valve is restricted	• Evacuate, leak test and charge the system • Replace the expansion valve
Low side high—high side low	• Internal leak in the compressor—worn	• Remove the compressor cylinder head and inspect the compressor. Replace the valve plate assembly if necessary. If the compressor pistons, rings or

Troubleshooting Basic Air Conditioning Problems (cont.)

Problem	Cause	Solution
Low side high—high side low (cont.)		cylinders are excessively worn or scored replace the compressor
	• Cylinder head gasket is leaking	• Install a replacement cylinder head gasket
	• Expansion valve is defective	• Replace the expansion valve
	• Drive belt slipping	• Adjust the belt tension
Low side high—high side high	• Condenser fins obstructed	• Clean the condenser fins
	• Air in the system	• Evacuate, leak test and charge the system
	• Expansion valve is defective	• Replace the expansion valve
	• Loose or worn fan belts	• Adjust or replace the belts as necessary
Low side low—high side high	• Expansion valve is defective	• Replace the expansion valve
	• Restriction in the refrigerant hose	• Check the hose for kinks—replace if necessary
	• Restriction in the receiver/drier	• Replace the receiver/drier
	• Restriction in the condenser	• Replace the condenser
Low side and high side normal (inadequate cooling)	• Air in the system	• Evacuate, leak test and charge the system
	• Moisture in the system	• Evacuate, leak test and charge the system

gauge set and install the dust caps on the service valves.

NOTE: *Multi-can dispensers are available which allow a simultaneous hook-up of up to four 1 lb. cans of R-12.*

CAUTION: *Never exceed the recommended maximum charge for the system. The maximum charge for systems using the 2-cylinder Tecumseh compressor is 2½ lb.; 2 lb. for those systems using the 5-cylinder Sankyo compressor.*

Battery

ELECTROLYTE LEVEL

The correct level should be at the bottom of the well inside each cell opening. The surface of the electrolyte should appear distorted, not flat. Only colorless, odorless, preferably distilled, water should be added. It is a good idea to add the water with a squeeze bulb to avoid splashing and spills. If water is frequently needed, the most likely cause is overcharging, caused by voltage regulator problems. If any acid should escape, it can be neutralized with a baking soda and water solution.

CAUTION: *Avoid sparks and smoking around the battery! It gives off explosive hydrogen gas. If you get acid on your skin or eyes, rinse it off immediately with lots of water. See a doctor if got in your eyes. In winter, add water only before driving to prevent the battery from freezing and cracking.*

NOTE: *Original equipment batteries with*

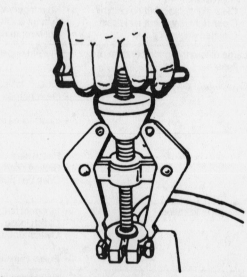

A small puller will easily remove the cables from the terminals

the ganged caps are often chronically wet on top, causing a lot of corrosion in the battery tray. The problem is insufficient venting. Solve it by removing the caps and drilling a tiny vent hole for each cell through the top of the cap.

Check the specific gravity of the battery. It should be between 1.20–1.26 at room temperature. Clean and tighten the terminal clamps and apply a thin coating of petroleum jelly to the terminals. This will help to retard corrosion. The terminals can be cleaned with a stiff wire brush or with a terminal cleaner made for

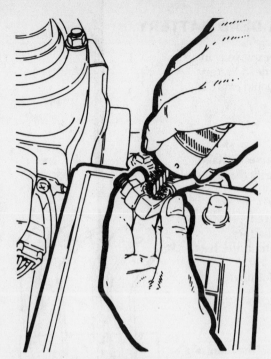

Clean the inside of the terminal clamp

the purpose. These are inexpensive and can be purchased in most any decently equipped parts store.

If water is added during freezing weather,

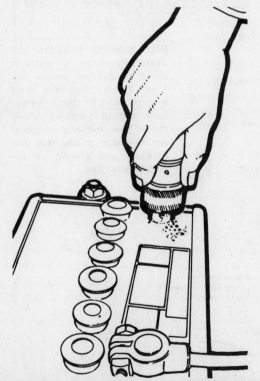

An inexpensive tool easily cleans the battery terminals

the truck should be driven several miles to allow the water to mix with the electrolyte. Otherwise the battery could freeze.

If the battery becomes corroded, a mixture of baking soda and water will neutralize the corrosion. This should be washed off after making sure that the caps are tight and securely in place. Rinse the solution off with cold water.

If a fast charger is used to charge the battery while the battery is in the truck, disconnect the battery first.

NOTE: *Keep flame or sparks away from the battery! It gives off explosive hydrogen gas, while it is being charged.*

Exhaust Manifold Heat Valve

The exhaust manifold heat valve should be inspected and lubricated every 30,000 miles.

On 6-cylinder engines, the valve is located in the center lower portion of the exhaust manifold, on the left hand side of the engine.

CAUTION: *Be sure that the manifold is cool before carrying out inspection and lubrication.*

1. To check the heat valve operation, turn the valve shaft by hand.

2. Lubricate the heat valve with one of the special heat valve lubricants made for this purpose. Do not use grease or oil.

3. Check valve operation again.

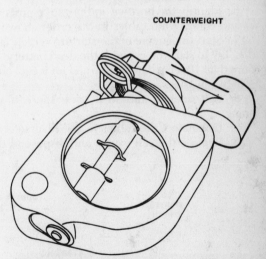

COUNTERWEIGHT

Typical exhaust manifold heat valve (heat riser); V8 shown, the others are similar

Tires and Wheels

Inspect the tire treads for cuts, bruises and other damage. Check the air valves to be sure that they are tight. Replace any missing valve caps.

JUMP STARTING A DEAD BATTERY

The chemical reaction in a battery produces explosive hydrogen gas. This is the safe way to jump start a dead battery, reducing the chances of an accidental spark that could cause an explosion.

Jump Starting Precautions

1. Be sure both batteries are of the same voltage.
2. Be sure both batteries are of the same polarity (have the same grounded terminal).
3. Be sure the vehicles are not touching.
4. Be sure the vent cap holes are not obstructed.
5. Do not smoke or allow sparks around the battery.
6. In cold weather, check for frozen electrolyte in the battery.
7. Do not allow electrolyte on your skin or clothing.
8. Be sure the electrolyte is not frozen.

Jump Starting Procedure

1. Determine voltages of the two batteries; they must be the same.
2. Bring the starting vehicle close (they must not touch) so that the batteries can be reached easily.
3. Turn off all accessories and both engines. Put both cars in Neutral or Park and set the handbrake.
4. Cover the cell caps with a rag—do not cover terminals.
5. If the terminals on the run-down battery are heavily corroded, clean them.
6. Identify the positive and negative posts on both batteries and connect the cables in the order shown.
7. Start the engine of the starting vehicle and run it at fast idle. Try to start the car with the dead battery. Crank it for no more than 10 seconds at a time and let it cool off for 20 seconds in between tries.
8. If it doesn't start in 3 tries, there is something else wrong.
9. Disconnect the cables in the reverse order.
10. Replace the cell covers and dispose of the rags.

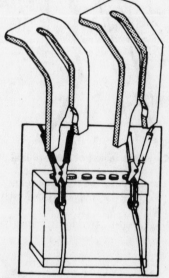

Side terminal batteries occasionally pose a problem when connecting jumper cables. There frequently isn't enough room to clamp the cables without touching sheet metal. Side terminal adaptors are available to alleviate this problem and should be removed after use.

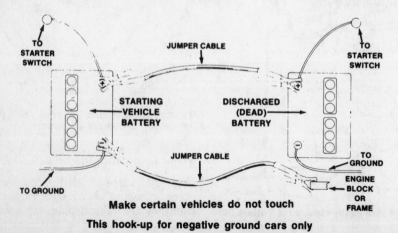

Make certain vehicles do not touch

This hook-up for negative ground cars only

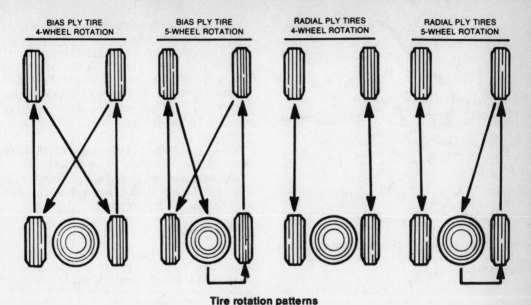

Tire rotation patterns

The tires should be checked frequently for proper air pressure. A chart in the glove compartment or on the driver's door pillar gives the recommended inflation pressure. Pressures can increase as much as 6 psi due to heat buildup. It is a good idea to have your own accurate gauge, and to check pressures weekly. Not all gauges on service station air pumps can be trusted.

Inspect tires for uneven wear that might indicate the need for front end alignment or tire rotation. Tires should be replaced when a tread wear indicator appears as a solid band across the tread.

When you buy new tires, give some thought to these points, especially if you are switching to larger tires or to another profile series (50, 60, 70, 78):

1. All four tires should be the same. Four wheel drive requires that all tires be the same size, type, and tread pattern to provide even traction on loose surfaces, to prevent driveline bind when conventional part time four wheel drive is used, and to prevent excessive wear on the center differential with full time four wheel drive.

2. The wheels must be the correct width for the tire. Tire dealers have charts of tire and rim compatibility. A mismatch can cause sloppy handling and rapid tread wear. The old rule of thumb is that the tread width should match

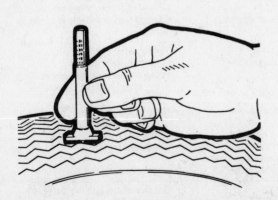

An easily acquired tool can be used to check tire tread depth

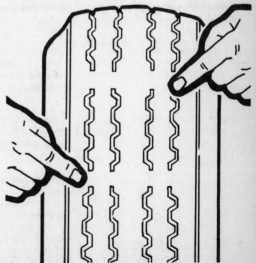

Wear indicators, ½ inch wide strips, are molded into the tires. They appear at the tread surface when tread depth is less than 1/16 inch

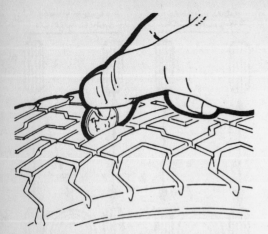

Tread depth can also be checked, roughly, using a penny. If the top of Lincoln's head is visible, replace the tire

the rim width (inside bead to inside bead) within an inch. For radial tires, the rim width should be 80% or less of the tire (not tread) width.

3. The height (mounted diameter) of the new tires can greatly change speedometer accuracy, engine speed at a given road speed, fuel mileage, acceleration, and ground clearance. Tire makers furnish full measurement specifications. Speedometer drive gears are available from car parts for correction.

NOTE: *Dimensions of tires marked the same*

size *may vary significantly, even among tires from the same maker.*

4. The spare tire should be usable, at least for low speed operation, with the new tires. You will probably have to remove the side mounted spare for clearance. This is especially true on 1972 and later models, since they have a wider tread and minimal tire-to-spare clearance.

5. There shouldn't be any body interference when loaded, on bumps, or in turning.

The only sure way to avoid problems with these points is to stick to tire and wheel sizes available as factory options.

TIRE ROTATION

Tire rotation is recommended to obtain maximum tread wear. The pattern you use depends on personal preference, and whether or not you have a usable spare. Radial tires should not be cross-switched. They last longer if their direction of rotation is not changed. Studded snow tires will lose their studs if their rotation direction is reversed.

NOTE: *Mark the wheel position or direction of rotation on radial, or studded snow tires before removing them.*

CAUTION: *Avoid overtightening the lug nuts to prevent damage to the brake disc or drum. Alloy wheels can also be cracked by overtightening. Use of a torque wrench is highly recommended. Tighten the lug nuts in a criss-cross sequence shown to 85 ft.lb.*

Troubleshooting Basic Wheel Problems

Problem	Cause	Solution
The car's front end vibrates at high speed	• The wheels are out of balance • Wheels are out of alignment	• Have wheels balanced • Have wheel alignment checked/adjusted
Car pulls to either side	• Wheels are out of alignment • Unequal tire pressure • Different size tires or wheels	• Have wheel alignment checked/adjusted • Check/adjust tire pressure • Change tires or wheels to same size
The car's wheel(s) wobbles	• Loose wheel lug nuts • Wheels out of balance • Damaged wheel • Wheels are out of alignment • Worn or damaged ball joint • Excessive play in the steering linkage (usually due to worn parts) • Defective shock absorber	• Tighten wheel lug nuts • Have tires balanced • Raise car and spin the wheel. If the wheel is bent, it should be replaced • Have wheel alignment checked/adjusted • Check ball joints • Check steering linkage • Check shock absorbers
Tires wear unevenly or prematurely	• Incorrect wheel size • Wheels are out of balance • Wheels are out of alignment	• Check if wheel and tire size are compatible • Have wheels balanced • Have wheel alignment checked/adjusted

Troubleshooting Basic Tire Problems

Problem	Cause	Solution
The car's front end vibrates at high speeds and the steering wheel shakes	• Wheels out of balance • Front end needs aligning	• Have wheels balanced • Have front end alignment checked
The car pulls to one side while cruising	• Unequal tire pressure (car will usually pull to the low side) • Mismatched tires • Front end needs aligning	• Check/adjust tire pressure • Be sure tires are of the same type and size • Have front end alignment checked
Abnormal, excessive or uneven tire wear See "How to Read Tire Wear"	• Infrequent tire rotation • Improper tire pressure • Sudden stops/starts or high speed on curves	• Rotate tires more frequently to equalize wear • Check/adjust pressure • Correct driving habits
Tire squeals	• Improper tire pressure • Front end needs aligning	• Check/adjust tire pressure • Have front end alignment checked

Tire Size Comparison Chart

"Letter" sizes			Inch Sizes	Metric-inch Sizes		
"60 Series"	"70 Series"	"78 Series"	1965–77	"60 Series"	"70 Series"	"80 Series"
		Y78-12	5.50-12, 5.60-12 6.00-12	165/60-12	165/70-12	155-12
		W78-13 Y78-13	5.20-13 5.60-13 6.15-13	165/60-13 175/60-13 185/60-13	145/70-13 155/70-13 165/70-13	135-13 145-13 155-13, P155/80-13
A60-13 B60-13	A70-13 B70-13	A78-13 B78-13	6.40-13 6.70-13 6.90-13	195/60-13 205/60-13	175/70-13 185/70-13	165-13 175-13
C60-13 D60-13 E60-13	C70-13 D70-13 E70-13	C78-13 D78-13 E78-13	7.00-13 7.25-13 7.75-13	215/60-13	195/70-13	185-13 195-13
			5.20-14 5.60-14 5.90-14	165/60-14 175/60-14	145/70-14 155/70-14	135-14 145-14
A60-14	A70-14 B70-14 C70-14	A78-14 B78-14 C78-14	6.15-14 6.45-14 6.95-14	185/60-14 195/60-14 205/60-14	165/70-14 175/70-14 185/70-14	155-14 165-14 175-14
D60-14 E60-14 F60-14 G60-14 H60-14 J60-14 L60-14	D70-14 E70-14 F70-14 G70-14 H70-14 J70-14 L70-14	D78-14 E78-14 F78-14, F83-14 G77-14, G78-14 H78-14 J78-14	7.35-14 7.75-14 8.25-14 8.55-14 8.85-14 9.15-14	215/60-14 225/60-14 235/60-14 245/60-14 255/60-14 265/60-14	195/70-14 200/70-14 205/70-14 215/70-14 225/70-14 235/70-14	185-14 195-14 205-14 215-14 225-14
	A70-15	A78-15	5.60-15	185/60-15	165/70-15	155-15
B60-15 C60-15	B70-15 C70-15 D70-15	B78-15 C78-15 D78-15	6.35-15 6.85-15	195/60-15 205/60-15	175/70-15 185/70-15	165-15 175-15
E60-15 F60-15 G60-15 H60-15 J60-15	E70-15 F70-15 G70-15 H70-15 J70-15 K70-15	E78-15 F78-15 G78-15 H78-15 J78-15	7.35-15 7.75-15 8.15-15/8.25-15 8.45-15/8.55-15 8.85-15/8.90-15 9.00-15	215/60-15 225/60-15 235/60-15 245/60-15 255/60-15 265/60-15	195/70-15 205/70-15 215/70-15 225/70-15 235/70-15 245/70-15	185-15 195-15 205-15 215-15 225-15 230-15
L60-15	L70-15 M70-15	L78-15, L84-15 M78-15 N78-15	9.15-15			235-15 255-15

Note: Every size tire is not listed and many size comparisons are approximate, based on load ratings. Wider tires than those supplied new with the vehicle, should always be checked for clearance.

FLUIDS AND LUBRICANTS

Fuel and Oil Recommendations

All 1975 and later models must use no-lead gasoline.

NOTE: *Be aware that your engine's fuel requirement can change with time, mainly due to carbon buildup changing the compression ratio. If your engine pings, knocks, or runs on, switch to a higher grade of fuel and check the ignition timing as soon as possible. Do not retard the timing from specification unless you still have trouble with the higher grade fuel, and then not more than 3°. Retarded timing will reduce power output and fuel mileage and increase engine temperature.*

Only oils labeled SF are approved under warranty for use. Select the viscosity rating to be used by your type of driving and the temperature range anticipated before the next oil change.

The multi-viscosity oils offer the important advantage of being adaptable to temperature extremes. They can allow easy starts at low temperatures, yet still give good protection at high speeds and warm temperatures. This is a decided advantage in changeable climate or in long distance touring.

NOTE: *If your engine takes a long time in building up oil pressure after starting in warm weather, when using 10W-30 or 10W-40 oil, the problem can often be solved by switching to 20W-40. This is not specifically recommended by AMC, but it is a proven method.*

Engine Oil
CHECKING THE OIL LEVEL

The engine oil should be checked on a regular basis, at least at every gas stop, or more often under severe usage. If the check is made at a gas stop, wait until the tank has been filled. If the level is checked immediately after stopping, a false low reading will result. The proper level is between the FULL and ADD marks on the dipstick, preferable at FULL.

1. Pull out the dipstick on the side of the engine. Do not take a reading yet, unless the engine has been off all night.

2. Wipe off the dipstick with a clean rag.

3. Replace the dipstick, count slowly to ten or do whatever you like for ten seconds, and remove it. Check the level on the dipstick.

4. If the level is at the ADD mark, adding one full quart at the filler (usually marked OIL) will bring it to the FULL mark. Never add a full quart if the level is not down to the ADD mark, because this overfilling will result in possible damage to engine seals or rapid oil consumption. See 'Oil and Fuel Recommendations' later in this chapter for the proper oils.

NOTE: *If you need to add oil when the level is down less than a full quart, you will have a problem storing partly full quart oil cans.*

Oil Viscosity Selector

Lowest Temperature Expected (deg F)	Multi-Viscosity (SAE)	Single-Viscosity (SAE)
Above 32	10W-30 10W-40 10W-50 20W-50	20W-20
Above 0	10W-30 10W-40 10W-50	10W*
Below 0	5W-20 5W-30	10W*

*Do not run above 65 mph with SAE 10W; oil consumption will be excessive.

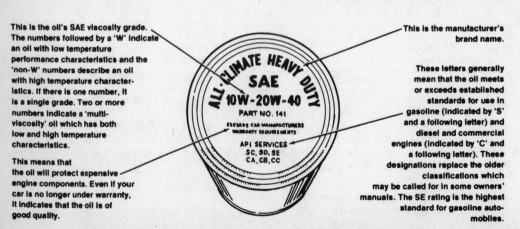

This is the oil's SAE viscosity grade. The numbers followed by a 'W' indicate an oil with low temperature performance characteristics and the 'non-W' numbers describe an oil with high temperature characteristics. If there is one number, it is a single grade. Two or more numbers indicate a 'multi-viscosity' oil which has both low and high temperature characteristics.

This means that the oil will protect expensive engine components. Even if your car is no longer under warranty, it indicates that the oil is of good quality.

This is the manufacturer's brand name.

These letters generally mean that the oil meets or exceeds established standards for use in gasoline (indicated by 'S' and a following letter) and diesel and commercial engines (indicated by 'C' and a following letter). These designations replace the older classifications which may be called for in some owners' manuals. The SE rating is the highest standard for gasoline automobiles.

ALL CLIMATE HEAVY DUTY
SAE
10W-20W-40
PART NO. 141
EXCEEDS CAR MANUFACTURERS WARRANTY REQUIREMENTS
API SERVICES
SC, SD, SE
CA, CB, CC

The top of the oil can will tell you all you need to know about the oil

The plastic covers that come with coffee cans are ideal for covering these cans.

5. Replace the dipstick, seating it firmly.

CHANGING THE ENGINE OIL AND FILTER

Assuming that the recommended oils are used, the oil and filter should be changed at the intervals shown in the 'Service Intervals' chart. This interval should be halved under severe usage such as dusty conditions, trailer towing, prolonged high speeds, or repeated short trips in freezing temperatures.

To change the oil and filter:

1. Operate the car until the engine is at normal operating temperature. if you don't, most

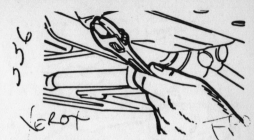

The oil drain plug is located at the lowest point of the pan

of the contaminants will stay in your engine. Stop the engine.

2. Slide a pan of at least five quarts capacity

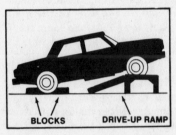

1. Warm the car up before changing your oil. Raise the front end of the car and support it on drive-on ramps or jackstands.

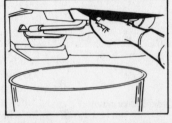

2. Locate the drain plug on the bottom of the oil pan and slide a low flat pan of sufficient capacity under the engine to catch the oil. Loosen the plug with a wrench and turn it out the last few turns by hand. Keep a steady inward pressure on the plug to avoid hot oil from running down your arm.

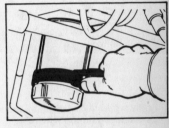

3. Remove the oil filter with a filter wrench. The filter can hold more than a quart of oil, which will be hot. Be sure the gasket comes off with the filter and clean the mounting base on the engine.

4. Lubricate the gasket on the new filter with clean engine oil. A dry gasket may not make a good seal and will allow the filter to leak.

5. Position a new filter on the mounting base and spin it on by hand. Do not use a wrench. When the gasket contacts the engine, tighten it another ½–1 turn by hand.

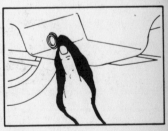

6. Using a rag, clean the drain plug and the area around the drain hole in the oil pan.

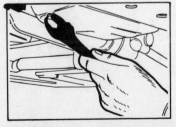

7. Install the drain plug and tighten it finger-tight. If you feel resistance, stop and be sure you are not cross-threading the plug. Finally, tighten the plug with a wrench.

8. Locate the oil cap on the valve cover. An oil spout is the easiest way to add oil, but a funnel will do just as well.

9. Start the engine and check for leaks. The oil pressure warning light will remain on for a few seconds; when it goes out, stop the engine and check the level on the dipstick.

Use an oil filter strap wrench to remove the old filter; install the new filter by hand

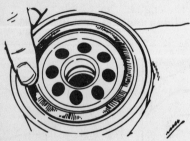

Apply a thin film of clean oil to the gasket to prevent its distortion during tightening

under the oil pan. Throw-away aluminum roasting pans work well.

3. Remove the drain plug from the engine oil pan, after wiping the plug area clean. If this is your first attempt at oil changing, make sure that you have the engine drain plug and not the one for the transmission or something else.

CAUTION: *Watch our for that hot oil! You will probably find the plug too hot to hold, too.*

4. Allow the oil to drain into the pan. Do not replace the plug before the oil has completely stopped draining.

5. Clean off the plug, particularly the threads, and replace it.

6. The filter is on the lower right side of the engine. use a filter wrench to loose it. These are available often for less than a dollar, at discount and auto supply stores. Unscrew and discard the old filter after wiping the area clean.

CAUTION: *Watch it! The filter is full of hot oil and is probably too hot to hold long, itself.*

7. If some brute has overtightened your filter, causing it to collapse when you use the filter wrench on it, drive a long punch through the cartridge as near the base as possible and use this as a lever to unscrew it.

8. Lubricate the new filter gasket with a few drops of engine oil, smeared around with a finger.

9. Screw the filter on by hand until the gasket makes contact. Then tighten the filter one half to a full turn by hand. If you overtighten the filter, you may have to resort to Step 7 to get it off next time.

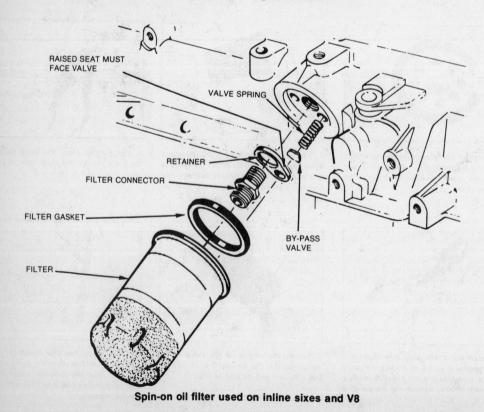

Spin-on oil filter used on inline sixes and V8

10. Remove the filler cap on top of the engine, after wiping the area clean.

11. Add the oil specified under 'Fuel and Oil Recommendations.' If you are adding oil from a bulk container (other than 1 qt cans), keep track of the number of quarts added. Overfilling could cause damage to engine seals. Replace the cap.

12. Check the oil level on the dipstick. Start the engine and look for leaks around the drain plug and filter.

13. Stop the engine and recheck the level. After all this is done, you note that you have a pan with foul looking oil to dispose of. Your best bet is to funnel the stuff into plastic milk containers, bleach bottles, antifreeze jugs, or the like. If you are on good terms with a gas station man, he might let you dump it into his used oil container for recycling. Otherwise you will be forced to return it to Mother Earth by slipping the containers into your trash barrel.

Manual Transmission

FLUID LEVEL CHECK

The transmission level should be checked when the oil is changed. Since your hands are apt to be pretty oily at these times, you

Manual Transmission Fluid Recommendations

Transmission	Fluid
HR-1	80W-90
SR-4	85W-90
T-150	80W-90
T-4	Dexron® II ATF
T-5	Dexron® II ATF
T-14	80W-90

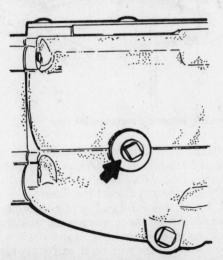

Manual transmission fill and drain plugs with the drain plug at the bottom center

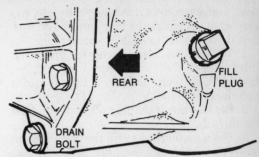

Manual transmission fill and drain plugs, using a tailshaft bolt as the drain plug

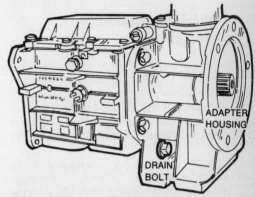

Manual transmission drain bolt location on Eagles

shouldn't mind this job. To check the level, remove the filler plug in the right side of the transmission case from under the car. There is a similar plug in the overdrive case at the rear of the transmission. With the car level, oil should drip out. If it runs our in a steady stream, let it run until it just drips. Any fluid required can be pumped in with a suction gun. All transmissions use SAE 80W-90 Gear oil, except the 1982 T4 and T5. These use Dexron*II automatic transmission fluid.

Pacer 3-Speed with Overdrive

The overdrive unit shares a common supply of lubricant with the manual transmission. The fluid level is checked at the transmission fill plug in the same manner as for manual transmissions without overdrive. The fluid level should be checked every 5,000 miles.

If lubricant is required, use only API GL-4 SAE 80W-140 gear lubricant.

CAUTION: *Don't use antifriction or limited slip differential lubricant in the transmission/overdrive unit.*

FLUID CHANGE

The manufacturer says that the transmission lubricant need never be changed, except for overhaul. However, if you bought your car used, or if you subject it to heavy duty use, you may want to change the lubricant. To do this, first drive the car until it is warm, then:

1. Wipe off the area around the drain and filler plugs for the transmission and overdrive. Remove both plugs and drain the oil into a container.

2. Replace the drain plug after cleaning off the threads.

3. Use a suction gun to fill the transmission or overdrive through the filler hole. The correct level is even with the bottom of the filler hoe. See 'Fluid level Checks,' earlier in the Chapter, for the proper lubricants.

Automatic Transmission

FLUID LEVEL CHECK

Check the level at oil change intervals. With the transmission at operating temperature, proceed as follows:

1. The normal operating temperature of 175°F is not obtained until the car has been driven several miles, making frequent starts and stops.

2. Park the car on a level surface. Set the parking brake.

3. With the engine idling, shift the selector lever through all gear positions.

4. Shift into Neutral.

5. Pull out the dipstick at the right rear of the engine. Wipe it off with a clean rag.

6. Replace the dipstick and push it in all the way.

7. Pull out the dipstick after ten seconds and take a reading. The level should be between the FULL and ADD ONE PINT marks.

8. If the level is at or below the ADD ONE PINT mark, add fluid through the dipstick tube to bring the level from ADD ONE PINT to FULL. Be very cautious not to overfill the transmission.

NOTE: *The proper transmission fluid is AMC or DEXRON®II automatic transmission fluid.*

FLUID AND FILTER CHANGE

The manufacturer says that the transmission fluid doesn't ever have to be changed, unless the car is used for heavy work such as trailering. In this case, the fluid is to be changed every 25,000 miles. A band adjustment is also required at the same interval for these cars.

NOTE: *See Chapter 6 for details of the band adjustment.*

1. Drive the car until it is thoroughly warm.

2. Unbolt the pan. It holds six or more quarts, so be ready.

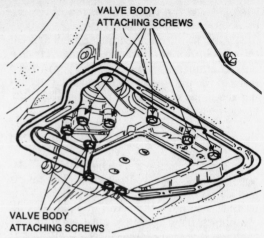

VALVE BODY ATTACHING SCREWS

VALVE BODY ATTACHING SCREWS

Automatic transmission filter location. Do not disturb the valve body screws when removing the filter

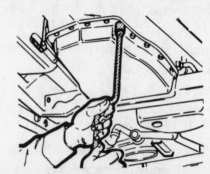

Many late model vehicles have no drain plug. Loosen the pan bolts and allow one corner of the pan to hang, so that the fluid will drain out

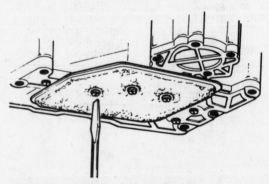

Removing automatic transmission filter

NOTE: *If the fluid removed smells burnt, serious transmission troubles, probably due to overheating should be suspected.*

3. Unscrew and discard the filter.

4. Install a new filter. The proper torque is 28 in.lb., though the torque wrench isn't absolutely necessary here.

5. Clean out the pan, being extremely careful not to leave any lint from rags inside.

6. Replace the pan with a new gasket.

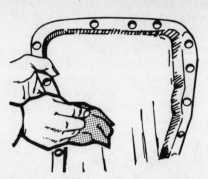

Clean the pan thoroughly with a safe solvent and allow it to air dry

Install a new pan gasket

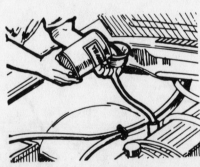

Fill the transmission with the required amount of fluid. Do not overfill. Start the engine and run the selector through all the shift points. Check the fluid and add as necessary

Tighten the bolts to 11 ft.lb. in a crisscross pattern. The torque wrench isn't absolutely essential.

7. Pour six quarts of DEXRON*II or AMC automatic transmission fluid through the dipstick tube.

8. Start the engine in Neutral and let it idle for two minutes or more.

9. Hold you foot on the Brake and shift through D, 2 and R and back to N.

10. Add enough fluid to bring the level to the ADD ONE PINT mark.

11. Operate the car until the transmission is thoroughly warmed up, then check the level as

explained previously under 'Fluid Level Checks.' Add fluid as necessary.

Brake Master Cylinder

The master cylinder is in the left rear of the engine compartment, on the firewall. With power brakes, there is a round container behind the cylinder. To check the fluid level as recommended at each oil change interval:

1. Clean off the area around the cap. Very small particles of dirt can cause serious difficulties in the brake system.

2. Remove the bolt retaining the cover, or, on later models, pry the wire retaining the cap to one side with a screwdriver. Take off the cover.

3. The proper level in each of the two reservoirs is within ¼" (6mm) of the top. Add fluid as necessary.

CAUTION: *Brake fluid dissolves paint.*

4. Replace the cover. Replace the retaining bolt or snap the retaining wire back in place.

CAUTION: *Use only high quality brake fluid designated for disc brake systems, even if you don't have discs. Lesser fluids can boil during heavy braking, causing complete loss of braking power. Make sure that brake fluid containers are sealed tightly; brake fluid can absorb moisture from the air.*

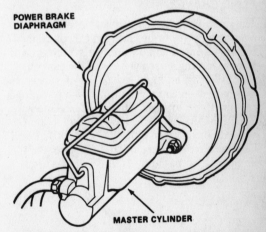

POWER BRAKE DIAPHRAGM

MASTER CYLINDER

Typical brake master cylinder; power brake models shown

Drive Axles

FLUID LEVEL CHECK

It is recommended that the front or rear axle lubricant level be checked at each engine oil change. The filler plug may be located either on the front or the rear of the housing, depending on the axle used. Sometimes it is an allen head plug. When the unit is warm, the level should be even with the plug hole; when cold, it

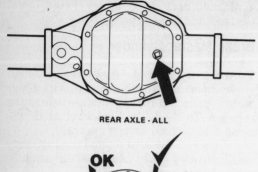

REAR AXLE - ALL

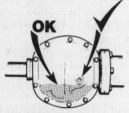

FRONT AXLE - EAGLE

Drive axle fill plugs

may be a bit below. A finger makes a fine dipstick. Lubricant may be added with a suction gun. Standard differentials may use SAE 80W GL-5 gear lubricant or the special lubricant made for limited slip differentials. Limited slip differentials must use the special lubricant or they will be damaged. If you don't want to go to the trouble of finding our, then the obvious solution is to use the special limited slip stuff.

FLUID CHANGE

The manufacturer says that the rear axle lubricant need never be changed except on models with limited slip differentials. However, if you are buying a used vehicle, if the car is used for trailering or high speeds, or if you have driven in deep water, you may wish to change the lubricant anyway. This must be done with a suction gun inserted in the filler hole, unless you axle has a drain plug. Refer to Fluid Level Checks, earlier along in this Chapter for the proper lubricants and level.

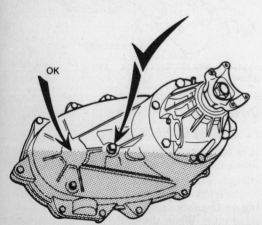

Transfer case drain and fill plug locations

Transfer Case

Drain and fill the transfer case at the interval recommended in the Maintenance Intervals chart. The drain and fill plugs are on the front of the case. Fill the case until the fluid is at the fill plug hole. Recommended fluid is: 1982 and later: Dexron*II automatic transmission fluid 1980–81: 10W-30 engine oil.

Manual Steering Gear

The level of lubricant in the steering gear box doesn't need to be checked unless you notice leakage. An oily film is not important, but escaping grease is. To check the level:

1. Wipe off the gearbox until you can see one cover bolt between the words CHECK LUBE. Sometimes there is a filler plug.

2. With the wheels turned all the way to the left, remove the cover bolt or filler plug.

CAUTION: *Don't remove the locknut in the center or you will mess up the gearbox adjustment. Don't take the cover off.*

3. If you can see grease, there is enough. If not, fill the chassis grease through the hole.

4. Torque the cover bolt to 25–40 ft.lb. if you have a torque wrench. If not, just pull it down firmly but gently.

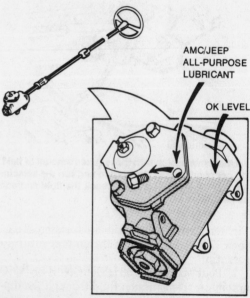

AMC/JEEP
ALL-PURPOSE
LUBRICANT

OK LEVEL

Manual steering gear fill hole location

Power Steering Reservoir

The belt driven power steering pump/reservoir is located at the from of the engine. To check the level, as recommended at oil change intervals, proceed as follows:

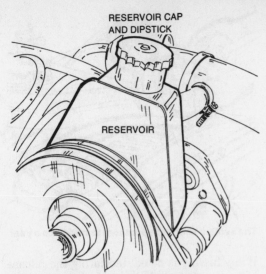

Power steering pump dipstick location

1. Wipe off the cap and surrounding area, after stopping the engine with the wheels straight.

CAUTION: *Very small dirt particles can cause trouble in any hydraulic system.*

2. Remove the cap.

3. If the cap has a dipstick, wipe it off with a clean rag, replace the cap, wait ten seconds, and take a reading. The level should be at FULL.

4. If you didn't get a dipstick, the level should be 1" below the top.

5. The correct fluid is DEXRON®II or AMC Automatic Transmission Fluid.

Coolant

COOLANT LEVEL CHECK

The coolant level should be maintained 1½–2" (38–51mm) below the bottom of the filler cap when the engine is cold. Since operating temperatures reach as high as +205°F (+96°C) for the four and six, and +190°F (+88°C) for the V8s, coolant could be forced out of the radiator if it is filled too high. The radiator coolant level should be checked regularly, such as every time you fill the vehicle with gas. Never open the radiator cap of an engine that hasn't had sufficient time to cool or the pressure can blow off the cap and send out a spray of scalding water.

On systems with a coolant recovery tank, maintain the coolant level at the level marks on the recovery bottle.

For best protection against freezing and overheating, maintain an approximate 50% water and 50% ethylene glycol antifreeze mixture in the cooling system. Do not mix different brands of antifreeze to avoid possible chemical damage to the cooling system.

Avoid using water that is known to have a high alkaline content or is very hard, except in emergency situations. Drain and flush the cooling system as soon as possible after using such water.

CAUTION: *Cover the radiator cap with a thick cloth before removing it from a radiator in a vehicle that is hot. Turn the cap counterclockwise slowly until pressure can be heard escaping. Allow all pressure to escape from the radiator before completely removing the radiator cap. It is best to allow the engine to cool if possible, before removing the radiator cap.*

NOTE: *Never add cold water to an overheated engine while the engine is not running.*

After filling the radiator, run the engine until it reaches normal operating temperature, to make sure that the thermostat has opened and all the air is bled from the system.

DRAINING, FLUSHING AND REFILLING

CAUTION: *When draining the coolant, keep in mind that cats and dogs are attracted by the ethylene glycol antifreeze, and are quite likely to drink any that is left in an uncovered container or in puddles on the ground. This will prove fatal in sufficient quantity. Always drain the coolant into a sealable container. Coolant should be reused unless it is contaminated or several years old.*

To drain the cooling system, allow the engine to cool down **BEFORE ATTEMPTING TO REMOVE THE RADIATOR CAP**. Then turn the cap until it hisses. Wait until all pressure is off the cap before removing it completely.

CAUTION: *To avoid burns and scalding, always handle a warm radiator cap with a heavy rag.*

1. At the dash, set the heater TEMP control lever to the fully HOT position.

2. With the radiator cap removed, drain the radiator by loosening the petcock at the bottom of the radiator. Locate any drain plugs in the block and remove them. Flush the radiator with water until the fluid runs clear.

3. Close the petcock and replace the plug(s), then refill the system with a 50/50 mix of ethylene glycol antifreeze. Fill the system to ¾–1¼" (19.05–31.75mm) from the bottom of the filler neck. Reinstall the radiator cap.

NOTE: *If equipped with a fluid reservoir tank, fill it up to the MAX level.*

4. Operate the engine at 2,000 rpm for a few minutes and check the system for signs of leaks.

Radiator Cap Inspection

Allow the engine to cool sufficiently before attempting to remove the radiator cap. Use a rag to cover the cap, then remove by pressing down and turning counterclockwise to the first stop.

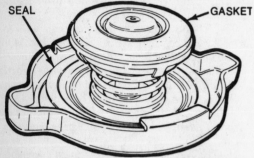

SEAL — GASKET

Check the radiator cap's rubber gasket and metal seal for deterioration at least once a year

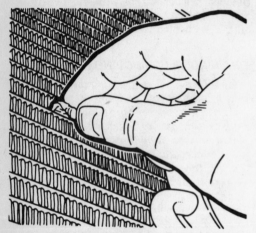

Keep the radiator fins clear for maximum cooling

Coolant protection can be checked with a simple float-type tester

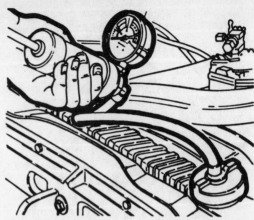

The system should be pressure tested once a year

If any hissing is noted (indicating the release of pressure), wait until the hissing stops completely, then press down again and turn counterclockwise until the cap can be removed.

CAUTION: *DO NOT attempt to remove the radiator cap while the engine is hot. Severe personal injury from steam burns can result.* Check the condition of the radiator cap gasket and seal inside of the cap. The radiator cap is designed to seal the cooling system under normal operating conditions which allows the build up of a certain amount of pressure (this pressure rating is stamped or printed on the cap). The pressure in the system raises the boiling point of the coolant to help prevent overheating. If the radiator cap does not seal, the boiling point of the coolant is lowered and overheating will occur. If the cap must be replaced, purchase the new cap according to the pressure rating which is specified for your vehicle.

Prior to installing the radiator cap, inspect and clean the filler neck. If you are reusing the old cap, clean it thoroughly with clear water. After turning the cap on, make sure the arrows align with the overflow hose.

Front Hub and Wheel Bearings

ADJUSTMENT

Before handling the bearings, there are a few things that you should remember to do and not to do.

NOTE: *Sodium based grease is not compatible with lithium based grease. Read the package labels and be careful not to mix the two types. If there is any doubt as to the type of grease used, completely clean the old grease from the bearing and hub before replacing.*

Remember to DO the following:

• Remove all outside dirt from the housing before exposing the bearing.

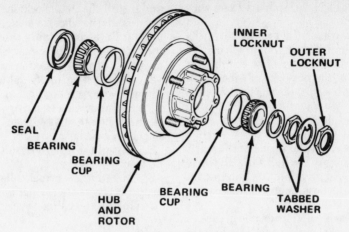

SEAL

BEARING

BEARING CUP

HUB AND ROTOR

BEARING CUP

BEARING

INNER LOCKNUT

OUTER LOCKNUT

TABBED WASHER

Hub and wheel bearings on 1980–86 models

• Treat a used bearing as gently as you would a new one.

• Work with clean tools in clean surroundings.

• Use clean, dry canvas gloves, or at least clean, dry hands.

• Clean solvents and flushing fluids are a must.

• Use clean paper when laying out the bearings to dry.

• Protect disassembled bearings from rust and dirt. Cover them up.

• Use clean rags to wipe bearings.

• Keep the bearings in oil-proof paper when they are to be stored or are not in use.

• Clean the inside of the housing before replacing the bearing.

Do NOT do the following:

• Don't work in dirty surroundings.

• Don't use dirty, chipped or damaged tools.

• Try not to work on wooden work benches or use wooden mallets.

• Don't handle bearings with dirty or moist hands.

• Do not use gasoline for cleaning. Use a safe solvent.

• Do not spin dry bearings with compressed air. They will be damaged.

• Do not spin dirty bearings.

• Avoid using cotton waste or dirty cloths to wipe bearings.

• Try not to scratch or nick bearing surfaces.

• Do not allow the bearing to come in contact with dirt or rust at any time.

4-WD

1. Raise the front of the vehicle and place jackstands under the axle.

2. Remove the wheel.

3. Remove the front hub grease cap and driving hub snapring. On models equipped with locking hubs, remove the retainer knob hub ring, agitator knob, snapring, outer clutch retaining ring and actuating cam body.

4. Remove the splined driving hub and the pressure spring. This may require slight prying with a screwdriver.

5. Remove the external snapring from the sindle shaft and remove the hub shaft drive gear.

6. Remove the wheel bearing locknut, lockring, adjusting nut and inner lockring.

7. On vehicles with drum brakes, remove the hub and drum assembly. This may require that the brake adjusting wheel be backed off a few turns. The outer wheel bearing and spring retainer will come off with the hub.

8. On vehicles with disc brakes, remove the caliper and suspend it out of the way by hanging it from a suspension or frame member with a length of wire. Do not disconnect the brake hose, and be careful to avoid stretching the hose. Remove the rotor and hub assembly. The outer wheel bearing and, on vehicles with locking hubs, the spring collar, will come off with the hub.

9. Carefully drive out the inner bearing and seal from the hub, using a wood block.

10. Inspect the bearing races for excessive wear, pitting or grooves. If they are cracked or grooved, or if pitting and excess wear is present, drive them out with a drift or punch.

11. Check the bearing for excess wear, pitting or cracks, or excess looseness.

NOTE: *If it is necessary to replace either the bearing or the race, replace both. Never replace just a bearing or a race. These parts wear in a mating pattern. If just one is replaced, premature failure of the new part will result.*

12. If the old parts are retained, thoroughly clean them in a safe solvent and allow them to

dry on a clean towel. Never spin dry them with compressed air.

13. On vehicles with drum brakes, cover the spindle with a cloth and thoroughly brush all dirt from the brakes. Never blow the dirt off the brakes, due to the presence of asbestos in the dirt, which is harmful to your health when inhaled.

14. Remove the cloth and thoroughly clean the spindle.

15. Thoroughly clean the inside of the hub.

16. Pack the inside of the hub with EP wheel bearing grease. Add grease to the hub until it is flush with the inside diameter of the bearing cup.

17. Pack the bearing with the same grease. A needle shaped wheel bearing packer is best for this operation. If one is not available, place a large amount of grease in the palm of your hand and slide the edge of the bearing cage through the grease to pick up as much as possible, then work the grease in as best you can with your fingers.

18. If a new race is being installed, very carefully drive it into position until it bottoms all around, using a brass drift. Be careful to avoid scratching the surface.

19. Place the inner bearing in the race and install a new grease seal.

20. Place the hub assembly onto the spindle and install the inner lockring and outer bearing. Install the wheel bearing nut and torque it to 50 ft.lb. while turning the wheel back and forth to seat the bearings. Back off the nut about ¼ turn (90°) maximum.

21. Install the lockwasher with the tab aligned with the keyway in the spindle and turn the inner wheel bearing adjusting nut until the peg on the nut engages the nearest hole in the lockwasher.

22. Install the outer locknut and torque it to 50 ft.lb.

23. Install the spring collar, drive flange, snapring, pressure spring, and hub cap.

24. Install the caliper over the rotor.

2-WD

1. Raise the front of the vehicle and place jackstands under the axle.

2. Remove the wheel.

3. Remove the front hub grease cap.

4. Remove the cotter pin and locknut.

5. Pull out on the brake drum slightly to free the outer bearing and remove the bearing.

6. Remove the drum and hub.

7. Using an awl, puncture the inner seal and pry it out. Discard the seal.

8. Remove the inner bearing.

9. Inspect the bearing races for excessive wear, pitting or grooves. If they are cracked or

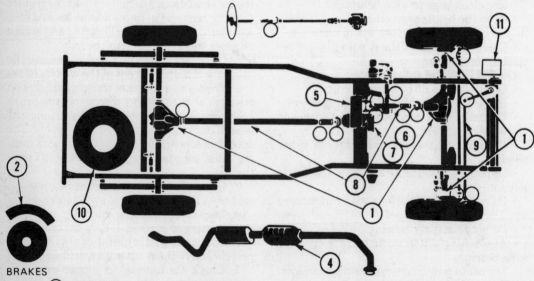

BRAKES

◯ INSPECTION/LUBRICATION POINTS

1. Check front and rear axle differential fluid level
1. Drain and change front and rear axle differential oil
2. Brake and chassis inspection lubrication ①
3. Lubricate body components ①
4. Check exhaust system ②
5. Check transfer case oil

5. Drain and change transfer case oil
6. Drain and change automatic transmission oil
7. Check manual transmission fluid level
8. Lubricate front and rear propeller shafts ③
9. Check and lubricate steering linkage ④
10. Check tire pressure in spare tire
11. Check windshield washer reservoir fluid level

Eagle chassis inspection and lubrication points

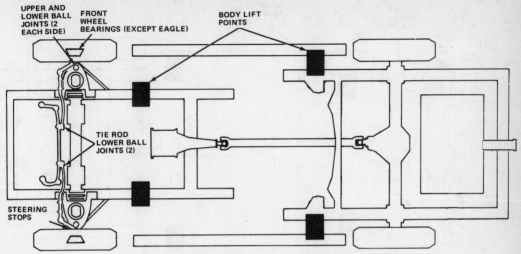

UPPER AND LOWER BALL JOINTS (2 EACH SIDE)

FRONT WHEEL BEARINGS (EXCEPT EAGLE)

BODY LIFT POINTS

TIE ROD LOWER BALL JOINTS (2)

STEERING STOPS

Chassis lubrication points on all except Eagle and Pacer

grooved, or if pitting and excess wear is present, drive them out with a drift or punch.

10. Check the bearing for excess wear, pitting or cracks, or excess looseness.

NOTE: *If it is necessary to replace either the bearing or the race, replace both. Never replace just a bearing or a race. These parts wear in a mating pattern. If just one is replaced, premature failure of the new part will result.*

11. If the old parts are retained, thoroughly clean them in a safe solvent and allow them to dry on a clean towel. Never spin dry them with compressed air.

12. On vehicles with drum brakes, cover the spindle with a cloth and thoroughly brush all dirt from the brakes. Never blow the dirt off the brakes, due to the presence of asbestos in the dirt, which is harmful to your health when inhaled.

13. Remove the cloth and thoroughly clean the spindle.

14. Thoroughly clean the inside of the hub.

15. Pack the inside of the hub with EP wheel bearing grease. Add grease to the hub until it is flush with the inside diameter of the bearing cup.

16. Pack the bearing with the same grease. A needle shaped wheel bearing packer is best for this operation. If one is not available, place a large amount of grease in the palm of your hand and slide the edge of the bearing cage through the grease to pick up as much as possible, then work the grease in as best you can with your fingers.

17. If a new race is being installed, very carefully drive it into position until it bottoms all around, using a brass drift. Be careful to avoid scratching the surface.

18. Place the inner bearing in the race and install a new grease seal.

19. Place the hub assembly onto the spindle and install the outer bearing. Install the wheel bearing nut and tighten it until the hub binds while turning. Back off the nut about $1/6$–$1/4$ turn to free the bearings. Install a new cotter pin.

20. Install the grease cap.

21. Install the wheel.

22. Lower the vehicle and install the hub cap.

PUSHING AND TOWING

Cars with automatic transmission may not be started by pushing or towing. Manual transmission cars may be started by pushing. The car need not be pushed very fast to start.

To push start a manual transmission car:

1. Make sure that the bumpers of the two cars align so as not to damage either one.

2. Turn on the ignition switch in the pushed car. Place the transmission in Second or Third gear and hold down the clutch pedal.

3. Have the car pushed to a speed of 10–15 mph.

4. Ease up on the clutch and press down on the accelerator slightly at the same time. If the clutch is engaged abruptly, damage to the push vehicle may result.

The car should not be towed to start, since there is a chance of the towed vehicle ramming the tow car. Models with automatic should not be towed over 30 mph, for more than 15 miles. If these recommendations must be exceeded, remove the driveshaft to prevent automatic transmission damage.

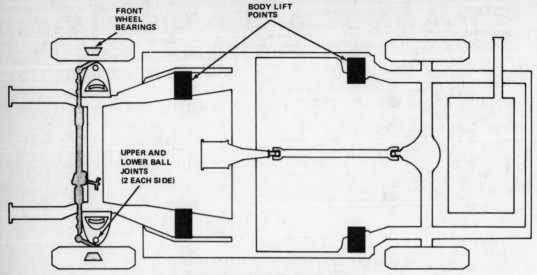

FRONT WHEEL BEARINGS

BODY LIFT POINTS

UPPER AND LOWER BALL JOINTS (2 EACH SIDE)

Pacer chassis lubrication points

JACKING AND HOISTING

The jack supplied with the car should never be used for any service operation other than tire changing. NEVER get under the car while it is supported only by the jack. They very often slip or topple over. Always block the wheels when changing tires.

Some of the service operations in this book require that one or both ends of the car be raised and supported safely. The best arrangement is a grease pit or a vehicle lift. It is understood that these items are not often found in the home garage, but there are reasonable and safe substitutes. Small hydraulic, screw, or scissors jacks are satisfactory for raising the car.

Heavy wooden blocks or adjustable jackstands should be used to support the car while it is being worked on. Drive-on trestles, or ramps, are also a handy and safe way to raise the car. These can be bought or constructed from suitable heavy timbers or steel.

In any case, it is always best to spend a little extra time to make sure that the car is lifted and supported safely.

CAUTION: *Concrete blocks are not recommended. They may break if the load is not evenly distributed. Boxes and milk crates of any description must not be used.*

OUTSIDE VEHICLE MAINTENANCE

Lock Cylinders

Apply graphite lubricant sparingly through the key slot. Insert the key and operate the lock several times to be sure that the lubricant is worked into the lock cylinder.

Door Hinges and Hinge Checks

Spray a silicone lubricant on the hinge pivot points to eliminate any binding conditions. Open and close the door several times to be sure that the lubricant is evenly and thoroughly distributed.

Tailgate

Spray a silicone lubricant on all of the pivot and friction surfaces to eliminate any squeaks or binds. Work the tailgate to distribute the lubricant

Body Drain Holes

Be sure that the drain holes in the doors and rocker panels are cleared of obstruction. A small screwdriver can be used to clear them of any debris.

TRAILER TOWING

Car vehicles have long been popular as trailer towing vehicles. Their strong construction, 4-wheel drive and wide range of engine/transmission combinations make them ideal for towing campers, boat trailers and utility trailers.

Factory trailer towing packages are available on most car vehicles. However, if you are installing a trailer hitch and wiring on your car, there are a few thing that you ought to know.

Trailer Weight

Trailer weight is the first, and most important, factor in determining whether or not your vehicle is suitable for towing the trailer you have in mind. The horsepower-to-weight ratio should be calculated. The basic standard is a ratio of 35:1. That is, 35 pounds of GVW for every horsepower.

To calculate this ratio, multiply you engine's rated horsepower by 35, then subtract the weight of the vehicle, including passengers and luggage. The resulting figure is the ideal maximum trailer weight that you can tow. One point to consider: a numerically higher axle ratio can offset what appears to be a low trailer weight. If the weight of the trailer that you have in mind is somewhat higher than the weight you just calculated, you might consider changing your rear axle ratio to compensate.

Hitch Weight

There are three kinds of hitches: bumper mounted, frame mounted, and load equalizing.

Bumper mounted hitches are those which attach solely to the vehicle's bumper. Many states prohibit towing with this type of hitch, when it attaches to the vehicle's stock bumper, since it subjects the bumper to stresses for which it was not designed. Aftermarket rear step bumpers, designed for trailer towing, are acceptable for use with bumper mounted hitches.

Frame mounted hitches can be of the type which bolts to two or more points on the frame, plus the bumper, or just to several points on the frame. Frame mounted hitches can also be of the tongue type, for Class I towing, or, of the receiver type, for classes II and III.

Load equalizing hitches are usually used for large trailers. Most equalizing hitches are welded in place and use equalizing bars and chains to level the vehicle after the trailer is hooked up.

The bolt-on hitches are the most common, since they are relatively easy to install.

Check the gross weight rating of your trailer. Tongue weight is usually figured as 10% of gross trailer weight. Therefore, a trailer with a

Recommended Equipment Checklist

Equipment	Class I Trailers Under 2,000 pounds	Class II Trailers 2,000-3,500 pounds	Class III Trailers 3,500-6,000 pounds	Class IV Trailers 6,000 pounds and up
Hitch	Frame or Equalizing	Equalizing	Equalizing	Fifth wheel Pick-up truck only
Tongue Load Limit**	Up to 200 pounds	200-350 pounds	350-600 pounds	600 pounds and up
Trailer Brakes	Not Required	Required	Required	Required
Safety Chain	3/16" diameter links	1/4" diameter links	5/16" diameter links	—
Fender Mounted Mirrors	Useful, but not necessary	Recommended	Recommended	Recommended
Turn Signal Flasher	Standard	Constant Rate or heavy duty	Constant Rate or heavy duty	Constant Rate or heavy duty
Coolant Recovery System	Recommended	Required	Required	Required
Transmission Oil Cooler	Recommended	Recommended	Recommended	Recommended
Engine Oil Cooler	Recommended	Recommended	Recommended	Recommended
Air Adjustable Shock Absorbers	Recommended	Recommended	Recommended	Recommended
Flex or Clutch Fan	Recommended	Recommended	Recommended	Recommended
Tires	***	***	***	***

NOTE: The information in this chart is a guide. Check the manufacturer's recommendations for your car if in doubt.

  *Local laws may require specific equipment such as trailer brakes or fender mounted mirrors. Check your local laws. Hitch weight is usually 10-15% of trailer gross weight and should be measured with trailer loaded.

 **Most manufacturer's do not recommend towing trailers of over 1,000 pounds with compacts. Some intermediates cannot tow Class III trailers.

***Check manufacturer's recommendations for your specific car/ trailer combination.

 —Does not apply

maximum gross weight of 2,000 lb. will have a maximum tongue weight of 200 lb. Class I trailers fall into this category. Class II trailers are those with a gross weight rating of 2,000–3,500 lb., while Class III trailers fall into the 3,500–6,000 lb. category. Class IV trailers are those over 6,000 lb. and are for use with fifth wheel trucks, only.

When you've determined the hitch that you'll need, follow the manufacturer's installation instructions, exactly, especially when it comes to fastener torques. The hitch will subjected to a lot of stress and good hitches come with hardened bolts. Never substitute an inferior bolt for a hardened bolt.

Wiring

Wiring the car for towing is fairly easy. There are a number of good wiring kits available and these should be used, rather than trying to design your own. All trailers will need brake lights and turn signals as well as tail lights and side marker lights. Most states require extra marker lights for overly wide trailers. Also, most states have recently required back-up lights for trailers, and most trailer manufacturers have been building trailers with back-up lights for several years.

Additionally, some Class I, most Class II and just about all Class III trailers will have electric brakes.

Add to this number an accessories wire, to operate trailer internal equipment or to charge the trailer's battery, and you can have as many as seven wires in the harness.

Determine the equipment on your trailer and buy the wiring kit necessary. The kit will contain all the wires needed, plus a plug adapter set which included the female plug, mounted on the bumper or hitch, and the male plug, wired into, or plugged into the trailer harness.

When installing the kit, follow the manufacturer's instructions. The color coding of the wires is standard throughout the industry.

One point to note, some domestic vehicles, and most imported vehicles, have separate turn signals. On most domestic vehicles, the brake lights and rear turn signals operate with the same bulb. For those vehicles with separate turn signals, you can purchase an isolation unit so that the brake lights won't blink whenever the turn signals are operated, or, you can go to your local electronics supply house and buy four diodes to wire in series with the brake and turn signal bulbs. Diodes will isolate the brake and turn signals. The choice is yours. The isolation units are simple and quick to install, but far more expensive than the diodes. The diodes, however, require more work to install properly, since they re-

quire the cutting of each bulb's wire and soldering in place of the diode.

One, final point, the best kits are those with a spring loaded cover on the vehicle mounted socket. This cover prevent dirt and moisture from corroding the terminals. Never let the vehicle socket hang loosely. Always mount it securely to the bumper or hitch.

Cooling
ENGINE

One of the most common, if not THE most common, problems associated with trailer towing is engine overheating.

With factory installed trailer towing packages, a heavy duty cooling system is usually included. Heavy duty cooling systems are available as optional equipment on most car vehicles, with or without a trailer package. If you have one of these extra capacity systems, you shouldn't have any overheating problems.

If you have a standard cooling system, without an expansion tank, you'll definitely need to get an aftermarket expansion tank kit, preferably one with at least a 2 quart capacity. These kits are easily installed on the radiator's overflow hose, and come with a pressure cap designed for expansion tanks.

Another helpful accessory is a Flex Fan. These fan are large diameter units are designed to provide more airflow at low speeds, with blades that have deeply cupped surfaces. The blades then flex, or flatten out, at high speed, when less cooling air is needed. These fans are far lighter in weight than stock fans, requiring less horsepower to drive them. Also, they are far quieter than stock fans.

If you do decide to replace your stock fan with a flex fan, note that if your car has a fan clutch, a spacer between the flex fan and water pump hub will be needed.

Aftermarket engine oil coolers are helpful for prolonging engine oil life and reducing overall engine temperatures. Both of these factors increase engine life.

While not absolutely necessary in towing Class I and some Class II trailers, they are recommended for heavier Class II and all Class III towing.

Engine oil cooler systems consist of an adapter, screwed on in place of the oil filter, a remote filter mounting and a multi-tube, finned heat exchanger, which is mounted in front of the radiator or air conditioning condenser.

TRANSMISSION

An automatic transmission is usually recommended for trailer towing. Modern automatics have proven reliable and, of course, easy to operate, in trailer towing.

The increased load of a trailer, however, causes an increase in the temperature of the automatic transmission fluid. Heat is the worst enemy of an automatic transmission. As the temperature of the fluid increases, the life of the fluid decreases.

It is essential, therefore, that you install an automatic transmission cooler.

The cooler, which consists of a multi-tube, finned heat exchanger, is usually installed in front of the radiator or air conditioning compressor, and hooked inline with the transmission cooler tank inlet line. Follow the cooler manufacturer's installation instructions.

Select a cooler of at least adequate capacity, based upon the combined gross weights of the car and trailer.

Cooler manufacturers recommend that you use an aftermarket cooler in addition to, and not instead of, the present cooling tank in your car radiator. If you do want to use it in place of the radiator cooling tank, get a cooler at least two sizes larger than normally necessary.

NOTE: *A transmission cooler can, sometimes, cause slow or harsh shifting in the transmission during cold weather, until the fluid has a chance to come up to normal operating temperature. Some coolers can be purchased with or retrofitted with a temperature bypass valve which will allow fluid flow through the cooler only when the fluid has reached operating temperature, or above.*

HOW TO BUY A USED CAR

Many people believe that a two or three year old, or older, car is a better buy than a new one. This may be true. The new car suffers the heaviest depreciation in the first few years, but is not old enough to present a lot of costly repairs. Whatever the age of the used car you want to buy, this section and a little patience will help you select one that should be safe and dependable.

Shopping Tips

1. First, decide what model you want and how much you want to spend.

2. Check the used car lots and your local newspaper ads. Privately owned cars are usually less expensive, however, you will not get a warranty that, in most cases, comes with a used car purchased from a dealer.

3. Never shop at night. The glare of the lights makes it easy to miss defects in the paint and faults in the body caused by accident or rust repair.

4. Once you've found a car that you're interested in, try to get the name and phone number of the previous owner. Contact that person for details about the car. If he or she refuses information about the car, shop elsewhere. A private seller can tell you about the car and its maintenance history, but there are few laws requiring honesty from private citizens who are selling used vehicles. There are laws forbidding the tampering with or turning back a vehicle's odometer mileage reading. These laws apply to both a private seller as well commercial dealers. The law also requires that the seller, or anyone transferring ownership of a vehicle, must provide the buyer with a signed statement indicating the mileage on the odometer at the time of transfer.

5. Write down the year, model and serial number of the car before you buy it. Then, dial 1–800–424–9393, the toll-free number of the National Highway Traffic Safety Administration, and ask if the car has ever been included on any manufacturer's recall list. If so, make sure the necessary repairs were made.

6. Use the Used car Checklist in this section, and check all the items on the used car that you are considering. Some items are more important than others. You've already determined how much money you can afford for repairs, and, depending on the price of the car, you should consider doing some of the needed repairs yourself. Beware, however, of trouble in areas involving operation, safety or emissions. Problems in the Used car Checklist are arranged as follows:

1–8: Two or more problems in this segment indicate a lack of maintenance. You should reconsider your selection.

9–13: Indicates a lack of proper care, however, these can usually be corrected with a tune-up or relatively simple parts replacement.

14–17: Problems in the engine or transmission can be very expensive. Walk away from any car with problems in these areas.

7. If you are satisfied with the apparent condition of the car, take it to an independent diagnostic center or mechanic for a complete checkout. If your state has a state inspection program, have it inspected immediately before purchase, or specify on the invoice that purchase is conditional on the car's passing a state inspection.

8. Road test the car. Refer to the Road Test Checklist in this section. If your original evaluation, and the road test agree, the rest is up to you.

Used car Checklist

NOTE: *The numbers on the illustration correspond to the numbers in this checklist.*

1. **Mileage:** Average mileage is about 12,000 miles per year. More than average may indicate hard usage. Catalytic converter equipped models may need converter service beyond the 50,000 mile mark.

2. **Paint:** Check around the tailpipe, molding and windows for overspray, indicating that the car has been repainted.

3. **Rust:** Check fenders, doors, rocker panels, window moldings, wheelwells, flooring and in the bed, for signs of rust. Any rust at all will be a problem. There is no way to stop the spread of rust, except to replace the part or panel.

4. **Body Appearance:** Check the moldings, bumpers, grille, vinyl roof, glass, doors, tail gate and body panels for overall condition. Check for misalignment, loose holddown clips, ripples, scratches in the glass, rips or patches in the top. Mismatched paint, welding in the bed, severe misalignment of body panels or ripples may indicate crash work.

5. **Leaks:** Get down under the car and take a good look. There are no "normal" leaks, other than water from the air conditioning condenser drain tube.

6. **Tires:** Check the tire air pressure. A common trick is to pump the tires up hard to make the car roll more easily. Check the tread wear and the spare tire condition. Uneven wear is a sign that the front end is, or was, out of alignment. See the Troubleshooting Chapter for indications of treadwear.

7. **Shock Absorbers:** Check the shocks by forcing downward sharply on each corner of the car. Good shocks will not allow the car to rebound more than twice after you let go.

8. **Interior:** Check the entire interior. You're looking for an interior condition that agrees with the overall condition of the car. Reasonable wear can be expected, but be suspicious of new seatcovers on sagging seats, new pedal pads, and worn armrests. These indicate an attempt to cover up hard usage. Pull back the carpets and/or mats and look for signs of water leaks or flooding. Look for missing hardware, door handles, control knobs, etc. Check lights and signal operations. Make sure that all accessories, such as air conditioner, heater, radio, etc., work. Air conditioning, especially automatic temperature control units, can be very expensive to repair. Check the operation of the windshield wipers.

9. **Belts and Hoses:** Open the hood and check all belts and hoses for wear, cracks, or weak spots. Check around hose connections for stains, indicating leaks.

10. **Battery:** Low electrolyte level, corroded terminals and/or a cracked battery case, indicate a lack of maintenance.

11. **Radiator:** Look for corrosion or rust in the coolant, indicating a lack of maintenance.

12. **Air Filter:** A dirty air filter element indicates a lack of maintenance.

13. **Spark Plug Wires:** Check the wires for cracks, burned spots or wear. Worn wires will have to be replaced.

14. **Oil Level:** If the level is low, chances are that the engine either uses an excessive amount of oil, or leaks. If the oil on the dipstick

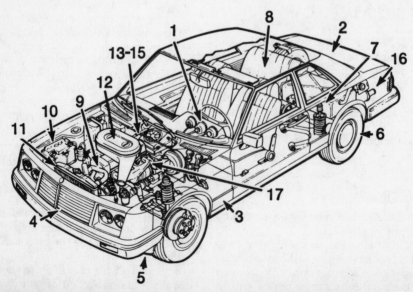

You should check these points when buying a used car. The "Used Car Checklist" gives an explanation of the numbered items

appears foamy or tan in color, a leakage of coolant into the oil is indicated. Stop here, and go elsewhere for your car. If the oil appears thin or has the smell of gasoline, stop here and go elsewhere for your car.

15. **Automatic Transmission:** Pull the transmission dipstick out when the engine is running in PARK. If the fluid is hot, the dipstick should read FULL. If the fluid is cold, the level will show about one pint low. The fluid itself should be bright red and translucent, with no burned odor. Fluid that is brown or black and has a burned odor is a sign that the transmission needs major repairs.

Capacities Chart
Gremlin, Hornet, Concord, Spirit

Year	Engine	Crankcase Incl. Filter (qt)	Transmission (pt.)				Drive Axle (pt.)	Fuel Tank (gal.)	Cooling System (qt)	
			3-sp	4-sp	5-sp	Auto			w/AC	wo/AC
1975	6-232	5.0	①	—	—	17.0	②	③	11.0	11.5
	6-258	5.0	①	—	—	17.0	②	③	11.0	11.5
	8-304	5.0	3.5	—	—	17.0	4.0	③	16.0	16.0
1976	6-232	5.0	①	—	—	17.0	②	③	11.0	11.5
	6-232	5.0	①	—	—	17.0	②	③	11.0	11.5
	8-304	5.0	3.5	—	—	17.0	4.0	③	16.0	16.0
1977	4-121	4.5	—	2.4	—	14.2	3.0	15.0	6.5	6.5
	6-232	5.0	3.5	3.5	—	17.0	3.0	③	11.0	④
	6-258	5.0	3.5	3.5	—	17.0	3.0	③	11.0	④
	8-304	5.0	3.5	—	—	17.0	4.0	③	16.0	16.0
1978	4-121	4.5	—	2.4	—	14.2	3.0	15.0	6.5	6.5
	6-232	5.0	3.0	3.5	—	17.0	3.0	③	11.0	14.0
	6-258	5.0	3.0	3.5	—	17.0	3.0	③	11.0	④
	8-304	5.0	3.0	—	—	17.0	4.0	③	18.0	18.0
1979	4-121	4.5	2.5	2.8	—	14.2	3.0	13.0	6.5	6.5
	6-232	5.0	2.5	2.8	—	17.0	②	21.0	11.0	14.0
	6-258	5.0	2.5	2.8	—	17.0	②	21.0	11.0	14.0
	8-304	5.0	2.5	2.8	—	17.0	②	21.0	18.0	18.0
1980	4-151	4.0	—	3.3	—	17.0	3.0	21.0	6.5	6.5
	6-258	5.0	—	3.3	—	17.0	3.0	21.0	11.0	11.0
1981	4-151	3.0	—	3.5	—	14.2	3.0	21.0	6.5	6.5
	6-258	5.0	—	3.5	—	17.0	3.0	21.0	11.0	14.0
1982	4-151	3.0	—	3.5	4.0	14.2	3.0	⑤	6.5	6.5
	6-258	5.0	—	3.5	4.0	17.0	3.0	⑤	11.0	14.5
1983	4-151	3.0	—	3.5	4.0	14.2	3.0	⑤	6.5	6.5
	6-258	5.0	—	3.5	4.0	17.0	3.0	⑤	11.0	14.5

① wo/overdrive: 3.5
  w/overdrive: 4.5
② 7⁹⁄₁₆″ ring gear: 3.0
  8⁷⁄₈″ ring gear: 4.0
③ Gremlin: 21
  Hornet & Concord: 22
④ Gremlin: 14.0
  Hornet & Concord: 11.5
⑤ Spirit: 21.0
  Concord: 22.0

Capacities Chart
Matador

| Year | Engine | Crank-case Incl. Filter (qt) | Transmission (pt.) | | | | Drive Axle (pt.) | Fuel Tank (gal.) | Cooling System (qt) | |
			3-sp	4-sp	5-sp	Auto			w/AC	wo/AC
1975	6-232	5.0	3.5	—	—	17.0	②	③	11.0	11.5
	6-258	5.0	3.5	—	—	17.0	②	③	11.0	11.5
	8-304	5.0	3.5	—	—	17.0	4.0	③	16.0	16.0
1976	6-258	5.0	3.5	—	—	17.0	4.0	③	①	①
	8-304	5.0	3.5	—	—	17.0	4.0	③	16.0	②
	8-360	5.0	—	—	—	19.0	4.0	③	④	④
	8-401	5.0	—	—	—	19.0	4.0	③	④	④
1977	6-258	5.0	—	—	—	17.0	4.0	③	①	①
	8-304	5.0	3.5	—	—	17.0	4.0	③	16.0	②
	8-360	5.0	—	—	—	19.0	4.0	③	④	④
1978	6-258	5.0	—	—	—	17.0	4.0	③	①	①
	8-304	5.0	3.5	—	—	16.4	4.0	③	16.0	②
	8-360	5.0	—	—	—	16.4	4.0	③	④	④

① Coupe: 14.0
   Sedan and SW: 11.0 wo/air cond.; 11.5 w/air cond.; 13.5 w/coolant recovery system
② 16.5 wo/coolant recovery; 19.5 w/coolant recovery
③ Sedan and SW: 21.5
   Coupe: 24.5
④ Coupe: 17.5
   Sedan and SW: 15.5 wo/air cond.; 15.5 w/air cond.; 18.5 w/coolant recovery system

Pacer

| Year | Engine | Crank-case Incl. Filter (qt) | Transmission (pt.) | | | | Drive Axle (pt.) | Fuel Tank (gal.) | Cooling System (qt) | |
			3-sp	4-sp	5-sp	Auto			w/AC	wo/AC
1975	6-232	5.0	①	—	—	17.0	3.0	22.0	11.0	11.5
	6-258	5.0	①	—	—	17.0	3.0	22.0	11.0	11.5
1976	6-232	5.0	①	3.5	—	17.0	3.0	22.0	14.0	14.0
	6-258	5.0	①	3.5	—	17.0	3.0	22.0	14.0	14.0
1977	6-232	5.0	3.5	3.5	—	17.0	3.0	22.0	14.0	14.0
	6-258	5.0	3.5	3.5	—	17.0	3.0	22.0	14.0	14.0
1978	6-232	5.0	3.0	3.5	—	17.0	3.0	20.0	14.0	14.0
	6-258	5.0	3.0	3.5	—	17.0	3.0	20.0	14.0	14.0
1979	6-258	5.0	2.5	2.8	—	17.0	3.0	21.0	14.0	14.0
1980	6-258	5.0	—	3.3	—	17.0	3.0	21.0	14.5	14.5

① wo/overdrive: 3.5
   w/overdrive: 4.5

Capacities Chart
Eagle

Year	Engine	Crank-case Incl. Filter (qt)	Transmission (pts.)			Transfer Case (pt.)	Drive Axle (pt.)		Fuel Tank (gal.)	Cooling System (qt)	
			4-sp	5-sp	Auto		Front	Rear		w/AC	wo/AC
1980	6-258	5.0	3.3	—	17.0	①	2.5	3.0	22.0	14.0	14.0
1981	4-151	4.0	3.5	—	14.2	4.0	2.5	3.0	22.0	6.5	6.5
	6-258	5.0	3.5	—	17.0	4.0	2.5	3.0	22.0	14.0	14.0
1982	4-151	3.0	3.5	4.0	17.0	6.0	2.5	3.0	②	6.5	6.5
	6-258	5.0	3.5	4.0	17.0	6.0	2.5	3.0	②	14.0	14.0
1983	4-151	3.0	3.5	4.0	14.2	6.0	2.5	3.0	②	6.5	6.5
	6-258	5.0	3.5	4.0	17.0	6.0	2.5	3.0	②	14.0	14.0
1984	4-150	4.0	3.5	4.0	17.0	6.0③	2.5	3.0	22.0	9.0	9.0
	6-258	5.0	3.5	4.0	17.0	6.0③	2.5	3.0	22.0	14.0	14.0
1985	6-258	5.0	3.5	4.0	17.0	6.0③	2.5	3.0	22.0	14.0	14.0
1986	6-258	5.0	3.5	4.0	17.0	6.0③	2.5	3.0	22.0	14.0	14.0

① Transfer cases built prior to 3/80: 3.0
  Transfer cases built after 3/80: 4.0
② Sedan and SW: 22.0
  SX/4 and Kammback: 21.0
③ Select-Shift housing: 5.0 oz

16. **Exhaust:** Check the color of the exhaust smoke. Blue smoke indicates excessive oil usage, usually due to major internal engine problems. Black smoke can indicate burned valves or carburetor problems. Check the exhaust system for leaks. A leaky system is dangerous and expensive to replace.

17. **Spark Plugs:** Remove one of the spark plugs. An engine in good condition will have spark plugs with a light tan or gray deposit on the electrodes. See the color Tune-Up section for a complete analysis of spark plug condition.

Road Test Check List

1. **Engine Performance:** The car should have good accelerator response, whether cold or warm, with adequate power and smooth acceleration through the gears.

2. **Brakes:** Brakes should provide quick, firm stops, with no squealing, pulling or fade.

3. **Steering:** Sure control with no binding, harshness or looseness, and no shimmy in the wheel should be encountered. Noise or vibration from the steering wheel means trouble.

4. **Clutch:** Clutch action should be quick and smooth with easy engagement of the transmission.

5. **Manual Transmission:** The transmission should shift smoothly and crisply with easy change of gears. No clashing and grinding should be evident. The transmission should not stick in gear, nor should there be any gear whine evident at road speed.

6. **Automatic Transmission:** The transmission should shift rapidly and smoothly, with no noise, hesitation or slipping. The transmission should not shift back and forth, but should stay in gear until an upshift or downshift is needed.

7. **Differential:** No noise or thumps should be present. No external leakage should be present.

8. **Driveshaft, Universal Joints:** Vibration and noise could mean driveshaft problems. Clicking at low speed or coast conditions means worn U-joints.

9. **Suspension:** Try hitting bumps at different speeds. A car that bounces has weak shock absorbers. Clunks mean worn bushings or ball joints.

10. **Frame:** Wet the tires and drive in a straight line. Tracks should show two straight lines, not four. Four tire tracks indicates a frame bent by collision damage. If the tires can't be wet for this purpose, have a friend drive along behind you and see if the car appears to be traveling in a straight line.

Preventive Maintenance Chart

1975–76

Interval	Item	Service
Every 5,000 miles	Engine oil and filter	Change
	Steering gear	Check level
	Power steering reservoir	Check level
	Heat riser	Lubricate
	Differentials	Check level
	Manual transmission	Check level
	Transfer case	Check level
	Automatic transmission	Check level
	All chassis lube fittings	EP chasis lube
	Drive belts	Check
	Air cleaner	Change filter
Every 10,000 miles	Driveshaft splines	EP chassis lube
Every 15,000 miles	Front and rear wheel bearings	Clean and repack
	U-joints	EP chassis lube
	Fuel filter	Replace
	PCV valve	Replace
	Oil filler cap	Clean
	Timing and dwell	Check
	Point, condenser, rotor	Replace
	Spark plugs	Replace
	EGR valve port	Clean
Every 25,000 miles	Automatic transmission	Change fluid and filter
Every 30,000 miles	Differentials	Change fluid
	Manual transmission	Change fluid
	Spark plug wires	Change

1977–79

Interval	Item	Service
Every 5,000 miles	Engine oil and filter	Change
	Steering gear	Check level
	Power steering reservoir	Check level
	Hear riser	Lubricate
	Differentials	Check level
	Manual transmission	Check level
	Transfer case	Check level
	Automatic transmission	Check level
	Drive belts	Check
	Air cleaner	Change filter
Every 10,000 miles	Driveshaft splines	EP chassis lube
Every 15,000 miles	All chassis lube fittings	EP chassis lube
	U-joints	EP chassis lube
	Fuel filter	Replace
	PCV valve	Replace
	Oil filler cap	Clean
	Timing and dwell	Check
	Point, condenser, rotor	Replace
	Spark plugs	Replace
	ERG valve port	Clean
Every 25,000 miles	Automatic transmission	Change fluid and filter
Every 30,000 miles	Differentials	Change fluid
	Manual transmission	Change fluid
	Spark plug wires	Change
	Front wheel bearings	Clean and repack

Preventive Maintenance Chart
1980–86

Interval	Item	Service
Every 5,000 miles	Engine oil and filter	Change
	Steering gear	Check level
	Power steering reservoir	Check level
	Heat riser	Lubricate
	Differentials	Check level
	Manual transmission	Check level
	Transfer case	Check level
	Automatic transmission	Check level
	Air cleaner	Change filter
	Drive belts	Check
Every 10,000 miles	Driveshaft splines	EP chassis lube
Every 15,000 miles	All chassis lube fittings	EP chassis lube
	U-joints	EP chassis lube
	Fuel filter	Replace
	PCV valve	Replace
	Oil filler cap	Clean
	Spark plugs	Replace
	EGR valve port	Clean
Every 25,000 miles	Automatic transmission	Change fluid and filter
Every 30,000 miles	Differentials	Change fluid
	Manual transmission	Change fluid
	Spark plug wires	Change
	Front wheel bearings	Clean and repack
	Transfer case	Change fluid

1987

Interval	Item	Service
Every 5,000 miles	Engine oil and filter	Change
	Steering gear	Check level
	Power steering reservoir	Check level
	Differentials	Check level
	Manual transmission	Check level
	Transfer case	Check level
	Automatic transmission	Check level
	Air cleaner	Change filter
	Drive belts	Check
Every 15,000 miles	All chassis lube fittings	EP chassis lube
	U-joints	EP chassis lube
	Fuel filter	Replace
	PCV valve	Replace
	Oil filler cap	Clean
	Spark plugs	Replace
Every 30,000 miles	Spark plug wires	Change
	Front wheel bearings	Clean and repack
Every 48,000 miles	Manual transmission	Change fluid
	Differentials	Change fluid
	Automatic transmission	Change fluid and filter
	Transfer case	Change fluid

Tune-Up and Performance Maintenance

Tune-up Specifications

Engine	Years	Spark Plugs Type	Gap (in.)	Distributor Point Gap (in.)	Dwell (deg.)	Ignition Timing (deg.) Man. Trans.	Auto. Trans.	Valve * Clearance In.	Exh.	Idle Speed MT	AT
4-121	1977	N-8L	0.035	0.018	47	12B	⑰	0.006–0.009	0.016–0.019	900	800
	1978	N-8L	0.035	0.018	47	12B	⑰	0.006–0.009	0.016–0.019	900	800
	1979	N-8L	0.035	0.018	47	12B	⑰	0.006–0.009	0.016–0.019	900	800
4-150	1984	RFN-14LY	0.035	Electronic		12B	12B	Hyd.	Hyd.	750	750
4-151	1980	R44TSX	0.060	Electronic		①	②	Hyd.	Hyd.	900	700
	1981	R44TSX	0.060	Electronic		③	④	Hyd.	Hyd.	900	700
	1982–83	R44TSX	0.060	Electronic		⑤	⑤	Hyd.	Hyd.	900	700
6-232	1975	N-12Y	0.035	Electronic		5B	5B	Hyd.	Hyd.	600	⑥
	1976	N-12Y	0.035	Electronic		8B	8B	Hyd.	Hyd.	850	⑥
	1977	N-12Y	0.035	Electronic		⑦	10B	Hyd.	Hyd.	⑧	⑥
	1978	N-13L	0.035	Electronic		8B	10B	Hyd.	Hyd.	600	550
	1979	N-13L	0.035	Electronic		8B	10B	Hyd.	Hyd.	600	550
6-258	1975	N-12Y	0.035	Electronic		3B	3B	Hyd.	Hyd.	600	⑥
	1976	N-12Y	0.035	Electronic		6B	8B	Hyd.	Hyd.	⑨	⑥
	1977	N-12Y	0.035	Electronic		⑩	⑪	Hyd.	Hyd.	600	⑥
	1978	1 bbl N-13L	0.035	Electronic		⑩	⑪	Hyd.	Hyd.	⑪	550
	1978	2 bbl N-13L	0.035	Electronic		6B	8B	Hyd.	Hyd.	600	600
	1979	1 bbl N-13L	0.035	Electronic		—	8B	Hyd.	Hyd.	—	700
	1979	2 bbl N-13L	0.035	Electronic		4B	8B	Hyd.	Hyd.	700	600
	1980	⑫	0.035	Electronic		6B	⑬	Hyd.	Hyd.	700	600
	1981	RFN-14LY	0.035	Electronic		⑭	⑮	Hyd.	hyd.	700	600
	1982–83	RFN-14LY	0.035	Electronic		⑯	⑯	Hyd.	Hyd.	750	650
	1984–87	RFN-14LY	0.035	Electronic		9B	9B	Hyd.	Hyd.	900	800
8-304	1975	N-12Y	0.035	Electronic		5B	5B	Hyd.	Hyd.	750	700

Tune-up Specifications

Engine	Years	Spark Plugs Type	Gap (in.)	Distributor Point Gap (in.)	Dwell (deg.)	Ignition Timing (deg.) Man. Trans.	Auto. Trans.	Valve * Clearance In.	Exh.	Idle Speed MT	AT
8-304	1976	N-12Y	0.035	Electronic		5B	⑱	Hyd.	Hyd.	750	700
	1977–78	N-12Y	0.035	Electronic		—	⑱	Hyd.	Hyd.	—	⑥
	1979	N-12Y	0.035	Electronic		5B	8B	Hyd.	Hyd.	800	600
8-360	1975	N-12Y	0.035	Electronic		5B	5B	Hyd.	Hyd.	750	700
	1976	N-12Y	0.035	Electronic		—	⑱	Hyd.	Hyd.	—	700
	1977	N-12Y	0.035	Electronic		—	⑱	Hyd.	Hyd.	—	⑥
	1978	N-12Y	0.035	Electronic		—	10B	Hyd.	Hyd.	—	⑲
8-401	1975	N-12Y	0.035	Electronic		5B	5B	Hyd.	Hyd.	750	700
	1976	N-12Y	0.035	Electronic		—	⑱	Hyd.	Hyd.	—	700

NOTE: The specifications on the underhood sticker often reflect changes made during production. If the specifications on your vehicle's sticker disagree with the specifications in this chart, use the sticker specifications.

*Valve clearance is set on a hot engine.

① Except California: 10B
  California: 12B
② Except California: 12B
  California: 10B
③ Eagle, exc. Calif.: 11B
  All other car models: 10B
④ Exc. Pacer and Calif. Eagle: 12B
  Pacer and Calif. Eagle: 8B
⑤ Eagle, except Calif.: 12B
  All California models: 8B
  All High Altitude models: 15B
  All other car models: 10B
⑥ Except Calif.: 550
  Calif.: 700
⑦ Except Calif.: 8B
  Calif.: 10B
⑧ Except Calif.: 600
  Calif.: 850
⑨ Matador Coupe and Sedan: 600
  All others: 850
⑩ Except High Altitude: 6B
  High Altitude: 10B
⑪ Except High Altitude: 8B
  High Altitude: 10B

⑫ Except Eagle: N-14LY
  Eagle: N-13L
⑬ Except Pacer and Calif. Eagle: 10B
  Pacer and Calif. Eagle: 8B
⑭ Concord and Spirit: 6B
  Eagle, except Calif. and High Altitude: 8B
  Calif., Eagles: 4B
  High Altitude Eagles: 15B
⑮ Concord and Spirit: 6B
  Eagle, except Calif. and High Altitude: 8B
  Calif. Eagles: 6B
  High Altitude Eagles: 15B
⑯ Concord and Spirit, except High Altitude: 15B
  High Altitude Concord and Spirit: 19B
  Eagle: 21B
⑰ Except Calif.: 12B
  Calif.: 8B
⑱ Except Calif.: 10B
  Calif.: 5B
⑲ Except Calif.: 600
  Calif.: 650

TUNE-UP PROCEDURES

In order to extract the full measure of performance and economy from your engine it is essential that it be properly tuned at regular intervals. A regular tune-up will keep your vehicle's engine running smoothly and will prevent the annoying minor breakdowns and poor performance associated with an untuned engine.

A complete tune-up should be performed every 12,000 miles or twelve months, whichever comes first. This interval should be halved if the vehicle is operated under severe conditions, such as trailer towing, prolonged idling, continual stop and start driving, or if starting or running problems are noticed. It is assumed that the routine maintenance described in Chapter 1 has been kept up, as this will have a decided effect on the results of a tune-up. All of the applicable steps of a tune-up should be followed in order, as the result is a cumulative one.

If the specifications on the tune-up sticker in the engine compartment disagree with the Tune-Up Specifications chart in this chapter, the figures on the sticker must be used. The sticker often reflects changes made during the production run.

Spark Plugs

Spark plugs ignite the air and fuel mixture in the cylinder as the piston reaches the top of the compression stroke. The controlled explosion

Troubleshooting Engine Performance

Problem	Cause	Solution
Hard starting (engine cranks normally)	• Binding linkage, choke valve or choke piston	• Repair as necessary
	• Restricted choke vacuum diaphragm	• Clean passages
	• Improper fuel level	• Adjust float level
	• Dirty, worn or faulty needle valve and seat	• Repair as necessary
	• Float sticking	• Repair as necessary
	• Faulty fuel pump	• Replace fuel pump
	• Incorrect choke cover adjustment	• Adjust choke cover
	• Inadequate choke unloader adjustment	• Adjust choke unloader
	• Faulty ignition coil	• Test and replace as necessary
	• Improper spark plug gap	• Adjust gap
	• Incorrect ignition timing	• Adjust timing
	• Incorrect valve timing	• Check valve timing; repair as necessary
Rough idle or stalling	• Incorrect curb or fast idle speed	• Adjust curb or fast idle speed
	• Incorrect ignition timing	• Adjust timing to specification
	• Improper feedback system operation	• Refer to Chapter 4
	• Improper fast idle cam adjustment	• Adjust fast idle cam
	• Faulty EGR valve operation	• Test EGR system and replace as necessary
	• Faulty PCV valve air flow	• Test PCV valve and replace as necessary
	• Choke binding	• Locate and eliminate binding condition
	• Faulty TAC vacuum motor or valve	• Repair as necessary
	• Air leak into manifold vacuum	• Inspect manifold vacuum connections and repair as necessary
	• Improper fuel level	• Adjust fuel level
	• Faulty distributor rotor or cap	• Replace rotor or cap
	• Improperly seated valves	• Test cylinder compression, repair as necessary
	• Incorrect ignition wiring	• Inspect wiring and correct as necessary
	• Faulty ignition coil	• Test coil and replace as necessary
	• Restricted air vent or idle passages	• Clean passages
	• Restricted air cleaner	• Clean or replace air cleaner filler element
	• Faulty choke vacuum diaphragm	• Repair as necessary
Faulty low-speed operation	• Restricted idle transfer slots	• Clean transfer slots
	• Restricted idle air vents and passages	• Clean air vents and passages
	• Restricted air cleaner	• Clean or replace air cleaner filter element
	• Improper fuel level	• Adjust fuel level
	• Faulty spark plugs	• Clean or replace spark plugs
	• Dirty, corroded, or loose ignition secondary circuit wire connections	• Clean or tighten secondary circuit wire connections
	• Improper feedback system operation	• Refer to Chapter 4
	• Faulty ignition coil high voltage wire	• Replace ignition coil high voltage wire
	• Faulty distributor cap	• Replace cap
Faulty acceleration	• Improper accelerator pump stroke	• Adjust accelerator pump stroke
	• Incorrect ignition timing	• Adjust timing
	• Inoperative pump discharge check ball or needle	• Clean or replace as necessary
	• Worn or damaged pump diaphragm or piston	• Replace diaphragm or piston

Troubleshooting Engine Performance (cont.)

Problem	Cause	Solution
Faulty acceleration (cont.)	• Leaking carburetor main body cover gasket	• Replace gasket
	• Engine cold and choke set too lean	• Adjust choke cover
	• Improper metering rod adjustment (BBD Model carburetor)	• Adjust metering rod
	• Faulty spark plug(s)	• Clean or replace spark plug(s)
	• Improperly seated valves	• Test cylinder compression, repair as necessary
	• Faulty ignition coil	• Test coil and replace as necessary
	• Improper feedback system operation	• Refer to Chapter 4
Faulty high speed operation	• Incorrect ignition timing	• Adjust timing
	• Faulty distributor centrifugal advance mechanism	• Check centrifugal advance mechanism and repair as necessary
	• Faulty distributor vacuum advance mechanism	• Check vacuum advance mechanism and repair as necessary
	• Low fuel pump volume	• Replace fuel pump
	• Wrong spark plug air gap or wrong plug	• Adjust air gap or install correct plug
	• Faulty choke operation	• Adjust choke cover
	• Partially restricted exhaust manifold, exhaust pipe, catalytic converter, muffler, or tailpipe	• Eliminate restriction
	• Restricted vacuum passages	• Clean passages
	• Improper size or restricted main jet	• Clean or replace as necessary
	• Restricted air cleaner	• Clean or replace filter element as necessary
	• Faulty distributor rotor or cap	• Replace rotor or cap
	• Faulty ignition coil	• Test coil and replace as necessary
	• Improperly seated valve(s)	• Test cylinder compression, repair as necessary
	• Faulty valve spring(s)	• Inspect and test valve spring tension, replace as necessary
	• Incorrect valve timing	• Check valve timing and repair as necessary
	• Intake manifold restricted	• Remove restriction or replace manifold
	• Worn distributor shaft	• Replace shaft
	• Improper feedback system operation	• Refer to Chapter 4
Misfire at all speeds	• Faulty spark plug(s)	• Clean or replace spark plug(s)
	• Faulty spark plug wire(s)	• Replace as necessary
	• Faulty distributor cap or rotor	• Replace cap or rotor
	• Faulty ignition coil	• Test coil and replace as necessary
	• Primary ignition circuit shorted or open intermittently	• Troubleshoot primary circuit and repair as necessary
	• Improperly seated valve(s)	• Test cylinder compression, repair as necessary
	• Faulty hydraulic tappet(s)	• Clean or replace tappet(s)
	• Improper feedback system operation	• Refer to Chapter 4
	• Faulty valve spring(s)	• Inspect and test valve spring tension, repair as necessary
	• Worn camshaft lobes	• Replace camshaft
	• Air leak into manifold	• Check manifold vacuum and repair as necessary
	• Improper carburetor adjustment	• Adjust carburetor
	• Fuel pump volume or pressure low	• Replace fuel pump
	• Blown cylinder head gasket	• Replace gasket
	• Intake or exhaust manifold passage(s) restricted	• Pass chain through passage(s) and repair as necessary
	• Incorrect trigger wheel installed in distributor	• Install correct trigger wheel

Troubleshooting Engine Performance (cont.)

Problem	Cause	Solution
Power not up to normal	• Incorrect ignition timing	• Adjust timing
	• Faulty distributor rotor	• Replace rotor
	• Trigger wheel loose on shaft	• Reposition or replace trigger wheel
	• Incorrect spark plug gap	• Adjust gap
	• Faulty fuel pump	• Replace fuel pump
	• Incorrect valve timing	• Check valve timing and repair as necessary
	• Faulty ignition coil	• Test coil and replace as necessary
	• Faulty ignition wires	• Test wires and replace as necessary
	• Improperly seated valves	• Test cylinder compression and repair as necessary
	• Blown cylinder head gasket	• Replace gasket
	• Leaking piston rings	• Test compression and repair as necessary
	• Worn distributor shaft	• Replace shaft
	• Improper feedback system operation	• Refer to Chapter 4
Intake backfire	• Improper ignition timing	• Adjust timing
	• Faulty accelerator pump discharge	• Repair as necessary
	• Defective EGR CTO valve	• Replace EGR CTO valve
	• Defective TAC vacuum motor or valve	• Repair as necessary
	• Lean air/fuel mixture	• Check float level or manifold vacuum for air leak. Remove sediment from bowl
Exhaust backfire	• Air leak into manifold vacuum	• Check manifold vacuum and repair as necessary
	• Faulty air injection diverter valve	• Test diverter valve and replace as necessary
	• Exhaust leak	• Locate and eliminate leak
Ping or spark knock	• Incorrect ignition timing	• Adjust timing
	• Distributor centrifugal or vacuum advance malfunction	• Inspect advance mechanism and repair as necessary
	• Excessive combustion chamber deposits	• Remove with combustion chamber cleaner
	• Air leak into manifold vacuum	• Check manifold vacuum and repair as necessary
	• Excessively high compression	• Test compression and repair as necessary
	• Fuel octane rating excessively low	• Try alternate fuel source
	• Sharp edges in combustion chamber	• Grind smooth
	• EGR valve not functioning properly	• Test EGR system and replace as necessary
Surging (at cruising to top speeds)	• Low carburetor fuel level	• Adjust fuel level
	• Low fuel pump pressure or volume	• Replace fuel pump
	• Metering rod(s) not adjusted properly (BBD Model Carburetor)	• Adjust metering rod
	• Improper PCV valve air flow	• Test PCV valve and replace as necessary
	• Air leak into manifold vacuum	• Check manifold vacuum and repair as necessary
	• Incorrect spark advance	• Test and replace as necessary
	• Restricted main jet(s)	• Clean main jet(s)
	• Undersize main jet(s)	• Replace main jet(s)
	• Restricted air vents	• Clean air vents
	• Restricted fuel filter	• Replace fuel filter
	• Restricted air cleaner	• Clean or replace air cleaner filter element
	• EGR valve not functioning properly	• Test EGR system and replace as necessary
	• Improper feedback system operation	• Refer to Chapter 4

TROUBLESHOOTING BASIC POINT-TYPE IGNITION SYSTEM PROBLEMS

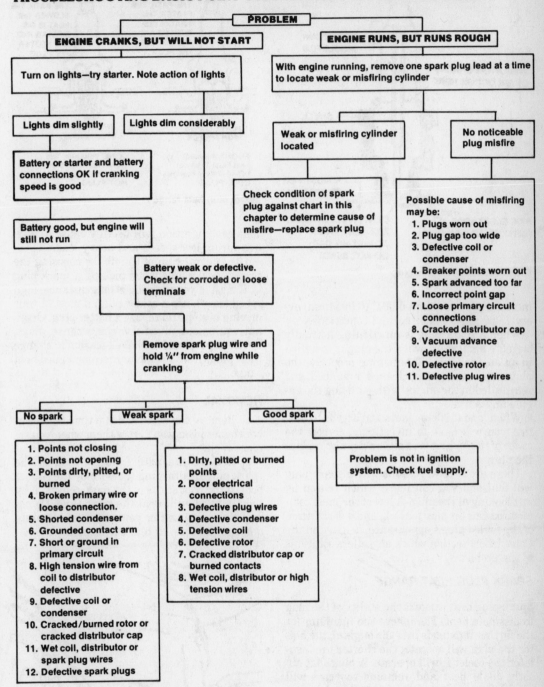

that results forces the piston down, turning the crankshaft and the rest of the drive train.

The average life of a spark plug is dependent on a number of factors; the mechanical condition of the engine; the type of fuel; driving conditions; and the driver.

When you remove the spark plugs, check their condition. They are a good indicator of the condition of the engine.

A small deposit of light tan or gray material on a spark plug that has been used for any period of time is to be considered normal. Additives in unleaded fuels may give a number of unusual color indications; for instance, MMT (a manganese anti-knock compound) will cause rust red deposits.

The gap between the center electrode and the side or ground electrode can be expected to

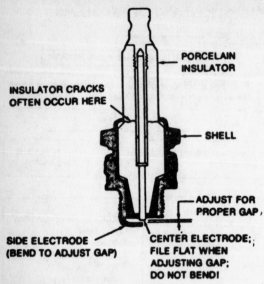

PORCELAIN INSULATOR

INSULATOR CRACKS OFTEN OCCUR HERE

SHELL

ADJUST FOR PROPER GAP

SIDE ELECTRODE (BEND TO ADJUST GAP)

CENTER ELECTRODE; FILE FLAT WHEN ADJUSTING GAP; DO NOT BEND!

Cross section of a spark plug

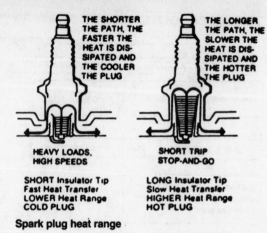

THE SHORTER THE PATH, THE FASTER THE HEAT IS DISSIPATED AND THE COOLER THE PLUG

THE LONGER THE PATH, THE SLOWER THE HEAT IS DISSIPATED AND THE HOTTER THE PLUG

HEAVY LOADS, HIGH SPEEDS

SHORT TRIP STOP-AND-GO

SHORT Insulator Tip
Fast Heat Transfer
LOWER Heat Range
COLD PLUG

LONG Insulator Tip
Slow Heat Transfer
HIGHER Heat Range
HOT PLUG

Spark plug heat range

increase not more than 0.001″ (0.0254mm) every 1,000 miles under normal conditions.

When a spark plug is functioning normally or, more accurately, when the plug is installed in an engine that is functioning properly, the plugs can be taken out, cleaned, regapped, and reinstalled in the engine without doing the engine any harm.

When, and if, a plug fouls and begins to misfire, you will have to investigate, correct the cause of the fouling, and either clean or replace the plug.

There are several reasons why a spark plug will foul and you can learn which reason by just looking at the plug. A few of the most common reasons for plug fouling, and a description of the fouled plug's appearance, is listed in the Color Insert section which also offers solutions to the problems.

SPARK PLUG HEAT RANGE

Spark plug heat range is the ability of the plug to dissipate heat. The longer the insulator (or the farther it extends into the engine), the hotter the plug will operate; the shorter the insulator the cooler it will operate. A plug that absorbs little heat and remains too cool will quickly accumulate deposits of oil and carbon since it is not hot enough to burn them off. This leads to plug fouling and consequently to misfiring. A plug that absorbs too much heat will have no deposits but, due to the excessive heat, the electrodes will burn away quickly and in some instances, preignition may result. Preignition takes place when plug tips get so hot that they glow sufficiently to ignite the fuel/air mixture before the actual spark occurs.

This early ignition will usually cause a pinging during low speeds and heavy loads.

The general rule of thumb for choosing the correct heat range when picking a spark plug is: if most of your driving is long distance, high speed travel, use a colder plug; if most of your driving is stop and to, use a hotter plug. Original equipment plugs are compromise plugs, but most people never have occasion to change their plugs from the factory recommended heat range.

REMOVAL

1. Remove the wires one at a time and number them so you won't cross them when you replace them.

2. Remove the wire from the end of the spark plug by grasping the wire by the rubber boot. If the boot sticks to the plug, remove it by twisting and pulling at the same time. Do not pull the wire itself or you will most certainly damage the core, or tear the connector.

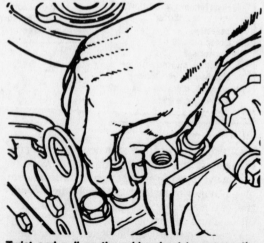

Twist and pull on the rubber boot to remove the spark plug wires; never pull on the wire itself

3. Use a spark plug socket to loosen all of the plugs about two turns.

4. If compressed air is available, blow off the area around the spark plug holes. Otherwise, use a rag or a brush to clean the area. Be careful not to allow any foreign material to drop into the spark plug holes.

5. Remove the plugs by unscrewing them the rest of the way from the engine.

INSPECTION

Check the plugs for deposits and wear. If they are not going to be replaced, clean the plugs thoroughly. Remember that any kind of deposit will decrease the efficiency of the plug. Plugs can be cleaned on a spark plug cleaning machine, which can sometimes be found in service stations, or you can do an acceptable job of cleaning with a stiff brush.

Check spark plug gap before installation. The ground electrode must be aligned with the center electrode and the specified size wire gauge should pass through the gap with a slight drag. If the electrodes are worn, it is possible to file them level.

INSTALLATION

1. Insert the plugs in the spark plug hole and tighten them hand tight. Take care not to crossthread them.

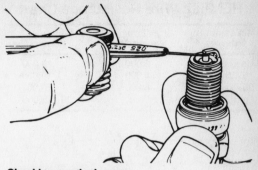

Checking spark plug gap

Plugs that are in good condition can be filed and re-used

2. Tighten the plugs to 11 ft.lb. on the 4-151; 25–30 ft.lb. on all other engines.

3. Install the spark plug wires on their plugs. Make sure that each wire is firmly connected to each plug.

CHECKING AND REPLACING SPARK PLUG CABLES

Visually inspect the spark plug cables for burns, cuts, or breaks in the insulation. Check the spark plug boots and the nipples on the distributor cap and coil. Replace any damages wiring. If no physical damage is obvious, the wires can be checked with an ohmmeter for excessive resistance.

When installing a new set of spark plug cables, replace the cables one at a time so there will be no mixup. Start by replacing the longest cable first. Install the boot firmly over the spark plug. Route the wire exactly the same as the original. Insert the nipple firmly into the tower on the distributor cap. Repeat the process for each cable.

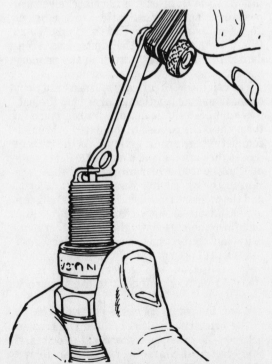

Bending the side electrode to adjust spark plug gap

HEI Plug Wire Resistance Chart

Wire Length (inches)	Minimum Ohms	Maximum Ohms
Up to 15	3,000	10,000
15–25	4,000	15,000
25–35	6,000	20,000
Over 35		25,000

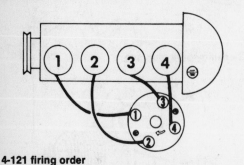

4-121 firing order

4-151 firing order

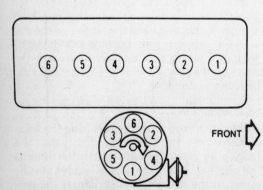

6-232, 258 firing order

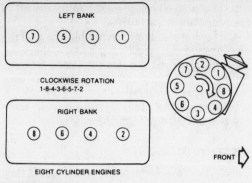

V8 firing order

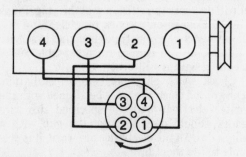

Distributor wiring and firing order: 4-150

Breaker Points and Condenser

The points function as a circuit breaker for the primary circuit of the ignition system. The ignition coil must boost the 12 volts of electrical pressure supplied by the battery to as much as 25,000 volts in order to fire the plugs. To do this, the coil depends on the points and the condenser to make a clean break in the primary circuit.

The coil has both primary and secondary circuits. When the ignition is turned on, the battery supplies voltage through the coil and onto the points. The points are connected to ground, completing the primary circuit. As the current passes through the coil, a magnetic field is created in the iron center core of the coil. As the cam in the distributor turns, the points open and the primary circuit collapses. The magnetic field in the primary circuit of the coil also collapses and cuts through the secondary circuit windings around the iron core. Because of the scientific phenomenon called electromagnetic induction, the battery voltage is increased to a level sufficient to fire the spark plugs.

When the points open, the electrical charge in the primary circuit jumps the gap created between the two open contacts of the points. If this electrical charge were not transferred elsewhere, the metal contacts of the points would melt and the gap between the points

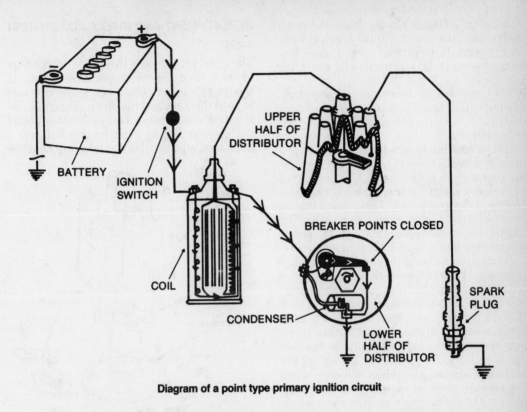

Diagram of a point type primary ignition circuit

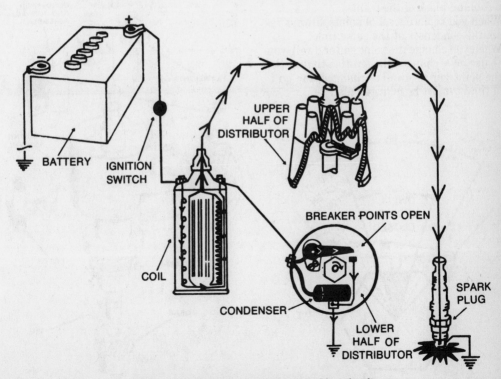

Diagram of a point type secondary ignition circuit

would start to change rapidly. If this gap is not maintained, the points will not break the primary circuit. If the primary circuit is not broken, the secondary circuit will not have enough voltage to fire the spark plugs.

The function of the condenser is to absorb excessive voltage from the points when they open and thus prevent the points from becoming pitted or burned.

It is interesting to note that the above cycle must be completed by the ignition system every time a spark plug fires. In a V8 engine, all of the spark plugs fire once for every two revolutions of the crankshaft. That means that in one revolution, 4 spark plugs fire. So, when the engine is at an idle speed of 800 rpm, the points are opening and closing 3,200 times a minute.

There are two ways to check the breaker point gap. It can be done with a feeler gauge or a dwell meter. Either way you set the points, you are basically adjusting the amount of time that the points remain open. The time is measured in degrees of distributor rotation. When you measure the gap between the breaker points with a feeler gauge, you are setting the maximum amount the points will open when the rubbing block on the points is on a high point of the distributor cam. When you adjust the points with a dwell meter, you are adjusting the number of degrees that the points will remain closed before they start to open as a high point of the distributor cam approaches the rubbing block of the points.

When you replace a set of points, always replace the condenser at the same time.

When you change the point gap or dwell, you will also have changed the ignition timing. So, if the point gap or dwell is changed, the ignition timing must be adjusted also.

REPLACEMENT AND DWELL ADJUSTMENT

4-121

The usual procedure is to replace the condenser each time the point set is replaced. Although this is not always necessary, it is easy to do at this time and the cost is negligible. Every time you adjust or replace breaker points, the ignition timing must be checked and, if necessary, adjusted. No special equipment oth-

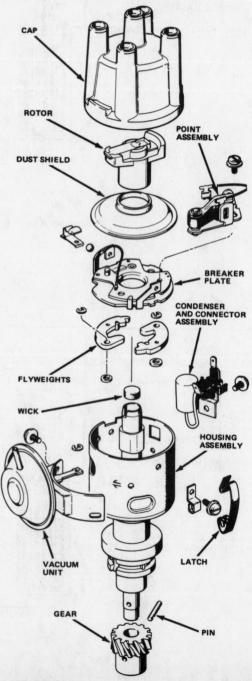

4-121 distributor

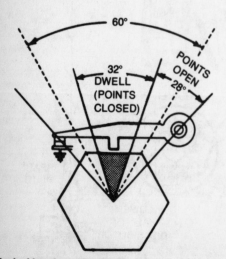

Typical breaker point dwell

NORMAL DWELL-NORMAL GAP

POINTS CLOSE — POINTS OPEN PLUGS FIRE

LARGE DWELL

SMALL GAP EXCESSIVE DWELL

SMALL DWELL

WIDE GAP INSUFFICIENT DWELL

Dwell angle

er than a feeler gauge is required for point replacement or adjustment, but a dwell meter is strongly advised.

1. Remove the distributor cap. You might have to unclip or detach some or all of the plug wires to remove the cap.

2. Clean the cap inside and out with a clean rag. Check for cracks and carbon paths. A carbon path shows up as a dark line, usually from one of the cap sockets inside terminals to a

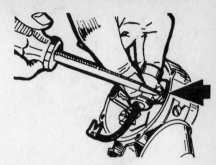

Removing the 4-121 condenser

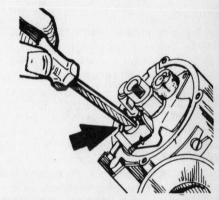

Removing the 4-121 ignition point holddown screws

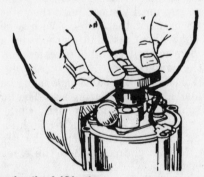

Removing the 4-121 rotor

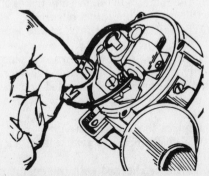

Removing the 4-121 ignition point wires

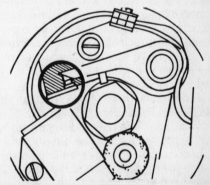

Once the points are installed, make certain that the contact surfaces are properly aligned. If there is misalignment, correct it by bending the STATIONARY arm, NOT THE MOVING ARM! Use a pair of needle-nosed pliers to bend the arm.

ground. Check the condition of the carbon button inside the center of the cap and the inside terminals. Replace the cap as necessary.

3. Pull the rotor up and off the shaft. Clean off the metal outer tip if it is burned or corroded. Don't file it. Replace the rotor as necessary or if one came with your tune-up kit.

4. The factory says that the points don't need to be replaced if metal transfer from one

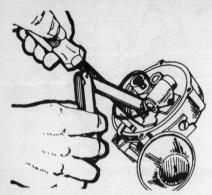

Adjusting the point gap on the 4-121

contact to the other doesn't exceed 0.020" (0.51mm). However, sad experience show that it is more economical and reliable in the long run to replace the point set while the distributor is open, than to have to do this at a later (and possible more inconvenient) time.

5. Pull off the two wire terminals from the point assembly. One wire comes from the condenser and the other comes from within the distributor. The terminals are usually held in place by spring tension only. There might be a clamp screw securing the terminals on some older versions. Loosen the point set holddown screw(s). Be very careful not to drop any of these little screws inside the distributor. If this happens, the distributor will probably have to be removed to get at the screw. If the holddown screw is lost elsewhere, it must be replaced with one that is no longer than the original to avoid interference with the distributor workings. Remove the point set, even if it is to be reused.

6. If the points are to be reused, clean them with a few strokes or a special point file. This is done with the points removed to prevent tiny metal filings getting into the distributor.

7. Loosen the condenser holddown screw and slide the condenser out of the clamp. This will save you a struggle with the clamp, condenser, and the tiny screw when you install the new one. If you have the type of clamp that is permanently fastened to the condenser, remove the screw and the condenser. Don't lose the screw.

8. Attend to the distributor cam lubricator. If you have the round kind, turn it around on its shaft at the first tune-up and replace it at the second. If you have the long kind, switch ends at the first tune-up and replace it at the second.

NOTE: *Don't oil or grease the lubricator. The foam is impregnated with a special lubricant.*

If you didn't get any lubricator at all, of if it

looks like someone took it off, don't worry. You don't really need it. Just rub a match head size dab of grease on the cam lobes.

9. Install the new condenser. If you left the clamp in place, just slide the new condenser into the clamp.

10. Replace the point set and leave the screw slightly loose. Replace the two wire terminals, making sure that the wired don't interfere with anything.

11. Check that the contacts meet squarely. If they don't, bend the tab supporting the fixed contact.

12. Turn the engine until a high point on the cam that opens the points contacts the rubbing block on the point arm. You can turn the engine by hand if you can get a wrench on the crankshaft pulley nut, or you can grasp the fan belt and turn the engine with the spark plugs removed.

CAUTION: *If you try turning the engine by hand, be very careful not to get your fingers pinched in the pulleys.*

On a stick shift car, you can push it forward in High gear. Another alternative is to bump the starter switch or use a remote starter switch.

13. There is a screwdriver slot near the contacts. Insert a screwdriver and lever the points open or closed until they appear to be at about the gap specified in the Tune-Up Specifications.

14. Insert the correct size feel gauge and adjust the gap until you can push the gauge in and out between the contacts with a slight drag, but without distributing the point arm. This operation takes a bit of experience to obtain the correct feel. Check by trying the gauges 0.001–0.002" (0.025–0.051mm) larger and smaller than the setting size. The larger one should disturb the point arm, while the smaller one should not drag at all. Tighten the point set holddown screw. Recheck the gap, because it often changes when the screw is tightened.

15. After all the point adjustments are complete, pull a white business card through (between) the contacts to remove any traces of oil. Oil will cause rapid contact burning.

NOTE: *You can adjust dwell at this point, if you wish. Refer to Step 18.*

16. Push the rotor firmly down into place. It will only go on one way. Tighten the V8 rotor screws. If the rotor is not installed properly, it will probably break when the starter is operated.

17. Replace the distributor cap.

18. If a dwell meter is available, check the dwell.

Dwell can be checked with the engine running or cranking. Decrease dwell by increasing the point gap; increase by decreasing the gap. Dwell angle is simply the number of degrees of distributor shaft rotation during which the points stay closed. Theoretically, if the point gap is correct, the dwell should also be correct or nearly so. Adjustment with a dwell meter produces more exact, consistent results since it is a dynamic adjustment. If dwell varies more than 3° from idle speed to 1,750 engine rpm, the distributor is worn.

19. If the engine won't start, check:

    a. That all the spark plug wires are in place.

    b. That the rotor has been installed.

    c. That the two (or three) wires inside the distributor are connected.

    d. That the points open and close when the engine turns.

    e. That the gap is correct and the holddown screw is tight.

20. After the first 200 miles or so on a new set of points, the point gap often closes up due to initial rubbing block wear. For best performance, recheck the dwell (or gap) at this time.

21. Since changing the gap affects the ignition point setting, the timing should be checked and adjusted as necessary after each point replacement or adjustment.

ELECTRONIC IGNITION

NOTE: *This book contains simple testing procedures for your car's electronic ignition. More comprehensive testing on this system and other electronic control systems on your car can be found in CHILTON'S GUIDE TO ELECTRONIC ENGINE CONTROLS, book part number 7535, available at your local retailer.*

American Motors Breakerless Inductive Discharge Ignition System

During the years 1975 through 1977, all American Motors built engines were equipped with the Breakerless Inductive Discharge (BID) ignition system. The system consists of an electronic ignition control unit, a standard type ignition coil, a distributor that contains an electronic sensor and trigger wheel instead of a cam, breaker points and condenser, and the usual high tension wires and spark plugs. There are no contacting (and thus wearing) surfaces between the trigger wheel and the sensor. The dwell angle remains the same and never requires adjustment. The dwell angle is determined by the control unit and the angle between the trigger wheel spokes.

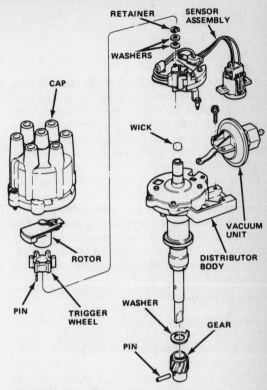

BID distributor

COMPONENTS

The AMC breakerless inductive discharge (BID) ignition system consists of five components:

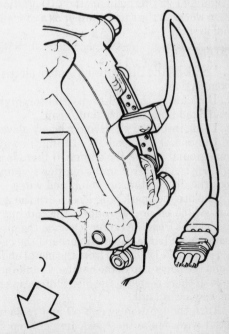

BID distributor sensor

Control unit
Coil
Breakerless distributor
Ignition cables
Spark plugs

The control unit is a solid state, epoxy sealed module with waterproof connectors. The control unit has a built-in current regulator, so no separate ballast resistor or resistance wire is needed in the primary circuit. Battery voltage is supplied to the ignition coil positive (+) terminal when the ignition key is turned to the ON or START position; low voltage coil primary current is also supplied by the control unit. In place of the points, cam, and condenser, the distributor has a sensor and trigger wheel. The sensor is a small coil which generates an electromagnetic field when excited by the oscillator in the control unit. This system was last used in 1977.

OPERATION

When the ignition switch is turned on, the control unit is activated. The control unit then sends an oscillating signal to the sensor, which cause the sensor to generate a magnetic field. When one of the trigger wheel teeth enters this field, the strength of the oscillation in the sensor is reduced. One the strength drops to a predetermined level, a demodulator circuit operates the control unit's switching transistor. The switching transistor is wired in series with the coil primary circuit; it switches the circuit off, inducing high voltage in the coil secondary winding when it gets the demodulator signal. From this point on, the BID ignition system works in the same manner as a conventional system.

SYSTEM TEST

1. Check all the BID ignition system electrical connections.
2. Disconnect the coil-to-distributor high tension lead from the distributor cap.
3. Using insulated pliers and a heavy glove, hold the end of the lead ½" (12.7mm) away from a ground. Crank the engine. If there is a spark, the trouble is not in the ignition system. Check the distributor cap, rotor, and wires.
4. Replace the spark plug lead. Turn the ignition switch off and disconnect the coil high tension cable from the center tower on the distributor cap. Place a paper clip around the cable ½-¾" (12.7-19.05mm) from the metal end. Ground the paper clip to the engine. Crank the engine. If there is spark, the distributor cap or rotor may be at fault.
5. Turn the ignition switch off and replace the coil wire. Make the spark test of Step 3 again. If there is no spark, check the coil high

tension wire with an ohmmeter. It should show 5–10,000Ω resistance. If not, replace it and repeat the spark test.
6. Detach the distributor sensor lead wire plug. Check the wire connector by trying a no. 16 (0.177" [4.5mm]) drill bit for a snug fit in the female terminals. Apply a light coat of Silicone Dielectric Compound or its equivalent to the male terminals. Fill the female cavities ¼ full. Reconnect the plug.
7. Repeat the test of Step 4.
8. If there was a spark in Step 7, detach the sensor lead plug and try a replacement sensor. Try the test again. If there is a spark, the sensor was defective.
9. Connect a multitester with a volt scale, between the coil positive terminal and an engine ground. With the ignition switch on, the volt scale should read battery voltage. If it is lower, there is a high resistance between the battery (through the ignition switch) and the coil.
10. Connect the multitester between the coil negative terminal and an engine ground. With the ignition switch on, the voltage should be 5–8v. If not, replace the coil. If you get a battery voltage reading, crank the engine slightly to move the trigger wheel tooth away from the sensor; voltage should drop to 5–8v.
11. Check the sensor resistance by connecting an ohmmeter to its leads. Resistance should be 1.6–2.4Ω.

COIL TESTING

Test the coil with a conventional coil checker or an ohmmeter. Primary resistance should be 1.25–1.40Ω and secondary resistance should be 9–12KΩ. The open output circuit should be more than 20 kilovolts. Replace the coil if it doesn't meet specifications.

DISTRIBUTOR OVERHAUL

NOTE: *If you must remove the sensor from the distributor for any reason, it will be necessary to have the special sensor positioning gauge in order to align it properly during installation.*

Disassembly

1. Scribe matchmarks on the distributor housing, rotor, and engine block. Disconnect the leads and vacuum lines from the distributor. Remove the distributor. Unless the cap is to be replaced, leave it connected to the spark plug cables and position it out of the way.
2. Remove the rotor and dust cap.
3. Place a small gear puller over the trigger wheel, so that its jaws grip the inner shoulders of the wheel and not its arms. Place a thick washer between the gear puller and the dis-

tributor shaft to act as a spacer; do not press against the smaller inner shaft.

4. Loosen the sensor holddown screw with a small pair of needlenosed pliers; it has a tamper proof head. Pull the sensor lead grommet out of the distributor body and pull out the leads from around the spring pivot pin.

5. Release the sensor securing spring by lifting it. Make sure that it clears the leads. Slide the sensor off the bracket. Remember, a special gauge is required for sensor installation.

6. Remove the vacuum advance unit securing screw. Slide the vacuum unit out of the distributor. Remove it only if it is to be replaced.

7. Clean the vacuum unit and sensor brackets. Lubrication of these parts is not necessary.

Assembly

1. Install the vacuum unit, if it was removed.

2. Assemble the sensor, sensor guide, flat washer, and retaining screw. Tighten the screw only far enough to keep the assembly together; don't allow the screw to project below the bottom of the sensor.

NOTE: *Replacement sensors come with a slotted head screw to aid in assembly. If the original sensor is being used, replace the tamperproof screw with a conventional one. Use the original washer.*

3. Secure the sensor on the vacuum advance unit bracket, making sure that the tip of the sensor is placed in the notch on the summing bar.

4. Position the spring on the sensor and route the leads around the spring pivot pin. Fit the sensor lead grommet into the slot on the distributor body. Be sure that the lead can't get caught in the trigger wheel.

5. Place the special sensor positioning gauge over the distributor shaft, so that the flat on the shaft is against the large notch on the gauge. Move the sensor until the sensor core fits into the small notch on the gauge. Tighten the sensor securing screw with the gauge in place (through the round hole in the gauge).

6. It should be possible to remove and install the gauge without any side movement of the sensor. Check this and remove the gauge.

7. Position the trigger wheel on the shaft. Check to see that the sensor core is centered between the trigger wheel legs and that the legs don't touch the core.

8. Bend a piece of 0.050" (1.27mm) gauge wire, so that it has a 90° angle and one leg ½" (12.7mm) long. Use the gauge to measure the clearance between the trigger wheel legs and the sensor boss. Press the trigger wheel on the

shaft until it just touches the gauge. Support the shaft during this operation.

9. Place 3 to 5 drops of SAE 20 oil on the felt lubricator wick.

10. Install the dust shield and rotor on the shaft.

11. Install the distributor on the engine using the matchmarks made during removal and adjust the timing. Use a new distributor mounting gasket.

American Motors Solid State Ignition (SSI) System

AMC introduced Solid State Ignition (SSI) as a running change on some 1977 Canadian models. It is standard equipment on all 1978 and later American Motors built engines.

The system consists of a sensor and toothed trigger wheel inside the distributor, and a permanently sealed electronic control unit which determines dwell, in addition to the coil, ignition wires, and spark plugs.

The trigger wheel rotates on the distributor shaft. As one of its teeth nears the sensor magnet, the magnetic field shifts toward the tooth. When the tooth and sensor are aligned, the magnetic field is shifted to its maximum, signaling the electronic control unit to switch off the coil primary current. This starts an elec-

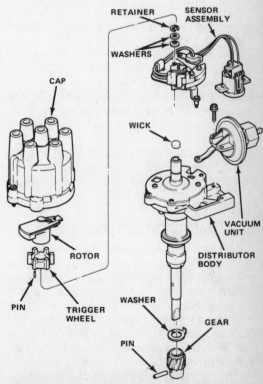

SSI distributor; 6 cylinder shown, the V8 is similar

tronic timer inside the control unit, which allows the primary current to remain off only long enough for the spark plug to fire. The timer adjusts the amount of time primary current is off according to conditions, thus automatically adjusting dwell. There is also a special circuit within the control unit to detect and ignore spurious signals. Spark timing is adjusted by both mechanical (centrifugal) and vacuum advance.

A wire of 1.35Ω resistance is spliced into the ignition feed to reduce voltage to the coil during running conditions. The resistance wire is bypassed when the engine is being started so that full battery voltage may be supplied to the coil. Bypass is accomplished by the I-terminal on the solenoid.

SECONDARY CIRCUIT TEST

1. Disconnect the coil wire from the center of the distributor cap.
NOTE: *Twist the rubber boot slightly in either direction, then grasp the boot and pull straight up. Do not pull on the wire, and do not use pliers.*
2. Hold the wire ½″ (12.7mm) from a ground with a pair of insulated pliers and a heavy glove. As the engine is cranked, watch for a spark.
3. If a spark appears, reconnect the coil wire. Remove the wire from one spark plug, and test for a spark as above.
CAUTION: *Do not remove the spark plug wires from cylinder 3 on the 4–150, or cylinder 3 or 5 on a 1977–79 6–258 or 1 or 5 on a 1980 and later 6–258, or cylinders 3 or 4 of an 8–360, when performing this test, as sensor damage could occur.*
4. If a spark occurs, the problem is in the fuel system or ignition timing. If no spark occurs, check for a defective rotor, cap, or spark plug wires.
5. If no spark occurs from the coil wire in Step 2, test the coil wire resistance with an ohmmeter. It should be 7,700–9,300Ω at +75°F (+24°C) or 12,000Ω maximum at +93°F (+34°C).

COIL PRIMARY CIRCUIT TEST

1. Turn the ignition On. Connect a multitester to the coil positive (+) terminal and a ground. If the voltage is 5.5–6.5 volts, go to Step 2. If above 7 volts, go to Step 4. If below 5.5 volts, disconnect the condenser lead and measure. If the voltage is now 5.5–6.5 volts, replace the condenser. If not, go to Step 6.
2. With the multitester connected as in Step 1, read the voltage with the engine cranking. If battery voltage is indicated, the circuit is okay. If not, go to Step 3.

3. Check for a short or open in the starter solenoid I-terminal wire. Check the solenoid for proper operation.
4. Disconnect the wire from the starter solenoid I-terminal, with the ignition On and the multitester connected as in Step 1. If the voltage drops to 5.5–6.5 volts, replace the solenoid. If not, connect a jumper between the coil negative (–) terminal and a ground. If the voltage drops to 5.5–6.5 volts, go to Step 5. If not, repair the resistance wire.
5. Check for continuity between the coil (–) terminal and D4, and D1 to ground. If the continuity is okay, replace the control unit. If not, check for an open wire and go back to Step 2.
6. Turn ignition Off. Connect an ohmmeter between the + coil terminal and dash connector AV. If above 1.40Ω, repair the resistance wire.
7. With the ignition Off, connect the ohmmeter between connector AV and ignition switch terminal 11. If less than 0.1Ω, replace the ignition switch or repair the wire, whichever is the cause. If above 0.1Ω, check connections, and check for defective wiring.

COIL TEST

1. Check the coil for cracks, carbon tracks, etc., and replace as necessary.
2. Connect an ohmmeter across the coil + and – terminals, with the coil connector removed. If 1.13–1.23Ω @ +75°F (+24°C), the coil is okay. If not, replace it.

CONTROL UNIT AND SENSOR TEST

1. With the ignition On, remove the coil high tension wire from the distributor cap and hold ½″ (12.7mm) from ground with insulated pliers. Disconnect the 4-wire connector at the control unit. If a spark occurs (normal), go to Step 2. If not, go to Step 5.
2. Connect an ohmmeter to D2 and D3. If the resistance is 400–800Ω (normal), go to Step 6. If not, go to Step 3.
3. Disconnect and reconnect the 3-wire connector at distributor. If the reading is now 400–800Ω, go to Step 6. If not, disconnect the 3-wire connector and go to Step 4.
4. Connect the ohmmeter across B2 and B3. If 300–800Ω, repair the harness between the 3-wire and 4-wire connectors. If not, replace the sensor.
5. Connect the ohmmeter between D1 and the battery negative terminal. If the reading is 0 (0.002Ω or less), go to Step 2. If above 0.002Ω, there is a bad ground in the cable or at the distributor. Repair the ground and retest.
6. Connect a multitester across D2 and D3. Crank the engine. If the needle fluctuates, the system is okay. If not, either the trigger wheel

is defective, or the distributor is not turning. Repair or replace as required.

IGNITION FEED TO CONTROL UNIT TEST

NOTE: *Do not perform this test without first performing the Coil Primary Circuit Test.*

1. With the ignition On, unplug the 2-wire connector at the module. Connect a multitester between F2 and ground. If the reading is battery voltage, replace the control unit and go to Step 3. If not, go to Step 2.

2. Repair the cause of the voltage reduction: either the ignition switch or a corroded dash connector. Check for a spark at the coil wire. If okay, stop. If not, replace the control unit and check for proper operation.

3. Reconnect the 2-wire connector at the control unit, and unplug the 4-wire connector at the control unit. Connect an ammeter between C1 and ground. If it reads 0.9–1.1 amps, the system is okay. If not, replace the module.

Delco High Energy Ignition (HEI) System — 4–151

The General Motors HEI system is a pulse triggered, transistor controlled, inductive discharge ignition system. The entire HEI system is contained within the distributor cap.

The distributor, in addition to housing the mechanical and vacuum advance mechanisms, contains the ignition coil (except on some inline six engines), the electronic control module, and the magnetic triggering device. The magnetic pick-up assembly contains a permanent magnet, a pole piece with internal teeth, and a pick-up coil (not to be confused with the ignition coil).

In the HEI system, as in other electronic ignition systems, the breaker points have been replaced with an electronic switch—a transistor, which is located within the control module. This switching transistor performs the same function the points did in a conventional ignition system; it simply turns coil primary current on and off at the correct time. Essentially then, electronic and conventional ignition systems operate on the same principle.

The module which houses the switching transistor is controlled (turned on and off) by a magnetically generated impulse induced in the pick-up coil. When the teeth of the rotating timer align with the teeth of the pole piece, the induced voltage in the pick-up coil signals the electronic module to open the coil primary circuit. The primary current then decreases, and a high voltage is induced in the ignition coil secondary windings, which is then directed through the rotor and spark plug wires to fire the spark plugs.

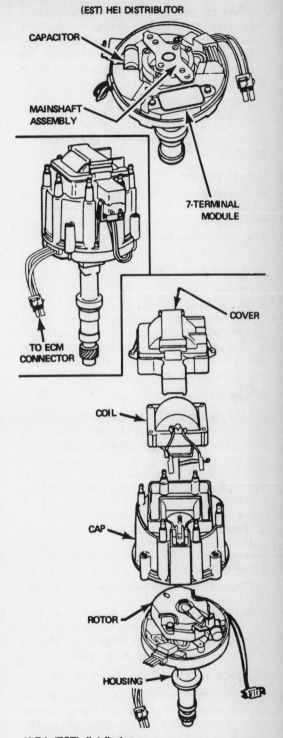

H.E.I. (EST) distributor

In essence, then, the pick-up coil module system simply replaces the conventional breaker points and condenser. The condenser found within the distributor is for radio suppression purposes only and has nothing to do with the ignition process. The module automatically controls the dwell period, increasing it with increasing engine speed. Since dwell is automatically controlled, it cannot be adjusted. The module itself is non-adjustable and non-repairable and must be replaced if found defective.

HEI SYSTEM PRECAUTIONS

Before going on to troubleshooting, it might be a good idea to take note of the following precautions.

Timing Light Use

Inductive pick-up timing lights are the best kind to use with HEI. Timing lights which connect between the spark plug and the spark plug wire occasionally (not always) give false readings.

Spark Plug Wires

The plug wires used with HEI systems are of a different construction than conventional wires. When replacing them, make sure you get the correct wires, since conventional wires won't carry the voltage. Also handle them carefully to avoid cracking or splitting them and never pierce them.

Tachometer Use

Not all tachometers will operate or indicate correctly when used on an HEI system. While some tachometers may give a reading, this does not necessarily mean the reading is correct. In addition, some tachometers hook up differently from others. If you can't figure out whether or not your tachometer will work on your truck, check with the tachometer manufacturer. Dwell readings have no significance at all.

HEI System Testers

Instruments designed specifically for testing HEI systems are available from several tool manufacturers. Some of these will even test the module itself. However, the test given in the following section will require only a multitester with volt and ohm scales.

TROUBLESHOOTING THE HEI SYSTEM

The symptoms of a defective component within the HEI system are exactly the same as those you would encounter in a conventional system. Some of these symptoms are:

Hard or no starting
Rough idle
Poor fuel economy
Engine misses under load or while accelerating

If you suspect a problem in the ignition system, there are certain preliminary checks which you should carry out before you begin to check the electronic portions of the system.

First, it is extremely important to make sure that the vehicle's battery is in good condition. A defective or poorly charged battery will cause the various components of the ignition system to read incorrectly when tested.

Second, make sure all of the wiring connections are clean and tight, not only at the battery, but also at the distributor cap, coil and module.

Since the major difference between electronic and point type ignition systems is in the distributor area, it is imperative to check the secondary ignition wires first. If the secondary system checks out okay, then the problem is probably not in the ignition system. To check the secondary system, perform a simple spark test. Remove on of the spark plug wires from the plug and insert a makeshift extension made of conductive metal, in the wire boot. Hold the wire and extension about ¼" (6.35mm) away from the block and crank the engine. If a normal spark occurs, then the problem is most likely not in the ignition system. Check for fuel system problems, or fouled spark plugs.

If, however, there is no spark or a weak spark, then further ignition system testing will have to be done. Troubleshooting techniques fall into two categories, depending on the nature of the problem. The categories are (1) Engine cranks, but won't start, and (2) Engine runs, but runs rough or cuts out.

Engine Fails to Start

If the engine won't start, perform a spark test as described earlier. If no spark occurs, check for the presence of normal battery voltage at the battery (BAT) terminal in the distributor cap. The ignition switch must be in the on position for this test. Either a multitester or a test light may be used for this test. Connect the test light wire to ground and the probe end to the BAT terminal at the distributor. If the light comes on, you have voltage to the distributor. If the light fails to come on, this indicates an open circuit in the ignition primary wiring leading to the distributor. In this case, you will have to check wiring continuity back to the ignition switch using test light. If there is battery voltage at the BAT terminal, but no spark at the plugs, then the problem lies within the distributor assembly. Go on to the distributor components test section.

Engine Runs, but Runs Roughly or Cuts Out

1. Make sure the plug wires are in good shape first. There should be no obvious cracks or breaks. You can check the plug wires with

an ohmmeter, but do not pierce the wires with a probe. Check the chart for the correct plug wire resistance.

2. If the plug wires are okay, remove the cap assembly, and check for moisture, cracks, chips, or carbon tracks, or any other high voltage leaks or failures. Replace the cap if you find any defects. Make sure the timer wheel rotates when the engine is cranked. If everything is all right so far, go on to the distributor components test section.

Distributor Components Testing

If the trouble has been narrowed down to the units within the distributor, the following tests can help pinpoint the defective component. An ohmmeter with both high and low ranges should be used. These tests are made with the cap assembly removed and the battery wire disconnected.

1. Connect an ohmmeter between the TACH and BAT terminals in the distributor cap. The primary coil resistance should be <1.0Ω (zero or nearly zero).

2. To check the coil secondary resistance, connect an ohmmeter between the rotor button and the BAT terminal. Then connect the ohmmeter between the ground terminal and the rotor button. The resistance in both cases should be between 6,000 and 30,000Ω.

3. Replace the coil only if the readings in steps 1 and 2 are infinite.

NOTE: *These resistance checks will not disclose shorted coil windings. This condition can be detected only with scope analysis or a suitably designed coil tester. If these instruments are unavailable, replace the coil with a known good coil as a final coil test.*

4. To test the pick-up coil, first disconnect the white and green module leads. Set the ohmmeter on the high scale and connect it between a ground and either the white or green lead. Any resistance measurement less than infinity requires replacement of the pick-up coil.

5. Pick-up coil continuity is tested by connecting the ohmmeter (on low range) between the white and green leads. Normal resistance is between 500 and 1500Ω. Move the vacuum advance arm while performing this test. This

will detect any break in coil continuity. Such a condition can cause intermittent misfiring. Replace the pick-up coil if the reading is outside the specific limits.

6. If no defects have been found at this time, and you still have a problem, then the module will have to be checked. If you do not have access to a module tester, the only possible alternative is a substitution test. If the module fails the substitution test, replace it.

COMPONENT REPLACEMENT

Integral Ignition Coil

1. Disconnect the feed and module wire terminal connectors from the distributor cap.
2. Remove the ignition set retainer.
3. Remove the 4 coil cover-to-distributor cap screws and coil cover.
4. Remove the 4 coil-to-distributor cap screws.
5. Using a blunt drift, press the coil wire spade terminals up out of distributor cap.
6. Lift the coil up out of the distributor cap.
7. Remove and clean the coil spring, rubber seal washer and coil cavity of the distributor cap.
8. Coat the rubber seal with a dielectric lubricant furnished in the replacement ignition coil package.
9. Reverse the above procedures to install.

Distributor Cap

1. Remove the feed and module wire terminal connectors from the distributor cap.
2. Remove the retainer and spark plug wires from the cap.
3. Depress and release the 4 distributor cap-

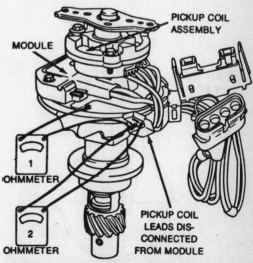

Ohmmeter 1 shows the connections for testing the pick-up coil. Ohmmeter 2 shows the connections for testing the pick-up coil continuity

HEI Plug Wire Resistance Chart

Wire Length (inches)	Minimum Ohms	Maximum Ohms
Up to 15	3,000	10,000
15–25	4,000	15,000
25–35	6,000	20,000
Over 35		25,000

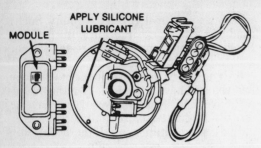

MODULE

APPLY SILICONE LUBRICANT

Module replacement; be sure to coat the mating surfaces with silicone lubricant

to-housing retainers and lift off the cap assembly.

4. Remove the 4 coil cover screws and cover.

5. Using a finger or a blunt drift, push the spade terminals up out of the distributor cap.

6. Remove all 4 coil screws and lift the coil, coil spring, and rubber seal washer out of the cap coil cavity.

7. Using a new distributor cap, reverse the above procedures to assembly, being sure to clean and lubricate the rubber seal washer with dielectric lubricant.

Rotor

1. Disconnect the feed and module wire connectors from the distributor.

2. Depress and release the 4 distributor cap to housing retainers and lift off the cap assembly.

3. Remove the two rotor attaching screws and rotor.

4. Reverse the above procedure to install.

Vacuum Advance

1. Remove the distributor cap and rotor as previously described.

2. Disconnect the vacuum hose from the vacuum advance unit.

3. Remove the two vacuum advance retaining screws, pull the advance unit outward, rotate, and disengage the operating rod from its tang.

4. Reverse the above procedure to install.

Module

1. Remove the distributor cap and rotor as previously described.

2. Disconnect the harness connector and pick-up coil spade connectors from the module. Be careful not to damage the wires when removing the connector.

3. Remove the two screws and module from the distributor housing.

4. Coat the bottom of the new module with dielectric lubricant supplied with the new module. Reverse the above procedure to install.

IGNITION TIMING

Ignition timing is the measurement, in degrees of crankshaft rotation, of the point at which the spark plugs fire in each of the cylinders. It is measured in degrees before or after Top Dead Center (TDC) of the compression stroke. Ignition timing is controlled by turning the distributor in the engine.

Ideally, the air/fuel mixture in the cylinder

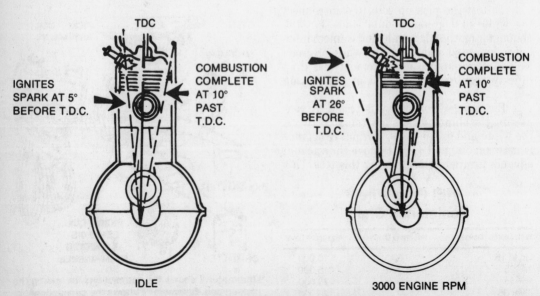

TDC

IGNITES SPARK AT 5° BEFORE T.D.C.

COMBUSTION COMPLETE AT 10° PAST T.D.C.

TDC

IGNITES SPARK AT 26° BEFORE T.D.C.

COMBUSTION COMPLETE AT 10° PAST T.D.C.

IDLE

3000 ENGINE RPM

Ignition timing at idle and at 3,000 rpm

will be ignited by the spark plug just as the piston passes TDC of the compression stroke. If this happens, this piston will be beginning the power stroke just as the compressed and ignited air/fuel mixture starts to expand. The expansion of the air/fuel mixture then forces the piston down on the power stroke and turns the crankshaft.

Because it takes a fraction of a second for the spark plug to ignite the gases in the cylinder, the spark plug must fire a little before the piston reaches TDC. Otherwise, the mixture will not be completely ignited as the piston TDC and the full benefit of the explosion will not be used by the engine. The timing measurement is given in degrees of crankshaft rotation before the piston reaches TDC (BTDC). If the setting for the ignition timing is 5° BTDC, the spark plug must fire 5° before that piston reaches TDC. This only holds true, however, when the engine is at idle speed.

As the engine speed increases, the pistons go faster. The spark plugs have to ignite the fuel even sooner if it is to be completely ignited when the piston reaches TDC. To do this, the distributor has a means to advance the timing of the spark as the engine speed increases. In some vehicles that were made before 1972, the advancing of the spark in the distributor was accomplished by weights alone. Others have a vacuum diaphragm to assist the weights. It is necessary to disconnect the vacuum line to the distributor when the engine is being timed.

If the ignition is set too far advanced (BTDC), the ignition and expansion of the fuel in the cylinder will occur too soon and tend to force the piston down while it is still traveling up. This causes engine ping. If the engine is too far retarded after TDC (ATDC), the piston will have already passed TDC and started on its way down when the fuel is ignited. This will cause the piston to be forced down for only a portion of its travel. This will result in poor engine performance and lack of power.

The timing is best checked with a timing light. This device is connected in series with the no. 1 spark plug. The current that fires the spark plug also causes the light to flash.

When the engine is running, the timing light is aimed at the marks on the engine and crankshaft pulley.

There are three basic types of timing lights available. The first is a simple neon bulb with two wire connections. One wire connects to the spark plug terminal and the other plugs into the end of the spark plug wire for the No. 1 cylinder, thus connecting the light in series with the spark plug. This type of light is pretty dim and must be held very close to the timing marks to be seen. Sometimes a dark corner has to be sought out to see the flash at all. This type of light is very inexpensive. The second type operates from the car battery – two alligator clips connect to the battery terminals, while an adapter enables a third clip to be connected to the No. 1 spark plug and wire. This type is a bit more expensive, but it provides a nice bright flash that you can see even in bright sunlight. It is the type most often seen in professional shops. The third type replaces the battery power source with 110 volt current.

NOTE: *Connect a tachometer to the BID or SSI ignition system in the conventional way; to the negative (distributor) side of the coil and to a ground. HEI distributor caps have a Tach terminal. Some tachometers may not work with a BID, SSI, or HEI ignition system and there is a possibility that some could be damaged. Check with the manufacturer of the tachometer to make sure it can be used.*

Timing should be checked at each tune-up and any time the points are adjusted or replaced. The timing marks consist of a notch on the rim of the crankshaft pulley and a graduated scale attached to the engine front (timing) cover. A stroboscopic flash (dynamic) timing light must be used, as a static light is too inaccurate for emission controlled engines.

IGNITION TIMING ADJUSTMENT

Point Type Ignition

NOTE: *Some early engines have 6v ignition systems. Make sure your tach/dwell and timing light have 6v capability.*

1. Locate the timing marks.
2. Clean off the timing marks so you can see them.
3. Mark the timing marks with a piece of

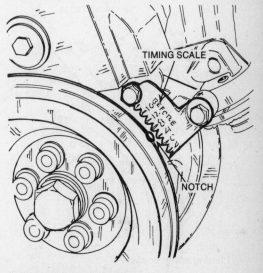

4-121 timing mark location

chalk or white paint. Mark the one on the engine that will indicate correct timing when it is aligned with the mark on the pulley or flywheel.

4. Attach a tachometer to the engine.

5. Attach a timing light according to the manufacturer's instructions. If the timing light has three wires, one is attached to the no. 1 spark plug lead with an adapter. The other two are connected to the battery. The red one goes to the positive side of the battery and the black one to the negative terminal.

6. Disconnect the vacuum line to the distributor at the distributor. Plug the end of the hose.

7. Check to make sure that all of the wires clear the fan and then start the engine.

8. If there is an idle speed solenoid, disconnect it.

9. Aim the timing light at the timing marks. If the marks that you put on the pulley and the engine are aligned, the timing is correct. Turn off the engine and remove the tachometer and the timing light. If the marks are not in alignment, proceed to the following steps.

10. Turn off the engine.

11. Loosen the distributor lockbolt just enough so that the distributor can be turned with a little effort.

12. Start the engine. Keep the cords of the timing light clear of the fan.

13. With the timing light aimed at the pulley and the marks on the engine, turn the distributor in the direction of rotor rotation to retard the spark, and in the opposite direction of rotor rotation to advance the spark. Line up the marks on the pulley and the engine.

14. When the marks are aligned, tighten the distributor lockbolt and recheck the timing with the timing light to make sure that the distributor did not move when you tightened the distributor lockbolt.

15. Turn off the engine and remove the timing light.

Electronic Ignition

1. Warm up the engine to normal operating temperature. Stop the engine and connect the timing light to the No. 1 (left front on V8, front on four or six) spark plug wire. Clean off the timing marks and mark the pulley notch and timing scale with white chalk.

2. Disconnect and plug the vacuum line at the distributor. This is done to prevent any distributor vacuum advance.

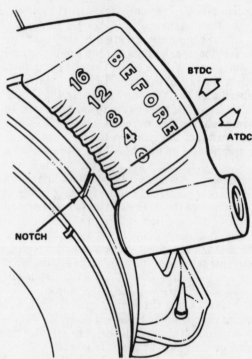

6-232, 258 timing mark location

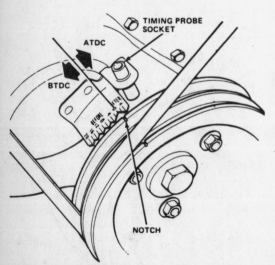

4-151 timing mark location

V8 timing mark location

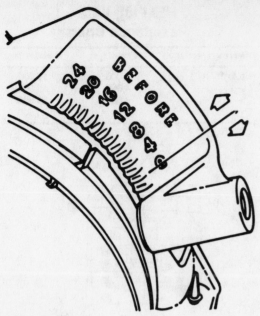

4-150 timing marks

3. Start the engine and adjust the idle to 500 rpm with the carburetor idle speed screw on 1975–77 vehicles. On 1978 and later models, set the idle speed to the figure shown on the underhood sticker. This is done to prevent any distributor centrifugal advance. If there is a throttle stop solenoid, disconnect it electrically.

4. Aim the timing light at the pointer marks. Be careful not to touch the fan, because it may appear to be standing still. If the pulley notch isn't aligned with the proper timing mark (refer to the Tune-Up Specifications chart), the timing will have to be adjusted.

NOTE: *TDC or Top Dead Center corresponds to 0°. B, or BTDC, or Before Top Dead Center, may be shown as A for Advanced on a V8 timing scale. R on a V8 timing scale means Retarded, corresponding to ATDC, or After Top Dead Center.*

5. Loosen the distributor clamp locknut. You can buy trick wrenches that make this task a lot easier. Turn the distributor slowly to adjust the timing, holding it by the base and not the cap. Turn counterclockwise to advance timing (toward BTDC), and clockwise to retard (toward TDC or ATDC).

6. Tighten the locknut. Check the timing again, in case the distributor moved slightly as you tightened it.

7. Replace the distributor vacuum line and correct the idle speed to that specified in the Tune-Up Specifications chart.

8. Stop the engine and disconnect the timing light.

VALVE LASH

4-121

Valve adjustment is one factor which determines how far the intake and exhaust valves open into the cylinder. If the valve clearance is too large, part of the lift of the camshaft will be used in removing the excessive clearance, therefore the valves will not open far enough. This has two ill effects; one, the valve gear will become noisy as the excess clearance is taken up and, two, the engine will perform poorly. This is because intake valves which don't open the full distance will admit a smaller air/fuel mixture into the cylinders. Exhaust valves which aren't opening the full amount create a greater back pressure in the cylinder which prevents the proper air/fuel mixture from entering the cylinder.

If the valve clearance is too small, the intake and exhaust valves will not fully seat on the cylinder head when they close. When a valve seats on the cylinder head it does two things; it seals the combustion chamber so that none of the gases in the cylinder can escape and it cools itself by transferring some of the heat absorbed from the combustion process through the cylinder head and into the cooling system. Therefore, if the valve clearance is too small, the engine will run poorly (due to gases escaping from the combustion chamber), and the valves will overheat and eventually warp (since they cannot properly transfer heat unless they fully seat on the cylinder head).

While all valve adjustments must be as accurate as possible, it is better to have the valve adjustment slightly loose than tight, as burned valves can result from too tight an adjustment.

The valves are operated by an overhead camshaft, driven by a toothed rubber belt, connected to the crankshaft. The cam lobes contact 'bucket' type tappets, which are set over the valve and valve springs, and force the valve and springs to move downward, moving the valve from its seat on the cylinder head. Both intake and exhaust valves are manual adjusted by a wedge type screw angled into the tappet, perpendicular to the valve stem. A flat area is milled onto the screw, which contacts the valve stem end. The threaded area locks to a threaded area within the tappet. Each turn changes the clearance 0.002" (0.051mm). When tappet adjustment is done, the flat side of the adjusting screw must be toward the valve stem end at the completion of the adjustment.

ADJUSTMENT

NOTE: *Valve adjustment must be made with the engine at normal operating temperature.*

1. Remove the TAC hose, the cylinder head cover, the spark plug wires and distributor cap.

2. Rotate the crankshaft to bring the number one cylinder to TDC (the beginning of its firing stroke). The position of the distributor rotor will assist in determining this position.

NOTE: *There is a mark on the edge of the*

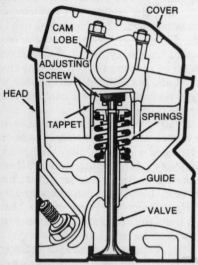

4-121 valve train

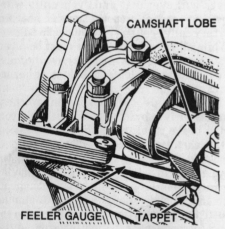

4-121 valve clearance measurement

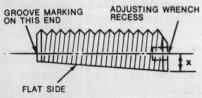

4-121 valve adjusting screw

HEI Plug Wire Resistance Chart

Wire Length (inches)	Minimum Ohms	Maximum Ohms
Up to 15	3,000	10,000
15–25	4,000	15,000
25–35	6,000	20,000
Over 35		25,000

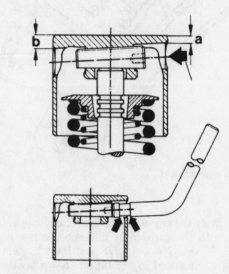

Adjuster mechanism on the 4-121

distributor housing at number one terminal position. Do not attempt to rotate the engine by turning the camshaft. Turn the crankshaft in the direction of normal rotation to avoid damage to the timing belt.

3. With number one cylinder on TDC of its firing stroke, the clearance of the exhaust valves on cylinders number one and three, and of the intake valves on cylinders number one and two, can be checked.

NOTE: *The front valve in each pair per cylinder is the intake valve. If the clearance requires adjustment, a special too is required to move the adjusting screw.*

4. Adjust the screw by turning one complete turn until it clicks, and continue until the proper clearance (0.006–0.009″ [0.15–0.22mm] for intake, and 0.016–0.019″ [0.40–0.48mm] for exhaust) is obtained.

5. After adjusting the clearance, use the special AMC gauge J-26860 to check the position of the screw in the tappet. If the gauge indicates the adjusting screw is turned too far into the tappet, the screw must be replaced. Five sizes of screws are available, identified by grooves on the end of the screws.

NOTE: *If the adjusting screws must be re-*

placed, *the tappets must be removed from the head. Note which tappets must be removed, then continue the adjustment procedure. When all eight adjustments are made, remove those tappets requiring screw replacement. Refer to camshaft removal and installation.*

6. Rotate the crankshaft 360°. The distributor rotor should be 180° opposite the mark on the distributor housing.

7. The clearance can now be checked on the exhaust valves for cylinders two and four, and the intake valve on cylinders three and four.

8. Reinstall the head cover, using a new gasket.

9. Reinstall the distributor cap and spark plug wiring. Reinstall the TAC flexible hose.

FUEL SYSTEM

This section contains only tune-up adjustment procedures for fuel systems. Descriptions, adjustments, and overhaul procedures for fuel system components can be found in the Fuel System section of Chapter 4.

Idle Speed and Mixture

Some of these adjustments procedures require that the air cleaner be kept in place. A flexible screwdriver will probably be needed to reach the carburetor screws.

4–121

The 4-cylinder engine uses a staged, two barrel carburetor. The primary barrel is smaller than the secondary barrel, and mechanical linkage progressively open the secondary barrel. Idle speed and mixture setting procedures are as follows:

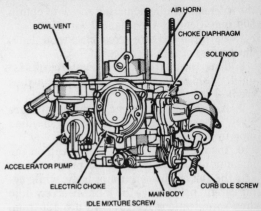

5210 2-bbl carburetor adjustments

NOTE: *To compensate for temperature and fuel variations, while performing idle mixture adjustments, don't idle the engine over three minutes at a time. If settings are not completed within three minutes, operate the engine at 2,000 rpm for one minute. Repeat as necessary until the proper adjustments are attained.*

1. Note position of the screw head slot in the limiter cap.

2. Remove the limiter cap by installing a sheet metal screw in the center of the cap and turning the screw clockwise.

3. Reset the idle screw to its approximate original position.

4. Attach a tachometer. Start engine and warm to operating temperature.

5. A throttle stop solenoid is used to adjust curb idle. With the solenoid wire connected, turn the adjusting screw of the solenoid in or out to obtain the specified setting of 30 rpm above the specified rpm.

6. Disconnect the solenoid wire and adjust

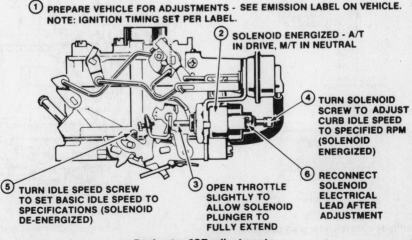

Rochester 2SE adjustments

the solenoid off idle adjusting screw to obtain 500 rpm. Connect the solenoid wire.

7. Turn the mixture screw clockwise (lean) until a loss of rpm is indicated.

8. Turn the mixture screw counterclockwise until the highest rpm reading is obtained at the best lean idle setting.

9. As a final adjustment, turn the mixture screw clockwise (leaner) until the specified drop in engine rpm is obtained.

10. Install a replacement limiter cap on the idle mixture screw, with the tab positioned inside the slot on the carburetor body, while being careful not to move the mixture screw. Idle drop specifications for 1977–78 are 120 rpm, except for high altitude manual transmission models (75 rpm). For 1979 models they are 120 for manual transmissions and 45 for automatic transmissions.

4-151

The air cleaner should be removed and associated vacuum hoses plugged, choke open, A/C compressor clutch wire disconnected (if equipped), and the deceleration valve supply hose plugged. Mixture is not adjustable.

1. Disconnect and plug the purge hose at the charcoal canister.

2. If equipped with a feedback system, connect a dwell meter to the single light blue wire which is taped to the mixture control solenoid wires at the carburetors. Set the meter on the six cylinder scale.

3. Connect a tachometer. There is a green wire above the heater fan motor for easy ta-chometer connection. Start the engine and allow it to reach normal operating temperature. On feedback models, the dwell meter should be fluctuating; the oscillation should be within 10° to 15° of needle movement. If not, the feedback system is not operating correctly and must be repaired.

4. Set the parking brake, shift automatic transmissions to Drive; if equipped with air conditioning, turn it on. Open the throttle to extend the solenoid plunger. Set idle speed by turning the solenoid idle screw. Turn off the A/C, if equipped.

5. Disconnect the anti-dieseling solenoid wire. Use the curb screw to adjust idle to specifications. Connect the solenoid wire.

1975–79 6-Cylinder and V8

Beginning with the 1977 models, special carburetors, incorporating an altitude compensating circuit to increase the air flow are used on cars that are sold for use at elevations above 4,000 feet. The single barrel YF-1 is manually adjusted for altitude while the two barrel 2150-2 had a automatic compensator system, controlled by an aneroid, which is sensitive to atmospheric pressures. At high altitudes, where the atmospheric pressure is lower, the aneroid expands and opens an altitude compensating valve, allowing extra air to enter the carburetor and lean our the fuel/air mixture.

NOTE: *The aneroid is factory calibrated an is not adjustable. With a change of altitude*

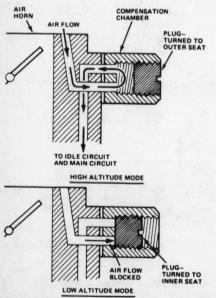

6 cylinder altitude compensator plug operation and adjustment

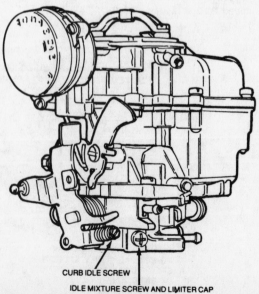

Carter YF carburetor adjustments

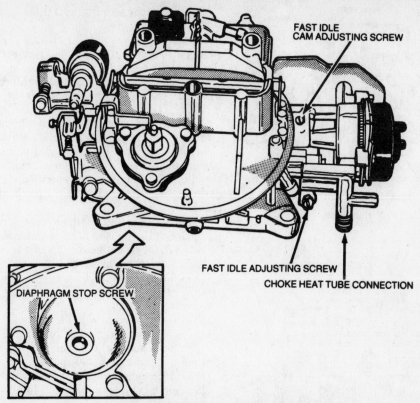

Autolite/Motorcraft 2100 left side

operation, ignition timing and carburetor adjustments must be reset on all models.

This adjustment is performed with the air cleaner installed. Do not allow the engine to idle more than three minutes at a time. If the idle/mixture adjustment is not completed by the end of three minutes, run the engine for one minute at 2,000 rpm. Return to the specified rpm and continue the adjustment.

1. Adjust the idle screw(s) to the full rich stop(s). Note the position of the screw head slot inside the limited cap slots.

2. Carefully remove the idle limiter cap(s) by installing a sheet metal screw in the center of the cap and turning clockwise. Discard the old caps. Return the screws to their original positions.

3. Install a tachometer on the engine.

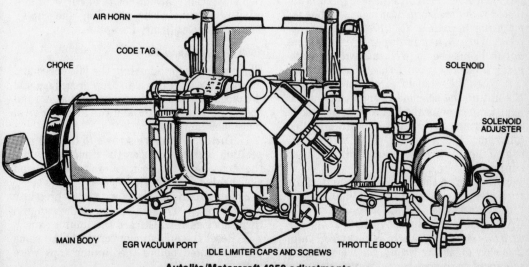

Autolite/Motorcraft 4350 adjustments

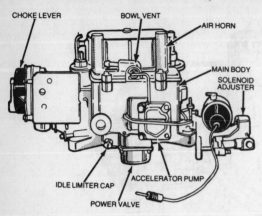

CHOKE LEVER · BOWL VENT · AIR HORN · MAIN BODY · SOLENOID ADJUSTER · IDLE LIMITER CAP · ACCELERATOR PUMP · POWER VALVE

Autolite/Motorcraft 2100 right side

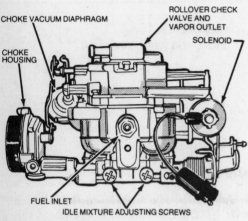

CHOKE VACUUM DIAPHRAGM · ROLLOVER CHECK VALVE AND VAPOR OUTLET · SOLENOID · CHOKE HOUSING · FUEL INLET · IDLE MIXTURE ADJUSTING SCREWS

BBD 2-bbl adjustments

4. Start the engine and allow it to reach normal operating temperature.

5. Adjust the idle speed to 30 rpm above the specified idle speed. See the Tune-Up Specifications chart.

NOTE: *On most engines the idle speed is adjusted with the throttle stop solenoid. Use the following procedure for idle speed adjustment. When setting idle speed, put the manual transmission in Neutral and the automatic transmission in Drive.*

a. With the solenoid wire connected, turn the nut on the solenoid plunger, idle speed adjusting screw, or the hex screw on the solenoid carriage in or out to obtain specified idle rpm.

b. Tighten the solenoid locknut, if so equipped.

c. Disconnect the solenoid wire and adjust curb idle speed screw to obtain 500 rpm.

d. Connect the solenoid wire.

CAUTION: *On the Carter BBD 2bbl., the curb idle and fast idle screws are side by side; it is easy to get the wrong one when setting idle speed on cars without a throttle stop sole-*

noid. *The screw for idle speed is the longer of the two.*

6. Starting from the full rich stop position, as noted in step 1, turn the mixture screw(s) clockwise (leaner) until the engine loses speed.

7. Turn the mixture screw(s) counterclockwise until the highest rpm reading is obtained.

NOTE: *On engines with two mixture screws, turn both the screws an equal number of turns unless the engine demands otherwise.*

8. If the idle speed has changed more than 30 rpm during the mixture adjustment, reset the idle to 30 rpm above the specified idle rpm as indicated in the 'Tune-Up Specifications' chart.

9. Turn the mixture adjustment screw(s) clockwise until the rpm drops as follows:
- 1975–76 6-cyl. automatic: 25 rpm
- 1975 6-cyl. manual: 25 rpm
- 1976 6-cyl. manual: 50 rpm
- 1975 6-cyl. manual w/EGR and catalytic converter: 35 rpm
- 1976 6-cyl. manual w/EGR: 50 rpm
- 1975–76 8-cyl. automatic: 20 rpm
- 1975 8-cyl. manual: 40 rpm
- 1976 8-cyl. manual: 100 rpm
- 1977–79 6-cyl. manual: 50 rpm
- 1977–78 6-cylinder automatic Matador: 175 rpm
- 1977–79 6-cyl. automatic high altitude: 25 rpm
- 1978–79 6-cyl. manual high altitude: 50 rpm
- 1978–79 6-cyl. 2-bbl automatic: 25 rpm
- 1977–79 6-cyl. 2-bbl manual: 50 rpm
- 1977–78 8-cyl. automatic: 20 rpm
- 1979 8-cyl. automatic: 40 rpm

10. Install new blue service idle limiter cap(s) over the idle mixture screw(s) with the limiter cap tang(s) positioned against the full rich stop(s). Be careful not to disturb the idle mixture setting while installing the cap(s). Press the cap(s) firmly into place.

1980 6-cylinder and V8

The procedure for adjusting the idle speed and mixture is called the lean drop procedure and is made with the engine operating at normal operating temperature and the air cleaner in place as follows:

1. Turn the mixture screws to the full rich position with the tabs on the limiters against the stops. Note the position of the screw head slot inside the limiter cap slots.

2. Remove the idle limiter caps by threading a sheet metal screw in center of the cap and turning clockwise. Discard the limiter caps.

3. Reset the adjustment screws to the same position noted before the limiter caps were removed.

4. Start the engine and allow it to reach normal operating temperature.

5. Adjust the idle speed to 30 rpm above the specified rpm. See the Tune-Up Specifications chart. On 6-cylinder engines with a throttle stop solenoid, turn the solenoid in or out to obtain the specified rpm. On V8 engines with a throttle stop solenoid, turn the hex screw on the throttle stop solenoid carriage to obtain the specified rpm. This is done with the solenoid wire connected. Tighten the solenoid locknut, if so equipped. Disconnect the solenoid wire and adjust the curb idle speed screw to obtain an idle speed of 500 rpm. Reconnect the solenoid wire.

6. Starting from the full rich stop position, as was determined before the limiter caps were removed, turn the mixture adjusting screws clockwise (leaner) until a loss of engine speed is noticed.

7. Turn the screws counterclockwise (richer) until the highest rpm reading is obtained at the best lean idle setting. The best lean idle setting is on the lean side of the highest rpm setting without changing rpm.

8. If the idle speed changed more than 30 rpm during the mixture adjustment procedure, reset the idle speed to 30 rpm above the specified rpm with the idle speed adjusting screw or the throttle stop solenoid and repeat the mixture adjustment.

9. Install new limiter caps over the mixture adjusting screws with the tabs positioned against the full rich stops. Be careful not to disturb the idle mixture setting while installing the caps.

1981–82 6-cylinder and V8

Idle mixture screws on these carburetors are sealed with plugs or dowel pins. A mixture adjustment must be undertaken ONLY when the carburetor is overhauled, the throttle body replaced, or the engine does not meet required emission standards. Since expensive testing equipment is needed to properly set the mixture, only the idle speed adjusting procedure is given below.

NOTE: *The adjustment is made with the manual transmission in neutral and the automatic in drive. Therefore, make certain that the vehicle's parking brake is set firmly, and that the wheels are blocked. It may be a good idea to have someone in the vehicle with their foot on the brake.*

1. Connect a tachometer, start engine and warm it to normal operating temperature. The choke and intake manifold heater (6-cylinder engine only) must be off.

2. If the engine speed is not within the OK range, turn the curb idle adjustment screw to obtain the specified curb idle rpm.

3. For the 6-cylinder engine (BBD carburetor): Disconnect the vacuum hose from the vacuum actuator and holding solenoid wire connector. Adjust the curb (slow) idle speed adjustment screw to obtain the specified curb (slow) idle rpm, if it is not within the OK range. Refer to the Emission Control Information label, and the Tune-Up Specifications Chart. Apply a direct source of vacuum to the vacuum actuator. Turn the vacuum actuator adjustment screw on the throttle lever until the specified rpm is obtained (900 rpm for manual transmissions, and 800 rpm for automatic transmissions). Disconnect the manifold vacuum source from the vacuum actuator. With the jumper wire, apply battery voltage (12v) to energize the holding solenoid. Turn the A/C on, if equipped.

NOTE: *The throttle must be opened manually to allow the Sol-Vac throttle positioner to be extended.*

With the Sol-Vac throttle positioner extended, the idle speed should be 650 rpm for automatic transmission equipped vehicles and 750 rpm for manual transmission equipped vehicles. If the idle speed is not within tolerance, adjust the Sol-Vac (hex-head adjustment screw) to obtain the specified rpm. Remove the jumper wire from the Sol-Vac holding solenoid wire connector. Connect the Sol-Vac holding solenoid wire connector. Connect the original hose to the vacuum actuator.

4. For four and eight cylinder engines, turn the nut on the solenoid plunger or the hex screw on the solenoid carriage to obtain the specified idle rpm. Tighten the locknut, if equipped. Disconnect the solenoid wire connector and adjust the curb idle screw to obtain a 500 rpm idle speed. Connect the solenoid wire connector. If the model 2150 carburetor (8-cylinder engine), is equipped with a dashpot, fully depress the dashpot stem with the throttle at the curb idle position, and measure the clearance between the stem and throttle lever. The clearance should be 0.032″ (0.8128mm). Adjust it by loosening the locknut and turning the dashpot.

1983 4–150

1. Fully warm up the engine.

2. Check the choke fast idle adjustment: Disconnect and plug the EGR valve vacuum hose. Position the fast idle adjustment screw on the second step of the fast idle cam with the transmission in neutral. Adjust the fast idle speed to 2,000 rpm for manual transmission and 2,300 rpm for automatic transmission. Al-

low the throttle to return to normal curb idle
and reconnect the EGR vacuum hose.

3. To adjust the Sol-Vac Vacuum Actuator:
Remove the vacuum hose from the vacuum actuator and plug the hose. Connect an external
vacuum source to the actuator and apply 10–
15 in.Hg. of vacuum to the actuator. Shift the
transmission to Neutral. Adjust the idle speed
to the following rpm using the vacuum actuator adjustment screw on the throttle lever: 850
rpm for automatic transmission 950 rpm for
manual transmission. The adjustment is made
with all accessories turned off.

NOTE: *The curb idle should always be adjusted after vacuum actuator adjustment.*

4. To adjust the curb idle: Remove the vacuum hose from the Sol-Vac vacuum actuator
and plug the hose. Shift the transmission into
Neutral. Adjust the curb idle using the ¼"
(6.35mm) hex-head adjustment screw on the
end of the Sol-Vac unit. Set the speed to 750
rpm for manual transmission, 700 rpm for automatic transmission. Reconnect the vacuum
hose to the vacuum actuator.

NOTE: *Engine speed will vary 10–30 rpm
during this mode due to the closed loop fuel
control.*

5. To adjust the TRC (Anti-Diesel): The TRC
screw is preset at the factory and should not require adjustment. However, to check adjust-

ment, the screw should be ¾ turn from closed
throttle position.

1983–84 6–258

SOL-VAC VACUUM ACTUATOR ADJUSTMENT

1. Disconnect and plug the vacuum hose to
the Sol-Vac vacuum actuator.

2. Disconnect the Sol-Vac electrical connector. Connect an external vacuum source to the
vacuum actuator and apply 10–15 in.Hg. of
vacuum.

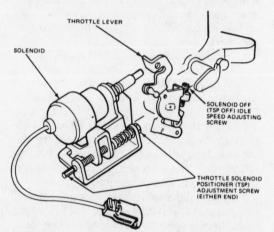

Location of idle speed adjustment—Motorcraft
2100, 2150, 4300, 4350 (all with TSP)

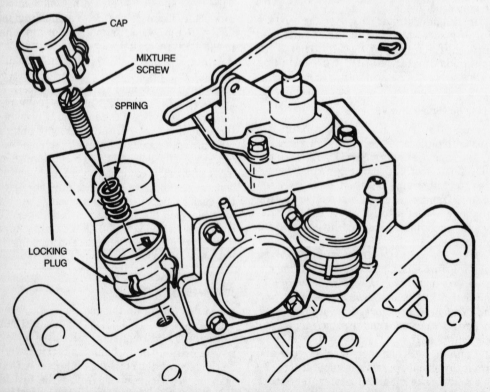

**Some 1980 and later 2150 models have 2-piece metal plugs and caps in place of plastic limiter caps on the
idle mixture adjusting screws. They should be carefully removed before attempting any adjustments.**

3. Open throttle for at least 3.0 seconds (1200 rpm); then close throttle.

4. Set the speed using the vacuum actuator adjustment screw on the throttle lever to obtain specified rpm.

5. Disconnect the external vacuum source. Reconnect the Sol-Vac vacuum hose and electrical connector.

SOL-VAC HOLDING SOLENOID ADJUSTMENT

NOTE: *The Sol-Vac vacuum actuator adjustment should always precede the Sol-Vac solenoid adjustment.*

1. Disconnect and plug the vacuum hose at the Sol-Vac vacuum actuator.

2. Disconnect the Sol-Vac electrical connector.

3. Energize the Sol-Vac holding solenoid with either of the two following methods:

    a. Apply battery voltage (12v) to the solenoid, or,

    b. Reconnect the Sol-Vac electrical connector and turn on the rear window defogger or turn on the air conditioner with the compressor disconnected.

4. Open throttle for at least 3.0 seconds (1,200 rpm) to allow the Sol-Vac holding solenoid to fully extend.

5. Set the speed using the ¼" (6.35mm) hex-head adjustment screw on the end of the Sol-Vac unit to obtain the specified rpm.

6. Reopen the throttle above 1,200 rpm to insure the correct holding position and reset the speed if necessary. Reconnect the vacuum hose to the Sol-Vac actuator. Reconnect the Sol-Vac electrical connector if disconnected.

1985–86
NOTE:

The carburetor choke and intake manifold heater must be off. This occurs when the engine coolant heats to approximately +160°F (71°C).

1. Have the engine at normal operating temperature. Connect a tachometer to the ignition coil negative (TACH) terminal.

2. Remove the vacuum hose from the Sol-Vac vacuum actuator unit. Plug the vacuum hose. Disconnect the holding solenoid wire connector.

3. Adjust the curb (slow) idle speed screw to obtain the correct curb idle speed. Refer to the specifications under Idle Speed or refer to the Emission Information label, under the hood, for the correct curb idle engine rpm.

4. Apply a direct source of vacuum to the vacuum actuator, using a hand vacuum pump or its equivalent. When the Sol-Vac throttle positioner is fully extended, turn the vacuum actuator adjustment screw on the throttler lever until the specified engine rpm is obtained. Disconnect the vacuum source from the vacuum actuator.

5. With a jumper wire, apply battery voltage (12v) to energize the holding solenoid.

NOTE: *The holding wire connector can be installed and either the rear window defroster or the air conditioner (with the compressor clutch wire disconnected) can be turned on to energize the holding solenoid.*

6. Hold the throttle open manually to allow the throttle positioner to fully extend.

NOTE: *Without the vacuum actuator, the throttle must be opened manually to allow the Sol-Vac throttle positioner to fully extend.*

7. If the holding solenoid idle speed is not within specifications, adjust the idle using the ¼" (6.35mm) hex-headed adjustment screw on the end of the Sol-Vac unit. Adjust to specifications.

8. Disconnect the jumper wire from the Sol-Vac holding solenoid wire connector, if used. Connect the wire connector to the Sol-Vac unit, if not connected. Install the original vacuum hose to the vacuum actuator.

9. Remove the tachometer and if disconnected, connect the compressor clutch wire. Install any other component that was previously removed.

Engine and Engine Overhaul

3

ENGINE ELECTRICAL

A conventional point-type ignition system is used on all 4–121 engines. All other engines are equipped with electronic ignition.

1975 through 1977 engines use the Breakerless Inductive Discharge (BID) ignition system. The system consists of an electronic ignition control unit, a standard type ignition coil, a distributor that contains an electronic sensor and trigger wheel instead of a cam, breaker points and condenser, and the usual high tension wires and spark plugs. There are no contacting (and thus wearing) surfaces between the trigger wheel and the sensor. The dwell angle remains the same and never requires adjustment. The dwell angle is determined by the control unit and the angle between the trigger wheel spokes. In 1978 the system was modified to include a different ignition module and dis-

Alternator and Regulator Specifications

Engine	Year	Alternator			Regulator	
		Manufacturer	Field Current @ 12V (amps)	Output (amps)	Manufacturer	Volts @ 75° F
4-121	1977–79	Delco-Remy	4.0–5.0	37 ③	Delco-Remy	13.7–14.2
4-150	1984	Delco-Remy	4.0–5.0	56 ①	Delco-Remy	13.9–14.9
4-151	1980–83	Delco-Remy	4.0–5.0	42 ②	Delco-Remy	12.0–15.5
6-232, 258	1975	Delco-Remy	1.8–2.5	37 ③	Delco-Remy	13.7–14.2
	1976–79	Delco-Remy	4.0–5.0	37 ②	Delco-Remy	12.0–15.5
6-258	1980–87	Delco-Remy	4.0–5.0	42 ②	Delco-Remy	13.9–14.9
8-304	1975	Motorola	1.8–2.5	37 ④	Motorola	12.7–15.3
	1976–77	Motorcraft	2.5–3.0	40 ⑤	Motorcraft	13.1–14.8
	1978–79	Delco-Remy	4.0–5.0	37 ②	Delco-Remy	12.0–15.5
8-360	1975	Motorola	1.8–2.5	37 ④	Motorola	12.7–15.3
	1976–77	Motorcraft	2.5–3.0	40 ⑤	Motorcraft	13.1–14.8
	1978	Delco-Remy	4.0–5.0	37 ②	Delco-Remy	12.0–15.5
8-401	1975	Motorola	1.8–2.5	37 ④	Motorola	12.7–15.3
	1976	Motorcraft	2.5–3.0	40 ⑤	Motorcraft	13.1–14.8

① Optional 68 and 78
② Optional 56, 63, 78 and 85
③ Optional 55 and 63
④ Optional 51 and 62
⑤ Optional 60
⑥ Optional 40 amp

Starter Specifications

Engine	Year	Manufacturer	Lock Test		Torque (ft. lb.)	No-Load Test			Brush Spring Tension (oz.)
			Amps	Volts		Amps	Volts	RPM	
4-121	1977–79	Bosch	Not Recommended			69	12.0	10,834	N.A.
4-150	1984	Delco	Not Recommended			67	12.0	8,500	30–40
4-151	1980–83	Delco	Not Recommended			70	9.0	11,900	N.A.
6-232, 6-258	1975–78	Autolite	600	3.4	13.0	65	12.0	9,250	35–40
6-258	1979–81	Motorcraft	Not Recommended			77	12.0	9,250	35–40
	1982–87	Motorcraft	Not Recommended			67	12.0	7,868	35–40
8-304	1975–79	Autolite	600	3.4	13.0	65	12.0	9,250	35–40
8-360	1975–78	Autolite	600	3.4	13.0	65	12.0	9,250	35–40
8-401	1975–76	Autolite	600	3.4	13.0	65	12.0	9,250	35–40

N.A.: Information Not Available

General Engine Specifications

Engine	Years	Fuel System Type	SAE net Horsepower @ rpm	SAE net Torque ft. lb. @ rpm	Bore x Stroke	Comp. Ratio	Oil Press. (psi.) @ 2000 rpm
4-121	1977–79	2-bbl	80 @ 5,000	105 @ 2,800	3.410 x 3.320	8.1:1	30
4-150	1984	1-bbl	83 @ 4,200	116 @ 2,600	3.876 x 3.188	9.2:1	40
4-151	1980–83	2-bbl	99 @ 4,000	134 @ 2,400	4.000 x 3.000	8.4:1	38
6-232	1975–78	1-bbl	100 @ 3,600	185 @ 1,800	3.750 x 3.500	8.0:1	50
6-258	1975–76	1-bbl	110 @ 3,500	195 @ 2,000	3.750 x 3.895	8.0:1	50
	1977–86	2-bbl	114 @ 3,600	196 @ 2,000	3.750 x 3.895	8.0:1	50
	1987	2-bbl	112 @ 3,000	210 @ 2,000	3.750 x 3.895	8.6:1	50
8-304	1975	2-bbl	150 @ 4,200	245 @ 2,500	3.750 x 3.753	8.4:1	50
	1976	2-bbl	120 @ 3,200	220 @ 2,200	3.750 x 3.753	8.4:1	50
	1977	2-bbl	121 @ 3,450	219 @ 2,000	3.750 x 3.753	8.4:1	50
	1978	2-bbl	130 @ 3,200	238 @ 2,000	3.750 x 3.753	8.4:1	50
	1979	2-bbl	125 @ 3,200	220 @ 2,400	3.750 x 3.753	8.4:1	50
8-360	1975	2-bbl	175 @ 4,000	285 @ 2,400	4.080 x 3.440	8.25:1	46
		4-bbl	195 @ 4,400	295 @ 2,900	4.080 x 3.440	8.25:1	46
		DE	220 @ 4,400	315 @ 3,100	4.080 x 3.440	8.25:1	46
	1976	2-bbl	140 @ 4,000	260 @ 2,400	4.080 x 3.440	8.25:1	46
		4-bbl	180 @ 4,400	280 @ 2,800	4.080 x 3.440	8.25:1	46
	1977	2-bbl	129 @ 3,700	245 @ 1,600	4.080 x 3.440	8.25:1	46
	1978	2-bbl	140 @ 3,350	278 @ 2,000	4.080 x 3.440	8.25:1	46
8-401	1975	4-bbl	255 @ 4,600	345 @ 3,300	4.165 x 3.680	8.25:1	46
	1976	4-bbl	215 @ 4,200	320 @ 2,800	4.165 x 3.680	8.25:1	46

1-bbl: one barrel carburetor
2-bbl: two barrel carburetor
DE: 4-bbl w/Dual Exhaust

Valve Specifications

Engine	Seat Angle (deg)	Face Angle (deg)	Spring Test Pressure (lbs. @ in.)	Spring Installed Height (in.)	Stem to Guide Clearance (in.)		Stem Diameter (in.)	
					Intake	Exhaust	Intake	Exhaust
4-121	45	45.33	①	②	0.0280–0.0330	0.0370–0.0410	0.3526–0.3531	0.3522–0.3528
4-150	45	44	212 @ 1.203	1.625	0.0010–0.0030	0.0010–0.0030	0.3110–0.3120	0.3110–0.3120
4-151	46	45	176 @ 1.250	1.660	0.0010–0.0027	0.0010–0.0027	0.3422	0.3422
6-232	③	④	⑤	⑥	0.0010–0.0030	0.0010–0.0030	0.3715–0.3725	0.3715–0.3725
6-258	③	④	⑦	⑧	0.0010–0.0030	0.0010–0.0030	0.3715–0.3725	0.3715–0.3725
8-304, 360, 401	③	④	218 @ 1.359 ⑨	1.812 ⑨	0.0010–0.0030	0.0010–0.0030	0.3715–0.3725	0.3715–0.3725

① Intake outer spring: 166.46 @ 1.30
   Intake inner spring: 39.02 @ 1.09
   Exhaust outer spring: 160.28 @ 1.32
   Exhaust inner spring: 37.15 @ 1.11
② Inner spring: 1.49
   Outer spring: 1.70
③ Intake: 30
   Exhaust: 44.5
④ Intake: 29
   Exhaust: 44
⑤ With rotators: 218 @ 1.875
   Without rotators: 195 @ 1.437
⑥ Intake: 1.786
   Exhaust: 2.110

⑦ 1975–76: with rotators, 218 @ 1.875
            without rotators: 195 @ 1.437
   1977–78: 208 @ 1.386
   1979–87: Intake, 195 @ 1.411
            Exhaust, 220 @ 1.188
⑧ 1975–78: 1.786
   1979–84: Intake, 1.786
            Exhaust, 1.625
   1985–87: 1.786
⑨ 1975–76 Police Special package for the 8-360 and 401:
   Intake: 270 @ 1.38
   Exhaust: 270 @ 1.19
   Installed height: 1.625

Camshaft Specifications

(All specifications in inches)

Engine	Journal Diameter					Bearing Clearance	Lobe Lift		End Play
	1	2	3	4	5		Int.	Exh.	
4-121	1.2579–1.2569	1.0220–1.0212	1.0220–1.0212	1.0220–1.0212	1.0220–1.0212	①	0.396	0.366	0.002–0.006
4-150	2.0300–2.0290	2.0200–2.0190	2.0100–2.0009	2.0000–1.9990	—	0.0010–0.0030	0.2650	0.2650	0
4-151	1.8690	1.8690	1.8690	—	—	0.0007–0.0027	0.3980	0.3980	0.0015–0.0050
6-232	2.0300–2.0290	2.0200–2.0190	2.0100–2.0090	2.0000–1.9990	—	0.0010–0.0030	0.2540	0.2540	0
6-258	2.0300–2.0290	2.0200–2.0190	2.0100–2.0090	2.0000–1.9990	—	0.0010–0.0030	②	②	0
8-304, 360, 401	2.1205–2.1195	2.0905–2.0895	2.0605–2.0595	2.0305–2.0295	2.0005–1.9995	0.0010–0.0030	0.2660 ③	0.2660 ③	0

① #1: 0.002–0.004
   #2–5: 0.002–0.003
② 1-bbl: 0.2540
   2-bbl thru 1984: 0.2480
   1985–87: 0.2531
③ 8-401: 0.286

Crankshaft and Connecting Rod Specifications
(All specifications in inches)

Engine	Crankshaft				Connecting Rod		
	Main Bearing Journal Dia.	Main Bearing Oil Clearance	Shaft End Play	Thrust on No.	Journal Dia.	Oil Clearance	Side Clearance
4-121	2.5177–2.5185	0.0012–0.0035	0.0039–0.0075	3	1.8701–1.9567	0.0009–0.0032	0.002–0.012
4-150	2.4996–2.5001	0.0010–0.0025	0.0015–0.0065	2	2.0934–2.0955	0.0010–0.0030	0.010–0.019
4-151	2.2988	0.0005–0.0022	0.0035–0.0085	5	1.8690	0.0007–0.0027	0.006–0.022
6-232	2.4986–2.5001	0.0010–0.0020	0.0015–0.0065	3	2.0934–2.0955	0.0010–0.0020	0.005–0.014
6-258	2.4986–2.5001	①	0.0015–0.0065	3	2.0934–2.0955	②	③
8-304, 360, 401	④	⑤	0.0030–0.0080	3	2.0934–2.0955	0.0010–0.0020	0.006–0.018

① 1975–80: 0.0010–0.0030
  1981: #1—0.0005–0.0026
       #2,3,4,5,6—0.0005–0.0030
       #7—0.0011–0.0035
  1982–87: 0.0010–0.0025
② 1975–76: 0.0010–0.0030
  1977–81: 0.0010–0.0025
  1982–87: 0.0010–0.0030

③ 1975–80: 0.005–0.014
  1981–87: 0.010–0.019
④ #1,2,3,4: 2.7474–2.7489
  #5: 2.7464–2.7479
⑤ #1,2,3,4—0.0010–0.0020
  #5—0.0020–0.0030

Piston and Ring Specifications
(All specifications in inches)

Engine	Ring Gap			Ring Side Clearance			Piston* Clearance
	#1 Compr.	#2 Compr.	Oil Control	#1 Compr.	#2 Compr.	Oil Control	
4-121	0.0098–0.0177	0.0098–0.0177	0.0098–0.0157	0.0012–0.0024	0.0012–0.0024	0.0012–0.0024	0.0007–0.0017
4-150	0.0100–0.0200	0.0100–0.0200	0.0100–0.0250	0.0017–0.0032	0.0017–0.0032	0.0010–0.0080	0.0009–0.0017
4-151	0.0027–0.0033	0.0090–0.0190	0.0150–0.0550	0.0025–0.0033	0.0025–0.0033	0.0025–0.0033	0.0025–0.0033
6-232	0.0100–0.0200	0.0100–0.0200	0.0150–0.0550	0.0015–0.0030	0.0015–0.0030	0.0010–0.0080	0.0009–0.0017
6-258	0.0100–0.0200	0.0100–0.0200	0.0100–0.0250	①	①	0.0010–0.0080	0.0009–0.0017
8-304	0.0100–0.0200	0.0100–0.0200	0.0100–0.0250	0.0015–0.0030	0.0015–0.0030	0.0011–0.0080	0.0010–0.0018
8-360	0.0100–0.0200	0.0100–0.0200	0.0150–0.0450	0.0015–0.0030	0.0015–0.0035	0.0000–0.0070	0.0012–0.0020 ②
8-401	0.0100–0.0200	0.0100–0.0200	0.0150–0.0550	0.0015–0.0030	0.0015–0.0035	0.0000–0.0070	0.0012–0.0020 ③

*Measured at the skirt
① 1975–80: 0.0015–0.0030
  1981–87: 0.0017–0.0032
② Police Special package: 0.0016–0.0024
③ Police Special package: 0.0014–0.0022

Torque Specifications
(All specifications in ft. lb.)

Engine	Cyl. Head	Conn. Rod	Main Bearing	Crankshaft Damper	Flywheel	Manifold Intake	Manifold Exhaust
4-121	65 cold 80 hot	41	①	181	65	18	18
4-150	80–90	30–35	75–85	75–85	50 ②	20–25	20–25
4-151	93–97	28–32	63–67	155–165	53–57	Bolt: 40 Nut: 30	Bolt: 40 Nut: 30
6-232	100–110	25–30	75–85	50–60	100–110	40–45	23–28
6-258	③	30–35	75–85	75–85	100–110	20–25	④
8-304	100–110	25–30	95–105	53–58	100–110	40–45	23–27
8-360	100–110	25–30	95–105	53–58	100–110	40–45	23–27
8-401	100–120	35–40	95–105	70–90	95–120	37–47	20–30

① #1–4: 58
#5: 47
② Plus a 60° turn
③ 1975–80: 105
1981–87: 85
④ 1975–79: 23
1980 and later (See illustration in text): Bolts #1 thru 11: 23
Bolts #12 & 13: 50

Troubleshooting Basic Charging System Problems

Problem	Cause	Solution
Noisy alternator	• Loose mountings • Loose drive pulley • Worn bearings • Brush noise • Internal circuits shorted (High pitched whine)	• Tighten mounting bolts • Tighten pulley • Replace alternator • Replace alternator • Replace alternator
Squeal when starting engine or accelerating	• Glazed or loose belt	• Replace or adjust belt
Indicator light remains on or ammeter indicates discharge (engine running)	• Broken fan belt • Broken or disconnected wires • Internal alternator problems • Defective voltage regulator	• Install belt • Repair or connect wiring • Replace alternator • Replace voltage regulator
Car light bulbs continually burn out— battery needs water continually	• Alternator/regulator overcharging	• Replace voltage regulator/alternator
Car lights flare on acceleration	• Battery low • Internal alternator/regulator problems	• Charge or replace battery • Replace alternator/regulator
Low voltage output (alternator light flickers continually or ammeter needle wanders)	• Loose or worn belt • Dirty or corroded connections • Internal alternator/regulator problems	• Replace or adjust belt • Clean or replace connections • Replace alternator or regulator

Troubleshooting Basic Starting System Problems

Problem	Cause	Solution
Starter motor rotates engine slowly	• Battery charge low or battery defective	• Charge or replace battery
	• Defective circuit between battery and starter motor	• Clean and tighten, or replace cables
	• Low load current	• Bench-test starter motor. Inspect for worn brushes and weak brush springs.
	• High load current	• Bench-test starter motor. Check engine for friction, drag or coolant in cylinders. Check ring gear-to-pinion gear clearance.
Starter motor will not rotate engine	• Battery charge low or battery defective	• Charge or replace battery
	• Faulty solenoid	• Check solenoid ground. Repair or replace as necessary.
	• Damage drive pinion gear or ring gear	• Replace damaged gear(s)
	• Starter motor engagement weak	• Bench-test starter motor
	• Starter motor rotates slowly with high load current	• Inspect drive yoke pull-down and point gap, check for worn end bushings, check ring gear clearance
	• Engine seized	• Repair engine
Starter motor drive will not engage (solenoid known to be good)	• Defective contact point assembly	• Repair or replace contact point assembly
	• Inadequate contact point assembly ground	• Repair connection at ground screw
	• Defective hold-in coil	• Replace field winding assembly
Starter motor drive will not disengage	• Starter motor loose on flywheel housing	• Tighten mounting bolts
	• Worn drive end busing	• Replace bushing
	• Damaged ring gear teeth	• Replace ring gear or driveplate
	• Drive yoke return spring broken or missing	• Replace spring
Starter motor drive disengages prematurely	• Weak drive assembly thrust spring	• Replace drive mechanism
	• Hold-in coil defective	• Replace field winding assembly
Low load current	• Worn brushes	• Replace brushes
	• Weak brush springs	• Replace springs

Troubleshooting Engine Mechanical Problems

Problem	Cause	Solution
External oil leaks	• Fuel pump gasket broken or improperly seated	• Replace gasket
	• Cylinder head cover RTV sealant broken or improperly seated	• Replace sealant; inspect cylinder head cover sealant flange and cylinder head sealant surface for distortion and cracks
	• Oil filler cap leaking or missing	• Replace cap
	• Oil filter gasket broken or improperly seated	• Replace oil filter
	• Oil pan side gasket broken, improperly seated or opening in RTV sealant	• Replace gasket or repair opening in sealant; inspect oil pan gasket flange for distortion
	• Oil pan front oil seal broken or improperly seated	• Replace seal; inspect timing case cover and oil pan seal flange for distortion

Troubleshooting Engine Mechanical Problems (cont.)

Problem	Cause	Solution
External oil leaks (cont.)	• Oil pan rear oil seal broken or improperly seated	• Replace seal; inspect oil pan rear oil seal flange; inspect rear main bearing cap for cracks, plugged oil return channels, or distortion in seal groove
	• Timing case cover oil seal broken or improperly seated	• Replace seal
	• Excess oil pressure because of restricted PCV valve	• Replace PCV valve
	• Oil pan drain plug loose or has stripped threads	• Repair as necessary and tighten
	• Rear oil gallery plug loose	• Use appropriate sealant on gallery plug and tighten
	• Rear camshaft plug loose or improperly seated	• Seat camshaft plug or replace and seal, as necessary
	• Distributor base gasket damaged	• Replace gasket
Excessive oil consumption	• Oil level too high	• Drain oil to specified level
	• Oil with wrong viscosity being used	• Replace with specified oil
	• PCV valve stuck closed	• Replace PCV valve
	• Valve stem oil deflectors (or seals) are damaged, missing, or incorrect type	• Replace valve stem oil deflectors
	• Valve stems or valve guides worn	• Measure stem-to-guide clearance and repair as necessary
	• Poorly fitted or missing valve cover baffles	• Replace valve cover
	• Piston rings broken or missing	• Replace broken or missing rings
	• Scuffed piston	• Replace piston
	• Incorrect piston ring gap	• Measure ring gap, repair as necessary
	• Piston rings sticking or excessively loose in grooves	• Measure ring side clearance, repair as necessary
	• Compression rings installed upside down	• Repair as necessary
	• Cylinder walls worn, scored, or glazed	• Repair as necessary
	• Piston ring gaps not properly staggered	• Repair as necessary
	• Excessive main or connecting rod bearing clearance	• Measure bearing clearance, repair as necessary
No oil pressure	• Low oil level	• Add oil to correct level
	• Oil pressure gauge, warning lamp or sending unit inaccurate	• Replace oil pressure gauge or warning lamp
	• Oil pump malfunction	• Replace oil pump
	• Oil pressure relief valve sticking	• Remove and inspect oil pressure relief valve assembly
	• Oil passages on pressure side of pump obstructed	• Inspect oil passages for obstruction
	• Oil pickup screen or tube obstructed	• Inspect oil pickup for obstruction
	• Loose oil inlet tube	• Tighten or seal inlet tube
Low oil pressure	• Low oil level	• Add oil to correct level
	• Inaccurate gauge, warning lamp or sending unit	• Replace oil pressure gauge or warning lamp
	• Oil excessively thin because of dilution, poor quality, or improper grade	• Drain and refill crankcase with recommended oil
	• Excessive oil temperature	• Correct cause of overheating engine
	• Oil pressure relief spring weak or sticking	• Remove and inspect oil pressure relief valve assembly
	• Oil inlet tube and screen assembly has restriction or air leak	• Remove and inspect oil inlet tube and screen assembly. (Fill inlet tube with lacquer thinner to locate leaks.)

Troubleshooting Engine Mechanical Problems (cont.)

Problem	Cause	Solution
Low oil pressure (cont.)	• Excessive oil pump clearance • Excessive main, rod, or camshaft bearing clearance	• Measure clearances • Measure bearing clearances, repair as necessary
High oil pressure	• Improper oil viscosity • Oil pressure gauge or sending unit inaccurate • Oil pressure relief valve sticking closed	• Drain and refill crankcase with correct viscosity oil • Replace oil pressure gauge • Remove and inspect oil pressure relief valve assembly
Main bearing noise	• Insufficient oil supply • Main bearing clearance excessive • Bearing insert missing • Crankshaft end play excessive • Improperly tightened main bearing cap bolts • Loose flywheel or drive plate • Loose or damaged vibration damper	• Inspect for low oil level and low oil pressure • Measure main bearing clearance, repair as necessary • Replace missing insert • Measure end play, repair as necessary • Tighten bolts with specified torque • Tighten flywheel or drive plate attaching bolts • Repair as necessary
Connecting rod bearing noise	• Insufficient oil supply • Carbon build-up on piston • Bearing clearance excessive or bearing missing • Crankshaft connecting rod journal out-of-round • Misaligned connecting rod or cap • Connecting rod bolts tightened improperly	• Inspect for low oil level and low oil pressure • Remove carbon from piston crown • Measure clearance, repair as necessary • Measure journal dimensions, repair or replace as necessary • Repair as necessary • Tighten bolts with specified torque
Piston noise	• Piston-to-cylinder wall clearance excessive (scuffed piston) • Cylinder walls excessively tapered or out-of-round • Piston ring broken • Loose or seized piston pin • Connecting rods misaligned • Piston ring side clearance excessively loose or tight • Carbon build-up on piston is excessive	• Measure clearance and examine piston • Measure cylinder wall dimensions, rebore cylinder • Replace all rings on piston • Measure piston-to-pin clearance, repair as necessary • Measure rod alignment, straighten or replace • Measure ring side clearance, repair as necessary • Remove carbon from piston

Valve actuating component noise	• Insufficient oil supply
	
	• Push rods worn or bent
	• Rocker arms or pivots worn
	
	• Foreign objects or chips in hydraulic tappets
	• Excessive tappet leak-down
	• Tappet face worn
	
	• Broken or cocked valve springs
		• Check for:
		  (a) Low oil level
		  (b) Low oil pressure
		  (c) Plugged push rods
		  (d) Wrong hydraulic tappets
		  (e) Restricted oil gallery
		  (f) Excessive tappet to bore clearance
		• Replace worn or bent push rods
		• Replace worn rocker arms or pivots
		• Clean tappets
		
		• Replace valve tappet
		• Replace tappet; inspect corresponding cam lobe for wear
		• Properly seat cocked springs; replace broken springs

Troubleshooting Engine Mechanical Problems (cont.)

Problem	Cause	Solution
Valve actuating component noise (cont.)	• Stem-to-guide clearance excessive	• Measure stem-to-guide clearance, repair as required
	• Valve bent	• Replace valve
	• Loose rocker arms	• Tighten bolts with specified torque
	• Valve seat runout excessive	• Regrind valve seat/valves
	• Missing valve lock	• Install valve lock
	• Push rod rubbing or contacting cylinder head	• Remove cylinder head and remove obstruction in head
	• Excessive engine oil (four-cylinder engine)	• Correct oil level

Troubleshooting the Cooling System

Problem	Cause	Solution
High temperature gauge indication— overheating	• Coolant level low	• Replenish coolant
	• Fan belt loose	• Adjust fan belt tension
	• Radiator hose(s) collapsed	• Replace hose(s)
	• Radiator airflow blocked	• Remove restriction (bug screen, fog lamps, etc.)
	• Faulty radiator cap	• Replace radiator cap
	• Ignition timing incorrect	• Adjust ignition timing
	• Idle speed low	• Adjust idle speed
	• Air trapped in cooling system	• Purge air
	• Heavy traffic driving	• Operate at fast idle in neutral intermittently to cool engine
	• Incorrect cooling system component(s) installed	• Install proper component(s)
	• Faulty thermostat	• Replace thermostat
	• Water pump shaft broken or impeller loose	• Replace water pump
	• Radiator tubes clogged	• Flush radiator
	• Cooling system clogged	• Flush system
	• Casting flash in cooling passages	• Repair or replace as necessary. Flash may be visible by removing cooling system components or removing core plugs.
	• Brakes dragging	• Repair brakes
	• Excessive engine friction	• Repair engine
	• Antifreeze concentration over 68%	• Lower antifreeze concentration percentage
	• Missing air seals	• Replace air seals
	• Faulty gauge or sending unit	• Repair or replace faulty component
	• Loss of coolant flow caused by leakage or foaming	• Repair or replace leaking component, replace coolant
	• Viscous fan drive failed	• Replace unit
Low temperature indication— undercooling	• Thermostat stuck open	• Replace thermostat
	• Faulty gauge or sending unit	• Repair or replace faulty component
Coolant loss—boilover	• Overfilled cooling system	• Reduce coolant level to proper specification
	• Quick shutdown after hard (hot) run	• Allow engine to run at fast idle prior to shutdown
	• Air in system resulting in occasional "burping" of coolant	• Purge system
	• Insufficient antifreeze allowing coolant boiling point to be too low	• Add antifreeze to raise boiling point
	• Antifreeze deteriorated because of age or contamination	• Replace coolant
	• Leaks due to loose hose clamps, loose nuts, bolts, drain plugs, faulty hoses, or defective radiator	• Pressure test system to locate source of leak(s) then repair as necessary

Troubleshooting the Cooling System (cont.)

Problem	Cause	Solution
Coolant loss—boilover (cont.)	• Faulty head gasket • Cracked head, manifold, or block • Faulty radiator cap	• Replace head gasket • Replace as necessary • Replace cap
Coolant entry into crankcase or cylinder(s)	• Faulty head gasket • Crack in head, manifold or block	• Replace head gasket • Replace as necessary
Coolant recovery system inoperative	• Coolant level low • Leak in system • Pressure cap not tight or seal missing, or leaking • Pressure cap defective • Overflow tube clogged or leaking • Recovery bottle vent restricted	• Replenish coolant to FULL mark • Pressure test to isolate leak and repair as necessary • Repair as necessary • Replace cap • Repair as necessary • Remove restriction
Noise	• Fan contacting shroud • Loose water pump impeller • Glazed fan belt • Loose fan belt • Rough surface on drive pulley • Water pump bearing worn • Belt alignment	• Reposition shroud and inspect engine mounts • Replace pump • Apply silicone or replace belt • Adjust fan belt tension • Replace pulley • Remove belt to isolate. Replace pump. • Check pulley alignment. Repair as necessary.
No coolant flow through heater core	• Restricted return inlet in water pump • Heater hose collapsed or restricted • Restricted heater core • Restricted outlet in thermostat housing • Intake manifold bypass hole in cylinder head restricted • Faulty heater control valve • Intake manifold coolant passage restricted	• Remove restriction • Remove restriction or replace hose • Remove restriction or replace core • Remove flash or restriction • Remove restriction • Replace valve • Remove restriction or replace intake manifold

NOTE: *Immediately after shutdown, the engine enters a condition known as heat soak. This is caused by the cooling system being inoperative while engine temperature is still high. If coolant temperature rises above boiling point, expansion and pressure may push some coolant out of the radiator overflow tube. If this does not occur frequently it is considered normal.*

Troubleshooting the Serpentine Drive Belt

Problem	Cause	Solution
Tension sheeting fabric failure (woven fabric on outside circumference of belt has cracked or separated from body of belt)	• Grooved or backside idler pulley diameters are less than minimum recommended • Tension sheeting contacting (rubbing) stationary object • Excessive heat causing woven fabric to age • Tension sheeting splice has fractured	• Replace pulley(s) not conforming to specification • Correct rubbing condition • Replace belt • Replace belt
Noise (objectional squeal, squeak, or rumble is heard or felt while drive belt is in operation)	• Belt slippage • Bearing noise • Belt misalignment • Belt-to-pulley mismatch • Driven component inducing vibration • System resonant frequency inducing vibration	• Adjust belt • Locate and repair • Align belt/pulley(s) • Install correct belt • Locate defective driven component and repair • Vary belt tension within specifications. Replace belt.

Troubleshooting the Serpentine Drive Belt (cont.)

Problem	Cause	Solution
Rib chunking (one or more ribs has separated from belt body)	• Foreign objects imbedded in pulley grooves	• Remove foreign objects from pulley grooves
	• Installation damage	• Replace belt
	• Drive loads in excess of design specifications	• Adjust belt tension
	• Insufficient internal belt adhesion	• Replace belt
Rib or belt wear (belt ribs contact bottom of pulley grooves)	• Pulley(s) misaligned	• Align pulley(s)
	• Mismatch of belt and pulley groove widths	• Replace belt
	• Abrasive environment	• Replace belt
	• Rusted pulley(s)	• Clean rust from pulley(s)
	• Sharp or jagged pulley groove tips	• Replace pulley
	• Rubber deteriorated	• Replace belt
Longitudinal belt cracking (cracks between two ribs)	• Belt has mistracked from pulley groove	• Replace belt
	• Pulley groove tip has worn away rubber-to-tensile member	• Replace belt
Belt slips	• Belt slipping because of insufficient tension	• Adjust tension
	• Belt or pulley subjected to substance (belt dressing, oil, ethylene glycol) that has reduced friction	• Replace belt and clean pulleys
	• Driven component bearing failure	• Replace faulty component bearing
	• Belt glazed and hardened from heat and excessive slippage	• Replace belt
"Groove jumping" (belt does not maintain correct position on pulley, or turns over and/or runs off pulleys)	• Insufficient belt tension	• Adjust belt tension
	• Pulley(s) not within design tolerance	• Replace pulley(s)
	• Foreign object(s) in grooves	• Remove foreign objects from grooves
	• Excessive belt speed	• Avoid excessive engine acceleration
	• Pulley misalignment	• Align pulley(s)
	• Belt-to-pulley profile mismatched	• Install correct belt
	• Belt cordline is distorted	• Replace belt
Belt broken (Note: identify and correct problem before replacement belt is installed)	• Excessive tension	• Replace belt and adjust tension to specification
	• Tensile members damaged during belt installation	• Replace belt
	• Belt turnover	• Replace belt
	• Severe pulley misalignment	• Align pulley(s)
	• Bracket, pulley, or bearing failure	• Replace defective component and belt
Cord edge failure (tensile member exposed at edges of belt or separated from belt body)	• Excessive tension	• Adjust belt tension
	• Drive pulley misalignment	• Align pulley
	• Belt contacting stationary object	• Correct as necessary
	• Pulley irregularities	• Replace pulley
	• Improper pulley construction	• Replace pulley
	• Insufficient adhesion between tensile member and rubber matrix	• Replace belt and adjust tension to specifications
Sporadic rib cracking (multiple cracks in belt ribs at random intervals)	• Ribbed pulley(s) diameter less than minimum specification	• Replace pulley(s)
	• Backside bend flat pulley(s) diameter less than minimum	• Replace pulley(s)
	• Excessive heat condition causing rubber to harden	• Correct heat condition as necessary
	• Excessive belt thickness	• Replace belt
	• Belt overcured	• Replace belt
	• Excessive tension	• Adjust belt tension

tributor, and was renamed Solid State Ignition (SSI).

The 4–151 uses the Delco-Remy High Energy Ignition (HEI) system.

Ignition Coil
REMOVAL AND INSTALLATION
All Except the 4–151

1. Disconnect the battery ground.
2. Disconnect the two small and one large wire from the coil.
3. Disconnect the condenser connector from the coil, if equipped.
4. Unbolt and remove the coil.
5. Installation is the reverse of removal.

4–151
1980–81

1. Remove the distributor cap.
2. Remove the three coil cover attaching screws and lift off the cover.
3. Remove the four coil attaching screws and lift off the coil.

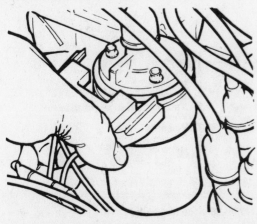

Coil typical of all engines except the 4-151. Early models had separate wires rather than the slip-on connector

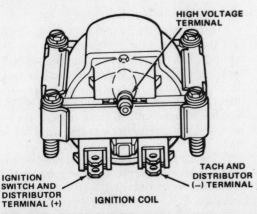

HIGH VOLTAGE TERMINAL

IGNITION SWITCH AND DISTRIBUTOR TERMINAL (+)

IGNITION COIL

TACH AND DISTRIBUTOR (–) TERMINAL

1980–81 4-151 ignition coil

4. Installation is the reverse of removal.
1982–83

1. Disconnect the harness at the coil.
2. Pulling on the boot, only, pull the coil-to-distributor cap wire from the coil.
3. Remove the three coil mounting screws and lift off the coil.
4. Installation is the reverse of removal.

Ignition Module
REMOVAL AND INSTALLATION

The ignition module is mounted next to the battery on all models. It is a sealed, weatherproof unit on all models.

Removing the module, on all models, is a matter of simply removing the fasteners that attach it to the fender or firewall and pulling apart the connectors. When unplugging the connectors, pull them apart with a firm, straight pull. NEVER PRY THEM APART! To pry them will cause damage. When reconnecting them, coat the mating ends with silicone dielectric grease to waterproof the connection. Press the connectors together firmly to overcome any vacuum lock caused by the grease.

NOTE: *If the locking tabs weaken or break, don't replace the unit. Just secure the connection with electrical tape or tie straps.*

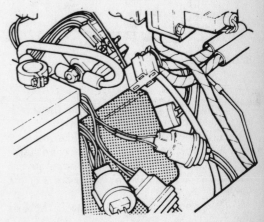

Ignition control module used on all but the 1987 4-150

Distributor
REMOVAL

1. Remove the high tension wires from the distributor cap terminal towers, noting their positions to assure correct reassembly. For diagrams of firing orders and distributor wiring, refer to the tune-up and troubleshooting section.

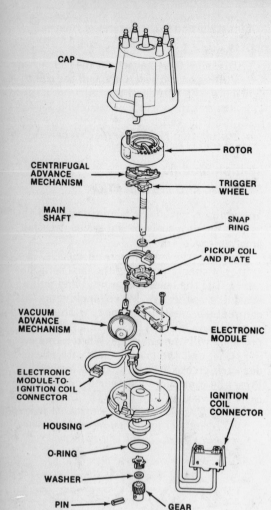

CAP

CENTRIFUGAL
ADVANCE
MECHANISM

MAIN
SHAFT

VACUUM
ADVANCE
MECHANISM

ELECTRONIC
MODULE-TO-
IGNITION COIL
CONNECTOR

HOUSING

O-RING

WASHER

PIN

ROTOR

TRIGGER
WHEEL

SNAP
RING

PICKUP COIL
AND PLATE

ELECTRONIC
MODULE

IGNITION
COIL
CONNECTOR

GEAR

HEI distributor

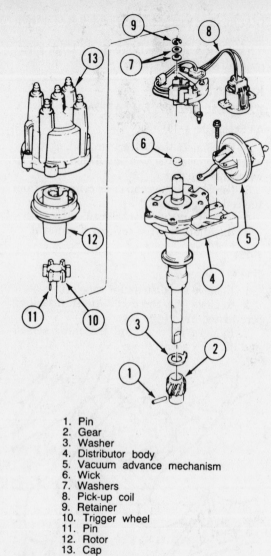

1. Pin
2. Gear
3. Washer
4. Distributor body
5. Vacuum advance mechanism
6. Wick
7. Washers
8. Pick-up coil
9. Retainer
10. Trigger wheel
11. Pin
12. Rotor
13. Cap

1984–86 4-150 distributor

2. Remove the primary lead from the terminal post at the side of the distributor.

NOTE: *The wire connector on 1978 and later models will contain a special conductive grease. Do not remove it. The same grease will also be found on the metal parts of the rotor.*

3. Disconnect the vacuum line if there is one.

4. Remove the two distributor cap retaining hooks or screws and remove the distributor cap.

5. Note the position of the rotor in relation to the base. Scribe a mark on the base of the distributor and on the engine block to facilitate reinstallation. Align the marks with the direction the metal tip of the rotor is pointing.

6. Remove the bolt that holds the distributor to the engine.

7. Lift the distributor assembly from the engine.

INSTALLATION, ENGINE NOT ROTATED

All Except the 4–150

1. Insert the distributor shaft and assembly into the engine. Line up the mark on the distributor and the one on the engine with the metal tip of the rotor. Make sure that the vacuum advance diaphragm is pointed in the same direction as it was pointed originally. This will be done automatically if the marks on the engine and the distributor are line up with the rotor.

2. Install the distributor holddown bolt and clamp. Leave the screw loose enough so that you can move the distributor with heavy hand pressure.

3. Connect the primary wire to the distribu-

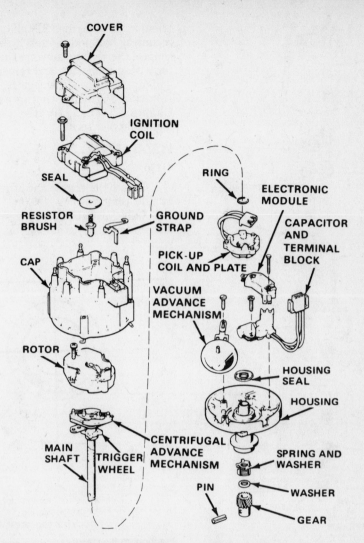

1980–81 4-151 ignition coil, located in the cap

tor side of the coil. Install the distributor cap on the distributor housing. Secure the distributor cap with the spring clips or the screw type retainers, whichever is used.

4. Install the spark plug wires. Make sure that the wires are pressed all of the way into the top of the distributor cap and firmly onto the spark plugs.

5. Adjust the point cam dwell and set the ignition timing. Refer to the tune-up section.

NOTE: *If the engine was turned while the distributor was removed, or if the marks were not drawn, it will be necessary to initially time the engine. Follow the procedure below.*

INSTALLATION, ENGINE ROTATED

All Except the 4–150

1. If the engine has been rotated while the distributor was out, you'll have to first put the engine on No. 1 cylinder at Top Dead Center firing position. You can either remove the valve cover or No. 1 spark plug to determine engine position. Rotate the engine with a socket wrench on the nut at the center of the front pulley in the normal direction of rotation. Either feel for air being expelled forcefully through the spark plug hole or watch for the engine to rotate up to the Top Center mark without the valves moving (both valves will be closed). If the valves are moving as you approach TDC or there is no air being expelled through the plug hole, turn the engine another full turn until you get the appropriate indication as the engine approaches TDC position.

2. Start the distributor into the engine with the matchmarks between the distributor body and the engine lined up. Turn the rotor slightly until the matchmarks on the bottom of the distributor body and the bottom of the distributor shaft near the gear are aligned.

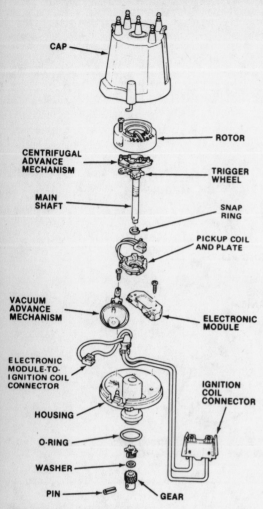

1982–83 4-151 distributor

tributor and engine. Install the distributor mounting bolt and tighten it finger tight. Reconnect the vacuum advance line and distributor wiring connector, and reinstall the gasket and cap. Reconnect the negative battery cable. Adjust the ignition timing as described in Chapter 2. Then, tighten the distributor mounting bolt securely.

INSTALLATION

4–150

1. Rotate the engine until the No.1 piston is at TDC compression.

2. Using a flat bladed screwdriver, in the distributor hole, rotate the oil pump gear so

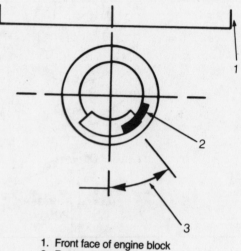

1. Front face of engine block
2. Rotor pre-positioned
3. 5 o'clock position (approx.)

Positioning the distributor rotor and shaft for installation, on the 4-150

Then, insert the distributor all the way into the engine. If you have trouble getting the distributor and camshaft gears to mesh, turn the rotor back and forth very slightly until the distributor can be inserted easily. If the rotor is not now lined up with the position of No. 1 plug terminal, you'll have to pull the distributor back out slightly, shift the position of the rotor appropriately, and then reinstall it.

3. Align the matchmarks between the dis-

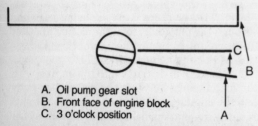

A. Oil pump gear slot
B. Front face of engine block
C. 3 o'clock position

Positioning the oil pump shaft for distributor installation on the 4-150

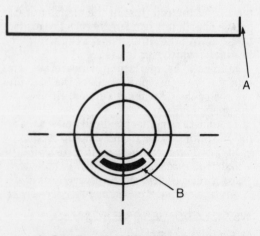

A. Front face of engine block
B. Rotor position when properly installed

Rotor position with the distributor properly installed on the 4-150

that the slot in the oil pump shaft is slightly past the 3:00 o'clock position, relative to the length of the engine block.

3. With the distributor cap removed, install the distributor with the rotor at the 5:00 o'clock position, relative to the oil pump gear shaft slot. When the distributor is comnpletely in place, the rotor should be at the 6:00 o'clock position. If not, remove the distributor and perform the entire procedure again.

4. Tighten the lockbolt.

Alternator

A variety of alternators were used:
- 1975: Motorola and Delco
- 1976: 6-cyl. – Delco
  8-cyl. – Motorcraft
- 1977–78: 4- & 6-cyl. – Delco
  8-cyl. – Motorcraft
- 1979: 4- & 6-cyl. – Delco
  8-cyl. – Bosch
- 1980: All Delco, exc. Eagle
  with heated rear window (Bosch)
- 1981–82: All Delco

The alternator needs no lubrication or adjustments except for drive belt tension.

ALTERNATOR PRECAUTIONS

Certain safety precautions should be observed concerning the alternator:

1. Do not polarize the unit.

2. Do not short across or ground any of the terminals.

3. Never operate the unit with the output terminal disconnected.

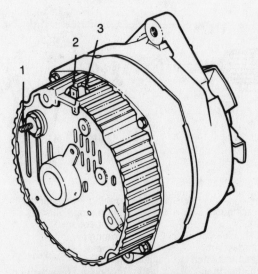

- Alternator "BAT" terminal to ground (1).
- Alternator No. 1 terminal to ground (2).
- Alternator No. 2 terminal to ground (3).

Typical Delco alternator

4. Make sure that the battery is installed with the correct polarity.

5. When connecting a booster battery or a charger, always connect positive terminal to positive terminal and negative terminal to negative terminal.

6. Disconnect the battery ground cable when working on any electrical equipment.

7. If any electric welding is done on the car, disconnect the alternator completely.

REMOVAL AND INSTALLATION

1. Disconnect the battery cables.
NOTE: *Always disconnect the ground cable first, and connect it last, and then you needn't fear sparks.*

2. Disconnect the alternator wires or wiring plug.

3. Remove the adjusting bolt.

4. Take off the drive belt.

5. Remove the mounting bolts and the alternator.

6. Reverse the procedure for installation.

7. Adjust the drive belt.

BELT TENSION ADJUSTMENT

The alternator drive belt, or any engine V-belt, is correctly tensioned when the longest span of belt between pulleys can be depressed about ½" (12.7mm) in the middle by moderate thumb pressure. To adjust, loosen the slotted adjusting bracket bolt. If the alternator hinge bolt(s) is very tight, it may be necessary to loosen it slightly to more the alternator. V8 engines have a hole in the alternator bracket, so that you can insert a big screwdriver and pry out on the the alternator. Some V8s have a square hole into which you can insert a ½" square socket drive. The best way is to pull the alternator out by hand to avoid overtightening.

CAUTION: *Be careful not to overtighten the belt, as this will damage the alternator bearings.*

Regulator

The regulator is sealed at the factory and thus cannot be adjusted. It is mounted to the fender well inside the engine compartment. To remove it, simply unplug it and remove the sheet metal screws holding it in place.

Starter

REMOVAL AND INSTALLATION

1. Disconnect the battery ground cable.

2. Disconnect the leads from the starter.

3. Unbolt and remove the starter.

4. Reverse the procedure on installation.

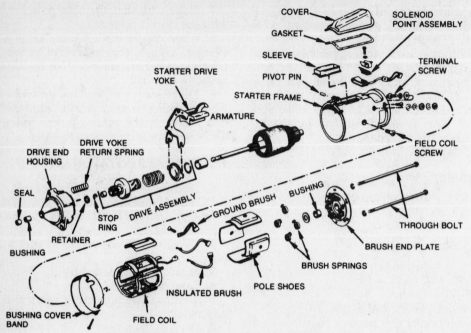

Starter used on all engines except the 4-150 and 4-151

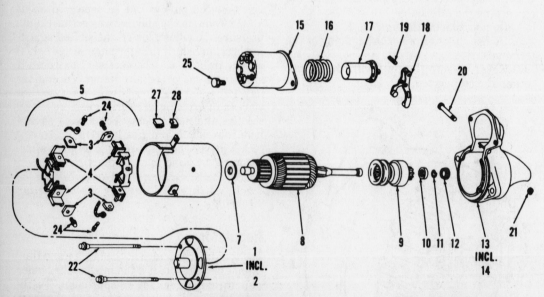

1. Frame—commutator end	11. Shift lever	21. Bushing—drive end
2. Brush and holder pkg.	12. Plunger return springer	22. Pinion stop collar
3. Brush	13. Shift lever shaft	23. Thrust collar
4. Brush holder	14. Lock washer	24. Grommet
5. Housing—drive end	15. Screw—Brush attaching	25. Grommet
6. Frame and field asm.	16. Screw—field lead to switch	26. Plunger pin
7. Solenoid switch	17. Screw—Switch attaching	27. Pinion stop retainer ring
8. Armature	18. Washer—brake	28. Lever shaft retaining ring
9. Drive asm.	19. Thru bolt	
10. Plunger	20. Bushing—commutator end	

4-151 starter

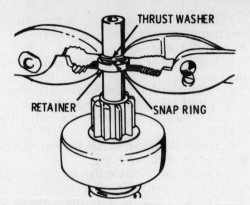

Installing starter drive snap ring

STARTER DRIVE REPLACEMENT

Autolite

1. Remove the cover of the starter drive's actuating lever arm. Remove the through bolts, starter drive gear housing, and the return spring of the drive gear's actuating lever.

2. Remove the pivot pin which retains the starter gear actuating lever and remove the lever and armature.

3. Remove the stopring retainer. Remove and discard the stopring which holds the drive gear to the armature shaft and then remove the drive gear assembly.

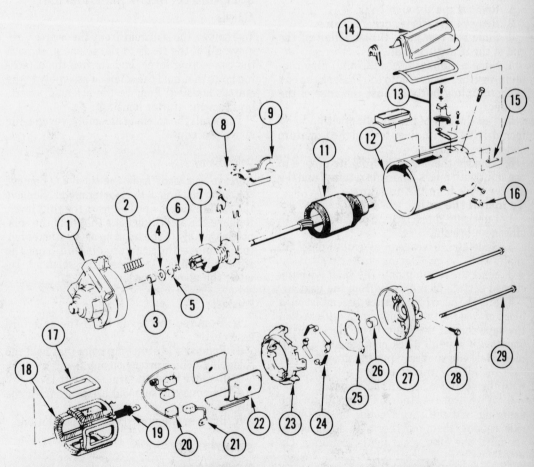

1. Drive end housing	11. Armature	21. Ground brush
2. Drive yoke return spring	12. Frame	22. Pole shoe
3. Bushing	13. Solenoid contact point assembly	23. Brush holder and insulator
4. Washer	14. Drive yoke cover	24. Springs
5. Retainer	15. Hold-in coil terminal	25. Insulator
6. Snapring	16. Field winding screw	26. Bushing
7. Pinion gear drive mechanism	17. Sleeve	27. Brush end plate
8. Drive yoke	18. Field winding	28. Terminal screw
9. Solenoid contact point actuator	19. Terminal	29. Through bolt
10. Moveable pole shoe	20. Insulated brush	

Starter motor used on the 4-150

To install the unit:

1. Lightly Lubriplate® the armature shaft splines and install the starter drive gear assembly on the shaft. Install a new stopring and stopring retainer.

2. Position the starter drive gear actuating lever to the frame and starter drive assembly. Install the pivot pin.

3. Fill the starter drive gear housing one quarter full of grease.

4. Position the drive actuating lever return spring and the drive gear housing to the frame, then install and tighten the through bolts. Be sure that the stopring retainer is properly seated in the drive housing.

Delco-Remy

1. Remove the through bolts.

2. Remove the starter drive housing.

3. Slide the two piece thrust collar off the end of the armature shaft.

4. Slide a standard ½″ (12.7mm) pipe coupling, or other spacer, onto the shaft so the end of the coupling butts against the edge of the retainer.

5. Tap the end of the coupling with a hammer, driving the retainer toward the armature end of the snapring.

6. Remove the snapring from its groove in the shaft with pliers. Slide the retainer and the starter drive from the armature.

To install the unit:

1. Lubricate the drive end of the shaft with silicone lubricant.

2. Slide the drive gear assembly onto the shaft, with the gear facing outward.

3. Slide the retainer onto the shaft with the cupped surface facing away from the gear.

4. Stand the whole starter assembly on a block of wood with the snapring positioned on the upper end of the shaft. Drive the snapring down with a small block of wood and a hammer. Slide the snapring into its groove.

5. Install the thrust collar onto the shaft with the shoulder next to the snapring.

6. With the retainer on one side of the snapring and the thrust collar on the other side, squeeze them together with a pair of pliers until the ring seats in the retainer. On models without a thrust collar, use a washer. Remember to remove the washer before installing the starter in the engine.

Prestolite

1. Slide the thrust collar off the armature shaft.

2. Using a standard ½″ (12.7mm) pipe connector, drive the snapring retainer off the shaft.

3. Remove the snapring from the groove, and then remove the drive assembly.

To install the unit:

1. Lubricate the drive end and splines with Lubriplate®.

2. Install the clutch assembly onto the shaft.

3. Install the snapring retainer with the cupped surface facing toward the end of the shaft.

4. Install the snapring into the groove. Use a new snapring if necessary.

5. Install the thrust collar onto the shaft with the shoulder against the snapring.

6. Force the retainer over the snapring in the same manner as was used for the Delco-Remy starters.

SOLENOID OR RELAY REPLACEMENT

Autolite

To remove the solenoid from the starter, remove all of the leads to the solenoid, remove the connecting lever, and remove the attaching bolts that hold the solenoid assembly to the starter housing. Remove the solenoid assembly from the starter housing.

To install the solenoid assembly, reverse the above procedure.

Delco-Remy

Remove the leads from the solenoid. Remove the drive housing of the starter motor. Remove the shift lever pin and bolt from the shift lever. Remove the attaching bolts that hold the solenoid assembly to the housing of the starter motor. Remove the starter solenoid from the starter housing. To install the solenoid, reverse the above procedure.

Prestolite

1. Remove the leads from the solenoid assembly.

2. Remove the attaching bolts that hold the solenoid to the starter housing.

3. Remove the bolt form the shift lever.

4. Remove the solenoid assembly from the starter housing.

5. Reverse the procedure for installation.

STARTER OVERHAUL

Autolite/Motorcraft

DISASSEMBLY

1. Remove the cover screw, the cover through-bolts, the starter drive end housing and the starter drive plunger lever return spring.

2. Remove the starter gear plunger lever pivot pin, the lever and the armature. Remove the stop ring retainer and the stop ring from

the armature shaft (discard the ring), then the starter drive gear assembly.

3. Remove the brush end plate, the insulator assembly and the brushes from the plastic holder, then lift out the brush holder. For reassembly, note the position of the brush holder with respect to the end terminal.

4. Remove the two ground brush-to-frame screws.

5. Bend up the sleeve's edges which are inserted in the frame's rectangular hole, then remove the sleeve and the retainer. Detach the field coil ground wire from the copper tab.

6. Remove the three coil retaining screws. Cut the field coil connection at the switch post lead, then remove the pole shoes and the coils from the frame.

7. Cut the positive brush leads from the field coils (as close to the field connection point as possible).

8. Check the armature and the armature windings for broken or burned insulation, open circuits or grounds.

9. Check the commutator for runout. If it is rough, has flat spots or is more than 0.005" (0.127mm) out of round, reface the commutator face.

10. Inspect the armature shaft and the two bearings for scoring and excessive wear, then replace (if necessary).

11. Inspect the starter drive. If the gear teeth are pitted, broken or excessively worn, replace the starter drive.

NOTE: *The factory brush length is ½" (12.7mm); the wear limit is ¼" (6.35mm).*

ASSEMBLY

1. Install the starter terminal, the insulator, the washers and the nut in the frame.

NOTE: *Be sure to position the screw slot perpendicular to the frame end surface.*

2. Position the coils and the pole pieces, with the coil leads in the terminal screw slot, then install the screws. When tightening the pole screws, strike the frame with several sharp hammer blows to align the pole shoes, then stake the screws.

3. Install the solenoid coil and the retainer, then bend the tabs to hold the coils to the frame.

4. Using resin core solder and a 300 watt iron, solder the field coils and the solenoid wire to the starter terminal. Check for continuity and ground connections of the assembled coils.

5. Position the solenoid coil ground terminal over the nearest ground screw hole and the ground brushes-to-starter frame, then install the screws.

6. Apply a thin coating of Lubriplate® on the armature shaft splines. Install the starter

motor drive gear assembly-to-armature shaft, followed by a new stop ring and retainer. Install the armature in the starter frame.

7. Position the starter drive gear plunger lever to the frame and the starter drive assembly, then install the pivot pin. Place some grease into the end housing bore. Fill it about ¼ full, then position the drive end housing to the frame.

8. Install the brush holder and the brush springs. The positive brush leads should be positioned in their respective brush holder slots, to prevent grounding problems.

9. Install the brush end plate. Be certain that the end plate insulator is in the proper position on the end plate. Install the two starter frame through-bolts and torque them to 55–75 in.lb.

10. Install the starter drive plunger lever cover and tighten the retaining screw.

Delco-Remy

DISASSEMBLY

1. Detach the field coil connectors from the motor solenoid terminal.

NOTE: *If equipped, remove solenoid mounting screws.*

2. Remove the through-bolts, the commutator end frame, the field frame and the armature assembly from drive housing.

3. Remove the overrunning clutch from the armature shaft as follows:

a. Slide the two piece thrust collar off the end of the armature shaft.

b. Slide a standard ½" (12.7mm) pipe coupling or other spacer onto the shaft, so that the coupling end butts against the retainer edge.

c. Using a hammer, tap the coupling end, driving the retainer towards the armature end of the snapring.

d. Using snapring pliers, remove the snapring from its groove in the shaft, then slide the retainer and the clutch from the shaft.

4. Disassemble the field frame brush assembly by releasing the V-spring and removing the support pin. The brush holders, the brushes and the springs can now be pulled out as a unit and the leads disconnected.

NOTE: *On the integral frame units, remove the brush holder from the brush support and the brush screw.*

5. If equipped, separate the solenoid from the lever housing.

CLEANING AND INSPECTION

1. Clean the parts with a rag. Do not immerse the parts in a solvent.

CAUTION: *Immersion in a solvent will dis-*

solve the grease that is packed in the clutch mechanism. It will damage the armature and the field coil insulation.

2. Test the overrunning clutch action. The pinion should turn freely in the overrunning direction but must not slip in the cranking direction. Check that the pinion teeth have not been chipped, cracked or excessively worn. Replace the unit (if necessary).

3. Inspect the armature commutator. If the commutator is rough or out of round, it should be machined and undercut.

NOTE: *Undercut the insulation between the commutator bars by* $\frac{1}{32}$" *(0.79375mm). The undercut must be the full width of the insulation and flat at the bottom. A triangular groove will not be satisfactory. Most late model starter motor use a molded armature commutator design. No attempt to undercut the insulation should be made or serious damage may result to the commutator.*

ASSEMBLY

1. Install the brushes into the holders, then install solenoid (if equipped).

2. Assemble the insulated and the grounded holder together. Using the V-spring, position and assemble the unit on the support pin. Push the holders and the spring to bottom of the support, then rotate the spring to engage the slot in the support. Attach the ground wire to the grounded brush and the field lead wire to the insulated brush, then repeat this procedure for other brush sets.

3. Assemble the overrunning clutch to the armature shaft as follows:

   a. Lubricate the drive end of the shaft with silicone lubricant.

   b. Slide the clutch assembly onto the shaft with the pinion outward.

   c. Slide the retainer onto the shaft with the cupped surface facing away from the pinion.

   d. Stand the armature up on a wood surface with the commutator downward. Position the snapring on the upper end of the shaft and drive it onto the shaft with a small block of wood and a hammer, then slide the snapring into groove.

   e. Install the thrust collar onto the shaft with the shoulder next to snapring.

   f. With the retainer on one side of the snapring and the thrust collar on the other side, squeeze two sets together (with pliers) until the ring seats in the retainer. On models without a thrust collar use a washer. Remember to remove the washer before continuing.

4. Lubricate the drive end bushing with silicone lubricant, then slide the armature and

the clutch assembly into place, while engaging the shift lever with the clutch.

NOTE: *On the non-integral starters, the shift lever may be installed in the drive gear housing first.*

5. Position the field frame over the armature and apply sealer (silicone) between the frame and the solenoid case. Position the frame against the drive housing, making sure the brushes are not damaged in the process.

6. Lubricate the commutator end bushing with silicone lubricant, place a washer on the armature shaft and slide the commutator end frame onto the shaft. Install the through-bolts and tighten.

7. Reconnect the field coil connections to the solenoid motor terminal. Install the solenoid mounting screws (if equipped).

8. Check the pinion clearance. It should be 0.010–0.140" (0.254–3.556mm) with the pinion in the cranking position, on all models.

Bosch

DISASSEMBLY

1. Disconnect the field coil wire from the solenoid terminal.

2. Remove the solenoid and work the plunger off the shift fork.

3. Remove the two end shield bearing cap screws, the cap and the washers.

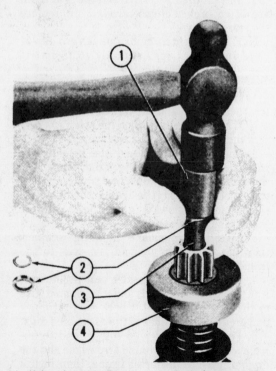

1. ½ in. pipe coupling
2. Snap-ring and retainer
3. Armature shaft
4. Drive assembly

Removing the starter drive

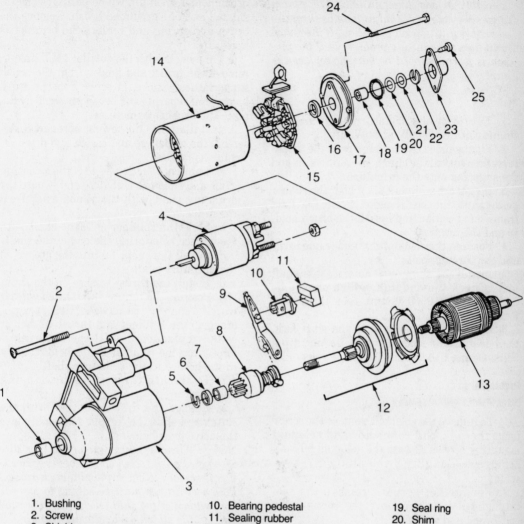

1. Bushing
2. Screw
3. Shield
4. Solenoid switch
5. Retainer
6. Stop ring
7. Bushing
8. Overrunning clutch drive
9. Fork
10. Bearing pedestal
11. Sealing rubber
12. Planetary gear system
13. Armature
14. Stator frame
15. Brush holder
16. Gasket
17. Commutator end shield
18. Bushing
19. Seal ring
20. Shim
21. Shim
22. Retaining washer
23. Closure cap
24. Hexagon screw
25. Screw

Bosch starter motor used on the 1986 4-150

4. Remove the two commutator end frame cover through-bolts, the cover, the two brushes and the brush plate.

5. Slide the field frame off over the armature. Remove the shift lever pivot bolt, the rubber gasket and the metal plate.

6. Remove the armature assembly and the shift lever from the drive end housing. Press the stop collar off the snapring, then remove the snapring, the clutch assembly, the clutch assembly and the drive end housing from the armature.

INSPECTION AND SERVICE

1. The brushes that are worn more than ½ the length of new brushes or are oil soaked, should be replaced. The new brushes are $^{11}/_{16}$" (17.4625mm) long.

2. Do not immerse the starter clutch unit in cleaning solvent. Solvent will wash the lubricant from the clutch.

3. Place the drive unit on the armature shaft, then, while holding the armature, rotate the pinion.

NOTE: *The drive pinion should rotate*

smoothly in one direction only. The pinion may not rotate easily but as long as it rotates smoothly it is in good condition. If the clutch unit does not function properly or if the pinion is worn, chipped or burred, replace the unit.

ASSEMBLY

1. Lubricate the armature shaft and the splines with SAE 10W or 30W oil.
2. Fit the drive end housing onto the armature, then install the clutch, the stop collar and the snapring onto the armature.
3. Install the shift fork pivot bolt, the rubber gasket and the metal plate. Slide the field frame into position and install the brush holder and the brushes.
4. Position the commutator end frame cover and the through-bolts.
5. Install the shim and the armature shaft lock. Check the endplay, which should be 0.002–0.012″ (0.05–0.30mm), then install the bearing cover.
6. Assemble the plunger to the shift fork, then install the solenoid with its mounting bolts. Connect the field wire to the solenoid.

Prestolite

DISASSEMBLY AND ASSEMBLY

1. To remove the solenoid, remove the screw from the field coil connector and solenoid mounting screws. Rotate the solenoid 90° and remove it along with the plunger return spring.
2. For further service, remove the two through-bolts, then remove the commutator end frame and washer.
3. To replace the clutch and drive assembly proceed as follows:
   a. Remove the thrust washer or the collar from the armature shaft.
   b. Slide a ⅝″ (15.875mm) deep socket or a piece of pipe of suitable size over the shaft and against the retainer as a driving tool. Tap the tool to remove the retainer off the snapring.
   c. Remove the snapring from the groove in the shaft. Check and make sure the snapring isn't distorted. If it is, it will be necessary to replace it with a new one upon reassembly.
   d. Remove the retainer and clutch assembly from the armature shaft.
4. The shift lever may be disconnected from the plunger at this time by removing the roll pin.
5. On models with the standard starter, the brushes may be removed by removing the

brush holder pivot pin which positions one insulated and one grounded brush. Remove the brush and spring and replace the brushes as necessary.
6. On models with the smaller 5MT starter, remove the brush and holder from the brush support, then remove the screw from the brush holder and separate the brush and holder. Replace the brushes as necessary.
7. Installation is the reverse of removal. Assemble the armature and clutch and drive assembly as follows:
   a. Lubricate the drive end of the armature shaft and slide the clutch assembly onto the armature shaft with the pinion away from the armature.
   b. Slide the retainer onto the shaft with the cupped side facing the end of the shaft.
   c. Install the snapring into the groove on the armature shaft.
   d. Install the thrust washer on the shaft.
   e. Position the retainer and thrust washer with the snapring in between. Using two pliers, grip the retainer and thrust washer or collar and squeeze until the snapring is forced into the retainer and is held securely in the groove in the armature shaft.
   f. Lubricate the drive gear housing bushing.
   g. Engage the shift lever yoke with the clutch and slide the complete assembly into the drive gear housing.

NOTE: *When the starter motor has been disassembled or the solenoid has been replaced, it is necessary to check the pinion clearance. Pinion clearance must be correct to prevent the buttons on the shift lever yoke from rubbing on the clutch collar during cranking.*

CHECKING PINION CLEARANCE

1. Disconnect the motor field coil connector from the solenoid motor terminal and insulate it carefully.
2. Connect one 12 volt battery lead to the solenoid switch terminal and the other to the starter frame.
3. Flash a jumper lead momentarily from the solenoid motor terminal to the starter frame. This will shift the pinion into cranking position and it will remain there until the battery is disconnected.
   Push the pinion back as far as possible to take up any movement, and check the clearance with a feeler gauge. The clearance should be 0.010–0.140″ (0.254–3.556mm).
4. There is no means for adjusting pinion clearance on the starter motor. If clearance does not fall within the limits, check for improper installation and replace all worn parts.

Battery

REMOVAL AND INSTALLATION

1. Remove the holddown screws from the battery box. Loosen the nuts that secure the cable ends to the battery terminals. Lift the battery cables from the terminals with a twisting motion.

2. If there is a battery cable puller available, make use of it. Lift the battery from the vehicle.

3. Before installing the battery in the vehicle, make sure that the battery terminals are clean and free from corrosion. Use a battery terminal cleaner on the terminals and on the inside of the battery cable ends. If a cleaner is not available, use a heavy sandpaper to remove the corrosion. A mixture of baking soda and water will neutralize any acid. Place the battery in the vehicle. Install the cables on the terminals. Tighten the nuts on the cable ends. Smear a light coating of grease on the cable ends and the tops of the terminals. This will prevent buildup of oxidized acid on the terminals and the cable ends. Install and tighten the nuts of the battery box.

ENGINE MECHANICAL

Design

4-121

During the 1977 model year, a four cylinder 2 liter (121 CID) engine, manufactured by Volkswagen, was introduced for the Gremlin. The engine is of overhead camshaft design, belt driven from the crankshaft. The cylinder head is cast aluminum alloy and has removable camshaft bearing caps. Valve lash is controlled by manual adjustment of a tapered adjusting screw, located at the base of the tappet, under the camshaft. The intake and exhaust manifolds are on the opposite sides of the cylinder head. The block is of cast iron and the crankshaft is set into five main bearings. Three grooved aluminum alloy pistons are used with full floating piston pins. The oil pump is located at the front of the block and is driven by the crankshaft.

4-150

The 4-150 engine used in 1984 models , replacing the 4-151, is a new design, developed from

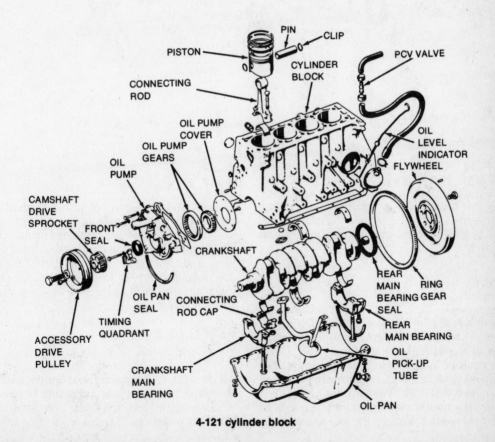

4-121 cylinder block

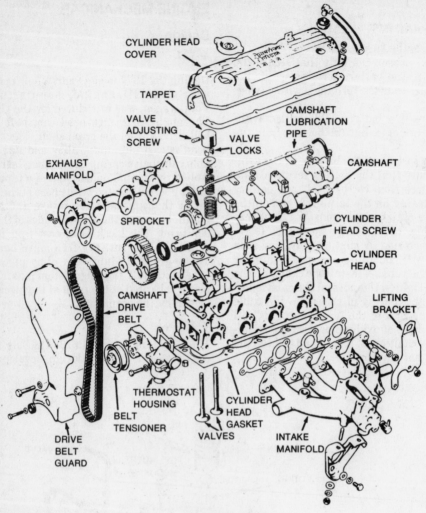

4-121 cylinder head

existing technology at work in the venerable 6–258. It is a four cylinder, overhead valve configuration with cast iron head and block. The crankshaft rides in 5 main bearings. Both manifolds are on the left side of the engine. The engine is thoroughly conventional in all respects.

4-151

Beginning in 1980, the 151 cubic inch engine, manufactured by Pontiac, replaced the 121. The 151 is an inline 4-cylinder engine with a cast iron cylinder head and block. The pistons are made of light weight cast aluminum. The cylinder head is of a crossflow design for more efficient combustion. The cam shaft, gear driven by the crankshaft, operates the overhead valves through hydraulic lifters and pushrods.

6-232
6-258

The 232 and 258 sixes are virtually identical in construction. The design was originally adopted in 1966 and has remained unchanged. They employ a cast iron cylinder head and block and are long stroke cycle, giving them a good torque curve for low end power. The engines are overhead valve with a seven main bearing crankshaft.

8-304
8-360
8-401

All the AMC V8s are similar in design, having five main bearing crankshafts and overhead valves with hydraulic lifters. The head and block are cast iron.

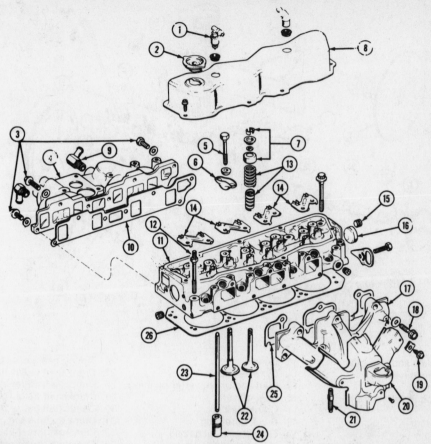

1. PCV valve
2. Oil filler cap
3. Intake manifold attaching bolts
4. Intake manifold
5. Rocker arm capscrew
6. Rocker arm
7. Valve spring retainer assembly
8. Cylinder head cover (rocker cover)
9. Coolant hose fitting
10. Intake manifold gasket
11. Cylinder head
12. Cylinder head stud bolt
13. Valve spring
14. Push rod guide
15. Cylinder head plug
16. Cylinder head core plug
17. Exhaust manifold
18. Exhaust manifold bolt
19. Oil level indicator tube attaching screw
20. Exhaust manifold heat shroud (heat shield)
21. Exhaust manifold to exhaust pipe stud
22. Valves
23. Push rod
24. Tappet
25. Exhaust manifold gasket
26. Cylinder head gasket

4-151 cylinder head

Engine Overhaul Tips

Most engine overhaul procedures are fairly standard. In addition to specific parts replacement procedures and complete specifications for your individual engine, this chapter also is a guide to accept rebuilding procedures. Examples of standard rebuilding practice are shown and should be used along with specific details concerning your particular engine.

Competent and accurate machine shop services will ensure maximum performance, reliability and engine life.

In most instances it is more profitable for the do-it-yourself mechanic to remove, clean and inspect the component, buy the necessary parts and deliver these to a shop for actual machine work.

On the other hand, much of the rebuilding work (crankshaft, block, bearings, piston rods, and other components) is well within the scope of the do-it-yourself mechanic.

TOOLS

The tools required for an engine overhaul or parts replacement will depend on the depth of your involvement. With a few exceptions, they will be the tools found in a mechanic's tool kit (see Chapter 1). More in-depth work will require any or all of the following:

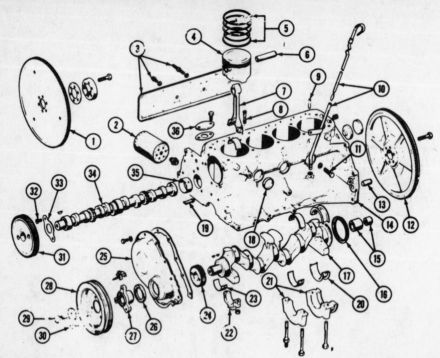

1. Drive plate and ring gear (automatic trans)
2. Oil filter
3. Push rod cover and bolts
4. Piston
5. Piston ring
6. Piston pin
7. Connecting rod
8. Connecting rod bolt
9. Dowel
10. Oil level indicator and tube
11. Block drain
12. Flywheel and ring gear (manual trans)
13. Dowel
14. Cylinder block
15. Pilot and/or converter bushing
16. Rear oil seal
17. Crankshaft
18. Block core plug
19. Timing gear oil nozzle
20. Main bearings
21. Main bearing caps
22. Connecting rod bearing cap
23. Connecting rod bearing
24. Crankshaft gear
25. Timing gear cover (front)
26. Timing gear cover oil seal
27. Crankshaft pulley hub
28. Crankshaft pulley
29. Crankshaft pulley hub bolt
30. Crankshaft pulley bolt
31. Crankshaft timing gear
32. Camshaft thrust plate screw
33. Camshaft thrust plate
34. Camshaft
35. Camshaft bearing
36. Oil pump driveshaft retainer plate, gasket and bolt

4-151 cylinder block

• a dial indicator (reading in thousandths) mounted on a universal base
  • micrometers and telescope gauges
  • jaw and screw-type pullers
  • scraper
  • valve spring compressor
  • ring groove cleaner
  • piston ring expander and compressor
  • ridge reamer
  • cylinder hone or glaze breaker
  • Plastigage®
  • engine stand

The use of most of these tools is illustrated in this chapter. Many can be rented for a one-time use from a local parts jobber or tool supply house specializing in automotive work.

Occasionally, the use of special tools is called for. See the information on Special Tools and Safety Notice in the front of this book before substituting another tool.

INSPECTION TECHNIQUES

Procedures and specifications are given in this chapter for inspecting, cleaning and assessing the wear limits of most major components. Other procedures such as Magnaflux® and Zyglo® can be used to locate material flaws and stress cracks. Magnaflux® is a magnetic process applicable only to ferrous materials. The Zyglo® process coats the material with a fluorescent dye penetrant and can be used on any material Check for suspected surface cracks can be more readily made using spot check dye. The dye is sprayed onto the suspected area, wiped off and the area sprayed with a developer. Cracks will show up brightly.

OVERHAUL TIPS

Aluminum has become extremely popular for use in engines, due to its low weight. Observe

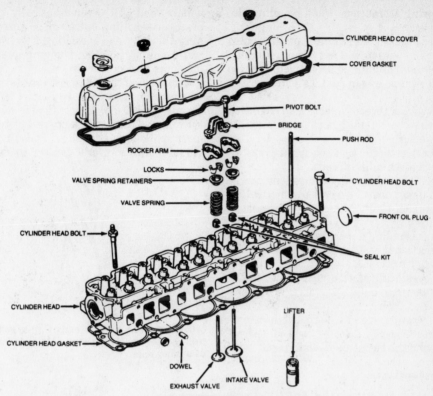

6-232 or 258 cylinder head

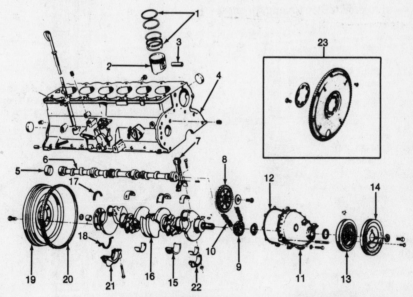

1. Piston rings
2. Piston
3. Piston pin
4. Block
5. Camshaft bearing
6. Camshaft
7. Connecting rod
8. Camshaft sprocket
9. Crankshaft sprocket
10. Timing chain
11. Timing case cover
12. Cover gasket
13. Vibration damper
14. Pulley
15. Main bearing
16. Crankshaft
17. Upper seal
18. Lower seal
19. Flywheel
20. Ring gear
21. Main bearing cap
22. Connecting rod bearing cap
23. Converter drive plate and spacer
   (with auto. trans.)

6-232 or 258 cylinder block

the following precautions when handling aluminum parts:

• Never hot tank aluminum parts (the caustic hot tank solution will eat the aluminum.

• Remove all aluminum parts (identification tag, etc.) from engine parts prior to the tanking.

• Always coat threads lightly with engine oil or antiseize compounds before installation, to prevent seizure.

• Never overtorque bolts or spark plugs especially in aluminum threads.

Stripped threads in any component can be repaired using any of several commercial repair kits (Heli-Coil®, Microdot®, Keenserts®, etc.).

When assembling the engine, any parts that will be frictional contact must be prelubed to provide lubrication at initial start-up. Any product specifically formulated for this purpose can be used, but engine oil is not recommended as a prelube.

When semi-permanent (locked, but removable) installation of bolts or nuts is desired, threads should be cleaned and coated with Loctite® or other similar, commercial nonhardening sealant.

REPAIRING DAMAGED THREADS

Several methods of repairing damaged threads are available. Heli-Coil® (shown here), Keenserts® and Microdot® are among the most

widely used. All involve basically the same principle—drilling out stripped threads, tapping the hole and installing a prewound insert—making welding, plugging and oversize fasteners unnecessary.

Two types of thread repair inserts are usually supplied: a standard type for most Inch Coarse, Inch Fine, Metric Course and Metric Fine thread sizes and a spark lug type to fit most spark plug port sizes. Consult the individual manufacturer's catalog to determine

Drill out the damaged threads with specified drill. Drill completely through the hole or to the bottom of a blind hole

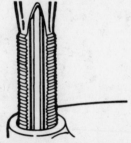

With the tap supplied, tap the hole to receive the thread insert. Keep the tap well oiled and back it out frequently to avoid clogging the threads

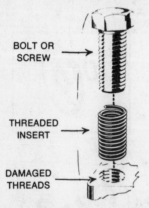

BOLT OR SCREW

THREADED INSERT

DAMAGED THREADS

Damaged bolt holes can be repaired with thread repair inserts

TANG

NOTCH

Standard thread repair insert (left) and spark plug thread insert (right)

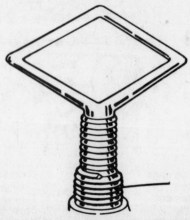

Screw the threaded insert onto the installation tool until the tang engages the slot. Screw the insert into the tapped hole until it is ¼–½ turn below the top surface. After installation break off the tang with a hammer and punch

Standard Torque Specifications and Fastener Markings

In the absence of specific torques, the following chart can be used as a guide to the maximum safe torque of a particular size/grade of fastener.

- There is no torque difference for fine or coarse threads.
- Torque values are based on clean, dry threads. Reduce the value by 10% if threads are oiled prior to assembly.
- The torque required for aluminum components or fasteners is considerably less.

U.S. Bolts

SAE Grade Number	1 or 2			5			6 or 7		
Number of lines always 2 less than the grade number.									
Bolt Size (Inches)—(Thread)	Maximum Torque			Maximum Torque			Maximum Torque		
	Ft./Lbs.	Kgm	Nm	Ft./Lbs.	Kgm	Nm	Ft./Lbs.	Kgm	Nm
¼—20	5	0.7	6.8	8	1.1	10.8	10	1.4	13.5
—28	6	0.8	8.1	10	1.4	13.6			
5/16—18	11	1.5	14.9	17	2.3	23.0	19	2.6	25.8
—24	13	1.8	17.6	19	2.6	25.7			
3/8—16	18	2.5	24.4	31	4.3	42.0	34	4.7	46.0
—24	20	2.75	27.1	35	4.8	47.5			
7/16—14	28	3.8	37.0	49	6.8	66.4	55	7.6	74.5
—20	30	4.2	40.7	55	7.6	74.5			
½—13	39	5.4	52.8	75	10.4	101.7	85	11.75	115.2
—20	41	5.7	55.6	85	11.7	115.2			
9/16—12	51	7.0	69.2	110	15.2	149.1	120	16.6	162.7
—18	55	7.6	74.5	120	16.6	162.7			
5/8—11	83	11.5	112.5	150	20.7	203.3	167	23.0	226.5
—18	95	13.1	128.8	170	23.5	230.5			
¾—10	105	14.5	142.3	270	37.3	366.0	280	38.7	379.6
—16	115	15.9	155.9	295	40.8	400.0			
7/8— 9	160	22.1	216.9	395	54.6	535.5	440	60.9	596.5
—14	175	24.2	237.2	435	60.1	589.7			
1— 8	236	32.5	318.6	590	81.6	799.9	660	91.3	894.8
—14	250	34.6	338.9	660	91.3	849.8			

Metric Bolts

Relative Strength Marking	4.6, 4.8			8.8		
Bolt Markings						
Bolt Size Thread Size x Pitch (mm)	Maximum Torque			Maximum Torque		
	Ft./Lbs.	Kgm	Nm	Ft./Lbs.	Kgm	Nm
6 x 1.0	2–3	.2–.4	3–4	3–6	.4–.8	5–8
8 x 1.25	6–8	.8–1	8–12	9–14	1.2–1.9	13–19
10 x 1.25	12–17	1.5–2.3	16–23	20–29	2.7–4.0	27–39
12 x 1.25	21–32	2.9–4.4	29–43	35–53	4.8–7.3	47–72
14 x 1.5	35–52	4.8–7.1	48–70	57–85	7.8–11.7	77–110
16 x 1.5	51–77	7.0–10.6	67–100	90–120	12.4–16.5	130–160
18 x 1.5	74–110	10.2–15.1	100–150	130–170	17.9–23.4	180–230
20 x 1.5	110–140	15.1–19.3	150–190	190–240	26.2–46.9	160–320
22 x 1.5	150–190	22.0–26.2	200–260	250–320	34.5–44.1	340–430
24 x 1.5	190–240	26.2–46.9	260–320	310–410	42.7–56.5	420–550

exact applications. Typical thread repair kits will contain a selection of prewound threaded inserts, a tap (corresponding to the outside diameter threads of the insert) and an installation tool. Spark plug inserts usually differ because they require a tap equipped with pilot threads and a combined reamer/tap section. Most manufacturers also supply blister-packed thread repair inserts separately in addition to a master kit containing a variety of taps and inserts plus installation tools.

Before effecting a repair to a threaded hole, remove any snapped, broken or damaged bolts or studs. Penetrating oil can be used to free frozen threads. The offending item can be removed with locking pliers or with a screw or stud extractor. After the hole is clear, the thread can be repaired, as follows:

Checking Engine Compression

A noticeable lack of engine power, excessive oil consumption and/or poor fuel mileage measured over an extended period are all indicators of internal engine war. Worn piston rings, scored or worn cylinder bores, blown head gaskets, sticking or burnt valves and worn valve seats are all possible culprits here. A check of each cylinder's compression will help you locate the problems.

As mentioned in the Tools and Equipment section of Chapter 1, a screw-in type compression gauge is more accurate that the type you simply hold against the spark plug hole, although it takes slightly longer to use. It's worth it to obtain a more accurate reading. Follow the procedures below.

1. Warm up the engine to normal operating temperature.

2. Remove all spark plugs.

3. Disconnect the high tension lead from the ignition coil.

4. On fully open the throttle either by operating the carburetor throttle linkage by hand or by having an assistant floor the accelerator pedal.

5. Screw the compression gauge into the no.1 spark plug hole until the fitting is snug. NOTE: *Be careful not to crossthread the plug hole. On aluminum cylinder heads use extra care, as the threads in these heads are easily ruined.*

6. Ask an assistant to depress the accelerator pedal fully. Then, while you read the compression gauge, ask the assistant to crank the engine two or three times in short bursts using the ignition switch.

7. Read the compression gauge at the end of each series of cranks, and record the highest of these readings. Repeat this procedure for each of the engine's cylinders. Compare the highest reading of each cylinder to the compression pressure specification in the Tune-Up Specifications chart in Chapter 2. The specs in this chart are maximum values.

A cylinder's compression pressure is usually acceptable if it is not less than 80% of maximum. The difference between any two cylinders should be no more than 12–14 pounds.

8. If a cylinder is unusually low, pour a tablespoon of clean engine oil into the cylinder through the spark plug hole and repeat the compression test. If the compression comes up after adding the oil, it appears that the cylinder's piston rings or bore are damaged or worn. If the pressure remains low, the valves may not be seating properly (a valve job is needed), or the head gasket may be blown near that cylinder. If compression in any two adjacent cylinders is low, and if the addition of oil doesn't help the compression, there is leakage past the head gasket. Oil and coolant water in the combustion chamber can result from this problem. There may be evidence of water droplets on the engine dipstick when a head gasket has blown.

Engine
REMOVAL AND INSTALLATION
4–121

NOTE: *It is recommended by the manufacturer that the engine be removed from the car separately, and the transmission remain in the car.*

1. Mark the hinge locations and remove the hood.

2. Drain the coolant and remove the air cleaner and TAC hose.

CAUTION: *When draining the coolant, keep in mind that cats and dogs are attracted by the ethylene glycol antifreeze, and are quite likely to drink any that is left in an uncovered container or in puddles on the ground. This will prove fatal in sufficient quantity. Always drain the coolant into a sealable container. Coolant should be reused unless it is contaminated or several years old.*

3. Detach the negative cable at the alternator bracket and battery.

4. Remove the fuel and vacuum lines from the engine. Plug the fuel line.

5. Disconnect the necessary wiring, the throttle cable, and automatic transmission valve linkage.

6. If you car has air conditioning, the system must be bled, the hoses disconnected, and the condenser moved. See Chapter 1.

7. Raise the car, disconnect and remove the starter motor and exhaust pipe support bracket. Unbolt the exhaust pipe from the manifold.

8. Remove the torque convertor nuts and fluid cooler lines, if the car has automatic transmission.

9. Disconnect the wiring at the backup lamp switch and from the alternator.

10. Remove the lower radiator hose and heater hose from the radiator.

11. Remove all the bell housing bolts, except the top center bolt.

12. Lower the car and remove the top radiator hose and the cold air induction manifold at the radiator.

13. Remove the radiator screws, move the radiator one inch to the left, rotate, and lift the radiator and shroud assembly out of the car. With air conditioning, first remove the condenser attaching bolts and more the condenser away from the radiator.

14. Remove any other heater hoses and wiring that are still attached to the car.

15. With power steering, disconnect the hoses from the steering gear. Remove the transmission filler tube support screws with automatic transmission.

16. Remove the engine support cushion nuts on both sides of the engine and attach a lifting device.

17. With the engine partially raised, support the transmission and remove the center bolt from the transmission bell housing. Carefully remove the engine from the car.

NOTE: *When mating the engine to the transmission bell housing, install three bolts for a more secure mounting until the engine is bolted into place.*

18. With the engine partially raised, support the transmission and install the center bolt in the transmission bell housing. Carefully install the engine in the car.

19. Install the engine support cushion nuts on both sides of the engine and remove the lifting device.

20. With power steering, connect the hoses to the steering gear. Install the transmission filler tube support screws with automatic transmission.

21. Install the heater hoses and any wiring that was disconnected from the car.

22. Install the radiator and the condenser.

23. Lower the car and install the top radiator hose and the cold air induction manifold at the radiator.

24. Install all remaining bell housing bolts.

25. Install the lower radiator hose.

26. Connect the wiring at the backup lamp switch and alternator.

27. Install the torque convertor nuts and fluid cooler lines, if the car has automatic transmission.

28. Raise the car, install the starter motor

and exhaust pipe support bracket. Connect the exhaust pipe at the manifold.

29. If you car has air conditioning, evacuate, charge and leak test the system. See Chapter 1.

30. Connect any remaining wiring, the throttle cable, and automatic transmission valve linkage.

31. Connect the fuel and vacuum lines at the engine.

32. Attach the negative cable at the alternator bracket and battery.

33. Fill the cooling system and install the air cleaner and TAC hose.

34. Install the hood.

4–150

1. Disconnect the battery ground cable.

2. Remove the air cleaner.

3. Remove the hood.

4. Drain the coolant.

CAUTION: *When draining the coolant, keep in mind that cats and dogs are attracted by the ethylene glycol antifreeze, and are quite likely to drink any that is left in an uncovered container or in puddles on the ground. This will prove fatal in sufficient quantity. Always drain the coolant into a sealable container. Coolant should be reused unless it is contaminated or several years old.*

5. Remove the lower radiator hose.

6. Remove the upper radiator hose.

7. Disconnect the coolant recovery hose.

8. Remove the fan shroud.

9. Disconnect the automatic transmission coolant lines.

10. Discharge the refrigerant system. See Chapter 1.

CAUTION: *Do this CAREFULLY, or let someone with experience do it for you. GREAT PERSONAL INJURY CAN OCCUR WHEN MISHANDLING REFRIGERANT GAS!*

11. Disconnect and remove the condenser. Cap all openings at once!

12. Remove the radiator.

13. Remove the fan and install a $5/16''$ x $1/2''$ (7.9375mm x 12.7mm) capscrew through the pulley and into the water pump flange to maintain the pulley-to-pump alignment.

14. Disconnect the heater hoses.

15. Disconnect the throttle linkage.

16. Disconnect the cruise control linkage.

17. Disconnect the oil pressure sending unit wire.

18. Disconnect the temperature sending unit wire.

19. Disconnect and tag all vacuum hoses connected to the engine.

20. Remove the air conditioning compressor.

21. Remove the power steering hoses at the gear.

22. Drain the power steering reservoir.

23. Remove the power brake vacuum check valve from the booster.

24. Raise and support the front end on jackstands.

25. Disconnect and tag the starter wires.

26. Remove the starter.

27. Disconnect the exhaust pipe at the manifold.

28. Remove the flywheel housing access cover.

29. On vehicles equipped with automatic transmission, matchmark the converter and flywheel and remove the attaching bolts.

30. Remove the upper flywheel housing-to-engine bolts and loosen the lower ones.

31. Remove the engine mount cushion-to-engine compartment bolts.

32. Attach a shop crane to the lifting eyes on the engine.

33. Raise the engine off the front supports.

34. Place a floor jack under the flywheel housing.

35. Remove the remaining flywheel housing bolts.

36. Lift the engine out of the vehicle.

37. Mount the engine on a work stand or cradle. Never let it rest on the oil pan.

To install the engine:

38. Lower the engine into place in the vehicle.

39. Lubricate the manual transmission input shaft with chassis lube before insertion into clutch splines.

40. Install the flywheel housing bolts. Torque the top flywheel housing-to-engine bolts to 27 ft.lb. and the bottom ones to 43 ft.lb.

41. Install the engine mount cushion-to-engine compartment bolts. Torque the front bracket support bolts to 33 ft.lb.

42. Remove the shop crane.

43. On vehicles equipped with automatic transmission, install the converter attaching bolts.

44. Install the flywheel housing access cover.

45. Connect the exhaust pipe at the manifold.

46. Install the starter.

47. Connect the wires.

48. Raise and support the front end on jackstands.

49. Install the power brake vacuum check valve on the booster.

50. Fill the power steering reservoir.

51. Connect the power steering hoses at the gear.

52. Install the air conditioning compressor,

53. Connect all vacuum hoses.

54. Connect all wires.

55. Connect the throttle linkage.

56. Connect the cruise control linkage.

57. Connect the heater hoses.

58. Install the fan.

59. Install the radiator.

60. Install the condenser.

61. Evacuate and charge the refrigerant system. See Chapter 1.

CAUTION: *Do this CAREFULLY, or let someone with experience do it for you. GREAT PERSONAL INJURY CAN OCCUR WHEN MISHANDLING REFRIGERANT GAS!*

62. Install the fan shroud.

63. Connect the automatic transmission coolant lines.

64. Install the upper radiator hose.

65. Connect the coolant recovery hose.

66. Install the lower radiator hose.

67. Fill the cooling system.

68. Install the hood.

69. Install the air cleaner.

70. Connect the battery ground cable.

4–151

1. Disconnect the battery.

2. Remove the air cleaner.

3. Jack up the vehicle and support it on jackstands.

4. Disconnect the exhaust pipe from the manifold.

5. Disconnect the oxygen sensor.

6. Disconnect the wires from the starter.

7. Unbolt the starter and remove it from the vehicle.

8. Disconnect the wires from the distributor and oil pressure sending unit.

9. Remove the engine mount nuts.

10. On vehicles with manual transmission, remove the clutch slave cylinder and flywheel inspection plate.

11. Remove the clutch or converter housing-to-engine bolts.

12. On vehicle with automatic transmission, disconnect the converter from the drive plate.

13. Lower the vehicle.

14. Support the transmission with a jack.

15. Tag all hoses at the carburetor and remove them.

16. Disconnect the mixture control solenoid wire from the carburetor, (not all vehicles have these).

17. Disconnect the wires from the alternator.

18. Disconnect the throttle cable from the bracket and the carburetor.

19. Disconnect the choke and solenoid wires at the carburetor.

20. Disconnect the temperature sender wire.

21. Drain the radiator at the drain cock, then remove the lower hose.

CAUTION: *When draining the coolant, keep in mind that cats and dogs are attracted by the ethylene glycol antifreeze, and are quite likely to drink any that is left in an uncovered container or in puddles on the ground. This will prove fatal in sufficient quantity. Always drain the coolant into a sealable container. Coolant should be reused unless it is contaminated or several years old.*

22. Remove the upper radiator hose and the heater hoses.

23. Remove the fan shroud, and radiator.

24. Remove the power steering hoses at the pump.

25. Attach a shop crane to the engine and lift it out of the vehicle.

NOTE: *The manual transmission may have to be raised slightly to allow a smooth separation.*

26. Lower the engine into the truck.

27. On vehicle with automatic transmission, Connect the converter to the drive plate.

28. Install the clutch or converter housing-to-engine bolts. Torque the bolts to 35 ft.lb.

29. On vehicles with manual transmission, Install the clutch slave cylinder and flywheel inspection plate. Torque the slave cylinder bolts to 18 ft.lb.

30. Install the engine mount nuts. Torque them to 34 ft.lb.

31. Connect the wires to the distributor and oil pressure sending unit.

32. Install the starter. Torque the mounting bolts to 27 ft.lb.; the bracket nut to 40 in.lb.

33. Connect the wires to the starter.

34. Connect the oxygen sensor.

35. Connect the exhaust pipe at the manifold. Torque the nuts to 35 ft.lb.

36. Install the power steering hoses at the pump.

37. Install the fan shroud, and radiator.

38. Install the upper radiator hose and the heater hoses.

39. Connect the temperature sender wire.

40. Connect the choke and solenoid wires at the carburetor.

41. Connect the throttle cable at the bracket and the carburetor.

42. Connect the wires to the alternator.

43. Connect the mixture control solenoid wire at the carburetor, (not all vehicles have these).

44. Install all hoses at the carburetor.

45. Lower the vehicle.

46. Install the air cleaner.

47. Connect the battery.

48. Fill the cooling system.

6–232, 258
8–304, 360, 401

NOTE: *The engine is removed without the transmission on all models except the Pacer.*

1. Mark the hood hinge locations, disconnect the underhood light, if equipped, and remove the hood.

2. Drain and coolant and engine oil. Remove the filter on the Pacer.

CAUTION: *When draining the coolant, keep in mind that cats and dogs are attracted by the ethylene glycol antifreeze, and are quite likely to drink any that is left in an uncovered container or in puddles on the ground. This will prove fatal in sufficient quantity. Always drain the coolant into a sealable container. Coolant should be reused unless it is contaminated or several years old.*

3. Disconnect and remove the battery and air cleaner. On Pacers, first run the wipers to the center of the windshield.

4. Disconnect an tag the alternator, ignition coil distributor temperature and oil sender wiring. On Pacers, also disconnect the brake warning switch wiring.

5. If equipped with TCS, remove the switch bracket and vacuum solenoid wire harness.

6. Disconnect and plug the hose from the fuel pump. On Pacers, also disconnect the automatic transmission fluid cooler line.

7. Disconnect the engine ground strap at the block and the starter cable at the starter. Remove the right front engine support cushion-to-bracket bolt.

8. If your car has air conditioning, the system must be bled, the hoses disconnected, and the system removed. See Chapter 1.

CAUTION: *Do not perform this operation if you are unfamiliar with A/C systems.*

9. Disconnect the return hose from the fuel filter. TAC hose from the manifold, carburetor vent hose, heater or A/C vacuum hose and/or power brake hose at intake manifold, and power brake vacuum check valve from booster, if equipped.

10. disconnect the throttle cable and throttle valve rod, if equipped.

11. Disconnect the radiator and heater hoses from the engine, automatic transmission cooler lines from the radiator, radiator shroud, fan, and spacer, and remove the radiator.

12. Install a $5/16''$x $1/2''$ bolt through the fan pulley into the water pump flange to maintain alignment (all but Pacer).

13. With power steering, disconnect the hoses, drain the reservoir, and cap the fittings.

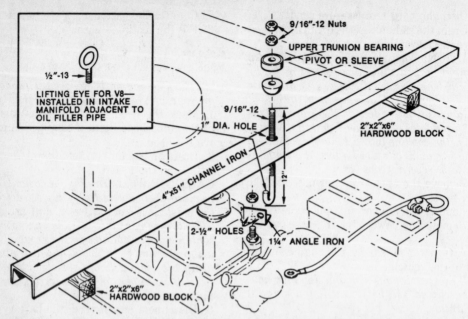

9/16"-12 Nuts

UPPER TRUNION BEARING

PIVOT OR SLEEVE

½"-13 →

**LIFTING EYE FOR V8—
INSTALLED IN INTAKE
MANIFOLD ADJACENT TO
OIL FILLER PIPE**

9/16"-12

1" DIA. HOLE

2"x2"x6"
HARDWOOD BLOCK

4"x51" CHANNEL IRON

12"

2-½" HOLES

1¼" ANGLE IRON

2"x2"x6"
HARDWOOD BLOCK

A lifting fixture can be fabricated as illustrated to facilitate oil pan and/or engine mount removal

With power brakes, remove the vacuum check valve from the booster.

14. On Pacers only, remove the carburetor and plug the fitting, remove the valve cover(s) and remove the vibration damper.

15. With automatic transmission, remove the filler tube.

16. Jack and support the front of the car. Remove the starter.

17. With automatic transmission on all except the Pacer, remove the converter cover, converter bolts (rotate the crankshaft for access), and the exhaust pipe/transmission linkage support.

With manual transmission on all but the Pacer, remove the clutch cover, bellcrank inner support bolts and springs, the bellcrank, outer bellcrank-to-strut retainer, and disconnect the back-up lamp wire harness at the firewall for access later.

On Pacers disconnect the transmission and clutch linkage, speedometer cable at the transmission remove the driveshaft (plug the transmission), and support the transmission with a jack. Remove the rear crossmember.

18. Attach the lifting device and support the engine. Remove the engine mount bolts.

19. Disconnect the exhaust pipe from the manifold.

20. On all but the Pacer, remove the upper converter or clutch housing bolts and loosen the lower bolts. Raise the car and move the jackstands to the jack pad area. Remove the A/C idler pulley and bracket, if equipped. Lift the engine off the front supports, support the

transmission, remove the lower transmission cover attaching bolts, and lift the engine out of the car.

On Pacers, lift the engine slightly and remove the front support cushions. Remove the transmission support, raise the front of the car so that the bottom of the bumper is three feet from the floor, and partially remove the engine/transmission assembly until the rear of the cylinder head clears the cowl Lower the car and remove the engine.

21. On installation with manual transmission, insert the transmission shaft into the clutch spline and align the clutch housing to the engine. Install and tighten the lower housing bolts.

With automatic transmission, align the converter housing to the engine and loosely install the bottom housing bolts. Then install the next higher bolts and tighten all four bolts.

With both transmissions, next, lower the engine onto the mounts, and install the mounting bolts.

On Pacers raise the car with a jack as in Step 20. Lower the engine/transmission assembly into the compartment. Raise the transmission into position with a jack and install the rear crossmember.

22. On all but the Pacer, install the upper converter or clutch housing bolts and loosen the lower bolts. Raise the car and move the jackstands to the jack pad area. Install the A/C idler pulley and bracket, if equipped. Lift the engine off the front supports, support the transmission, install the lower transmission

cover attaching bolts, and lift the engine out of the car.

On Pacers, lift the engine slightly and install the front support cushions. Install the transmission support, raise the front of the car so that the bottom of the bumper is three feet from the floor, and partially install the engine/transmission assembly until the rear of the cylinder head clears the cowl Lower the car and install the engine.

23. Connect the exhaust pipe from the manifold.

24. Install the engine mount bolts.

25. With automatic transmission on all except the Pacer, install the converter cover, converter bolts (rotate the crankshaft for access), and the exhaust pipe/transmission linkage support.

With manual transmission on all but the Pacer, install the clutch cover, bellcrank inner support bolts and springs, the bellcrank, outer bellcrank-to-strut retainer, and connect the back-up lamp wire harness at the firewall.

On Pacers connect the transmission and clutch linkage, speedometer cable at the transmission and install the driveshaft. Install the rear crossmember.

26. Install the starter.

27. With automatic transmission, install the filler tube.

28. On Pacers only, install the carburetor, valve cover(s) and vibration damper.

29. With power steering, connect the hoses. With power brakes, install the vacuum check valve on the booster.

30. Install the fan, spacer, and radiator. Connect the radiator and heater hoses, automatic transmission cooler lines and install the radiator shroud.

31. Connect the throttle cable and throttle valve rod, if equipped.

32. Connect the return hose to the fuel filter. Connect the TAC hose to the manifold, carburetor vent hose, heater or A/C vacuum hose and/or power brake hose at intake manifold, and power brake vacuum check valve to booster, if equipped.

33. Evacuate, charge and leak test the air conditioning system. See Chapter 1.

34. Connect the engine ground strap at the block and the starter cable at the starter. Install the right front engine support cushion-to-bracket bolt.

35. Connect the hose at the fuel pump. On Pacers, also connect the automatic transmission fluid cooler line.

36. If equipped with TCS, install the switch bracket and vacuum solenoid wire harness.

37. Connect the alternator, ignition coil distributor temperature and oil sender wiring. On Pacers, also connect the brake warning switch wiring.

38. Install and connect the battery and install the air cleaner.

39. Fill the cooling system and engine oil.

40. Install the hood. Connect the underhood light, if equipped.

Rocker Shafts and Rocker Studs
REMOVAL AND INSTALLATION
4-150

1. Remove the rocker arm cover. The cover seal is RTV sealer. Break the seal with a clean putty knife or razor blade. Don't attempt to remove the cover until the seal is broken. To remove the cover, pry where indicated at the bolt holes.

2. Remove the two capscrews at each bridge and pivot assembly. It's best to remove the capscrews alternately, a little at a time each to avoid damage to the bridge.

3. Remove the bridges, pivots and rocker arms. Keep them in order.

4. Install the rocker arms and bridge and pivot assemblies. Tighten the capscrews to 19 ft.lb.

5. Clean the mating surfaces of the cover and head.

6. Run a ⅛″ (3.175mm) bead of RTV sealer around the mating surface of the head. Install

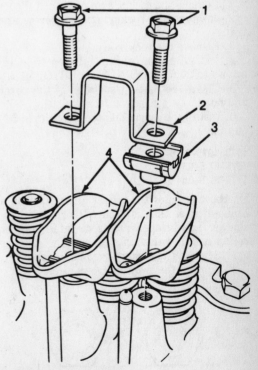

4-150 rocker arm removal

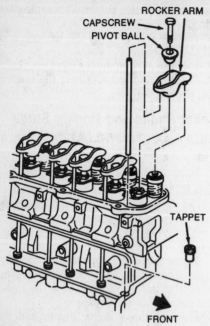

4-151 rocker arm assembly

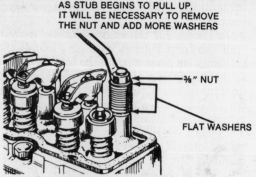

AS STUB BEGINS TO PULL UP, IT WILL BE NECESSARY TO REMOVE THE NUT AND ADD MORE WASHERS

Extracting a pressed-in rocker stud

Ream the stud bore for oversize rocker studs

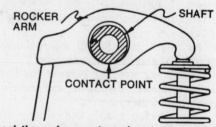

Check the rocker arm-to-rocker shaft contact area

the cover within 10 minutes! Don't allow any of the RTV material to drop into the engine! In the engine it will form and set and possibly block and oil passage. Torque the cover bolts to 36–60 in.lb.

4–151

1. Remove the rocker arm cover.
2. Remove the rocker arm capscrew and ball.
3. Remove the rocker arm.
4. Install rocker arms. Tighten the capscrews to 20 ft.lb. DO NOT OVERTORQUE!
5. Clean the mating surfaces of the cover and head.
6. Install the cover. Tighten the bolts to 36–60 in.lb.

1973, 1975–78 6–232
1975–87 6–258
1973–81 8–304

On these engines the rocker arms pivot on a bridged pivot that is secured with two capscrews. The bridged pivots maintain proper rocker arm-to-valve tip alignment.

1. Remove the rocker cover and gasket.
2. Remove the two capscrews at each

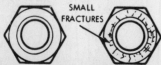

Stress cracks in the rocker nuts

bridged pivot, backing off each capscrew one turn at a time to avoid breaking the bridge.
3. Remove each bridged pivot and corresponding pair of rocker arms and place them on a clean surface in the same order as they are removed.
NOTE: *Bridged pivots, capscrews, rockers, and pushrods must all be reinstalled in their original positions.*
4. Clean all the parts in a suitable solvent and use compressed air to blow out the oil passages in the pushrods and the rocker arms. Replace any excessively worn parts.
5. Install rocker arms, pushrods and bridged pivots in the same positions from which they were removed.
NOTE: *Be sure that the bottom end of each pushrod is centered in the plunger which they were removed. Be sure that the bottom end of each pushrod is centered in the plunger cap of each hydraulic valve tappet.*
6. Install the capscrews and tighten them

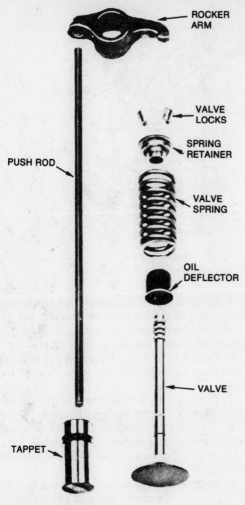

6-232, 258 valve train

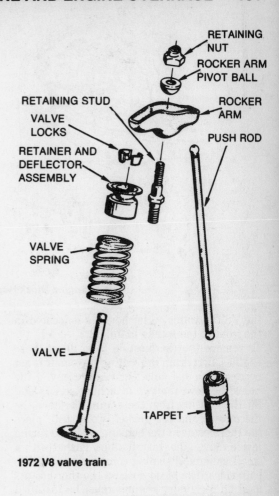

1972 V8 valve train

one turn at a time, alternating between the two screws on each bridge. Tighten the capscrews to 21 ft.lb. on the Sixes and 10 ft.lb. on the 304 V8.

7. Install the rocker cover(s) with new gasket(s).

Thermostat

REMOVAL AND INSTALLATION

CAUTION: *When draining the coolant, keep in mind that cats and dogs are attracted by the ethylene glycol antifreeze, and are quite likely to drink any that is left in an uncovered container or in puddles on the ground. This will prove fatal in sufficient quantity. Always drain the coolant into a sealable container. Coolant should be reused unless it is contaminated or several years old.*

The thermostat is located in the water outlet housing at the front or on top of the engine. On

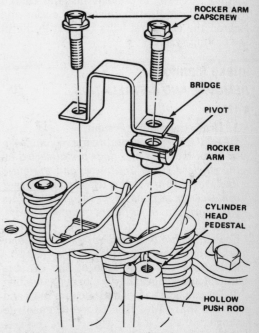

6 cylinder rocker arm assembly; V8 is almost identical

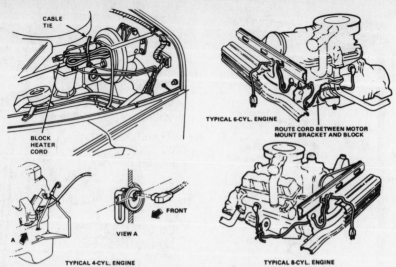

Engine Block Heater Installation

the V8 the water outlet housing is located in the front of the intake manifold.

To remove the thermostats from all of these engines, first drain the cooling system. It is not necessary to disconnect or remove any of the hoses. Remove the two attaching screws and lift the housing from the engine. Remove the thermostat and the gasket. To install, place the thermostat in the housing with the spring inside the engine. Install a new gasket with a small amount of sealing compound applied to both sides. The bleed hose on the thermostats used on 6-cylinder engines must be installed up (at 12 o'clock), to prevent 'burping' caused by trapped air. Install the water outlet and tighten the attaching bolts to 30 ft.lb. Refill the cooling system.

Intake Manifold

REMOVAL AND INSTALLATION

4–121

1. Drain the cooling system.

CAUTION: *When draining the coolant, keep in mind that cats and dogs are attracted by the ethylene glycol antifreeze, and are quite likely to drink any that is left in an uncovered container or in puddles on the ground. This will prove fatal in sufficient quantity. Always drain the coolant into a sealable container. Coolant should be reused unless it is contaminated or several years old.*

2. Remove the EGR tube at the exhaust manifold and remove the air cleaner assembly.

3. Disconnect the fuel and vacuum lines and plug the main fuel line to avoid gasoline leakage.

4. Remove the accelerator cable and the air hose from the diverter valve.

5. Remove the fuel pump and the power brake cylinder vacuum hose. Loosen the air conditioner compressor mounting bracket, if so equipped. Do not discharge the system.

6. Remove the water inlet and outlet hoses from the manifold and the PCV hose at the block.

7. Remove the wires from the carburetor, accessories and from the ignition coil.

8. Remove the manifold bracket lower screw, loosen and remove the manifold nuts, and remove the manifold and lift bracket from the engine.

9. Remove the gasket and clean the mating surfaces on the manifold and the cylinder head.

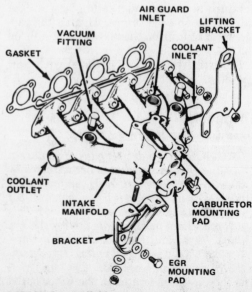

4-121 intake manifold

10. Install the a new gasket on the cylinder head.

11. Install the manifold and lift bracket on the engine. Don't tighten the manifold retaining nuts until the EGR tube is connected to the exhaust manifold. Install, but don't tighten, the manifold bracket lower screw.

12. Install the wires on the carburetor, accessories and ignition coil.

13. Install the water inlet and outlet hoses on the manifold and connect the PCV hose at the block.

14. Install the fuel pump and the power brake cylinder vacuum hose. Tighten the air conditioner compressor mounting bracket, if so equipped.

15. Install the accelerator cable and connect the air hose at the diverter valve.

16. Connect the fuel and vacuum lines.

17. Connect the EGR tube at the exhaust manifold and Install the air cleaner assembly. Then tighten the manifold retaining nuts to 18 ft.lb. torque and the bracket lower screw to 30 ft.lb.

18. Fill the cooling system.

19. Operate the engine for 3 to 5 minutes and check for leaks.

4-150

NOTE: *It may be necessary to remove the carburetor from the intake manifold before the manifold is removed.*

1. Disconnect the negative battery cable. Drain the radiator.

CAUTION: *When draining the coolant, keep in mind that cats and dogs are attracted by the ethylene glycol antifreeze, and are quite likely to drink any that is left in an uncovered container or in puddles on the ground. This will prove fatal in sufficient quantity. Always drain the coolant into a sealable container. Coolant should be reused unless it is contaminated or several years old.*

2. Remove the air cleaner. Disconnect the fuel pipe. Remove the carburetor as required.

3. Disconnect the coolant hoses from the intake manifold.

4. Disconnect the throttle cable from the bellcrank.

5. Disconnect the PCV valve vacuum hose from the intake manifold.

6. If equipped, remove the vacuum advance CTO valve vacuum hoses.

7. Disconnect the system coolant temperature sender wire connector (located on the intake manifold). Disconnect the air temperature sensor wire, if equipped.

8. Disconnect the vacuum hose from the EGR valve.

9. On vehicles equipped with power steering remove the power steering pump and its mounting bracket. Do not detach the power steering pump hoses.

10. Disconnect the intake manifold electric heater wire connector, as required.

11. Disconnect the throttle valve linkage, if equipped with automatic transmission.

12. Disconnect the EGR valve tube from the intake manifold.

13. Remove the intake manifold attaching screws, nuts and clamps. Remove the intake manifold. Discard the gasket.

14. Clean the mating surfaces of the manifold and cylinder head.

NOTE: *If the manifold is being replaced, ensure all fittings, etc., are transferred to the replacement manifold.*

15. Install the intake manifold. Install the intake manifold attaching screws, nuts and clamps. Torque manifold fasteners to 23 ft.lb.

16. Connect the EGR valve tube to the intake manifold.

17. Connect the throttle valve linkage, if equipped with automatic transmission.

18. Connect the intake manifold electric heater wire connector, as required.

19. On vehicles equipped with power steering install the power steering pump and its mounting bracket.

20. Connect the vacuum to from the EGR valve.

21. Connect the system coolant temperature sender wire connector (located on the intake manifold). Connect the air temperature sensor wire, if equipped.

22. If equipped, install the vacuum advance CTO valve vacuum hoses.

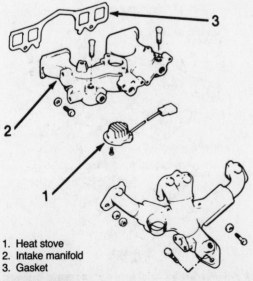

1. Heat stove
2. Intake manifold
3. Gasket

4-150 manifolds

23. Install the carburetor. Torque the mounting bolts to 14 ft.lb.
24. Connect the PCV valve vacuum hose to the intake manifold.
25. Connect the throttle cable to the bellcrank.
26. Connect the fuel pipe.
27. Connect the coolant hoses to the intake manifold.
28. Install the air cleaner.
29. Connect the negative battery cable.
30. Fill the cooling system.

4–151

1. Remove the negative cable.
2. Remove the air cleaner and the PCV valve hose.
CAUTION: *DO NOT remove the block drain plugs or loosen the radiator draincock the with system hot and under pressure because serious burns from the coolant can occur.*
3. Drain the cooling system.
CAUTION: *When draining the coolant, keep in mind that cats and dogs are attracted by the ethylene glycol antifreeze, and are quite likely to drink any that is left in an uncovered container or in puddles on the ground. This will prove fatal in sufficient quantity. Always drain the coolant into a sealable container. Coolant should be reused unless it is contaminated or several years old.*
4. Tag and remove the vacuum hoses (ensure the distributor vacuum advance hose is removed).
5. Disconnect the fuel pipe and electrical wire connections from the carburetor.
6. Disconnect the carburetor throttle linkage. Remove the carburetor and the carburetor spacer.
7. Remove the bellcrank and throttle linkage brackets and move them to one side for clearance.
8. Remove the heater hose at the intake manifold.
9. Remove the alternator. Note the position of spacers for installation.
10. Remove the manifold-to-cylinder head bolts and remove the manifold.
11. Position the replacement gasket and install the replacement manifold on the cylinder head. Start all bolts.

12. Tighten all bolts with 37 ft.lb.
13. Connect the heater hose to the intake manifold.
14. Install the bellcrank and throttle linkage brackets.
15. Connect the carburetor throttle linkage to the brackets and bellcrank.
16. Install the carburetor spacer and tighten the bolts with 15 ft.lb.
17. Install the carburetor and gasket. Tighten the nuts with 15 ft.lb.
18. Install the fuel pipe and electrical wire connections. Install the vacuum hoses.
19. Install the battery negative cable.
CAUTION: *Use extreme caution when the engine is operating. Do not stand in a direct line with the fan. Do not put your hands near pulleys, belts or fan. Do not wear loose clothing.*
20. Refill the cooling system. Start the engine and inspect for leaks.
21. Install the air cleaner and the PCV valve hose.

6–232
6–258

The intake manifold and exhaust manifold are mounted externally on the left side of the engine and are attached to the cylinder head. The intake and exhaust manifolds are removed as a unit. On some engines, an exhaust gas recirculation valve is mounted on the side of the intake manifold.

1. Remove the air cleaner and carburetor.
2. Disconnect the accelerator cable from the accelerator bellcrank.
3. Disconnect the PCS vacuum hose from the intake manifold.
4. Disconnect the distributor vacuum hose

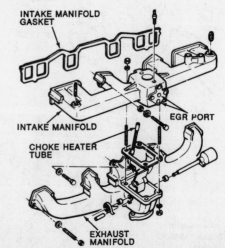

6 cylinder intake and exhaust manifold through 1980

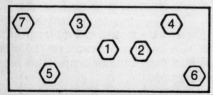

4-151 intake manifold bolt torque sequence

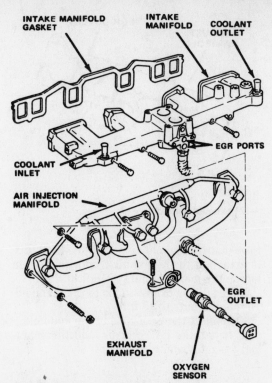

1981–82 6 cylinder intake and exhaust manifold assemblies

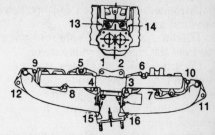

6 cylinder manifold torque sequences through 1980

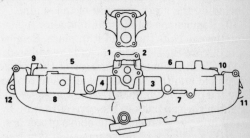

1981–82 6 cylinder manifold torque sequences

and electrical wires at the TCS solenoid vacuum valve.

5. Remove the TCS solenoid vacuum valve and bracket from the intake manifold. In some cases it might not be necessary to remove the TCS unit.

6. If so equipped, disconnect the EGR valve vacuum hoses.

7. Remove the power steering mounting bracket and pump and set it aside without disconnecting the hoses.

8. Remove the EGR valve, if so equipped.

9. Disconnect the exhaust pipe from the manifold flange. Disconnect the spark CTO hoses and remove the oxygen sensor.

10. Remove the manifold attaching bolts, nuts and clamps.

11. Separate the intake manifold and exhaust manifold from the engine as an assembly. Discard the gasket.

12. If either manifold is to be replaced, they should be separated at the heat riser area.

13. Clean the mating surfaces of the manifolds and the cylinder head before replacing the manifolds. Replace them in reverse order of the above procedure with a new gasket. Tighten the bolts and nuts to the specified torque in the proper sequence.

14. Connect the exhaust pipe to the manifold flange. Torque the nuts to 20 ft.lb. Connect the spark CTO hoses and install the oxygen sensor.

15. Install the EGR valve, if so equipped.

16. Install the power steering mounting bracket and pump.

17. If so equipped, connect the EGR valve vacuum hoses.

18. Install the TCS solenoid vacuum valve and bracket to the intake manifold.

19. Connect the distributor vacuum hose and electrical wires at the TCS solenoid vacuum valve.

20. Connect the PCS vacuum hose to the intake manifold.

21. Connect the accelerator cable to the accelerator bellcrank.

22. Install the air cleaner and carburetor.

8–304, 360, 401

1. Drain the coolant from the radiator.
CAUTION: *When draining the coolant, keep in mind that cats and dogs are attracted by the ethylene glycol antifreeze, and are quite likely to drink any that is left in an uncovered container or in puddles on the ground. This will prove fatal in sufficient quantity. Always drain the coolant into a sealable container. Coolant should be reused unless it is contaminated or several years old.*

2. Remove the air cleaner assembly.

3. Disconnect the spark plug wires. Remove the spark plug wire brackets from the valve covers, and the bypass valve bracket.

4. Disconnect the upper radiator hose and the by-pass hose from the intake manifold. Disconnect the heater hose from the rear of the manifold.

5. Disconnect the ignition coil bracket and lay the coil aside.

6. Disconnect the tCS solenoid vacuum valve from the right side valve cover.

7. Disconnect all lines, hoses, linkages and wires from the carburetor and intake manifold and TCS components as required.

8. Disconnect the air delivery hoses at the air distribution manifolds.

9. Disconnect the air pump diverter valve and lay the valve and the bracket assembly, including the hoses, forward of the engine.

10. Remove the intake manifold after removing the cap bolts that hold it in place. Remove and discard the side gaskets and the end seals.

11. Clean the mating surfaces of the intake manifold and the cylinder head before replacing the intake manifold. Use new gaskets and tighten the cap bolts to the correct torque. Install in reverse order of the above procedure.

NOTE: *There is no specified tighten sequence for this intake manifold. Start at the center bolts and work outward.*

12. Connect the air pump diverter valve.

13. Connect the air delivery hoses at the air distribution manifolds.

14. Connect all lines, hoses, linkages and wires to the carburetor and intake manifold and TCS components as required.

15. Install the TCS solenoid vacuum valve to the right side valve cover.

16. Install the ignition coil bracket.

17. Connect the upper radiator hose and the by-pass hose to the intake manifold. Connect the heater hose to the rear of the manifold.

18. Connect the spark plug wires. Install the spark plug wire brackets on the valve covers, and the bypass valve bracket.

19. Install the air cleaner assembly.

20. Fill the cooling system.

Exhaust Manifold

REMOVAL AND INSTALLATION

4–121

1. Remove the TAC cold air induction manifold assembly and components.

2. Disconnect the EGR tube from the manifold.

3. Remove the exhaust pipe from the manifold.

4. Remove the manifold retaining nuts and washers.

5. Remove the manifold and gasket from the engine.

6. Clean the mating surfaces of the manifold and the head.

7. Install a new gasket on the head and install the manifold. Install, but do not tighten,

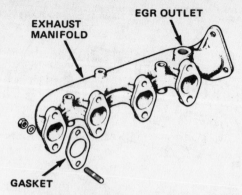

4-121 exhaust manifold

the exhaust manifold nuts until the EGR tube is attached to the exhaust manifold, then torque the manifold nuts to 18 ft.lb.

8. Install the exhaust pipe to the manifold. Torque the nuts to 18 ft.lb.

9. Connect the EGR tube to the manifold.

10. Install the TAC cold air induction manifold assembly and components.

4–150

1. Remove the intake manifold.

2. Disconnect the EGR tube.

3. Disconnect the exhaust pipe at the manifold.

4. Disconnect the oxygen sensor wire.

5. Support the manifold and remove the nuts from the studs.

6. If a new manifold is being installed, transfer the oxygen sensor. Torque the sensor to 35 ft.lb.

7. Thoroughly clean the gasket mating surfaces of the manifold and head.

8. Install the manifold, using a new gasket. Torque the nuts to 23 ft.lb.

9. Connect the oxygen sensor wire.

10. Connect the exhaust pipe at the manifold.

11. Connect the EGR tube.

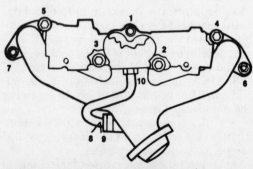

4-150 exhaust manifold installation

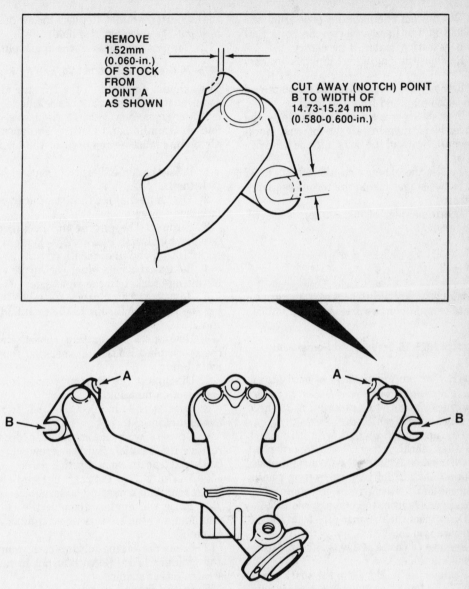

REMOVE
1.52mm
(0.060-in.)
OF STOCK
FROM
POINT A
AS SHOWN

CUT AWAY (NOTCH) POINT
B TO WIDTH OF
14.73-15.24 mm
(0.580-0.600-in.)

A

A

B

B

Exhaust manifold modification on the 4-150

12. Install the intake manifold.

NOTE: *On some 1984 4–150 engines, the manifold end studs can be bent or broken if the manifold is misaligned. To remedy this:*

a. Remove the manifold.

b. Replace any bent or broken studs.

c. Using a straightedge, check the flatness of the manifold mating surface. If a 0.015″ (0.38mm) flat feeler gauge can be inserted between the straightedge and the manifold, at any point, replace the manifold.

d. Modify the original or replacement manifold by grinding the mounting flanges as shown in the accompanying illustration.

e. Install the manifold

4–151

1. Remove the air cleaner and the hot air tube.

2. Remove the Pulsair system from the exhaust manifold.

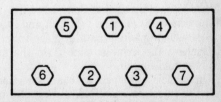

5   1   4

6   2   3   7

4-151 exhaust manifold torque sequence

3. Disconnect the exhaust pipe from the manifold at the flange. Spray the bolts first with penetrating sealer, if necessary.

4. Remove the engine oil dipstick bracket bolt.

5. Remove the exhaust manifold bolts and remove the manifold from the head.

6. To install, place a new gasket against the cylinder head, then install the exhaust manifold over it. Start all the bolts into the head finger tight.

7. Torque the exhaust manifold bolts to 37 ft.lb. in two stages, using the torque sequence illustrated.

8. The remainder of installation is the reverse removal.

6–232
6–258

The exhaust manifold is removed along with the intake manifold. See previous instructions.

V8, Except 1975–76 Gremlin and Hornet w/Air Pump

NOTE: *The mating surfaces of both the exhaust manifold and the cylinder head are machined smooth, thus eliminating any need for a gasket between them.*

1. Disconnect the wires from the spark plugs after marking them for firing order.

2. On models equipped with air injection, disconnect the air delivery hoses from the injection manifold. Remove the injection manifold and nozzles from the exhaust manifold.

3. Disconnect the exhaust pipe from the exhaust manifold flange.

4. Remove the bolts and washers used to retain the manifold.

5. Remove the shields from the spark plugs. On 1977 and later Hornets and Concords only, before removing the right side manifold, remove the transmission filler tube bolt and tube.

6. Remove the exhaust manifold from cylinder head.

7. Clean the machined surfaces of the manifold and head.

8. Install the exhaust manifold on the cylinder head.

9. Install the shields on the spark plugs. On 1977 and later Hornets and Concords only, install the transmission filler tube bolt and tube. Use a new O-ring when installing the tube.

10. Connect the exhaust pipe from the exhaust manifold flange.

11. On models equipped with air injection, install the injection manifold and nozzles on the exhaust manifold. Connect the air delivery hoses at the injection manifold.

12. Connect the wires at the spark plugs.

1975–76 Gremlin and Hornet V8 With Air Pump

The exhaust manifold on the left side may be removed in the same manner s detailed for other V8 engines; however, the right side manifold on Gremlins and Hornets equipped with air pumps must be removed in the following order:

1. Raise the car and securely support it with jackstands.

2. Disconnect the exhaust pipe from the manifold flange.

3. Support the engine at the vibration damper, by placing a jack with a block of wood on its lifting pad underneath it.

4. Remove the bolts which secure the engine mounting bracket on the right side.

5. Remove the air cleaner assembly, including the tube which runs to the manifold heat stove.

6. Disconnect the battery cables. Remove the spark plug leads after marking them for installation.

7. Disconnect the air supply hose from the air injection manifold.

8. Remove the air injection tubes from the exhaust manifold.

9. On cars with automatic transmissions, remove the dipstick and the screw which secures the transmission dipstick tube.

10. Working from the rear, unscrew the exhaust manifold mounting bolts.

11. Raise the engine. Remove the exhaust manifold and the air injection manifold as an assembly.

12. Clean the joining surfaces of the manifold and cylinder head. Be careful not to nick or scratch either surface.

13. Install the exhaust manifold and the air injection manifold as an assembly.

14. On cars with automatic transmissions, install the dipstick and the screw which secures the transmission dipstick tube.

15. Install the air injection tubes.

16. Connect the air supply hose at the air injection manifold.

17. Connect the battery cables. Install the spark plug leads.

18. Install the air cleaner assembly, including the tube which runs to the manifold heat stove.

19. Install the bolts which secure the engine mounting bracket on the right side.

20. Remove the jack.

21. Connect the exhaust pipe at the manifold flange.

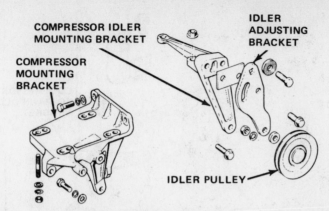

Compressor mounting on the 6-258 for 1977–80 all, and 1981, except Calif.

22. Raise the car and securely support it with jackstands.

Air Conditioning Compressor
REMOVAL AND INSTALLATION

1. Isolate the compressor. See Chapter 1.
2. Remove both service valves and cap the valves and compressor ports immediately.
3. Loosen the power steering pump and remove the drive belt.
4. Remove the power steering pump and brackets and lay the pump aside, without disconnecting the hoses.

5. Loosen the idler pulley eccentric and remove the compressor drive pulley.
6. Disconnect the clutch wire.
7. Unbolt and remove the compressor.
8. Install the compressor.
9. Disconnect the clutch wire.
10. Install the compressor drive pulley and adjust the belt tension.
11. Install the power steering pump and brackets.
12. Install and adjust the power steering drive belt.
13. Install both service valves and remove the caps.

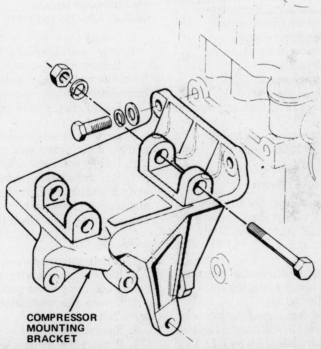

Compressor mounting on the 1981 California 6-258 and all 1982–87 models

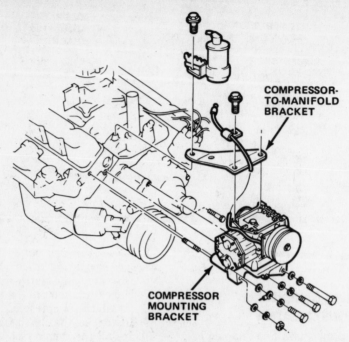

V8 compressor mounting

14. Purge the compressor of air and open the service valves. See Chapter 1.

4–151

1. Isolate the compressor. See Chapter 1.
2. Remove both service valves and cap the valves and compressor ports immediately.
3. Loosen and remove the drive belt.
4. Disconnect the clutch wire.
5. Unbolt and remove the compressor.
6. Install the compressor.
7. Connect the clutch wire.
8. Install and adjust the drive belt.
9. Install both service valves and remove the caps.
10. Purge the compressor of air and open service valves. See Chapter 1.

1975–80 6–232, 258
1981 6–232, 258, except California

1. Isolate the compressor. See Chapter 1.
2. Remove both service valves and cap the valves and compressor ports immediately.
3. Remove the alternator belt and adjusting bolt.
4. Remove the upper alternator mounting bolt and loosen the lower mounting bolt.
5. Remove the idler pulley.
6. Disconnect the compressor clutch wire. Remove the compressor mounting nuts and lift out the compressor. BE CAREFUL; IT'S HEAVY!
7. For installation, install the compressor, alternator and belt, idler pulley, and adjust the drive belts.
8. Install the service valves and purge the compressor of air. Open the valves.
9. Connect the clutch wire.

1981 California Models
1982–87 All 4–150 and 6–258

1. Isolate the compressor. See Chapter 1.
2. Disconnect the battery ground.
3. Remove the discharge and suction hoses from the compressor and cap all openings immediately.
4. Loosen the alternator and remove the drive belts.
5. Remove the alternator from its brackets and set it out of the way.
6. Unbolt and remove the compressor.
7. For installation, install the compressor and alternator, connect the hoses and install and tension the drive belts. Connect the compressor clutch wire. Open the valves.

8–304, 360, 401

1. Isolate the compressor. See Chapter 1.
2. Remove both service valves and cap the valves and compressor ports immediately.
3. Loosen the alternator and remove the drive belts.
4. Remove the alternator mounting bracket.
5. Remove the compressor clutch wire.
6. Remove the compressor and mounting bracket as an assembly.

7. For installation, install the compressor and mounting bracket, install the alternator bracket, connect the clutch wire, install the belts, idler pulley, and adjust the drive belts.

8. Install the service valves and purge the compressor of air. Open the valves.

Radiator

REMOVAL AND INSTALLATION

1. Raise the hood and remove the radiator cap. Be sure the engine is cold.

2. Drain the radiator. If the coolant appears to be clean, drain it into a clean container and save it for re-use.

CAUTION: *When draining the coolant, keep in mind that cats and dogs are attracted by the ethylene glycol antifreeze, and are quite likely to drink any that is left in an uncovered container or in puddles on the ground. This will prove fatal in sufficient quantity. Always drain the coolant into a sealable container. Coolant should be reused unless it is contaminated or several years old.*

3. Remove the upper and lower radiator hoses. Disconnect the coolant recovery hose, if so equipped.

4. On four cylinder models, remove the ambient air intake from the radiator support.

5. On four cylinder air conditioned models, remove the charcoal canister and the bracket.

6. Remove the fan shroud, if so equipped.

7. On automatic transmission models, disconnect and plug the fluid cooler lines. Remove battery on Pacers for access.

8. Remove the radiator attaching screws and bolts and lift out the radiator.

9. Install the radiator.

10. On automatic transmission models, connect and plug the fluid cooler lines. Install battery on Pacers.

11. Install the fan shroud, if so equipped.

12. On 4–121 air conditioned models, install the charcoal canister and the bracket.

13. On 4–121 models, install the ambient air intake from the radiator support.

14. Install the upper and lower radiator hoses. Connect the coolant recovery hose, if so equipped.

15. Fill the cooling system.

16. Install the radiator cap.

Water Pump

REMOVAL AND INSTALLATION

The water pump is a centrifugal unit having a non-adjustable packless seal. It is non-serviceable and must be replace of defective. No maintenance is required.

4–121

1. Drain the cooling system. Disconnect the negative (–) cable from the battery. Remove the fan shroud.

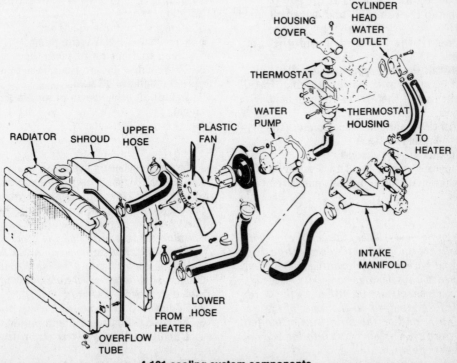

4-121 cooling system components

CAUTION: *When draining the coolant, keep in mind that cats and dogs are attracted by the ethylene glycol antifreeze, and are quite likely to drink any that is left in an uncovered container or in puddles on the ground. This will prove fatal in sufficient quantity. Always drain the coolant into a sealable container. Coolant should be reused unless it is contaminated or several years old.*

2. Rotate the crankshaft until the camshaft and crankshaft are at TDC for number one cylinder.

3. If equipped with power steering, loosen the pump and remove the belt. Loosen the air conditioner idler pulley and remove the belt, if so equipped.

4. Loosen the alternator and air pump.

5. Remove the fan, spacer, and pulley.

6. Remove the belt guard and air pump bracket.

7. Remove the camshaft and drive belt idler pulley.

8. Disconnect all the hoses from the pump except the hose from the thermostat.

9. Remove the water pump attaching bolts and pull the pump out of the hose from the thermostat.

10. Clean the gasket from the block, install a new gasket on the pump or block.

11. Insert the pump into the thermostat hose, install the pump attaching bolts and torque the small bolts to 7 ft.lb. and the large bolts to 16 ft.lb.

12. Connect all the hoses at the pump.

13. Install the camshaft and drive belt idler pulley.

14. Install the belt guard and air pump bracket.

15. Install the fan, spacer, and pulley.

16. If equipped with power steering, install the belt. Install the air conditioner belt, if so equipped.

17. Fill the cooling system. Connect the negative (–) battery cable.

18. Install the fan shroud.

19. Operate engine for 3 to 5 minutes with the heater on to check for leaks and correct fluid level.

4–150

NOTE: *Some 4–150 engines with air conditioning are equipped with a serpentine drive belt and have a reverse rotating water pump coupled with a viscous fan drive assembly. The components are identified by the words REVERSE stamped on the cover of the viscous drive and on the inner side of the fan. The word REV is also cast into the body of the water pump.*

1. Drain the cooling system.

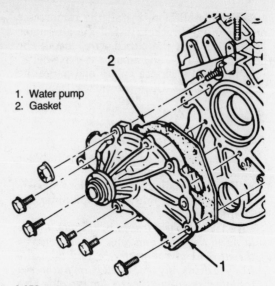

1. Water pump
2. Gasket

4-150 water pump

CAUTION: *When draining the coolant, keep in mind that cats and dogs are attracted by the ethylene glycol antifreeze, and are quite likely to drink any that is left in an uncovered container or in puddles on the ground. This will prove fatal in sufficient quantity. Always drain the coolant into a sealable container. Coolant should be reused unless it is contaminated or several years old.*

2. Disconnect the hoses at the pump.

3. Remove the drive belts.

4. Remove the power steering pump bracket.

5. Remove the fan and shroud.

6. Unbolt and remove the pump.

7. Clean the mating surfaces thoroughly.

8. Using a new gasket, install the pump and torque the bolts to 13 ft.lb.

9. Install all other parts in reverse order of removal.

4–151

1. Drain the cooling system.

CAUTION: *When draining the coolant, keep in mind that cats and dogs are attracted by the ethylene glycol antifreeze, and are quite likely to drink any that is left in an uncovered container or in puddles on the ground. This will prove fatal in sufficient quantity. Always drain the coolant into a sealable container. Coolant should be reused unless it is contaminated or several years old.*

2. Remove all drive belts.

3. Remove the fan and pump pulley.

4. Unbolt and remove the pump from the engine.

5. Clean the gasket surfaces, coat the new

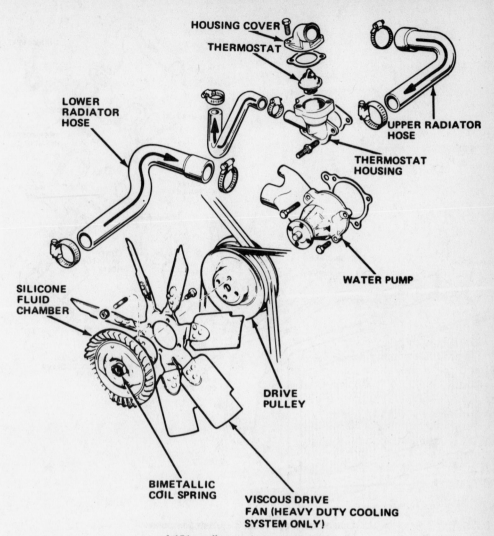

4-151 cooling system components

gasket with non-hardening type sealer and position the gasket on the block.

6. Coat the threaded areas of the bolts with waterproof sealer and install the pump. Torque the bolts to 25 ft.lb.

7. Install the pulley and fan. Tighten the fan and hub bolts to 18 ft.lb.

8. Install the drive belts. The belts should be adjusted so that a ½″ (12.7mm) deflection is present when they are depressed mid-point along their longest straight run.

6–232, 258

1. Drain the cooling system.
CAUTION: *When draining the coolant, keep in mind that cats and dogs are attracted by the ethylene glycol antifreeze, and are quite likely to drink any that is left in an uncovered container or in puddles on the ground. This will prove fatal in sufficient quantity. Always*
drain the coolant into a sealable container. Coolant should be reused unless it is contaminated or several years old.

2. Disconnect all hoses at the pump.

3. Remove the drive belts.

4. Remove the fan shroud attaching screws.

5. Unbolt the fan and fan drive assembly and remove along with the shroud. On some models it may be easier to turn the shroud ½ turn.

6. Unbolt and remove the pump.
NOTE: *Engines built for sale in California having a single, serpentine drive belt and viscous fan drive, have a reverse rotating pump and drive. These components are identified by the word REVERSE stamped on the drive cover and inner side of the fan, and REV cast into the water pump body. Never interchange standard rotating parts with these.*

7. Installation is the reverse of removal. Al-

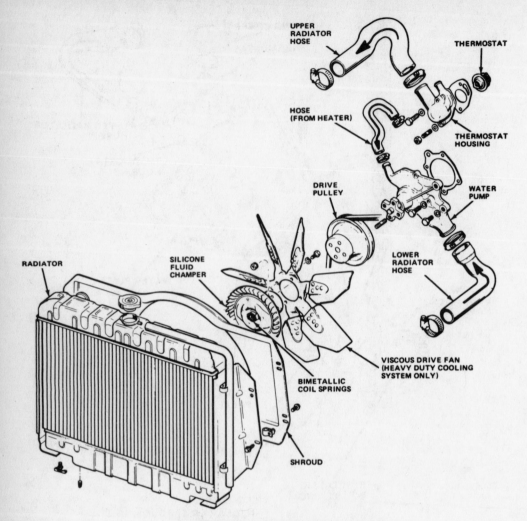

Late model 6-cyl. cooling system components

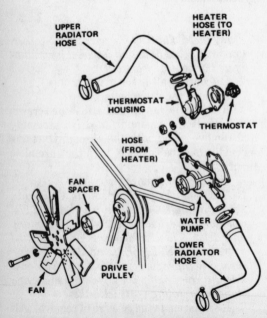

Early 6-cylinder cooling system components

ways use a new gasket coated with sealer. Torque the water pump bolts to 13 ft.lb.; the fan bolts to 18 ft.lb.

8–304, 360, 401

1. Drain the cooling system.
CAUTION: *When draining the coolant, keep in mind that cats and dogs are attracted by the ethylene glycol antifreeze, and are quite likely to drink any that is left in an uncovered container or in puddles on the ground. This will prove fatal in sufficient quantity. Always drain the coolant into a sealable container. Coolant should be reused unless it is contaminated or several years old.*
2. Disconnect all hoses at the pump.
3. Loosen all drive belts.
4. Remove the shroud, but reinsert one bolt to hold the radiator.
5. Remove the fan and hub.
6. If the vehicle is equipped with A/C install a double nut on the compressor bracket-to-water pump stud and remove the stud.

7. Remove, but do not disconnect the alternator and bracket.

8. If so equipped, remove the nuts that attach the power steering pump to the rear half of the pump bracket.

9. Remove the two bolts that attach the front half to the rear half of the bracket.

10. Remove the remaining upper screw from the inner air pump support bracket, loosen the lower bolt and drop the bracket away from the power steering front bracket.

11. Remove the front half of the power steering bracket from the water pump mounting stud.

12. Unbolt and remove the water pump.

13. Install the pump. Always use a new gasket coated with sealer. Torque the pump-to-timing case bolts to 48 in.lb. and the pump-to-block bolts to 25 ft.lb.

14. Install the front half of the power steering bracket to the water pump mounting stud. Torque the power steering pulley nut to 60 ft.lb.

15. Install the upper screw from the inner air pump support bracket, and tighten the lower bolt.

16. If so equipped, install the nuts that attach the power steering pump to the rear half of the pump bracket.

17. Install the two bolts that attach the front half to the rear half of the bracket.

18. Install the alternator and bracket.

19. If the vehicle is equipped with A/C install a double nut on the compressor bracket-to-water pump stud and install the stud.

20. Install the fan and hub.

21. Install the shroud.

22. Adjust all drive belts.

1. Radiator upper hose
2. Thermostat housing cover
3. Gasket
4. Thermostat
5. Gasket
6. Drive pulley
7. Viscous drive fan
8. Coolant recovery bottle
9. Radiator
10. Shroud
11. Bimetallic coil spring
12. Silicone fluid chamber
13. Stud
14. Hose (from heater)
15. Water pump
16. Bypass hose

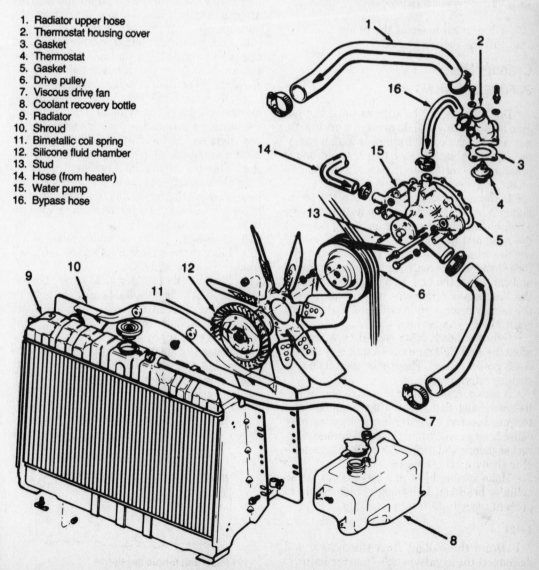

Late model V8 cooling system components

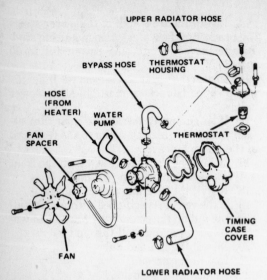

Early V8 cooling system components

23. Connect all hoses at the pump.
24. Fill the cooling system.

Cylinder Head

BEFORE BEGINNING

• Don't loosen the head bolts until the engine is thoroughly cool, to prevent warping. Do not remove block drain plugs or loosen radiator draincock with the system hot and under pressure, as serious burns from coolant can occur.

• If the head sticks, operate the starter to loosen it by compression or rap it upward with a soft hammer. Do not force anything between the head and the block.

• Resurfacing (milling or grinding) the cylinder head will increase the compression ratio, and can affect the emission output, as well as the fuel octane requirement. For this reason the factory recommends replacing rather than resurfacing cylinder heads.

• Cylinder heads bolts should be retorqued after the first 500 miles or so unless a special AMC gasket is used. The special gasket doesn't require retorquing.

• It is important to note that each engine has its own head bolt tightening sequence and torque. Incorrect tightening procedure may cause head warpage and compression loss. Correct sequence and torque for each engine model is shown in this chapter.

• Make sure to blow any coolant out of the cylinder head bolt holes before reassembly to prevent inaccurate torque readings.

4–121

1. Drain the coolant from the system and disconnect the negative cable from the battery.

CAUTION: *When draining the coolant, keep in mind that cats and dogs are attracted by the ethylene glycol antifreeze, and are quite likely to drink any that is left in an uncovered container or in puddles on the ground. This will prove fatal in sufficient quantity. Always drain the coolant into a sealable container. Coolant should be reused unless it is contaminated or several years old.*

2. Remove the air cleaner assembly, vacuum hoses and flexible hoses from the cylinder head area.

3. Remove the radiator hoses, radiator bypass hose and the heater hoses.

4. Remove the accessory drive belts, camshaft drive belt cover, and the camshaft drive belt. Loosen the compressor mounting bracket if equipped with A/C.

5. Remove the fan belt, fan blades, spacer and pulley. Remove the air pump and also the alternator pivot bolt. Do not disconnect the wire harness from the alternator.

6. Remove the air pump front bracket, and the exhaust pipe from the manifold. Remove the air hose from the diverter valve and remove the EGR tube to bell housing screw.

7. Disconnect the remaining wires to the electrical units of the cylinder head, marking the wires for connection during assembly.

8. Remove the fuel line at the bottom of the intake manifold, and remove the screw from the bottom of the manifold bracket.

9. Disconnect the power brake vacuum hose. Remove the remaining fuel vapor control hoses, PCV hoses, and the remaining vacuum lines.

10. Disconnect the accelerator cable.

11. Remove the coolant inlet and outlet hoses from the intake manifold.

12. Remove the cylinder head cover. Loosen and remove the head bolts. Loosen the bolts in the reverse order of the tightening sequence, in two passes. Remove the cylinder head, manifolds and carburetor as a unit.

13. Clean the machined surfaces of the cylinder head and the engine block. With a straight edge and feeler gauge, check the flatness of the mating surfaces. There should not be a distortion of over 0.002″ (0.051mm) on both surfaces.

14. After the necessary services have been done to the cylinder head and/or the block as-

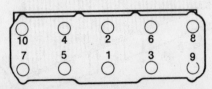

4-121 head bolt torque sequence

sembly, prepare the mating surfaces by cleaning thoroughly.

15. Install a new head gasket, and place the head on the block with the aid of locating dowels. Torque the cylinder head according to the torque sequence illustration, and in three stages.

16. Install the coolant inlet and outlet hoses on the intake manifold.

17. Connect the accelerator cable.

18. Connect the power brake vacuum hose. Install the fuel vapor control hoses, PCV hoses, and the vacuum lines.

19. Attach the fuel line at the bottom of the intake manifold, and install the screw in the bottom of the manifold bracket.

20. Connect the wires to the electrical units of the cylinder head.

21. Install the air pump front bracket, and the exhaust pipe at the manifold. Install the air hose at the diverter valve and install the EGR tube-to-bell housing screw.

22. Install the fan belt, fan blades, spacer and pulley. Install the air pump and also the alternator pivot bolt.

23. Install the accessory drive belts, camshaft drive belt cover, and the camshaft drive belt.

24. Install the radiator hoses, radiator by-pass hose and the heater hoses.

25. Install the air cleaner assembly, vacuum hoses and flexible hoses at the cylinder head area.

26. Fill the cooling system and connect the negative battery cable.

27. Temporarily install the head cover. Start the engine and allow it to warm up for five minutes.

28. When the engine has warmed up to operating temperature, stop the engine and remove the top engine cover.

29. Following the head torque sequence, loosen the first head bolt ⅛ of a turn and retorque the bolt to 80 ft.lb. Proceed to the second bolt and repeat the procedure fro each head bolt until all the bolts have been retorqued to the new specification.

30. Check the engine for leakage.

4–150

1. Disconnect the battery ground.
2. Drain the cooling system.
CAUTION: *When draining the coolant, keep in mind that cats and dogs are attracted by the ethylene glycol antifreeze, and are quite likely to drink any that is left in an uncovered container or in puddles on the ground. This will prove fatal in sufficient quantity. Always drain the coolant into a sealable container.*

Coolant should be reused unless it is contaminated or several years old.

3. Disconnect the hoses at the thermostat housing.

4. Remove the air cleaner.

5. Remove the rocker arm cover. The cover seal is RTV sealer. Break the seal with a clean putty knife or razor blade. Don't attempt to remove the cover until the seal is broken. To remove the cover, pry where indicated at the bolt holes.

6. Remove the rocker arms. Keep them in order!

7. Remove the pushrods. Keep them in order!

8. Remove the power steering pump bracket.

9. Suspend the pump out of the way.

10. Remove the intake and exhaust manifolds.

11. Remove the air conditioning compressor drive belt.

12. Loosen the alternator drive belt.

13. Remove the compressor/alternator bracket mounting bolt.

14. Unbolt the compressor and suspend it out of the way. DO NOT DISCONNECT THE REFRIGERANT LINES!

15. Remove the spark plugs.

16. Disconnect the temperature sending unit wire.

17. Remove the head bolts.

18. Lift the head off the engine and place it on a clean workbench.

19. Remove the head gasket.

NOTE: *Some head bolts used on the spark plug side of the 1984 4–150 were improperly hardened and may break under the head during service or at head installation while torquing the bolts. Engines with the defective bolts are serial numbers 310U06 through 310U14. Whenever a broken bolts is found, replace all bolts on the spark plug side of the head with bolt #400 6593.*

20. Thoroughly clean the gasket mating surfaces. Remove all traces of old gasket material. Remove all carbon deposits from the combus-

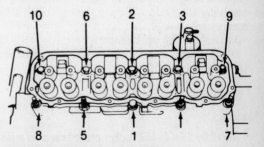

4-150 head bolt torque sequence

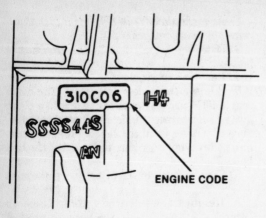

ENGINE CODE

Engine code location

tion chambers. Lay a straightedge across the head and check for flatness. Total deviation should not exceed 0.001″ (0.0254mm).

21. Do not apply sealant to the head or block. Coat both sides of the gasket with sealer. The gasket should be stamped TOP for installation. Place the gasket on the block.

22. Install the head on the block.

23. Coat the bolt labeled 8 in the torque sequence illustration, with Permatex #2®, or equivalent. Install all the bolts. Tighten the bolts in three equal steps, in the sequence shown, to 85 ft.lb. Torque #8 to 75 ft.lb.

24. Connect the temperature sending unit wire.

25. Install the spark plugs.

26. Install the compressor.

27. Install the compressor/alternator bracket mounting bolt.

28. Adjust the alternator drive belt.

29. Install the air conditioning compressor drive belt.

30. Install the intake and exhaust manifolds.

31. Install the power steering pump bracket.

32. Install the pushrods. Keep them in order!

33. Install the rocker arms. Keep them in order!

34. Thoroughly clean the mating surfaces of the head and rocker cover. Run a ⅛″ (3.175mm) bead of RTV sealer along the length of the sealing surface of the head. Position the cover on the head within 10 minutes of applying the sealer. Torque the cover bolts, in a crisscross pattern, to 55 in.lb.

35. Install the air cleaner.

36 Connect the hoses at the thermostat housing.

37. Connect the battery ground.

38. Fill the cooling system.

4–151

NOTE: *The 4–151 rocker cover is sealed with RTV silicone gasket material. Do not use a conventional gasket.*

1. Drain the cooling system and disconnect the hoses at the thermostat housing.

CAUTION: *When draining the coolant, keep in mind that cats and dogs are attracted by the ethylene glycol antifreeze, and are quite likely to drink any that is left in an uncovered container or in puddles on the ground. This will prove fatal in sufficient quantity. Always drain the coolant into a sealable container. Coolant should be reused unless it is contaminated or several years old.*

2. Remove the cylinder head cover (valve cover), the gasket, the rocker arm assembly, and the pushrods.

3. Remove the intake and exhaust manifold from the cylinder head.

4. Disconnect the spark plug wires and remove the spark plugs to avoid damaging them.

5. Disconnect the temperature sending unit wire, ignition coil and bracket assembly and battery ground cable from the engine.

6. Remove the cylinder head bolts, the cylinder head and gasket from the block.

7. Thoroughly clean the gasket mating surfaces. Remove all traces of old gasket material. Remove all carbon deposits from the combustion chambers. Lay a straightedge across the head and check for flatness. Total deviation should not exceed 0.001″ (0.0254mm).

8. Do not apply sealant to the head or block. Coat both sides of the gasket with sealer. The gasket should be stamped TOP for installation. Place the gasket on the block.

9. Install the head on the block. Insert the bolts and tighten them, in sequence, to the proper torque.

10. Install the pushrods and the rocker arm assembly.

11. Install the intake and exhaust manifold on the cylinder head.

12. Install the spark plugs and connect the spark plug wires.

13. Connect the temperature sending unit wire, ignition coil and bracket assembly and battery ground cable at the engine.

14. Connect the hoses at the thermostat housing.

15. Thoroughly clean the mating surfaces of the head and rocker cover. Run a ⅛″ (3.175mm) bead of RTV sealer along the length of the sealing surface of the head, inboard of the bolt holes. Position the cover on

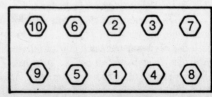

4-151 head bolt torque sequence

the head within 10 minutes of applying the sealer. Torque the cover bolts, in a crisscross pattern, to 55 in.lb.

16. Fill the cooling system.

6–232
6–258

NOTE: *On Pacers, run the wipers to the center of the windshield to ease valve cover removal.*

1. Drain the cooling system and disconnect the hoses at the thermostat housing.

CAUTION: *When draining the coolant, keep in mind that cats and dogs are attracted by the ethylene glycol antifreeze, and are quite likely to drink any that is left in an uncovered container or in puddles on the ground. This will prove fatal in sufficient quantity. Always drain the coolant into a sealable container. Coolant should be reused unless it is contaminated or several years old.*

2. Remove the cylinder head cover (valve cover), the gasket, the rocker arm assembly, and the pushrods.

NOTE: *The pushrods must be replaced in their original positions.*

3. Remove the intake and exhaust manifold from the cylinder head.

If equipped with power steering, remove the power steering pump bracket and Air Guard pump and set them aside. Don't disconnect the hoses.

4. Disconnect the spark plug wires and the spark plugs to avoid damaging them.

5. Disconnect the temperature sending unit wire, ignition coil and bracket assembly from the engine.

If the vehicle is equipped with air conditioning, remove the drive belt idler pulley bracket from the cylinder head. Loosen the alternator drive belt and remove the bolts from the compressor mounting bracket. Set the compressor aside, all hoses attached.

6. Remove the cylinder head bolts, the cylinder head and gasket from the block.

7. Thoroughly clean the gasket mating surfaces. Remove all traces of old gasket material. Remove all carbon deposits from the combustion chambers. Lay a straightedge across the head and check for flatness. Total deviation should not exceed 0.001″ (0.0254mm).

8. Do not apply sealant to the head or block. Coat both sides of the gasket with sealer. The gasket should be stamped TOP for installation. Place the gasket on the block.

9. Install the head on the block. Insert the bolts and tighten them, in sequence, to the proper torque, in three progressive passes. Torque all bolts to 85 ft.lb., except #11 in the torque sequence, which should be coated with sealer and torqued to 75 ft.lb.

NOTE: *Some head bolts used on the spark plug side of the 1984 6–258 were improperly hardened and may break under the head during service or at head installation while torquing the bolts. Engines with the defective bolts are serial numbers 310C06 through 310C14. Whenever a broken bolts is found, replace all seven bolts on the spark plug side of the head with bolt #400 6593.*

10. Connect the temperature sending unit wire, ignition coil and bracket assembly at the engine.

11. Install the spark plugs and connect the spark plug wires.

12. Install the intake and exhaust manifold on the cylinder head.

13. Install the the rocker arm assembly, and the pushrods.

NOTE: *The pushrods must be replaced in their original positions.*

14. Install the cylinder head cover (valve cover) and the gasket.

15. Connect the hoses at the thermostat housing.

16. Fill the cooling system

8–304, 360, 401

1. Drain the cooling system and cylinder block.

CAUTION: *When draining the coolant, keep in mind that cats and dogs are attracted by the ethylene glycol antifreeze, and are quite likely to drink any that is left in an uncovered container or in puddles on the ground. This will prove fatal in sufficient quantity. Always drain the coolant into a sealable container. Coolant should be reused unless it is contaminated or several years old.*

2. When removing the right cylinder head, it may be necessary to remove the heater core housing from the firewall.

3. Remove the valve cover(s) and gasket(s).

4. Remove the rocker arm assemblies and the pushrods.

NOTE: *The valve train components must be replaced in their original positions.*

5. Remove the spark plugs to avoid damaging them.

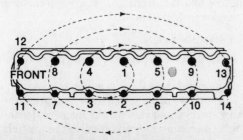

6 cylinder head bolt torque sequence

6. Remove the intake manifold with the carburetor still attached.

7. Remove the exhaust pipes at the flange of the exhaust manifold. When replacing the exhaust pipes it is advisable to install new gaskets at the flange.

8. Loosen all of the drive belts.

9. Disconnect the battery ground cable and alternator bracket from the right cylinder head.

10. Disconnect the air pump and power steering pump brackets from the left cylinder head.

11. Remove the cylinder head bolts and lift the head(s) from the cylinder block.

12. Remove the cylinder head gasket from the head or the block.

13. Thoroughly clean the gasket mating surfaces. Remove all traces of old gasket material. Remove all carbon deposits from the combustion chambers. Lay a straightedge across the head and check for flatness. Total deviation should not exceed 0.001″ (0.0254mm).

14. Do not apply sealant to the head or block. Coat both sides of the gasket with sealer. The gasket should be stamped TOP for installation. Place the gasket on the block.

15. Install the head on the block. Insert the bolts and tighten them, in sequence, to the proper torque, in three progressive passes. Torque all bolts to 80 ft.lb.

16. Connect the air pump and power steering pump brackets to the left cylinder head.

17. Connect the battery ground cable and alternator bracket to the right cylinder head.

18. Adjust all of the drive belts.

19. Install the exhaust pipes at the flange of the exhaust manifold. When replacing the exhaust pipes it is advisable to install new gaskets at the flange.

20. Install the intake manifold with the carburetor still attached.

21. Install the spark plugs.

22. Install the rocker arm assemblies and the pushrods.

NOTE: *The valve train components must be replaced in their original positions.*

23. Install the valve cover(s) and gasket(s).

24. Install the heater core housing on the firewall.

25. Fill the cooling system and cylinder block.

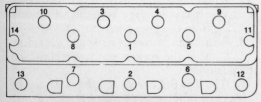

V8 head bolt torque sequence

Valves and Springs

NOTE: *Fabricate a valve arrangement board to use when you remove the valves, which will indicate the port in which each valve was originally installed (and which cylinder head on V8 models). Also note that the valve keys, rotators, caps, etc. should be arranged in a manner which will allow you to install them on the valve on which they were originally used.*

REMOVAL

4–121

1. Remove the cylinder head.

2. Make a wooden fixture according to the dimensions shown in the accompanying illustration. Attach the fixture to the bottom of the head with ⅜″ x ¾″ (10mm x 83mm) bolts and nuts, to hold the valves against their seats while the valve springs are compressed.

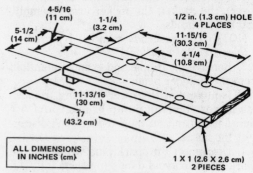

Fabricated cylinder head fixture for the 4-121

3. Remove the camshaft from the head.

4. Loosely install a nut to one camshaft bearing stud next to each valve.

5. Lift the tappets from their bores, keeping them in order for installation.

6. Place a 21mm deep socket on each retainer and strike it sharply with a hammer to loosen the valve locks.

7. Using spring compressor J-26809, compress the valve springs. Remove the locks, retainers, springs and oil deflectors.

8. When all of the parts are removed from all the valves, remove the home made retaining tool and remove the valves. Keep them in order for installation.

All Except the 4–121

1. The head must be removed from the engine.

2. Remove the rocker arm assemblies.

3. Using a spring compressor, compress the valve springs and remove the keepers (locks). Relax the compressor and remove the washers

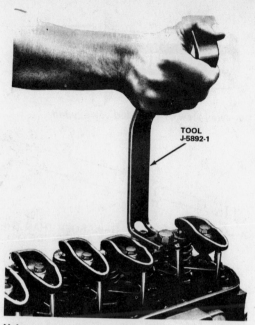

Using a valve spring compressor

TOOL
J-5892-1

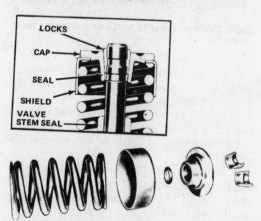

LOCKS
CAP
SEAL
SHIELD
VALVE
STEM SEAL

Typical upper valve train components

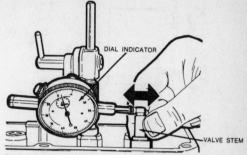

DIAL INDICATOR

VALVE STEM

Check the valve stem-to-guide clearance

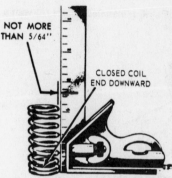

NOT MORE
THAN 5/64''

CLOSED COIL
END DOWNWARD

Check the valve spring free length and squareness

Check the valve spring test pressure

or rotators, the springs, and the lower washers (on some engines). Keep all parts in order.

INSPECTION AND REFACING

1. Clean the valves with a wire wheel.
2. Inspect the valves for warping, cracks or wear.
3. The valves may be refaced if not worn or pitted excessively.
4. Using a valve guide cleaner chucked into a drill, clean all of the valve guides. Check the valve stem diameter and the guide diameter with micrometers. The guide must be reamed and an insert pressed in, or they may be knurled to bring up interior metal, restoring their diameter. Oversized valve stems are available to compensate for wear.

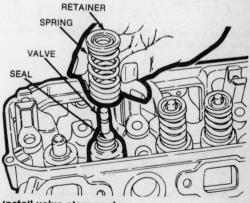

RETAINER
SPRING
VALVE
SEAL

Install valve stem seals

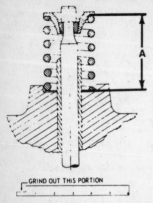

GRIND OUT THIS PORTION

Measure the valve spring installed height (A) with a modified steel rule

Valve spring installed height (A)

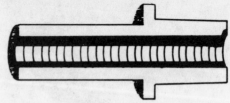

Cut-away view of a knurled valve guide

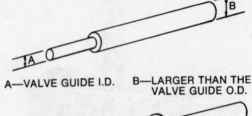

A—VALVE GUIDE I.D.   B—LARGER THAN THE VALVE GUIDE O.D.

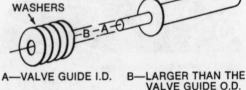

WASHERS

A—VALVE GUIDE I.D.   B—LARGER THAN THE VALVE GUIDE O.D.

Valve guide installation tool using washers for installation

NOTE: *AMC recommends that, if the 4–121 guides are worn excessively, the head should be replaced. Inserts are not available.*

5. Install each valve into its respective port (guide) of the cylinder head.

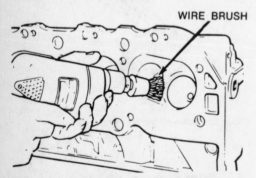

WIRE BRUSH

Remove the carbon from the cylinder head with a wire brush and electric drill

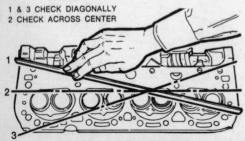

1 & 3 CHECK DIAGONALLY
2 CHECK ACROSS CENTER

Check the cylinder head for warpage

6. Mount a dial indicator so that the stem is at 90° to the valve stem, as close to the valve guide as possible.

7. Move the valve off its seat, and measure the valve guide-to-stem clearance by rocking the stem back and forth to actuate the dial indicator.

8. In short, the refacing of valves and other such head work is most easily done at a machine shop. The quality and time saved easily justifies the cost.

9. Inspect the springs for obvious signs of wear. Check their installed height and tension using the values in the Valve Specifications Chart in this chapter.

REFACING

CAUTION: *On the 4–121, reface only the intake valves. Never attempt to reface the exhaust valves. Exhaust valves are sodium-filled and refacing could be hazardous! When refacing the intake valves, the face width should not exceed 3.5mm.*

Using a valve grinder, resurface the valves according to specifications in this chapter. All machine work should be performed by a competent, professional machine shop.

NOTE: *Valve face angle is not always identical to valve seat angle.*

A minimum margin of $\frac{1}{32}$" (0.79375mm) should remain after grinding the valve. The

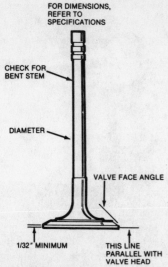

FOR DIMENSIONS, REFER TO SPECIFICATIONS

CHECK FOR BENT STEM

DIAMETER

VALVE FACE ANGLE

1/32" MINIMUM

THIS LINE PARALLEL WITH VALVE HEAD

Critical valve dimensions

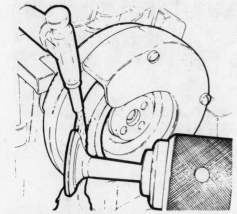

Valve grinding by machine

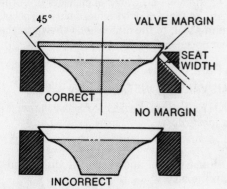

45°

VALVE MARGIN

SEAT WIDTH

CORRECT

NO MARGIN

INCORRECT

Valve seat width and centering

valve stem top should also be squared and resurfaced, by placing the stem in the V-block of the grinder, and turning it while pressing lightly against the grinding wheel. Be sure to chamfer the edge of the tip so that the squared edges don't dig into the rocker arm or cam.

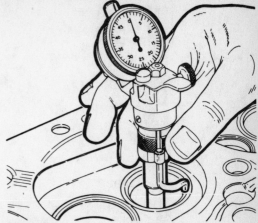

Check the valve seat concentricity with a dial gauge

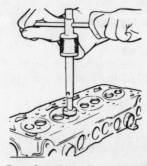

Reaming the valve seat with a hand reamer

LAPPING

This procedure should be performed after the valves and seats have been machined, to insure that each valve mates to each seat precisely.

1. Invert the cylinder head, lightly lubricate the valve stems, and install the valves in the head as numbered.

2. Coat valve seats with fine grinding com-

Lapping the valves by hand

HAND DRILL

ROD

SUCTION CUP

Home-made valve lapping tool

BREAK SHARP CORNER

Close-up of a hand reamer

pound, and attach the lapping tool suction cup to a valve head.

NOTE: *Moisten the suction cup.*

3. Rotate the tool between your palms, changing position and lifting the tool often to prevent grooving.

4. Lap the valve until a smooth, polished seat is evident.

5. Remove the valve and tool, and rinse away all traces of grinding compound.

VALVE SPRING TESTING

Place the spring on a flat surface next to a square. Measure the height of the spring, and rotate it against the edge of the square to measure distortion. If spring height varies (by comparison) by more than $1/16''$ (1.5875mm) or if distortion exceeds $1/16''$ (1.5875mm), replace the spring.

In addition to evaluating the spring as above, test the spring pressure at the installed and compressed (installed height minus valve lift) height using a valve spring tester. Spring pressure should be ± 1 lb. of all other springs in either position.

INSTALLATION

1. Coat all parts with clean engine oil. Install all parts in their respective locations. The spring is installed with the closely wound coils toward the valve head. Always use new valve seals.

2. Use a spring compressor to install the keepers and slowly release the compressor after the keepers are in place.

3. Release the spring compressor. Tap the end of the stem with a wood mallet to insure that the keepers are securely in place.

4. Install all other parts in reverse order of removal.

Valve Seats
INSPECTION AND REFACING

All engines have integral seats. Check the condition of the seats for excessive wear, pitting or cracks. Remove all traces of deposits from the seats. The seats may be refaced with a special grinding tool, to the dimensions shown in the Valve Specifications Chart.

Oil Pan
REMOVAL AND INSTALLATION

NOTE: *It is much easier to remove the engine in most cases.*

4-121

1. Raise the car and support it with stands. Drain the oil.

2. Install an engine lifting device and support weight of the engine, while removing the engine bracket to mount cushion nuts. Loosen the strut and bracket screws.

3. Raise the engine approximately 2″ and remove the crossmember to sill attaching parts.

4. Remove the steering gear idler bracket from the frame rail.

5. Pry the crossmember down and insert

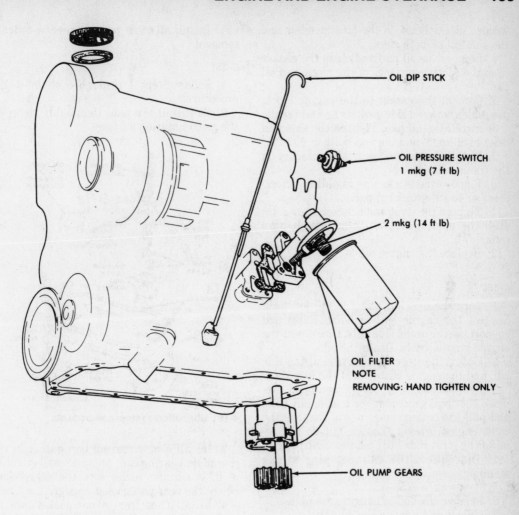

OIL DIP STICK

OIL PRESSURE SWITCH
1 mkg (7 ft lb)

2 mkg (14 ft lb)

OIL FILTER
NOTE
REMOVING: HAND TIGHTEN ONLY

OIL PUMP GEARS

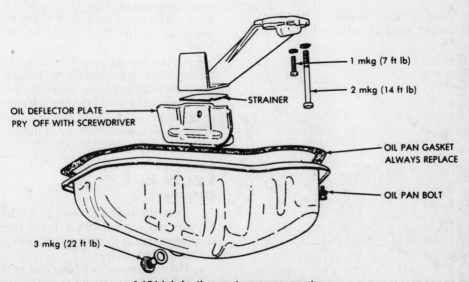

1 mkg (7 ft lb)

2 mkg (14 ft lb)

STRAINER

OIL DEFLECTOR PLATE
PRY OFF WITH SCREWDRIVER

OIL PAN GASKET
ALWAYS REPLACE

OIL PAN BOLT

3 mkg (22 ft lb)

4-121 lubrication system components

wooden blocks between the crossmember and the side sill on both sides.

6. Remove the oil pan and clean the gasket from the mating surfaces of the block and oil pan.

7. Cement the gasket to the engine block; use sealer between side gaskets and end seals.

8. Install the oil pan. Tighten the side pan bolts to 80 in.lb. and the end bolts to 90 in.lb.

9. Install the steering gear idler bracket on the frame rail.

10. Remove the blocks and install the cross-member-to-sill attaching parts.

11. Tighten the strut and bracket screws. Install the engine bracket-to-mount cushion nuts.

12. Replace the engine oil.

4–150

1. Turn the steering wheel to full left lock. Support the engine with a hoist. Raise and support the car at the side sills. Disconnect the engine ground cable. Drain the oil.

2. Unbolt the steering idler arm at the side sill, and the engine cushions at the brackets.

3. Remove the sway bar, if equipped. Remove the front crossmember-to-side sill bolts and pull the crossmember down. Remove the right engine bracket. Loosen but do not remove the strut rods at the lower control arm.

4. Disconnect the exhaust pipe at the manifold.

5. Remove the starter.

6. Remove the bellhousing access plate.

7. Unbolt and remove the oil pan.

8. Clean the gasket surfaces thoroughly.

9. Install a replacement seal at the bottom of the timing case cover and at the rear bearing cap.

10. Using new gaskets coated with sealer, install the pan and torque the bolts to 10 ft.lb.

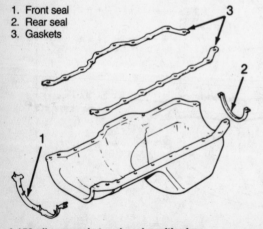

1. Front seal
2. Rear seal
3. Gaskets

4-150 oil pan gasket and seal positioning

11. Install all other parts in reverse order of removal.

4–151

1. Follow Steps 1 through 6 of the 4–121 procedure.

2. To install the pan, thoroughly clean all the gasket mating surfaces.

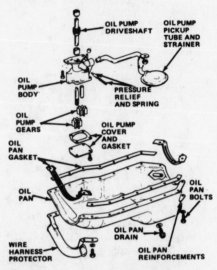

4-151 lubrication system components

3. Install a new rear oil pan gasket in the rear main bearing cap. Apply a small quantity of RTV silicone sealer into the depressions where the rear pan gasket engages the block.

4. Install a new from oil pan gasket onto the timing gear cover. Press the tips into the holes in the cover.

5. Install the side gaskets onto the block, not the oil pan. Retain them with a thin film of grease. Apply a ¼″ (6mm) long bead of RTV silicone sealer to the split lines of the front and side gaskets; the bead should be ⅛″ (3mm) wide.

6. Install the oil pan onto the engine. The timing cover bolts should be installed last. They are installed at an angle; the holes will line up after the rest of the pan bolts have been snugged down. The bolts should be tightened to 6 ft.lb. all around. The rest of installation is the reverse of removal.

6–232, 258
8–304, 360, 401
Except Pacer

1. Turn the steering wheel to full left lock. Support the engine with a hoist. Raise and support the car at the side sills. Disconnect the engine ground cable.

2. Unbolt the steering idler arm at the side sill, and the engine cushions at the brackets.

3. Remove the sway bar, if equipped. Remove the front crossmember-to-side sill bolts and pull the crossmember down. Remove the right engine bracket. Loosen but do not remove the strut rods at the lower control arm.

4. Drain the engine oil.

5. Remove the starter.

6. Remove the oil pan bolts and pan. Remove the front and rear seats, and clean the gasket surfaces.

7. Install the new pan front seal to the timing cover, and apply sealer to end tabs. Cement new pan side gaskets to the block, and apply sealer to the ends of the gasket.

8. Coat the inside surface of the new rear seal with soap, and apply sealer to end tabs. Install the seal in the rear main cap.

9. Coat front and rear seal contact surfaces with engine oil, and install the pan. The remainder of the installation is the reverse of removal.

Pacer

1. Drain the engine oil.

2. Install an engine lifting device and support the weight of the engine.

3. Disconnect the steering shaft flexible joint and hold it aside with a length of wire.

4. Raise and support the car.

5. Remove the front engine support through bolts.

6. Disconnect the front brake lines at the wheel cylinders.

7. Disconnect the upper ball joints from the spindles. Make sure the shock absorbers are attached securely.

8. Remove the upper control arm and move it aside.

9. Support the front crossmember with a jack.

10. Remove the nuts from the front crossmember rear mounts and swing the crossmember down and froward.

11. Follow Steps 5–9 of the preceding 6-cylinder and V8 procedure.

12. Install and assemble the remaining components in the reverse order of removal, tightening the ¼″ oil pan screws to 7 ft.lb., the $\frac{5}{16}$″ oil pan screws to 11 ft.lb., the crossmember attaching nuts to 50 ft.lb., the upper control arm cross shaft bolt and nut to 60 ft.lb., and the engine mount and steering shaft nuts to 25 ft.lb. Fill the crankcase with oil and bleed the brakes.

Oil Pump

REMOVAL AND INSTALLATION

CAUTION: *Anytime the oil pump cover is removed or the pump disassembled, the pump must be primed by filling the spaces around the gears with petroleum jelly. Do not use grease.*

4-121

The oil pump is on the lower front of the engine block. It consists of two gears with meshing teeth, one with internal teeth and the other with external teeth. Oil pressure is controlled by a pressure relief valve and spring assembly. The inner gear is driven by the crankshaft at twice the speed of distributor driven oil pumps. To service the oil pump assembly, removal is necessary. Proceed as follows:

1. Remove the fan shroud.

2. Raise the car and support it on stands.

3. Loosen the crankshaft pulley screws but don't remove them.

4. Loosen and remove the power steering pump belt, air conditioner and alternator belt.

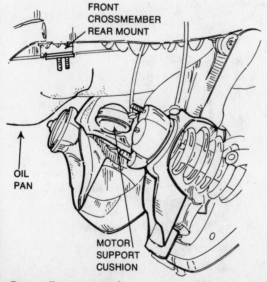

FRONT CROSSMEMBER REAR MOUNT

OIL PAN

MOTOR SUPPORT CUSHION

Pacer oil pan removal

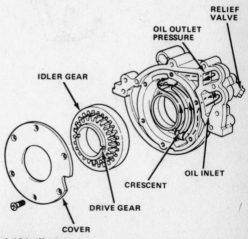

RELIEF VALVE

OIL OUTLET PRESSURE

IDLER GEAR

OIL INLET

CRESCENT

DRIVE GEAR

COVER

4-121 oil pump

5. Remove the crankshaft pulley. Attach a crankshaft sprocket wrench using all of the pulley screws and remove the crankshaft screw.

6. Remove the camshaft drive sprocket from the crankshaft.

7. Remove the oil pump screws and the front oil pan screws and remove the oil pump by prying in the slots with a large screwdriver.

8. Replace the gasket and the crankshaft seal. Trim the edges of the gasket.

9. Rotate the crankshaft so the oil pump lugs are either vertical or horizontal.

10. Cut off the oil pan gasket flush with the front of the block.

11. Align the gears of the oil pump with the crankshaft lugs and carefully tap the pump on as far as possible.

12. Apply silicone sealant to the edges of the pump and the oil pan and to the pump sealing surfaces. Tighten the screws to 87 in.lb.

13. Install the crankshaft seal with a seal installing tool.

14. Install the camshaft drive sprocket and the crankshaft accessory drive pulley, making sure the pins align with the holes. Install the crankshaft screw.

15. Install the camshaft drive belt, belt guard, accessory drive belts and the fan shroud. Start the engine and check for leaks or low oil pressure, and adjust the timing.

CAUTION: *An oil filter with a built-in bypass valve must be used on the 4–121 engine.*

4–150

1. Disconnect the battery ground.

2. Raise and support the car on jackstands.

3. Drain the oil.

4. Disconnect the exhaust pipe at the manifold.

5. Remove the starter.

6. Remove the bellhousing access plate.

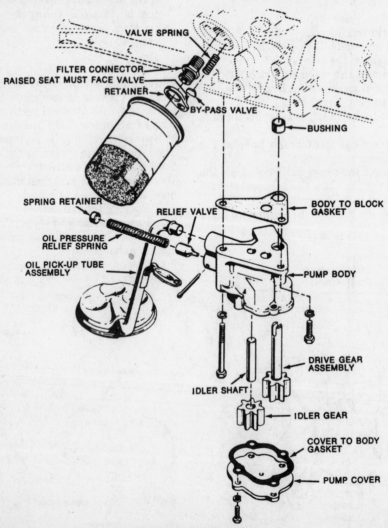

6 cylinder oil pump and filter

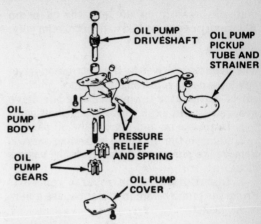

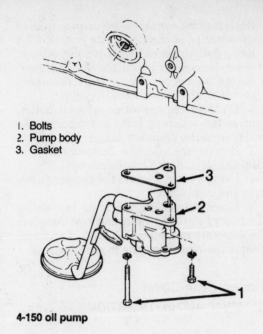

1. Bolts
2. Pump body
3. Gasket

4-150 oil pump

4-151 oil pump

7. Unbolt and remove the oil pan.

8. Clean the gasket surfaces thoroughly.

9. Install a replacement seal at the bottom of the timing case cover and at the rear bearing cap.

10. Using new gaskets coated with sealer, install the pan and torque the bolts to 10 ft.lb.

11. Install all other parts in reverse order of removal.

4–151

1. Remove the engine oil pan. (See previous procedure).

2. Remove the two bolts and one nut, and carefully lower the pump.

3. Install in reverse order. To ensure imme-

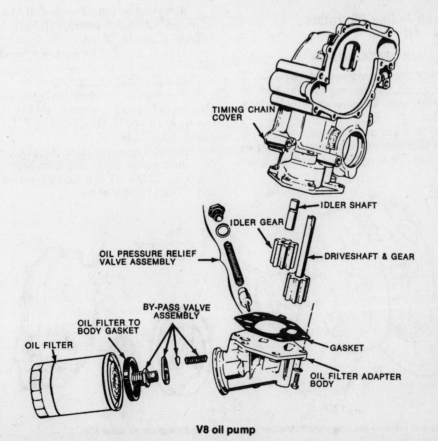

V8 oil pump

diate oil pressure on start-up, the oil pump gear cavity can be packed with petroleum jelly.

6–232, 258

The oil pump is driven by the distributor driveshaft. Oil pump replacement does not, however affect distributor timing because the drive gear remains in mesh with the camshaft gear.

1. Drain the oil and remove the oil pan.
2. Remove the oil pump attaching screws. Remove the pump and gasket from the engine block.
3. Installation is the reverse removal. Prime the pump before installation; use a new cover gasket.

8–304, 360, 401

The oil pump is located in, and is part of, the timing cover. The pump is driven by the distributor driveshaft. Oil pump replacement does not, however, affect distributor timing.

1. Remove the retaining bolts and separate the oil pump cover, complete with filter and gasket, from the timing cover.
2. The drive gear and shaft and the idler gear will slide out of the timing cover after removal of the pump cover.
3. Prime the pump before installation, and use a new gasket.

Crankshaft Pulley (Vibration Damper)

REMOVAL AND INSTALLATION

1. Remove the fan shroud, as required. If necessary, drain the cooling system and remove the radiator. Remove drive belts from pulley.

CAUTION: *When draining the coolant, keep in mind that cats and dogs are attracted by the ethylene glycol antifreeze, and are quite likely to drink any that is left in an uncovered container or in puddles on the ground. This will prove fatal in sufficient quantity. Always drain the coolant into a sealable container. Coolant should be reused unless it is contaminated or several years old.*

2. On those engines with a separate pulley, remove the retaining bolts and separate the pulley from the vibration damper.
3. Remove the vibration damper/pulley retaining bolt from the crankshaft end.
4. Using a puller, remove the damper/pulley from the crankshaft.
5. Upon installation, align the key slot of the pulley hub to the crankshaft key. Complete the assembly in the reverse order of removal. Torque the retaining bolts to specifications.

Timing Case Cover

REMOVAL AND INSTALLATION

4–150

NOTE: *Special tools are needed for this job.*

1. Remove the drive belts and fan shroud.
2. Unscrew the vibration damper bolts and washer.
3. Using a puller, remove the vibration damper.
4. Remove the fan assembly. If the fan is equipped with a fan clutch DO NOT LAY IT DOWN! If you lay it down, the fluid will leak out of the clutch and irreversibly damage the fan.
5. Disconnect the battery ground.
6. Remove the air conditioning compressor/alternator bracket assembly and lay it out of the way. DO NOT DISCONNECT THE REFRIGERANT LINES!
7. Unbolt the cover from the block and oil pan. Remove the cover and front seal.
8. Cut off the oil pan side gasket end tabs and oil pan front seal tabs.

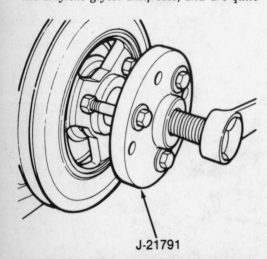

J-21791

Using a puller to remove the crankshaft damper

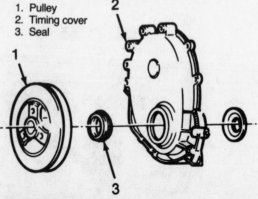

1. Pulley
2. Timing cover
3. Seal

4-150 timing cover assembly

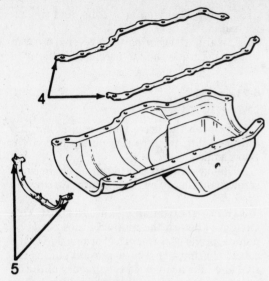

4-150 oil pan and gaskets

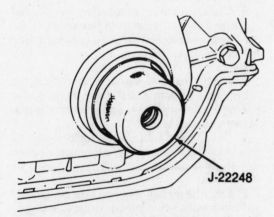

Timing cover centering tool installed on a 4-150

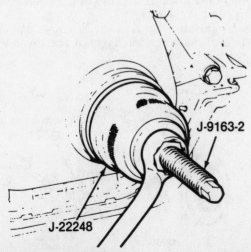

Oil seal installation tool

9. Clean all gasket mating surfaces thoroughly.

10. Remove the seal from the cover.

11. Apply sealer to both sides of the new case cover gasket and position it on the block.

12. Cut the end tabs off the new oil pan side gaskets corresponding to those cut off the original gasket and attach the tabs to the oil pan with gasket cement.

13. Coat the front cover seal end tab recesses generously with RTV sealant and position the side seal in the cover.

14. Apply engine oil to the seal-to-pan contact surface.

15. Position the cover on the block.

16. Insert alignment tool J-22248 into the crankshaft opening in the cover.

17. Install the cover bolts. Tighten the cover-to-block bolts to 5 ft.lb.; the cover-to-pan bolts to 11 ft.lb.

18. Remove the alignment tool and position the new front seal on the tool with the seal lip facing outward. Apply a light film of sealer to the outside diameter of the seal. Lightly coat the crankshaft with clean engine oil.

19. Position the tool and seal over the end of the crankshaft and insert the Draw Screw J-9163-2 into the installation tool.

20. Tighten the nut until the tool just contacts the cover.

21. Remove the tools and apply a light film of engine oil on the vibration damper hub contact surface of the seal.

22. With the key inserted in the keyway in the crankshaft, install the vibration damper, washer and bolt. Lubricate the bolt and tighten it to 108 ft.lb.

23. Install all other parts in reverse order of removal.

4–151

1. Disconnect the battery ground.

2. Remove the crankshaft pulley hub.

3. Remove the alternator bracket.

4. Remove the fan and radiator shroud.

5. Remove the oil pan-to-timing case cover bolts.

6. Pull the cover forward just enough to allow cutting the oil pan front seal flush with the block on both sides of the cover. Use a sharp knife or razor.

7. Remove the front cover.

8. Clean the gasket surface on the block and cover.

9. Cut the tabs from the new oil pan front seal.

10. Install the seal on the cover, pressing the tips into the holes provided in the cover.

11. Coat a new gasket with sealer and place on the cover.

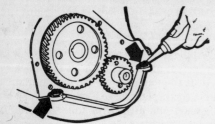

Applying sealer to the 4-151 front cover prior to installation

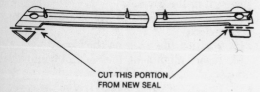

CUT THIS PORTION FROM NEW SEAL

4-151 oil pan seal modification

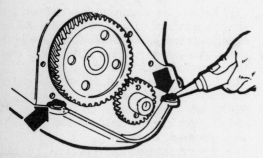

Applying RTV sealant on 4-151 engines

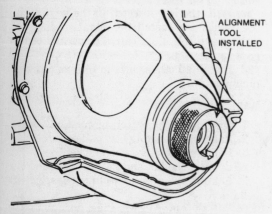

ALIGNMENT TOOL INSTALLED

Timing case cover alignment tool installed on 4-151 engines

12. Apply a ⅛″ (3.175mm) bead of RTV sealant to the joint formed at the oil pan and block.

13. Install an aligning tool such as tool J-23042 in the timing case cover seal.

NOTE: *It is important that an aligning tool is used to avoid seal damage and to ensure a tight, even seal fit.*

14. Position the cover on the block and partially retighten the two oil pan-to-cover bolts.

15. Install the remaining bolts, and tighten all bolts to 45 in.lb.

16. Install all other parts in reverse order of removal. Torque the fan assembly bolts to 18 ft.lb.

6-232, 6-258

COVER REMOVED

1. Remove the drive belts, engine fan and hub assembly, the accessory pulley, and vibration damper.

2. Remove the oil pan to timing chain cover screws and the screws that attach the cover to the block.

3. Raise the timing chain cover just high enough to detach the retaining nibs of the oil pan neoprene seal from the bottom side of the cover. This must be done to prevent pulling the seal end tabs away from the tongues of the oil pan gaskets which would cause a leak.

4. Remove the timing chain cover and gasket from the engine.

5. Use a razor blade to cut off the oil pan seal end tabs flush with the front face of the cylinder block and remove the seal. Clean the timing chain cover, oil pan, and cylinder block surfaces.

6. Apply seal compound (Perfect Seal, or equivalent) to both sides of the replacement timing case cover gasket and position the gasket on cylinder block.

7. Cut the end tabs off the replacement oil pan gasket corresponding to the pieces cut off the original gasket. Cement these pieces on the oil pan.

8. Coat the oil pan seal end tabs generously with Permatex® No. 2 or equivalent, and position the seal on the timing case cover.

9. Position the timing case cover on the engine. Place Timing Case Cover Alignment Tool and Seal Installer J-22248 in the crankshaft opening of the cover.

10. Install the cover-to-block screws and oil pan-to-cover screws. Tighten the cover-to-

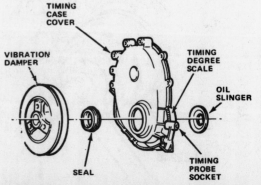

TIMING CASE COVER

VIBRATION DAMPER

TIMING DEGREE SCALE

OIL SLINGER

SEAL

TIMING PROBE SOCKET

6 cylinder timing case cover

block screws to 60 in.lb. and the oil pan-to-cover screws to 11 ft.lb.

11. Remove the cover aligning tool and position the replacement oil seal aligning tool in the case. Position the replacement oil seal on the tool with the seal lip facing outward. Apply a light film of Perfect Seal, or equivalent, on the outside diameter of the seal.

12. Insert the draw screw from Tool J-9163 into the seal installing tool. Tighten the nut against the tool until the tool contacts the cover.

13. Remove the tools and apply a light film of engine oil to the seal lip.

14. Install the vibration damper and tighten the retaining screw to 80 ft.lb.

15. Install the damper pulley. Tighten the capscrews to 20 ft.lb.

16. Install the engine fan and hub assembly.

17. Install the drive belt(s).

COVER INSTALLED

1. Remove the drive belts.
2. Remove the vibration damper pulley.
3. Remove the vibration damper.
4. Remove the oil seal with Tool J-9256.
5. Position the replacement oil seal on the Timing Case Cover Alignment Tool and Seal Installer J-22248 with the seal lip facing outward. Apply a light film of Perfect Seal, or equivalent, to the outside diameter of the seal.
6. Insert the draw screw from Tool J-9163 into the seal installing tool. Tighten the nut against the tool until the tool contacts the cover.
7. Remove the tools. Apply a light film of engine oil to the seal lip.
8. Install the vibration damper and tighten the retaining bolt to 80 ft.lb.
9. Install the damper pulley. Tighten the capscrews to 20 ft.lb.
10. Install the drive belt(s).

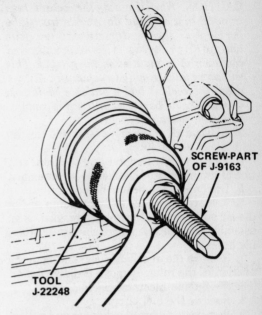

Timing case oil seal installation, 6-258 engines

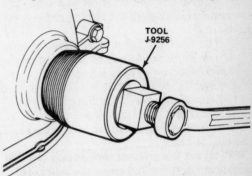

6-258 timing case cover oil seal removal

8–304, 360, 401

1. Remove the negative battery cable.
2. Drain the cooling system and disconnect the radiator hoses and by-pass hose.

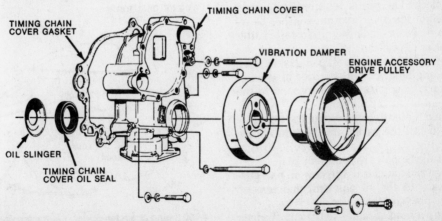

V8 timing case cover assembly, through 1976. 1977 and later are identical except for seal location

CAUTION: *When draining the coolant, keep in mind that cats and dogs are attracted by the ethylene glycol antifreeze, and are quite likely to drink any that is left in an uncovered container or in puddles on the ground. This will prove fatal in sufficient quantity. Always drain the coolant into a sealable container. Coolant should be reused unless it is contaminated or several years old.*

3. Remove all of the drive belts and the fan and spacer assembly.

4. Remove the alternator and the front portion of the alternator bracket as an assembly.

5. Disconnect the heater hose.

6. Remove the power steering pump and/or the air pump, and the mounting bracket as an assembly. Do not disconnect the power steering hoses.

7. Remove the distributor cap and note the position of the rotor. Remove the distributor. (See the Engine Electrical Section).

8. Remove the fuel pump.

9. Remove the vibration damper and pulley.

10. Remove the two front oil pan bolts and the bolts which secure the timing chain cover to the engine block.

NOTE: *The timing gear cover retaining bolts vary in length and must be installed in the same locations from which they were removed.*

11. Remove the cover by pulling forward until it is free of the locating dowel pins.

12. Clean the gasket surface of the cover and the engine block.

13. Pry out the original seal from inside the timing chain cover and clean the seal bore.

14. Drive the new seal into place from the inside with a block of wood until it contacts the outer flange of the cover.

15. Apply a light film of motor oil to the lips of the new seal.

16. Before reinstalling the timing gear cover, remove the lower locating dowel pin from the engine block. The pin is required for correct alignment of the cover and must either be reused or a replacement dowel pin installed after the cover is in position.

17. Cut both sides of the oil pan gasket flush with the engine block with a razor blade.

18. Trim a new gasket to correspond to the amount cut off at the oil pan.

19. Apply sealer to both sides of the new gasket and install the gasket on the timing case cover.

20. Install the new front oil pan seal.

21. Align the tongues of the new oil pan gasket pieces with the oil pan seal and cement them into place on the cover.

22. Apply a bead of sealer to the cutoff edges of the original oil pan gaskets.

23. Place the timing case cover into position and install the front oil pan bolts. Tighten the bolts slowly and evenly until the cover aligns with the upper locating dowel.

24. Install the lower dowel through the cover and drive it into the corresponding hole in the engine block.

25. Install the cover retaining bolts in the same locations from which they were removed. Tighten to 25 ft.lb.

26. Assemble the remaining components in the reverse order of removal.

Timing Chain or Gear and Sprocket or Pulley

REMOVAL AND INSTALLATION

4–150

1. Remove the timing case cover.

2. Rotate the crankshaft so that the timing marks on the cam and crank sprockets align next to each other, as illustrated.

3. Remove the oil slinger from the crankshaft.

4. Remove the cam sprocket retaining bolt and remove the sprocket and chain. The crank sprocket may also be removed at this time. If the tensioner is to be removed, the oil pan must be removed. first.

5. Prior to installation, turn the tensioner lever to the unlock (down) position.

6. Pull the tensioner block toward the tensioner to compress the spring. Hold the block and turn the tensioner lever to the lock (up) position. The camshaft sprocket bolt should be torqued to 50 ft.lb.

7. Install the sprockets and chain together, as a unit. Make sure the timing marks are aligned.

To verify that the timing chain is correctly installed:

a. Turn the crankshaft to place the **camshaft** timing mark at approximately the one o'clock position.

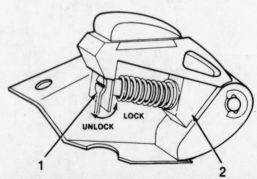

4-150 timing chain tensioner. 1 is the tensioner lever, 2 is the block

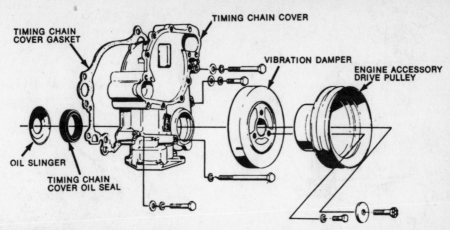

TIMING CHAIN COVER GASKET

TIMING CHAIN COVER

VIBRATION DAMPER

ENGINE ACCESSORY DRIVE PULLEY

OIL SLINGER

TIMING CHAIN COVER OIL SEAL

8-304, 360, 401 timing case, cover and seal. The unit for engines through 1976 is shown. 1977 and later engines are identical except for the seal location

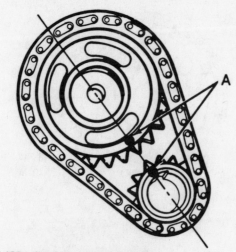

A

4-150 valve timing mark alignment

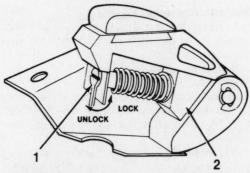

LOCK

UNLOCK

1

2

4-150 timing chain tensioner. 1 is the tensioner lever, 2 is the block

b. At this point, there should be a tooth on the **crankshaft** sprocket meshed with the chain at the three o'clock position.

c. Count the number of timing chain pins between the two timing marks on the right

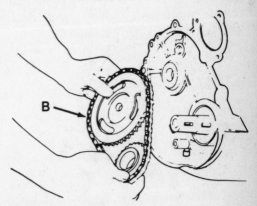

B

Installing the timing chain and sprockets on the 4-150

side (your right, facing the engine). There should be 20 pins.

8. Install the oil pan, slinger and timing cover.

4-151

NOTE: *Removal of the camshaft gear requires a special adapter #J-971 and the use of a press. Camshaft removal is necessary.*

1. Place the adapter on the press and place the camshaft through the opening.

2. Press the shaft out of the gear using a socket or other suitable tool.

CAUTION: *The thrust plate must be in position so that the woodruff key does not damage the gear when the shaft is pressed out.*

3. To install the gear firmly support the shaft at the back of the front journal in an arbor press using pressplate adapters J-21474-13 or J-21795-1.

4. Place the gear spacer ring and thrust plate over the end of the shaft, and install the woodruff key in the shaft keyway.

5. Install the camshaft gear and press it

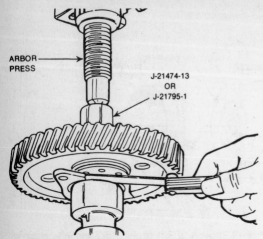

Installing the 4-151 camshaft timing gear and measuring the thrust plate end clearance

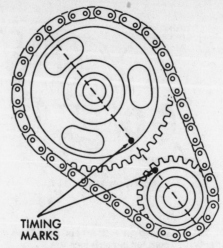

Aligning the 6 cylinder timing marks

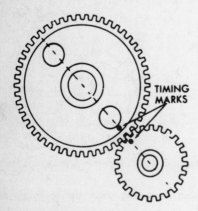

Aligning the 4-151 timing marks

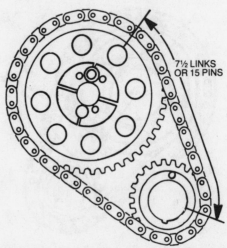

Correct timing chain installation for the 6 cylinder

onto the shaft until it bottoms against the gear spacer ring. The end clearance of the thrust plate should be 0.0015–0.0050″ (0.0381–0.127mm). If less than 0.0015″ (0.0381mm), the spacer ring should be replaced.

6–232
6–258

1. Remove the drive belts, engine fan and hub assembly, accessory pulley, vibration damper and timing chain cover.

2. Remove the oil seal from the timing chain cover.

3. Remove the camshaft sprocket retaining bolt and washer.

4. Rotate the crankshaft until the timing mark on the crankshaft sprocket is closest to and in a center line with the timing pointer of the camshaft sprocket.

5. Remove the crankshaft sprocket, camshaft sprocket and timing chain as an assembly. Disassemble the chain and sprockets.

Installation is as follows:

1. Assemble the timing chain, crankshaft sprocket and camshaft sprocket with the timing marks aligned.

2. Install the assembly to the crankshaft and the camshaft.

3. Install the camshaft sprocket retaining bolt and washer and tighten to 45–55 ft.lb.

4. Install the timing chain cover and a new oil seal.

5. Install the vibration damper, accessory pulley, engine fan and hub assembly and drive belts. Tighten the belts to the proper tension.

8–304, 360, 401

1. Remove the timing chain cover and gasket.

2. Remove the crankshaft oil slinger.

3. Remove the camshaft sprocket retaining bolt. and washer, distributor drive gear and fuel pump eccentric.

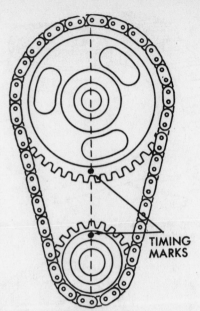

Aligning the V8 timing marks

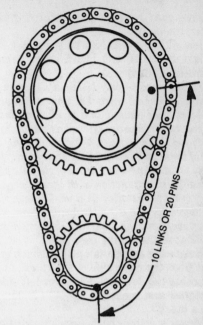

Correct timing chain installation on the V8

4. Rotate the crankshaft until the timing mark on the crankshaft sprocket is adjacent to, and on a center line with, the timing mark on the camshaft sprocket.

5. Remove the crankshaft sprocket, camshaft sprocket and timing chain as an assembly.

6. Clean all of the gasket surfaces.

Installation is as follows:

1. Assemble the timing chain, crankshaft sprocket and camshaft sprocket with the timing marks on both sprockets aligned.

2. Install the assembly to the crankshaft and the camshaft.

3. Install the fuel pump eccentric, distribu-

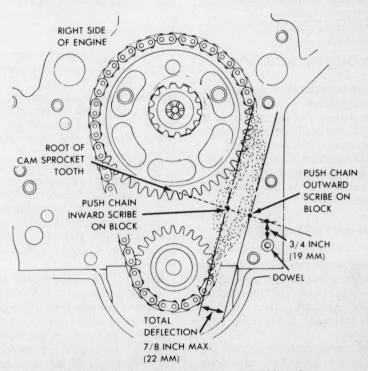

Measuring timing chain deflection on 8-304 engines

tor drive gear, washer and retaining bolt. Tighten the bolt to 25–35 ft.lb.

4. Install the crankshaft oil slinger.

5. Install the timing chain cover using a new gasket and oil seal.

NOTE: *In mid-year 1979, a new timing chain, camshaft sprocket and crankshaft sprocket were phased into production on all V8 engines. These are offered as replacement parts for older engines. When installing any one of these parts on an older engine, all three parts must be installed. None of the new parts is usable in conjunction with the older parts. They must be installed as a set. To determine the necessity for a replacement of an older chain, perform the following deflection test:*

1. Remove the timing case cover.

2. Rotate the sprockets until all slack is removed from the right side of the chain.

3. Locate the dowel on the lower left side of the engine and measure up ¾" (19.05mm). Make a mark.

4. Measure across the chain with a straightedge from the mark to a point at the bottom of the camshaft sprocket.

5. Grab the chain at the point where the straightedge crosses it. Push the chain left (inward) as far as it will go. Make a mark on the block at this point. Push the chain to the right as far as it will go. Make another mark. Measure between the two marks. Total deflection should not exceed ⅞" (22.23mm).

6. Replace the chain and sprockets if deflection is not within specifications.

7. Replace the timing case cover.

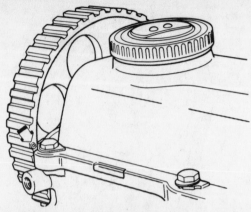

Aligning the camshaft timing dot with the edge of the cylinder head on the 4-121

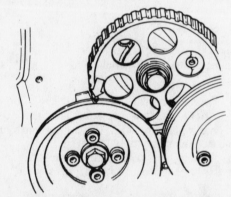

Aligning the timing marks on the crankshaft and intermediate shaft on the 4-121

4–121 Timing Belt and Sprockets

This engine used a toothed rubber belt to drive the camshaft. Belt tension is controlled by an adjustable idler pulley. The distributor is at the rear of the cylinder head and is driven by a gear pressed on the rear of the camshaft.

CAUTION: *Do not turn the engine backwards. Damage to the drive belt teeth could result. Turn the engine by the crankshaft bolt, not the camshaft.*

BELT REMOVAL AND INSTALLATION

1. Rotate the crankshaft in the normal direction of rotation, until the timing mark on the pulley is pointing to the zero position on the degree scale on the block. The timing mark on the rear of the camshaft pulley should be aligned with the pointer on the cylinder head cover.

2. Loosen the accessory pulley attaching bolts. Remove the V belts and the cam drive belt shield.

3. Loosen the adjuster retaining screw to allow the belt to slacken and remove the belt.

4. To replace the belt, install the belt on the crankshaft pulley, and position it on the tensioner pulley. Slip the belt over the camshaft pulley using hand pressure only, while maintaining the pulleys at their respective timing marks.

NOTE: *Do not pry the belt with metal tools. The belt drive surface can be damaged and premature belt failure can result.*

5. Turn the offset adjusting nut on the tensioning pulley counterclockwise to increase the belt tension. The belt is properly tensioned when the drive side of the belt can be twisted 90° with finger pressure.

NOTE: *When checking belt tension, apply tension on the crankshaft with a wrench, in a counterclockwise direction, to get all the slack on one side of the belt.*

6. With pressure on the tensioning pulley nut, tighten the retaining nut to 29 ft.lb. torque. Recheck the belt tension.

7. Install the drive belt shield. Install the al-

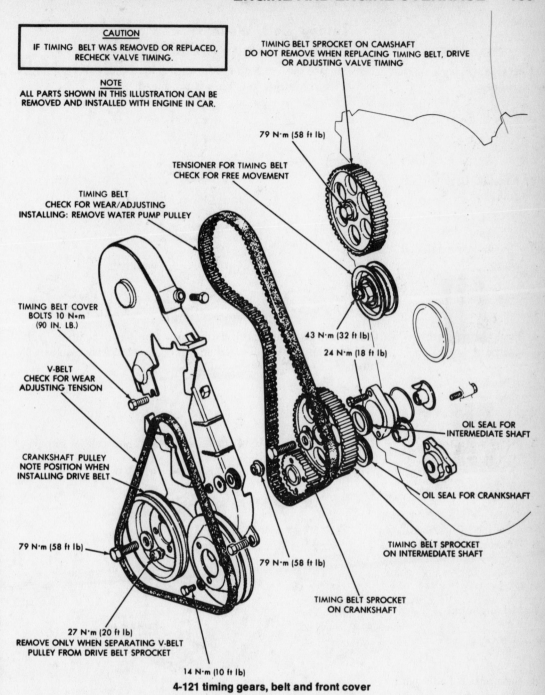

CAUTION
IF TIMING BELT WAS REMOVED OR REPLACED, RECHECK VALVE TIMING.

NOTE
ALL PARTS SHOWN IN THIS ILLUSTRATION CAN BE REMOVED AND INSTALLED WITH ENGINE IN CAR.

TIMING BELT SPROCKET ON CAMSHAFT
DO NOT REMOVE WHEN REPLACING TIMING BELT, DRIVE OR ADJUSTING VALVE TIMING

79 N·m (58 ft lb)

TENSIONER FOR TIMING BELT
CHECK FOR FREE MOVEMENT

TIMING BELT
CHECK FOR WEAR/ADJUSTING
INSTALLING: REMOVE WATER PUMP PULLEY

TIMING BELT COVER
BOLTS 10 N·m
(90 IN. LB.)

V-BELT
CHECK FOR WEAR
ADJUSTING TENSION

43 N·m (32 ft lb)
24 N·m (18 ft lb)

OIL SEAL FOR
INTERMEDIATE SHAFT

CRANKSHAFT PULLEY
NOTE POSITION WHEN
INSTALLING DRIVE BELT

OIL SEAL FOR CRANKSHAFT

79 N·m (58 ft lb)

TIMING BELT SPROCKET
ON INTERMEDIATE SHAFT

79 N·m (58 ft lb)

TIMING BELT SPROCKET
ON CRANKSHAFT

27 N·m (20 ft lb)
REMOVE ONLY WHEN SEPARATING V-BELT
PULLEY FROM DRIVE BELT SPROCKET

14 N·m (10 ft lb)

4-121 timing gears, belt and front cover

ternator belts and adjust their tension. Tighten the accessory pulley bolts to 15 ft.lb.

8. Start the engine and adjust the ignition timing.

CAMSHAFT SPROCKET REMOVAL AND INSTALLATION

1. Remove the drive belt.
2. Insert a bar or other suitable tool through

the camshaft pulley to prevent it from turning.

3. Remove the pulley retaining bolt. Remove the pulley, woodruff key, and washer from the camshaft.

4. To replace the pulley reverse the disassembly procedure. Hold the camshaft pulley and torque the retaining bolt to 58 ft.lb.

5. Refer to Belt Removal and Installation for installation and tensioning.

Timing Belt Wear

DESCRIPTION	FLAW CONDITIONS
1. Hardened back surface rubber	Back surface glossy. Non-elastic and so hard that even if a finger nail is forced into it, no mark is produced.

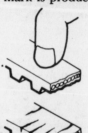

2. Cracked back surface rubber

3. Cracked or exfoliated' canvas

4. Badly worn teeth (initial stage) — Canvas on load side tooth flank worn (Fluffy canvas fibers, rubber gone and color changed to white, and unclear canvas texture)

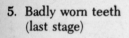

5. Badly worn teeth (last stage) — Canvas on load side tooth flank worn down and rubber exposed (tooth width reduced)

6. Cracked tooth bottom

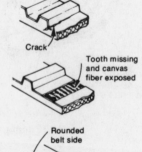

7. Missing tooth

8. Side of belt badly worn

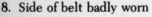

NOTE: *Normal belt should have clear-cut sides as if cut by a sharp knife.*

9. Side of belt cracked

4-121 timing belt wear diagnosis

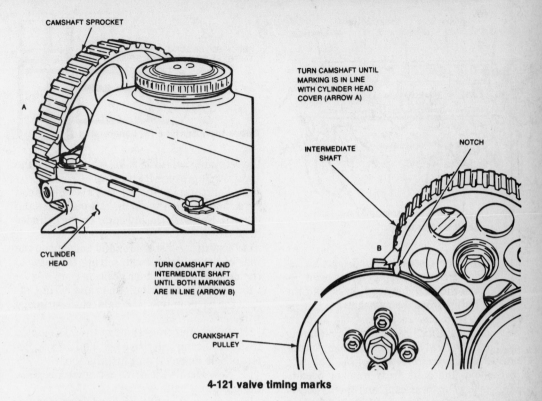

TURN CAMSHAFT UNTIL
MARKING IS IN LINE
WITH CYLINDER HEAD
COVER (ARROW A)

CAMSHAFT SPROCKET

A

CYLINDER
HEAD

TURN CAMSHAFT AND
INTERMEDIATE SHAFT
UNTIL BOTH MARKINGS
ARE IN LINE (ARROW B)

INTERMEDIATE
SHAFT

NOTCH

B

CRANKSHAFT
PULLEY

4-121 valve timing marks

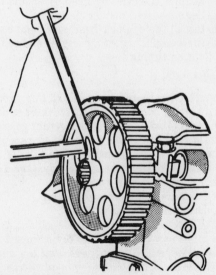

Removing the 4-121 camshaft pulley

CRANKSHAFT SPROCKET REMOVAL AND INSTALLATION

1. Raise and support the from of the car with stands.
2. Remove the camshaft drive belt.
3. Remove the accessory drive pulley from the crankshaft pulley using a no. 40 Torx head bit to remove the pulley screws.
4. The sprocket retaining bolt can be loosened and removed from the crankshaft. Hold the pulley from turning while the bolt is loosened.
5. Remove the pulley from the crankshaft.
6. Install in the pulley so that the indexing hole in the pulley engages with the pin on the crankshaft.
7. Hold the pulley from turning. Install the retaining bolt and torque to 181 ft.lb.
8. Install the drive belt. See Belt Removal and Installation for tensioning.
9. Replace the belt guard. Replace the accessory drive pulley and torque the attaching bolts to 15 ft.lb.
10. Complete the assembly in the reverse order of disassembly. Start the engine and reset the ignition timing.

Camshaft

REMOVAL AND INSTALLATION

NOTE: *Caution must be taken when performing this procedure. Camshaft bearings are coated with babbit material, which can be damaged by scraping the cam lobes across the bearing.*

4–121

1. Remove the air cleaner assembly, and the distributor cap with the wires attached.
2. Remove the accessory belts, and the belt guard. Loosen and remove the camshaft drive belt.

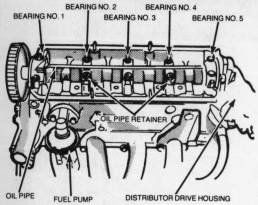

4-121 camshaft and bearings

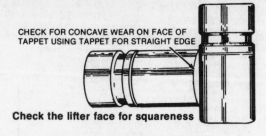

CHECK FOR CONCAVE WEAR ON FACE OF TAPPET USING TAPPET FOR STRAIGHT EDGE

Check the lifter face for squareness

3. Remove the distributor and housing assembly from the rear of the cylinder head.

4. Remove the cylinder head cover, and the camshaft pulley from the camshaft.

NOTE: *Use a tool to prevent the sprocket from turning while removing the retaining bolt, and protect the head surface by wrapping a cloth around the end of the tool.*

5. Remove the bolts from number 5 camshaft bearing cap (rear cap), and them remove the retaining nuts from caps 1, 3, and 5. Next remove the nuts on bearing caps number 2 and 4, backing off each nut ¼ turn at a time to relieve tension on the camshaft. Remove the oil pipe retainers from the bolts on bearing caps number 2 and 4.

6. Remove all the camshaft bearing caps from the cylinder head. Keep them in order.

7. Remove the camshaft from the cylinder head.

NOTE: *The distributor drive fear should be removed from the camshaft with a puller. It can be replaced by driving the gear on the camshaft with the use of a block or wood and a hammer. Note the gear location before removal.*

8. The tappets may be removed for service by lifting them our of their bores in the cylinder head.

9. On installation, lubricate the camshaft lobes and bearing surfaces and install the shaft into the cylinder head. Install the camshaft bearing caps on their respective seats, and install the retaining nuts on cap numbers 2 and 4, tightening to 13 ft.lb.

10. Torque numbers 3 and 5 retaining nuts to 13 ft.lb. Install the bolts in bearing cap number 5 and torque to 7 ft.lb.

11. Install a replacement seal on the camshaft and tighten the number 1 bearing cap to 13 ft.lb. torque. Install the oil pipe and tighten the nuts to 13 ft.lb.

12. Install the camshaft sprocket and torque the retaining bolt to 58 ft.lb., while holding the sprocket to prevent its turning.

13. Temporarily install the cylinder head cover and position the camshaft pulley timing mark in line with the indicator on the cylinder head cover.

14. Install the distributor and housing on the rear of the cylinder head, setting the rotor to the number one cylinder position.

15. Install the distributor cap and wiring, attach the vacuum line, and connect the primary wire.

16. Rotate the crankshaft to the TDC mark. Install the camshaft drive belt and adjust. Refer to Belt Removal and Installation.

17. Reassemble the drive belt guard, replace the accessory belts and adjust.

18. Remove the cylinder head cover and adjust the tappet to camshaft clearance.

19. Install the cylinder head cover and complete the assembly. Start the engine and adjust the ignition timing.

4–150

CAUTION: *To remove perform this procedure the air conditioning system must be discharged. Mishandling of refrigerant gas can cause severe personal injury. If you are not completely familiar with the handling of refrigerant systems, have the system discharged by someone who is.*

1. Disconnect the battery ground.

2. Drain the cooling system.

CAUTION: *When draining the coolant, keep in mind that cats and dogs are attracted by the ethylene glycol antifreeze, and are quite likely to drink any that is left in an uncovered container or in puddles on the ground. This will prove fatal in sufficient quantity. Always drain the coolant into a sealable container. Coolant should be reused unless it is contaminated or several years old.*

3. Remove the radiator, discharge the refrigerant system (See Chapter 1) and remove the condenser.

4. Remove the fuel pump.

5. Matchmark the distributor and engine for installation. Note the rotor position by marking it on the distributor body. Unbolt and remove the distributor and wires.

J-21884

Using a special tool to remove the lifters from a
4-150

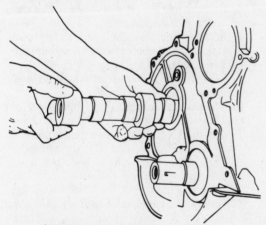

Removing the 4-150 camshaft

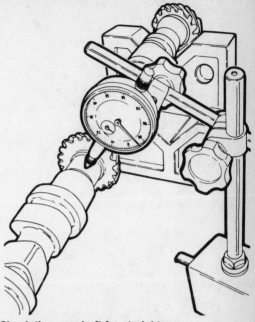

Check the camshaft for straightness

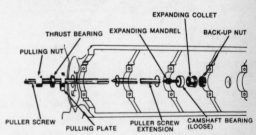

EXPANDING COLLET

THRUST BEARING   EXPANDING MANDREL   BACK-UP NUT

PULLING NUT

PULLER SCREW   PULLER SCREW   CAMSHAFT BEARING
    EXTENSION   (LOOSE)
PULLING PLATE

Camshaft bearing removal and installation tool
(OHV engines only)

6. Remove the rocker arm cover.

7. Remove the rocker arm assemblies.

8. Remove the pushrods.

NOTE: *Keep everything in order for installation.*

9. Using a tool J-21884, or equivalent, remove the hydraulic lifters.

10. Remove the pulley, vibration damper and timing case cover. Remove the crankshaft oil slinger.

NOTE: *If the camshaft sprocket appears to*

Check the camshaft end-play with a feeler gauge

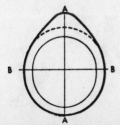

Camshaft lobe measurement

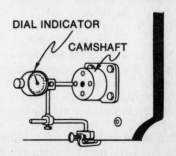

DIAL INDICATOR

CAMSHAFT

Check the camshaft end-play with a dial indicator

Check the camshaft gear backlash

Check the camshaft gear run-out

have been rubbing against the cover, check the oil pressure relief holes in the rear cam journal for debris.

11. Remove the timing chain and sprockets.

12. Slide the camshaft from the engine.

13. Inspect all parts for wear and damage. Lubricate all moving parts with engine oil supplement.

14. Slide the camshaft into the engine, carefully, to avoid damage to the bearing surfaces.

15. Install the timing chain and sprockets. Make sure that all camshaft timing marks align. Torque the camshaft sprocket bolt to 50 ft.lb.

16. Install the timing case cover.

17. Using a tool J-21884, or equivalent, install the hydraulic lifters.

18. Install the pushrods.

19. Install the rocker arm assemblies.

20. Install the rocker arm cover.

21. Install the distributor and wires. When installing the distributor, make sure that all matchmarks align. It may be necessary to rotate the oil pump drive tang with a long bladed screwdriver to facilitate installation of the distributor.

NOTE: *If the distributor is not installed correctly, or removed later, the complete installation procedure must be done again.*

22. Install the fuel pump.

23. Install the radiator.

24. Install the condenser and evacuate and charge the refrigerant system. (See Chapter 1).

25. Fill the cooling system.

26. Connect the battery ground.

4–151

1. Remove the air cleaner.

2. Drain the cooling system.

CAUTION: *When draining the coolant, keep in mind that cats and dogs are attracted by the ethylene glycol antifreeze, and are quite likely to drink any that is left in an uncovered container or in puddles on the ground. This will prove fatal in sufficient quantity. Always drain the coolant into a sealable container. Coolant should be reused unless it is contaminated or several years old.*

3. Remove the timing gear cover.

4. Disconnect the radiator hoses at the radiator. Remove the radiator.

5. Remove the two camshaft thrust plate screws through the holes in the camshaft gear.

6. Remove the tappets.

7. Remove the distributor, oil pump drive and fuel pump.

8. Remove the camshaft and gear assembly by pulling out through front of the block. Support the shaft carefully when removing it to prevent damaging the camshaft bearings.

9. Thoroughly coat the camshaft journals with a high quality engine oil supplement such as STP or its equivalent.

10. Install the camshaft assembly in engine block. Use care to prevent damaging the bearings or the camshaft.

11. Turn the crankshaft and camshaft so that the valve timing marks on the gear teeth are aligned. The engine is now in number four cylinder firing position. Install the camshaft thrust plate-to-block screws and tighten to 75 in.lb.

Removing 4-151 camshaft thrust plate screws

12. Install the timing gear cover and gasket.

13. Line up the keyway in the hub with the key on crankshaft and slide the hub onto the shaft. Install the center bolt and tighten to 160 ft.lb.

14. Install the valve tappets, pushrods, pushrod cover, oil pump shaft and gear assembly and the fuel pump. Install the distributor according to the following procedure:

a. Turn the crankshaft 360° to the firing position of the number one cylinder (number one exhaust and intake valve tappets both on base circle [heel] of the camshaft and the timing notch on the vibration damper is indexed with the top dead center mark [TDC] on the timing degree scale).

b. Install the distributor and align the shaft so that the rotor arm points toward the number one cylinder spark plug contact.

15. Install the rocker arms and pivot balls over the pushrods. With the tappets on the base circle (heel) of camshaft, tighten the rocker arm capscrews to 20 ft.lb. Do not overtighten.

16. Install the cylinder head cover.

17. Install the intake manifold.

18. Install the radiator and lower radiator hose.

19. Install the belt, fan and shroud. Tighten the fan bolts to 18 ft.lb.

20. Install the upper radiator hose.

21. Tighten the belts.

6–232
6–258

1. Drain the cooling system and remove the radiator. With air conditioning, remove the condenser and receiver assembly as a unit, without disconnecting any lines or discharging the system.

CAUTION: *When draining the coolant, keep in mind that cats and dogs are attracted by the ethylene glycol antifreeze, and are quite likely to drink any that is left in an uncovered container or in puddles on the ground. This will prove fatal in sufficient quantity. Always drain the coolant into a sealable container. Coolant should be reused unless it is contaminated or several years old.*

2. Remove the valve cover and gasket, the rocker assemblies, pushrods, cylinder head and gasket and the lifters.

NOTE: *The valve train components must be replaced in their original locations.*

3. Remove the drive belts, cooling fan, fan hub assembly, vibration damper and the timing chain cover.

4. Remove the fuel pump and distributor assembly, including the spark plug wires.

5. Rotate the crankshaft until the timing mark of the crankshaft sprocket is adjacent to, and on a center line with, the timing mark of the camshaft sprocket.

6. Remove the crankshaft sprocket, camshaft sprocket, and the timing chain as an assembly.

7. Remove the front bumper or grille as required and carefully slide out the camshaft.

8. Coat all parts with engine oil supplement.

9. Slide the camshaft into place.

10. Install the front bumper and/or grille.

11. Install the crankshaft sprocket, camshaft sprocket, and the timing chain as an assembly.

12. Rotate the crankshaft until the timing mark of the crankshaft sprocket is adjacent to, and on a center line with, the timing mark of the camshaft sprocket.

13. Install the fuel pump and distributor assembly, including the spark plug wires.

14. Install the drive belts.

15. Install the cooling fan and fan hub assembly.

16. Install the vibration damper.

17. Install the cylinder head and gasket and the lifters.

18. Install the rocker assemblies and pushrods.

19. Install the valve cover and gasket.

20. Install the the timing chain cover.

21. With air conditioning, install the condenser and receiver.

NOTE: *The valve train components must be replaced in their original locations.*

22. Install the radiator and fill the cooling system.

8–304, 360, 401

1. Disconnect the battery cables.

2. Drain the radiator and both banks of the block. Remove the lower hose at the radiator, the by-pass hose at the pump, the thermostat

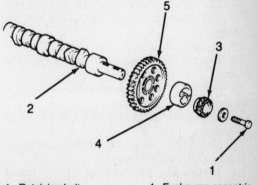

1. Retaining bolt
2. Camshaft
3. Distributor drive gear
4. Fuel pump eccentric
5. Sprocket

8–304, 360, 401 camshaft and related parts

housing and the radiator. With air conditioning, remove the condenser and receiver assembly as a unit, without disconnecting any lines or discharging the system.

CAUTION: *When draining the coolant, keep in mind that cats and dogs are attracted by the ethylene glycol antifreeze, and are quite likely to drink any that is left in an uncovered container or in puddles on the ground. This will prove fatal in sufficient quantity. Always drain the coolant into a sealable container. Coolant should be reused unless it is contaminated or several years old.*

3. Remove the distributor, all wires, and the coil from the manifold.

4. Remove the intake manifold as an assembly.

5. Remove the valve covers, rocker arms and pushrods.

6. Remove the lifters.

NOTE: *The valve train components must be replaced in their original locations.*

7. Remove the cooling fan and hub assembly, fuel pump, and heater hose at the water pump.

8. Remove the alternator and bracket as an assembly. Just move it aside, do not disconnect the wiring.

9. Remove the crankshaft pulley and the damper. Remove the lower radiator hose at the water pump.

10. Remove the timing chain cover.

11. Remove the distributor/oil pump drive gear, fuel pump eccentric, sprockets and the timing chain.

12. Remove the grille.

13. Remove the camshaft carefully by sliding it forward out of the engine.

14. Coat all parts with engine oil supplement.

15. Slide the camshaft, carefully, into the engine.

16. Install the grille.

17. Install the distributor/oil pump drive gear, fuel pump eccentric, sprockets and the timing chain.

18. Install the timing chain cover.

19. Install the crankshaft pulley and the damper.

20. Install the lower radiator hose at the water pump.

21. Install the alternator and bracket as an assembly.

22. Install the cooling fan and hub assembly.

23. Install the fuel pump.

24. Install the heater hose at the water pump.

25. Install the lifters.

NOTE: *The valve train components must be replaced in their original locations.*

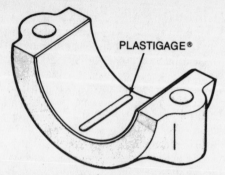

Plastigage® installed on the lower bearing shell

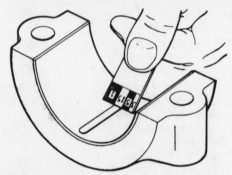

Measure Plastigage® to determine main bearing clearance

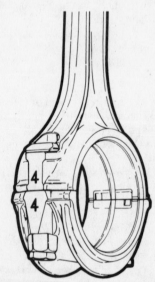

Match the connecting rod to the cylinder with a number stamp

26. Install the valve covers, rocker arms and pushrods.

27. Install the intake manifold as an assembly.

28. Install the distributor, all wires, and the coil on the manifold.

29 Install the radiator.

30. With air conditioning, install the condenser and receiver assembly.

31. Install the thermostat and housing.
32. Install the by-pass hose at the pump.
33. Install the lower hose at the radiator.
34. Fill the cooling system.
35. Connect the battery cables.

Pistons and Connecting Rods

REMOVAL

NOTE: *In most cases, this procedure is easier with the engine out of the vehicle.*

1. Remove the head(s).
2. Remove the oil pan.
3. Rotate the engine to bring each piston, in turn, to the bottom of its stroke. With the piston bottomed, use a ridge reamer to remove the ridge at the top of the cylinder. DO NOT CUT TOO DEEPLY!
4. Matchmark the rods and caps. If the pistons are to be removed from the connecting rod, mark the cylinder number on the piston with a silver pencil or quick drying paint for proper cylinder identification and cap-to-rod location. Remove the connecting rod capnuts and lift off the rod caps, keeping them in order. Install a guide hose over the threads of the rod bolts. This is to prevent damage to the bearing journal and rod bolt threads.
5. Using a hammer handle, push the piston and rod assemblies up out of the block.

PISTON PIN REMOVAL AND INSTALLATION

Use care at all times when handling and servicing connecting rods and pistons. To prevent possible damage to these units, do not clamp the rod or piston in a vise since they may become distorted. Do not allow the pistons to strike against one another, against hard objects or bench surfaces, since distortion of the piston contour or nicks in the soft aluminum material may result.

1. Remove the piston rings using a suitable piston ring remover.
2. Remove the piston pin lockring, if used. Install the guide bushing of the piston pin removing and installing tool.
3. Install the piston and connecting rod assembly on a support, and place the assembly in an arbor press. Press the pin out of the connecting rod, using the appropriate piston pin tool.
4. Assembly is the reverse of disassembly. Use new lockrings where needed.

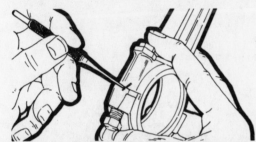

Match the connecting rod and cap with scribe marks

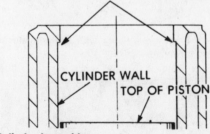

RIDGE CAUSED BY CYLINDER WEAR

CYLINDER WALL

TOP OF PISTON

Cylinder bore ridge

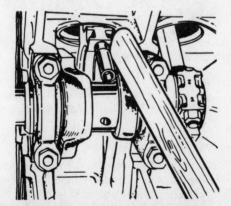

Push the piston out with a hammer handle

Install the piston pin lock-rings (if used)

Measure the cylinder bore with a dial gauge

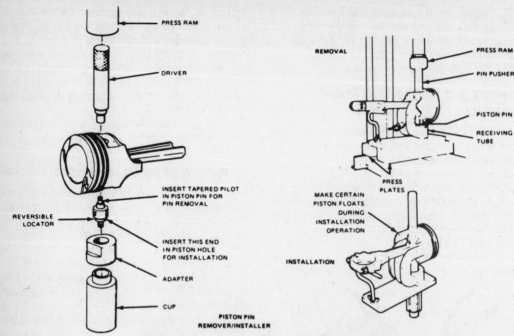

Piston pins must be pressed in with an arbor press

INSPECTION

Cylinder Block

Check the cylinder walls for evidence of rust, which would indicate a cracked block. Check the block face for distortion with a straight-edge. Maximum distortion variance is 0.005″

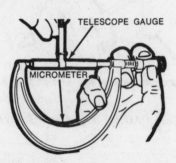

Measure the telescope gauge with a micrometer to determine the cylinder bore

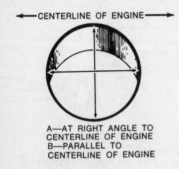

Cylinder bore measuring points

Check the main bearing saddle alignment

(0.127mm). The block cannot be planed, so it will have to be replaced if too distorted. Using a micrometer, check the cylinders for out-of-roundness.

Connecting Rods and Bearings

Wash connecting rods in cleaning solvent and dry with compressed air. Check for twisted or bent rods and inspect for nicks or cracks. Replace connecting rods that are damaged.

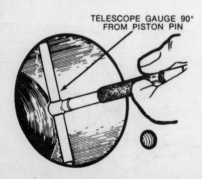

Measure the cylinder bore with a telescope gauge

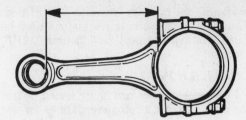

Check the connecting rod length (arrow)

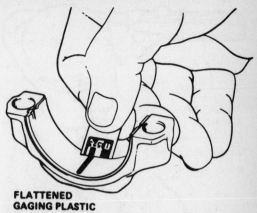

**FLATTENED
GAGING PLASTIC**

Checking the connecting rod bearing clearance with Plastigage®

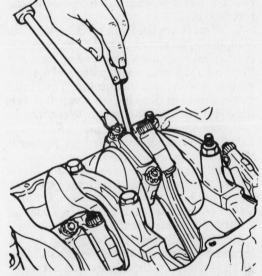

Checking rod side clearance with a flat feeler gauge. Use a small prybar to spread the rods

Inspect journals for roughness and wear. Slight roughness may be removed with a fine grit polishing cloth saturated with engine oil. Burrs may be removed with a fine oil stone by moving the stone on the journal circumference. Do not move the stone back and forth across the journal. If the journals are scored or ridged, the crankshaft must be replaced.

The connecting rod journals should be checked for out-of-round and correct size with a micrometer.

NOTE: *Crankshaft rod journals will normally be standard size. If any undersized bearings are used, the size will be stamped on a counterweight.*

If plastic gauging material is to be used:

1. Clean oil from the journal bearing cap, connecting rod and outer and inner surfaces of the bearing inserts. Position the insert so that the tang is properly aligned with the notch in the rod and cap.

2. Place a piece of plastic gauging material in the center of lower bearing shell.

3. Remove the bearing cap and determine the bearing clearances by comparing the width of the flattened plastic gauging material at its

widest point with the graduation on the container. The number within the graduation on the envelope indicates the clearance in thousandths of an inch or millimeters. If this clearance is excessive, replace the bearing and recheck the clearance with the plastic gauging material. Lubricate the bearing with engine oil before installation. Repeat the procedure on the remaining connecting rod bearings. All rods must be connected to their journals when rotating the crankshaft, to prevent engine damage.

Pistons

Clean varnish from piston skirts and pins with a cleaning solvent. DO NOT WIRE BRUSH ANY PART OF THE PISTON. Clean the ring grooves with a groove cleaner and make sure oil ring holes and slots are clean.

Inspect the piston for cracked ring lands, skirts or pin bosses, wavy or worn ring lands, scuffed or damaged skirts, eroded areas at the top of the piston. Replace pistons that are damaged or show signs of excessive wear. Inspect

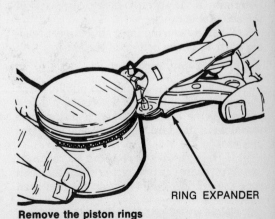

RING EXPANDER

Remove the piston rings

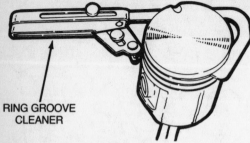

RING GROOVE
CLEANER

Clean the piston ring grooves

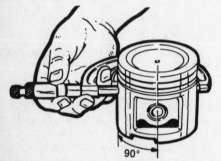

90°

Measure the piston prior to fitting

the grooves for nicks or burrs that might cause the rings to hang up.

Measure piston skirt (across center line of piston pin) and check piston clearance.

MEASURING THE OLD PISTONS

Check used piston-to-cylinder bore clearance as follows:

1. Measure the cylinder bore diameter with a telescope gauge.

2. Measure the pistons for size or taper, measurements must be made with the piston pin removed.

3. Subtract the piston diameter from the cylinder bore diameter to determine piston-to-bore clearance.

4. Compare the piston-to-bore clearances obtained with those clearances recommended. Determine if the piston-to-bore clearance is in the acceptable range.

5. When measuring taper, the largest reading must be at the bottom of the skirt.

SELECTING NEW PISTONS

1. If the used piston is not acceptable, check the service piston size and determine if a new piston can be selected. (Service pistons are available in standard, high limit and standard oversize.

2. If the cylinder bore must be reconditioned, measure the new piston diameter, then hone the cylinder bore to obtain the preferred clearance.

3. Select a new piston and mark the piston

to identify the cylinder for which it was fitted. (On some vehicles, oversize pistons may be found. These pistons will be 0.254mm (0.010") oversize).

CYLINDER HONING

1. When cylinders are being honed, follow the manufacturer's recommendations for the use of the hone.

2. Occasionally, during the honing operation, the cylinder bore should be thoroughly cleaned and the selected piston checked for correct fit.

3. When finish-honing a cylinder bore, the hone should be moved up and down at a sufficient speed to obtain a very fine uniform surface finish in a cross-hatch pattern of approximately 45–65° included angle. The finish marks should be clean but not sharp, free from imbedded particles and torn or folded metal.

4. Permanently mark the piston for the cylinder to which it has been fitted and proceed to hone the remaining cylinders.

NOTE: *Handle the pistons with care. Do not attempt to force the pistons through the cylinders until the cylinders have been honed to the correct size. Pistons can be distorted through careless handling.*

5. Thoroughly clean the bores with hot water and detergent. Scrub well with a stiff bristle brush and rinse thoroughly with hot water. It is extremely essential that a good cleaning operation be performed. If any of the abrasive material is allowed to remain in the cylinder bores, it will rapidly wear the new rings and cylinder bores. The bores should be swabbed several times with light engine oil and a clean cloth and then wiped with a clean dry cloth. CYLINDERS SHOULD NOT BE CLEANED

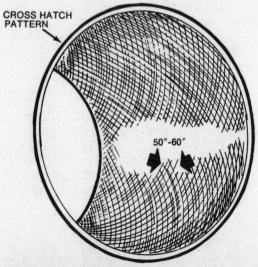

CROSS HATCH
PATTERN

50°-60°

Cylinder bore after honing

WITH KEROSENE OR GASOLINE. Clean the remainder of the cylinder block to remove the excess material spread during the honing operation.

CHECKING CYLINDER BORE

Cylinder bore size can be measured with inside micrometers or a cylinder gauge. The most wear will occur at the top of the ring travel.

Reconditioned cylinder bores should be held to not more than 0.025mm (0.001″) taper.

If the cylinder bores are smooth, the cylinder walls should not be deglazed. If the cylinder walls are scored, the walls may have to be honed before installing new rings. It is important that reconditioned cylinder bores be thoroughly washed with a soap and water solution to remove all traces of abrasive material to eliminate premature wear.

RING TOLERANCES

When installing new rings, ring gap and side clearance should be checked as follows:

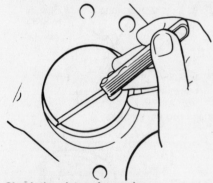

Check the piston ring end gap

Piston Ring and Rail Gap

Each ring and rail gap must be measured with the ring or rail positioned squarely and at the bottom of the ring travel area of the bore.

Side Clearance

Each ring must be checked for side clearance in its respective piston groove by inserting a

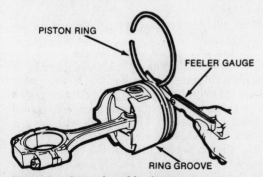

Check the piston ring side clearance

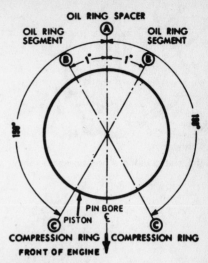

Proper ring gap spacing

feeler gauge between the ring and its upper land. The piston grooves must be cleaned before checking the ring for side clearance specifications. To check oil ring side clearance, the oil rings must be installed on the piston.

RING INSTALLATION

For service ring specifications and detailed installation productions, refer to the instructions furnished with the parts package.

PISTON ASSEMBLY AND INSTALLATION

1. Using a ring expander, install new rings in the grooves, with their gaps staggered to be 270° apart.

2. Using a straightedge, check the rods for straightness. Check, also, for cracks. Before assembling the block, it's a good idea to have the

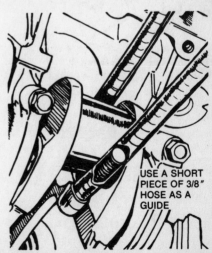

USE A SHORT PIECE OF 3/8″ HOSE AS A GUIDE

Use lengths of vacuum hose or rubber tubing to protect the crankshaft journals and cylinder walls during piston installation

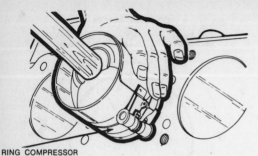

RING COMPRESSOR

Install the piston using a ring compressor

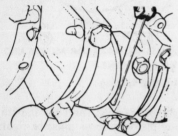

Check the connecting rod side clearance with a feeler gauge

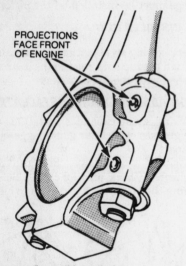

PROJECTIONS FACE FRONT OF ENGINE

4-121 connecting rod installation

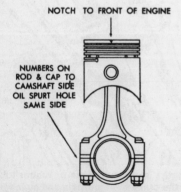

NOTCH TO FRONT OF ENGINE

NUMBERS ON ROD & CAP TO CAMSHAFT SIDE OIL SPURT HOLE SAME SIDE

6 cylinder piston and connecting rod

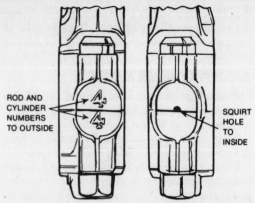

ROD AND CYLINDER NUMBERS TO OUTSIDE

SQUIRT HOLE TO INSIDE

4-151 connecting rod numbering and oil squirt hole

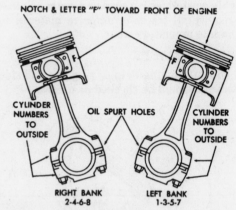

NOTCH & LETTER "F" TOWARD FRONT OF ENGINE

CYLINDER NUMBERS TO OUTSIDE

OIL SPURT HOLES

CYLINDER NUMBERS TO OUTSIDE

RIGHT BANK 2-4-6-8

LEFT BANK 1-3-5-7

V8 piston and rod assemblies

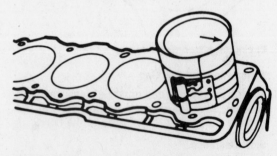

On the 4-150, the arrow on the piston crown faces front

block checked for cracks with Magnaflux® or its equivalent.

3. Install the pins and retainers.

4. Coat the pistons with clean engine oil and apply a ring compressor. Position the assembly over the cylinder bore and slide the piston into the cylinder slowly, taking care to avoid nicking the walls. The pistons will have a mark on the crown, such as a groove or notch or stamped symbol. This mark indicates the side of the piston which should face front. Lower the piston slowly, until it bottoms on the

crankshaft. A good idea is to cover the rod studs with length of rubber hose to avoid nicking the crank journals. Assemble the rod caps at this time. Check the rod bearing clearances using Plastigage®, going by the instructions on the package.

5. Install the bearing caps with the stamped numbers matched. Torque the caps to the figure shown in the Torque Specifications Chart. See the accompanying illustrations for proper piston and rod installation.

Rear Main Bearing Oil Seal

REPLACEMENT

4–121

The rear main bearing oil seal consists of a single piece of formed neoprene with a single lip. To replace the seal, proceed as follows.

1. Remove the transmission assembly. If manual transmission, remove the pressure plate and flywheel.

2. Remove the crankshaft seal from its seat in the block, while exercising care not to scratch the seal contacting area of the crankshaft.

3. Install the seal, after lubricating the lip with engine oil, into the recess of the block, until the seal bottoms. The seal should be about $1/32''$ (0.79mm) below the surface of the block.

4. Install the flywheel and components. Install the transmission assembly, adjust as necessary, start the engine and check for oil leakage.

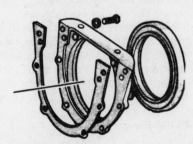

4-121 rear main oil seal

4–150

1. Remove the transmission.
2. Remove the flywheel.
3. Pry out the seal from around the crankshaft flange.
4. Coat the inner lip of the new seal with clean engine oil.
5. Gently tap the new seal into place, flush with the block, using a rubber or plastic mallet.
6. Install the flywheel.
7. Install the transmission.

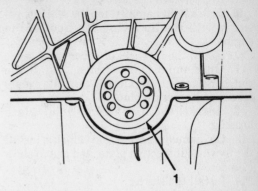

4-150 rear main seal. 1 is the actual seal surface

4–151

NOTE: *The seal is a one piece unit that can be removed and installed without removing the oil pan or crankshaft.*

1. Raise and support the vehicle on jackstands.

2. Remove the transmission and transfer case as an assembly.

3. Disconnect and remove the starter.

4. On manual transmission vehicles, remove the flywheel inspection plate, and clutch slave cylinder.

5. Remove the flywheel or drive plate housing.

6. On manual transmission, remove the clutch assembly by backing out the bolts evenly around the pressure plate.

7. Remove the flywheel or drive plate. It is a good idea to match mark the flywheel location for assembly.

8. Using a small bladed screwdriver, pry the rear seal out from around the crankshaft hub. Be careful to avoid damaging the sealing groove or hub.

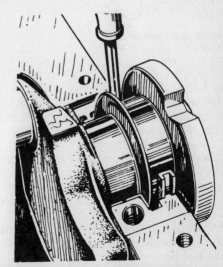

4-151 upper rear main oil seal removal

9. With a light hammer, tap the seal into position with the lip facing the front of the engine.

10. Install the flywheel or drive plate.

11. On manual transmission, install the clutch assembly by tightening the bolts evenly around the pressure plate.

12. Install the flywheel or drive plate housing.

13. On manual transmission vehicles, install the flywheel inspection plate, and clutch slave cylinder.

14. Install the starter.

15. Install the transmission and transfer case as an assembly.

6–232, 258
8–304, 360, 401

This seal is a two piece neoprene type with a single lip.

1. Raise and support the vehicle on jackstands.

2. Remove the oil pan.

3. Remove the rear main bearing cap and discard the lower seal.

4. Loosen all remaining main bearing caps.

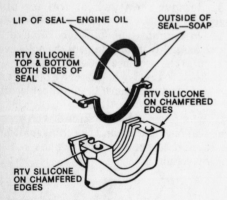

LIP OF SEAL—ENGINE OIL

OUTSIDE OF SEAL—SOAP

RTV SILICONE TOP & BOTTOM BOTH SIDES OF SEAL

RTV SILICONE ON CHAMFERED EDGES

RTV SILICONE ON CHAMFERED EDGES

6 and V8 rear main oil seal

5. Using a center punch, carefully drive the upper half of the seal out of the block just far enough to graph with a pliers and pull out.

6. Remove the oil pan front and rear seals and the side gaskets.

7. Clean all gasket surfaces.

8. Wipe clean the sealing surface of the crankshaft and coat it lightly with engine oil.

9. Coat the lip of the upper seal with engine oil and install it in the block. The lip faces forward.

10. Coat both end tabs of the lower seal with RTV silicone sealer. Do not get any RTV sealer on the seal lip.

11. Coat the outer curved surface of the seal with liquid soap. Coat the seal lip with engine oil.

12. Install the seal into the cap, pressing firmly.

13. Coat both chamferred edges of the cap with RTV sealer.

CAUTION: *Do not allow any RTV sealer to get on the mating surfaces of the cap or block as this will affect bearing clearance.*

14. Install the rear main cap.

15. Tighten all main bearing cap bolts gradually to 80 ft.lb.

16. Replace the oil pan.

Crankshaft

REMOVAL

4–121

NOTE: *On engines equipped with automatic transmissions, mark the converter-to-flexplate position prior to disassembly.*

1. Remove the engine from the car.

2. Remove the rear main seal.

3. Install the engine on a work stand.

4. Remove the timing belt cover.

5. Remove the accesory drive pulley.

6. Loosen the tensioner and remove the timing belt.

7. Using tool J-26876, or equivalent, remove the belt drive pulley from the crankshaft. Leave the pulley attached to the tool.

8. Remove the oil pump.

9. Remove the oil pan. Remove all traces of the gasket from the pan and block.

10. Remove the oil pick-up tube.

11. Matchmark and number the connecting rod bearing caps and remove the caps, two at a time, rotating the crankshaft to make them accesible. Place them on a clean work surface.

12. Number the main bearing caps and remove them. Place them on a clean work surface.

13. Lift out the crankshaft.

4–151

1. Remove the engine and mount it on a work stand.

2. Remove the spark plugs.

3. Remove the fan and pulley.

4. Remove the vibration damper and hub.

5. Remove the oil pan and oil pump.

6. Remove the timing case cover.

7. Remove the crankshaft timing gear.

8. Remove the connecting rod bearing caps. Mark each for reassembly.

9. Remove the main bearing caps, marking each for reassembly.

10. Remove the crankshaft.

4–150
6–232, 258
8–304, 360, 401

1. Remove the engine from the vehicle and mount it on a work stand.
2. Drain the oil.
3. Remove the flywheel or torque converter, match marking the pieces for installation.
4. Remove all drive belts.
5. Remove the fan and hub assembly.
6. Remove the crankshaft pulley and vibration damper.
7. Remove the timing case cover.
8. Remove the oil pan.
9. Remove the oil pump and pickup.
10. Remove the rod bearing caps, marking them for installation.
11. Remove the main bearing caps, marking them for installation.
12. Lift out the crankshaft.

NOTE: *A replacement oil pickup tube must be used. Do not attempt to install the original. Make sure the plastic button is inserted in the bottom of the pickup screen. Always use a new rear main seal. If new bearings are installed, check clearances with Plastigage®.*

INSPECTION

1. Check the crankshaft for wear or damage to the bearing surfaces of the journals. Crankshafts that are damaged can be reconditioned by a professional machine shop.
2. Using a dial indicator, check the crank-shaft journal runout. Measure the crankshaft journals with a micrometer to determine the correct size rod and main bearings to be used. Whenever a new or reconditioned crankshaft

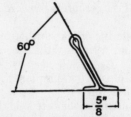

Home-made bearing roll-out pin

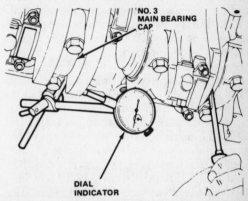

Check the crankshaft end-play with a dial indicator

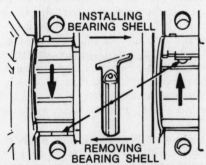

Remove or install the upper bearing insert using a roll-out pin

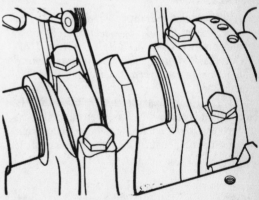

Check the crankshaft end-play with a feeler gauge

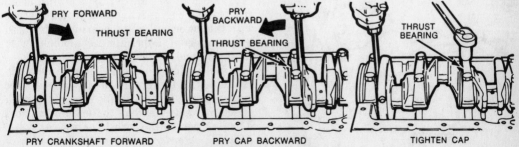

Aligning the thrust bearing

is installed, new connecting rod bearings and main bearings should be installed.

3. Clean all oil passages in the block (and crankshaft if it is being reused).

NOTE: *A new rear main seal should be installed any time the crankshaft is removed or replaced.*

4. Wipe the oil from the crankshaft journal and the outer and inner surfaces of the bearing shell.

5. Place a piece of plastic gauging material in the center of the bearing.

6. Use a floor jack or other means to hold the crankshaft against the upper bearing shell. This is necessary to obtain accurate clearance readings when using plastic gauging material.

7. Install the bearing cap and bearing. Place engine oil on the cap bolts and install. Torque the bolts to specification.

8. Remove the bearing cap and determine the bearing clearance by comparing the width of the flattened plastic gauging material at its widest point with the graduations on the gauging material container. The number within the graduation on the envelope indicates the clearance in millimeters or thousandths of an inch. If the clearance is greater than allowed, REPLACE BOTH BEARING SHELLS AS A SET. Recheck the clearance after replacing the shells.

INSTALLATION

NOTE: *Main bearing clearances must be corrected by the use of selective upper and lower shells. UNDER NO CIRCUMSTANCES should the use of shims behind the shells to compensate for wear be attempted.*

1. Install new bearing upper halves in the block. If the crankshaft has been turned to resurface the journals, undersized bearing must be used to compensate. Lay the crankshaft in the block.

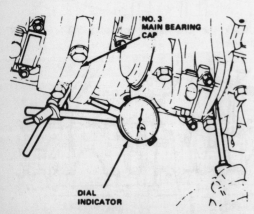

Checking crankshaft endplay with a dial indicator

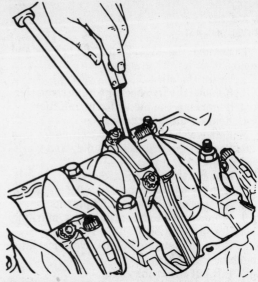

Checking rod side clearance with a flat feeler gauge. Use a small prybar to spread the rods

2. Install the lower bearing halves in the caps.

3. Use Plastigage⋇ to check bearing fit.

4. When the bearings are properly fitted, install and torque the bearing caps.

5. Check crankshaft endplay to determine the need for thrust washers.

6. While you're at it, it's a good idea to replace the rear main seal at this time.

7. Install sufficient oil pan bolts in the block to align with the connecting rod bolts. Use rubber bands between the bolts to position the connecting rods as required. Connecting rod position can be adjusted by increasing the tension on the rubber bands with additional turns around the pan bolts or thread protectors.

8. Position the upper half of main bearings in the block and lubricate them with engine oil.

9. Position crankshaft keyway in the same position as removed and lower it into block. The connecting rods will follow the crank pins into the correct position as the crankshaft is lowered.

10. Lubricate the thrust flanges with clean engine oil or engine rebuilding oil. Install caps with the lower half of the bearings lubricated with engine oil. Lubricate the cap bolts with engine oil and install, but do not tighten.

11. With a block of wood, bump the shaft in each direction to align the thrust flanges of the main bearing. After bumping the shaft in each direction, wedge the shaft to the front and hold it while torquing the thrust bearing cap bolts.

NOTE: *In order to prevent the possibility of cylinder block and/or main bearing cap dam-*

age, the main bearing caps are to be tapped into their cylinder block cavity using a wood or rubber mallet before the bolts are installed. Do not use attaching bolts to pull the main bearing caps into their seats. Failure to observe this information may damage the cylinder block or a bearing cap.

12. Torque all main bearing caps to specification. Check crankshaft endplay, using a flat feeler gauge.

13. Remove the connecting rod bolt thread protectors and lubricate the connecting rod bearings with engine oil.

14. Install the connecting rod bearing caps in their original position. Torque the nuts to specification.

15. Install all parts in reverse order of removal. See related procedures in this chapter for component installation.

Flywheel/Flex Plate and Ring Gear

NOTE: Flex plate is the term for a flywheel mated with an automatic transmission.

REMOVAL AND INSTALLATION

All Engines

NOTE: The ring gear is replaceable only on engines mated with a manual transmission. Engine with automatic transmissions have ring gears which are welded to the flex plate.

1. Remove the transmission and transfer case.

2. Remove the clutch, if equipped, or torque converter from the flywheel. The flywheel bolts should be loosened a little at a time in a cross pattern to avoid warping the flywheel. On vehicles with manual transmission, replace the pilot bearing in the end of the crankshaft if removing the flywheel.

3. The flywheel should be checked for cracks and glazing. It can be resurfaced by a machine shop.

4. If the ring gear is to be replaced, drill a hole in the gear between two teeth, being careful not to contact the flywheel surface. Using a cold chisel at this point, crack the ring gear and remove it.

5. Polish the inner surface of the new ring gear and heat it in an oven to about 600°F (316°C). Quickly place the ring gear on the flywheel and tap it into place, making sure that it is fully seated.

NOTE: Never heat the ring gear past 800°F (426°C), or the tempering will be destroyed.

6. Position the flywheel on the end of the crankshaft. Torque the bolts a little at a time, in a cross pattern, to the torque figure shown in the Torque Specifications Chart.

7. Install the clutch or torque converter.

8. Install the transmission and transfer case.

EXHAUST SYSTEM

CAUTION: When working on exhaust systems, ALWAYS wear protective goggles! Avoid working on a hot exhaust system!

Muffler

REMOVAL AND INSTALLATION

NOTE: The following applies to exhaust systems using clamped joints. Most later model, original equipment systems use welded joints at the muffler. These joints will, of course, have to be cut.

1. Raise and support the rear end on jackstands, placed under the frame, so that the axle hangs freely.

2. Remove the muffler clamps.

3. Remove the tailpipe hanger clamp.

4. Spray the joint liberally with a penetrant/rust dissolver compound such as Liquid Wrench, WD-40, or equivalent.

5. If the tailpipe cannot be pulled or twisted free from the muffler, drive a chisel between the muffler and tailpipe at several places to free it.

6. Disconnect the muffler hanger.

7. If the pipe leading into the muffler is not to be replaced, and cannot be pulled free of the muffler, heat the joint with an oxyacetylene torch until it is cherry red. Place a block of wood against the front of the muffler and drive it rearward to disengage it from the pipe.

If the pipe is being replaced, use a chisel to free it.

CAUTION: When using a torch, make certain that no combustibles or brake or fuel lines are in the immediate area of the torch.

8. When installing the new muffler, make sure that the locator slot and tab at the tailpipe joint index each other.

9. Drive the muffler onto the front pipe.

10. Position the system, without muffler clamps, under the car and install the hangers. Make certain that there is sufficient clearance between the system components and the floor pan and axle. Then, install the muffler clamps and tighten the hangers.

NOTE: Install the muffler clamps so that the shafts of the U-bolts covers the slots in the joint flanges.

Front Exhaust Pipe (Head Pipe)

REMOVAL AND INSTALLATION

1. Raise and support the front end on jackstands.

SPECIAL TOOLS

 B.Vi. 28-01

 Mot. 521-01

 J-22248

 Mot. 582

 Mot. 251-01

 J-9163

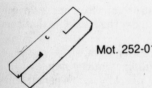 Mot. 252-01

 Mot. 788

 Mot. 853

 Mot. 789

 Mot. 851

 B.Vi. 859

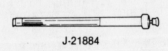 J-21884

 Mot. 854

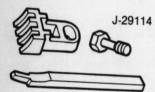 J-29114

 Mot. 852

 Mot. 861

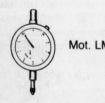 Mot. LM

 Mot. 855

2. Disconnect any oxygen sensor wires or air injection pipes.

3. Disconnect the front pipe at the manifold(s).

4. Disconnect the rear end of the pipe from the muffler or catalytic converter.

5. Installation is the reverse of removal. Torque the pipe-to-manifold nuts to 17 ft.lb. on 4-cylinder engines, or 20 ft.lb. on the 6- and 8-cylinder engines. Make sure the pipe is properly aligned.

Rear Exhaust Pipe or Tailpipe
REMOVAL AND INSTALLATION

NOTE: *Some vehicle use an intermediate pipe, also called a rear exhaust pipe. This pipe connects the front pipe with the muffler, or runs between the converter and muffler.*

1. Raise and support the rear end on jackstands.

2. If just the intermediate pipe is being replaced, cut it at the joints and collapse and remove the remainder from the front pipe and muffler or converter. If adjoining parts are also being replaced, the pipe may be chiseled off.

3. If just the tailpipe is being replaced, cut it just behind the muffler and collapse and remove the remainder from the muffler flange. Remove the tailpipe hanger.

4. When installing any pipe, position it in the system and make sure that it is properly aligned and has sufficient clearance at the floor pan. Position U-bolts so that the bolt shafts cover any slots in the pipe flanges.

When the system is correctly aligned, tighten all U-bolts and hangers.

Catalytic Converter
REMOVAL AND INSTALLATION

1. Raise and support the rear end on jackstands.

2. Disconnect the downstream air injection tube at the converter.

3. On the 4-cylinder engine, the front pipe is bolted to the converter at a facing flange. On the 6- and 8-cylinder engines, the front pipe and converter are clamped together at a slip-fit joint. On all engines, the rear joint of the converter is a slip-fit.

4. To avoid damaging any components, it will probably be necessary to heat any slip-fit joint with an oxyacetylene torch, until the joint is cherry red. Then, place a block of wood against the converter and drive it off of the pipe.

CAUTION: *When using a torch, make certain that no combustibles or brake or fuel lines are in the immediate area of the torch.*

5. Position the replacement converter in the system and install the rear clamp. Hand tighten the nuts.

6. On 4-cylinder engines: bolt the flanges together at the front end. Tighten the bolts to 25 ft.lb. Tighten the rear clamp nuts to 45 ft.lb.

7. On 6- and 8-cylinder engines, install the front clamp, make sure that the converter is properly positioned and tighten the front and rear clamp nuts to 45 ft.lb.

8. Install the downstream air injection tube and tighten the clamps to 36–48 in.lb.

9. Lower the car.

Emission Controls and Fuel System

Emission Control Systems Usage

System	Application
Positive Crankcase Ventilation	1965 and later gasoline engines
Air injection	1965 and later gasoline engines
Thermostatically controlled air cleaner	All 1971 and later engines
Transmission controlled spark (TCS)	All AMC engines
Exhaust Gas Recirculation (EGR)	All 1971 and later engines
Evaporative emission control canister	All 1971 and later engines
Catalytic Converter.	1979 and later gasoline engines
Vacuum throttle modulation	1975 and later gasoline engines

Troubleshooting Basic Fuel System Problems

Problem	Cause	Solution
Engine cranks, but won't start (or is hard to start) when cold	• Empty fuel tank • Incorrect starting procedure • Defective fuel pump • No fuel in carburetor • Clogged fuel filter • Engine flooded • Defective choke	• Check for fuel in tank • Follow correct procedure • Check pump output • Check for fuel in the carburetor • Replace fuel filter • Wait 15 minutes; try again • Check choke plate
Engine cranks, but is hard to start (or does not start) when hot— (presence of fuel is assumed)	• Defective choke	• Check choke plate
Rough idle or engine runs rough	• Dirt or moisture in fuel • Clogged air filter • Faulty fuel pump	• Replace fuel filter • Replace air filter • Check fuel pump output
Engine stalls or hesitates on acceleration	• Dirt or moisture in the fuel • Dirty carburetor • Defective fuel pump • Incorrect float level, defective accelerator pump	• Replace fuel filter • Clean the carburetor • Check fuel pump output • Check carburetor
Poor gas mileage	• Clogged air filter • Dirty carburetor • Defective choke, faulty carburetor adjustment	• Replace air filter • Clean carburetor • Check carburetor
Engine is flooded (won't start accompanied by smell of raw fuel)	• Improperly adjusted choke or carburetor	• Wait 15 minutes and try again, without pumping gas pedal • If it won't start, check carburetor

EMISSION CONTROLS

Description

There are three types of automotive pollutants: crankcase fumes, exhaust gases and gasoline evaporation. The equipment that is used to limit these pollutants is commonly called emission control equipment.

Crankcase Emission Controls

The crankcase emission control equipment consists of a positive crankcase ventilation valve (PCV), a closed or open oil filler cap and hoses to connect this equipment.

When the engine is running, a small portion of the gases which are formed in the combustion chamber during combustion, leak by the piston rings and enter the crankcase. Since these gases are under pressure, they tend to escape from the crankcase and enter the atmosphere. If these gases were allowed to remain in the the crankcase for any length of time, they would contaminate the engine oil and cause sludge to build up. If the gases were allowed to escape into the atmosphere, they would pollute the air, as they contain unburned hydrocarbons. The crankcase emission control equipment recycles these gases back into the engine combustion chamber where they are burned.

Crankcase gases are recycled in the following manner: while the engine is running, clean filtered air is drawn into the crankcase either directly through the oil filler cap, or through the carburetor air filter and then through a hose leading to the oil filler cap. As the air passes through the crankcase, it picks up the combustion gases and carries them out of the crankcase, up through the PCV valve and into the intake manifold. After they enter the intake manifold, they are drawn into the combustion chamber and burned.

The most critical component in the system is the PCV valve. This vacuum controlled valve regulates the amount of gases which are recycled into the combustion chamber. At low engine speeds, the valve is partially closed, limiting the flow of gases into the intake manifold. As engine speed increases, the valve opens to admit greater quantities of the gases into the intake manifold. If the valve should become blocked or plugged, the gases will be prevented from escaping from the crankcases by the normal route. Since these gases are under pressure, they will find their own way out of the crankcase. This alternate route is usually a weak oil seal or gasket in the engine. As the gas escapes by the gasket, it also creates an oil leak. Besides causing oil leaks, a clogged PCV valve also allows these gases to remain in the crankcase for an extended period of time, promoting the formation of sludge in the engine.

The above explanation and the troubleshooting procedure which follows applies to all engines with PCV systems.

TROUBLESHOOTING

With the engine running, pull the PCV valve and hose from the engine. Block off the end of the valve with your finger. The engine speed should drop at least 50 rpm when the end of the valve is blocked. If the engine speed does not drop at least 50 rpm, then the valve is defective and should be replaced.

REMOVAL AND INSTALLATION

1. Pull the PCV valve and hose from the engine.
2. Remove the PCV valve from the hose. Inspect the inside of the PCV valve from the hose. If it is dirty, disconnect if from the intake manifold and clean it.
3. If the PCV valve hose was removed, connect it to the intake manifold.

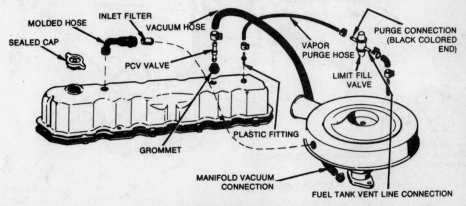

Typical PCV system

4. Connect the PCV valve to its hose.

5. Install the PCV valve on the engine.

Air Injection System

DESCRIPTION

The exhaust emission air injection system consists of a belt driven air pump which directs compressed air through connecting hoses to a steel distribution manifold into stainless steel injection tubes in the exhaust port adjacent to each exhaust valve. The air, with its normal oxygen content, reacts with the hot, but incompletely burned exhaust gases and permits further combustion in the exhaust port or manifold.

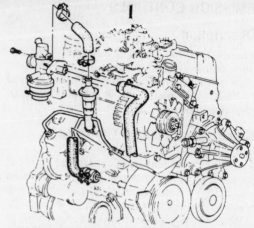

4-150 AIR diverter valve and manifold

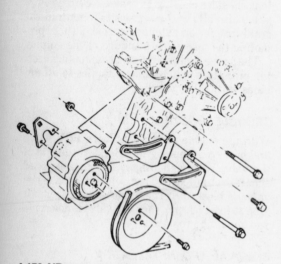

4-150 AIR pump mounting

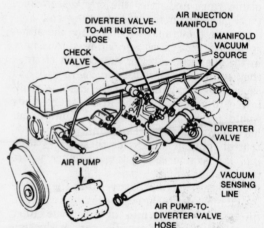

Typical air pump system, except V8

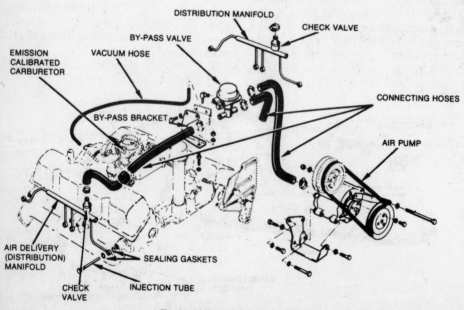

Typical V8 air pump system

Air Pump

The air injection pump is a positive displacement vane type which is permanently lubricated and requires little periodic maintenance. The only serviceable parts on the air pump are the filter, exhaust tube, and relief valve. The relief valve relieves the air flow when the pump pressure reaches a preset level. This occurs at high engine rpm. This serves to prevent damage to the pump and to limit maximum exhaust manifold temperatures.

Pump Air Filter

The air filter attached to the pump is a replaceable element type. The filter should be replaced every 12,000 miles under normal conditions and sooner under off-road use. Some models draw their air supply through the carburetor air filter.

Air Delivery Manifold

The air delivery manifold distributes the air from the pump to each of the air delivery tubes in a uniform manner. A check valve is integral with the air delivery manifold. Its function is to prevent the reverse flow of exhaust gases to the pump should the pump fail. This reverse flow would damage the air pump and connecting hose.

Air Injection Tubes

The air injection tubes are inserted into the exhaust ports. The tubes project into the exhaust ports, directing air into the vicinity of the exhaust valve.

Anti-Backfire Valve

The anti-backfire diverter valve prevents engine backfire by briefly interrupting the air being injected into the exhaust manifold during periods of deceleration or rapid throttle closure. The valve opens when a sudden increase in manifold vacuum overcomes the diaphragm spring tension. With the valve in the open position, the air flow from the air pump is directed to the atmosphere.

On the 1972 6–232, the anti-backfire valve is what is commonly called a gulp valve. During rapid deceleration the valve is opened by the sudden high vacuum condition in the intake manifold and gulps air into the intake manifold.

Both of these valves prevent backfiring in the exhaust manifold. Both valves also prevent an over right fuel mixture from being burned in the exhaust manifold, which would cause backfiring and possible damage to the engine.

COMPONENT REMOVAL AND INSTALLATION

Air Pump

CAUTION: *Never place the pump is a vise or attempt to dismantle it. The pump has no internal parts that are replaceable and it is serviced as a unit. Never pry or hammer on the pump housing.*

1. Loosen the bolts on the pump pulley.
2. Loosen the air pump attachment racket. On V8 models with air conditioning, loosen the power steering pump to aid in drive belt removal.
3. Detach the air supply hoses at the pump.
4. Remove the drivebelt and pulley from the hub.
5. Unfasten the bolts on the bracket and remove the pump.

Installation is as follows:

1. Place the pump on its mounting bracket and install, but so not tighten the attachment volts.
2. With the rotor shaft used as a center, fit the pulley into the hub and install the drive belt over the pulley.
3. Tighten the pulley attachment bolts, using care not to snap them off.
4. Adjust the pump until the belt is secure. Tighten the mounting bolts and the adjusting screw to 18–22 ft.lb.; do not overtighten.
5. Attach the hoses and clamps.

Air Pump Relief Valve

1. Use a gear pulley and a steel bridge to remove the relief valve from the pump.
2. Remove the pressure plug from the new relief valve assembly.
3. Insert the relief valve into it housing mounting hole.
4. Place a block of wood over the valve. Use a hammer to tap the valve until it lightly registers against the housing. Use care not to distort the housing.
5. Press the pressure plug into the center of the relief valve.

Centrifugal Filter Fan

NOTE: *Never attempt to clean the filter fan. It is impossible to remove the fan without destroying it.*

1. Remove the air pump from the car, as detailed above.
2. Gently pry the outer disc off and pull off the remaining portion. Be careful that no fragments from the fan enter the pump air intake.
3. Install a new filter fan pulling it into place with the pump pulley and attaching bolts.
4. Alternately tighten the bolts so that the

fan is drawn down evenly. Be sure that the outer edge of the fan fits into the pump housing.

CAUTION: *Never hammer or press the fan into place; damage to it and the pump will result.*

5. Install the pump on the car.

NOTE: *For the first 20–30 minutes of operation, the fan may squeal until its lip has worn in. This is normal and does not indicate a damaged pump.*

Exhaust Tube

1. Remove the exhaust tube by grasping it (never the pump body) in a vise or a pair of pliers. Pull the tube out with a gentle twisting motion.

2. Install the new exhaust tube by tapping it into the hole with a hammer and a wooden block. Be careful not to damage its end.

3. Tap it until 7/8" (22.23mm) of the tube remains above the pump cover.

NOTE: *Do not clamp the pump in a vise while installing the exhaust tube.*

By-Pass (Diverter Valve)

1. Disconnect the hoses from the valve.

2. Remove the screws that attach the valve bracket to the engine. Remove the valve and bracket assembly.

3. Installation is the reverse of removal.

Air Injection Manifold and Check Valve Assembly

6–232, 258

1. Remove the intake/exhaust manifold assembly, after disconnecting the hoses from the air injection manifold.

2. Place the assembly in a vise and unfasten the retaining nuts on the air injection manifold at each cylinder exhaust port.

3. Lightly tap the injection tubes, then pull the injection manifold away from the exhaust manifold.

4. If the tubes have become fused to the injection manifold, remove them by applying heat while rotating them with pliers.

Installation of the injection manifold and tubes is performed as follows:

1. Insert new air injection tubes into the exhaust manifold.

NOTE: *The shorter tubes of into the Nos. 3 and 4 cylinders.*

2. Using a new gasket, assemble the exhaust/intake manifold to the engine.

3. Using new gaskets, install the air injection manifold on to the exhaust manifold in the reverse order of removal.

V8

1. Detach the air delivery hose at the check valve.

2. Unfasten the air injection manifold attachment nuts from the cylinder head. Carefully, ease the air injection manifold away from the heat.

NOTE: *On some models it may be necessary to lower the bottom steering shaft clamp to gain access to the left rear mounting bolt; or to disconnect the right engine support and raise the engine to remove the right air injection manifold assembly.*

3. On newer cars, the air injection tubes and the manifold are removed as an assembly.

4. On older models, or if the tubes are hard to remove, use a screw extractor to twist the tube out gradually.

NOTE: *Some interference may be encountered because of the normal carbon buildup on the tubes. Injection tubes which are removed with a screw extractor must be replaced with new ones.*

5. Installation is the reverse of removal.

TROUBLESHOOTING

CAUTION: *Do not hammer on, pry, or bend the pump housing while tightening the drive belt or testing the pump.*

Belt Tension and Air Leaks

1. Check the pump drive belt tension. There should be about 1/2" (12.7mm) play in the longest span of belt between pulleys.

2. Turn the pump by hand. If it has seized, the belt will slip, producing noise. Disregard any chirping, squealing, or rolling sounds from inside the pump; these are normal when it is turned by hand.

3. Check the hoses and connections for leaks. Hissing or a blast of air is indicative of a leak. Soapy water, applied lightly around the area in question, is a good method for detecting leaks.

Air Output Tests

1. Disconnect the air supply hose at the antibackfire valve.

2. Connect a vacuum pressure gauge to the air supply hose.

NOTE: *If there are two hoses plug the second one.*

3. With the engine at normal operating temperature, increase the idle speed and watch the gauge.

Exhaust Gas Recirculation (EGR) System

The EGR system consists of a diaphragm actuated flow control valve (EGR valve), coolant temperature override switch, low temperature

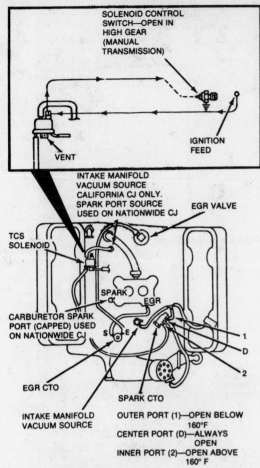

8 cylinder TCS system

SOLENOID CONTROL SWITCH—OPEN IN HIGH GEAR (MANUAL TRANSMISSION)

IGNITION FEED

VENT

INTAKE MANIFOLD VACUUM SOURCE CALIFORNIA CJ ONLY. SPARK PORT SOURCE USED ON NATIONWIDE CJ

EGR VALVE

TCS SOLENOID

SPARK

EGR

CARBURETOR SPARK PORT (CAPPED) USED ON NATIONWIDE CJ

S E

1

D

2

EGR CTO

SPARK CTO

INTAKE MANIFOLD VACUUM SOURCE

OUTER PORT (1)—OPEN BELOW 160°F
CENTER PORT (D)—ALWAYS OPEN
INNER PORT (2)—OPEN ABOVE 160° F

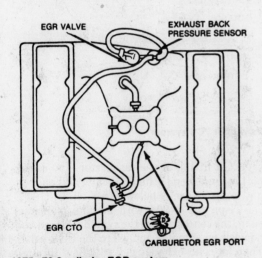

EGR VALVE

EXHAUST BACK PRESSURE SENSOR

EGR CTO

CARBURETOR EGR PORT

1975–79 8 cylinder EGR system

EGR

EGR VALVE

EXHAUST BACK-PRESSURE SENSOR

OUTER E-PORT

INNER S-PORT

EGR CTO

FRONT

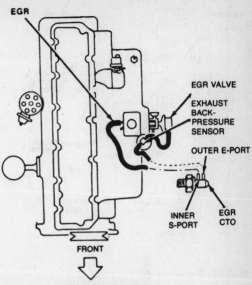

1975–79 6 cylinder EGR system

VACUUM SIGNAL DUMP VALVE (NOT USED ON 49 STATE 304 ENGINES)

THERMAL VACUUM SWITCH

FORWARD DELAY VALVE

EGR VALVE

ORIFICE PLATE

CARBURATOR

EGR CTO SWITCH

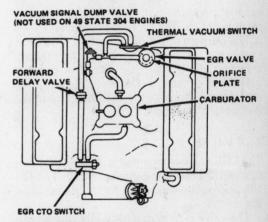

1980–86 8-cylinder EGR system

CARBURETOR

EXHAUST CROSS FLOW

EGR CTO

EGR ADAPTER

EGR VALVE

DELAY VALVE

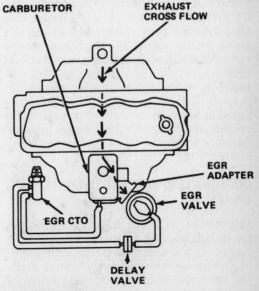

4-151 EGR system

vacuum signal modulator, high temperature vacuum signal modulator.

All 1977 and later California units have a back pressure sensor which modulates EGR signal vacuum according to the rise or fall of

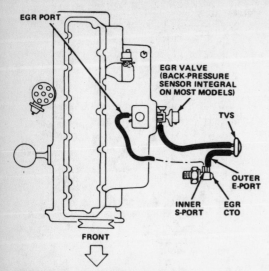

1980–82 6 cylinder EGR system

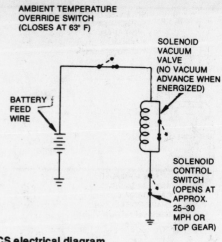

TCS electrical diagram

exhaust pressure in the manifold. A restrictor plate is not used in these applications.

The purpose of the EGR system is to limit the formation of nitrogen oxides by diluting the fresh air intake charge with a metered amount of exhaust gas, thereby reducing the peak temperatures of the burning gases in the combustion chambers.

EGR VALVE

The EGR valve is mounted on a machined surface at the rear of the intake manifold on the V8s and on the side of the intake manifold on the sixes.

The valve is held in a normally closed position by a coil spring located above the diaphragm. A special fitting is provided at the carburetor to route ported (above the throttle plates) vacuum through hose connections to a fitting located above the diaphragm on the valve. A passage in the intake manifold directs exhaust gas from the exhaust crossover passage (V8) or from below the riser area (Sixes) to the EGR valve. When the diaphragm is actuated by vacuum, the valve opens and meters exhaust gas through another passage in the intake manifold to the floor of the intake manifold below the carburetor.

COOLANT TEMPERATURE OVERRIDE SWITCH

This switch is located in the intake manifold at the coolant passage adjacent to the oil filler tube on the V8s or at the left side of the engine block (formerly the drain plug) on the Sixes. The outer port of the switch is open and not used. The inner port is connected by a host to

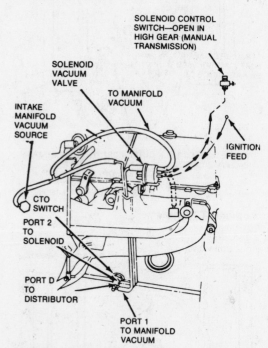

6 cylinder TCS system

the EGR fitting at the carburetor. The center port is connected to the EGR valve. When coolant temperature is below 115°F (46°C) (160°F [71°C] on the 8–304 with manual transmission), the center port of the switch is closed and no vacuum signal is applied to the EGR valve. Therefore, no exhaust gas will flow through the valve. When the coolant temperature reaches 115°F (46°C), both the center port and the inner port of the switch are open and a vacuum signal is applied to the EGR valve. This vacuum signal is, however, subject to regulation by the low and high temperature signal modulators.

LOW TEMPERATURE VACUUM SIGNAL MODULATOR

This unit is located just to the right of the radiator behind the grill opening. The low temperature vacuum signal modulator vacuum hose is connected by a plastic T-fitting to the EGR vacuum signal hose. The modulator is open when ambient temperatures are below 60°F (16°C). This causes a weakened vacuum signal to the EGR valve and a resultant decrease in the amount of exhaust gas being recirculated.

HIGH TEMPERATURE VACUUM SIGNAL MODULATOR

This unit is located at the right front fender inner panel. The high temperature vacuum signal modulator is connected to the EGR vacuum signal hose by a plastic T-fitting. The modulator opens when the underhood air temperatures reach 115°F (46°C) and it causes a weakened vacuum signal to the EGR valve, thus reducing the amount of exhaust gases being recirculated.

COMPONENT REMOVAL AND INSTALLATION

EGR Valve

1. Remove the air cleaner assembly from the carburetor.
2. Unfasten the vacuum line from the top of the EGR valve.
3. Loosen and remove the two screws which secure the valve to the manifold.
4. Remove the EGR valve, complete with its gasket.
5. Installation of the EGR valve is the reverse of its removal. Always use a new gasket. Tighten the valve securing bolts to 13 ft.lb.

Valve and Passage Cleaning

1. Remove the EGR valve.
2. Use a wire brush to clean all the deposits from the stainless steel pintle.
3. Press down on the pintle to open the EGR valve and them release it to close the valve. Replace the valve assembly if it will not close fully.

4. Inspect the manifold passages. If necessary, clean them with a spiral wire brush.
NOTE: *On 6-cylinder engines, deposits will build up most rapidly in the upper passage. If the deposits cannot be removed with the wire brush, use a $\frac{9}{16}$" (14mm) drill bit. Rotate the drill by hand, after coating it with heavy grease.*
5. Install the EGR valve with a new gasket.

Thermostatically Controlled Air Cleaner System (TAC)

This system consists of a heat shroud which is integral with the right side exhaust manifold, a hot air hose and a special air cleaner assembly equipped with a thermal sensor and a vacuum motor and air valve assembly.

The thermal sensor incorporates an air bleed valve which regulates the amount of vacuum applied to the vacuum motor, controlling the air valve position to supply either heated air

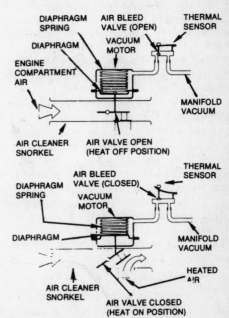

Vacuum controlled thermostatic air cleaner

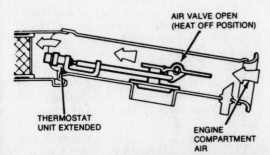
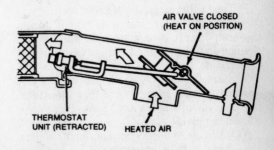

Non-vacuum controlled thermostatic air cleaner

from the exhaust manifold or air from the engine compartment.

During the warm-up period when underhood temperatures are low, the air bleed valve is closed and sufficient vacuum is applied to the vacuum motor to hold the air valve in the closed (heat on) position.

As the temperature of the air entering the air cleaner approaches approximately 115°F (46°C), the air bleed valve opens to decrease the amount of vacuum applied to the vacuum motor. The diaphragm spring in the vacuum motor then moves the air valve into the open (heat off) position, allowing only underhood air to enter the air cleaner.

The air valve in the air cleaner will also open, regardless of air temperature, during heavy acceleration to obtain maximum air flow through the air cleaner.

TROUBLESHOOTING

Non Vacuum-Operated Air Door Test

1. Unfasten the temperature sensing valve and snorkle assembly from the air cleaner. Place it in a container of cold water. Make sure that the thermostat is completely covered with water.

2. Place a thermometer, of known accuracy, in the water. Heat the water slowly and watch the temperature.

3. At 105°F or less, the door should be closed (manifold heat position).

4. Continue heating the water until it reaches 130°F. The door should be fully open to the outside air position.

5. If the door does not open at or near this temperature, check it for binding or a detached spring. If the door doesn't open or close properly, the sensor is defective and must be replaced.

NOTE: *This usually requires that the entire snorkle assembly must be replaced.*

Vacuum-Operated Air Door Test

1. Either start with a cold engine or remove the air cleaner from the engine for at least half an hour. While cooling the air cleaner, leave the hood open.

2. Tape a thermometer, of know accuracy, to the inside of the air cleaner so that it is near the temperature sensor unit. Install the air cleaner on the engine but do not fasten its securing nut.

3. Start the engine. With the engine cold and the outside temperature less than 90°F, the door should be in the 'heat-on' position (closed to outside air).

NOTE: *Due to the position of the air cleaner on some cars, a mirror may be necessary when observing the position of the air door.*

4. Operate the throttle rapidly to ½–¾ of its opening and release it. The air door should open to allow outside air to enter and then close again.

5. Allow the engine to warm up to normal temperature. Watch the door. When it opens to the outside air, remove the cover from the air cleaner. The temperature should be over 90°F and no more than 130°F; 115°F is about normal. If the door does not work within these temperature ranges, or fails to work at all, check for linkage or door binding.

If there is no binding and the air door is not working, proceed with the vacuum test below. If these indicate no faults in the vacuum motor and the door is not working, the temperature sensor is defective and must be replaced.

Vacuum Motor Test

NOTE: *Be sure that the vacuum hose that runs between the temperature switch and the vacuum motor is not pinched by the retaining clip under the air cleaner. This could prevent the air door from closing.*

1. Check all of the vacuum lines and fittings for leaks. Correct any leaks. If none are found, proceed with the test.

2. Remove the hose which runs from the sensor to the vacuum motor. Run a hose directly from the manifold vacuum source to the vacuum motor.

3. If the motor closes the air door, it is functioning properly and the temperature sensor is defective.

4. If the motor does not close the door and no binding is present in its operations, the vacuum motor is defective and must be replaced.

NOTE: *If an alternate vacuum source is applied to the motor, insert a vacuum gauge in the line by using a T-fitting. Apply at least 9 in.Hg of vacuum in order to operate the motor.*

Distributor Controls

DUAL DIAPHRAGM DISTRIBUTOR TEST

1. Connect a timing light to the engine. Check the ignition timing.

NOTE: *First disconnect any spark control devices, distributor vacuum valves, etc. If these are left connected, inaccurate results may be obtained.*

2. Remove the retard hose from the distributor and plug it. Increase the engine speed. The timing should advance. It it fails to do so, then the vacuum unit is faulty and must be replaced.

3. Check the timing with the engine at normal idle speed. Unplug the retard hose and connect it to the vacuum unit. The timing

should instantly be retarded from 4–10. If this does not occur, the retard diaphragm has a leak and the vacuum unit must be replaced.

Vacuum Throttle Modulating System (VTM)

This system is designed to reduce the level of hydrocarbon emission during rapid throttle closure at high speed. It is used on some 49 states models, and all models with a V8 engine.

The system consists of a deceleration valve located at the right front of the intake manifold, and a throttle modulating diaphragm located at the carburetor base. The valve and the diaphragm are connected by a vacuum hose and the valve is connected to direct manifold vacuum. During deceleration, manifold vacuum acts to delay, slightly, the closing of the throttle plate.

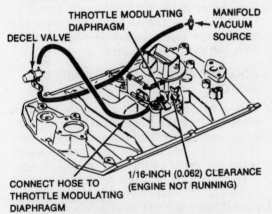

THROTTLE MODULATING DIAPHRAGM   MANIFOLD VACUUM SOURCE
DECEL VALVE
1/16-INCH (0.062) CLEARANCE (ENGINE NOT RUNNING)
CONNECT HOSE TO THROTTLE MODULATING DIAPHRAGM

Typical vacuum throttle modulating system

To adjust:

1. Run the engine to normal operating temperature and set the idle speed to specification. Shut off the engine.
2. Position the throttle lever against the curb idle adjusting screw.
3. Measure the clearance between the throttle modulating diaphragm plunger and the throttle lever. A clearance of $^1/_{16}$" (1.5875mm) should exist.
4. Adjust the clearance, if necessary, by loosening the jam nut and turning the diaphragm assembly.

DECELERATION VALVE TEST

NOTE: *Timing, idle speed and air fuel mixture should be correct before beginning this test.*

1. Connect a vacuum gauge to the distributor vacuum advance line.

2. If the carburetor has a dashpot, tape its plunger down so that it cannot touch the throttle lever at idle.
3. Speed the engine up to about 2,000 rpm and retain this speed for about ten seconds.
4. Release the throttle, allowing the engine to return to normal idle.
5. The vacuum reading should rise to about 20 in.Hg and stay there for one second. It should take about three seconds for the reading to return to normal, the valve should be adjusted.

To check for a leaking valve diaphragm:

1. Remove the vacuum gauge and connect it to the manifold vacuum line with a T-connector.
2. Clamp shut the valve-to-distributor vacuum line and, with the engine at normal idle speed, check the vacuum reading.
3. Clamp the line shut between the deceleration valve and the T-connection. Check the vacuum gauge reading again.
4. If the second reading is higher than the first, the valve diaphragm is leaking and the valve should be replaced.

Deceleration Valve Adjustment

If the deceleration valve test indicted a need for adjustment, proceed as follows:

1. Remove the cover to gain access to the adjusting screw.
2. If an increase in valve opening time is desired, turn the adjusting screw counterclockwise.
3. If a decrease in time is desired, turn the adjusting screw clockwise.

NOTE: *Each complete turn of the adjusting screw equals ½ in.Hg.*

4. After finishing the adjustments, retest the valve. If the valve cannot be adjusted, it is defective and must be replaced.

Transmission Controlled Spark System

The purpose of this system is to reduce the emission of oxides of nitrogen by lowering the peak combustion pressure and temperature during the power stroke.

The system incorporates the following components:

AMBIENT TEMPERATURE OVERRIDE SWITCH

This switch, located at the firewall, senses ambient temperatures and completes the electrical circuit from the battery to the solenoid vacuum valve when the ambient temperatures are above 63°F (17°C).

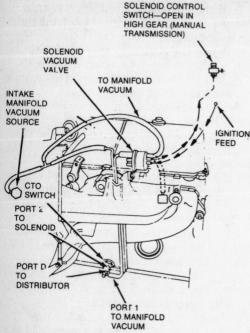

Inline six TCS system

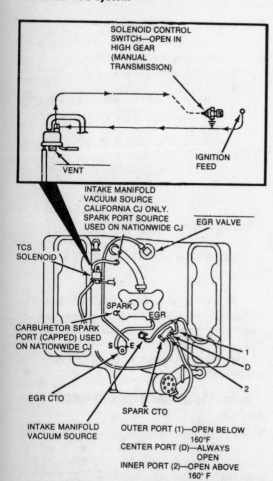

V8 TCS system

SOLENOID VACUUM VALVE

This valve is attached to the ignition coil bracket at the right side of the engine (V8 engines) or to a bracket at the rear of the intake manifold (Sixes). When the valve is energized, carburetor vacuum is blocked off and the distributor vacuum line is vented to the atmosphere through a port in the valve, resulting in no vacuum advance. When the valve is de-energized, vacuum is applied to the distributor resulting in normal vacuum advance.

SOLENOID CONTROL SWITCH

This switch is located in the transmission valve body. It opens or closes in relation to car speed and gear range. When the transmission is in high gear, the switch opens and breaks the ground circuit to the solenoid vacuum valve. In lower gear ranges the switch closes and completes the ground circuit to the solenoid vacuum valve. With a manual transmission, the switch is operated by the transmission shifter shaft. With automatic transmissions, the switch is controlled by the speedometer gear speed. Under speeds of 25 mph, the switch is activated.

COOLANT TEMPERATURE OVERRIDE SWITCH

This switch is used only on the 8–304. It is threaded into the thermostat housing. The switch reacts to coolant temperatures to route either intake manifold or carburetor vacuum to the distributor vacuum advance diaphragm.

When the coolant temperature is below 160°F (71°C), intake manifold vacuum is applied through a hose connection to the distributor advance diaphragm, resulting in full vacuum advance.

When the coolant temperature is above 160°F (71°C), intake manifold vacuum is blocked off and carburetor vacuum is then applied through the solenoid vacuum valve to the distributor advance diaphragm, resulting in decreased vacuum advance.

The relationship between distributor vacuum advance and the operation of the TCS system and coolant temperature override switch can be determined by referring to the Emission Control Distributor Vacuum Application Charts.

Transmission Controlled Spark System Test
MANUAL TRANSMISSION SYSTEM TEST

1. Connect a vacuum gauge between the distributor and the solenoid vacuum valve, using a T-connector.

Emission Controlled Distributor Vacuum Application Chart for Vehicles Equipped with TCS

Manual Transmission Gear		Automatic Transmission Vehicle Speed (mph)	Ambient Temperature Deg. F	Coolant Temperature Deg. F	Vacuum Applied to Distributor
3-sp	4-sp				
1–2	1–2–3	Under 25	Below 63	Below 160	Manifold
1–2	1–2–3	Under 25	Below 63	Above 160	Ported
1–2	1–2–3	Under 25	Above 63	Above 160	None
1–2	1–2–3	Under 25	Above 63	Below 160	Manifold
3	4	25–30	Below 63	Below 160	Manifold
3	4	25–30	Below 63	Above 160	Ported
3	4	25–30	Above 63	Above 160	Ported
3	4	25–30	Above 63	Below 160	Manifold

NOTE: *This won't work unless the temperature switch on the front crossmember is above 63°F.*

2. Start the engine. With the transmission in Neutral, the vacuum gauge should ready zero.

3. Increase engine speed to between 1,000–1,500 rpm with the clutch pedal depressed. The vacuum reading should remain at zero.

4. With the clutch still depressed, place the transmission in High gear. Increase engine speed, as before. The vacuum gauge should now read at least 6 in.Hg. If it does not, proceed further with testing.

5. Unfasten the transmission switch lead from the solenoid vacuum valve terminal. Connect the lead in series with a low amperage test lamp and the positive side of the battery.

6. Move the shift lever through all of the gears. The test lamp should remain on until high gear is entered.

7. If the lamp stays on when the transmission is in High, either the switch is defective or the circuit is grounded. If it fails to come on at all, the switch is defective or the circuit has a loose wire.

8. If the transmission switch is functioning properly but the system check indicates that something is still wrong, check the temperature switch.

AUTOMATIC TRANSMISSION SYSTEM TEST

NOTE: *The spark control system is controlled by a switch which operates on transmission governor oil pressure.*

1. Disconnect the electrical lead from the terminal of the governor pressure switch.

NOTE: *The switch may easily be reached with the hood opened. On sixes, the switch is located on the right rear of the cylinder block; on V8's, it is attached to a bracket at the rear of the right hand rocker cover.*

2. Connect a 12V test light in series, between the lead and the terminal on the switch.

CAUTION: *Use a low amperage test light, so that the switch contacts will not be damaged.*

3. Raise the car, block the front wheels (if they are not off the ground), and securely support it so that the rear wheels are free to turn.

4. Apply the service brakes. Start the engine. The test light should glow.

5. Place the gear selector in Drive, release the brake pedal and slowly depress the gas pedal.

6. Watch the speedometer and the test light; between 33–37 mph the switch should open and the test light should go out.

7. If the light does not go out within this speed range, adjust the switch by turning the $1/16''$ allen screw on the switch terminal. Turn the screw clockwise to increase or counterclockwise to decrease the switch cut-out sped. The switch should be adjusted to open at 35 mph.

8. If the switch cannot be adjusted, replace it.

9. If the switch is working properly, but the TCS system is not working, the solenoid vacuum valve is probably defective.

TRANSMISSION SWITCH TEST

1. Leave the rear wheels of the car off the ground as in the system test above.

2. Disconnect the transmission switch leads. Connect a low amperage test lamp in series with the switch and the positive side of the battery.

3. Accelerate to the speed specified in Step 3 of the system test and watch the test lamp. It should remain on until the specified speed is reached. If the lamp fails to go out or if it does not light at all, the switch if defective and must be replaced.

4. If the switch is working properly, reconnect it and go on with the next test.

VACUUM ADVANCE SOLENOID TEST

1. Disconnect the vacuum advance solenoid leads. Connect a vacuum gauge to the solenoid hose as in the system test.

2. Place the transmission in Neutral and start the engine. Increase engine speed. The gauge should indicate the presence of a vacuum.

3. Connect the hot lead to a 12V power source. Ground the other lead. Increase the engine speed again. The solenoid should energize, resulting in a vacuum reading of zero.

4. Replace the vacuum advance solenoid if it is faulty. If it is not, reconnect the wiring and go on with the next appropriate test.

AMBIENT TEMPERATURE OVERRIDE SWITCH TEST

1. Disconnect the ambient temperature switch leads.

2. Replace the switch in the circuit with a jumper wire.

3. Repeat the system test. If the vacuum gauge now reads zero or below the specified speed, i.e., the solenoid energized, the temperature switch is defective.

4. If the switch proves no to be defective when tested in Step 3, reconnect it after removing the jumper lead.

5. Cool the switch, using either ice, cold water, or an aerosol spray, to below 63°F. Repeat the system test. If there is no vacuum below the specified speed, the switch is stuck closed and must be replaced.

Carburetor

The carburetors used on engines equipped with emission controls have specific flow characteristics that differ from the carburetors used on vehicles not equipped with emission control devices. The carburetors are identified by number. The correct carburetor should be used when replacement is necessary.

ANTI-DIESELING SOLENOID TEST

NOTE: *Anti-dieseling solenoids are also referred to as, 'throttle stop' or 'idle stop' solenoids.*

1. Turn the ignition key on and open the throttle. The solenoid plunger should extend (solenoid energized).

2. Turn the ignition off. The plunger should retract, allowing the throttle to close.

NOTE: *With the anti-dieseling solenoid de-energized, the carburetor idle speed adjusting screw must make contact with the throttle shaft to prevent the throttle plates from jamming in the throttle bore when the engine is turned off.*

3. If the solenoid is functioning properly and the engine is still dieseling, check for one of the following:

    a. High idle or engine shut off speed.

    b. Engine timing not set to specifications. Correct any of these problems, as necessary.

4. If the solenoid fails to function as outlined in steps 1–2, disconnect the solenoid leads; the solenoid should de-energize. If it does not, it is jammed and must be replaced.

5. Connect the solenoid to a 12 V power source and to ground. Open the throttle so that the plunger can extend. I it does not, the solenoid is defective.

6. If the solenoid is functioning correctly and no other source of trouble can be found, the fault probably lies in the wiring between the solenoid and the ignition switch or in the ignition switch itself.

Electric Assist Choke

An electric assist choke is used to more accurately match the choke operation to engine requirements. It provides extra heat to the choke bimetal spring to speed up the choke valve opening after the underhood air temperature reaches 95°F ± 15°F (35°C). Its purpose is to reduce the emission of carbon monoxide (CO) during the engine's warmup period.

A special AC terminal is provided at the alternator to supply a 7 volt power source for the electric choke. A thermostatic switch within the choke cover closes when the underhood air temperature reaches 95°F ± 15°F (35°C) and allows current to flow to a ceramic heating element. The circuit is completed through the choke cover ground strap and choke housing to the engine. As the heating element warms up, heat is absorbed by an attached metal plate which in turn heats the coke bimetal spring.

After the engine is turned off, the thermostatic switch remains closed until the underhood temperature drops below approximately 65°F (18°C). Therefore, the heating element will immediately begin warming up when the engine is restarted, if the underhood temperature is above 65°F (18°C).

ELECTRICALLY ASSISTED CHOKE TEST

1. Detach the electrical lead from the choke cap.

2. Use a jumper lead to connect the terminal on the choke cap and the wire terminal, so that the electrical circuit is still completed.

3. Start the engine.

4. Hook up a test light between the connector on the choke lead and ground.

5. The test light should glow. If it does not, current is not being supplied to the electrically assisted choke.

6. Connect the test light between the terminal on the alternator and the terminal on the choke cap. If the light now glows, replace the lead, since it is not passing current to the choke assist.

CAUTION: *Do not ground the terminal on the alternator while performing Step 6.*

7. If the light still does not glow, the fault lies somewhere in the electrical system.

If the electrically assisted choke receives power, but still does not appear to be functioning properly, reconnect the choke lead and proceed with the rest of the test.

8. Tape the bulb end of a thermometer to the metallic portion of the choke housing.

9. If the electrically assisted choke operates below 55°F (13°C), it is defective and must be replaced.

10. Allow the engine to warm up to between 80°F and 110°F (27–43°C); at these temperatures the choke should operate for about 1½ minutes.

11. It if does not operate for this length of time, check the bi-metallic spring to see of it is connected to the tang on the choke lever.

12. If the spring is connected and the choke is not operating properly, replace the cap assembly.

Fuel Tank Vapor Emission Control System

A closed fuel tank system is used on some 1975–78, and all 1979 and later models, to route raw fuel vapor from the fuel tank into the PCV system (sixes) or air cleaner snorkle (V8s), where it is burned along with the fuel/air mixture. The system prevents raw fuel vapors from entering the atmosphere.

The fuel vapor system consists of internal fuel tank venting, a vacuum-pressure fuel tank filler cap, an expansion tank or charcoal filled canister, liquid limit fill valve, and internal carburetor venting.

Fuel vapor pressure in the fuel tank forces the vapor through vent lines to the expansion tank or charcoal filled storage canister. The vapor then travels through a single vent line to the limit fill valve, which regulates the vapor flow to the valve cover or air cleaner.

LIMIT FILL VALVE

This valve is essentially a combination vapor flow regulator and pressure relief valve. It regulates vapor flow from the fuel tank vent line into the valve cover. The valve consists of a housing, a spring loaded diaphragm and a diaphragm cover. As tank vent pressure increases, the diaphragm lifts, permitting vapor to flow through. The pressure at which this oc-

curs is 4–6 in.H_2O column. This action regulates the flow of vapors under severe conditions, but generally prohibits the flow of vapor during normal temperature operation, thus minimizing driveability problems.

LIQUID CHECK VALVE

The liquid check valve prevents liquid fuel from entering the vapor lines leading to the storage canister. The check valve incorporates a float and needle valve assembly. If liquid fuel should enter the check valve, the float will rise and force the needle upward to close the vent passage. With no liquid fuel present in the check valve, fuel vapors pass freely from the tank, through the check valve, and on to the storage canister.

TROUBLESHOOTING

There are several things to check for it a malfunction of the evaporative emission control system is suspected.

1. Leaks may be traced by using an infrared hydrocarbon tester. Run the test probe along the lines and connections. The meter will indicate the presence of a leak by a high hydrocarbon (HC) reading. This method is much more accurate than a visual inspection which would indicate only the presence of a leak large enough to pass liquid.

2. Leaks may be caused by any of the following, so always check these areas when looking for them:

    a. Defective or worn lines.

    b. Disconnected or pinched lines.

    c. Improperly routed lines.

    d. A defective filler cap.

NOTE: *It if become necessary to replace any of the lines used in the evaporative emission control system, use only hoses which are fuel resistant or are marked 'EVAP'.*

3. If the fuel tank has collapsed, it may be the fault of clogged or pinched vent lines, a defective vapor separator, or a plugged or incorrect fuel filler cap.

4. To test the filler cap, clean it and place it against the mouth. Blow into the relief valve housing. If the cap passes pressure with light blowing or if it fails to release with hard blowing, it is defective and must be replaced.

General Motors Computer Controlled Catalytic Converter (C-4) System, and Computer Command Control (CCC) System

INTRODUCTION

The GM designed Computer Controlled Catalytic Converter System (C-4 System), was in-

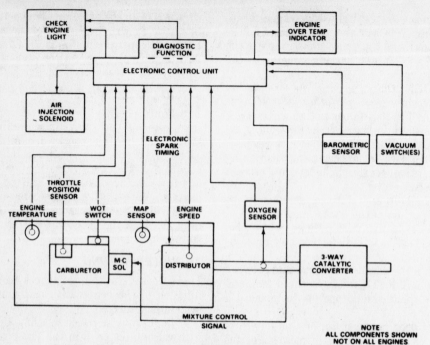

GM Computer Controlled Catalytic Converter (C-4) system

troduced in 1979 and used on 4–151 engines through 1980. The C-4 System primarily maintains the ideal air/fuel ratio at which the catalytic converter is most effective. Some versions of the system also control ignition timing of the distributor.

The Computer Command Control System (CCC System), introduced on some 1980 California models and used on all 1981 and later carbureted car lines, is an expansion of the C-4 System. The CCC System monitors up to fifteen engine/vehicle operating conditions which uses to control up to nine engine and emission control systems. In addition to maintaining the ideal air/fuel ratio for the catalytic converter and adjusting ignition timing, the CCC System also controls the Air Management System so that the Catalytic converter can operate at the highest efficiency possible. The system also controls the lockup on the transmission torque converter clutch (certain automatic transmission models only), adjust idle speed over a wide range of conditions, purges the evaporative emissions charcoal canister, controls the EGR valve operation and operates the early fuel evaporative (EFE) system. Not all engines use all of the above sub systems.

There are two operation modes for both the C-4 System and the CCC System: closed loop and open loop fuel control. Closed loop fuel control means the oxygen sensor is controlling the carburetor's air/fuel mixture ratio. Under open loop fuel control operating conditions (wide open throttle, engine and/or oxygen sensor cold), the oxygen has no effect on the air/fuel mixture.

NOTE: *On some engines, the oxygen sensor will cool off while the engine is idling, putting the system into open loop operation. To restore closed loop operation, run the engine at part throttle and accelerate from idle to part throttle a few times.*

COMPUTER CONTROLLED CATALYTIC CONVERTER (C-4) SYSTEM OPERATION

Major components of the system include an Electronic Control Module (ECM), an oxygen sensor, and electronically controlled variable mixture carburetor, and a three-way oxidation/reduction catalytic converter.

The oxygen sensor generates a voltage which varies with exhaust gas oxygen content. Lean mixtures (more oxygen) reduce voltage; rich mixtures (less oxygen) increase voltage. Voltage output is sent to the ECM.

An engine temperature sensor installed in the engine coolant outlet monitors coolant temperatures. Vacuum control switches and throttle position sensors also monitor engine conditions and supply signals to the ECM.

The Electronic Control Module (ECM) monitors the voltage input of the oxygen sensor along with information from other input signals. It processes these signals and generates a control signal sent to the carburetor. The control signal cycles between ON (lean command) and OFF (rich command). The amount of On and OFF time is a function of the input voltage sent to the ECM by the oxygen sensor. The ECM has a calibration unit called a PRO (Programmable Read Only Memory) which contains the specific instructions for a given engine application. In other words, the PROM assembly is a replaceable component which plugs into a socket on the ECM and requires a special tool for removal and installation.

NOTE: *Electronic Spark Timing (EST) allows continuous spark timing adjustments to be made by the ECM. Engines with EST can easily be identified by the absence of vacuum and mechanical spark advance mechanisms on the distributor. Engines with EMR systems may be recognized by the presence of five connectors, instead of the HEI module's usual four.*

To maintain good idle and driveability under all conditions, other input signals are used to modify the ECM output signal. Besides the sensors and switches already mentioned, these input signals include the manifold absolute pressure (MAP) or vacuum sensors and the barometric pressure (BARO) sensor. The MAP or vacuum sensors sense changes in manifold vacuum, while the BARO sensor senses changes in barometric pressure. One important function of the BARO sensor is the maintenance of good engine performance at various altitudes. These sensors act as throttle position sensors on some engines. See the following paragraph for description.

A Rochester Dualjet carburetor is used with the C-4 system. It may be an E2SE, E2SME, E4MC or E4ME model, depending on engine application. An electronically operated mixture control solenoid is installed in the carburetor float bowl. The solenoid controls the air/fuel mixture metered to the idle and main metering systems. Air metering to the idle system is controlled by an idle air bleed valve. It follows the movement of the mixture solenoid to control the amount of air bled into the idle system, enrichening or leaning out the mixture as appropriate. Air/fuel mixture enrichment occurs when the fuel valve is open and the air bleed is closed. All cycling of this system, which occurs ten times per second, is controlled by the ECM. A throttle position switch informs the ECM of open or closed throttle operation. A number of different switches are used, varying with application. The 4-cylinder engine (151 cu. in.) uses two vacuum switches to sense open throttle and closed throttle operation.

COMPUTER COMMAND CONTROL (CCC) SYSTEM OPERATION

The CCC has many components in common with the C-4 system (although they should probably not be interchanged between systems). These include the Electronic Control Module (ECM), which is capable of monitoring and adjusting more sensors and components than the ECM used on the C-4 System, an oxygen sensor, an electronically controlled variable mixture carburetor, a three-way catalytic converter, throttle position and coolant sensors, a barometric pressure (BARO) sensor, a manifold absolute pressure (MAP) sensor, a 'check engine' light on the instrument cluster, and an Electronic Spark Control (ESC) which retards ignition spark under some conditions (detonation, etc.).

Components used almost exclusively by the CCC System include the Air Injection Reaction (AIR) Management System, charcoal canister purge solenoid, EGR valve control, vehicle speed sensor (located in the instrument cluster), transmission torque converter clutch solenoid (automatic transmission models only), idle speed control, and early fuel evaporate (EFE) system.

See the operation descriptions under C-4 System for those components (except the ECM) the CCC System shares with the C-4 System.

The CCC System ECM, in addition to monitoring sensors and sending a control signal to the carburetor, also control the following components or sub systems: charcoal canister urge, AIR Management System, idle speed control, automatic transmission converter lockup, distributor ignition timing, EGR valve control, EFE control, and the air conditioner compressor clutch operation. The CCC ECM is equipped with a PROM assembly similar to the one used in the C-4 ECM. See above description.

The AIR Management System is an emission control which provides additional oxygen either to the catalyst or the cylinder head ports (in some cases exhaust manifold). An AIR Management System, composed of an air switching valve and/or an air control valve, controls the air pump flow and is itself controlled by the ECM. A complete description of the AIR system is given elsewhere in this unit repair section. The major difference between the CCC AIR System and the systems used on other cars is that the flow of air from the air pump is controlled electrically by the ECM, rather than the vacuum signal.

The charcoal canister purge control is an electrically operated solenoid valve controlled by the ECM. When energized, the purge control solenoid blocks vacuum from reaching the canister purge valve. When the ECM de-energized the purge control solenoid, vacuum is allowed to reach the canister and operate the purge valve. This releases the fuel vapors collected in the canister into the induction system.

The EGR valve control solenoid is activated by the ECM in similar fashion to the canister purge solenoid. When the engine is cold, the ECM energized the solenoid, which blocks the vacuum signal to the EGR valve. When the engine is warm, the ECM de-energized the solenoid and the vacuum signal is allowed to reach and activate the EGR valve.

The Transmission Converter Clutch (TCC) lock is controlled by the ECM through an electrical solenoid in the automatic transmission. When the vehicle speed sensor in the instrument panel signals the ECM that the vehicle has reached the correct speed, the ECM energizes the solenoid which allows the torque converter to mechanically couple the engine to the transmission. When the brake pedal is pushed or during deceleration, passing, etc., the ECM returns the transmission to fluid drive.

The Early Fuel Evaporative (EFE) system is used on some engines to provide rapid heat to the engine induction system to promote smooth start-up and operation. There are two types of system: vacuum servo and electrically heated. They use different means to achieve the same end, which is to pre-heat the incoming air/fuel mixture. They are controlled by the ECM.

BASIC TROUBLESHOOTING

NOTE: *The following explains how to activate the Trouble Code signal light in the instrument cluster and gives an explanation of what each code means. This is not a full C-4 of CCC System troubleshooting and isolation procedure.*

Before suspecting the C-4 or CCC System or any of its components as faulty, check the ignition system including distributor, timing, spark plugs and wires. Check the engine compression, air cleaner, and emission control components not controlled by the ECM. Also check the intake manifold, vacuum hoses and hose connectors for leaks and the carburetor for tightness.

The following systems could indicate a possible problem with the C-4 or CCC System.

1. Detonation.
2. Stalls or rough idle, cold.
3. Stalls or rough idle, hot.
4. Missing.
5. Hesitation.
6. Surges.
7. Poor gasoline mileage.
8. Sluggish or spongy.
9. Hard Starting, cold.
10. hard starting, hot.
11. Objectionable exhaust odors.
12. Cuts out.

As a bulb and system check, the 'Check Engine' light will come on when the ignition switch is turned to the ON position but the engine is not started. The 'Check Engine' light will also produce the trouble code or codes by a series of flashes which translate as follows. When the diagnostic test lead (C-4) or terminal (CCC) under the dash is grounded, with the ignition in the ON position and the engine not running, the 'Check Engine' light will flash once, pause, then flash twice in rapid succession. This is a code 12, which indicates that the diagnostic system is working. After a longer pause, the code 12 will repeat itself two more times. The cycle will then repeat itself until the engine is started or the ignition is turned off.

When the engine is started, the 'Check Engine' light will remain on for a few seconds, then turn off. If the 'Check Engine' light remains on, the self-diagnostic system has detected a problem. If the test lead (C-4) or test terminal (CCC) is then grounded, the trouble code will flash three times. If more than one problem is found, each trouble code will flash three times. Trouble codes will flash in numerical order (lowest code number to highest). The trouble codes series will repeat as long as the test lead or terminal is grounded.

A trouble code indicates a problem with a given circuit. For example, trouble code 14 indicated a problem in the cooling sensor circuit. This includes the coolant sensor, its electrical harness, and the Electronic Control Module (ECM).

Since the self-diagnostic system cannot diagnose every possible fault in the system, the absence of a trouble code does not mean the system is trouble free. To determine problems within the system which do not activate a trouble code, a system performance check must be mad. This job should be left to a qualified technician.

In the case of a intermittent fault in the system, the 'Check Engine' light will go out when the fault goes away, but the trouble code will remain in the memory of the ECM. Therefore, if a trouble code can be obtained even though the 'Check Engine' light is not on, the trouble code must be evaluated. It must be determined if the fault is intermittent or if the engine must be at certain operating conditions (under load, etc.) before the 'Check Engine' light will come on. Some trouble codes will not be recorded in

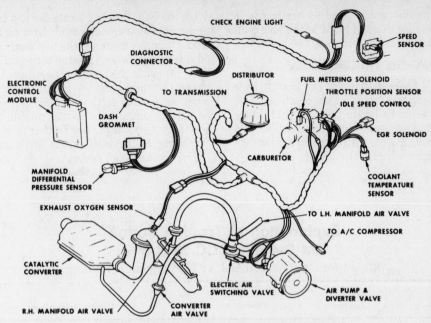

GM Computer Command Control (CCC) system

the ECM until the engine has been operated at part throttle for about 5 too 18 minutes.

On the C-4 System, The ECM erases all trouble codes every time the ignition is turned off. In the case of intermittent faults, a long term memory is desirable. This can be produced by connecting the orange connector/lead from terminal 'S' of the ECM directly to the battery (or to a 'hot' fuse panel terminal). This terminal must be disconnected after diagnosis is complete or it will drain the battery.

On the CCC System, a trouble code will be stored until terminal 'R' of the ECM has been disconnected from the battery for 10 seconds.

An easy way to erase the computer memory on the CCC System is to disconnect the battery terminals from the battery. If this method is used, don't forget to reset clocks and electronic

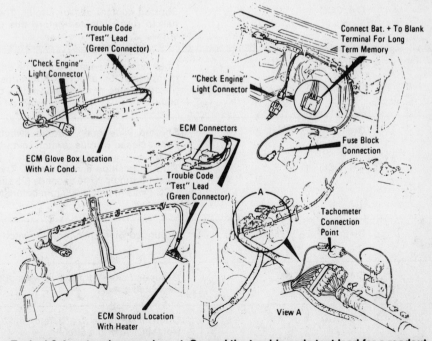

Typical C-4 system harness layout. Ground the trouble code test lead for a readout

preprogramable radios. Another method is to remove the fuse marked ECM in the fuse panel. Not all models have such a fuse.

ACTIVATING THE TROUBLE CODE

On the C-4 System, activate the trouble code by grounding the trouble code test lead. Use the illustration to locate the test lead under the instrument panel (usually a white and black wire or a wire with a green connector). Run a jumper wire fro the lead to ground.

On the CCC System, locate the test terminal under the instrument panel. Ground the test lead. On many systems, the test lead is situated side by dies with a ground terminal In addition, on some models, the partition between the test terminal and the ground terminal has a cut out section so that a spade terminal can be used to connect the two terminals.

NOTE: *Ground the test lead or terminal according to the instructions given in 'Basic Troubleshooting', above.*

Explanation of Trouble Codes
GM C-4 and CCC Systems

Ground test lead or terminal AFTER engine is running.

Trouble Code	Applicable System	Notes	Possible Problem Area
12	C-4, CCC		No tachometer or reference signal to computer (ECM). This code will only be present while a fault exists, and will not be stored if the problem is intermittent.
13	C-4, CCC		Oxygen sensor circuit. The engine must run for about five minutes at part throttle (and under road load—CCC equipped cars) before this code will show.
13 & 14 (at same time)	C-4		See code 43.
14	C-4, CCC		Shorted coolant sensor circuit. The engine has to run 2 minutes before this code will show.
15	C-4, CCC		Open coolant sensor circuit. The engine has to operate for about five minutes at part throttle (some models) before this code will show.
21	C-4		Shorted wide open throttle switch and/or open closed-throttle switch circuit (when used).
	C-4, CCC		Throttle position sensor circuit. The engine must be run up to 10 seconds (25 seconds—CCC System) below 800 rpm before this code will show.
21 & 22 (at same time)	C-4		Grounded wide open throttle switch circuit.
22	C-4		Grounded closed throttle or wide open throttle switch circuit.
23	C-4, CCC		Open or grounded carburetor mixture control (M/C) solenoid circuit.

Explanation of Trouble Codes (cont.)
GM C-4 and CCC Systems

Ground test lead or terminal AFTER engine is running.

Trouble Code	Applicable System	Notes	Possible Problem Area
24	CCC		Vehicle speed sensor (VSS) circuit. The car must operate up to five minutes at road speed before this code will show.
32	C-4, CCC		Barometric pressure sensor (BARO) circuit output low.
32 & 55 (at same time)	C-4		Grounded +8V terminal or V(REF) terminal for barometric pressure sensor (BARO), or faulty ECM computer.
34	C-4		Manifold absolute pressure (MAP) sensor output high (after ten seconds and below 800 rpm).
	CCC		Manifold absolute pressure (MAP) sensor circuit or vacuum sensor circuit. The engine must run up to five minutes below 800 RPM before this code will set.
35	CCC		Idle speed control (ISC) switch circuit shorted (over ½ throttle for over two seconds).
41	CCC		No distributor reference pulses to the ECM at specified engine vacuum. This code will store in memory.
42	CCC		Electronic spark timing (EST) bypass circuit grounded.
43	C-4		Throttle position sensor adjustment (on some models, engine must run at part throttle up to ten seconds before this code will set).
44	C-4, CCC		Lean oxygen sensor indication. The engine must run up to five minutes in closed loop (oxygen sensor adjusting carburetor mixture), at part throttle and under road load (drive car) before this code will set.
44 & 55 (at same time)	C-4, CCC		Faulty oxygen sensor circuit.
45	C-4, CCC	Restricted air cleaner can cause code 45.	Rich oxygen sensor system indication. The engine must run up to five minutes in closed loop (oxygen sensor adjusting carburetor mixture), at part throttle under road load before this code will set.
51	C-4, CCC		Faulty calibration unit (PROM) or improper PROM installation in electronic control module (ECM). It takes up to thirty seconds for this code to set.

Explanation of Trouble Codes (cont.)
GM C-4 and CCC Systems
Ground test lead or terminal AFTER engine is running.

Trouble Code	Applicable System	Notes	Possible Problem Area
52 & 53	C-4		"Check Engine" light off: Intermittent ECM computer problem. "Check Engine" light on: Faulty ECM computer (replace).
52	C-4, CCC		Faulty ECM computer.
53	CCC		Faulty ECM computer.
54	C-4, CCC		Faulty mixture control solenoid circuit and/or faulty ECM computer.
55	C-4		Faulty throttle position sensor or ECM computer. Faulty ECM computer.
55	CCC		Grounded +8 volt supply (terminal 19 of ECM computer connector), grounded 5 volt reference (terminal 21 of ECM computer connector), faulty oxygen sensor circuit or faulty ECM computer.

American Motors Feedback System

American Motors introduced feedback systems on all cars (except Eagle) in 1980. Two different, but similar, systems are used. The four cylinder engine used the G.M. C-4 feedback system, which is covered earlier in this section. Component usage is identical to that of the 4–151 engine, including an oxygen sensor, a vacuum switch (which is closed at idle and partial throttle positions), a wide open throttle switch, a coolant temperature sensor (set to open at 150°F [66°C]), and Electronic Control Module (ECM) equipped with modular Programmable Read Only memory (PROM), and a mixture control solenoid installed in the air horn on the E2SE carburetor. A 'Check Engine' light is included on the instrument panel as a service and diagnostic indicator.

The 6-cylinder engine is equipped with a Computerized Emission Control (CEC) System.

In 1980 CEC components include an oxygen sensor; two vacuum switches (one ported and one manifold) to detect three operating conditions; idle, partial throttle, and wide open throttle; a coolant temperature switch; a Micro Computer Unit (MCY), the control unit for the system which monitors all data and sends an output signal to the carburetor; and a stepper motor installed in the main body of the BBD carburetor, which varies the position of the two metering pins controlling the size of the air bleed orifices in the carburetor. The MCU also interrupts signals from the distributor (rpm voltage) to monitor engine rpm.

On 1981 and later models with CEC, the number of sensors has been increased. Three vacuum operated electric switches, two mechanically operated switches, one engine coolant switch and an air temperature operated switch are used to detach and send engine operating data to the MCU concerning the following engine operating conditions: cold engine start-up and operation; wide open throttle; idle (closed throttle); and partial and deep throttle.

Both AMC systems are conventional in operation. As in other feedback systems, two modes of operation are possible; open loop and closed loop. Open loop operation occurs during engine starting, cold engine operation, cold oxygen sensor operation, engine idling, wide open throttle operation, and low battery voltage operation. In open loop, a fixed air/fuel mixture signal is provided by the ECM or MCU to the carburetor, and oxygen sensor data is ignored. Closed loop operation occurs at all other times, and in this mode all signals are used by the control unit to determine the optimum air/fuel mixture.

OXYGEN SENSOR REPLACEMENT

1. Disconnect the two wire plug.
2. Remove the sensor from the exhaust manifold on the four cylinder, or the exhaust pipe on the six.
3. Clean the threads in the manifold or pipe.
4. Coat the threads of the replacement sensor with an electrically conductive antiseize compound. Do not use a conventional antiseize compound, which may electrically insulate the sensor.
5. Install the sensor. Installation torque is 25 ft.lb. for the four cylinder, 31 ft.lb. for the 6-cylinder.
6. Connect the sensor lead. Do not push the rubber boot into the sensor body more than ½" (12.7mm) above the base.
7. If the sensors' pigtail is broken, replace the sensor. The wires cannot be spliced or soldered.

VACUUM SWITCH REPLACEMENT

The vacuum switches are mounted in a bracket bolted to the left inner fender panel in the engine compartment. They are not replaceable individually; the complete unit must be replaced.

1. Tag all the vacuum hoses, then disconnect them from switches. Disconnect the electrical plugs. The four cylinder has two plugs and the six has one.
2. Remove the switch and bracket assembly from the fender panel.
3. Installation is the reverse.

CONTROL UNIT REPLACEMENT

The control unit, whether ECM or MCU is mounted in the passenger compartment, beneath the right side of the instrument panel.

1. The ECM is installed in a mounting bracket; remove it from the bracket. The MCU is attached with bolts; remove the bolts and remove the unit.
2. Disconnect the electrical plugs.
3. Installation is the reverse. The 4-cylinder ECM is electrically insulated from the chassis; do not ground the ECM bracket!

MIXTURE CONTROL SOLENOID REPLACEMENT

The E2SE mixture control solenoid is installed in the air horn.

1. Remove the air cleaner case.
2. Disconnect the solenoid electrical plug.
3. Remove the solenoid retaining screw.
4. Remove the solenoid from the air horn.
5. Before installation, coat the rubber seal on the end of the stem with silicone grease or light engine oil. Install the solenoid, accurately aligning the stem with the recess at the bottom of the bowl. Use a new gasket. Connect the electrical plug and install the air cleaner.

STEPPER MOTOR REPLACEMENT

The BBD stepper motor is installed in the side of the main body of the carburetor.

1. Remove the air cleaner case.
2. Disconnect the electrical plug.
3. Remove the retaining screw and remove the motor from the side of the carburetor. Be careful not to drop the metering pins or the spring when removing the motor.
4. Installation is the reverse.

Catalytic Converter

The catalytic converter is a muffler like device inserted in the exhaust system. Exhaust gases flow through the converter where a chemical change takes place, reducing carbon monoxide and hydrocarbons to carbon dioxide and water; the latter two elements being harmless. The catalysts promoting this reaction are platinum and palladium coated beads of alumina. Because of the chemical reaction which does take place in the converter, the temperature of the converter during operation is higher than the exhaust gases when they leave the engine. However, insulation keeps the outside skin of the converter about the same temperature as the muffler. An improperly adjusted carburetor or ignition problem which would permit unburned fuel to enter the converter could produce excessive heat. Excessive heat in the converter could result in bulging or other distortion of the converter's shape. If the converter is heat damaged and must be replaced, the ignition or carburetor problem must be corrected for.

Choke Heat By-Pass Valve (CHBPV) 1976 and Later V8

When the engine is first started and begins to warm up, heated air from the exhaust crossover passage in the intake manifold is routed through a heat tube to the choke housing containing the thermostatic spring for regulating the choke flap. A thermostatic by-pass valve, which is integral with the choke heat tube, helps prevent premature choke valve opening during the early part of the warmup period. This is important when ambient temperatures are relatively low and adverse driveability could occur if the choke was opened too soon.

The thermostatic by-pass valve regulates the temperature of the hot airflow to the choke housing by allowing outside unheated air to enter the heat tube. A thermostatic disc in the valve is calibrated to close the valve at 75°F (24°C) and open it at 55°F (13°C).

Fuel Return System

The purpose of the fuel return system is to reduce high temperature fuel vapor problems. The system consists of a fuel return line to the fuel tank and special fuel filter with an extra outlet nipple to which the return line is connected. During normal operation, a small amount of fuel is returned to the fuel tank. During periods of high underhood temperatures, vaporized fuel in the fuel line is returned to the fuel tank and not passed through the carburetor.

NOTE: *The extra nipple on the special fuel filter should be positioned upward to ensure proper operation of the system.*

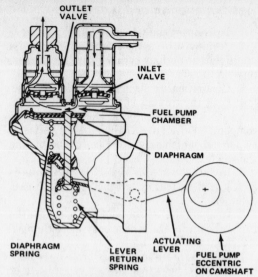

Fuel pump typical of all models, except the 4-151

FUEL SYSTEM

Fuel Pump

REMOVAL AND INSTALLATION

1. Disconnect the inlet and outlet fuel lines, and any vacuum lines.
2. Remove the two fuel pump body attaching nuts and lockwashers.
3. Pull the pump and gasket, or O-ring, free of the engine. Make sure that the mating surfaces of the fuel pump and the engine are clean.
4. Cement a new gasket to the mounting flange of the fuel pump.

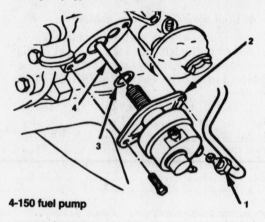

4-150 fuel pump

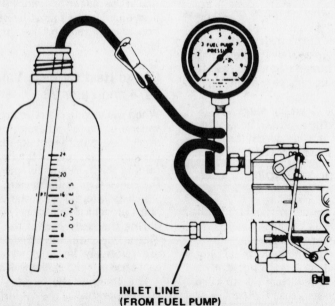

INLET LINE (FROM FUEL PUMP)

Fuel pump pressure and volume test

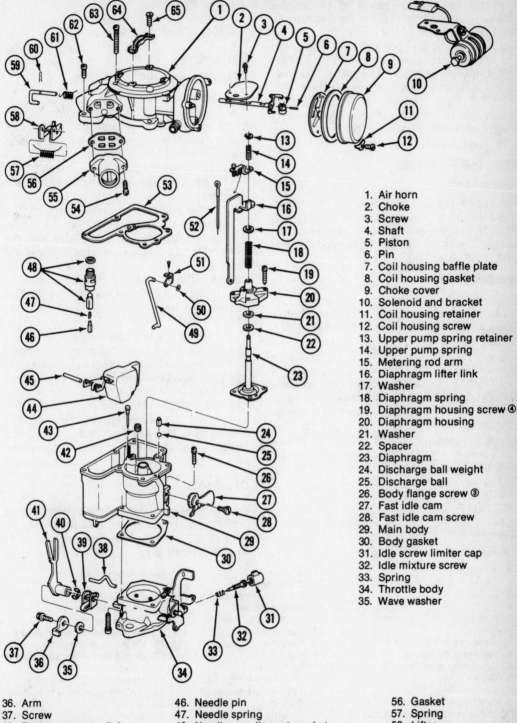

1. Air horn
2. Choke
3. Screw
4. Shaft
5. Piston
6. Pin
7. Coil housing baffle plate
8. Coil housing gasket
9. Choke cover
10. Solenoid and bracket
11. Coil housing retainer
12. Coil housing screw
13. Upper pump spring retainer
14. Upper pump spring
15. Metering rod arm
16. Diaphragm lifter link
17. Washer
18. Diaphragm spring
19. Diaphragm housing screw ④
20. Diaphragm housing
21. Washer
22. Spacer
23. Diaphragm
24. Discharge ball weight
25. Discharge ball
26. Body flange screw ③
27. Fast idle cam
28. Fast idle cam screw
29. Main body
30. Body gasket
31. Idle screw limiter cap
32. Idle mixture screw
33. Spring
34. Throttle body
35. Wave washer

36. Arm
37. Screw
38. Pump connector link
39. Throttle shaft arm
40. Retainer
41. Lever
42. Metering rod jet
43. Low speed jet
44. Float
45. Float pin

46. Needle pin
47. Needle spring
48. Needle, needle seat, gasket
49. Choke connector rod
50. Choke connector rod retainer
51. Lever
52. Metering rod
53. Air horn gasket
54. Screw ②
55. Chamber

56. Gasket
57. Spring
58. Lifter
59. Bellcrank
60. Retainer
61. Spring
62. Air horn screw (short)
63. Air horn screw (long)
64. Stud support
65. Screw

Carter YF with altitude compensator

5. Position the fuel pump on the engine block so that the lever of the fuel pump rests on the fuel pump cam of the camshaft.

6. Secure the fuel pump to the block with the two cap screws and lock washers.

7. Connect the intake and outlet fuel lines to the fuel pump, and any vacuum lines.

NOTE: *When installing the 4–121 pump, be sure that the pushrod is positioned properly against the actuating lover or the pump may be damaged when the screws are tightened.*

FUEL PUMP TESTING

Volume Check

Disconnect the fuel line from the carburetor. Place the open end in a suitable container. Start the engine and operate it at normal idle speed. The pump should deliver at least one pint in 30 seconds.

Pressure Check

Disconnect the fuel line at the carburetor. Disconnect the fuel return line from the fuel filter if so equipped, and plug the nipple on the filter. Install a T-fitting on the open end of the fuel line and refit the line to the carburetor. Plug a pressure gauge into the remaining opening of the T-fitting. The hose leading to the pressure gauge should not be any longer than 6" (152.5mm). Start the engine and let it run at idle speed. Bleed any air out of the hose between the gauge and the T-fitting. On pumps with a fuel return line, the line must be plugged. Start the engine. Fuel pressures are as follows:

4–121: 4.00–6.00psi @ idle
4–150: 4.00–5.00psi @ idle
4–151: 6.50–8.00psi @ idle
6–232: 3.00–5.00psi @ idle
6–258: 3.00–5.00psi @ idle

8–304: 4.00–6.00psi @ idle
8–360: 4.00–6.00psi @ idle
8–401: 4.00–6.00psi @ idle

Carburetors

REMOVAL AND INSTALLATION

1. Remove the air cleaner.
2. Disconnect the fuel and vacuum lines. It might be a good idea to tag them to avoid confusion when the time comes to put them back.
3. Disconnect the choke rod.
4. Disconnect the accelerator linkage.
5. Disconnect the automatic transmission linkage.
6. Unbolt and remove the carburetor.
7. Remove the base gasket.
8. Before installation, make sure that the carburetor and manifold sealing surfaces are clean.
9. Install a new carburetor base gasket.
10. Install the carburetor and start the fuel and vacuum lines.
11. Bolt down the carburetor evenly.
12. Tighten the fuel and vacuum lines.
13. Connect the accelerator and automatic transmission linkage. If the transmission linkage was disturbed, it will have to be adjusted. The procedure is in Chapter 6.
14. Connect the choke rod.
15. Install the air cleaner. Adjust the idle speed and mixture as described in Chapter 2. Depending on the vintage, it may not be necessary (or possible) to adjust the idle mixture.

OVERHAUL

Whenever wear or dirt causes a carburetor to perform poorly, there are two possible solutions to the problem. The simplest is to trade on the old unit for a rebuilt one. The other,

1. Air horn	22. Spacer	43. Low speed jet
2. Choke	23. Diaphragm	44. Float
3. Screw	24. Discharge ball weight	45. Float pin
4. Shaft	25. Discharge ball	46. Needle pin
5. Piston	26. Body flange screw ③	47. Needle spring
6. Pin	27. Fast idle cam	48. Needle, needle seat, gasket
7. Solenoid and bracket	28. Fast idle cam screw	49. Choke connector rod
8. Coil housing screw	29. Main body	50. Choke connector rod retainer
9. Coil housing retainer	30. Body gasket	51. Lever
10. Choke cover	31. Idle screw limiter cap	52. Metering rod
11. Coil housing gasket	32. Idle mixture screw	53. Air horn gasket
12. Coil housing baffle plate	33. Spring	54. Spring
13. Upper pump spring retainer	34. Throttle body	55. Lifter
14. Upper pump spring	35. Wave washer	56. Bellcrank
15. Metering rod arm	36. Arm	57. Retainer
16. Diaphragm lifter link	37. Screw	58. Spring
17. Washer	38. Pump connector link	59. Air horn screw (short)
18. Diaphragm spring	39. Throttle shaft arm	60. Air horn screw (long)
19. Diaphragm housing screw ④	40. Retainer	61. Stud support
20. Diaphragm housing	41. Lever	62. Screw
21. Washer	42. Metering rod jet	

Carter YF without altitude compensator

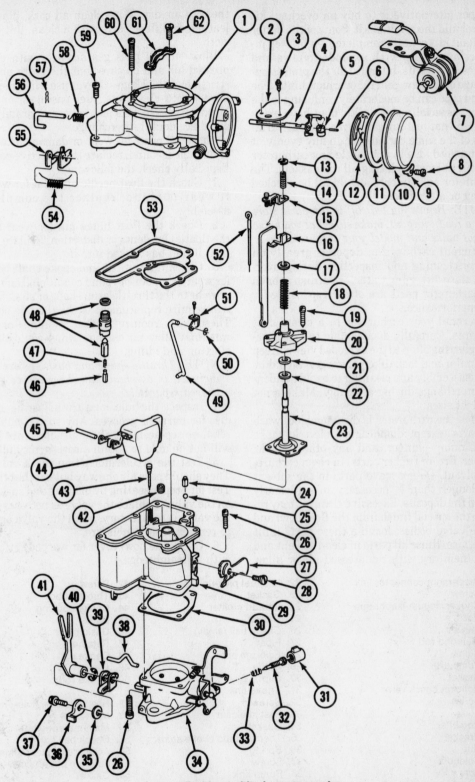

Carter YF without altitude compensator

cheaper alternative is to buy an overhaul kit and rebuild the original kit. Some of the better overhaul kits contain complete step-by-step instructions along with exploded views and gauges. Other kits, intended for the professional, have only a few general overhaul hints. The second type can be moderately confusing to the novice, especially since a kit may have extra parts so that one kit can cover several variations of the same carburetor. In any evenly, it is not a good idea to dismantle any carburetor without at least replacing all the gaskets. The carburetor adjustments should all be checked during or after overhaul

NOTE: *Before you tear off to the parts store for a rebuilding kit, make sure that you know what make and model your carburetor is.*

Efficient carburetion depends greatly on careful cleaning and inspection during overhaul, since dirt, gum, water, or varnish in or on the carburetor parts are often responsible for poor performance.

Overhaul your carburetor in a clean, dust free area. Carefully disassemble the carburetor, referring often to the exploded views. Keep all similar and lookalike pars segregated during disassembly and cleaning to avoid accidental interchange during assembly. Make a not of all jet sizes.

When the carburetor is disassembled, wash all parts (except diaphragms, electric choke units, pump plunger, and any other plastic, leather, fire, or rubber parts) in clean carburetor solvent. Do not leave parts in the solvent any longer than is necessary to sufficiently loosen the deposits. Excessive cleaning may remove the special finish from the float bowl and choke valve bodies, leaving these parts unfit for service. Rinse all parts in clean solvent and blow them dry with compressed air or allow them to air dry. Wipe clean all cork, plastic, leather, and fiber parts with a clean, lint-free cloth.

Blow our all passages and jets with compressed air and be sure that there are no restrictions or blockages. Never use wire or similar tools to clean jets, fuel passages, or air bleeds. Clean all jets and valves separately to avoid accidental interchange.

Check all parts for wear or damage. If wear or damage is found, replace the defective parts. Especially check the following:

1. Check the float needle and seat for wear. If wear is found, replace the complete assembly.

2. Check the float hinge pin for wear and the float(s) for dents or distortion. Replace the float if fuel has leaked into it.

3. Check the throttle and choke shaft bores for wear or an out-of-round condition. Damage or wear to the throttle arm, shaft, or shaft bore will require replacement of the throttle body. These parts require a close tolerance of fit; wear may allow air leakage, which could affect starting and idling.

NOTE: *Throttle shafts and bushings are not included in overhaul kits. They can be purchased separately.*

4. Inspect the idle mixture adjusting needles for burrs or grooves. Any such condition requires replacement of the needle, since you will not be able to obtain a satisfactory idle.

5. Test the accelerator pump check valves. They should pass air one way but not the other. Test for proper seating by blowing and sucking on the valve. Replace the valve as necessary. If the valve is satisfactory, wash the valve again to remove breath moisture.

6. Check the bowl cover for warped surfaces with a straightedge.

1. Diaphragm connector link	22. Idle fuel pick-up tube	42. Screw
2. Screw	23. Gasket	43. Throttle body
3. Choke vacuum diaphragm	24. Venturi cluster	44. Choke housing
4. Hose	25. Gasket	45. Baffle
5. Valve	26. Check ball (small)	46. Gasket
6. Metering rod	27. Float	47. Retainer
7. S-link	28. Fulcrum pin	48. Choke coil
8. Pump arm	29. Baffle	49. Lever
9. Gasket	30. Clip	50. Choke rod
10. Rollover check valve	31. Choke link	51. Clip
11. Screw	32. Screw	52. Needle and seat assembly
12. Lock	33. Fast idle cam	53. Main body
13. Rod lifter	34. Gasket	54. Main metering jet
14. Bracket	35. Thermostatic choke shaft	55. Check ball (large)
15. Nut	36. Spring	56. Accelerator pump plunger
16. Solenoid	37. Screw	57. Fulcrum pin retainer
17. Screw	38. Pump link	58. Gasket
18. Air horn retaining screw (short)	39. Clip	59. Spring
19. Air horn retaining screw (long)	40. Gasket	60. Air horn
20. Pump lever	41. Limiter cap	61. Lever
21. Venturi cluster screw		

Carter BBD

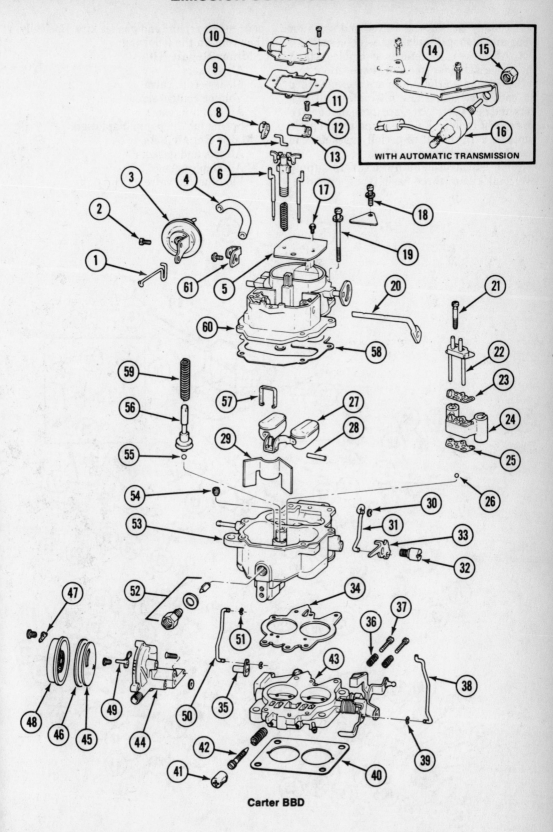

WITH AUTOMATIC TRANSMISSION

Carter BBD

7. Closely inspect the valves and seats for wear and damage, replacing as necessary.

8. After the carburetor is assembled, check the choke valve for freedom of operation.

Carburetor overhaul kits are recommended for each overhaul. These kit contain all gaskets and new parts to replace those that deteriorate most rapidly. Failure to replace all parts supplied with the kit (especially gaskets) can result in poor performance later.

Some carburetor manufacturers supply overhaul kits of three basic types: minor repair; major repair; and gasket kits. Basically, they contain the following:

Minor Repair Kits
- All gaskets
- Float needle valve
- Volume control screw
- All diaphragms
- Spring for the pump diaphragm

Major Repair Kits
- All jets and gaskets
- All diaphragms
- Float needle valve

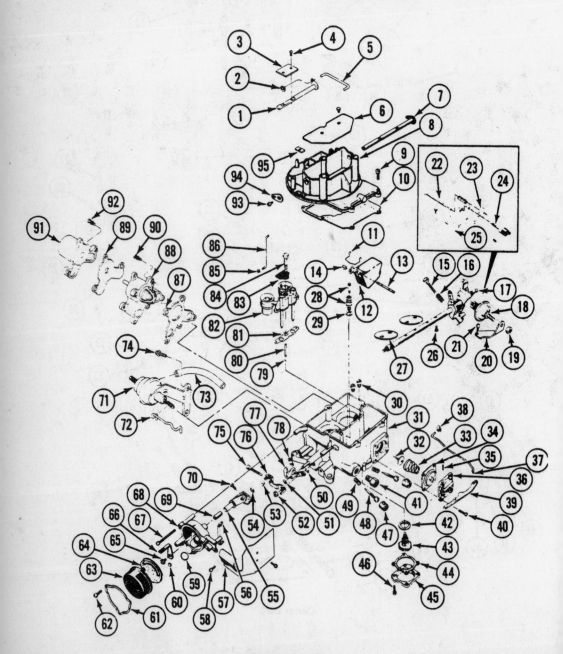

Motorcraft 2150

- Volume control screw
- Pump ball valve
- Main jet carrier
- Float
- Complete intermediate rod
- Intermediate pump lever
- Complete injector tube
- Some cover holddown screws and washers

Gasket Kits
- All gaskets

After cleaning and checking all components, reassemble the carburetor, using new parts and referring to the exploded view. When reassembling, make sure that all screws and jets are tight in their seats, but do not overtighten as the tips will be distorted. Tighten all screws gradually, in rotation. Do not tighten needle valves into their seats; uneven jetting will result. Always use new gaskets. BE sure to adjust the float level when reassembling.

Carburetor Adjustments

CARTER YF

The YF carburetor is a singe barrel downdraft carburetor with a diaphragm type accelerator pump and diaphragm operated metering rods.

1. Compensator choke shaft
2. Retainer
3. Compensator choke valve
4. Choke valve screw
5. Compensator choke rod
6. Choke valve
7. Choke shaft
8. Air horn
9. Air horn retaining screw ④
10. Air horn gasket
11. Float shaft retainer
12. Float and lever assembly
13. Float shaft
14. Needle retaining clip
15. Curb idle adjusting screw
16. Curb idle adjusting screw spring
17. Throttle shaft and lever assembly
18. Dashpot
19. Dashpot locknut
20. Dashpot bracket
21. Dashpot bracket
    retaining screw
22. Adjusting screw
23. Carriage
24. Electric solenoid
25. Mounting bracket
26. Throttle valve
    retaining screw ④
27. Throttle valve ②
28. Needle and seat assembly
29. Needle seat gasket
30. Main jet ②
31. Main body
32. Elastomer valve
33. Pump return spring
34. Pump diaphragm
35. Pump lever pin
36. Pump cover
37. Pump rod
38. Pump rod retainer
39. Pump lever
40. Pump cover retaining screw ④
41. Fuel inlet fitting
42. Power valve gasket
43. Power valve
44. Power valve cover gasket
45. Power valve cover
46. Power valve cover
    retaining screw ④
47. Idle limiter cap ②
48. Idle mixture
    screw ②
49. Idle mixture
    screw spring ②
50. Retainer
51. Retainer
52. Fast idle lever
    retaining nut
53. Fast idle lever pin
54. Retainer
55. Thermostatic
    choke shaft
56. Fast idle cam rod
57. Choke shield
58. Choke shield retaining screw ②
59. Piston passage plug
60. Heat passage plut
61. Choke cover retaining clamp
62. Choke cover retaining screw ③
63. Choke cover
64. Choke cover gasket
65. Thermostat lever retaining screw
66. Thermostat lever
67. Choke housing retaining screw ③
68. Choke housing
69. Choke shaft bushing
70. Fast idle cam lever adjusting screw
71. Choke diaphragm
72. Hose
73. Link
74. Screw
75. Fast idle speed adjusting screw
76. Fast idle lever
77. Fast idle cam
78. Choke housing gasket
79. Pump discharge check ball
80. Pump discharge weight
81. Booster venturi gasket
82. Booster venturi assembly
83. Air distribution plate
84. Pump discharge screw
85. Retainer
86. Choke rod
87. Gasket
88. Compensation chamber
89. Gasket
90. Screw
91. Aneroid
92. Screw
93. Choke lever retaining screw
94. Choke plate lever
95. Choke rod seal

Motorcarft 2150

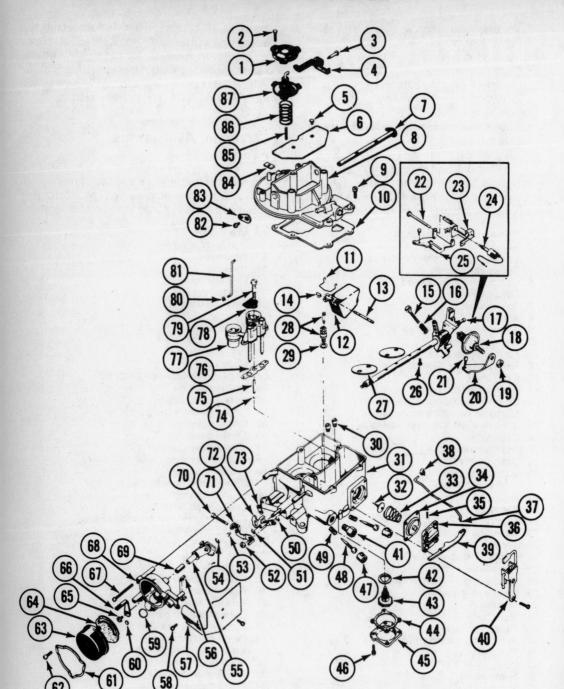

1. Modulator cover
2. Modulator retaining screw ③
3. Pivot pin
4. Modulator arm
5. Choke valve retaining screw ②
6. Choke valve
7. Choke shaft
8. Air horn
9. Air horn retaining screw ④
10. Air horn gasket
11. Float and lever assembly

12. Float shaft retainer
13. Float shaft
14. Needle retaining clip
15. Curb idle adjusting screw
16. Curb idle adjusting screw spring
17. Throttle shaft and lever assembly
18. Dashpot
19. Dashpot locknut
20. Dashpot bracket
21. Dashpot bracket retaining screw
22. Adjusting screw

Motorcraft 2100

CHILTON'S
FUEL ECONOMY
& TUNE-UP TIPS

55 WAYS TO IMPROVE FUEL ECONOMY

Tune-up • Spark Plug Diagnosis • Emission Controls

Fuel System • Cooling System • Tires and Wheels

General Maintenance

CHILTON'S FUEL ECONOMY & TUNE-UP TIPS

Fuel economy is important to everyone, no matter what kind of vehicle you drive. The maintenance-minded motorist can save both money and fuel using these tips and the periodic maintenance and tune-up procedures in this Repair and Tune-Up Guide.

There are more than 130,000,000 cars and trucks registered for private use in the United States. Each travels an average of 10-12,000 miles per year, and, and in total they consume close to 70 billion gallons of fuel each year. This represents nearly ⅔ of the oil imported by the United States each year. The Federal government's goal is to reduce consumption 10% by 1985. A variety of methods are either already in use or under serious consideration, and they all affect you driving and the cars you will drive. In addition to "down-sizing", the auto industry is using or investigating the use of electronic fuel delivery, electronic engine controls and alternative engines for use in smaller and lighter vehicles, among other alternatives to meet the federally mandated Corporate Average Fuel Economy (CAFE) of 27.5 mpg by 1985. The government, for its part, is considering rationing, mandatory driving curtailments and tax increases on motor vehicle fuel in an effort to reduce consumption. The government's goal of a 10% reduction could be realized — and further government regulation avoided — if every private vehicle could use just 1 less gallon of fuel per week.

How Much Can You Save?

Tests have proven that almost anyone can make at least a 10% reduction in fuel consumption through regular maintenance and tune-ups. When a major manufacturer of spark plugs sur-

TUNE-UP

1. Check the cylinder compression to be sure the engine will really benefit from a tune-up and that it is capable of producing good fuel economy. A tune-up will be wasted on an engine in poor mechanical condition.

2. Replace spark plugs regularly. New spark plugs alone can increase fuel economy 3%.

3. Be sure the spark plugs are the correct type (heat range) for your vehicle. See the Tune-Up Specifications.

Heat range refers to the spark plug's ability to conduct heat away from the firing end. It must conduct the heat away in an even pattern to avoid becoming a source of pre-ignition, yet it must also operate hot enough to burn off conductive deposits that could cause misfiring.

The heat range is usually indicated by a number on the spark plug, part of the manufacturer's designation for each individual spark plug. The numbers in bold-face indicate the heat range in each manufacturer's identification system.

Periodically, check the spark plugs to be sure they are firing efficiently. They are excellent indicators of the internal condition of your engine.

Manufacturer	Typical Designation
AC	R **45** TS
Bosch (old)	WA **145** T30
Bosch (new)	HR **8** Y
Champion	RBL **15** Y
Fram/Autolite	4**15**
Mopar	P-**62** PR
Motorcraft	BRF-**42**
NGK	BP **5** ES-15
Nippondenso	W **16** EP
Prestolite	14GR **5** 2A

On AC, Bosch (new), Champion, Fram/Autolite, Mopar, Motorcraft and Prestolite, a higher number indicates a hotter plug. On Bosch (old), NGK and Nippondenso, a higher number indicates a colder plug.

4. Make sure the spark plugs are properly gapped. See the Tune-Up Specifications in this book.

5. Be sure the spark plugs are firing efficiently. The illustrations on the next 2 pages show you how to "read" the firing end of the spark plug.

6. Check the ignition timing and set it to specifications. Tests show that almost all cars have incorrect ignition timing by more than 2°.

veyed over 6,000 cars nationwide, they found that a tune-up, on cars that needed one, increased fuel economy over 11%. Replacing worn plugs alone, accounted for a 3% increase. The same test also revealed that 8 out of every 10 vehicles will have some maintenance deficiency that will directly affect fuel economy, emissions or performance. Most of this mileage-robbing neglect could be prevented with regular maintenance.

Modern engines require that all of the functioning systems operate properly for maximum efficiency. A malfunction anywhere wastes fuel. You can keep your vehicle running as efficiently and economically as possible, by being aware of your vehicle's operating and performance characteristics. If your vehicle suddenly develops performance or fuel economy problems it could be due to one or more of the following:

PROBLEM	POSSIBLE CAUSE
Engine Idles Rough	Ignition timing, idle mixture, vacuum leak or something amiss in the emission control system.
Hesitates on Acceleration	Dirty carburetor or fuel filter, improper accelerator pump setting, ignition timing or fouled spark plugs.
Starts Hard or Fails to Start	Worn spark plugs, improperly set automatic choke, ice (or water) in fuel system.
Stalls Frequently	Automatic choke improperly adjusted and possible dirty air filter or fuel filter.
Performs Sluggishly	Worn spark plugs, dirty fuel or air filter, ignition timing or automatic choke out of adjustment.

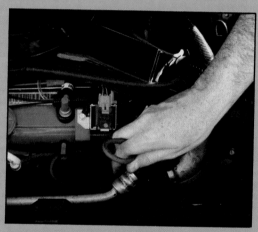

Check spark plug wires on conventional point type ignition for cracks by bending them in a loop around your finger.

Be sure that spark plug wires leading to adjacent cylinders do not run too close together. (Photo courtesy Champion Spark Plug Co.)

7. If your vehicle does not have electronic ignition, check the points, rotor and cap as specified.

8. Check the spark plug wires (used with conventional point-type ignitions) for cracks and burned or broken insulation by bending them in a loop around your finger. Cracked wires decrease fuel efficiency by failing to deliver full voltage to the spark plugs. One misfiring spark plug can cost you as much as 2 mpg.

9. Check the routing of the plug wires. Misfiring can be the result of spark plug leads to adjacent cylinders running parallel to each other and too close together. One wire tends to pick up voltage from the other causing it to fire "out of time".

10. Check all electrical and ignition circuits for voltage drop and resistance.

11. Check the distributor mechanical and/or vacuum advance mechanisms for proper functioning. The vacuum advance can be checked by twisting the distributor plate in the opposite direction of rotation. It should spring back when released.

12. Check and adjust the valve clearance on engines with mechanical lifters. The clearance should be slightly loose rather than too tight.

SPARK PLUG DIAGNOSIS

Normal

APPEARANCE: This plug is typical of one operating normally. The insulator nose varies from a light tan to grayish color with slight electrode wear. The presence of slight deposits is normal on used plugs and will have no adverse effect on engine performance. The spark plug heat range is correct for the engine and the engine is running normally.

CAUSE: Properly running engine.

RECOMMENDATION: Before reinstalling this plug, the electrodes should be cleaned and filed square. Set the gap to specifications. If the plug has been in service for more than 10-12,000 miles, the entire set should probably be replaced with a fresh set of the same heat range.

Oil Deposits

APPEARANCE: The firing end of the plug is covered with a wet, oily coating.

CAUSE: The problem is poor oil control. On high mileage engines, oil is leaking past the rings or valve guides into the combustion chamber. A common cause is also a plugged PCV valve, and a ruptured fuel pump diaphragm can also cause this condition. Oil fouled plugs such as these are often found in new or recently overhauled engines, before normal oil control is achieved, and can be cleaned and reinstalled.

RECOMMENDATION: A hotter spark plug may temporarily relieve the problem, but the engine is probably in need of work.

Incorrect Heat Range

APPEARANCE: The effects of high temperature on a spark plug are indicated by clean white, often blistered insulator. This can also be accompanied by excessive wear of the electrode, and the absence of deposits.

CAUSE: Check for the correct spark plug heat range. A plug which is too hot for the engine can result in overheating. A car operated mostly at high speeds can require a colder plug. Also check ignition timing, cooling system level, fuel mixture and leaking intake manifold.

RECOMMENDATION: If all ignition and engine adjustments are known to be correct, and no other malfunction exists, install spark plugs one heat range colder.

Photos Courtesy Fram Corporation

Carbon Deposits

APPEARANCE: Carbon fouling is easily identified by the presence of dry, soft, black, sooty deposits.

CAUSE: Changing the heat range can often lead to carbon fouling, as can prolonged slow, stop-and-start driving. If the heat range is correct, carbon fouling can be attributed to a rich fuel mixture, sticking choke, clogged air cleaner, worn breaker points, retarded timing or low compression. If only one or two plugs are carbon fouled, check for corroded or cracked wires on the affected plugs. Also look for cracks in the distributor cap between the towers of affected cylinders.

RECOMMENDATION: After the problem is corrected, these plugs can be cleaned and reinstalled if not worn severely.

MMT Fouled

APPEARANCE: Spark plugs fouled by MMT (Methycyclopentadienyl Maganese Tricarbonyl) have reddish, rusty appearance on the insulator and side electrode.

CAUSE: MMT is an anti-knock additive in gasoline used to replace lead. During the combustion process, the MMT leaves a reddish deposit on the insulator and side electrode.

RECOMMENDATION: No engine malfunction is indicated and the deposits will not affect plug performance any more than lead deposits (see Ash Deposits). MMT fouled plugs can be cleaned, regapped and reinstalled.

High Speed Glazing

APPEARANCE: Glazing appears as shiny coating on the plug, either yellow or tan in color.

CAUSE: During hard, fast acceleration, plug temperatures rise suddenly. Deposits from normal combustion have no chance to fluff-off; instead, they melt on the insulator forming an electrically conductive coating which causes misfiring.

RECOMMENDATION: Glazed plugs are not easily cleaned. They should be replaced with a fresh set of plugs of the correct heat range. If the condition recurs, using plugs with a heat range one step colder may cure the problem.

Ash (Lead) Deposits

APPEARANCE: Ash deposits are characterized by light brown or white colored deposits crusted on the side or center electrodes. In some cases it may give the plug a rusty appearance.

CAUSE: Ash deposits are normally derived from oil or fuel additives burned during normal combustion. Normally they are harmless, though excessive amounts can cause misfiring. If deposits are excessive in short mileage, the valve guides may be worn.

RECOMMENDATION: Ash-fouled plugs can be cleaned, gapped and reinstalled.

Detonation

APPEARANCE: Detonation is usually characterized by a broken plug insulator.

CAUSE: A portion of the fuel charge will begin to burn spontaneously, from the increased heat following ignition. The explosion that results applies extreme pressure to engine components, frequently damaging spark plugs and pistons.

Detonation can result by over-advanced ignition timing, inferior gasoline (low octane) lean air/fuel mixture, poor carburetion, engine lugging or an increase in compression ratio due to combustion chamber deposits or engine modification.

RECOMMENDATION: Replace the plugs after correcting the problem.

Photos Courtesy Champion Spark Plug Co.

EMISSION CONTROLS

13. Be aware of the general condition of the emission control system. It contributes to reduced pollution and should be serviced regularly to maintain efficient engine operation.

14. Check all vacuum lines for dried, cracked or brittle conditions. Something as simple as a leaking vacuum hose can cause poor performance and loss of economy.

15. Avoid tampering with the emission control system. Attempting to improve fuel econ-

FUEL SYSTEM

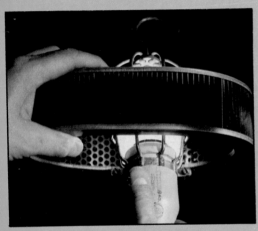

Check the air filter with a light behind it. If you can see light through the filter it can be reused.

Extremely clogged filters should be discarded and replaced with a new one.

18. Replace the air filter regularly. A dirty air filter richens the air/fuel mixture and can increase fuel consumption as much as 10%. Tests show that ⅓ of all vehicles have air filters in need of replacement.

19. Replace the fuel filter at least as often as recommended.

20. Set the idle speed and carburetor mixture to specifications.

21. Check the automatic choke. A sticking or malfunctioning choke wastes gas.

22. During the summer months, adjust the automatic choke for a leaner mixture which will produce faster engine warm-ups.

COOLING SYSTEM

29. Be sure all accessory drive belts are in good condition. Check for cracks or wear.

30. Adjust all accessory drive belts to proper tension.

31. Check all hoses for swollen areas, worn spots, or loose clamps.

32. Check coolant level in the radiator or expansion tank.

33. Be sure the thermostat is operating properly. A stuck thermostat delays engine warm-up and a cold engine uses nearly twice as much fuel as a warm engine.

34. Drain and replace the engine coolant at least as often as recommended. Rust and scale

TIRES & WHEELS

38. Check the tire pressure often with a pencil type gauge. Tests by a major tire manufacturer show that 90% of all vehicles have at least 1 tire improperly inflated. Better mileage can be achieved by over-inflating tires, but never exceed the maximum inflation pressure on the side of the tire.

39. If possible, install radial tires. Radial tires deliver as much as ½ mpg more than bias belted tires.

40. Avoid installing super-wide tires. They only create extra rolling resistance and decrease fuel mileage. Stick to the manufacturer's recommendations.

41. Have the wheels properly balanced.

omy by tampering with emission controls is more likely to worsen fuel economy than improve it. Emission control changes on modern engines are not readily reversible.

16. Clean (or replace) the EGR valve and lines as recommended.

17. Be sure that all vacuum lines and hoses are reconnected properly after working under the hood. An unconnected or misrouted vacuum line can wreak havoc with engine performance.

23. Check for fuel leaks at the carburetor, fuel pump, fuel lines and fuel tank. Be sure all lines and connections are tight.

24. Periodically check the tightness of the carburetor and intake manifold attaching nuts and bolts. These are a common place for vacuum leaks to occur.

25. Clean the carburetor periodically and lubricate the linkage.

26. The condition of the tailpipe can be an excellent indicator of proper engine combustion. After a long drive at highway speeds, the inside of the tailpipe should be a light grey in color. Black or soot on the insides indicates an overly rich mixture.

27. Check the fuel pump pressure. The fuel pump may be supplying more fuel than the engine needs.

28. Use the proper grade of gasoline for your engine. Don't try to compensate for knocking or "pinging" by advancing the ignition timing. This practice will only increase plug temperature and the chances of detonation or pre-ignition with relatively little performance gain.

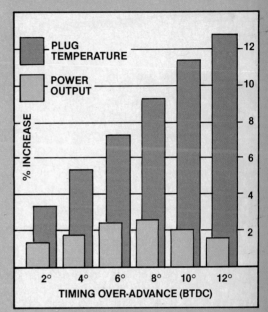

Increasing ignition timing past the specified setting results in a drastic increase in spark plug temperature with increased chance of detonation or preignition. Performance increase is considerably less. (Photo courtesy Champion Spark Plug Co.)

that form in the engine should be flushed out to allow the engine to operate at peak efficiency.

35. Clean the radiator of debris that can decrease cooling efficiency.

36. Install a flex-type or electric cooling fan, if you don't have a clutch type fan. Flex fans use curved plastic blades to push more air at low speeds when more cooling is needed; at high speeds the blades flatten out for less resistance. Electric fans only run when the engine temperature reaches a predetermined level.

37. Check the radiator cap for a worn or cracked gasket. If the cap does not seal properly, the cooling system will not function properly.

42. Be sure the front end is correctly aligned. A misaligned front end actually has wheels going in differed directions. The increased drag can reduce fuel economy by .3 mpg.

43. Correctly adjust the wheel bearings. Wheel bearings that are adjusted too tight increase rolling resistance.

Check tire pressures regularly with a reliable pocket type gauge. Be sure to check the pressure on a cold tire.

GENERAL MAINTENANCE

Check the fluid levels (particularly engine oil) on a regular basis. Be sure to check the oil for grit, water or other contamination.

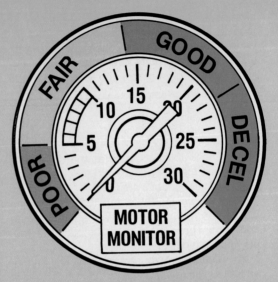

A vacuum gauge is another excellent indicator of internal engine condition and can also be installed in the dash as a mileage indicator.

44. Periodically check the fluid levels in the engine, power steering pump, master cylinder, automatic transmission and drive axle.

45. Change the oil at the recommended interval and change the filter at every oil change. Dirty oil is thick and causes extra friction between moving parts, cutting efficiency and increasing wear. A worn engine requires more frequent tune-ups and gets progressively worse fuel economy. In general, use the lightest viscosity oil for the driving conditions you will encounter.

46. Use the recommended viscosity fluids in the transmission and axle.

47. Be sure the battery is fully charged for fast starts. A slow starting engine wastes fuel.

48. Be sure battery terminals are clean and tight.

49. Check the battery electrolyte level and add distilled water if necessary.

50. Check the exhaust system for crushed pipes, blockages and leaks.

51. Adjust the brakes. Dragging brakes or brakes that are not releasing create increased drag on the engine.

52. Install a vacuum gauge or miles-per-gallon gauge. These gauges visually indicate engine vacuum in the intake manifold. High vacuum = good mileage and low vacuum = poorer mileage. The gauge can also be an excellent indicator of internal engine conditions.

53. Be sure the clutch is properly adjusted. A slipping clutch wastes fuel.

54. Check and periodically lubricate the heat control valve in the exhaust manifold. A sticking or inoperative valve prevents engine warm-up and wastes gas.

55. Keep accurate records to check fuel economy over a period of time. A sudden drop in fuel economy may signal a need for tune-up or other maintenance.

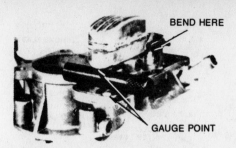

Float level adjustment: Carter YF, 1971 and later 6-232, 258

Float Adjustment

1. Invert the air horn assembly and check the clearance from the top of the float tot he surface of the air horn with a T-scale. The air horn should be held at eye level when gauging and the float arm should be resting on the needle pin.

2. Do not exert pressure on the needle valve when measuring or adjusting the float. Bend the float arm as necessary to adjust the float level.

Float drop adjustment: Carter YF, 1971 and later 6-232, 258

Float Drop Adjustment

1. Hold the air horn up with the float hanging free.

2. Measure the distance between the top of the float at the extreme out end and the air horn under surface.

3. Adjust by bending the tab at the rear of the float lever.

Metering Rod Adjustment

1. Back out the idle speed adjusting screw until the throttle plate is seated fully in its bore.

23. Carriage	55. Lever and shaft
24. Electric solenoid	56. Fast idle cam rod
25. Mounting bracket	57. Choke shield
26. Throttle valve retaining screw ④	58. Choke shield retaining screw ②
27. Throttle valve ②	59. Piston passage plug
28. Needle and seat assembly	60. Heat passage plug
29. Needle seat gasket	61. Choke cover retaining clamp
30. Main jet ②	62. Choke cover retaining screw ③
31. Main body	63. Choke cover
32. Elastomer valve	64. Choke cover gasket
33. Pump return spring	65. Thermostat lever retaining screw
34. Pump diaphragm	66. Thermostat lever
35. Pump lever pin	67. Choke housing retaining screw ③
36. Pump cover	68. Choke housing
37. Pump rod	69. Choke shaft bushing
38. Pump rod retainer	70. Fast idle speed adjusting screw
39. Pump lever	71. Fast idle lever
40. Bowl vent bellcrank	72. Fast idle cam
41. Fuel inlet fitting	73. Choke housing gasket
42. Power valve gasket	74. Pump discharge check ball
43. Power valve	75. Pump discharge weight
44. Power valve cover gasket	76. Booster venturi gasket
45. Power valve cover	77. Booster venturi assembly
46. Power valve cover	78. Air distribution plate
retaining screw ④	79. Pump discharge screw
47. Idle limiter cap ②	80. Retainer
48. Idle mixture screw ②	81. Choke rod
49. Idle mixture screw spring ②	82. Choke lever retaining screw
50. Retainer	83. Choke plate lever
51. Retainer	84. Choke rod seal
52. Fast idle lever retaining nut	85. Stop screw
53. Fast idle lever pin	86. Modulator return spring
54. Retainer	87. Modulator diaphragm assembly

Motorcraft 2100

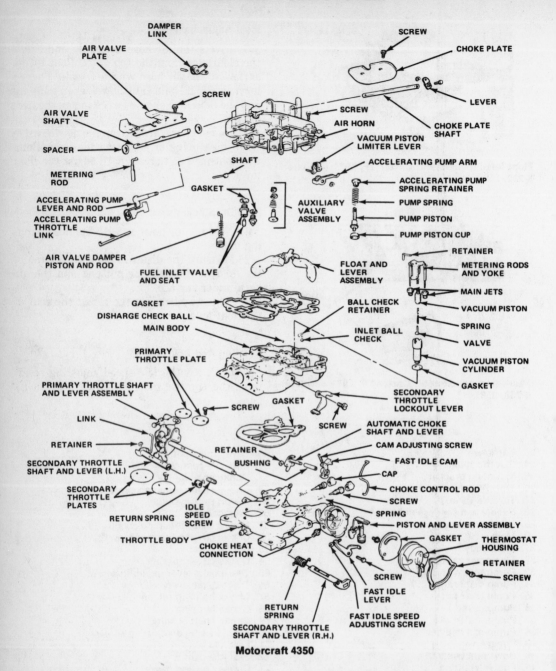

Motorcraft 4350

2. Press down on the upper end of the diaphragm shaft until the diaphragm bottoms in the vacuum chamber.

3. The metering rod should contact the bottom of the metering rod well and lifter link at the outer end nearest the springs and at the supporting link. The eyelet of the rod should slide freely on the pin of the metering rod arm.

4. On models not equipped with an adjusting screw, adjust by bending the metering rod pin tab.

5. On models with an adjusting screw, turn the screw until the metering rod just bottoms

in the body casting. For final adjustment, turn the screw one additional turn clockwise.

Fast Idle Cam Adjustment

1. Open the throttle side enough to allow full closing of the choke valve. Be sure that the fast idle screw is not contacting the fast idle cam.

2. Close the throttle valve and the fast idle cam should revolve to the fast idle position.

3. If adjustment is necessary, bend the choke rod at its upper angle.

4. Position the fast idle screw on the second

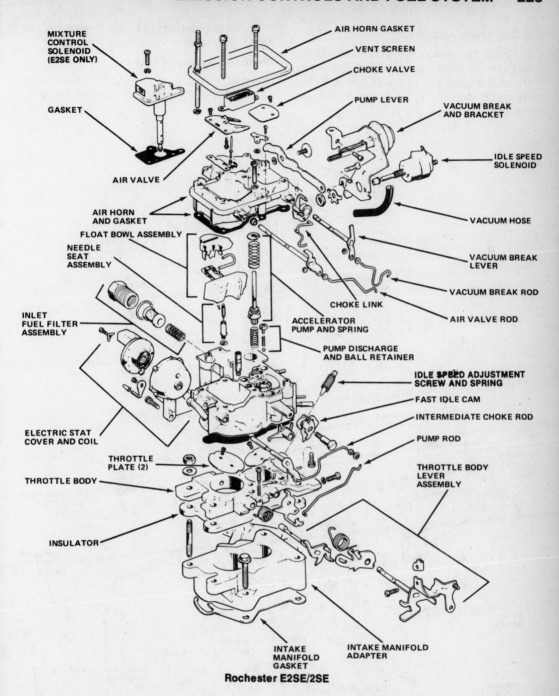

MIXTURE
CONTROL
SOLENOID
(E2SE ONLY)

AIR HORN GASKET

VENT SCREEN

CHOKE VALVE

PUMP LEVER

VACUUM BREAK
AND BRACKET

GASKET

IDLE SPEED
SOLENOID

AIR VALVE

AIR HORN
AND GASKET

VACUUM HOSE

FLOAT BOWL ASSEMBLY

NEEDLE
SEAT
ASSEMBLY

VACUUM BREAK
LEVER

VACUUM BREAK ROD

CHOKE LINK

AIR VALVE ROD

INLET
FUEL FILTER
ASSEMBLY

ACCELERATOR
PUMP AND SPRING

PUMP DISCHARGE
AND BALL RETAINER

IDLE SPEED ADJUSTMENT
SCREW AND SPRING

FAST IDLE CAM

INTERMEDIATE CHOKE ROD

ELECTRIC STAT
COVER AND COIL

PUMP ROD

THROTTLE
PLATE (2)

THROTTLE BODY
LEVER
ASSEMBLY

THROTTLE BODY

INSULATOR

INTAKE
MANIFOLD
GASKET

INTAKE MANIFOLD
ADAPTER

Rochester E2SE/2SE

step of the fast idle cam and against the shoulder of the high step. Measure the specified clearance between the lower edge of the choke plate and the air horn wall. Bent the choke rod to adjust.

5. Fast idle speed may be checked with the engine warmed up. Speed adjustment is made by bending the choke rod at the lower angle. The speed is given with the adjusting screw on the second step and against the highest step. Adjustment is made with the adjusting screw.

NOTE: *EGR hoses must be blocked off and TCS solenoid vacuum valve wires must be disconnected to do this.*

Choke Unloader Adjustment

With the throttle valve held wide open and the choke valve held in the closed position, vend the unloader lug on the choke trip lever to obtain the specified clearance between the lower edge of the choke valve and the air horn wall.

Automatic Choke Adjustment

1. Loosen the choke cover retaining screws.
2. Turn the choke over so that the index mark on the cover lines up with the specified mark on the choke housing. Never set it more

that two graduations in either direction of the specified setting.

Electrically Assisted Choke

Starting with the 1976 models, some single barrel Carter YF carburetors use an electrical-

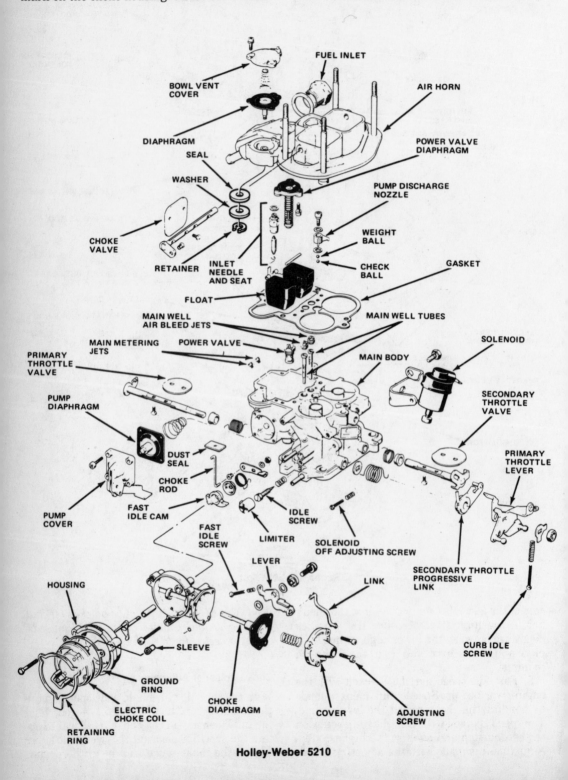

Holley-Weber 5210

ly assisted choke to reduce hydrocarbon and carbon monoxide exhaust emissions during warm-up.

Once underhood temperatures reach 95°F (15°F), a bimetallic switch located in the choke cap closes, allowing a ceramic heating element to draw power from a special tap on the alternator.

This causes the choke valve to open faster than normal, thus reducing CO emission during engine warm-up.

After the engine is shut off, the bimetallic

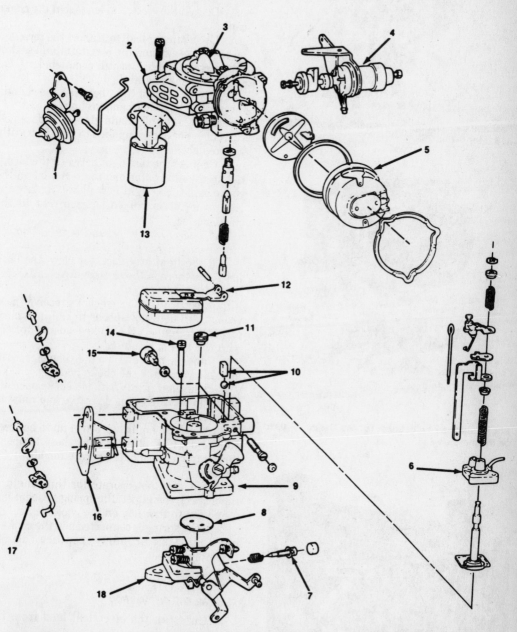

1. Vacuum break
2. Air horn
3. Choke plate
4. Sole-vac throttle positioner
5. Choke assembly
6. Accelerator pump assembly
7. Idle mixture screw with O-ring
8. Throttle plate
9. Main body
10. Accelerator pump check ball and weight
11. Main metering jet
12. Float assembly
13. Mixture control solenoid
14. Low speed jet
15. Accelerator pump vent valve
16. Wide open throttle (WOT) switch
17. Throttle shaft and lever
18. Throttle body

Carter YFA

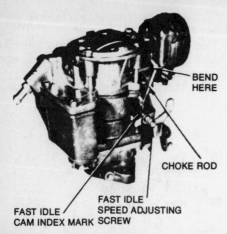

BEND HERE

CHOKE ROD

FAST IDLE SPEED ADJUSTING SCREW

FAST IDLE CAM INDEX MARK

Fast idle cam linkage adjustment: Carter YF, 1971 and later 6-232, 258

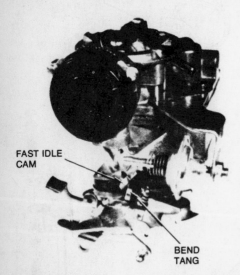

FAST IDLE CAM

BEND TANG

Choke unloader adjustment for the Carter YF used on the 6-cyl. engine

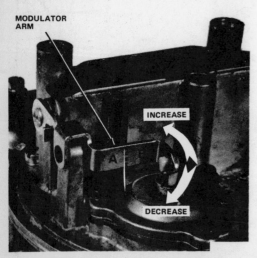

MODULATOR ARM

INCREASE

A

DECREASE

2100 initial choke valve clearance adjustment

switch remains closed until underhood temperature drops below 65°F. Thus, if the engine is turned off for only a short time or if the ambient temperature is above 65°F, the choke will function for only a limited period of time.

TESTING

1. Detach the electrical lead from the choke cap.
2. Use a jumper lead to connect the terminal on the choke cap and the wire terminal, so that the electrical circuit is still completed.
3. Start the engine.
4. Hook up a test light between the connector on the choke lead and ground.
5. The test light should glow. If it does not, current is not being supplied to the electrically assisted choke.
6. Connect the test light between the terminal on the alternator and the terminal on the choke cap. If the light now glows, replace the lead, since it is not passing current to the choke assist.

CAUTION: *Do not ground terminal on the alternator while performing Step 6.*

7. If the light still does not glow, the fault lies somewhere in the electrical system. Check the system out.

If the electrically assisted choke receives power, but still does not appear to be functioning properly, reconnect the choke lead and proceed with the rest of the test.

8. Tape the bulb end of a thermometer to the metallic portion of the choke housing.
9. If the electrically assisted choke operates below 55°F (13°C), it is defective and must be replaced.
10. Allow the engine to warm-up to between 80°F and 110°F (27–43°C); at these temperatures the choke should operate for about 1½ minutes.
11. If it does not operate for this length of time, check the bimetallic spring to see if it is connected to the tang on the choke lever.
12. If the spring is connected and the choke is not operating properly, replace the cap assembly.

REMOVAL AND INSTALLATION

1. Unfasten the electrical lead from the choke cover.
2. Remove the choke cover retaining screws and clamp.
3. Remove the choke cover and gasket from the carburetor.
4. Installation is performed in the reverse order of removal. Adjust the choke cover.

CARTER BBD 2-BBL

Float Adjustment

1. Remove the carburetor air horn.
2. Gently hold the lip of the float against its needle to raise the float.
3. Measure float level by placing a straight-edge across the float bowl. Float level should be maintained at 0.250" (6.35mm), plus or minus 0.032" (0.81mm). Release the floats.
4. If necessary, adjust by bending the float lips as required.

NOTE: *Do not bend float lip while it is resting against the needle as this may deform the synthetic needle tip and cause a false setting.*

5. Install the air horn.

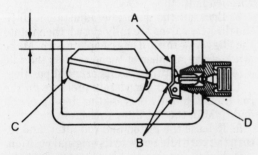

A. Apply slight pressure
B. Bend to adjust
C. Float
D. Gasket

Float adjustment on the Carter BBD

Fast Idle Adjustment

NOTE: *Perform this adjustment with the carburetor installed on the engine. If the car is equipped with a transmission controlled spark (TCS) system and/or an exhaust gas recirculation (EGR) system, be sure that both are disconnected before attempting to set fast idle speed.*

1. Start engine and allow it to reach normal operating temperature.
2. Connect a tachometer to the engine.
3. Set the fast idle adjusting screw so that it contacts the second step of the fast idle cam and rests against the shoulder of the high step.
4. Rotate the fast idle adjusting screw until a fast idle speed of 1,700 rpm is obtained.
5. Remove the tach and return the engine to normal idle speed after the adjustment is completed.

Automatic Choke Adjustment

NOTE: *This adjustment may be made with the carburetor either on or off the engine.*

1. Loosen the choke cover retaining screws.
2. Rotate the choke cover in the direction of its arrow to the setting specified in the chart below.
3. Tighten the retaining screws.
4. If the car stumbles or stalls at the specified choke setting during engine warm-up, adjust the setting to (richer or leaner) until the car runs properly.

NOTE: *Never set the choke more than two notches in either direction of the recommended setting.*

Choke Unloader Adjustment

1. Hold the throttle in the wide open position and apply pressure on the choke plate toward the closed position.
2. measure the distance between the lower edge of the choke plate and the air horn wall (see the 'Carburetor Specifications' chart).
3. If necessary, adjust by bending the unloader tang where it contacts the fast idle cam. Bend toward the cam to increase clearance, and away from the cam to decrease clearance.

NOTE: *Do not bend the unloader tang down from the horizontal plane. After adjusting, make sure that the unloader tang maintains*

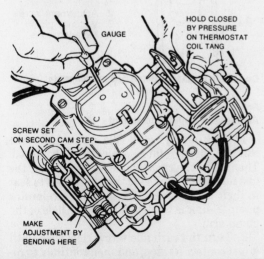

BBD fast idle cam adjustment

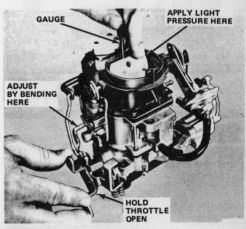

BBD choke unloader adjustment

at least a 0.070" (1.78mm) clearance from the flange of the main body at wide open throttle position.

4. Operate the throttle and make sure that the unloader does not bind against the carburetor or linkage. Also make sure the wide open throttle can be reached by fully depressing the gas pedal. If not, remove excess padding from beneath the floor mat or reposition the throttle cable bracket.

Initial Choke Valve Adjustment

1. Remove the choke cover.

2. Using a vacuum source which holds a minimum of 19 in.Hg, pull the diaphragm in against its stop.

3. Open the throttle valve slightly so that the fast idle screw locates on the high step of the cam.

4. hold the choke bimetallic coil tang in the

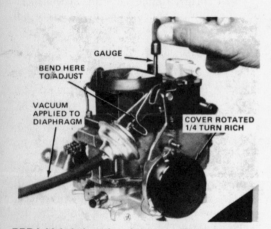

GAUGE

BEND HERE
TO ADJUST

VACUUM
APPLIED TO
DIAPHRAGM

COVER ROTATED
1/4 TURN RICH

BBD initial choke valve clearance adjustment

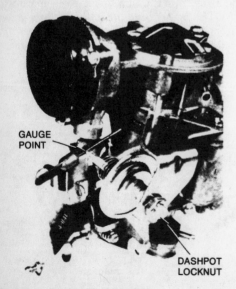

GAUGE
POINT

DASHPOT
LOCKNUT

Dashpot adjustment: Carter YF

closed position and measure the clearance between the choke plate and the air horn wall. The distance should be 0.128" (3.25mm), plus or minus 0.010" (0.254mm).

5. Adjust as necessary by bending the 'S' shaped section of the diaphragm connector link.

Vacuum Step-Up Piston Gap Adjustment

1. Remove the step-up piston cover plate and gasket from the carburetor air horn.

2. Adjust the gap in the step-up piston to 0.040" (1.016mm), plus or minus 0.015" (0.38mm) using the allen head screw on top of the piston. Turning the screw clockwise richens the fuel mixture and turning counterclockwise leans it out.

3. Back off the curb idle adjustment until the throttle valves are fully closed, then rotate the idle screw inward one complete turn. Make a not of the number of turns so that the idle screw can be returned to its original position.

4. While keeping moderate pressure on the rod lifter tab, fully depress the step-up piston and tighten the rod lifter lockscrew.

5. Release the piston and rod lifter, and return the curb idle screw to its original position.

6. Install the step-up piston cover plate and gasket.

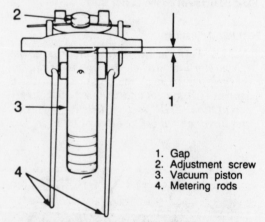

2

3

1

4

1. Gap
2. Adjustment screw
3. Vacuum piston
4. Metering rods

Carter BBD vacuum piston gap adjustment

Accelerator Pump Adjustment

1. Back off the curb idle screw until the throttle valves (plates) are completely closed. Then, open the choke valve (plate) so that the fast idle cam permits the throttle valves to seat in their bores. Make sure that the accelerator pump 'S' link is located in the outer hole of the pump arm.

2. Turn the curb idle screw clockwise until it just contact its stop, and then continue to rotate two complete turns.

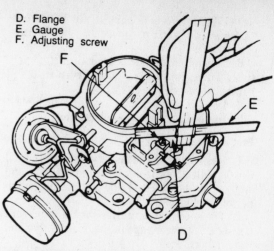

D. Flange
E. Gauge
F. Adjusting screw

Carter BBD accelerator pump adjustment

3. Measure the distance between the surface of the air horn and the top of the accelerator pump shaft. This distance should be 0.500" (12.7mm).

4. Adjust the pump travel as necessary, by loosening the pump arm adjusting lockscrew and rotating the sleeve until the proper measurement is obtained. Then, tighten the lockscrew.

AUTOLITE/MOTORCRAFT 2100 and 2150

The Model 2100 2150 2-barrel carburetors have an air horn assembly that covers the main body and houses the choke plate and the internal fuel bowl vents. The throttle plate, accelerator pump assembly, power valve assembly, and fuel bowl are contained in the main body. The automatic choke is also attached to the main body. Each bore contains a main and booster venturi, a main fuel discharge, an ac-celerating pump discharge, an idle fuel discharge, and a throttle plate. They are used on V8 engines.

Float Level (Dry)

The dry float level measurement is a preliminary check and must be followed by a wet float level measurement with the carburetor mounted on the engine.

1. With the air horn removed and the fuel inlet needle seated lightly, gently raise the float and measure the distance between the main body gasket surface (gasket removed) and the top of the float.

2. If necessary, bend the float tab to obtain the correct level.

Float Level (Wet)

1. Remove the screws that hold the air horn to the main body and break the seal between the air horn and main body. Leave the air horn and gasket loosely in place on top of the main body.

2. Start the engine and allow it to idle for at least 3 minutes.

3. After the engine has idled long enough to stabilize the fuel level, remove the air horn assembly.

4. With the engine idling, use a T-scale to measure the distance surface to the surface of the fuel. The scale must be held at least ¼" (6mm) away from any vertical surface to ensure proper measurement.

5. If any adjustment is required, stop the engine to avoid a fire from fuel spraying on the engine.

6. Bend the float tab upward to raise the level and downward to lower the level.

CAUTION: *Be sure to hold the fuel inlet needle off its seat when bending the float tab so as not to damage the Viton tip.*

7. Each time the float level is changed, the

Float level adjustment for the Autolite Model 2100 and 2150 2-bbl carburetor

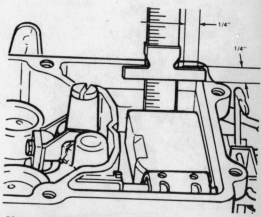

Motorcraft 2150 wet float adjustment

air horn must be temporarily positioned and the engine started to stabilize the fuel level before again checking it.

Initial Choke Valve Clearance Adjustment

1. Loosen the choke cover screws. Rotate the cover ¼ turn counterclockwise.

2. Disconnect the choke heat inlet tube. Align the fast idle speed adjusting screw with the indexed (second) step of the fast idle cam.

3. Start the engine without moving the accelerator linkage.

4. Turn the fast idle cam lever adjusting screw out 3 full turns. Measure the clearance between the lower edge of the choke valve and the air horn wall.

5. Adjust by grasping the modulator arm with a pair of pliers and twisting with a second pair of pliers. Twist to the front to increase the clearance and toward the rear to decrease the clearance.

CAUTION: *Be very careful not to damage the nylon piston rod of the modulator assembly.*

6. Stop the engine and connect the heat tube. Turn the fast idle cam lever in 3 full turns.

7. Don't reset the choke cover until the fast idle cam linkage adjustment is done.

Fast Idle Cam

1. Push down on the fast idle cam lever until the fast idle screw is in contact with the second step of the fast idle cam and against the shoulder of the high step.

2. The specified clearance should be present between the lower edge of the choke valve and the air horn wall.

3. The adjustment is made by turning the fast idle cam lever screw.

4. The choke cover may now be adjusted.

2100 initial choke valve clearance adjustment

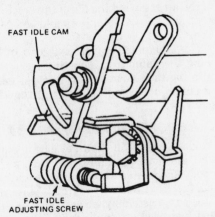

Fast idle cam index setting—Autolite (Motorcraft) 2100

Choke Unloader (Dechoke)

1. With the throttle held completely open, move the choke valve to the closed position.

2. Measure the distance between the lower

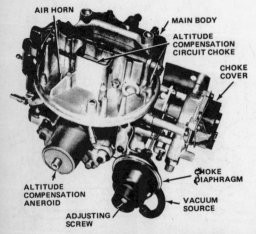

2150 initial choke valve clearance adjustment

Dashpot adjustment: Autolite 2100

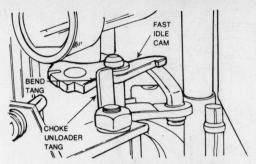

Motorcraft 2150 choke unloader adjustment

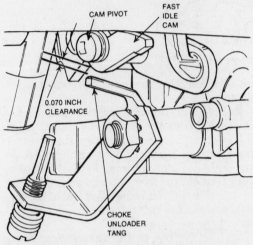

Motorcraft 2150 choke unloader/fast idle cam clearance

edge of the choke valve and the air horn wall.

3. Adjust by bending the tang on the fast idle speed lever which is located on the throttle shaft.

NOTE: *Final unloader adjustment must be performed on the car and the throttle should be opened by using the accelerator pedal of the car. This is to be sure that full throttle operation is achieved.*

Accelerator Pump

The accelerator pump operating rod must be positioned in the proper holes of the accelerator pump lever and the throttle overtravel lever to assure contact pump travel. If adjusting is required, additional holes are provided in the throttle overtravel lever.

Fast Idle

Adjust the fast idle setting with the engine at operating temperature. The fast idle screw should be resting against the second step of the fast idle cam. Adjust by turning the fast idle screw.

AUTOLITE/MOTORCRAFT 4300 and 4350 4-BBL

The model 4300/4350 4-barrel carburetor is composed of three main assemblies: the air horn, the main body, and the throttle body. The air horn assembly serves as the fuel bowl cover as well as the housing for the choke valve and shaft. It contains the accelerator pump

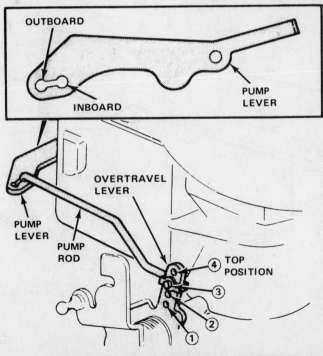

2100, 2150 accelerator pump adjustment points

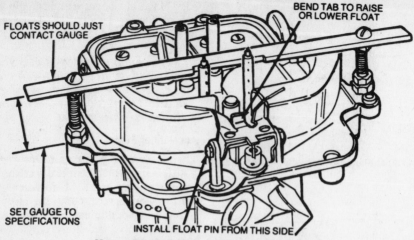

FLOATS SHOULD JUST
CONTACT GAUGE

BEND TAB TO RAISE
OR LOWER FLOAT

SET GAUGE TO
SPECIFICATIONS

INSTALL FLOAT PIN FROM THIS SIDE

Motorcraft 4300, 4350 float level adjustment

linkage, fuel inlet seat, float and lever, booster venturi, and internal fuel bowl vents.

The main body houses the fuel metering passages, accelerator pump mechanism, and the power valve.

The throttle body contains the primary and secondary throttle valve and shafts, the curb idle adjusting screw, the fast idle adjusting screw, the idle mixture adjusting screws, and the automatic choke assembly. It is used on V8 engines.

Float Adjustment, 4300

1. Adjustments to the fuel level are best made with the carburetor removed from the engine and the carburetor cleaned upon disassembly.

2. Invert the air horn assembly and remove the gasket from the surface.

3. Use a T-scale to measure the distance from the float to the air horn casting. Position the scale horizontally over the flat surface of both floats at the free ends and parallel to the air horn casting. Hold the lower end of the vertical scale in full contact with the smooth surface of the air horn.

CAUTION: *The end of the vertical scale must not come into contact with any gasket sealing ridges while measuring the float level.*

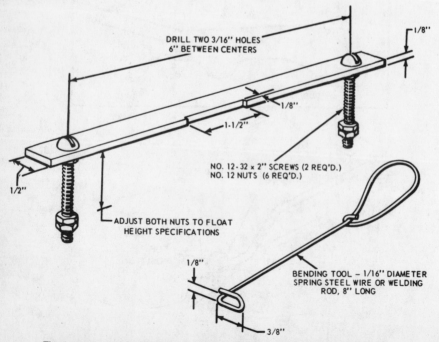

DRILL TWO 3/16" HOLES
6" BETWEEN CENTERS

1/8"

1/8"

1-1/2"

1/2"

NO. 12-32 x 2" SCREWS (2 REQ'D.)
NO. 12 NUTS (6 REQ'D.)

ADJUST BOTH NUTS TO FLOAT
HEIGHT SPECIFICATIONS

1/8"

BENDING TOOL – 1/16" DIAMETER
SPRING STEEL WIRE OR WELDING
ROD, 8" LONG

3/8"

Float gauge and bending tool details—Autolite (Motorcraft) 4300, 4350

4. The free end of each float should just touch the horizontal scale, of one float is lower than the other; twist the float and lever assembly slightly to correct.

5. Adjust the float level by bending the tab which contact the needle and seat assembly.

Float Adjustment, 4350

1. Invert the air horn assembly and remove the gasket.

2. Measure the distance from the floats to the air horn rim using a T-scale. Position the horizontal scale over the flat surface of both floats at the free ends, parallel to the air horn casting. Hold the lower end of the vertical scale in full contact with the smooth area of the casting, midway between the main discharge nozzles.

CAUTION: *Do not allow the end of the vertical scale to contact any gasket sealing ridge while measuring the float setting.*

3. The free end of the floats should just touch the horizontal scale. Float-to-air horn casting distance should be $^{29}/_{64}''$ (11.5mm). Bend the vertical tab on the float arm to adjust the distance.

Initial Choke Valve Clearance Adjustment

1. Remove the choke thermostatic spring housing.

2. Bend a wire gauge (0.035" [0.89mm] diameter) at a 90° angle about 1.8" (45.7mm) from one end.

3. Block the throttle open so that the fast idle screw does not contact the fast idle cam.

4. Insert the bend end of the wire gauge between the lower edge of the piston slot and the upped edge of the righthand slot in the choke housing.

5. Pull the choke piston lever counterclockwise until the gauge is snug in the piston slot. Hod the wire in place by exerting light pressure in a rearward direction on the choke piston lever. Check the distance from the lower edge of the choke valve to the air horn wall.

6. Adjustment is done by loosening the hex head screw (left hand thread) on the choke valve shaft and rotating the choke shaft.

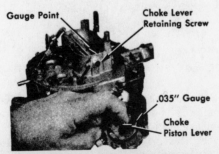

4300 initial choke valve clearance adjustment

Fast Idle Cam Adjustment, 4300

1. Loosen the screws on the choke thermostatic spring cover and rotate the housing ¼ turn counterclockwise. Tighten the screws.

2. Open the throttle and allow the choke valve to close completely.

3. Push down on the fast idle cam counterweight until the fast idle screw is in contact with the second step of the cam and against the high step.

4. Measure the clearance between the lower edge of the choke valve and the air horn wall.

5. Adjust the turning the fast idle cam adjusting screw.

6. Return the housing to its original position.

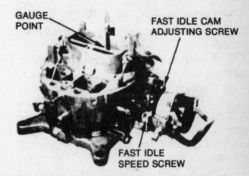

Fast idle adjustment: Autolite 4300, 8-360, 401

Fast Idle Cam Adjustment, 4350

1. Run the engine to normal operating temperature. Connect an accurate tachometer to the engine.

2. Disconnect and plug the EGR and TCS vacuum lines.

3. Position the fast idle screw against the first step of the fast idle screw. Adjust the fast idle screw to give a reading of 1600 rpm.

4. Return the linkage to its normal position, unplug and reconnect the vacuum lines.

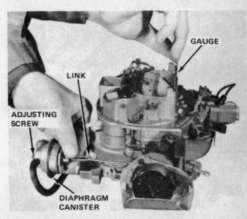

Measuring the initial choke valve clearance on the 4350

Adjusting the initial choke valve clearance on the 4350

Choke Unloader (Dechoke) Adjustment

1. Open the throttle fully and hold it in this position.
2. Rotate the choke valve toward the closed position.
3. Check the clearance between the lower edge of the choke valve and the air horn wall.
4. Adjust by bending the unloader tang on the fast idle speed lever toward the cam to increase the clearance and away to decrease the clearance.

CAUTION: *Do not bend the unloader tang down from the horizontal. After adjustment, there should be at least 0.070" (1.78mm) clearance from the choke housing with the throttle fully open.*

Accelerator Pump Stroke Adjustment

The accelerator pump should not need adjustment as its stroke is preset in compliance with exhaust emission control standards. If for any reason the stroke must be altered, it may be done by repositioning the link in the desired holes.

Fast Idle Sped

The fast idle speed is adjusted with the engine at operating temperature and the fast idle screw on the second step of the fast idle cam. Adjust by turning the fast idle screw in or out as required.

NOTE: *To adjust the fast idle speed, you must plug the EGR valve vacuum line and disconnect the TCS solenoid wire.*

Dashpot Adjustment

Some carburetors are equipped with a dashpot to prevent stalling. The dashpot adjustment procedure for these carburetors is as follows:

1. Be sure that the throttle valves are closed tightly and that the diaphragm stem is fully depressed.

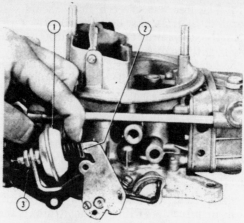

| 1. Dashpot | 3. Locknut |
| 2. 3/32 in. gap | |

Dashpot adjustment on Holley 4-bbl carburetors

2. Measure the clearance between the dashpot stem and the throttle lever with a feeler gauge. For the proper clearance specification, see the chart.
3. If the clearance is not correct, adjust it by loosening the locknut and rotating the dashpot until the proper clearance is obtained. Tighten the locknut.

ROCHESTER E2SE

This carburetor is used on the 4–151 engine.

Float Adjustment

1. Remove the air horn.
2. Hold the float retainer and push down lightly on the float.

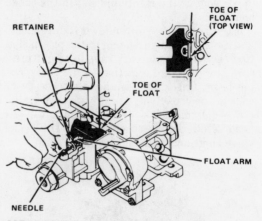

2SE and E2SE float adjustment

3. Using a T-scale, at a point ³/₁₆" (4.76mm) from the end of the float, measure the distance from the top surface of the float bowl to the top of the float. The distance should be 0.208" (5.28mm) with manual trans., 0.256" (6.5mm)

with automatic trans., and 0.208″ (5.28mm) for all Calif. E2SE models.

4. Bend the float arm as necessary to adjust.

Fast Idle Adjustment

1. Make sure the choke coil adjustment is correct and that the fast idle speed is correct.

2. Obtain a Choke Angle Gauge, tool #J-26701-1. Rotate the degree scale to the 0° mark opposite the pointer.

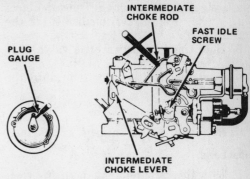

2SE, E2SE choke coil lever adjustment

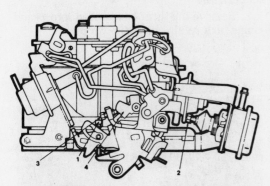

1. Idle speed screw
2. Vacuum diaphagm
3. Fast idle screw
4. Fast idle cam

2SE adjustment points

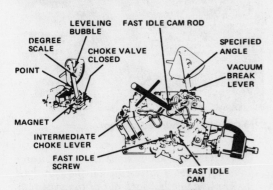

2SE, E2SE fast idle cam position adjustment

3. With the choke valve completely closed, place the magnet on the tool squarely on the choke plate. Rotate the bubble unit until it is centered.

4. Rotate the degree scale until the 25° mark is opposite the pointer. On carburetors with choke cover sticker number 70172, the angle is 18°.

5. Place the fast idle screw on the second step of the cam.

6. Close the choke plate by pushing on the intermediate choke lever.

7. Push the vacuum brake lever toward the open choke position until the lever is against the rear tang on the choke lever.

8. Adjust by bending the fast idle cam rod until the bubble is centered.

Choke Setting Adjustment

NOTE: *Once the rivets and choke cover are removed, a choke cover retainer kit is necessary for assembly.*

1. Remove the rivets, retainers, choke cover and coil following the instructions found in the cover retainer kit.

2. Position the fast idle adjustment screw on the highest step of the fast idle cam.

3. Push on the intermediate choke lever and close the choke plate.

4. Insert the proper plug gauge, 0.050–0.080″ (1.27–2.03mm) for manual trans. and 0.85″ (21.6mm) for automatic trans., in the hole adjacent to the coil lever. The edge of the lever should barely contact the plug gauge.

5. Bend the intermediate choke rod to adjust.

Choke Unloader Adjustment

1. Obtain a Carburetor Choke Angle Gauge, tool #J-26701-1. Rotate the scale on the gauge until the 0 mark is opposite the pointer.

2. Close the choke plate completely and set the magnet squarely on top of it.

3. Rotate the bubble until it is centered.

4. Rotate the degree scale until the 32°

2SE, E2SE choke unloader adjustment

mark is opposite the pointer. On carburetors with choke cover sticker number 70172 the setting is 19°.

5. Hold the primary throttle valve wide open.

6. Bend the throttle lever tang until the bubble is centered.

HOLLEY 5210-C

This carburetor is used on the 4–121 engine.

Float Level

1. With the carburetor air horn inverted, and the float tang resting lightly on the inlet

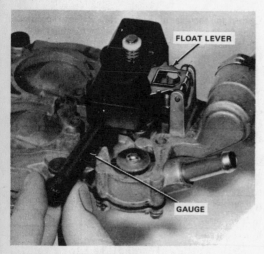

5210-C float level adjustment

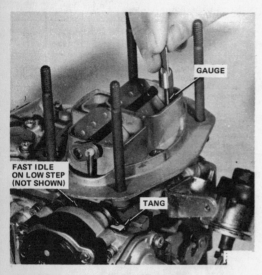

5210-C fast idle cam index adjustment

needle, insert the specified gauge between the air horn and the float.

2. Bend the float tang is an adjustment is needed.

Fast Idle Cam Adjustment

1. Place the fast idle screw on the second step of the fast idle cam and against the shoulder of the high step.

2. Place the specified drill or gauge on the down side of the choke plate.

3. To adjust, bend the choke lever tang.

Choke Plate Pulldown (Vacuum Break) Adjustment

THROUGH 1979

1. Remove the three hex headed screws and ring which retain the choke cover.

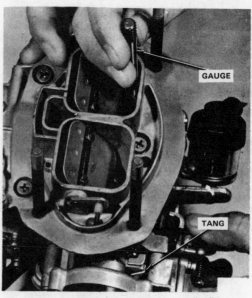

5210-C choke unloader adjustment

CAUTION: *Do not remove the choke water housing screw if adjusting on the car. Pull the choke assembly back out of the way.*

2. Push the diaphragm shaft against the stop. Push the coil lever clockwise.

3. Insert the specified size gauge on the down side of the primary choke plate.

4. Take the slack out of the linkage and turn the adjusting screw with a $\frac{5}{32}$" Allen wrench.

1980

1. Attach a hand vacuum pump to the vacuum break diaphragm; apply vacuum and seat the diaphragm.

2. Push the fast idle cam lever down to close the choke plate.

3. Take any slack our of the linkage in the open choke position.

4. Insert the specified gauge between the lower edge of the choke plate and the air horn wall.

5. If the clearance is incorrect, turn the vac-

5210-C initial choke valve clearance adjustment

uum break adjusting screw, located in the break housing, to adjust.

Secondary Vacuum Break Adjustment

THROUGH 1978 ONLY

1. Remove the three screws and the choke coil assembly.
2. Place the cam follower on the highest step of the fast idle cam.
3. Seat the diaphragm by applying an outside source of vacuum.
4. Push the inside choke coil lever counterclockwise for 1977; clockwise for 1978, to close the choke valve.
5. Place a gauge of the size specified in the chart between the lower edge of the choke valve and the air horn wall.
6. Bend the vacuum break rod to adjust.
7. Replace and adjust the choke.

Choke Unloader Adjustment

1. Position the throttle lever at the wide open position.
2. Insert a gauge of the size specified in the chart between the lower edge of the choke valve and the air horn wall.
3. Bend the unloader tang for adjustment.

Secondary Throttle Stop Screw Adjustment

1. Back off the screw until it doesn't touch the throttle lever.
2. Turn the screw in until it touches the secondary throttle lever. Turn it in ¼ turn more.

Fast Idle Speed Adjustment

1. The engine must be normal operating temperature with the air cleaner off.
2. With the engine running, position the fast idle screw on the high step of the cam for

GM cars, or on the second step against the shoulder of the high step for AMC cars. Plug the EGR Port on the carburetor.

3. Adjust the speed by turning the fast idle screw.

CARTER YFA

This carburetor is used on the 4–150

Float and Fuel Level Adjustment

1. Remove the top of the carburetor and the gasket.

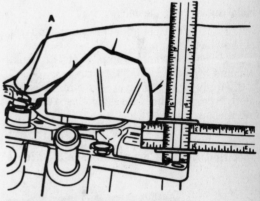

Measuring float clearance on the 4-150

2. Invert the carburetor top and check the clearance from the top of the float to the bottom edge of the air horn with a float level gauge. Hold the carburetor top at eye level when making the check. The float arm should be resting on the inlet needle pin. To adjust, bend the float arm. DO NOT BEND THE TAB AT THE END OF THE ARM! See the Carburetor Specifications chart for the correct clearance.

Fast Idle Linkage Adjustment

NOTE: *This adjustment is performed with the air cleaner removed.*

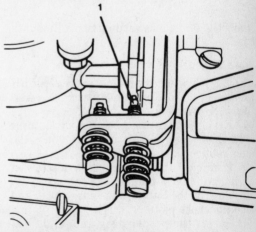

Carter YFA fast idle adjustment

1. Run the engine to normal operating temperature. Connect a tachometer according to the maker's instructions.

2. Disconnect and plug the EGR valve vacuum hose.

3. Position the fast idle adjustment screw on the second stop of the fast idle cam with the transmission in neutral.

4. Adjust the fast idle speed to 2300 rpm for auto. trans. and 2000 rpm for man. trans.

5. Idle the engine and reconnect the EGR hose.

Initial Choke Valve Clearance

1. Position the fast idle screw on the top step of the fast idle cam.

2. Using a vacuum pump, seat the choke vacuum break.

3. Apply light closing pressure in the choke plate to position the plate as far closed as possible without forcing it.

4. Measure the distance between the air horn wall and the choke plate. If it is not that specified in the Carburetor Specifications

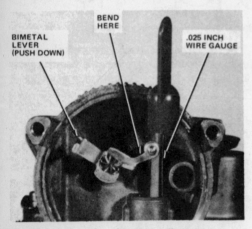

YF initial choke valve clearance adjustment

Chart, bend the choke vacuum break link until it is.

Choke Setting Adjustment

NOTE: *Once the rivets and choke cover are removed, a choke cover retainer kit is necessary for assembly.*

1. Remove the rivets, retainers, choke cover and coil following the instructions found in the cover retainer kit.

2. Position the fast idle adjustment screw on the highest stop of the fast idle cam.

3. Push on the intermediate choke lever and close the choke plate.

4. Insert the proper plug gauge, 0.050–0.080″ (1.27–2.032mm) for manual trans. and

0.85″ (21.59mm) for automatic trans., in the hole adjacent to the coil lever. The edge of the lever should barely contact the plug gauge.

5. Bend the intermediate choke rod to adjust.

Unloader Adjustment

1. Obtain a Carburetor Choke Angle Gauge, tool #J-26701-A. Rotate the scale on the gauge until the 0 mark is opposite the pointer.

2. Close the choke plate completely and set the magnet squarely on top of it.

3. Rotate the bubble until it is centered.

4. Rotate the degree scale until the 32° mark is opposite the pointer. On carburetors with choke cover sticker number 70172 the setting is 19°.

5. Hold the primary throttle valve wide open.

6. Bend the throttle lever tang until the bubble is centered.

Metering Rod Adjustment

1. Remove the air horn and gasket.

2. Make sure that the idle speed adjustment

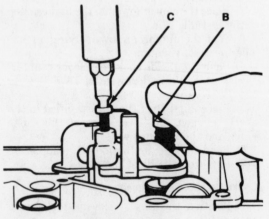

B. Diaphragm shaft
C. Adjustment screw

Metering rod adjustment

screw allows the throttle plate to close tightly in the bore.

3. Press down on the top of the pump diaphragm shaft until it bottoms.

4. In this position, adjust the metering rod by turning the adjusting screw counterclockwise, until the metering rod lightly bottoms in the main metering jet.

5. Turn the adjusting screw 1 full turn more.

6. Install the air horn and gasket, and adjust the curb idle speed.

Carburetor Specification Charts
Carter BBD

Engine	Years	Float Level Dry (in.)	Step-Up Piston Gap (in.)	Fast Idle Cam Setting (in.)	Fast Idle rpm	Choke Unloader (in.)	Initial Choke Valve Clearance (in.)	Automatic Choke Setting
6-258	1977–78	¼	³⁄₆₄	³⁄₃₂	1,700	⁹⁄₆₄	⅛	2 rich
	1979	¼	0.035	0.110	①	0.280	②	1 rich
	1980	¼	③	0.080–0.110	④	0.280	⑤	⑥
	1981	¼	⑦	0.080–0.110	⑧	0.280	⑨	⑥
	1982	¼	0.035	0.095	1,850	0.280	0.140	1 rich
	1983–84	¼	0.035	0.095	⑧	0.280	0.140	1 rich
	1985–87	¼	0.035	0.095	⑧	0.280	0.140	TR

TR: Tamper Resistant
① Except High Altitude: 1,600
  High Altitude: 1,500
② MT: 0.150
  AT: 0.140
③ Except High Altitude Eagle 0.035
  High Altitude Eagle: 0.025
④ MT: 1,700
  AT: 1,950
⑤ Eagle w/AT, except High Altitude: 0.128
  All w/MT: 0.140
  High Altitude Eagle w/AT and all 2-wd w/AT: 0.150

⑥ All w/MT: 1 rich
  High Altitude Eagle: Index
  All others: 2 rich
⑦ Eagle w/MT, except Calif.: 0.025
  All others: 0.035
⑧ MT: 1,700
  AT: 1,850
⑨ High Altitude Eagle: 0.140
  All others: 0.128

Carter YF

Engine	Years	Float Level (in.)	Float Drop (in.)	Dashpot Setting (in.)	Fast Idle rpm	Choke Unloader (in.)	Initial Choke Valve Clearance (in.)	Automatic Choke Setting
6-232, 258	1975	0.476	1.375	0.075	1,600	0.275	0.205	①
	1976	0.476	1.375	0.075	1,600	0.275	0.205	①
	1977	0.476	1.375	—	②	0.275	0.215 ④	③
	1978	0.476	1.375	—	②	0.275	0.215 ④	③
	1979	0.476	1.375	—	②	0.275	0.215	1 rich

① MT: 2 rich   ③ Except Calif., and High Altitude w/AT: 1 rich
  AT: 1 rich   Calif.: Index
② MT: 1,500   High Altitude w/AT: 2 rich
  AT: 1,600   ④ High Altitude: 0.221

Carter YFA

Engine	Years	Float Level (in.)	Initial Choke Valve Clearance (in.)	Fast Idle Cam Setting (in.)	Choke Unloader (in.)	Fast Idle Speed rpm	Automatic Choke Setting
4-150	1984	³⁹⁄₆₄	¹⁵⁄₆₄	¹¹⁄₆₄	¹⁵⁄₆₄	2,000 MT 2,300 AT	TR

MT: Manual Transmission
AT: Automatic Tranmission
TR: Tamper Resistant

Rochester 2SE/E2SE

Engine	Years	Float Level (in.)	Choke Coil Lever (in.)	Fast Idle Cam Clearance (in.)	Choke Vacuum Break (in.)		Choke Unloader (in.)	Air Valve Rod (deg.)
					Primary	Secondary		
4-151	1980–83	①	5/64	1/8	9/64	②	17/64	2

① 2SE/E2SE Man. Trans. and Calif.: 13/64
2SE Auto. Trans.: 1/4
E2SE Auto. Trans.: 13/64
② Man. Trans.: 3/64–5/64
Auto. Trans.: 5/64

Autolite/Motorcraft 2100

Engine	Years	Float Level Dry (in.)	Float Level Wet (in.)	Dashpot Setting (in.)	Fast Idle rpm	Choke Unloader (in.)	Initial Choke Valve Clearance (in.)	Automatic Choke Setting
8-304	1975	2/5	25/32	9/64	2,200	9/32	0.130	2 rich

Motorcraft 2100/2150

Engine	Years	Float Level Dry (in.)	Float Level Wet (in.)	Fast Idle Cam Setting (in.)	Fast Idle rpm	Choke Unloader (in.)	Initial Choke Valve Clearance (in.)	Automatic Choke Setting
8-304, 360	1976	①	②	③	1,600	0.250	④	⑤
	1977	0.313	0.780	⑥	⑦	0.250	④	⑧
	1978	0.555	0.780	⑨	⑪	⑫	⑬	⑩
	1979	0.313	0.780	0.113	⑭	0.300	0.125	1 rich

① MT: 0.547
AT: 0.476
② AT: 0.780
MT: 0.937
③ AT: 0.130
MT: 0.120
④ AT, except High Altitude: 0.140
High Altitude AT: 0.104
MT: 0.130
⑤ AT: 1 rich
MT: 2 rich
⑥ Except Calif. and High Altitude: 0.136
Calif.: 0.130
High Altitude: 0.089
⑦ Except Calif. 8-304: 1,600
Calif. 8-304: 1,800

⑧ 8-360, all High Altitude, and Calif. 8-304: 1 rich
All others: Index
⑨ Except Calif. and High Altitude: 0.126
Calif.: 0.120
High Altitude: 0.078
⑩ 8-304, except High Altitude: Index
8-360, except High Altitude: 1 rich
High Altitude: 2 rich
⑪ Except Calif. 8-304 and High Altitude 8-360: 1,600
Calif. 8-304 and High Altitude 8-360: 1,800
⑫ Except High Altitude: 0.250
High Altitude: 0.170 min.
⑬ Except High Altitude: 0.136
High Altitude: 0.089
⑭ MT: 1,500
AT: 1,600

Autolite 4350

Engine	Years	Float Level (in.)	Aux. Inlet (in.)	Fast Idle Cam Setting (in.)	Fast Idle rpm	Choke Unloader (in.)	Initial Choke Valve Clearance (in.)	Automatic Choke Setting
8-401	1975–76	0.050	0.900	0.135	1,600	0.325	0.130	2 rich

Holley-Weber 5210

Engine	Years	Float Level (in.)	Initial Choke Valve Clearance (in.)	Fast Idle Cam Setting (in.)	Choke Unloader (in.)	Fast Idle Speed (rpm)	Choke Cover Setting
4-121	1977–78	0.420	①	②	0.300	1,800	③
	1979	0.420	④	⑤	0.300	1,800	③

① MT, except High Altitude: 0.191
High Altitude w/MT: 0.180
AT: 0.202
② MT, except High Altitude: 0.193
High Altitude w/MT: 0.177
AT: 0.204
③ Except High Altitude: 1 rich
High Altitude: Index
④ MT, except High Altitude: 0.266
High Altitude w/MT: 0.177
AT: 0.191
⑤ MT, except High Altitude: 0.191
High Altitude w/MT: 0.173
AT, except Calif.: 0.204
Calif. w/AT: 0.193

Chassis Electrical

UNDERSTANDING AND TROUBLESHOOTING ELECTRICAL SYSTEMS

Electrical problems generally fall into one of three areas:

1. The component that is not functioning is not receiving current.
2. The component itself is not functioning.
3. The component is not properly grounded.

Problems that fall into the first category are by far the most complicated. It is the current supply system to the component which contains all the switches, relays, fuses, etc.

The electrical system can be checked with a test light and a jumper wire. A test light is a device that looks like a pointed screwdriver with a wire attached to it. It has a light bulb in its handle. A jumper wire is a piece of insulated wire with an alligator clip attached to each end. To check the system you must follow the wiring diagram of the vehicle being worked on. A wiring diagram is a road map of the car's electrical system.

If a light bulb is not working, you must follow a systematic plan to determine which of the three causes is the problem.

1. Turn on the switch that controls the inoperable bulb.
2. Disconnect the power supply wire from the bulb.
3. Attach the ground wire on the test light to a good metal ground.
4. Touch the probe end of the test light to the end of the power supply wire that was disconnected from the bulb. If the bulb is receiving current, the test light will glow.

NOTE: *If the bulb is one which works only when the ignition key is turned on (turn signal), make sure the key is turned on.*

5. If the test light does not go on, then the problem is in the circuit between the battery and the bulb. As mentioned before, this includes all the switches, fuses, and relays in the system. Turn to the wiring diagram and find the bulb on the diagram. Follow the wire that runs back to the battery. The problem is an open circuit between the battery and the bulb. If the fuse is blown and, when replaced, immediately blows again, there is a short circuit in the system which must be located and repaired. If there is a switch in the system, bypass it with a jumper wire. This is done by connecting one end of the jumper wire to the power supply wire into the switch and the other end of the jumper wire to the wire coming out of the switch. Again, consult the wiring diagram. If the test light lights with the jumper wire installed, the switch or whatever was bypassed is defective.

NOTE: *Never substitute the jumper wire for the bulb, as the bulb is the component required to use the power from the source.*

6. If the bulb in the test light goes on, then the current is getting to the bulb that is not working in the car. This eliminates the first of the three possible causes. Connect the power supply wire and connect a jumper wire from the bulb to a good metal ground. Do this with the switch which controls the bulb turned on, and also the ignition switch turned on if it is required for the light to work. If the bulb works with the jumper wire installed, then it has a bad ground. This is usually caused by the metal area on which the bulb mounts to the car being coated with some type of foreign matter.

7. If neither test located the source of the trouble, then the light bulb itself is defective.

The above test procedure can be applied to any of the components of the chassis electrical system by substituting the component that is not working for the light bulb. Remember that for any electrical system to work, all connections must be clean and tight.

Troubleshooting Basic Turn Signal and Flasher Problems

Most problems in the turn signals or flasher system can be reduced to defective flashers or bulbs, which are easily replaced. Occasionally, problems in the turn signals are traced to the switch in the steering column, which will require professional service.

F = Front   R = Rear   • = Lights off   ○ = Lights on

Problem	Solution
Turn signals light, but do not flash	• Replace the flasher
No turn signals light on either side	• Check the fuse. Replace if defective. • Check the flasher by substitution • Check for open circuit, short circuit or poor ground
Both turn signals on one side don't work	• Check for bad bulbs • Check for bad ground in both housings
One turn signal light on one side doesn't work	• Check and/or replace bulb • Check for corrosion in socket. Clean contacts. • Check for poor ground at socket
Turn signal flashes too fast or too slow	• Check any bulb on the side flashing too fast. A heavy-duty bulb is probably installed in place of a regular bulb. • Check the bulb flashing too slow. A standard bulb was probably installed in place of a heavy-duty bulb. • Check for loose connections or corrosion at the bulb socket
Indicator lights don't work in either direction	• Check if the turn signals are working • Check the dash indicator lights • Check the flasher by substitution
One indicator light doesn't light	• On systems with 1 dash indicator: See if the lights work on the same side. Often the filaments have been reversed in systems combining stoplights with taillights and turn signals. Check the flasher by substitution • On systems with 2 indicators: Check the bulbs on the same side Check the indicator light bulb Check the flasher by substitution

Troubleshooting Basic Lighting Problems

Problem	Cause	Solution
Lights		
One or more lights don't work, but others do	· Defective bulb(s) · Blown fuse(s) · Dirty fuse clips or light sockets · Poor ground circuit	· Replace bulb(s) · Replace fuse(s) · Clean connections · Run ground wire from light socket housing to car frame
Lights burn out quickly	· Incorrect voltage regulator setting or defective regulator · Poor battery/alternator connections	· Replace voltage regulator · Check battery/alternator connections
Lights go dim	· Low/discharged battery · Alternator not charging · Corroded sockets or connections · Low voltage output	· Check battery · Check drive belt tension; repair or replace alternator · Clean bulb and socket contacts and connections · Replace voltage regulator
Lights flicker	· Loose connection · Poor ground · Circuit breaker operating (short circuit)	· Tighten all connections · Run ground wire from light housing to car frame · Check connections and look for bare wires
Lights "flare"—Some flare is normal on acceleration—if excessive, see "Lights Burn Out Quickly"	· High voltage setting	· Replace voltage regulator
Lights glare—approaching drivers are blinded	· Lights adjusted too high · Rear springs or shocks sagging · Rear tires soft	· Have headlights aimed · Check rear springs/shocks · Check/correct rear tire pressure
Turn Signals		
Turn signals don't work in either direction	· Blown fuse · Defective flasher · Loose connection	· Replace fuse · Replace flasher · Check/tighten all connections
Right (or left) turn signal only won't work	· Bulb burned out · Right (or left) indicator bulb burned out · Short circuit	· Replace bulb · Check/replace indicator bulb · Check/repair wiring
Flasher rate too slow or too fast	· Incorrect wattage bulb · Incorrect flasher	· Flasher bulb · Replace flasher (use a variable load flasher if you pull a trailer)
Indicator lights do not flash (burn steadily)	· Burned out bulb · Defective flasher	· Replace bulb · Replace flasher
Indicator lights do not light at all	· Burned out indicator bulb · Defective flasher	· Replace indicator bulb · Replace flasher

HEATING AND AIR CONDITIONING

The following procedures for servicing the components of the heater apply to those cars which have air conditioning as well as those without it.

Blower Motor

REMOVAL AND INSTALLATION

Matador

1. Disconnect the motor wires, inside the engine compartment.

2. Remove the attaching screws from the motor mounting plate.

3. Remove the motor and fan assembly.

Gremlin
Hornet
Concord
Spirit
Eagle

1. Drain about two quarts of coolant from the radiator.

CAUTION: *When draining the coolant, keep in mind that cats and dogs are attracted by*

Troubleshooting Basic Dash Gauge Problems

Problem	Cause	Solution
Coolant Temperature Gauge		
Gauge reads erratically or not at all	• Loose or dirty connections • Defective sending unit • Defective gauge	• Clean/tighten connections • Bi-metal gauge: remove the wire from the sending unit. Ground the wire for an instant. If the gauge registers, replace the sending unit. • Magnetic gauge: disconnect the wire at the sending unit. With ignition ON gauge should register COLD. Ground the wire; gauge should register HOT.
Ammeter Gauge—Turn Headlights ON (do not start engine). Note reaction		
Ammeter shows charge Ammeter shows discharge Ammeter does not move	• Connections reversed on gauge • Ammeter is OK • Loose connections or faulty wiring • Defective gauge	• Reinstall connections • Nothing • Check/correct wiring • Replace gauge
Oil Pressure Gauge		
Gauge does not register or is inaccurate	• On mechanical gauge, Bourdon tube may be bent or kinked • Low oil pressure • Defective gauge • Defective wiring • Defective sending unit	• Check tube for kinks or bends preventing oil from reaching the gauge • Remove sending unit. Idle the engine briefly. If no oil flows from sending unit hole, problem is in engine. • Remove the wire from the sending unit and ground it for an instant with the ignition ON. A good gauge will go to the top of the scale. • Check the wiring to the gauge. If it's OK and the gauge doesn't register when grounded, replace the gauge. • If the wiring is OK and the gauge functions when grounded, replace the sending unit
All Gauges		
All gauges do not operate All gauges read low or erratically All gauges pegged	• Blown fuse • Defective instrument regulator • Defective or dirty instrument voltage regulator • Loss of ground between instrument voltage regulator and car • Defective instrument regulator	• Replace fuse • Replace instrument voltage regulator • Clean contacts or replace • Check ground • Replace regulator
Warning Lights		
Light(s) do not come on when ignition is ON, but engine is not started	• Defective bulb • Defective wire • Defective sending unit	• Replace bulb • Check wire from light to sending unit • Disconnect the wire from the sending unit and ground it. Replace the sending unit if the light comes on with the ignition ON.
Light comes on with engine running	• Problem in individual system • Defective sending unit	• Check system • Check sending unit (see above)

Troubleshooting the Heater

Problem	Cause	Solution
Blower motor will not turn at any speed	• Blown fuse • Loose connection • Defective ground • Faulty switch • Faulty motor • Faulty resistor	• Replace fuse • Inspect and tighten • Clean and tighten • Replace switch • Replace motor • Replace resistor
Blower motor turns at one speed only	• Faulty switch • Faulty resistor	• Replace switch • Replace resistor
Blower motor turns but does not circulate air	• Intake blocked • Fan not secured to the motor shaft	• Clean intake • Tighten security
Heater will not heat	• Coolant does not reach proper temperature • Heater core blocked internally • Heater core air-bound • Blend-air door not in proper position	• Check and replace thermostat if necessary • Flush or replace core if necessary • Purge air from core • Adjust cable
Heater will not defrost	• Control cable adjustment incorrect • Defroster hose damaged	• Adjust control cable • Replace defroster hose

Troubleshooting Basic Windshield Wiper Problems

Problem	Cause	Solution
Electric Wipers		
Wipers do not operate— Wiper motor heats up or hums	• Internal motor defect • Bent or damaged linkage • Arms improperly installed on linking pivots	• Replace motor • Repair or replace linkage • Position linkage in park and reinstall wiper arms
Wipers do not operate— No current to motor	• Fuse or circuit breaker blown • Loose, open or broken wiring • Defective switch • Defective or corroded terminals • No ground circuit for motor or switch	• Replace fuse or circuit breaker • Repair wiring and connections • Replace switch • Replace or clean terminals • Repair ground circuits
Wipers do not operate— Motor runs	• Linkage disconnected or broken	• Connect wiper linkage or replace broken linkage
Vacuum Wipers		
Wipers do not operate	• Control switch or cable inoperative • Loss of engine vacuum to wiper motor (broken hoses, low engine vacuum, defective vacuum/fuel pump) • Linkage broken or disconnected • Defective wiper motor	• Repair or replace switch or cable • Check vacuum lines, engine vacuum and fuel pump • Repair linkage • Replace wiper motor
Wipers stop on engine acceleration	• Leaking vacuum hoses • Dry windshield • Oversize wiper blades • Defective vacuum/fuel pump	• Repair or replace hoses • Wet windshield with washers • Replace with proper size wiper blades • Replace pump

the ethylene glycol antifreeze, and are quite likely to drink any that is left in an uncovered container or in puddles on the ground. This will prove fatal in sufficient quantity. Always drain the coolant into a sealable container.

Coolant should be reused unless it is contaminated or several years old.

2. Disconnect the heater hoses from the heater core tubes the plug the core tubes.

3. Disconnect the blower wires.

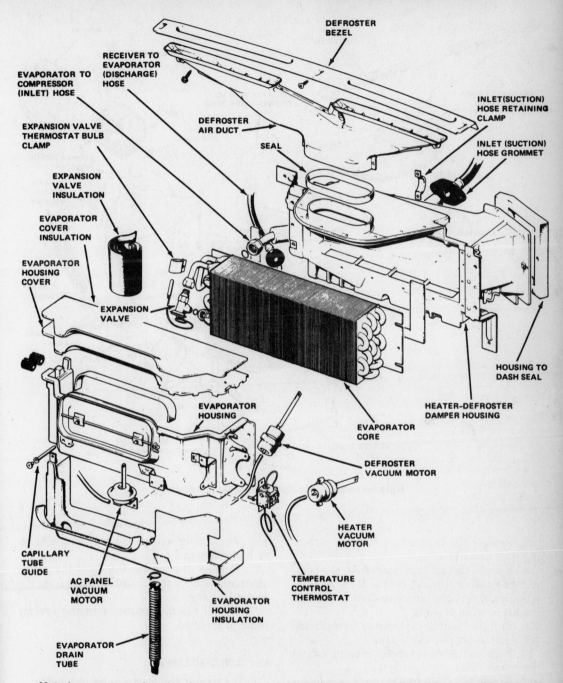

Matador evaporator housing, heater core and defroster/damper on models with air conditioning

4. Remove the cover retaining nut and remove the motor and fan assembly.

5. To install, reverse the removal procedure.

Pacer

CARS NOT EQUIPPED WITH AIR CONDITIONING

1. Disconnect the negative battery cable.

2. Remove the right side windshield finish molding.

3. Remove the instrument panel crash pad.

4. Remove the right scuff plate and cowl trim panel.

5. Remove the lower instrument panel-to-right A-pillar attaching screws.

6. Pull the instrument panel to the rear and replace the lower attaching screw in the right A-pillar. Allow the instrument panel to rest on the screw.

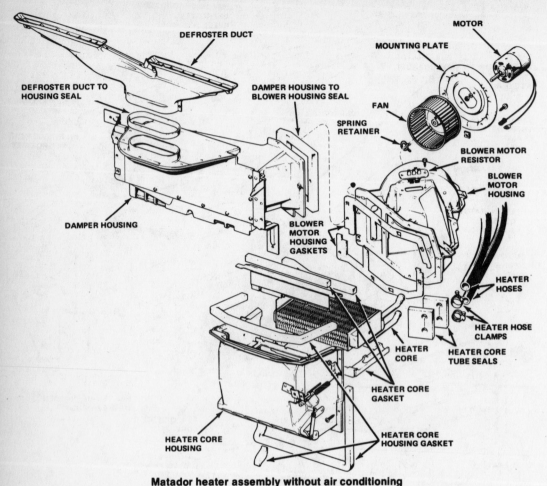

Matador heater assembly without air conditioning

7. Remove the heater core housing attaching nuts and screw.

8. Remove the vacuum hoses from the heater core housing clip and set the lines aside.

9. Disconnect the blend-air door cable from the heater core housing.

10. Pull the heater core housing forward and set atop the upper control arm.

11. Remove the blower motor ground wire at the relay.

12. Disconnect the wires at the blower motor resistor.

13. Remove the blower motor housing brace.

14. Loosen the heater housing-to-dash panel attaching nuts.

15. Pull the blower housing to the rear and downward.

16. Disconnect the vacuum hoses from the vacuum motors.

17. Remove the blower housing.

18. Remove the blower housing cover.

19. Disconnect the white blower wire inside the housing.

20. Remove the blower motor mounting plate-to-housing screws and remove the blower motor assembly.

21. Remove the blower fan from the motor shaft and remove the mounting plate from the motor housing.

22. Install the blower motor in the reverse order of removal.

AIR CONDITIONED CARS

1. Disconnect the negative battery cable.

2. Remove the right scuff plate and cowl trim panel.

3. Remove the radio overlay cover.

4. Remove the instrument panel crash pad.

5. Remove the instrument panel-to-right A-pillar attaching screws.

6. Remove the two upper instrument panel-to-lower instrument panel attaching screws above the glove box.

7. Disconnect the blend-air door cable from the heater core housing.

8. Remove the housing brace-to-floorpan screw.

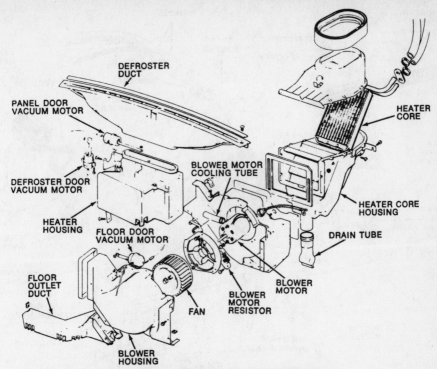

Pacer heater assembly without air conditioning

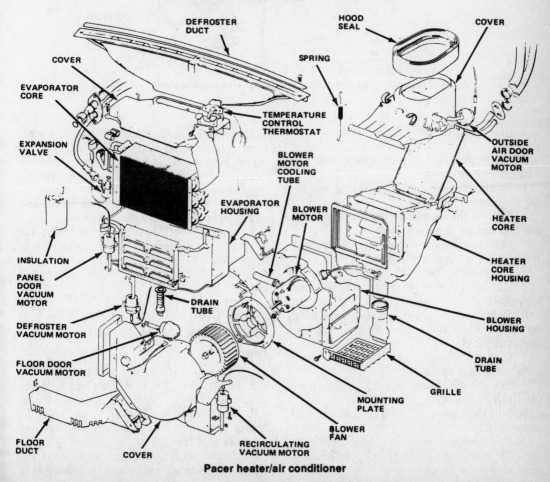

Pacer heater/air conditioner

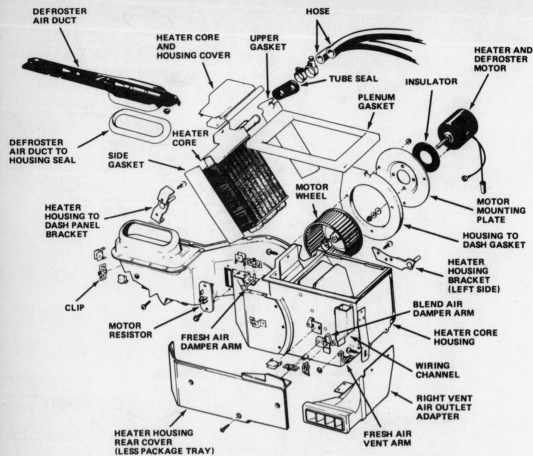

Heater assembly without air conditioning for all except Matador and Pacer

9. Disconnect the wire at the blower motor resistor.

10. Disconnect the vacuum hoses from the vacuum motors.

11. Remove the heater core housing attaching nuts and screw.

12. Remove the vacuum hoses from the housing clip and set the lines aside.

13. Pull the heater core housing forward and set it atop the upper control arm.

14. Remove the floor outlet duct.

15. Disconnect the wires from the blower motor relay.

16. Remove the blower housing attaching screw located in the engine compartment on the dash panel.

17. Loosen the evaporator housing-to-dash panel attaching screw.

18. Remove the blower housing-to-dash panel attaching screw.

19. Pull the blower housing to the rear and downward.

20. Pull the right side of the instrument panel to the rear and remove the blower housing from under the panel.

21. Remove the floor door vacuum motor attaching screws and motor to gain access to the blower housing cover attaching screws.

22. Remove the blower housing cover attaching screws and remove the cover.

23. Remove the blower motor mounting plate and remove the blower motor assembly.

24. Remove the blower fan from the motor shaft and the mounting plate from the body of the motor.

25. Install the motor in reverse order of removal.

Heater Core

REMOVAL AND INSTALLATION

Matador

1. Disconnect the negative battery cable.

2. Drain about 2 quarts of coolant from the cooling system.

3. Disconnect the heater hoses from the heater core in the engine compartment and plug the core tubes.

4. On air conditioned cars, disconnect the blend-air damper cable at the heater core

housing and remove the fuse panel. On non-A/
C cars, disconnect the blend-air damper door
and fresh air door cables.

5. Remove the lower instrument finish panel and remove the glove box door and liner.

6. Remove the right windshield pillar and
corner finish moldings for access to the upper
right heater core housing mounting screws.

7. On air conditioned cars, remove the vacuum motor hoses.

8. Remove the remaining heater core housing attaching screws.

9. On air conditioned cars, remove the capscrew retaining the instrument panel to the
right body pillar. Pull the right side of the instrument panel slightly rearward.

10. Remove the heater core housing and
heater core. Remove the heater core from the
housing.

11. Install the heater core and housing in the
reverse order of removal.

Gremlin
Hornet
Concord
Spirit
Eagle

1. Disconnect the negative battery cable
and drain 2 qts. of coolant.

2. Disconnect the heater hoses and plug the
hoses and core fittings.

3. Disconnect the blower wires and remove
the motor and fan assembly.

4. Remove the housing attaching nut from
the stud in the engine compartment.

5. Remove the package shelf, if so equipped.

6. Disconnect the wire at the resistor, located below the glove box.

7. Remove the instrument panel center bezel, air outlet, and duct on A/C models.

8. Disconnect the air and defroster cables
from the damper levers.

9. Remove the right side windshield pillar
molding, the instrument panel upper sheet
metal screws and the cap screw at the right
door post.

10. Remove the right cowl trim panel and
door sill plate.

11. Remove the right kick panel and heater
housing attaching screws.

12. Pull the right side of the instrument panel outward slightly and remove the housing.

13. Remove the core, defroster and blower
housing.

14. Remove the core from the housing.

15. Installation is the reverse of removal.

Pacer

1. Drain about two quarts of coolant from
the radiator.

2. Disconnect the heater hoses from the

heater core tubes and install plugs in the heater hoses.

3. Remove the vacuum hoses from the heater core housing cover clip and move the lines
aside.

4. Remove the heater core housing cover
screws.

5. Disconnect the overcenter spring from
the cover and remove the cover.

6. Remove the heater core-to-housing attaching screws and remove the heater core.

7. Install the heater core in the reverse order of removal.

Control Head
REMOVAL AND INSTALLATION
Matador
1975-77

1. Disconnect the battery ground cable.

2. Remove the instrument cluster bezel.

3. Remove the clock or clock opening cover.

4. If equipped, remove the fuel economy
gauge.

5. Remove the control head attaching
screws.

6. Pull the control head out slightly and disconnect the cables, vacuum hoses and wires.
It's a good idea to label the hoses and wires so
that you'll remember where they go.

7. Installation is the reverse of removal. Adjust the cables as necessary.

1978

1. Disconnect the battery ground cable.

2. Remove the right side remote mirror
control.

3. Remove the instrument cluster bezel.

4. Remove the clock or clock opening cover.

5. If equipped, remove the fuel economy
gauge.

6. Remove the control head attaching
screws.

7. Pull the control head out slightly and disconnect the cables, vacuum hoses and wires.
It's a good idea to label the hoses and wires so
that you'll remember where they go.

8. Installation is the reverse of removal. Adjust the cables as necessary.

NOTE: *The fan switch attaching screw is accessible on the back of the panel after panel
removal.*

1975–78 Gremlin
1975–77 Hornet
1978 Concord
1978 AMX
WITHOUT AIR CONDITIONING

1. Disconnect the battery ground cable.

2. Remove the instrument panel center
housing.

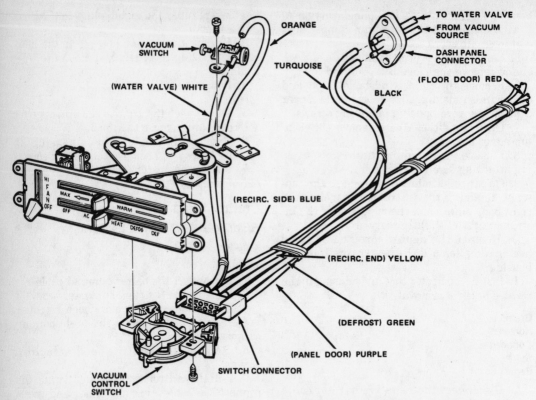

Control head and vacuum lines for 1975–78 models, with air conditioning, except Pacer

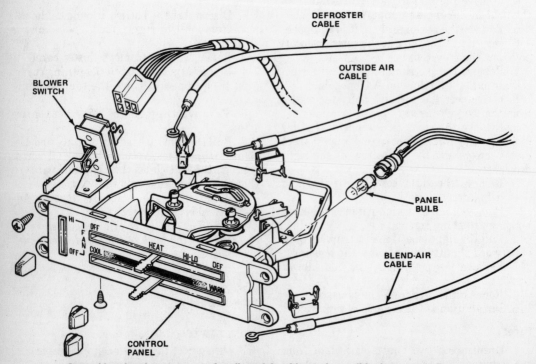

Control head and components for all models without air conditioning, except Pacer

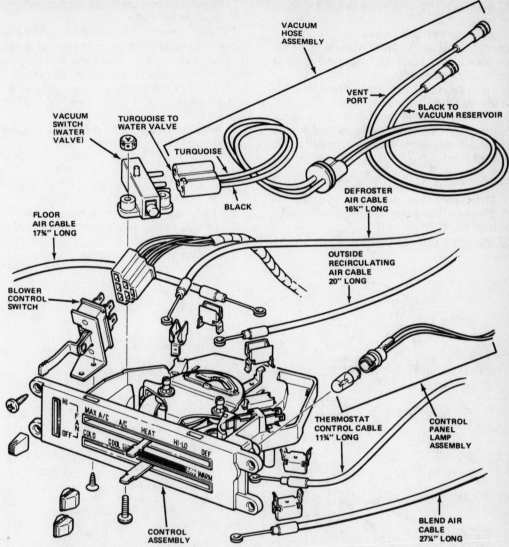

Control head and vacuum components for 1979–86 models with air conditioning, except Pacer

3. Remove the radio.

4. Remove the control head attaching screws.

5. Pull the control head out slightly and disconnect the cables, vacuum hoses and wires. It's a good idea to label the hoses and wires so that you'll remember where they go.

6. Installation is the reverse of removal. Adjust the cables as necessary.

WITH AIR CONDITIONING

1. Disconnect the battery ground cable.

2. Remove the instrument panel center housing.

3. Remove the AC thermostat control knob and attaching nut.

4. Remove the control head attaching screws.

5. Remove the center upper discharge duct.

6. Remove the radio.

7. Pull the control head out slightly and disconnect the cables, vacuum hoses and wires. It's a good idea to label the hoses and wires so that you'll remember where they go.

8. Installation is the reverse of removal. Adjust the cables as necessary.

1979–80 AMX
1979–83 Spirit
1979–83 Concord
1980–86 Eagle

WITHOUT AIR CONDITIONING

1. Disconnect the battery ground cable.

2. Remove the instrument panel center housing.

3. Remove the control head attaching screws.

4. Pull the control head out slightly and disconnect the cables, vacuum hoses and wires. It's a good idea to label the hoses and wires so that you'll remember where they go.

5. Installation is the reverse of removal. Adjust the cables as necessary.

NOTE: *On 1980–86 models, the control cables must be attached with the colored tape in the center of the clips that are attached to the control head.*

WITH AIR CONDITIONING

1. Disconnect the battery ground cable.

2. Remove the instrument panel center housing.

3. Remove the control head attaching screws.

4. Remove the center upper discharge duct.

5. Remove the radio.

6. Pull the control head out slightly and disconnect the cables, vacuum hoses and wires. It's a good idea to label the hoses and wires so that you'll remember where they go.

NOTE: *The fan switch attaching screw is accessible on the back of the panel after panel removal.*

7. Installation is the reverse of removal. Adjust the cables as necessary.

Pacer

1977–78

1. Disconnect the battery ground cable.

2. Remove the instrument panel center housing.

3. Remove the radio.

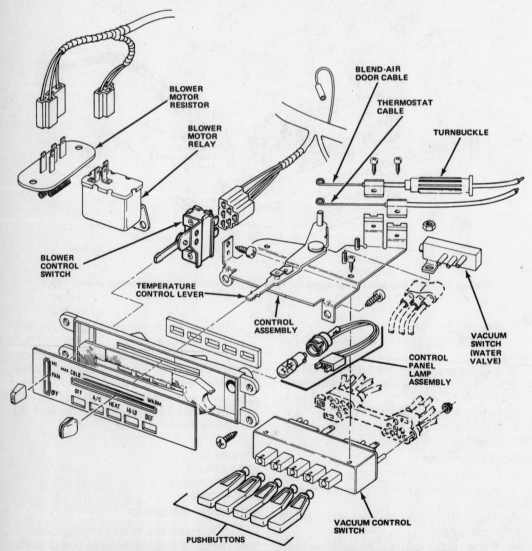

Control head and components for Pacer with air conditioning, through 1979

4. Remove the control head attaching screws.

5. Pull the control head out slightly and disconnect the cables, vacuum hoses and wires. It's a good idea to label the hoses and wires so that you'll remember where they go.

6. Installation is the reverse of removal. Adjust the cables as necessary.

1979–80

1. Disconnect the battery ground cable.
2. Remove the radio.
3. Remove the control panel attaching screws.
4. Pull the control panel out and disconnect the vacuum hoses, wires and cables. Tag them for proper installation.
5. Installation is the reverse of removal. Adjust the cables as necessary.

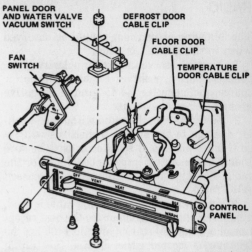

Control head for Pacer without air conditioning, through 1979

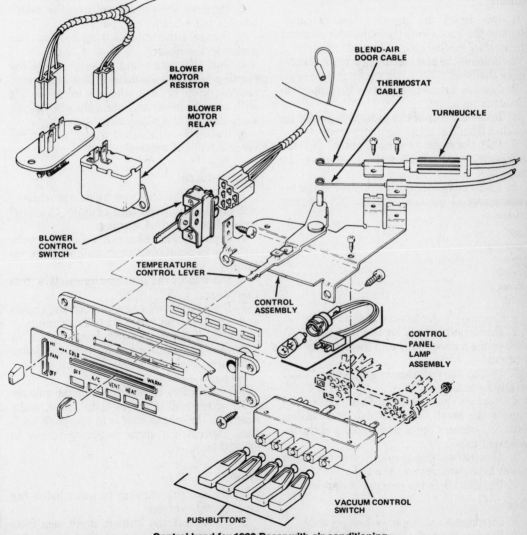

Control head for 1980 Pacer with air conditioning

RADIO

The following precautions should be observed when working on a car radio:

1. Always observe the proper polarity of the connections; i.e., positive (+) goes to the power source and negative (–) to ground (negative ground electrical system).

2. Never operate the radio without a speaker; damage to the output transistors will result. If a replacement speaker is used, be sure that it is the correct impedance (ohms) for the radio. The impedance is stamped on the case of AMC radios.

3. If a new antenna or antenna cable is used, adjust the antenna trimmer fro the best reception of a weak AM station around 1400 kc; the trimmer is located either behind the tuning knob or on the bottom of the radio case.

REMOVAL AND INSTALLATION

Matador

1. Disconnect the negative battery cable. Remove the knobs from the radio and unfasten the control shafts retaining nuts.

2. Remove the bezel securing screws, and remove the bezel.

3. Loosen, but do not remove, the upper radio securing screw.

4. Raise the rear of the radio to separate its bracket from the upper securing screw.

5. Pull the radio forward slightly, and disconnect all of the leads from it. Remove the radio.

6. Radio installation is performed in the reverse order of removal. Adjust the antenna trimmer.

AMX
Concord
Eagle
Gremlin
Hornet
Spirit

1. Disconnect the battery ground cable.

2. On Gremlins and Hornets through 1977, remove the package tray and the ash tray and bracket.

3. Pull off the radio knobs and remove shaft retaining nuts.

4. Remove the bezel retaining screws and remove the bezel. On 1978 and later models with A/C, remove the center housing of the instrument panel.

5. Disconnect the speaker, antenna, and power leads, and remove the radio.

6. Installation is the reverse of removal.

Pacer

1. Disconnect the negative battery cable.

2. Remove the radio knobs, attaching nuts, cluster bezel, and overlay cover.

3. Loosen the radio-to-instrument panel attaching screw.

4. Lift the rear of the radio and pull forward slightly. Disconnect the electrical connections and the antenna and remove the radio.

5. Installation is the reverse of removal.

WINDSHIELD WIPERS

Motor

REMOVAL AND INSTALLATION

AMX
Concord
Eagle
Gremlin
Hornet
Matador Sedan and Wagon
Spirit

1. Remove the wire arms and blades.

2. Remove the screws holding the motor adapter plate to the dash panel.

3. Separate the wiper wiring harness connector at the motor.

4. Pull the motor and linkage out of the opening to expose the drive link-to-crank stud retaining clip. Raise up the lock tab of the clip with a screwdriver and slide the clip off the stud. Remove the wiper motor assembly.

5. Install the windshield wiper motor in the reverse order of removal.

Matador Coupe

1. Remove the wire arm/blade assemblies.

2. Open the hood and remove the cowl screen from the cowl opening.

3. Separate the linkage drive arm from the motor arm crankpin, by unfastening the retaining clip.

4. Disconnect the two multiconnectors from the motor.

5. Remove the wiper motor securing screws and withdraw the motor from the opening.

NOTE: *If the output arm hangs up on the firewall panel during motor removal, rotate the arm clockwise by hand, so that it clears the panel opening.*

6. Installation is performed in the reverse order of removal. Prior to installation, make sure that the output arm is in the 'park' position. Tighten the motor retaining screws to 90–120 in.lb.

Pacer

1. Remove the vacuum canister mounting bracket and canister.

2. Disconnect the linkage drive arm from the motor output arm crankpin by removing the retaining clip.

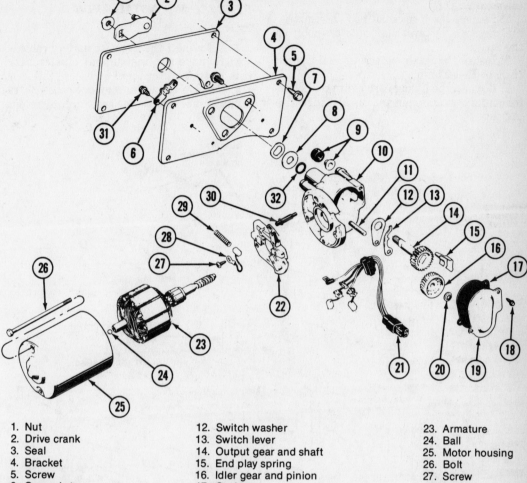

1. Nut
2. Drive crank
3. Seal
4. Bracket
5. Screw
6. Ground strap
7. Spring washer
8. Plain washer
9. Grommet
10. Gear housing
11. Shaft
12. Switch washer
13. Switch lever
14. Output gear and shaft
15. End play spring
16. Idler gear and pinion
17. Gasket
18. Screw
19. Cover
20. Push nut
21. Brushes and harness
22. End head
23. Armature
24. Ball
25. Motor housing
26. Bolt
27. Screw
28. Brush
29. Spring
30. Parking lever pin
31. Screw
32. Seal

Wiper motor and transmission

3. On vehicles equipped with air conditioning:

a. Remove the two nuts on the left side of the heater housing.

b. Remove the one nut on the right side on the heater housing.

c. Remove the screw from the heater housing support.

4. On vehicles not equipped with air conditioning:

a. Remove the two nuts and one screw on the left side of the heater housing.

b. Remove the one nut on the right side of the heater housing.

c. Remove the screw from the heater housing support. Pull the heater housing forward.

5. Remove the wiper motor mounting plate attaching screws and remove the wiper motor assembly from the cowl.

6. Disconnect the two wire connectors from the wiper motor.

7. Remove the wiper motor attaching screws and remove the wiper motor.

8. Install the wiper motor in the reverse order of removal.

Wiper Linkage

REMOVAL AND INSTALLATION

1. Remove the wiper arms and blades.

2. Remove the screws retaining the right and left pivot shaft bodies to the cowl.

3. Disconnect the linkage drive arm from

the motor output arm crankpin by removing the retaining clip.

4. Remove the pivot shaft body assembly.

5. Position the pivot shaft body assembly on the car.

6. Install the retaining screws and tighten them to 50–70 in.lb.

7. Connect the linkage drive arm to the motor output arm crankpin and install the retaining clip.

INSTRUMENT CLUSTER
REMOVAL AND INSTALLATION

Pacer

1. Disconnect the negative battery cable.

2. Remove the instrument cluster bezel with a straight, firm pull.

3. Remove the radio control knobs and retaining nuts. Remove the radio overlay retaining screws.

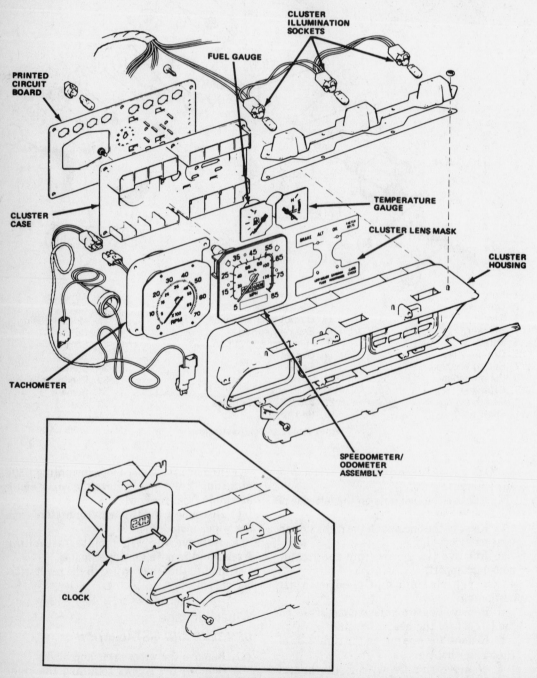

Pacer instrument cluster

4. Remove the headlight switch overlay retaining screws. Pull the headlight switch overlay back and disconnect the speedometer cable.

5. Remove the instrument cluster retaining screws. Tilt the cluster down and disconnect the instrument panel wire harness connectors.

6. If equipped with automatic transmission, disconnect the gear selector dial cable from the steering column.

7. Remove the cluster assembly.

8. Reverse the above procedure to install.

1975–76 Gremlin and Hornet

1. Disconnect the battery negative cable.

2. Cover the steering column with a cloth to prevent scratching of painted surfaces.

3. Remove the package tray (if equipped) and disconnect the speedometer cable.

4. Remove the control knobs and retaining nuts from the wiper control and headlight switches.

5. Remove the screws attaching the instrument cluster housing to the instrument panel.

6. Rotate the instrument cluster forward, disconnect all electrical connections and lamps, disconnect the vacuum line from the fuel economy gauge (if equipped), and remove the cluster.

7. Position the instrument cluster on the instrument panel and connect all electrical connections and lamps, connect the vacuum line to the fuel economy gauge (if equipped).

8. Install the cluster housing-to-instrument panel attaching screws.

9. Install the wiper control and headlight switch retaining nuts and control knobs.

10. Connect the speedometer cable and install the package tray.

11. Remove the protective cloth cover from the steering column.

12. Connect the battery negative cable.

1975–76 Matador

1. Remove the radio control knobs and attaching nuts.

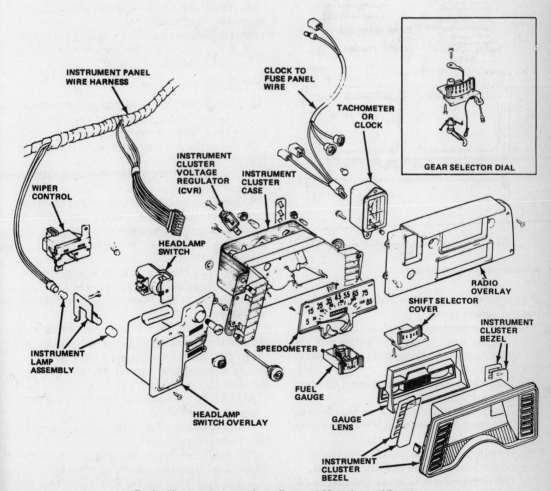

Typical instrument panel on all except Matador and Pacer

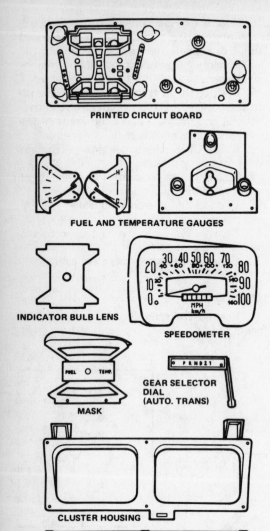

PRINTED CIRCUIT BOARD

FUEL AND TEMPERATURE GAUGES

INDICATOR BULB LENS

SPEEDOMETER

MASK

GEAR SELECTOR DIAL (AUTO. TRANS)

CLUSTER HOUSING

LENS

Matador instrument cluster

2. Remove the remote mirror control attaching nut (if equipped).

3. Remove the ten bezel attaching screws.

4. Tilt the bezel toward the interior of the car and disconnect all electrical connections.

5. Remove the bezel.

6. Remove the clock, clock opening cover, or fuel economy gauge.

7. Reach through the clock access opening and disconnect the speedometer cable from the cluster.

8. If equipped with automatic transmission, remove the lower instrument finish panel.

9. Disconnect the shift quadrant control cable from the steering column (if equipped).

10. Remove the instrument cluster mounting screws.

11. Tilt the cluster toward interior of car, disconnect all electrical connections, and remove the instrument cluster.

12. Position the instrument cluster in the panel and connect all electrical connections.

13. Install the cluster mounting screws.

14. Connect the shift quadrant control cable (if equipped).

NOTE: *Adjust the shift quadrant cable as outlined in the Torque-Command Transmission section.*

15. Install the lower instrument finish panel (if removed).

16. Reach through the clock access opening and connect the speedometer cable.

17. Install the clock, clock opening cover, or fuel economy gauge.

18. Position the bezel and connect all electrical connections.

19. Install the ten bezel attaching screws.

20. Install the radio attaching nuts and control knobs.

21. Install the remote mirror control attaching nut (if equipped).

NOTE: *The control knob aligning tabs must fit in the control shaft slots when installing the control knobs.*

1977 Gremlin and Hornet

1. Disconnect the battery negative cable.

2. Remove the package tray (if equipped) to gain access to the speedometer cable.

3. Cover the steering column with a cloth to prevent scratches.

4. Disconnect the speedometer cable (screw-on type).

5. Remove the top and side screws from the instrument panel and tilt the cluster forward slightly to gain access for disconnecting the headlamp switch and the wiper control harness connectors.

NOTE: *Lift the two locking tabs to disconnect the headlamp switch connector.*

6. Disconnect the fiber-optic ashtray lamp, if equipped.

7. Disconnect the harness connectors and remove the instrument cluster assembly.

8. Position the instrument cluster on the instrument panel and connect all the electrical connections and lamps.

NOTE: *Be sure to connect the headlamp switch ground wire.*

9. Connect the fiber optic ashtray lamp to the cluster, if removed.

10. Install the cluster housing to the instrument panel with the attaching screws.

11. Connect the speedometer cable and install the package tray.

12. Remove the protective cloth cover from the steering column.

13. Connect the battery negative cable.

14. Reset the clock, if equipped.

1977–78 Matador

1. Remove the radio control knobs and attaching nuts.

2. Remove the right remote mirror control attaching nut, if equipped.

3. Remove the bezel attaching screws.

4. Tilt the bezel toward interior of car and disconnect all electrical connections.

5. Remove the bezel. Cover the steering column with a cloth to prevent scratching the column.

6. Remove the clock housing attaching screws, pull the assembly away from the cluster, and disconnect the bulbs and electrical leads. Remove the assembly.

7. Using the clock access opening, disconnect the speedometer cable by depressing the locking tab and moving the cable away from the instrument cluster.

8. Disconnect the gear selector dial cable from the steering column.

9. Remove the cluster mounting screws and disconnect the electrical connections.

10. Remove the cluster.

11. Position the cluster and connect the electrical components.

12. Install the cluster mounting screws.

13. Connect the gear selector dial cable.

14. Connect the speedometer cable.

15. Connect the clock electrical connector and install the bulbs and clock (or cover).

16. Install the instrument cluster bezel.

17. Install the right mirror remote control, if removed.

18. Install the radio attaching nuts and control knobs.

19. Connect the battery negative cable.

20. Reset the clock, if equipped.

1978 Gremlin, Concord

1. Disconnect the battery negative cable.

2. Cover the steering column to protect against scratching.

3. Remove the bezel attaching screws across the top, above radio and behind the glove box door.

4. Tip the bezel outward at the top and disengage the tabs along the bottom edge.

5. Unplug the glove box lamp connector, if equipped.

6. Depress the speedometer cable locking tab and move the cable away from the cluster.

7. Push down on the three illumination lamp housings above the bezel until the lamp housings are clear from the instrument panel.

8. Disconnect the headlamp switch and wiper control connectors and the switch illumination lamp.

NOTE: *Lift the two locking tabs to disconnect the headlamp switch connector.*

9. Twist and remove the cluster illumination lamp sockets.

10. Disconnect the instrument cluster connectors.

11. Remove the clock or tachometer screws, if equipped. It is not necessary to remove the clock adjusting knob.

12. Disconnect the clock or tachometer feed wires from the circuit board, if equipped.

13. Remove the cluster housing and circuit board-to-bezel screws.

14. Remove the cluster housing and circuit board assembly from bezel. If equipped with a clock or tachometer, move it aside as required.

15. Position the instrument cluster on the instrument cluster bezel. Move the clock or tachometer aside as required.

16. Install the cluster housing mounting screws.

NOTE: *The clock ground wire terminal must contact the foil on the circuit board beneath the clock mounting boss.*

17. Connect the clock or tachometer feed wires to the circuit board, if removed.

18. Install the clock or tachometer screws.

19. Connect the instrument cluster connectors.

20. Install the cluster illumination lamp sockets.

21. Connect the headlamp and wiper switch connectors and the switch illumination lamp.

22. Align the tabs at the bottom of the bezel with the openings, and raise the bezel. It may be necessary to press down on the illumination housings for clearance. Do not push the bezel into the final position.

23. Connect the speedometer cable.

24. Connect the glove box lamp wires, if removed.

25. Push the bezel forward into the installed position and install the screws.

26. Remove the protective cloth, connect the battery and reset the clock, if equipped.

1979–86 All Models

1. Disconnect the battery negative cable.

2. Cover the steering column to protect against scratching.

3. Remove the lower steering column cover.

4. Unscrew the speedometer cable connector from the speedometer.

5. Remove the gear selector dial actuator cable from the steering column shift shroud, if the automobile is equipped with a column shift automatic transmission.

6. Remove the bezel attaching screws across the top, above the radio and behind the glove box door.

7. Tip the bezel outward at the top and disengage the tabs along the bottom edge.

8. Unplug the glove box lamp connector, if equipped.

9. Push down on the three illumination lamp housings above the bezel until the lamp housings clear the instrument panel.

10. Disconnect the headlamp switch and wiper control connectors and the switch illumination lamp.

NOTE: *Lift the two locking tabs to disconnect the headlamp switch connector.*

11. Twist and remove the cluster illumination lamp sockets.

12. Disconnect the instrument cluster connectors.

13. Remove the clock or tachometer screws, if equipped. It is not necessary to remove the clock adjusting knob.

14. Disconnect the clock or tachometer feed wires from the circuit board, if equipped.

15. Remove the cluster housing and circuit board-to-bezel screws.

16. Remove the cluster housing and circuit board assembly from the bezel. If equipped with a clock or tachometer, move it aside as required.

17. Position the instrument cluster on the instrument cluster bezel. Move the clock or tachometer aside as required.

18. Install the cluster housing mounting screws.

NOTE: *The clock ground and feed wire terminals must contact the foil beneath the circuit board mounting screws.*

19. Connect the clock or tachometer feed wires to the circuit board, if removed.

20. Install the clock or tachometer screws.

21. Connect the instrument cluster connectors.

22. Install the cluster illumination lamp sockets.

23. Connect the headlamp and wiper switch connectors and the switch illumination lamp.

24. If the automobile is equipped with a column shift automatic transmission, use a piece of wire to fish the gear selector dial actuator cable through the grommet in the instrument panel reinforcement and attach it to the shift column shroud. Adjust the cable, if necessary.

25. Align the tabs at the bottom of the bezel with the openings, and raise the bezel. It may be necessary to press down on the illumination housings for clearance. Do not push the bezel into the final position.

26. Connect the glove box lamp wires, if removed.

27. Push the bezel forward into the installed position and install the screws.

NOTE: *Make sure the gear selector dial actuator cable is adjusted in neutral.*

28. Connect the speedometer cable and tighten it securely.

29. Install the lower steering column cover.

30. Remove the protective cloth, connect the battery and reset the clock, if equipped.

SEAT BELT SYSTEMS

Disabling the Interlock System

Since the legal requirement for seat belt/starter interlock systems was dropped during the 1975 model year, those systems installed on cars built earlier may now be legally disconnected. However, the seat belt warning light is still required to operate.

1. Remove the pink wire and terminal from the two terminal connector at the emergency starter relay, located on the right inner fender panel, under the hood.

2. Cut off the pink wire close to the taped junction of the wire harness.

3. Remove the yellow wire and terminal.

4. Install the yellow wire into the two terminal connector at the location where the pink wire and terminal was removed from the three terminal connector at the starter relay.

5. From under the right side of the dash and along the right side of the glove box area, locate the interlock logic module and remove it from its bracket. Cut off the yellow with black tracer wire close to the taped junction of the wire harness and cut off the remaining end as close to the logic module as possible. Reinstall the logic module on its dash bracket.

6. The warning light should be off when the occupied seat belt is buckled and the car placed in gear with the ignition switch on.

NOTE: *Most models require the seating of both the driver and front seat passenger, prior to buckling of the belts or turning of the ignition system, due to the programming of the logic module for the seat belt warning light to go out. These series can be identified by a buff colored logic module. Other series are equipped with a green colored logic module which allows non-sequential operation and independent use of the seat belts.*

HEADLIGHTS

REMOVAL AND INSTALLATION

1. Remove the headlight cover (surrounding trim panel).

NOTE: *The screws directly above and to one side of the headlight are for adjusting the vertical and horizontal headlight aim. Don't confuse these with the headlight cover retaining screws.*

2. Loosen the screws holding the headlight retainer ring in place.

3. Rotate the retainer ring to disengage the ring from the screws. Remove the ring.

4. Pull the headlight out and pull the wire plug off the back.

There are currently only 3 types of headlights commonly in use on U.S. cars:

    a. Four lamp system high beam.

    b. Four lamp system combined high and low beam.

    c. Two lamp system combined high and low beam.

5. Push the plug onto the new headlight. Position the headlight. There are lugs on the headlight to make it impossible to put it in wrong.

6. Replace the retainer ring and tighten the screws.

7. Replace the headlight cover.

NOTE: *When aiming the headlights, each combined high and low beam should be within 6" (152.4mm) to the right of the vertical centerline of the light and within 2" (51mm) above or below the horizontal centerline, at a distance of 25 ft. (8m) The high beams of a four lamp system should be within 2" (51mm) below the horizontal centerline and within 6" (152.4mm) right or left from the vertical centerline. Some state inspection laws may not allow this much leeway in adjustment.*

PRINTED CIRCUIT BOARD

Current is supplied to the instruments and the instrument panel lights through a printed circuit which is attached to the rear of the instrument cluster. The disconnect plug is part of the panel wiring harness and connects to pins attached to the printed circuit. A keyway located on the printed circuit board insures that the plug is always mounted correctly.

CAUTION: *Never pry under the plug to remove it, or damage to the printed circuit will result.*

An instrument voltage regulator is wired in series with the gauges to supply a constant five volts to them. It is integral with the temperature gauge.

REMOVAL AND INSTALLATION

1. Disconnect the cable from the negative (–) battery terminal.

2. Cover the steering column with a clean cloth, so that it will not be scratched.

3. If equipped with a parcel shelf, unfasten the two screws which secure it at either end, remove the screws which secure it to the center support bracket and withdraw the shelf from underneath the instrument panel.

4. Working from underneath the dash, disconnect the speedometer cable.

5. Remove the knobs from the headlight and wiper switches.

6. Remove the 5 screws that are located around the cluster bezel and partially withdraw the cluster/bezel assembly from the panel.

7. Disconnect all of the wiring and lights from the back of the cluster and remove the cluster/bezel assembly the rest of the way.

8. Installation is performed in the reverse order of removal.

FUSE LINK

The fuse link is a short length of special, Hypalon (high temperature) insulated wire, integral with the engine compartment wiring harness and should not be confused with standard wire. It is several wire gauges smaller than the circuit which it protects. Under no circumstances should a fuse link replacement repair be made using a length of standard wire cut from bulk stock or from another wiring harness.

To repair any blown fuse link use the following procedure:

1. Determine which circuit is damaged, its location and the cause of the open fuse link. If the damaged fuse link is one of three fed by a common No. 10 or 12 gauge feed wire, determine the specific affected circuit.

2. Disconnect the negative battery cable.

3. Cut the damaged fuse link from the wiring harness and discard it. If the fuse link is one of three circuits fed by a single feed wire, cut it out of the harness at each splice end and discard it.

4. Identify and procure the proper fuse link and butt connectors for attaching the fuse link to the harness.

5. To repair any fuse link in a 3-link group with one feed:

    a. After cutting the open link out of the harness, cut each of the remaining undamaged fuse links close to the feed wire weld.

    b. Strip approximately ½" (12.7mm) of insulation from the detached ends of the two good fuse links. Then insert two wire ends into one end of a butt connector and carefully push one stripped end of the replacement

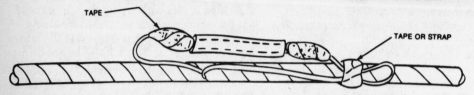

REMOVE EXISTING VINYL TUBE SHIELDING
REINSTALL OVER FUSE LINK BEFORE CRIMPING
FUSE LINK TO WIRE ENDS

TAPE

TAPE OR STRAP

TYPICAL REPAIR USING THE SPECIAL #17 GA. (9.00" LONG-YELLOW) FUSE LINK REQUIRED FOR THE AIR/COND. CIRCUITS

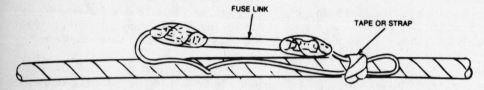

FUSE LINK

TAPE OR STRAP

TYPICAL REPAIR FOR ANY IN-LINE FUSE LINK USING THE SPECIFIED GAUGE FUSE LINK FOR THE SPECIFIC CIRCUIT

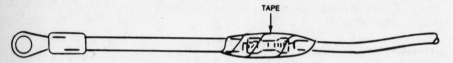

TAPE

TYPICAL REPAIR USING THE EYELET TERMINAL FUSE LINK OF THE SPECIFIED GAUGE FOR ATTACHMENT TO A CIRCUIT WIRE END

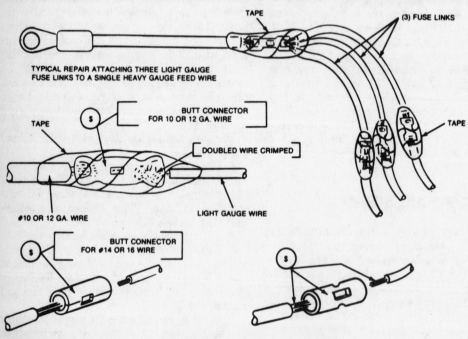

TAPE

(3) FUSE LINKS

TYPICAL REPAIR ATTACHING THREE LIGHT GAUGE
FUSE LINKS TO A SINGLE HEAVY GAUGE FEED WIRE

BUTT CONNECTOR
FOR 10 OR 12 GA. WIRE

TAPE

DOUBLED WIRE CRIMPED

TAPE

#10 OR 12 GA. WIRE

LIGHT GAUGE WIRE

BUTT CONNECTOR
FOR #14 OR 16 WIRE

FUSIBLE LINK REPAIR PROCEDURE

General fuse link repair procedure

fuse link into the same end of the butt connector and crimp all three firmly together.
NOTE: *Care must be taken when fitting the three fuse links into the butt connector as the internal diameter is a snug fit for three wires. Make sure to use a proper crimping tool. Pli-*

ers, side cutters, etc. will not apply the proper crimp to retain the wires and withstand a pull test.

c. After crimping the butt connector to the three fuse links, cut the weld portion from the feed wire and strip approximately ½"

(12.7mm) of insulation from the cut end. Insert the stripped end into the open end of the butt connector and crimp very firmly.

d. To attach the remaining end of the replacement fuse link, strip approximately ½" (12.7mm) of insulation from the wire end of the circuit from which the blown fuse link was removed, and firmly crimp a butt connector or equivalent to the stripped wire. Then, insert the end of the replacement link into the other end of the butt connector and crimp firmly.

e. Using rosin core solder with a consistency of 60 percent tin and 40 percent lead, solder the connectors and the wires at the repairs and insulate with electrical tape.

6. To replace any fuse link on a single circuit in a harness, cut out the damaged portion, strip approximately ½" (12.7mm) of insulation from the two wire ends and attach the appropriate replacement fuse link to the stripped wire ends with two proper size butt connectors. Solder the connectors and wires and insulate with tape.

7. To repair any fuse link which has an eyelet terminal on one end such as the charging circuit, cut off the open fuse link behind the weld, strip approximately ½" (12.7mm) of insulation from the cut end and attach the appropriate new eyelet fuse link to the cut stripped wire with an appropriate size butt connector. Solder the connectors and wires at the repair and insulate with tape.

8. Connect the negative battery cable to the battery and test the system for proper operation.

NOTE: *Do not mistake a resistor wire for a fuse link. The resistor wire is generally longer and has print stating 'Resistor-don't cut or splice.'*

When attaching a single No. 16, 17, 18 or 20 gauge fuse link to a heavy gauge wire, always double the stripped wire end of the fuse link before inserting and crimping it into the butt connector for positive wire retention.

FUSE BOX LOCATION

• 1975 and later Pacer: On the left of the glove box
• 1975–78 Gremlin and Hornet: Next to the parking brake mechanism
• 1975–78 Except Pacer, Gremlin and Hornet: In the glove box
• 1979–86 All models: Next to the parking brake mechanism

WIRING DIAGRAMS

Wiring diagrams have been left out of this book. As cars have become more complex, and available with longer and longer option lists, wiring diagrams have grown in size and complexity also. It has become virtually impossible to provide a readable reproduction in a reasonable number of pages. Information on ordering wiring diagrams from the vehicle manufacturer can be obtained from your dealer.

Drive Train

+6

UNDERSTANDING THE MANUAL TRANSMISSION AND CLUTCH

Because of the way an internal combustion engine breathes, it can produce torque, or twisting force, only within a narrow speed range. Most modern, overhead valve engines must turn at about 2,500 rpm to produce their peak torque. By 4,500 rpm they are producing so little torque that continued increases in engine speed produce no power increases.

The manual transmission and clutch are employed to vary the relationship between engine speed and the speed of the wheels so that adequate engine power can be produced under all circumstances. the clutch allows engine torque to be applied to the transmission input shaft gradually, due to mechanical slippage. the car can, consequently, be started smoothly from a full stop.

The transmission changes the ratio between the rotating speeds of the engine and the wheels by the use of gears. 3-speed or 4-speed transmissions are most common. the lower gears allow full engine power to be applied to the rear wheels during acceleration at low speeds.

The clutch drive plate is a thin disc, the center of which is splined to the transmission input shaft. Both sides of the disc are covered with a layer of material which is similar to brake lining and which is capable of allowing slippage without roughness or excessive noise.

The clutch cover is bolted to the engine flywheel and incorporates a diaphragm spring which provides the pressure to engage the clutch. the cover also houses the pressure plate. the driven disc is sandwiched between the pressure plate and the smooth surface of the flywheel when the clutch pedal is released, thus forcing it to turn at the same speed as the engine crankshaft.

The transmission contains a mainshaft which passes all the way through the transmission, from the clutch to the driveshaft. This shaft is separated at one point, so that front and rear portions can turn at different speeds.

Power is transmitted by a countershaft in the lower gears and reverse. the gears of the countershaft mesh with gears on the mainshaft, allowing power to be carried from one to the other. All the countershaft gears are integral with that shaft, while several of the mainshaft gears can either rotate independently of the shaft or be locked to it. Shifting from one gear to the next causes one of the gears to be freed from rotating with the shaft and locks another to it. Gears are locked and unlocked by internal dog clutches which slide between the center of the gear and the shaft. The forward gears usually employ synchronizers; friction members which smoothly bring gear and shaft to the same speed before the toothed dog clutches are engaged.

The clutch is operating properly if:

1. It will stall the engine when released with the vehicle held stationary.

2. The shift lever can be moved freely between first and reverse gears when the vehicle is stationary and the clutch disengaged.

A clutch pedal free play adjustment is incorporated in the linkage. If there is about 1–2″ (25.4–50.8mm) of motion before the pedal begins to release the clutch, it is adjusted properly. Inadequate free play wears all parts of the clutch releasing mechanisms and may cause slippage. Excessive free play may cause inadequate release and hard shifting of gears.

Some clutches use a hydraulic system in place of mechanical linkage. If the clutch fails to release, fill the clutch master cylinder with fluid to the proper level and pump the clutch pedal to fill the system with fluid. Bleed the system in the same way as a brake system. If leaks are located, tighten loose connections or overhaul the master or slave cylinder as necessary.

MANUAL TRANSMISSION

A lightweight Warner SR4 4-speed was introduced in six cylinder models in late 1976 and is used in all 1980–81 models. The four cylinder uses a Warner HR-1 4-speed transmission through 1979. The SR4 transmission has a cast aluminum case and extension housing, while the HR-1 has a cast iron case and an aluminum extension housing. The SR4 and HR-1 have internal, non-adjustable shift linkage. In 1982 a new Warner (T4) four speed and an optional Warner (T5) five speed transmission were introduced. Both are lightweight and feature an integral mounted shift mechanism.

NOTE: *SR4 and HR-1 transmissions have metric fasteners in most threaded holes.*

An identification tag, containing Warner and American Motors part numbers, is located at the rear of the transmission. The Warner model number is also usually cast into the side of the case.

The model 150T 3-speed transmission was also used through 1979. A nine character identification code is stamped on the left front case flange, but does not give the model number.

The 150T can readily be identified by its nine bolt top cover which is narrower in the front. Unlike the Warner transmissions, it does not have a drain plug: lubricant is drained by removing the lower extension housing bolt. Warner 3-speeds have a rectangular top cover, usually with four or six bolts.

Transmission

REMOVAL AND INSTALLATION

All except Eagle

NOTE: *Open the hood to avoid damage when the rear crossmember is removed. If the over-drive and transmission are to be separated, first engage then disengage the overdrive with the clutch pedal depressed and the engine running.*

1. Matchmark the driveshaft and rear axle yoke for correct installation. Split the rear universal joint and slide the driveshaft off the back of the transmission. Support the transmission with a jack.

2. Detach the column shift mechanism linkage from the transmission, and disconnect the clutch linkage and speedometer cable; disconnect the back-up light switch wiring, and TCS switch wiring, also.

On a floorshift, remove the shift lever. Remove the boot and unbolt the lever. Detach the column reverse lockup rod. Pull the lever and gauge out together. Support the engine.

3. Disconnect the overdrive wiring. Remove the rear transmission support cushion bolts. Also remove the starter on four cylinder models.

4. On Pacers with overdrive, remove the cotter pin from the parking brake equalizer and disconnect the front cable from the equalizer. Remove the cable adjuster and hooks from the floorpan bracket and lower equalizer and rear brake cables to provide clearance. Also, remove the ground strap from the floorpan.

NOTE: *On V8 models with dual exhaust or dual catalytic converters, exhaust pipes must be disconnected from manifolds and lowered so to gain working clearance.*

5. On HR1s, remove the throwout lever protective boot and disengage the clutch cable from the lever. Also remove the inspection cover at the front of the clutch housing.

6. Remove the transmission support crossmember except on Pacers; remove the crossmember with the transmission on those models. Remove the two lower studs which hold the transmission to the bell housing and replace

Manual Transmission Application Chart

Transmission Types	Years	Models
Tremec T-150 3-sp	1976–79	Standard on all models
Tremec T-176 4-sp	1980	All CJ-5 and CJ-7 w/8-304
	1981	Some CJ-5, CJ-7 w/6-258
		All models w/8-304
	1982–83	All models w/6-258
	1984–86	Standard on some models with 6-258
Warner SR-4 4-sp	1980	CJ-7 w/6-258
	1981	All CJ-5, CJ-7 w/4-151
		Some CJ-5 and CJ-7 w/6-258
Warner T-4 4-sp	1982–83	Standard on all models w/4-151
	1984–86	Standard on all models w/4-150
		Standard on some models w/6-258
Warner T-5 5-sp	1982–83	Optional on CJ-5 w/4-151
		Optional on CJ-7 and Scrambler w/6-258
	1984–86	Optional on all models

Troubleshooting the Manual Transmission and Transfer Case

Problem	Cause	Solution
Transmission shifts hard	• Clutch adjustment incorrect • Clutch linkage or cable binding • Shift rail binding	• Adjust clutch • Lubricate or repair as necessary • Check for mispositioned selector arm roll pin, loose cover bolts, worn shift rail bores, worn shift rail, distorted oil seal, or extension housing not aligned with case. Repair as necessary.
	• Internal bind in transmission caused by shift forks, selector plates, or synchronizer assemblies • Clutch housing misalignment • Incorrect lubricant • Block rings and/or cone seats worn	• Remove, dissemble and inspect transmission. Replace worn or damaged components as necessary. • Check runout at rear face of clutch housing • Drain and refill transmission • Blocking ring to gear clutch tooth face clearance must be 0.030 inch or greater. If clearance is correct it may still be necessary to inspect blocking rings and cone seats for excessive wear. Repair as necessary.
Gear clash when shifting from one gear to another	• Clutch adjustment incorrect • Clutch linkage or cable binding • Clutch housing misalignment • Lubricant level low or incorrect lubricant • Gearshift components, or synchronizer assemblies worn or damaged	• Adjust clutch • Lubricate or repair as necessary • Check runout at rear of clutch housing • Drain and refill transmission and check for lubricant leaks if level was low. Repair as necessary. • Remove, disassemble and inspect transmission. Replace worn or damaged components as necessary.
Transmission noisy	• Lubricant level low or incorrect lubricant • Clutch housing-to-engine, or transmission-to-clutch housing bolts loose • Dirt, chips, foreign material in transmission • Gearshift mechanism, transmission gears, or bearing components worn or damaged • Clutch housing misalignment	• Drain and refill transmission. If lubricant level was low, check for leaks and repair as necessary. • Check and correct bolt torque as necessary • Drain, flush, and refill transmission • Remove, disassemble and inspect transmission. Replace worn or damaged components as necessary. • Check runout at rear face of clutch housing
Jumps out of gear	• Clutch housing misalignment • Gearshift lever loose • Offset lever nylon insert worn or lever attaching nut loose • Gearshift mechanism, shift forks, selector plates, interlock plate, selector arm, shift rail, detent plugs, springs or shift cover worn or damaged • Clutch shaft or roller bearings worn or damaged	• Check runout at rear face of clutch housing • Check lever for worn fork. Tighten loose attaching bolts. • Remove gearshift lever and check for loose offset lever nut or worn insert. Repair or replace as necessary. • Remove, disassemble and inspect transmission cover assembly. Replace worn or damaged components as necessary. • Replace clutch shaft or roller bearings as necessary

Troubleshooting the Manual Transmission and Transfer Case (cont.)

Problem	Cause	Solution
Jumps out of gear (cont.)	• Gear teeth worn or tapered, synchronizer assemblies worn or damaged, excessive end play caused by worn thrust washers or output shaft gears	• Remove, disassemble, and inspect transmission. Replace worn or damaged components as necessary.
	• Pilot bushing worn	• Replace pilot bushing
Will not shift into one gear	• Gearshift selector plates, interlock plate, or selector arm, worn, damaged, or incorrectly assembled	• Remove, disassemble, and inspect transmission cover assembly. Repair or replace components as necessary.
	• Shift rail detent plunger worn, spring broken, or plug loose	• Tighten plug or replace worn or damaged components as necessary
	• Gearshift lever worn or damaged	• Replace gearshift lever
	• Synchronizer sleeves or hubs, damaged or worn	• Remove, disassemble and inspect transmission. Replace worn or damaged components.
Locked in one gear—cannot be shifted out	• Shift rail(s) worn or broken, shifter fork bent, setscrew loose, center detent plug missing or worn	• Inspect and replace worn or damaged parts
	• Broken gear teeth on countershaft gear, clutch shaft, or reverse idler gear	• Inspect and replace damaged part
	Gearshift lever broken or worn, shift mechanism in cover incorrectly assembled or broken, worn damaged gear train components	• Disassemble transmission. Replace damaged parts or assemble correctly.
Transfer case difficult to shift or will not shift into desired range	• Vehicle speed too great to permit shifting	• Stop vehicle and shift into desired range. Or reduce speed to 3–4 km/h (2–3 mph) before attempting to shift.
	• If vehicle was operated for extended period in 4H mode on dry paved surface, driveline torque load may cause difficult shifting	• Stop vehicle, shift transmission to neutral, shift transfer case to 2H mode and operate vehicle in 2H on dry paved surfaces
	• Transfer case external shift linkage binding	• Lubricate or repair or replace linkage, or tighten loose components as necessary
	• Insufficient or incorrect lubricant	• Drain and refill to edge of fill hole with SAE 85W-90 gear lubricant only
	• Internal components binding, worn, or damaged	• Disassemble unit and replace worn or damaged components as necessary
Transfer case noisy in all drive modes	• Insufficient or incorrect lubricant	• Drain and refill to edge of fill hole with SAE 85W-90 gear lubricant only. Check for leaks and repair if necessary. Note: If unit is still noisy after drain and refill, disassembly and inspection may be required to locate source of noise.
Noisy in—or jumps out of four wheel drive low range	• Transfer case not completely engaged in 4L position	• Stop vehicle, shift transfer case in Neutral, then shift back into 4L position
	• Shift linkage loose or binding	• Tighten, lubricate, or repair linkage as necessary
	• Shift fork cracked, inserts worn, or fork is binding on shift rail	• Disassemble unit and repair as necessary
Lubricant leaking from output shaft seals or from vent	• Transfer case overfilled	• Drain to correct level
	• Vent closed or restricted	• Clear or replace vent if necessary

Troubleshooting the Manual Transmission and Transfer Case (cont.)

Problem	Cause	Solution
Lubricant leaking from output shaft seals or from vent (cont.)	• Output shaft seals damaged or installed incorrectly	• Replace seals. Be sure seal lip faces interior of case when installed. Also be sure yoke seal surfaces are not scored or nicked. Remove scores, nicks with fine sandpaper or replace yoke(s) if necessary.
Abnormal tire wear	• Extended operation on dry hard surface (paved) roads in 4H range	• Operate in 2H on hard surface (paved) roads

these two studs with two long pilot studs on 150Ts and SR4s. On the HR1, remove the catalytic converter support bracket attaching bolts from the transmission rear support.

7. Remove the two top studs and slide the transmission assembly along the pilot studs and out of the car. On HR1s, support the engine and remove the clutch housing to engine bolts and remove the clutch and transmission as an assembly.

Installation is as follows:

1. Fill the slots in the inner groove of the throwout bearing with light temperature grease and soak the crankshaft pilot bushing wick in engine oil. Fit the throwout bearing and the sleeve assembly in the clutch fork. Center the bearing over the clutch lever. Shift 150Ts and SR4s into first gear.

2. Install two pilot studs in the clutch housing, instead of the lower clutch housing cap screws on 150Ts and SR4s.

3. Carefully slide the transmission into place. Be careful not to damage the clutch driven plate splines while mating them with the transmission input shaft. It may be necessary to raise the front of the engine for the HR1.

4. Install the upper screws, which attach the case to the housing. Remove the pilot studs and install the lower cap screws.

5. If the car is equipped with a floor shift, install the shift lever retainer and shift rods, if removed.

6. Attach the speedometer cable, connect the back-up light switch wires and the transmission controlled spark (TCS) wire, if so equipped. On the HR1, connect the clutch cable and adjust as necessary. Also install the inspection cover and the catalytic converter bracket bolts.

7. Raise the transmission. Attach the rear crossmember and support to the transmission. Fasten the crossmember to the side sills and finger tighten the bolts. Install and tighten the crossmember-to-support bolts. Tighten the crossmember stud nuts. Install the parking brake cables and ground strap on Pacer.

8. Attach the exhaust pipes to the exhaust manifolds, on V8 engines, if they were removed.

9. Install the front U-joint yoke on the transmission. Do the same for the rear U-joint at the differential. Be sure the alignment marks made earlier line up.

10. Connect the shift rods on the column shift transmissions and the reverse lockup rod on the floorshift transmission. Check the transmission oil level and add lubricant, as needed.

11. Remove the supports and lower the car.

12. Install the shift lever if the car is a floorshift transmission.

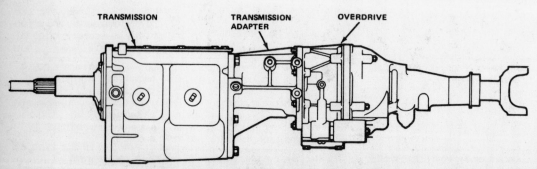

Pacer overdrive unit attached to the transmission

13. Adjust the shift linkage, if it was disturbed.

1980–81 Eagle

1. Shift the transmission into neutral.

2. Remove the screws attaching the gearshift lever bezel and boot to the floorpan.

3. Slide the bezel and boot upward on the gearshift lever to provide access to the lever attaching bolts.

4. Remove the bolts attaching the gearshift lever to the lever mounting cover on the transmission adapter housing and remove the gearshift lever.

5. Remove the bolts attaching the gearshift lever mounting cover to the transmission adapter and remove the mounting cover to provide access to the transfer case upper mounting stud nut in the transmission adapter housing.

6. Remove the nut from the transfer case upper mounting stud located inside the transmission adapter housing.

7. Raise the automobile.

8. Remove the skid plate.

9. Remove the speedometer adapter retainer bolt and remove the retainer, adapter, and cable. Discard the adapter O-ring and plug the adapter opening in the transfer case to prevent excessive oil spillage.

NOTE: *Mark the position of the speedometer adapter for assembly alignment reference before removing it.*

10. Mark the driveshafts and axle yokes for assembly alignment reference and disconnect the driveshafts at the transfer case.

11. Disconnect the back-up lamp switch wire.

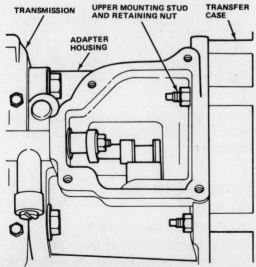

Eagle offset lever and retaining nut

12. Place a support stand under the engine.

13. Support the transmission and transfer case using a transmission jack.

14. Remove the rear crossmember.

15. Remove the catalytic converter bracket from the transfer case.

16. Remove the bolts attaching the transmission to the clutch housing.

17. Remove the transmission and transfer case as assembly.

18. Remove the nuts from the transfer case mounting studs and remove the transmission from the transfer case.

19. Install the transmission on the transfer case. Install and tighten all the transfer case mounting stud nuts to 26 ft.lb. torque.

20. Support the transmission/transfer case assembly on a transmission jack.

21. Align the transmission clutch shaft with the throwout bearing and clutch disc splines and seat the transmission against the clutch housing.

22. Install and tighten the transmission-to-clutch housing attaching bolts to 55 ft.lb. torque.

23. Connect the driveshafts to the transfer case yokes. Tighten the clamp strap bolts to 15 ft.lb. torque.

24. Install the rear crossmember. Tighten the crossmember attaching bolts to 30 ft.lb. torque.

25. Connect the back-up lamp switch wire.

26. Install the replacement O-ring on the speedometer adapter and install the adapter and cable, and the retainer. Tighten the retainer bolt to 100 in.lb. torque.

CAUTION: *Do not attempt to reuse the original adapter O-ring. The ring is designed to swell in service to improve its sealing qualities and could be cut or torn during installation if reuse is attempted.*

27. Attach the catalytic converter bracket to transfer case. Tighten the retaining nuts to 26 ft.lb. torque.

28. Check and correct the lubricant levels in the transmission and transfer case if necessary.

29. Install the skid plate. Tighten the skid plate attaching bolts to 30 ft.lb. torque.

30. Remove the stand used to support the engine and remove the transmission jack if not removed previously.

31. Lower the automobile.

32. Clean the mating surfaces of the gearshift lever mounting cover and the transmission adapter housing.

33. Apply RTV type sealant to the gearshift lever mounting cover and install the cover on the transmission adapter housing. Tighten the cover bolts to 13 ft.lb. torque.

34. Install the gearshift lever on the mounting cover. Be sure the lever is engaged with the shift rail before tightening the lever attaching bolts. Tighten the lever attaching bolts to 18 ft.lb. torque.

35. Position the gearshift lever boot and bezel in the floorpan and install the bezel attaching screws.

1982–86 Eagle

1. Shift the transmission into neutral.

2. Remove the screws attaching the gearshift lever bezel and boot to the floorpan.

3. Slide the bezel and boot upward on the gearshift lever to provide access to the lever attaching bolts.

4. Remove the bolts attaching the gearshift lever to lever mounting cover on transmission adapter housing and remove the gearshift lever.

5. Remove the bolts attaching the gearshift lever mounting cover to the transmission adapter and remove the mounting cover to provide access to the transfer case upper mounting stud nut in the transmission adapter housing.

6. Remove the nut from the transfer case upper mounting stud located inside the transmission adapter housing.

7. Raise the automobile.

8. Remove the skid plate.

9. Remove the speedometer adapter retainer bolt and remove the retainer, adapter, and cable. Discard the adapter O-ring and plug the adapter opening in the transfer case to prevent excessive oil spillage.

NOTE: *Mark the position of the speedometer adapter for assembly alignment reference before removing it.*

10. Mark the driveshafts and axle yokes for assembly alignment reference and disconnect the driveshafts at the transfer case.

11. Disconnect the back-up lamp switch wire.

12. Place a support stand under the engine.

13. Support the transmission and transfer case using a transmission jack.

14. Remove the rear crossmember.

15. Remove the catalytic converter bracket from the transfer case and the brace rod from the bracket.

16. Remove the bolts attaching the transmission to the clutch housing.

17. Remove the transmission and transfer case as assembly.

18. Remove the nuts from the transfer case mounting studs and remove the transmission from the transfer case.

19. Install the transmission on transfer case. Install and tighten all the transfer case mounting stud nuts to 26 ft.lb. torque.

20. Support the transmission/transfer case assembly on a transmission jack.

21. Align the transmission clutch shaft with the throwout bearing and clutch disc splines and seat the transmission against the clutch housing.

22. Install and tighten the transmission-to-clutch housing attaching bolts to 55 ft.lb. torque.

23. Connect the driveshafts to the transfer case yokes. Tighten the clamp strap bolts to 15 ft.lb. torque.

24. Install the brace rod and the rear crossmember. Tighten the attaching bolts to 30 ft.lb. torque.

25. Connect the back-up lamp switch wire.

26. Install a replacement O-ring on the speedometer adapter and install the adapter and cable, and retainer. Tighten the retainer bolt to 100 in.lb. torque.

CAUTION: *Do not attempt to reuse the original adapter O-ring. The ring is designed to swell in service to improve its sealing qualities and could be cut or torn during installation if reuse is attempted.*

27. Attach the catalytic converter bracket to the transfer case. Tighten the retaining nuts to 26 ft.lb. torque.

28. Check and correct the lubricant levels in the transmission and transfer case, if necessary.

29. Install the skid plate. Tighten the skid plate attaching bolts to 30 ft.lb. torque.

30. Remove the stand used to support the engine and remove the transmission jack if not removed previously.

31. Lower the automobile.

32. Clean the mating surfaces of the gearshift lever mounting cover and the transmission adapter housing.

33. Apply RTV type sealant to the gearshift lever mounting cover and install the cover bolts to 13 ft.lb. torque.

34. Install the gearshift lever on the mounting cover. Be sure the lever is engaged with the shift rail before tightening the lever attaching bolts. Tighten the lever attaching bolts to 18 ft.lb. torque.

35. Position the gearshift lever boot and bezel in the floorpan and install the bezel attaching screws.

Linkage Adjustment
PACER

Column Shift Linkage Adjustment

1. Detach the shift rods from the shift levers. Insert a $3/16''$ (4.76mm) drill through the column shift lever holes.

2. Shift into Reverse and lock the column

with the ignition key. Position the First/Reverse shift lever in Reverse.

3. Adjust the shift rod trunnion to a free pin fit in the outer shift lever. Tighten the trunnion locknuts.

4. Unlock the column and move the gearshift to Neutral. Both of the transmission out shift levers should be in the Neutral detent.

5. Repeat Step 3 for the Second/Third shift rod trunnion.

6. Withdraw the drill from the column levers. Shift through all gears and check for a free crossover into Neutral.

7. Shift into Reverse and lock the column. The column should lock without any binding.

Floor Shift Linkage Adjustment

1. Place the transmission shift levers in Neutral.

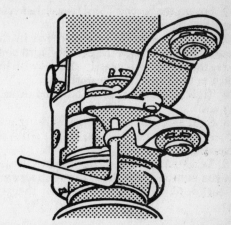

Aligning shift levers on column shift models

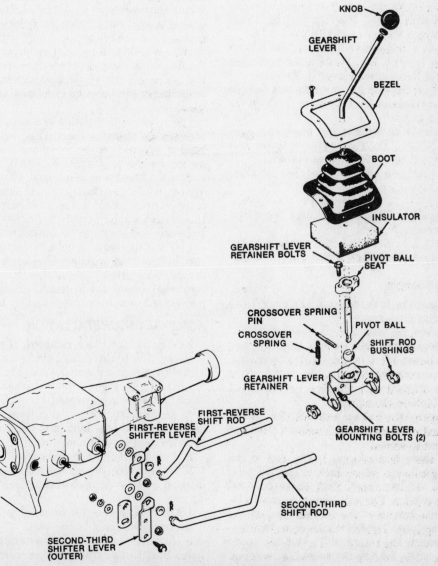

Three speed floor shift linkage

2. Loosen the Second/Third transmission lever attaching nut and adjusting bolt.

3. With the First/Reverse shift rod in the Neutral position, align the Second/Third shift rod so that its notch is exactly aligned with the notch in the First/Reverse shift rod.

4. Tighten the adjustment bolt and attaching nut.

5. Shift through all of the gears being particularly careful for binding in the First-to-Second shift.

6. To adjust the back-up light switch, loosen the jam nuts and then slide the switch forward or backward, as necessary. Tighten the jam nuts.

ALL EXCEPT PACER

Column Shift

1. Disconnect the shift rods from the transmission shift levers. Insert a $3/16''$ (4.76mm) drill through the column shift lever holes.

2. Shift into Reverse and lock the column with the ignition key. Position the transmission First/Reverse shift lever in Reverse.

3. Adjust the shift rod trunnion to a free pin fir in the transmission shift lever. Tighten the trunnion locknuts.

4. Unlock the column and move the gearshift to Neutral. Both of the transmission shift lever should be in the Neutral detent.

5. Repeat step three for the Second/Third shift rod trunnion.

6. Remove the drill from the column levers. Shift through all gears and check for a free crossover into Neutral.

7. Shift into Reverse and lock the column. The column should lock without any binding.

3-Speed Floorshift

1. Place the transmission shift levers in their neutral positions.

2. Loosen the second/third lever adjuster.

3. Keeping the first/reverse shift rod and transmission lever in the neutral position, align the second/third rod so the shift notch is exactly aligned with the first/reverse shift notch. Tighten the adjuster.

4. Operate the linkage and check for full engagement of all gears and a smooth crossover from first to second.

5. If there is a reverse lockup rod to the steering column, loosen both of the locknuts about ½'' (12.7mm) each. Shift into reverse and lock the column. You may have to rotate the lever at the bottom of the column up into the locked position. Tighten the lower locknut until it contacts the trunnion. Tighten the upper locknut while holding the trunnion centered.

Unlock the column and shift through gears. Shift into reverse and lock the binding.

PACER OVERDRIVE

The Laycock de Normanville overdrive unit for the Pacer is an electro-hydraulic actuated, planetary gear type, mounted to a special adapter at the rear of the transmission.

When the overdrive is in the direct drive position (overdrive switched off), and the car is driven forward, power from the transmission mainshaft is transmitted through the freewheel rollers and unidirectional clutch to the overdrive output shaft. When the car is backing up or during periods of engine braking, torque is transmitted through the clutch sliding member which is held by spring pressure against the tapered portion of the output shaft. When the overdrive is actuated, the clutch sliding member is pressed by hydraulic pressure against the brake disc (ring), which locks the sun wheel. As a result, the output shaft of the overdrive rotates at a higher speed than the mainshaft thereby accomplishing a 30% reduction in engine speed in relation to vehicle speed.

The overdrive is actuated by a switch located beneath the steering wheel. This switch energizes a solenoid on the overdrive unit, via a switch on the transmission, which is cut in only when Third gear is engaged. The solenoid has two windings: a heavy control winding and a lower current, hold winding. When actuated, the control winding opens the overdrive control valve, whereupon the control winding is cut off and the valve is held in the open position by the hold winding. The control valve regulates the pressurized oil flow from the cam operated pump to the hydraulic pistons which operate the overdrive clutch sliding member.

REMOVAL AND INSTALLATION

NOTE: *To facilitate removal, the vehicle should first be driven in Third gear with the overdrive engaged, and then coasted for a few seconds with the overdrive disengaged and the clutch pedal depressed.*

1. Remove the transmission from the vehicle as previously outlined in the Transmission Removal and Installation section.

2. Disconnect the solenoid cables.

3. If the overdrive unit has not already been drained, remove the six bolts and the overdrive oil pan.

CAUTION: *Be careful to avoid spilling hot transmission fluid on the skin.*

4. Remove the bolts which retain the overdrive unit to the transmission intermediate

Troubleshooting Basic Clutch Problems

Problem	Cause
Excessive clutch noise	Throwout bearing noises are more audible at the lower end of pedal travel. The usual causes are: • Riding the clutch • Too little pedal free-play • Lack of bearing lubrication A bad clutch shaft pilot bearing will make a high pitched squeal, when the clutch is disengaged and the transmission is in gear or within the first 2″ of pedal travel. The bearing must be replaced. Noise from the clutch linkage is a clicking or snapping that can be heard or felt as the pedal is moved completely up or down. This usually requires lubrication. Transmitted engine noises are amplified by the clutch housing and heard in the passenger compartment. They are usually the result of insufficient pedal free-play and can be changed by manipulating the clutch pedal.
Clutch slips (the car does not move as it should when the clutch is engaged)	This is usually most noticeable when pulling away from a standing start. A severe test is to start the engine, apply the brakes, shift into high gear and SLOWLY release the clutch pedal. A healthy clutch will stall the engine. If it slips it may be due to: • A worn pressure plate or clutch plate • Oil soaked clutch plate • Insufficient pedal free-play
Clutch drags or fails to release	The clutch disc and some transmission gears spin briefly after clutch disengagement. Under normal conditions in average temperatures, 3 seconds is maximum spin-time. Failure to release properly can be caused by: • Too light transmission lubricant or low lubricant level • Improperly adjusted clutch linkage
Low clutch life	Low clutch life is usually a result of poor driving habits or heavy duty use. Riding the clutch, pulling heavy loads, holding the car on a grade with the clutch instead of the brakes and rapid clutch engagement all contribute to low clutch life.

flange. Pull the unit straight to the rear until it clears the transmission mainshaft.

5. Reverse the above procedure to install. Install the overdrive oil pan with a new gasket. After installation of the transmission and overdrive assembly, fill the transmission (which automatically fills the overdrive), to the proper level with the correct lubricant. Check the lubricant level in the transmission after driving 6–9 miles.

CLUTCH

NOTE: *Several different clutch assemblies have been used over the years. For correct clutch identification, see the accompanying illustrations.*

REMOVAL AND INSTALLATION

4–121

1. Remove the transmission.
2. Mark the clutch cover and flywheel for reassembly. Remove the cover and driven plate

by loosening the bolts alternately and in several stages to avoid cover distortion.

Inspect the flywheel surface for heat cracks, scoring, or blue heat marks. Check the flywheel capscrews for proper torque. It will be

1977–79 4-121 clutch driven plate

necessary to lock-up the flywheel ring gear with a block or flywheel holding clamp tool before tightening these capscrews.

To install:

3. Align the driven plate and the cover on the flywheel with the marks made during removal and install the cover bolts finger tight. Make sure the cover is engaged with the flywheel dowel pins.

4. Using a clutch alignment tool, align the driven plate. Tighten the cover bolts to 23 ft.lb.

5. Install the transmission and the clutch housing assembly. It may be necessary to raise the front of the engine.

6. Position the rear crossmember on the side sills and finger tighten the bolts. Install the transmission-to-crossmember bolts. Tighten the crossmember nuts.

7. The remainder of the installation is the reverse of removal. Be sure, when installing the gearshift lever that the shift rail insert is facing straight down and the offset on the side of the lever fork is facing the right side of the extension housing before installing the lever.

4–150

CAUTION: *The clutch driven disc contains asbestos, which has been determined to be a cancer causing agent. Never clean clutch surfaces with compressed air! Avoid inhaling any dust from any clutch surface! When cleaning clutch surfaces, use a commercially available brake cleaning fluid.*

1. Remove the transmission.

2. Remove the starter.

3. Remove the throwout bearing and sleeve assembly.

4. Remove the bell housing.

5. Mark the clutch cover, pressure plate and the flywheel with a center punch so that these parts can be later installed in the same position.

6. Remove the clutch cover-to-flywheel attaching bolts. When removing these bolts, loosen them in rotation, one or two turns at a time, until the spring tension is released. The clutch cover is a steel stamping which could be warped by improper removal procedures, resulting in clutch chatter when reused.

7. Remove the clutch assembly from the flywheel.

8. The clutch release bearing (throwout bearing) is lubricated at time of assembly and no attempt should be made to lubricate it. Put a small amount of grease in the pilot bushing.

9. Install the driven plate with the short end of the hub toward the flywheel. Use a spare transmission mainshaft or an aligning arbor to align the pressure plate assembly and the driven plate.

10. Leave the arbor in place while tightening the pressure plate screws evenly a turn or two at a time. Torque the bolts to 40 ft.lb.

11. Install the bellhousing. Torque the bolts to 40 ft.lb.

12. Install the throwout bearing and sleeve assembly.

13. Install the starter.

14. Install the transmission.

4–151

1. Remove the starter, disconnect the slave cylinder spring at the throwout lever, and remove the transmission.

2. Remove the clutch housing to engine bolts. Remove the housing.

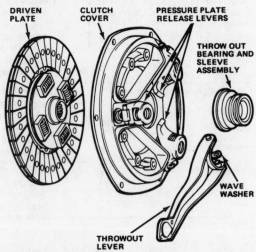

1975–76 9 inch clutch assembly

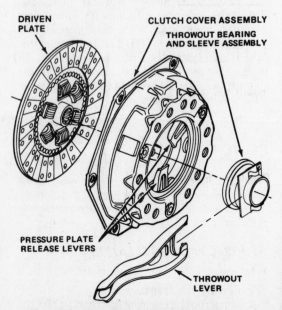

1975–76 10 inch clutch assembly

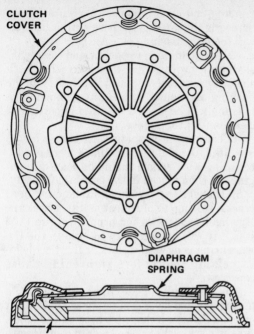

CLUTCH COVER

DIAPHRAGM SPRING

PRESSURE PLATE

Clutch pressure plate for: 1977–78 all 3-sp; 1979 Spirit 6-cyl. with 150T 3-sp or SR4 4-sp; 1980 Spirit 6-cyl. with 4-sp; 1981 all 6-cyl.; 1982 Eagle 6-cyl.

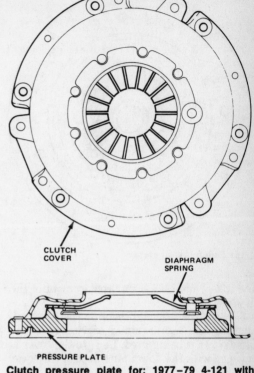

CLUTCH COVER

DIAPHRAGM SPRING

PRESSURE PLATE

Clutch pressure plate for: 1977–79 4-121 with HR-1 4-sp; 1980–82 all 4-cyl.

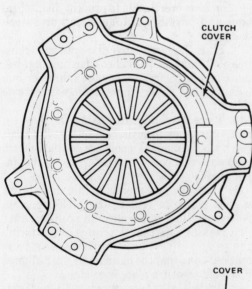

CLUTCH COVER

COVER

PRESSURE PLATE

DIAPHRAGM SPRING

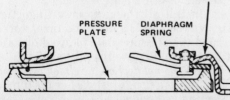

Clutch pressure plate for: 1977 all 4-sp; 1978 all SR4 4-sp; 1979 all Pacer and Concord, and AMX 8-cyl. with SR4 4-sp.; 1980 Pacer, AMX, Concord 6-cyl. with SR4 4-sp; 1982 Spirit and Concord 6-cyl.

1977–82 clutch driven plate for 6 and 8 cylinder

3. Remove the throwout bearing.

4. Matchmark the clutch cover and flywheel for installation. Loosen the clutch cover bolts alternately and evenly, to avoid distortion, and remove the clutch cover and disc.

5. Inspect the parts for signs of overheating (blue color), scoring, or abnormal wear. Overheated parts should be replaced. Deep scoring or wear may require replacement of the disc

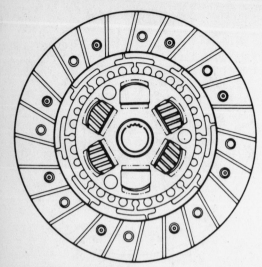

4-151 clutch driven plate

and cover, and refacing or replacement of the flywheel.

6. Place the disc and cover on the flywheel, aligning the marks made previously if the same cover is being used. Be sure the cover is engaged with the dowel pins. Install the cover bolts finger tight.

7. Align the disc with an alignment tool.

8. Tighten the cover bolts alternately and evenly to 23 ft.lb. Remove the alignment tool.

9. Install the throwout bearing, clutch housing, and transmission. The housing-to-engine bolts and transmission-to-housing bolts should be tightened to 54 ft.lb.

6–232, 258
8–304, 360, 401

1. Remove the transmission and the starter.

2. Disconnect the clutch linkage at the release lever.

3. Remove the capscrews that hold the bellhousing (clutch housing) to the engine. It may be necessary to more the rear of the engine up or down to gain wrench clearance.

NOTE: *Any shims between the housing and engine must be replaced in exactly the same place to prevent misalignment.*

4. Remove the throwout lever, washer, bearing and sleeve assembly.

5. Matchmark the clutch cover, pressure plate, and flywheel before removal to ensure proper balance.

6. Loosen each clutch cover capscrew a few turns at a time until spring tension is released, then remove the cover, pressure plate, and disc.

7. Check the pilot bushing in the end of the crankshaft for scoring or looseness. If it is necessary to replace the bushing, use either an ex-

panding end slide hammer or a suitable tap. Screwing the tap into the bore until it bottoms will force the bushing out. Another way to remove the bushing is to pack it and the crankshaft cavity with grease, then insert the clutch shaft aligning tool (dummy pilot shaft) into the bushing and tap it with a soft hammer. The bushing will be pushed out. It is important to clean out all the grease.

Lubricate the bushing with grease before installing the clutch. Sometimes there is a lubricating wick, which should be soaked in engine oil, then placed in the crankshaft cavity.

8. Inspect the flywheel surface for heat cracks, scoring, or blue heat marks. Check the flywheel capscrews for proper torque (105 ft.lb.). It will be necessary to lock-up the flywheel ring gear with a block or flywheel holding clamp tool before tightening these capscrews.

The throwout (release) linkage consists of a forked, pivoted lever contacting the bearing at one end and the linkage pushrod on the other. A return spring keeps the lever in contact with the ball pivot.

The throwout bearing itself is prelubricated and cannot be repacked if dry. A bad bearing results in uneven clutch pedal pressure and a grinding, rattling noise when the pedal is depressed. Replace any noisy throwout bearings as soon as is practicable to prevent disintegration and possible transmission or clutch damage.

9. Slide the new clutch disc onto the transmission input shaft to check for binding. Remove any burrs from either the splines or hub using emery paper, then clean with a safe solvent.

10. Place the clutch disc against the flywheel and secure it by inserting a dummy pilot shaft (such shafts, made of wood, are available from automotive jobbers) or an old transmission input shaft.

11. Place the new pressure plate (it's always a good policy to replace the pressure plate when installing a new disc) in position, after first making sure that the clutch disc is facing the proper direction (the flywheel side is marked), and that the matchmarks are aligned if the old pressure plate is used.

12. Install all the capscrews fingertight. Tighten the screws a little at a time, working around the pressure plate to avoid distorting it, to 40 ft.lb. Remove the pilot shaft.

NOTE: *Do not depress the clutch pedal until the transmission is installed or the throwout bearing will fall out.*

13. Install the clutch housing, throwout bearing and transmission. Hook up the clutch linkage and check the adjustment.

PEDAL FREE PLAY ADJUSTMENT

4–121

The clutch pedal free play is adjusted by varying the length of the control cable. The preferred free play is 1⅛″ (28.6mm).

1. To adjust the cable, loosen the cable locknut at the rear of the cable and pull the cable forward until the free play is eliminated from the throwout lever.

2. Rotate the adjuster nut toward the rear of the cable until the nut tabs contact the clutch housing.

3. Release the cable housing and turn the adjuster nut until the tabs engage the slots on the clutch housing.

4. Tighten the clutch cable locknut. Recheck clutch pedal free play.

6-Cylinder and V8

A free play measurement of ⅞–1⅛″ (22.23–28.6mm) is acceptable. Adjust the free play by

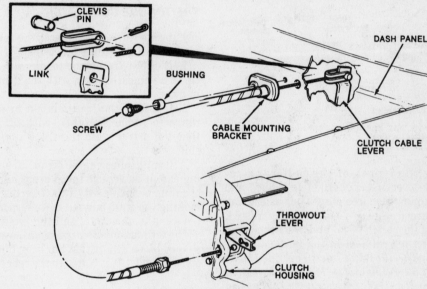

1977–79 4-121 clutch linkage

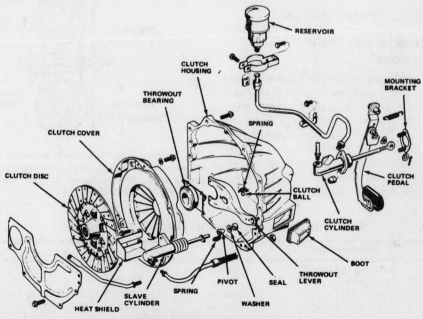

Hydraulic clutch components

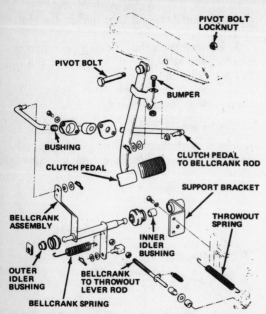

Clutch pedal and linkage assemblies for 6 and 8 cylinder through 1980

sion uses a light fluid as the medium for the transmission of power. This fluid also works in the operation of various hydraulic control circuits and as a lubricant. Because the transmission fluid performs all of these three functions, trouble within the unit can easily travel from one part to another. For this reason, and because of the complexity and unusual operating principles of the transmission, a very sound understanding of the basic principles of operation will simplify troubleshooting.

THE TORQUE CONVERTER

The torque converter replaces the conventional clutch. It has three functions:

1. It allows the engine to idle with the vehicle at a standstill, even with the transmission in gear.

2. It allows the transmission to shift from range to range smoothly, without requiring that the driver close the throttle during the shift.

3. It multiplies engine torque to an increasing extent as vehicle speed drops and throttle opening is increased. This has the effect of making the transmission more responsive and reduces the amount of shifting required.

The torque converter is a metal case which is shaped like a sphere that has been flattened on opposite sides. It is bolted to the rear end of the

varying the length of the bellcrank-to-throwout lever rod. Lengthen to reduce and shorten to increase free play. The easiest way to measure free play is to hold a yardstick alongside the clutch pedal and press the pedal down until you can feel spring tension.

NOTE: *The 1981 and later 6-cylinder models and all 4–150 and 4–151 models have a hydraulic clutch which requires no adjustment.*

AUTOMATIC TRANSMISSION

Understanding Automatic Transmissions

The automatic transmission allows engine torque and power to be transmitted to the rear wheels within a narrow range of engine operating speeds. The transmission will allow the engine to turn fast enough to produce plenty of power and torque at very low speeds, while keeping it at a sensible rpm at high vehicle speeds. The transmission performs this job entirely without driver assistance. The transmis-

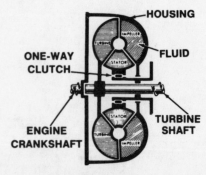

The torque converter housing is roated by the engine's crankshaft, and turns the impeller. The impeller spins the turbine, which gives motion to the turbine shaft, driving the gears

Automatic Transmission Application Chart

Transmission Type	Years	Models
Turbo Hydra-Matic 400	1976–79	CJ-7
Chrysler 904	1981	CJ-7 w/4-151
Chrysler 999	1980–81	CJ-7 w/6-258 and 8-304
	1982–86	CJ-7 and Scrambler w/6-258
	1987	Wrangler w/6-258

engine's crankshaft. Generally, the entire metal case rotates at engine speed and serves as the engine's flywheel.

The case contains three sets of blades. One set is attached directly to the case. This set forms the torus or pump. Another set is directly connected to the output shaft, and forms the turbine. The third set is mounted on a hub which, in turn, is mounted on a stationary shaft through a one-way clutch. This third set is known as the stator.

A pump, which is driven by the converter hub at engine speed, keeps the torque converter full of transmission fluid at all times. Fluid flows continuously through the unit to provide cooling.

Under low speed acceleration, the torque converter functions as follows:

The torus is turning faster than the turbine. It picks up fluid at the center of the converter and, through centrifugal force, slings it outward. Since the outer edge of the converter moves faster than the portions at the center, the fluid picks up speed.

The fluid then enters the outer edge of the turbine blades. It then travels back toward the center of the converter case along the turbine blades. In impinging upon the turbine blades, the fluid loses the energy picked up in the torus.

If the fluid were now to immediately be returned directly into the torus, both halves of the converter would have to turn at approximately the same speed at all times, and torque input and output would both be the same.

In flowing through the torus and turbine, the fluid picks up two types of flow, or flow in two separate directions. It flows through the turbine blades, and it spins with the engine. The stator, whose blades are stationary when the vehicle is being accelerated at low speeds, converts one type of flow into another. Instead of allowing the fluid to flow straight back into the torus, the stator's curved blades turn the fluid almost 90° toward the direction of rotation of the engine. Thus the fluid does not flow as fast toward the torus, but is already spinning when the torus picks it up. This has the effect of allowing the torus to turn much faster than the turbine. This difference in speed may be compared to the difference in speed between the smaller and larger gears in any gear train. The result is that engine power output is higher, and engine torque is multiplied.

As the speed of the turbine increases, the fluid spins faster and faster in the direction of engine rotation. As a result, the ability of the stator to redirect the fluid flow is reduced. Under cruising conditions, the stator is eventually forced to rotate on its one-way clutch in the direction of engine rotation. Under these conditions, the torque converter begins to behave almost like a solid shaft, with the torus and turbine speeds being almost equal.

THE PLANETARY GEARBOX

The ability of the torque converter to multiply engine torque is limited. Also, the unit tends to be more efficient when the turbine is rotating at relatively high speeds. Therefore, a planetary gearbox is used to carry the power output of the turbine to the driveshaft.

Planetary gears function very similarly to conventional transmission gears. However, their construction is different in that three elements make up one gear system, and, in that all three elements are different from one another. The three elements are: an outer gear that is shaped like a hoop, with teeth cut into the inner surface; a sun gear, mounted on a shaft and located at the very center of the outer gear; and a set of three planet gears, held by

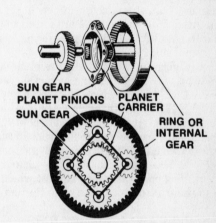

Planetary gears are similar to manual transmission gears but are composed of three parts

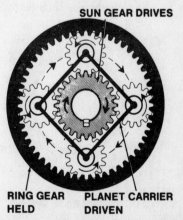

Planetary gears in the maximum reduction (low) range. The ring gear is held and a lower gear ration is obtained

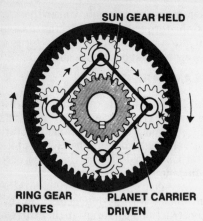

SUN GEAR HELD

RING GEAR DRIVES   PLANET CARRIER DRIVEN

Planetary gears in the minimum reduction (drive) range. The ring gear is allowed to revolve, providing a higher gear ratio

pins in a ring-like planet carrier, meshing with both the sun gear and the outer gear. Either the outer gear or the sun gear may be held stationary, providing more than one possible torque multiplication factor for each set of gears. Also, if all three gears are forced to rotate at the same speed, the gearset forms, in effect, a solid shaft.

Most modern automatics use the planetary gears to provide either a single reduction ratio of about 1.8:1, or two reduction gears: a low of about 2.5:1, and an intermediate of about 1.5:1. Bands and clutches are used to hold various portions of the gearsets to the transmission case or to the shaft on which they are mounted. Shifting is accomplished, then, by changing the portion of each planetary gearset which is held to the transmission case or to the shaft.

THE SERVOS AND ACCUMULATORS

The servos are hydraulic pistons and cylinders. They resemble the hydraulic actuators used on many familiar machines, such as bulldozers.

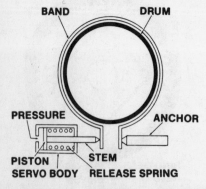

BAND   DRUM

PRESSURE   ANCHOR

PISTON   STEM
SERVO BODY   RELEASE SPRING

Servos, operated by pressure, are used to apply or release the bands, to either hold the ring gear or allow it to rotate

Hydraulic fluid enters the cylinder, under pressure, and forces the piston to move to engage the band or clutches.

The accumulators are used to cushion the engagement of the servos. The transmission fluid must pass through the accumulator on the way to the servo. The accumulator housing contains a thin piston which is sprung away from the discharge passage of the accumulator. When fluid passes through the accumulator on the way to the servo, it must move the piston against spring pressure, and this action smooths out the action of the servo.

THE HYDRAULIC CONTROL SYSTEM

The hydraulic pressure used to operate the servos comes from the main transmission oil pump. This fluid is channeled to the various servos through the shift valves. There is generally a manual shift valve which is operated by the transmission selector lever and an automatic shift valve for each automatic upshift the transmission provides: i.e., 2-speed automatics have a low/high shift valve, while 3-speeds have a 1–2 valve, and a 2–3 vavle.

There are two pressures which effect the operation of these valves. One is the governor pressure which is affected by vehicle speed. The other is the modulator pressure which is affected by intake manifold vacuum or throttle position. Governor pressure rises with an increase in vehicle speed, and modulator pressure rises as the throttle is opened wider. By responding to these two pressures, the shift valves cause the upshift points to be delayed with increased throttle opening to make the best use of the engine's power output.

Most transmissions also make use of an auxiliary circuit for downshifting. This circuit may be actuated by the throttle linkage or the vacuum line which actuates the modulator, or by a cable or solenoid. It applies pressure to a special downshift surface on the shift valve or valves.

The transmission modulator also governs the line pressure, used to actuate the servos. In this way, the clutches and bands will be actuated with a force matching the torque output of the engine.

Transmission

REMOVAL AND INSTALLATION

1975–76

1. Disconnect the fan shroud (if equipped).
2. Disconnect the transmission fill tube at the upper bracket.
3. Raise the car on hoist.

CAUTION: *It is necessary that the hood be*

Lockup Torque Converter Service Diagnosis

Problem	Cause	Solution

No lockup	• Faulty oil pump
	• Sticking governor valve
	• Valve body malfunction
	   (a) Stuck switch valve
	   (b) Stuck lockup valve
	   (c) Stuck fail-safe valve
	• Failed locking clutch
	• Leaking turbine hub seal
	• Faulty input shaft or seal ring
		• Replace oil pump
		• Repair or replace as necessary
		• Repair or replace valve body or its internal components as necessary
		
		• Replace torque converter
		• Replace torque converter
		• Repair or replace as necessary

Will not unlock	• Sticking governor valve
	• Valve body malfunction
	   (a) Stuck switch valve
	   (b) Stuck lockup valve
	   (c) Stuck fail-safe valve
		• Repair or replace as necessary
		• Repair or replace valve body or its internal components as necessary

Stays locked up at too low a speed in direct	• Sticking governor valve
	• Valve body malfunction
	   (a) Stuck switch valve
	   (b) Stuck lockup valve
	   (c) Stuck fail-safe valve
		• Repair or replace as necessary
		• Repair or replace valve body or its internal components as necessary

Locks up or drags in low or second	• Faulty oil pump
	• Valve body malfunction
	   (a) Stuck switch valve
	   (b) Stuck fail-safe valve
		• Replace oil pump
		• Repair or replace valve body or its internal components as necessary

Sluggish or stalls in reverse	• Faulty oil pump
	• Plugged cooler, cooler lines or fittings
	• Valve body malfunction
	   (a) Stuck switch valve
	   (b) Faulty input shaft or seal ring
		• Replace oil pump as necessary
		• Flush or replace cooler and flush lines and fittings
		• Repair or replace valve body or its internal components as necessary

Loud chatter during lockup engagement (cold)	• Faulty torque converter • Failed locking clutch • Leaking turbine hub seal	• Replace torque converter • Replace torque converter • Replace torque converter
Vibration or shudder during lockup engagement	• Faulty oil pump • Valve body malfunction • Faulty torque converter • Engine needs tune-up	• Repair or replace oil pump as necessary • Repair or replace valve body or its internal components as necessary • Replace torque converter • Tune engine
Vibration after lockup engagement	• Faulty torque converter • Exhaust system strikes underbody • Engine needs tune-up • Throttle linkage misadjusted	• Replace torque converter • Align exhaust system • Tune engine • Adjust throttle linkage
Vibration when revved in neutral Overheating: oil blows out of dip stick tube or pump seal	• Torque converter out of balance • Plugged cooler, cooler lines or fittings • Stuck switch valve	• Replace torque converter • Flush or replace cooler and flush lines and fittings • Repair switch valve in valve body or replace valve body
Shudder after lockup engagement	• Faulty oil pump • Plugged cooler, cooler lines or fittings • Valve body malfunction • Faulty torque converter • Fail locking clutch • Exhaust system strikes underbody • Engine needs tune-up • Throttle linkage misadjusted	• Replace oil pump • Flush or replace cooler and flush lines and fittings • Repair or replace valve body or its internal components as necessary • Replace torque converter • Replace torque converter • Align exhaust system • Tune engine • Adjust throttle linkage

Troubleshooting Basic Automatic Transmission Problems

Problem	Cause	Solution
Fluid leakage	• Defective pan gasket	• Replace gasket or tighten pan bolts
	• Loose filler tube	• Tighten tube nut
	• Loose extension housing to transmission case	• Tighten bolts
	• Converter housing area leakage	• Have transmission checked professionally
Fluid flows out the oil filler tube	• High fluid level	• Check and correct fluid level
	• Breather vent clogged	• Open breather vent
	• Clogged oil filter or screen	• Replace filter or clean screen (change fluid also)
	• Internal fluid leakage	• Have transmission checked professionally
Transmission overheats (this is usually accompanied by a strong burned odor to the fluid)	• Low fluid level	• Check and correct fluid level
	• Fluid cooler lines clogged	• Drain and refill transmission. If this doesn't cure the problem, have cooler lines cleared or replaced.
	• Heavy pulling or hauling with insufficient cooling	• Install a transmission oil cooler
	• Faulty oil pump, internal slippage	• Have transmission checked professionally
Buzzing or whining noise	• Low fluid level	• Check and correct fluid level
	• Defective torque converter, scored gears	• Have transmission checked professionally
No forward or reverse gears or slippage in one or more gears	• Low fluid level	• Check and correct fluid level
	• Defective vacuum or linkage controls, internal clutch or band failure	• Have unit checked professionally
Delayed or erratic shift	• Low fluid level	• Check and correct fluid level
	• Broken vacuum lines	• Repair or replace lines
	• Internal malfunction	• Have transmission checked professionally

Transmission Fluid Indications

The appearance and odor of the transmission fluid can give valuable clues to the overall condition of the transmission. Always note the appearance of the fluid when you check the fluid level or change the fluid. Rub a small amount of fluid between your fingers to feel for grit and smell the fluid on the dipstick.

If the fluid appears:	It indicates:
Clear and red colored	• Normal operation
Discolored (extremely dark red or brownish) or smells burned	• Band or clutch pack failure, usually caused by an overheated transmission. Hauling very heavy loads with insufficient power or failure to change the fluid, often result in overheating. Do not confuse this appearance with newer fluids that have a darker red color and a strong odor (though not a burned odor).
Foamy or aerated (light in color and full of bubbles)	• The level is too high (gear train is churning oil)
	• An internal air leak (air is mixing with the fluid). Have the transmission checked professionally.
Solid residue in the fluid	• Defective bands, clutch pack or bearings. Bits of band material or metal abrasives are clinging to the dipstick. Have the transmission checked professionally.
Varnish coating on the dipstick	• The transmission fluid is overheating

open to avoid damage to the hood and air cleaner when the rear crossmember is removed.

4. Remove the inspection cover from the front of the converter housing.

5. Rotate the torque converter until the drain plug is accessible. Remove the plug and drain the converter.

6. Remove the transmission fill tube.

7. Remove the starter.

8. Mark the rear universal joint and yoke for alignment reference during installation.

9. Remove the driveshaft.

10. Disconnect the catalytic converter(s) (if equipped) and front exhaust pipes to provide working clearance.

11. Disconnect the front exhaust pipe brace from the transmission.

12. Disconnect the speedometer cable, throttle and shift linkage, neutral safety, TCS switch wires, fluid cooler lines, and the governor pressure oil line from the transmission to the TCS control switch.

13. Mark the converter drive plate and converter for alignment reference during installation.

14. Remove the bolts which attach the converter to the drive plate.

15. Place the transmission jack under the transmission.

16. Remove the crossmember from the side sill and rear support cushion.

17. Remove the support cushion and adapter from the extension housing.

18. Remove the bolts which attach the transmission to the engine.

19. Move the transmission and converter a sufficient distance to clear the crankshaft.

20. Maintain pressure against the converter and lower the assembly until the transmission housing clears the engine.

21. If the torque converter is removed, insert Pump Aligning Tool J-24033 (Models 904-998) or J-24045 (Model 727) into the pump.

22. Engage the pump rotor.

23. Rotate the tool until the drilled holes in the tool are vertical.

24. Remove the tool.

25. Rotate the converter until the pump drive slots are vertical, and carefully install the converter into pump.

26. Place the assembly on a transmission jack.

27. Raise the transmission assembly and align the converter with the drive plate. Refer to the marks made during removal.

28. Raise the transmission and slide it forward.

29. Raise, lower, or tilt the transmission to

align the converter housing pilot holes with the dowels in the engine.

30. Install the two lower converter housing attaching bolts and pull the housing up snugly.

31. Install the remaining attaching bolts.

32. Tighten all the converter housing attaching bolts to 28 ft.lb. torque.

33. Install the rear crossmember, rear support cushion and adapter.

34. Remove the transmission jack.

35. Install the screws which attach the torque converter to the drive plate.

36. Install the drain plug.

37. Install the inspection cover.

38. Install the starter.

39. Conncect the neutral safety switch, TCS switch, throttle and shift linkages, fluid cooler lines, and speedometer cable.

40. Install the transmission filler tube in the transmission.

41. Install the driveshaft. Refer to the alignment marks made during removal.

42. Connect the front exhaust pipes, catalytic coverter(s) (if equipped), and lower the car.

43. Connect the filler tube upper bracket.

44. Fill the transmission to the correct level.

45. Adjust the manual throttle linkage.

46. Road test the car for proper transmission operation.

1977–79

4–121 ENGINES

1. Open the hood.

CAUTION: *The hood must remain open to avoid damaging the hood and air cleaner when the rear crossmember is removed.*

2. Disconnect the fan shroud.

3. Remove the bolt attaching the transmission filler tube to the rear of the engine.

4. Place the gearshift lever in Neutral.

5. Raise and support the car on jackstands.

6. Mark the driveshaft and yoke for assembly alignment reference.

7. Remove the driveshaft.

8. Remove the starter motor.

9. Remove the speedometer adapter and cable assembly. Cover the adapter bore in the case after removal.

10. Disconnect the gearshift and throttle linkage. On cars with column shift, remove the bolt attaching the linkage bellcrank bracket to the converter housing.

11. Remove the cover at the front of the converter housing.

12. Mark the converter drive plate and converter for assembly alignment reference.

13. Remove the bolts attaching the converter to the drive plate. Rotate the crankshaft and

drive plate using a ratchet handle and socket or box end wrench on the crankshaft front pulley bolt to gain access to the drive plate-to-converter bolts.

NOTE: *The crankshaft pulley bolt is a metric size and requires a 24mm socket or wrench. However, a $^{15}/_{16}$" (23.8mm) socket or wrench may also be used.*

14. Support the transmission using a transmission jack. Retain the transmission on the jack using a safety chain.

15. Lower the transmission slightly and disconnect the oil cooler lines at the transmission.

16. Remove the bolt attaching the rear support cushion to the rear support cushion bracket (bracket is attached to transmission extension housing).

17. Remove the rear crossmember-to-frame side sill attaching nuts and remove the crossmember and support cushion as assembly.

18. Place the support stand under the front of the engine.

19. Remove the bolts attaching the catalytic converter support bracket to the transmission.

20. Remove the bolts attaching the transmission and filler tube to the engine.

NOTE: *The transmission-to-engine block bolts are metric size bolts.*

21. Move the transmission and converter rearward until clear of the crankshaft.

22. Hold the converter in position and lower the transmission until the converter housing clears the engine.

CAUTION: *If the transmission was removed to correct a malfunction that generated sludge or heavy accumulations of metal or friction material particles, the oil cooler and cooler lines must be thoroughly flushed and the torque converter replaced. Do not attempt to flush the converter if it is contaminated.*

23. If the torque converter was removed, insert Pump Aligning Tool J-24033 into the pump rotor and engage the tool slots with the pump rotor drive lugs.

24. Rotate the aligning tool until the hole in tool is vertical then remove the tool.

25. Rotate the converter until the pump drive slots in the converter hub are vertical.

26. Carefully insert the converter hub into the oil pump. Be sure the drive lugs of the pump inner rotor are completely engaged with the drive slots in the converter hub.

27. Raise the transmission and align the converter with the drive plate. Refer to the alignment marks made during removal.

28. Move the transmission forward and raise, lower, or tilt the transmission to align the converter housing pilot holes with the dowels in the engine block.

NOTE: *If the downward angle at the rear of*

the engine is not sufficient to permit transmission installation, raise the front of the engine to increase the downward angle.

29. Install two, transmission-to-engine lower attaching bolts and tighten the bolts to pull the transmission to the engine.

30. Install the drive plate-to-converter attaching bolts. Tighten them to 26 ft.lb. torque.

31. Install the remaining transmission-to-engine attaching bolts. Tighten the bolts to 54 ft.lb. torque.

32. Connect the oil cooler lines.

33. Raise the transmission, position the rear crossmember, install the crossmember attaching nuts and tighten the nuts to 30 ft.lb. torque.

34. Install the rear support cushion-to-support cushion bracket bolt and tighten the bolt to 49 ft.lb. torque.

35. Remove the safety chain and transmission jack.

36. Install the cover at the front of the converter housing.

37. Install the starter motor.

38. Connect the neutral start switch wires to the switch terminal.

39. Connect the gearshift and throttle linkage. On cars with column shift, position the linkage bellcrank bracket on the converter housing and install the bracket attaching bolt.

40. Install the speedometer cable and adapter assembly. Be sure the adapter is correctly indexed.

41. Install the catalytic converter support bracket bolt.

42. Lower the car.

43. Fill the transmission to the correct fluid level.

44. Adjust the gearshift lever, then the throttle linkage.

NOTE: *The gearshift lever adjusting trunnion is located on the steering column shift lever.*

45. Road test the car to check transmission operation.

6–232, 258
8–304, 360, 401

1. Disconnect the fan shroud if equipped.

2. Disconnect the transmission fill tube at the upper bracket.

3. Open the hood.

CAUTION: *It is necessary that the hood be open to avoid damaging the hood and air cleaner when the rear crossmember is removed.*

4. Raise and support the car on jackstands.

5. Remove the inspection cover from the converter housing.

6. On 6-cylinder cars, remove the screws at-

taching the clamp to the exhaust pipe support bracket and slide the clamp off the bracket.

7. Remove the transmission fill tube.

8. Mark the driveshaft and rear axle yoke for assembly alignment reference.

9. Remove the driveshaft.

10. On 8-cylinder cars, disconnect the exhaust pipes at the exhaust manifolds.

11. Remove the speedometer adapter and cable assembly. Cover the adapter bore in the case after adapter removal.

12. Disconnect the gearshift and throttle linkage.

13. Disconnect the wires at the neutral start switch.

14. Disconnect the TCS switch oil line at the transmission fitting.

15. Mark the converter drive plate and converter for assembly alignment reference.

16. Remove the bolts attaching the converter to the drive plate. Rotate the crankshaft and drive plate using the ratchet handle and socket on the crankshaft front pulley bolt to gain access to the drive plate bolts.

17. Support the transmission using a transmission jack. Retain the transmission on the jack using a safety chain.

18. Lower the transmission slightly and disconnect the oil cooler lines at the transmission.

19. Remove the bolts attaching the rear support cushion to the transmission.

20. Remove the rear crossmember-to-frame side sill attaching nuts and remove the crossmember. On Pacers, remove the ground strap.

21. Remove the bolts attaching the converter support bracket to the transmission.

22. Remove the bolts attaching the transmission to the engine.

23. Move the transmission and converter rearward to clear the crankshaft.

24. Hold the converter in position and lower the assembly until the converter housing clears the engine.

CAUTION: *If the transmission was removed to correct a malfunction that generated sludge or heavy accumulations of metal particles or friction material, the oil cooler and cooler lines must be flushed thoroughly and the torque converter replaced. Do not attempt to flush the converter if it is contaminated.*

25. If the torque converter was removed, insert Pump Aligning Tool J-24033 in the pump rotor until the rotor drive lugs engage the slots in tool.

26. Rotate the tool until the drilled hole in the tool is vertical and remove the tool.

27. Rotate the converter until the pump drive slots in the converter hub are vertical and carefully insert the converter hub into the pump. Be sure the drive lugs of the pump inner rotor are properly engaged in the drive slots of the converter hub.

28. Raise the transmission and align the converter with the drive plate. Refer to the assembly alignment marks.

29. Pull the transmission forward.

30. Raise, lower, or tilt the transmission to align the converter housing pilot holes with the dowels in the engine.

31. Install the two converter housing lower attaching bolts and tighten the bolts to pull the housing to the engine.

32. Install the drive plate-to-converter attaching bolts.

33. Install the remaining converter housing-to-engine attaching bolts and tighten all bolts to 28 ft.lb. torque.

34. Connect the oil cooler lines.

35. Install the rear support cushion on the transmission.

36. Raise the transmission, position the rear crossmember, and install the crossmember attaching nuts. On Pacers, install the ground strap.

37. Remove the safety chain and transmission jack.

38. Install the inspection cover.

39. On 6-cylinder cars, install the exhaust pipe support bracket.

40. Install the starter.

41. Connect the wires to the neutral switch.

42. Connect the gearshift and throttle linkage.

43. Install the speedometer cable and adapter assembly. Be sure the adapter is correctly indexed.

44. Install the driveshaft. Refer to the alignment marks made during removal.

45. On 8-cylinder cars, connect the front exhaust pipes and the catalytic converter support bracket bolts.

46. Lower the car.

47. Fill the transmission to the correct level.

48. Adjust the gearshift selector lever linkage.

49. Road test the car to check transmission operation.

1980–81

4–151

1. Open the hood.

CAUTION: *The hood must remain open to avoid damaging the hood and air cleaner when the rear crossmember is removed.*

2. Disconnect the fan shroud.

3. Remove the bolt attaching the transmission fill tube to the engine.

4. Place the gearshift lever in Neutral.

5. Raise and support the car on jackstands.

6. Mark the driveshaft and yoke for assem-

bly alignment reference. On Eagle models, also remove the skid plate.

7. Remove the driveshafts.

8. Remove the starter motor. On Eagle models, also remove the stiffening braces.

9. Remove the speedometer adapter and cable assembly. Cover the adapter bore after removal.

10. Disconnect the gearshift and throttle linkage. On automobiles with column shift, remove the bolt attaching linkage bellcrank bracket to the converter housing.

11. Remove the cover at the front of the converter housing.

12. Mark the converter drive plate and the converter for assembly alignment reference.

13. Remove the bolts attaching the converter to the drive plate. Rotate the crankshaft and drive plate using the ratchet handle and socket or box end wrench on the crankshaft front pulley bolt to gain access to the drive plate-to-converter bolts.

NOTE: *The crankshaft pulley bolt is a metric size bolt.*

14. Support the transmission using a transmission jack. Retain the transmission on the jack using a safety chain.

NOTE: *On Eagle models, both the transmission and transfer case must be properly supported on the transmission jack and retained with a safety chain.*

15. Disconnect the oil cooler lines at the transmission.

16. Remove the bolt attaching the rear support cushion to the rear support cushion bracket (bracket is attached to transmission extension housing).

17. Remove the rear crossmember attaching nuts and remove the crossmember and support cushion as assembly.

18. Place a support stand under the front of the engine.

19. Remove the bolts attaching the catalytic converter support bracket to the transmission, if equipped.

20. Remove the fill tube.

21. Remove the bolts attaching the transmission to the engine.

NOTE: *The transmission-to-engine block bolts are metric size bolts.*

22. Move the transmission (and transfer case, if equipped) and converter rearward until clear of the crankshaft.

23. Hold the converter in position and lower the transmission until the transmission converter housing clears the engine.

CAUTION: *If the transmission was removed to correct a malfunction that generated sludge or heavy accumulations of metal or friction material particles, the oil cooler and cooler lines must be thoroughly flushed and*

the torque converter replaced. Do not attempt to flush the converter if it is contaminated.

24. If the torque converter was removed, insert Pump Aligning Tool J-24033 into the pump rotor and engage the tool slots with the pump rotor drive lugs.

25. Rotate the aligning tool until the hole in the tool is vertical, then remove the tool.

26. Rotate the converter until the pump drive slots in the converter hub are vertical.

27. Carefully insert the converter hub into the oil pump. Be sure the drive lugs of the pump inner rotor are completely engaged with the drive slots in the converter hub.

28. Raise the transmission and align the converter with the drive plate. Refer to the alignment marks made during removal.

29. Move the transmission forward and raise, lower, or tilt the transmission to align the transmission converter housing dowel holes with the dowels in the engine block.

NOTE: *If the downward angle at the rear of the engine is not sufficient to permit transmission installation, raise the front of the engine to increase the downward angle.*

30. Install two transmission-to-engine lower attaching bolts and tighten the bolts evenly to pull the transmission to the engine.

31. Install the drive plate-to-converter attaching bolts. Tighten the bolts to 40 ft.lb. torque.

NOTE: *Coat the threads of the drive plate-to-converter attaching bolts with Loctite*271 or equivalent.*

32. Install the remaining transmission-to-engine attaching bolts. Tighten the bolts to 54 ft.lb. torque.

33. Connect the oil cooler lines.

34. Install rear crossmember and support cushion. Tighten attaching nuts to 30 ft.lb. torque.

35. Install the rear support cushion-to-support cushion bracket bolt. Tighten the bolt to 48 ft.lb. torque.

36. Remove the safety chain and transmission jack.

37. Install the converter housing inspection cover.

38. Install the starter motor. On Eagle models also install the stiffening brace and skid plate.

39. Connect the neutral start switch wires to the switch terminal.

40. Connect the gearshift and throttle linkage. On automobiles with column shift, position the linkage bellcrank bracket on the converter housing and install the bracket attaching bolt.

41. Install the speedometer cable and adapter assembly. Be sure the adapter is correctly indexed.

42. Connect the catalytic converter, if equipped. On Eagle models, add the correct quantity of transfer case lubricant.

43. Lower the automobile.

44. Fill the transmission to the correct fluid level.

45. Check and adjust the gearshift lever and throttle linkage if necessary.

NOTE: *The gearshift lever adjusting trunnion is located at the lower end of the steering column.*

46. Road test the automobile to check transmission operation.

6–258

1. Disconnect the fan shroud, if equipped.

2. Disconnect the transmission fill tube at the upper bracket.

3. Open the hood.

CAUTION: *It is necessary that the hood be open to avoid damaging the hood and air cleaner when the rear crossmember is removed.*

4. Raise and support the automobile on jackstands.

5. Remove the inspection cover from the converter housing.

6. On Spirit and Concord, remove the screw attaching the exhaust pipe clamp to the exhaust pipe support bracket and slide the clamp off the bracket.

7. Remove the transmission fill tube.

8. Remove the starter. On Eagle models, also remove the stiffening braces.

9. Mark the driveshaft(s) and yoke(s) for assembly alignment reference.

10. Remove the driveshaft(s).

11. On Eagle models, disconnect the exhaust pipe and move it aside for working clearance.

12. Remove the speedometer adapter and cable assembly. Discard the adapter and cable seals, they are not reuseable. Cover the adapter bore after removal.

13. Disconnect the gearshift and throttle linkage.

14. Disconnect the wires at the neutral start switch.

15. Mark the converter drive plate and converter for assembly alignment reference.

16. Remove the bolts attaching the converter to the drive plate. Rotate the crankshaft and drive plate using a ratchet handle and socket on the crankshaft from the pulley bolt to gain access to the drive plate bolts.

17. On Eagle models, remove the skid plate and stiffening brace.

18. Support the transmission (and transfer case on Eagle models) using a transmission jack. Retain the transmission on the jack using a safety chain.

19. Disconnect the oil cooler lines at the transmission.

20. Remove the bolts attaching the rear support cushion to the transmission.

21. Remove the rear crossmember.

22. Remove the bolts attaching the transmission to the engine.

23. Move the transmission and converter rearward to clear the crankshaft.

24. Hold the converter in position and lower the transmission assembly until the converter housing clears the engine.

CAUTION: *If the transmission was removed to correct a malfunction that generated sludge or heavy accumulations of metal particles or friction material, the oil cooler and cooler lines must be flushed thoroughly and the torque converter replaced. Do not attempt to flush the converter if it is contaminated.*

25. If the torque converter was removed, insert Pump Aligning Tool J-24033 in the pump rotor until the rotor drive lugs engage the slots in the tool.

26. Rotate the tool until the drilled hole in the tool is vertical and remove the tool.

27. Rotate the converter until the pump drive slots in converter hub are vertical and carefully insert the converter hub into the pump. Be sure the drive lugs of the pump inner rotor are properly engaged in the drive slots of the converter hub.

28. Raise the transmission (and transfer case on Eagle models) and align the converter with the drive plate. Refer to the assembly alignment marks.

29. Move the transmission forward.

30. Raise, lower, or tilt the transmission to align the converter housing pilot holes with the dowels in the engine block.

31. Install two transmission lower attaching bolts and tighten the bolts evenly to pull the transmission to the engine.

32. Install the drive plate-to-converter attaching bolts.

33. Install the remaining transmission attaching bolts and tighten all bolts to 28 ft.lb. torque.

34. Connect the oil cooler lines.

35. Install the rear support cushion on the transmission, if removed.

36. Install the rear crossmember.

37. Remove the safety chain and transmission jack.

38. Install the inspection cover.

39. On Spirit and Concord, install the exhaust pipe clamp on the support bracket.

40. Install the starter. On Eagle models, also install the stiffening braces.

41. Connect the wires to the neutral switch.

42. Connect the gearshift and throttle linkage.

43. Install the speedometer cable and adapter assembly. Be sure the adapter is correctly indexed.

44. On Eagle models, connect the exhaust pipes, attach the stiffening brace and install the skid plate.

45. Install the driveshaft(s). Refer to the alignment marks made during removal. On Eagle models, add the correct quantity of transfer case lubricant.

46. Lower the automobile.

47. Fill the transmission to correct level.

48. Check and adjust the gearshift and throttle linkage if necessary.

49. Road test the automobile to check transmission operation.

1982
4–151

1. Open the hood.
CAUTION: *The hood must remain open to avoid damaging the hood and air cleaner when the rear crossmember is removed.*

2. Disconnect the fan shroud.

3. Remove the bolt attaching the transmission fill tube to the engine.

4. Place the gearshift lever in Neutral.

5. Raise and support the automobile on jackstands.

6. Mark the driveshaft and yoke for assembly alignment reference. On Eagle models, also remove the skid plate.

7. Remove the driveshafts.

8. On Eagle models, disconnect the exhaust system at the exhaust manifold, loosen the exahust system hangers and move the exhaust system as necessary to gain work space.

9. Remove the starter motor. On Eagle models, also remove the stiffening braces.

10. Remove the speedometer adapter and cable assembly. Cover the adapter bore after removal.

11. Disconnect the gearshift and throttle linkage. On automobiles with column shift, remove the bolt attaching the linkage bellcrank bracket to the converter housing.

12. Remove the cover at the front of the converter housing.

13. Mark the converter drive plate and converter for assembly alignment reference.

14. Remove the bolts attaching the converter to the drive plate. Rotate the crankshaft and drive plate using a ratchet handle and socket or box end wrench on the crankshaft front pulley bolt to gain access to the drive plate-to-converter bolts.
NOTE: *The crankshaft pulley bolt is a metric size bolt.*

15. Support the transmission using a transmission jack. Retain the transmission on the jack using a safety chain.

CAUTION: *On Eagle models, both the transmission and transfer case must be properly supported on the transmission jack and retained with a safety chain.*

16. Disconnect the oil cooler lines at the transmission.

17. Remove the bolt attaching the rear support cushion to the rear support cushion bracket (bracket is attached to transmission extension housing).

18. Remove the rear crossmember attaching nuts and remove the crossmember and support cushion as assembly.

19. Place the support stand under the front of the engine.

20. Remove the bolts attaching the catalytic converter support bracket to the transmission, if equipped.

21. Remove the fill tube.

22. Remove the bolts attaching the transmission to the engine.
NOTE: *The transmission-to-engine block bolts are metric size bolts.*

23. Move the transmission (and transfer case, if equipped) and converter rearward until clear of the crankshaft.

24. Hold the converter in position and lower the transmission until the transmission converter housing clears the engine.
CAUTION: *If the transmission was removed to correct a malfunction that generated sludge or heavy accumulations of metal or friction material particles, the oil cooler and cooler lines must be thoroughly flushed and the torque converter replaced. Do not attempt to flush the converter if it is contaminated.*

25. If the torque converter was removed, insert Pump Aligning Tool J-24033 into the pump rotor and engage the tool slots with the pump rotor drive lugs.

26. Rotate the aligning tool until the hole in tool is vertical, then remove the tool.

27. Rotate the converter until the pump drive slots in the converter hub are vertical.

28. Carefully insert the converter hub into the oil pump. Be sure the drive lugs of the pump inner rotor are completely engaged with the drive slots in the converter hub.

29. Raise the transmission and align the converter with the drive plate. Refer to the alignment marks made during removal.
CAUTION: *On Eagle models, both the transmission and transfer case must be supported on a transmission jack and retained with a safety chain.*

30. Move the transmission forward and raise, lower, or tilt the transmission to align the transmission converter housing dowel holes with the dowels in the engine block.
NOTE: *If the downward angle at the rear of the engine is not sufficient to permit trans-*

mission installation, raise the front of the engine to increase the downward angle.

31. Install two transmission-to-engine lower attaching bolts and tighten the bolts evenly to pull the transmission to the engine.

32. Install the drive plate-to-converter attaching bolts. Tighten the bolts to 40 ft.lb. torque.

NOTE: *Coat the threads of the drive plate-to-converter attaching bolts with Loctite*271, or equivalent.*

33. Install the remaining transmission-to-engine attaching bolts. Tighten the bolts to 54 ft.lb. torque.

34. Connect the oil cooler lines.

35. Install the driveshaft using the reference marks made during disassembly.

36. Install the rear crossmember and support cushion. Tighten the attaching nuts to 30 ft.lb. torque.

37. Install the rear support cushion-to-support cushion bracket bolt. Tighten the bolt to 48 ft.lb. torque.

38. Remove the safety chain and transmission cover.

39. Install the converter housing inspection cover.

40. Install the starter motor. On Eagle models also install the stiffening brace and skid plate.

41. Connect the neutral start switch wires to the switch terminal.

42. Connect the gearshift and throttle linkage. On automobiles with column shift, position the linkage bellcrank bracket on the converter housing and install the bracket attaching bolt.

43. Install the speedometer cable and adapter assembly. Be sure the adapter is correctly indexed.

44. Connect the catalytic converter, if equipped. On Eagle models, add the correct quantity of transfer case lubricant.

45. Lower the automobile.

46. Fill the transmission to the correct fluid level.

47. Check and adjust the gearshift lever and throttle linkage, if necessary.

NOTE: *The gearshift lever adjusting trunnion is located at the lower end of the steering column.*

48. Road test the automobile to check transmission operation.

6-258

1. Disconnect the fan shroud, if equipped.

2. Disconnect the transmission fill tube at upper bracket.

3. Open the hood.

CAUTION: *It is necessary that the hood be open to avoid damaging the hood and air cleaner when the rear crossmember is removed.*

4. Raise and support the car on jackstands.

5. Remove the inspection cover from the converter housing.

6. On Spirit and Concord, remove the screw attaching the exhaust pipe clamp to the exhaust pipe support bracket and slide the clamp off the bracket.

7. Remove the transmission fill tube.

8. Remove the starter. On Eagle models, also remove the stiffening braces.

9. Mark the driveshaft(s) and yoke(s) for assembly alignment reference.

10. Remove the driveshaft(s).

11. On Eagle models, disconnect the exhaust pipe and move it aside for working clearance.

12. Remove the speedometer adapter and cable assembly. Discard the adapter and cable seals, they are not reuseable. Cover the adapter bore after removal.

13. Disconnect the gearshift and throttle linkage.

14. Disconnect the wires at the neutral start switch.

15. Mark the converter drive plate and converter for assembly alignment reference.

16. Remove the bolts attaching the converter to the drive plate. Rotate the crankshaft and drive plate using a ratchet handle and socket on the crankshaft front pulley bolt to gain access to the drive plate bolts.

17. On Eagle models, remove the skid plate and stiffening braces.

CAUTION: *Support the transmission (and transfer case on Eagle models) using a transmission jack. Retain the transmission on the jack using a safety chain.*

18. Disconnect the oil cooler lines at the transmission.

19. Remove the bolts attaching the rear support cushion to the transmission.

20. Remove the rear crossmember.

21. Remove the bolts attaching the transmission to the engine.

22. Move the transmission and converter rearward to clear the crankshaft.

23. Hold the converter in position and lower the transmission assembly until the converter housing clears the engine.

24. If the torque converter was removed, insert Pump Aligning Tool J-24033 in the pump rotor until the rotor drive lugs engage the slots in the tool.

25. Rotate the tool until the drilled hole in the tool is vertical and remove the tool.

26. Rotate the converter until the pump drive slots in the converter hub are vertical and carefully insert the converter hub into the pump. Be sure the drive lugs of the pump inner

rotor are properly engaged in the drive slots of the converter hub.

27. Raise the transmission (and transfer case on Eagle models) and align the converter with the drive plate. Refer to the assembly alignment marks.

28. Move the transmission forward.

29. Raise, lower, or tilt the transmission to align the converter housing pilot holes with the dowels in the engine block.

30. Install the two transmission lower attaching bolts and tighten the bolts evenly to pull the transmission to the engine.

31. Install the drive plate-to-converter attaching bolts.

32. Install the remaining transmission attaching bolts and tighten all bolts to 28 ft.lb. torque.

33. Connect the oil cooler lines.

34. Install the rear support cushion on the transmission, if removed.

35. Install the rear crossmember.

36. Remove the safety chain and transmission jack.

37. Install the inspection cover.

38. On Spirit and Concord, install the exhaust pipe clamp on the support bracket.

39. Install the starter. On Eagle models, also install the stiffening braces.

40. Connect the wires to the neutral switch.

41. Connect the gearshift and throttle linkage.

42. Install the speedometer cable and adapter assembly. Be sure the adapter is correctly indexed.

43. On Eagle models, connect the exhaust pipes, attach the stiffening brace and install the skid plate.

44. Install the driveshaft(s). Refer to the alignment marks made during removal. On Eagle models, add the correct quantity of transfer case lubricant.

45. Lower the automobile.

46. Fill the transmission to the correct level.

47. Check and adjust the gearshift and throttle linkage, if necessary.

48. Road test the automobile to check transmission operation.

Adjustments

LOW AND REVERSE BAND

All 904
1978 and Later 998

1. Drain the fluid and remove the pan.

2. On 6-cylinder models:

  a. Remove the adjusting screw locknut.

  b. Tighten the adjusting screw to 41 in.lb. On some early Pacers, and all 998, torque the screw to 72 in.lb.

  c. Back the adjusting screw out 7 turns. (3¼ turns on early 1975 Pacers).

  d. Hold the adjusting screw, install the locknut, and tighten the locknut to 35 ft.lb. NOTE: *Heavy duty fleet versions of the 258 six and 304 V8 use the same transmission as the 360 and 401 V8. Thus, these models would follow the adjustment procedure for the 360 and 401 V8.*

3. On V8 models:

  a. Loosen the locknut and back it off 5 turns.

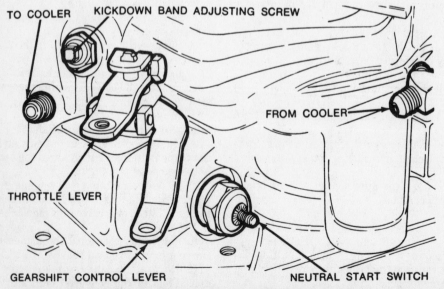

Automatic transmission external adjustments and controls

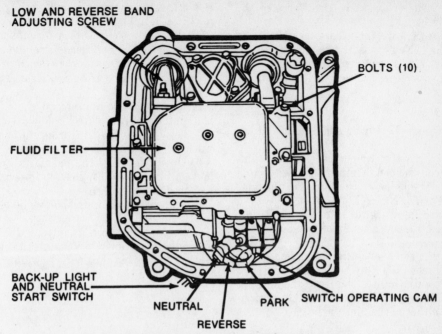

LOW AND REVERSE BAND
ADJUSTING SCREW

BOLTS (10)

FLUID FILTER

BACK-UP LIGHT
AND NEUTRAL
START SWITCH

NEUTRAL

PARK   SWITCH OPERATING CAM

REVERSE

Low and reverse band adjusting screw locations

b. Tighten the adjusting screw to 72 in.lb.

c. Back the adjusting screw out 4 turns with the 304 V8 and 2 turns with the 360 and 401 V8's.

d. Hold the adjusting screw and tighten the locknut to 35 ft.lb.

4. Install the pan with a new gasket. Tighten the screws to 150 in.lb. Fill the transmission as explained in Chapter 1.

LOW AND REVERSE BAND

**All 727,
1975–77 998**

1. Raise the car, drain the transmission, and remove the pan.

2. Loosen the locknut on the adjusting screw and back off the locknut about 5 turns. Be sure the adjusting screw is free to turn.

3. Tighten the adjusting screw to exactly 72 in.lb. of torque.

4. Back off the adjusting screw exactly to specification. Hold the adjusting screw to keep it from turning and tighten the locknut to 30–35 ft.lb.

  • 998 4 turns
  • 727 2 turns

5. Install the pan using a new gasket. Tighten the pan bolts to 150 in.lb. Refill the transmission with DEXRON®II fluid.

KICK-DOWN BAND

The adjustment screw for the kickdown band is located on the left side of the transmission, above the throttle and manual linkage levers.

1. Loosen the locknut and back it off 5 turns.

2. Using a torque wrench, tighten the screw to 72 in.lb.

3. Back off the adjusting screw:
  • 998 and 727, 1972–77 2½ turns
  • 904 2 turns
  • 998, 1978 and later 2 turns
      1978 2½ turns

4. Hold the adjusting screw and tighten the locknut to 29 ft.lb.

Neutral Safety and Backup Light Switch

This switch prevents the engine from being started in any transmission position other

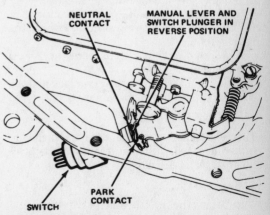

NEUTRAL
CONTACT

MANUAL LEVER AND
SWITCH PLUNGER IN
REVERSE POSITION

PARK
CONTACT

SWITCH

Neutral start and back-up light switch with the pan removed

than Neutral or Park. It also operates the backup lights.

On all American Motors cars, a combination backup light/Neutral safety switch is mounted on the left side of the transmission case. This switch cannot be adjusted; failure requires replacement.

TESTING

1. Unfasten the wiring connector from the switch.

2. Use a 12V test lamp to check for continuity between the center pin of the switch and the transmission case. The lamp should light only in Park or Neutral.

3. If the lamp lights in other positions, check the transmission linkage adjustments before replacing the switch.

4. To test the backup light function of the switch repeat Step 2 by bridging the outside pins to test continuity. The lamp should light only in Reverse. There should not be continuity from either of the pins to the case.

REPLACEMENT

1. Place a container under the switch to catch transmission fluid. Unscrew the switch.

2. Shift to Park and then Neutral while checking to see that the operating fingers for the switch are centered in the case opening.

3. Screw a new switch and a new seal into the transmission. Tighten the switch to 24 ft.lb.

4. Retest continuity. Add to the transmission fluid, as required. See Chapter 1 for details.

Adjustments

SHIFT LINKAGE

The function of this adjustment is to make sure that the transmission is fully engaged in each range position. If this is not the case, there could be severe damage due to slippage.

1. With the engine off, place the selector in Park and the transmission shifting lever in the Park detent.

2. Adjust the shift rod, as necessary, for a free pin fit.

3. See that the steering column lock and the Neutral safety switch operate properly.

THROTTLE LINKAGE

This adjustment positions a valve which controls shift speed, shift firmness, and part-throttle downshift sensitivity.

All Except 4-151

1. Detach the throttle control rod spring and hook it so that the throttle control lever is held forward against its stop.

2. Block the choke open and set the carburetor throttle linkage off the fast idle cam.

NOTE: *On models with a throttle solenoid valve, energize the solenoid and open the throttle halfway so that the solenoid will lock and then return the throttle to the idle position.*

3. Loosen, but do not remove, the retaining bolt on the throttle control rod adjusting link.

4. On V8's, remove the spring clip and nylon washer; leave them in place on sixes.

5. On sixes, pull on the end of the link to remove all lash. On V8s, push on the end of the link to remove all lash.

6. Tighten the retaining bolt while performing Step 5.

7. Replace the throttle control rod spring in its original location. On V8s, install the nylon washer and spring clip on the retaining rod before replacing the spring.

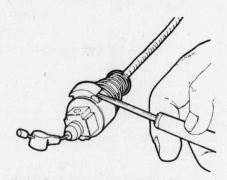

4 cylinder T-shaped cable adjuster clamp

4-151

1. Remove the air cleaner.

2. Remove the spark plug separator from the throttle cable bracket and move the separator and bracket out of the way.

3. Raise the car and support it on jackstands. Remove the strut rod bushing heat shield from the bottom of the transmission and hold the throttle control lever rearward against its stop using a spring.

4. Lower the car and block the choke open, then set the carburetor linkage completely off the fast idle cam.

5. Turn the ignition key to the ON position to energize the throttle stop solenoid.

6. Unlock the throttle control cable by releasing the T-shaped clamp. Release the clamp by prying it up with a screwdriver.

7. Grasp the cable outer sheath and pull it and the cable forward to remove any load on the throttle cable bellcrank, which is part of the carburetor linkage.

8. Adjust the cable by moving the cable.

Transfer Case Application Chart

Transfer Case Type	Years	Models
New Process NP-207	1987	All models
Warner Quadra-Trac®	1976–79	Standard on CJ-7 w/automatic trans.

TRANSFER CASE

REMOVAL AND INSTALLATION

Manual Transmission

NOTE: *Steps 1 through 6, below, pertain to models with the SR-4 transmission only.*

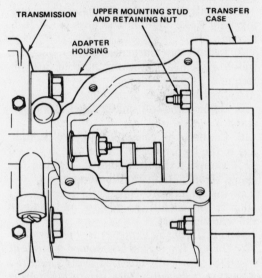

Transfer case mounting stud location on models mated to the SR4 transmission

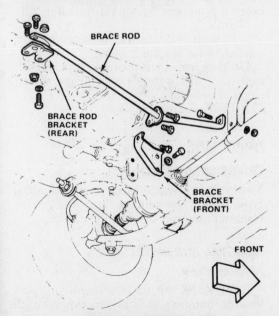

Manual transmission brace and bracket

1. Shift the transmission into neutral.
2. Remove the screws attaching the gearshift lever bezel to the floorpan or console, if equipped.
3. Side the bezel and boot upward on the gearshift to provide access to the lever attaching bolts.
4. Remove the bolts attaching the gearshift lever to the lever mounting cover on the transmission adapter housing and remove the lever.
5. Remove the bolts attaching the gearshift lever mounting cover to the transmission adapter housing and remove the cover.
6. Remove the nut from the transfer case mounting stud located inside the transmission adapter housing.
7. Raise the automobile.
8. Remove the skid plate and rear brace rod at the transfer case.
9. Remove the speedometer adapter retainer attaching bolt and remove the retainer, adapter, and cable. Plug the adapter opening in the transfer case to prevent excessive oil spillage.

NOTE: *Mark the position of the speedometer adapter for assembly reference before removing it.*

10. Mark the driveshafts and axle yokes for assembly alignment reference and disconnect the driveshafts at the transfer case.
11. On 1982 models, remove the transfer case shift motor vacuum harness.
12. Support the transfer case with a transmission jack.
13. Remove the nuts from the transfer case mounting stud nuts.
14. Align the transmission output and transfer case input shafts and install the transfer case on the transmission adapter housing.
15. Install and tighten the transfer case mounting stud nuts to 33 ft.lb. torque.
16. Remove the jack used to support the transfer case.
17. Align and connect the driveshafts to the axle yokes. Tighten the clamp strap bolts to 15 ft.lb. torque.
18. Install the replacement O-ring on the speedometer adapter and install the adapter and cable and retainer. Tighten the retainer bolt to 100 in.lb. torque.

CAUTION: *Do not attempt to reuse the original adapter O-ring. The O-ring is designed to swell in service to improve its sealing qual-*

ities and could be cut or torn during installation if reuse is attempted.

19. Install the skid plate and rear brace rod. Torque the retaining bolts to 30 ft.lb. torque.

20. On 1982 models install the transfer case shift motor vacuum harness.

21. Check and correct the lubricant levels in the transmission and transfer case if necessary.

22. Lower the automobile.

NOTE: *Steps 23 through 26, below, pertain to models with the SR-4 transmission only.*

23. Install the nut on the transfer case mounting stud located inside the transmission adapter housing. Tighten the nut to 33 ft.lb. torque.

24. Install the gearshift lever on the mounting cover on the transmission adapter housing.

25. Install the gearshift lever on the mounting cover. Be sure lever is engaged with the shift rail before tightening the lever attaching bolts.

26. Position the gearshift lever boot and bezel on the floorpan or console, if equipped, and install the bezel attaching screws.

Automatic Transmission.

1. Raise the automobile.

2. Support the engine and transmission with a support stand or transmission jack.

3. Disconnect the catalytic converter support bracket at the adapter housing.

4. Remove the skid plate and rear brace rod at the transfer case.

5. Remove the speedometer cable and adapter from the transfer case. Discard the adapter O-ring; it is not reusable.

6. Mark the driveshafts and transfer case yokes for assembly reference.

7. Disconnect the driveshafts at the yokes. Secure the shafts to the underside of the automobile.

8. Disconnect the gearshift and throttle linkage at the transmission.

9. Lower the rear crossmember.

10. Remove the transfer case-to-adapter housing stud nuts and remove the transfer case.

11. Install the transfer case on the adapter housing. Do not damage the output shaft splines during installation.

12. Install the transfer case-to-adapter housing stud nuts. Tighten the nuts to 33 ft.lb. torque.

13. Install the rear crossmember. Tighten the crossmember attaching nuts to 30 ft.lb. torque.

14. Install the rear brace rod.

15. Remove the transmission jack or support stand.

16. Connect the gearshift and throttle linkage to the transmission.

17. Connect the driveshafts. Tighten the clamp strap bolts to 15 ft.lb. torque.

18. Install a new O-ring on the speedometer adapter and install the adapter and cable in the transfer case.

NOTE: *Do not attempt to reuse the old adapter O-ring. The O-ring is designed to swell in service to provide improved sealing qualities and could be cut or torn if reinstallation is attempted.*

19. Install the skid plate and stiffening brace, if equipped. Tighten the retaining bolts to 30 ft.lb.

20. Connect the catalytic converter support bracket to the adapter housing.

21. Check and adjust the transfer case lubricant level and transmission linkage adjustments if necessary.

22. Lower the automobile.

DRIVE LINE

Driveshaft and U-Joints

Two types of driveshafts are used, designated types 1 and 2, depending on the type of bearing cap retaining ring. See the illustration.

REMOVAL AND INSTALLATION

All Except Eagle

1. Mark the rear universal joint yoke and bearing retainers so that you can reinstall them in their original positions.

2. Remove the U-bolts, being careful not to

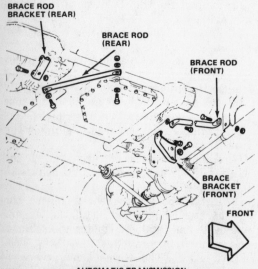

BRACE ROD
BRACKET (REAR)

BRACE ROD
(REAR)

BRACE ROD
(FRONT)

BRACE
BRACKET
(FRONT)

FRONT

AUTOMATIC TRANSMISSION
Automatic transmission brace and bracket

lose the round bearing retainer caps, which are filled with little needle bearings. Don't make any attempt to remove the large nut holding the yoke to the front of the rear axle assembly.

3. Slide the driveshaft back and remove it.

4. On installation, slide the front yoke on the transmission output shaft splines far enough to align the rear universal joint.

5. Align the marks you made in Step 1.

6. Install the rear U-bolts and tighten them evenly to 15 ft.lb. A torque wrench isn't essential here, but remember that 15 ft.lb. isn't very much. You can crush the bearings and retainer caps if you get carried away.

Eagle

NOTE: *Both driveshafts are secured at the transfer case end and the axle yoke end by*

Troubleshooting Basic Driveshaft and Rear Axle Problems

When abnormal vibrations or noises are detected in the driveshaft area, this chart can be used to help diagnose possible causes. Remember that other components such as wheels, tires, rear axle and suspension can also produce similar conditions.

BASIC DRIVESHAFT PROBLEMS

Problem	Cause	Solution
Shudder as car accelerates from stop or low speed	• Loose U-joint • Defective center bearing	• Replace U-joint • Replace center bearing
Loud clunk in driveshaft when shifting gears	• Worn U-joints	• Replace U-joints
Roughness or vibration at any speed	• Out-of-balance, bent or dented driveshaft • Worn U-joints • U-joint clamp bolts loose	• Balance or replace driveshaft • Replace U-joints • Tighten U-joint clamp bolts
Squeaking noise at low speeds	• Lack of U-joint lubrication	• Lubricate U-joint; if problem persists, replace U-joint
Knock or clicking noise	• U-joint or driveshaft hitting frame tunnel • Worn CV joint	• Correct overloaded condition • Replace CV joint

BASIC REAR AXLE PROBLEMS

First, determine when the noise is most noticeable.

Drive Noise: Produced under vehicle acceleration.

Coast Noise: Produced while the car coasts with a closed throttle.

Float Noise: Occurs while maintaining constant car speed (just enough to keep speed constant) on a level road.

Road Noise

Brick or rough surfaced concrete roads produce noises that seem to come from the rear axle. Road noise is usually identical in Drive or Coast and driving on a different type of road will tell whether the road is the problem.

Tire Noise

Tire noises are often mistaken for rear axle problems. Snow treads or unevenly worn tires produce vibrations seeming to originate elsewhere. **Temporarily** inflating the tires to 40 lbs will significantly alter tire noise, but will have no effect on rear axle noises (which normally cease below about 30 mph).

Engine/Transmission Noise

Determine at what speed the noise is most pronounced, then stop the car in a quiet place. With the transmission in Neutral, run the engine through speeds corresponding to road speeds where the noise was noticed. Noises produced with the car standing still are coming from the engine or transmission.

Front Wheel Bearings

While holding the car speed steady, lightly apply the footbrake; this will often decease bearing noise, as some of the load is taken from the bearing.

Rear Axle Noises

Eliminating other possible sources can narrow the cause to the rear axle, which normally produces noise from worn gears or bearings. Gear noises tend to peak in a narrow speed range, while bearing noises will usually vary in pitch with engine speeds.

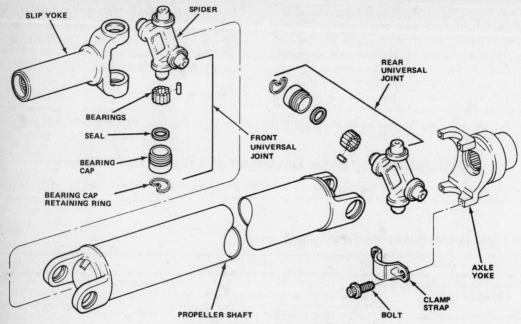

Type 1 driveshaft assembly

straps. The straps are retained by Torx head bolts.

1. Shift into Neutral. Raise and support the car.

2. Matchmark the driveshaft(s) at the transfer case and axle yoke for alignment reference.

3. Remove the retaining straps with a Torx bit tool of the proper size. Remove the driveshaft(s).

4. To install, align the matchmarks made during removal to assure proper balance. Seat the universal joints in the yokes and install the straps, tightening to 17 ft.lb.

U-JOINT OVERHAUL

NOTE: *The four end bearings or roller retainers are held in the yoke ends by snaprings on the front U-joint. The rear U-joint has 4 retainers held by U-bolts.*

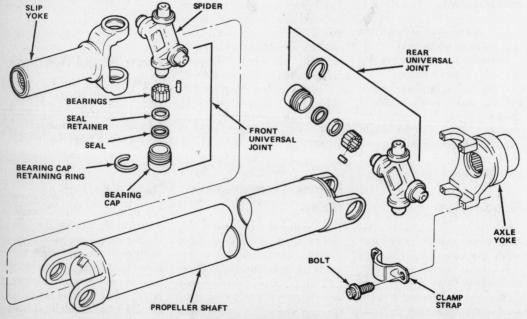

Type 2 driveshaft assembly

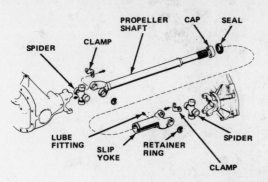 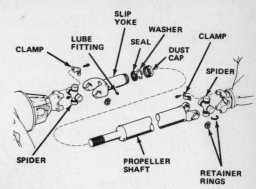

Eagle driveshafts

1. The snaprings can be pried out with a screwdriver.

2. Place the assembly in a vise with a $\frac{9}{16}$" socket against the bearing retainer on one side and a $1\frac{1}{8}$" socket against the yoke on the other side.

3. Tighten the vise slowly; the bearing retainer will be forced out into the big socket.

4. Clamp the protruding bearing retainer gently in the vise and remove it. Watch our for the little needle bearings inside.

5. Remove the other bearings retainers in the same way.

6. Wash all the parts in a safe solvent and check carefully for wear. These parts aren't very expensive and aren't serviced often, so replace any doubtful parts. The 4-armed part is called a cross or a spider.

7. Pack enough high quality grease into each bearing retainer so that you can install the needle bearings without them falling out.

8. Install the cross into the yoke and put the end bearing retainer in place.

9. Place the yoke in a vise and press the bearing retainer, using a $\frac{9}{16}$" socket, past the outside of the yoke.

10. Install the snaprings, making sure that they are securely seated.

EAGLE FRONT AXLE

Axle, Shaft, Shaft Seal and Bearing

REMOVAL AND INSTALLATION

NOTE: *The procedure for replacing the axle shafts and seals on 4-wheel drive models calls for removal of the axle first.*

1. Raise and support the front of the car. Install protectors over the halfshaft boots. Remove the halfshaft-to-axle flange bolts, and tie the halfshafts out of the way.

2. Matchmark the driveshaft and the axle yoke. Remove the driveshaft.

Front Drive Axle Application Chart

Axle Type	Years	Models
Dana 30	1971–87	All models

3. Support the axle on stands. Remove the five axle-to-engine mounting bolts.

4. Lower the axle partway and remove the vent hose. Remove the axle.

5. Remove the differential cover and drain the oil. Remove the axle shaft C-clips.

6. Remove the axle shafts.

7. Carefully remove the shaft seal using a screwdriver.

8. Two different bearings are used; the left side uses a ball bearing, and the right side uses a needle bearing. The ball bearing may be removed using a brass drift and a hammer. The needle bearing should be removed using a needle bearing removal too.

NOTE: *If the proper bearing removal tool is not available, remove the differential and remove the needle bearing using $\frac{15}{16}$" socket and a 3 ft. ratchet extension.*

9. Install the bearings, using drivers of the appropriate type and size.

10. Oil the lips of the new seal and install into the housing using a driver of the correct size.

11. Install the axle shaft and C-clips.

12. Apply a bead of silicone seal to the differential cover and install the cover.

13. Fill the axle with 2.5 pints of 85W-90 GL-5 gear oil.

14. Move the axle into place under the car. Raise it sufficiently to connect the vent hose, then raise it fully into place and install the mounting bolts. Tighten to 50 lbs.

15. Install the driveshaft, aligning the marks made during removal. Install the halfshaft to axle flange bolts, tightening to 45 ft.lb.

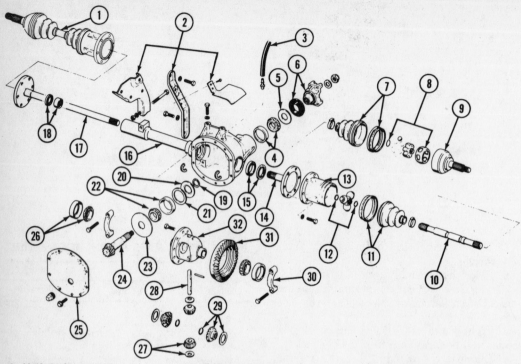

1. Half-shaft assembly
2. Axle mounting brackets
3. Vent hose
4. Pinion and front bearing cup
5. Washer
6. Yoke and seal
7. Outer boot and retainer
8. Rzeppa joint assembly
9. Spindle
10. Half-shaft
11. Inner boot and retainer
12. Tri-pot joint assembly
13. Tri-pot housing
14. Axle shaft (short)
15. Ball bearing and seal
16. Axle housing
17. Axle shaft (long)
18. Needle bearing and seal
19. Preload shim
20. Washer
21. Depth shim
22. Pinion rear bearing and cup
23. Slinger
24. Pinion gear
25. Cover
26. Differential bearing and cup
27. Differential pinion and thrust washer
28. Pinion mate shaft
29. Side gear, thrust washer and lockring
30. Bearing cap
31. Ring gear
32. Differential case

Eagle front drive axle

REAR AXLE

Two sizes of differential assemblies are used on American Motors cars; $7^9/_{16}$" (192mm) and $8^7/_8$" (225mm) ring gear units. A Twin-Grip limited slip differential is available as an option on both units.

A letter code used to identify the axle ratio will be found on most differentials, stamped on the right axle tube housing boss, on the rear side, adjacent to the dowel hole. Some earlier cars have either a metal tag attached to one of the bolts of the differential housing cover or the code letter stamped on the right differential housing cover flange. It may be necessary to remove the cover from the differential to locate the letter. The codes and the axle ratio are listed in dealer parts books and shop manuals.

NOTE: *The $7^9/_{16}$" (192mm) axle can be identified by the cover mounted filler plug, and*

Rear Axle Application Chart

Axle Type	Years	Models
AMC $7^9/_{16}$" ring gear	1984–86	All models
AMC $8^7/_8$" ring gear	1973–83	All models

the $8^7/_8$" (225mm) axle by the front filler on the housing.

Axle Shaft, Bearing and Seal
REMOVAL AND INSTALLATION

1. The hub and drum are separate units and are removed after the wheel is removed. The hub and axle shaft are serrated together on the taper. An axle shaft key assures proper alignment during assembly.

2. With the wheel on the ground and the parking brake applied, remove and discard the

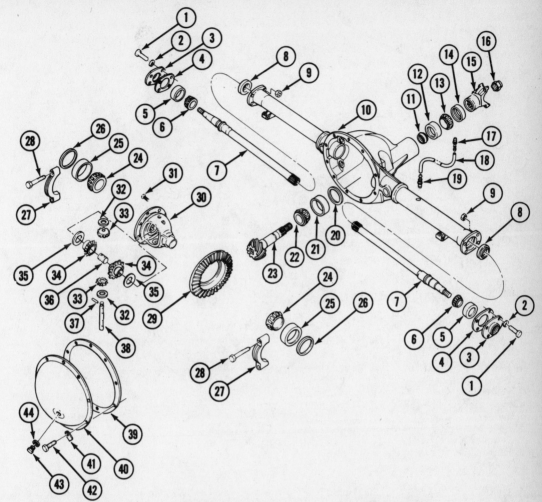

1. Bolt
2. Washer
3. Axle shaft oil seal and retainer assembly
4. Axle shaft bearing shim
5. Axle shaft bearing cup
6. Axle shaft bearing
7. Axle shaft
8. Axle shaft inner oil seal
9. Nut
10. Axle housing
11. Collapsible spacer
12. Pinion bearing cup-front
13. Pinion bearing-front
14. Pinion oil seal
15. Universal joint yoke

16. Pinion nut
17. Breather
18. Breather hose
19. Breather
20. Pinion depth adjusting shim
21. Pinion rear bearing cup
22. Pinion bearing-rear
23. Pinion gear
24. Differential bearing
25. Differential bearing cup
26. Differential bearing shim
27. Differential bearing cap
28. Differential bearing cap bolt
29. Ring gear

30. Differential case
31. Ring gear bolt
32. Differential pinion washer
33. Differential pinion
34. Differential side gear
35. Differential side gear thrust washer
36. Differential pinion shaft thrust block
37. Differential pinion shaft pin
38. Differential pinion shaft
39. Axle housing cover gasket
40. Axle housing cover
41. Axle identification tag
42. Bolt
43. Axle housing cover fill plug
44. Washer

7⁹/₁₆ inch ring gear rear axle with standard differential

axle shaft nut cotter pin and remove the nut. Raise the car and remove the wheel. Release the parking brakes and remove the drum.

3. Attach a puller to the rear hub and remove the hub. The use of a 'Knock-out', or slide hammer, puller should be discouraged, since it may result in damage to the axle shaft or wheel bearings.

4. Disconnect the parking brake cable at the equalizer.

5. Disconnect the brake tube at the wheel cylinder and remove the brake support plate assembly, oil seal, and axle shims. Note that the axle shims are located on the left side only.

6. Using a screw type puller, remove the axle shaft and bearings from the axle housing.

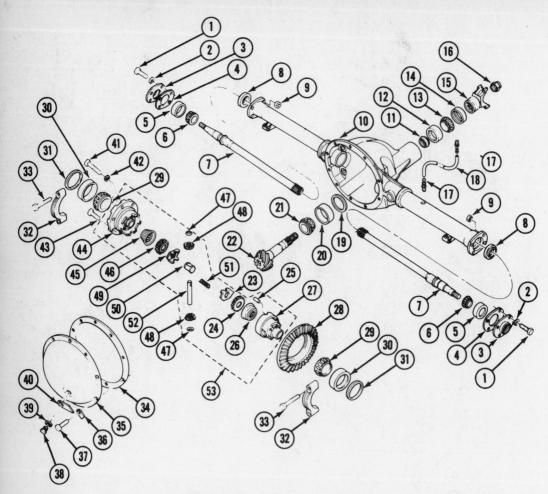

1. Bolt
2. Washer
3. Axle shaft oil seal
4. Axle shaft bearing shim
5. Axle shaft bearing cup
6. Axle shaft bearing
7. Axle shaft
8. Axle shaft inner oil seal
9. Nut
10. Axle housing
11. Collapsible spacer
12. Pinion bearing cup-front
13. Pinion bearing-front
14. Pinion oil seal
15. Universal joint yoke
16. Pinion nut
17. Breather
18. Breather hose
19. Pinion depth
    adjusting shim

20. Pinion bearing cup-rear
21. Pinion bearing-rear
22. Pinion gear
23. Retainer clip
24. Differential side gear
25. Differential pinion shaft pin
26. Clutch cone
27. Differential case
28. Ring gear
29. Differential bearing
30. Differential bearing cup
31. Differential bearing shim
32. Differential bearing cap
33. Differential bearing cap bolt
34. Axle housing cover gasket
35. Axle housing cover
36. Axle identification tag
37. Bolt
38. Axle housing cover fill plug

39. Washer
40. Twin grip identification tag
41. Differential case bolt
42. Washer
43. Ring gear bolt
44. Differential case
45. Clutch cone
46. Differential side gear
47. Differential pinion thrust washer
48. Differential pinion
49. Retainer clip
50. Differential pinion shaft thrust block
51. Spring
52. Differential pinion shaft
53. Differential serviced
    as assembly only

Twin-Grip differential

CAUTION: *On Twin-Grip* axles, rotating
*the differential with one shaft removed will
misalign the side gear splines, preventing installation of the replacement shaft.*

7. Remove the axle shaft inner oil seal and
install new seals at assembly.

8. The bearing is a press fit and should be
removed with an arbor press.

9. The axle shaft bearings have no provision
for lubrication after assembly. Before installing the bearings, they should be packed with a
good quality wheel bearing lubricant.

10. Press the axle shaft bearings onto the axle shaft with the small diameter of the cone toward the outer (tapered) end of the shaft.

11. Soak the inner axle shaft seal in light lubricating oil. Coat the outer surface of the seal retainer with sealant.

12. Install the inner oil seal.

13. Install the axle shafts, indexing the splined end with the differential side gears.

14. Install the outer bearing cup.

15. Install the brake support plate. Sealant should be applied to the axle housing flange and brake support mounting plate.

16. Install the original shims, oil seal and brake support plate. Torque the nuts to 30–35 ft.lb.

NOTE: *The oil seal and retainer go between the axle housing flange and the brake support plate on 9" (228.6mm) brakes or 7⁹/₁₆" (192mm) axle. On 10" (254mm) brakes or 8⅞" (225mm) axle, they go on the outside of the brake support plate.*

17. To adjust the axle shaft end play, strike the axle shafts with a lead mallet to seal the bearings. Install a dial indicator on the brake support plate and check the play while pushing and pulling the axle shaft. End play should be 0.004–0.008" (0.10–0.20mm), with 0.006" (0.15mm) desirable. Add shims to the left side only to decrease the play and remove shims to increase the play.

18. Slide the hub onto the axle shafts aligning the serrations and the keyway onto the hub with the axle shaft key.

19. Replace the hub and drum, install the wheel, lower the car onto the floor and tighten the axle shaft nut to 250 ft.lb. If the cotter pin hole is not aligned with a castellation on the nut, tighten the nut to the next castellation.

NOTE: *A new hub must be installed whenever a new axle shaft is installed.*

20. Install two thrust washers on the shaft. Tighten the new hub onto the shaft until the hub is 1.19" (30.2mm) from the end of the shaft on 7⁹/₁₆" (192mm) differentials, and 1.31" (33.2mm) on 8⅞" (225mm) models. Remove the nut; remove one thrust washer. Install the nut and torque to 250 ft.lb. New hubs do not have serrations on the axle shaft mating surface. The serrations are cut when the hub is installed to the axle shaft.

20. Connect the parking brake cable at the equalizer.

21. Connect the brake tube at the wheel cylinder and bleed the brakes.

Suspension and Steering

FRONT SUSPENSION

The front suspension on all models except Pacer is an independent linked type with the coil springs located between seats in the wheelwell panels and seats in the upper control arms. Rubber insulators between the springs and seats reduce noise transmission to the body.

Direct acting, telescopic shock absorbers are located inside the coil springs and the control arms are attached to the body via rubber bushings.

The suspension system is a double ball joint design, both upper and lower control arms each having one joint.

On all models, strut rods serve to support the lower control arms. Stabilizer bars are used on some models.

The Pacer front suspension is different from all other AMC cars. The coil spring is mounted between the two control arms; seated at the bottom on the lower control arm and at the top in the suspension/engine mount crossmember. The crossmember is isolated from the rest of the body structure by rubber mounting points. The shock absorbers are mounted inside the coil spring. The steering knuckle is attached to the upper and lower control arms by upper and lower ball joints. A front stabilizer bar is optional.

Wheel Alignment Specifications

AMX

Year	Caster (deg.) Range	Pref.	Camber (deg.) Range	Pref.	Toe-in (in.)	King Pin Incl. (deg.)
All	0 to 2½P	1¼P	0 to ¾P	⅜P	1/16 to 3/16	7¾

Gremlin/Hornet/Spirit/Concord

Year	Caster (deg.) Range	Pref.	Camber (deg.) Range	Pref.	Toe-in (in.)	King Pin Incl. (deg.)
1975–77	½N to ½P	0	①	②	1/16 to 3/16	7¾
1978	½P to 1½P	1P	①	②	1/16 to 3/16	7¾
1979–80	0 to 2½P	1¼P	0 to ¾P	⅜P	1/16 to 3/16	7¾
1981–82	0 to 2½P	1¼P	③	④	1/16 to 3/16	7¾
1983	3½P to 5P	4¼P	⑤	⑥	1/16 to 3/16	7¾

① Left: ⅛P to ⅝P
  Right: 0 to ½P
② Left: ⅜P
  Right: ¼P
③ Left: ⅛P to ¾P
  Right: ⅛P to ½P
④ Left: 7/16P
  Right: 5/16P
⑤ Left: ⅛P to ¾P
  Right: ⅛N to ½P
⑥ Left: 7/16P
  Right: 3/16P

Wheel Alignment Specifications

Matador

Year	Caster (deg.)		Camber (deg.)		Toe-in (in.)	King Pin Incl. (deg.)
	Range	Pref.	Range	Pref.		
1975–77	½P to 1½P	1P	①	②	¹⁄₁₆ to ³⁄₁₆	7¾
1978	0 to 2P	1P	①	②	¹⁄₁₆ to ³⁄₁₆	7¾

① Left: ⅛P to ⅝P
 Right: 0 to ½P
② Left: ⅜P
 Right: ¼P

Pacer

Year	Caster (deg.)		Camber (deg.)		Toe-in (in.)	King Pin Incl. (deg.)
	Range	Pref.	Range	Pref.		
1975–77	½P to 1½P	1P	①	②	¹⁄₁₆ to ³⁄₁₆	7¾
1978	1P to 3P	2P	①	②	¹⁄₁₆ to ³⁄₁₆	7¾
1979–80	1P to 3½P	2¼P	0 to ¾P	⅜P	¹⁄₁₆ to ³⁄₁₆	7¾

① Left:⅛P to ⅝P
 Right: 0 to ½P
② Left: ⅜P
 Right: ¼P

Eagle

Year	Caster (deg.)		Camber (deg.)		Toe-out (in.)	King Pin Incl. (deg.)
	Range	Pref.	Range	Pref.		
1980	3P to 5P	4P	⅜N to ⅜P	0	¹⁄₁₆ to ³⁄₁₆	11½
1981–82	2P to 3P	2½P	⅛N to ⅝P	¼P	①	11½
1983	3P to 5P	2½P	⅛N to ⅝P	¼P	¹⁄₁₆ to ³⁄₁₆	11½
1984–87	2P to 3½P	2¾P	⅛N to ⅝P	¼P	¹⁄₁₆ to ³⁄₁₆	11½

① 1981: ¹⁄₁₆ to ³⁄₁₆
 1982: ¹⁄₁₆ out to ¹⁄₁₆ in

NOISE DIAGNOSIS

The Noise Is	Most Probably Produced By
• Identical under Drive or Coast	• Road surface, tires or front wheel bearings
• Different depending on road surface	• Road surface or tires
• Lower as the car speed is lowered	• Tires
• Similar with car standing or moving	• Engine or transmission
• A vibration	• Unbalanced tires, rear wheel bearing, unbalanced driveshaft or worn U-joint
• A knock or click about every 2 tire revolutions	• Rear wheel bearing
• Most pronounced on turns	• Damaged differential gears
• A steady low-pitched whirring or scraping, starting at low speeds	• Damaged or worn pinion bearing
• A chattering vibration on turns	• Wrong differential lubricant or worn clutch plates (limited slip rear axle)
• Noticed only in Drive, Coast or Float conditions	• Worn ring gear and/or pinion gear

Troubleshooting Basic Steering and Suspension Problems

Problem	Cause	Solution
Hard steering (steering wheel is hard to turn)	• Low or uneven tire pressure • Loose power steering pump drive belt • Low or incorrect power steering fluid • Incorrect front end alignment • Defective power steering pump • Bent or poorly lubricated front end parts	• Inflate tires to correct pressure • Adjust belt • Add fluid as necessary • Have front end alignment checked/adjusted • Check pump • Lubricate and/or replace defective parts
Loose steering (too much play in the steering wheel)	• Loose wheel bearings • Loose or worn steering linkage • Faulty shocks • Worn ball joints	• Adjust wheel bearings • Replace worn parts • Replace shocks • Replace ball joints
Car veers or wanders (car pulls to one side with hands off the steering wheel)	• Incorrect tire pressure • Improper front end alignment • Loose wheel bearings • Loose or bent front end components • Faulty shocks	• Inflate tires to correct pressure • Have front end alignment checked/adjusted • Adjust wheel bearings • Replace worn components • Replace shocks
Wheel oscillation or vibration transmitted through steering wheel	• Improper tire pressures • Tires out of balance • Loose wheel bearings • Improper front end alignment • Worn or bent front end components	• Inflate tires to correct pressure • Have tires balanced • Adjust wheel bearings • Have front end alignment checked/adjusted • Replace worn parts
Uneven tire wear	• Incorrect tire pressure • Front end out of alignment • Tires out of balance	• Inflate tires to correct pressure • Have front end alignment checked/adjusted • Have tires balanced

NOTE: *The front end alignment must be checked after any disassembly procedure.*

Shock Absorber

REPLACEMENT

NOTE: *When installing new shock absorbers, purge them of air by extending them in their normal position and compressing them while inverted. Do this several times. It is normal for there to be more resistance to extension than to compression.*

Except Pacer

1. Remove the two lower shock absorber attaching nuts. Remove the washers and the grommets.
2. Remove the upper mounting bracket nuts and bolts.
3. Remove the bracket, complete with shock.
4. Remove the upper attaching nut and separate the shock from the mounting bracket.
5. For adjustable shocks: To adjust the shock, compress the piston completely. Holding the upper part of the shock, turn the shock until the lower arrow is aligned with the de-

sired setting. A click will be heard when the desired setting is reached.

Install the shock as follows:

1. Fit the grommets, washers, upper mounting bracket and nut on the shock, in the reverse order of removal. Tighten the nut to 8 ft.lb.
2. Fully extend the shock and install two grommets on the lower mounting studs.
3. Lower the shock through the hole in the wheel arch. Fit the lower attachment studs through the lower spring seat.
4. Install the grommets, washers, and nuts. Tighten the nuts to 15 ft.lb.
5. Secure the upper mounting bracket with its attachment nuts and bolts. Tighten them to 20 ft.lb.

Pacer

1. Remove the shock absorber upper locknut.
2. Raise the car and remove the nuts from the lower shock absorber mounting studs.
3. Remove the shock along with the lower grommet and jounce bumper retainer from the shock absorber piston rod.

4. Install the retainer on the new shock and the lower grommet on the piston rod.

5. Extend the piston to full length and insert the shock through the lower control arm.

6. Install the locknuts on the lower mounting studs and lower the car.

7. Install the grommet, retainer, and locknut on the piston rod, making sure the grommet seats properly in the hole in the crossmember.

Spring

REMOVAL AND INSTALLATION

Except Pacer

1. Remove the shock absorber.

2. Install a spring compressor through the upper spring seat opening and bolt it to the lower spring seat using the lower shock absorber mounting holes.

3. Remove the lower spring seat pivot retaining nuts, then tighten the compressor tool to compress the spring about 1" (25.4mm).

4. Jack up the front of the car and support it on axle stands at the subframe (allowing the control arms to hang free).

5. Remove the front wheel and pull the lower spring seat out away from the car, then slowly release the spring tension and remove the coil spring and lower spring seat.

To install:

1. Place the spring compressor through the coil spring and tape the rubber spring cushion to the small diameter end of the spring (upper).

2. Place the lower spring seat against the spring with the end of the coil against the formed shoulder in the seat. The shoulder and coil end face inwards, toward the engine, when the spring is installed.

3. Place the spring up against the upper seat, then align the lower spring seat pivot so that the retaining studs will enter the holes in the upper control arm.

4. Compress the coil spring and install the spring.

5. Then install the wheel and tire and lower the car to the floor (to place weight on suspension).

6. Install and tighten lower spring seat spindle retaining nuts and tighten them to 35 ft.lb.

7. Remove the spring compressor and install the shock absorber.

Pacer

1. Disconnect the upper end of the shock absorber.

2. Raise the front end of the car and support it.

3. Disconnect the lower end of the shock absorber and remove it.

4. Disconnect the stabilizer bar at the lower control arm, if so equipped.

5. Remove the wheel, brake drum, or caliper and rotor. Do not allow the brake hose to support the weight of the caliper; use a length of wire to suspend the caliper from the frame.

6. Remove the two bolts that attach the steering arm to the steering knuckle and more the steering arm aside.

7. Use a spring compressor to compress the coil spring.

8. Remove the cotter pin and nut from the lower ball joint stud and disengage the stud from the steering knuckle with a puller.

9. Move the steering knuckle, steering spindle, and support plate, or anchor plate assembly, aside to provide working clearance. Do not allow the brake hose to support the weight of these components. Use wire to hand the components from the upper control arm.

10. Move the lower control arm aside and remove the spring.

To install the front coil spring:

11. Position the upper end of the spring in the spring seat of the front crossmember. Align the cut-off end of the bottom coil with the formed shoulder is the spring seat. The top coil is flat and does not use an insulator. Use a floor jack or jackstand to support the spring until the spring compressor is installed. Install the spring compressor.

12. Assemble the remaining components of the front suspension in the reverse order of removal. Tighten the ball joint stud nut to 75 ft.lb., the steering arm-to-knuckle attaching bolts to 80 ft.lb. through 1976, 55 ft.lb. 1977 and later, the shock absorber lower mounting nuts to 20 ft.lb., and the stabilizer bar locknut to 8 ft.lb.

Upper Control Arm

REMOVAL AND INSTALLATION

Except Pacer

1. Remove the shock absorber and compress the soil spring approximately 2" (51mm) using the procedure under Front Spring Removal and Installation.

2. Jack up the front of the car and support the body on jackstands placed under the subframes (allow the control arms to hang free).

3. Remove the wheel and the upper ball joint cotter pin and retaining nut.

4. Separate the ball joint stud from the steering knuckle using a ball joint removal tool.

5. Remove the inner pivot bolts then remove the control arm.

6. To install, reverse the removal procedure. Do not tighten the pivot bolts nuts until the

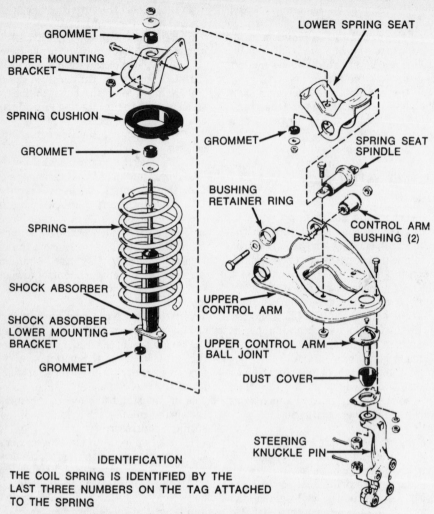

GROMMET

UPPER MOUNTING BRACKET

SPRING CUSHION

GROMMET

SPRING

SHOCK ABSORBER

SHOCK ABSORBER LOWER MOUNTING BRACKET

GROMMET

LOWER SPRING SEAT

GROMMET

SPRING SEAT SPINDLE

BUSHING RETAINER RING

CONTROL ARM BUSHING (2)

UPPER CONTROL ARM

UPPER CONTROL ARM BALL JOINT

DUST COVER

STEERING KNUCKLE PIN

IDENTIFICATION
THE COIL SPRING IS IDENTIFIED BY THE
LAST THREE NUMBERS ON THE TAG ATTACHED
TO THE SPRING

Upper control arm and shock absorber for all except Eagle and Pacer

full weight of the car is on the wheels. The ball joint stud nut must be tightened to 40 ft.lb., through 1975 and 75 ft.lb. thereafter, the lower spring seat pivot retaining nuts to 35 ft.lb., and the control arm inner pivot bolts to 45 ft.lb. through 1976, 80 ft.lb. 1977 and later.

Pacer

1. Raise and support the front of the vehicle.
2. Remove the wheel and tire.
3. Remove the cotter pin, locknut, and retaining nuts from the upper ball joint stud.
4. Loosen the stud from the steering knuckle with a ball joint removal tool.
5. Support the lower control arm with a floor jack.
6. Disengage the stud from the steering knuckle.
7. Remove the retaining nuts that attache the cross-shaft to the front crossmember and remove the upper control arm assembly.
8. Install the upper control arm in the re-

verse order of removal, tightening the cross-shaft retaining nuts to 80 ft.lb., the upper ball joint stud to 75 ft.lb., and if new bushings were installed, tighten the nuts to 60 ft.lb. after the car is lowered to the floor.

Lower Control Arm

REMOVAL AND INSTALLATION

Except Eagle and Pacer

NOTE: *The inner end of the lower control arm is attached to a removable crossmember. The outer end is attached to the steering knuckle pin and ball joint assembly.*

1. Jack up the car and support it on axle stands under the subframes.
2. Remove the brake drum or caliper and rotor from the spindle.
3. Disconnect the steering arm from the knuckle pin.
4. Remove the lower ball joint stud cotter pin and nut.

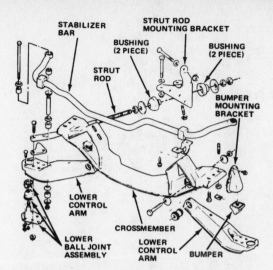

Lower control arm assembly for all except Eagle and Pacer

5. Separate the ball joint from the knuckle pin using a ball joint removal tool.

6. Disconnect the sway bar from the control arm.

7. Unbolt the strut rod.

8. Remove the inner pivot bolt and the control arm.

9. To install, reverse the removal procedure; do not tighten inner pivot bolt until car weight is on wheels. Tighten ball joint retaining nut to 40 ft.lb. through 1976, 75 ft.lb. thereafter, strut rod bolts to 75 ft.lb., sway bar bolts to 8

ft.lb., steering arm bolts to 65 ft.lb. through 1979, 55 ft.lb. thereafter, and control arm inner pivot bolt to 95 ft.lb. through 1976, 110 ft.lb. thereafter.

Eagle

1. Remove the wheel cover. Remove and discard the cotter pin. Remove the nut lock and the hub pin.

2. Raise and support the front of the car. Remove the wheel. Remove the brake caliper from the knuckle and suspend if from the body of a length of wire; do not allow it to hand by the hose. Remove the rotor.

3. Remove the lower ball joint cotter pin and retaining nut. Discard the cotter pin.

4. Separate the ball joint stud from the steering knuckle using a ball joint removal tool.

5. Remove the halfshaft flange bolts and remove the half shaft.

6. Remove the strut rod-to-control arm bolts. Disconnect the stabilizer bar from the arm.

7. Remove the inner pivot bolt and remove the control arm.

8. To install, place the control arm into position and install the inner pivot bolt, but do not tighten the pivot bolt yet.

9. Install the ball joint stud into the steering knuckle. Install the nut and tighten to 75 ft.lb. Continue to tighten until the holes align and install a new cotter pin.

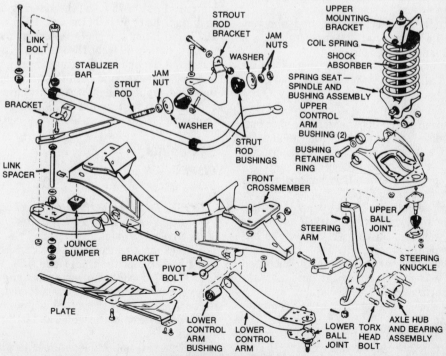

Eagle front suspension

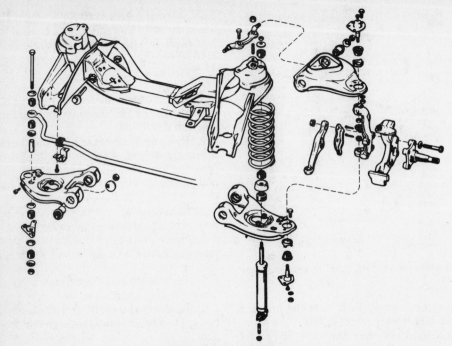

Pacer front suspension

10. Connect the stabilizer bar to the arm; tighten the bolts to 7 ft.lb. Install the strut rod; tighten to 45 ft.lb.

11. Install the halfshaft-to-axle flange bolts; tighten to 45 ft.lb.

12. Place a jack under the lower control arm. Raise the jack carefully to compress the spring slightly. Tighten the control arm pivot bolt to 110 ft.lb.

13. Install the rotor, caliper, and hub nut. Tighten the hub nut to 180 ft.lb. Install the nut lock and a new cotter pin.

14. Install the wheel. Check and adjust the front end alignment as necessary.

Pacer

1. Disconnect the upper end of the shock absorber, raise the front end of the car and disconnect the lower end of the shock absorber and remove the shock absorber.

2. Disconnect the stabilizer bar at the lower control arm, if so equipped.

3. Remove the wheel, brake drum, or caliper and rotor. Do not allow the brake hose to support the weight of the caliper. Use wire to support it from the frame.

4. Remove the two bolts attaching the steering arm to the steering knuckle and more the steering arm aside.

5. Install a spring compressor and compress the spring.

6. Remove the cotter pin and nut from the lower ball joint stud. Remove the ball joint from the steering knuckle using a ball joint removal tool.

7. Move the steering knuckle assembly out of the way. Support the assembly with wire from the upper control arm.

8. Remove the two pivot bolts that attache the lower arm to the front crossmember and remove the lower control arm.

9. Install the lower control arm in the reverse order of removal, tightening the ball joint stud nut to 75 ft.lb., the steering arm attaching bolts to 80 ft.lb. through 1976, 55 ft.lb. 1977 and later, the shock absorber lower attaching nuts to 20 ft.lb., the stabilizer bar locknut to 8 ft.lb., and lastly, after the car has been lowered to the ground with the wheel and tire installed, tighten the lower control arm pivot bolts to 95 ft.lb. through 1976, and 110 ft.lb. thereafter.

Ball Joints
INSPECTION
Except Pacer

NOTE: *Be sure that the front wheel bearings are adjusted to specification before checking the upper ball joint.*

1. Jack up the front of the car and place jackstands under the frame side sills.

NOTE: *The control arms must hang free if an accurate reading is to be obtained.*

2. Check the lower ball joints by grasping the lower portion of the wheel and pulling it in and out.

3. If there is noticeable lateral free play, the lower ball joint is worn and must be replaced.

NOTE: *The lower ball joints and control*

arms must be replaced as assemblies on Eagles.

4. To check the condition of the upper ball joint, place a dial indicator with its plunger against the tire scrub bead (just outside the whitewall).

5. Move the upper portion of the wheel and tire toward the car's center, while watching the dial indicator.

6. Move the wheel and tire back out while watching the indicator.

7. The upper ball joint should be replaced it is total movement is greater than 0.160" (4.06mm).

NOTE: *The upper ball joints and control arms must be replaced as assemblies on 1980 Eagles. On 1981 and later Eagles the upper ball joints are replaceable separately.*

Pacer

1. Check that the front wheel bearings are adjusted properly.

2. Remove the lubrication plug from the lower ball joints. Insert a piece of stiff wire until it contacts the ball. Mark the wire even with the edge of the plug hole.

3. Measure from the end of the wire to the mark. If it exceeds $7/16$" (11.11mm), the ball joint should be replaced.

4. Place a jack under the lower control arm and lift the wheel off the floor.

5. Push the top of the tire in and out. If there is any looseness, replace the upper ball joint.

6. Pry the upper control arm up and down. If there is any looseness, replace the upper ball joint.

REMOVAL AND INSTALLATION

NOTE: *On Eagles, do not attempt to replace the ball joints separately. If the ball joints are worn, the control arms and ball joints must be replaced as complete assemblies.*

Lower Ball Joint

1. On all vehicles except Pacer, place a 2" x 4" x 5" (51mm x 102mm x 127mm) block of wood on the side sill so that it supports the control arm.

2. Jack up the front end of the car and place jackstands underneath the frame side sills to support the body.

3. Remove the wheel and the brake drum. On cars equipped with disc brakes, remove the caliper and rotor.

4. Disconnect the lower control arm strut rod, on models other than Pacer. Disconnect the stabilizer bar, if so equipped.

5. Separate the steering arm from the steering knuckle.

6. Remove the ball stud retaining nut, after removing its cotter pin.

7. Install a ball joint removal tool then loosen the ball stud in the knuckle pin. Leave the tool in place on the stud.

8. Place a jackstand under the lower control arm.

9. Chisel the heads off the rivets which secure the ball joint to the control arm. Use a punch to remove the rivets.

10. Remove the tool from the ball stud.

11. Remove the ball stud from the knuckle pin and remove the joint from the control arm.

Installation of a new lower ball joint is as follows:

1. Position the new ball joint so that its securing holes align with the rivet holes in the control arm.

2. Install the special $5/16$" bolts, used to secure the ball joint, loosely.

CAUTION: *Use only the hardened $5/16$" bolts supplied with the ball joint replacement kit; standard bolts are not strong enough.*

3. Install the steering strut and stop on the lower control arm. Tighten their bolts to 75 ft.lb.

4. Tighten the $5/16$" ball joint securing bolts to 25 ft.lb.

5. Apply chassis grease to the steering stops and fit the knuckle pin and retaining nut on the ball stud; tighten the nut to 40 ft.lb. through 1976, 75 ft.lb. through 1976, 75 ft.lb. thereafter, and 75 ft.lb. on all Pacers. Install a new cotter pin.

6. Complete the installation procedure in the reverse order of removal and then check front end alignment.

Upper Ball Joint

1. Perform Steps 1–3 of the 'Lower Ball Joint Removal' procedure.

NOTE: *It is not necessary to remove the brake drum in Step 3. On 1981 and later Eagle models temporarily reinstall two lug nuts to retain each brake rotor. This eliminates repositioning rotors and calipers prior to reassembly.*

2. News, perform Steps 6–9 of the Lower Ball Joint Removal' procedure to the upper ball joint.

3. Separate the upper ball joint from the knuckle pin.

Installation of a new upper ball joint is as follows:

1. Perform Steps 1–2 of the 'Lower Ball Joint Installation' procedure.

2. Skip Step 3 and go on to Steps 4–5 of the 'Lower Ball Joint Installation' procedure.

3. Complete the installation in the reverse order of removal and check front end alignment.

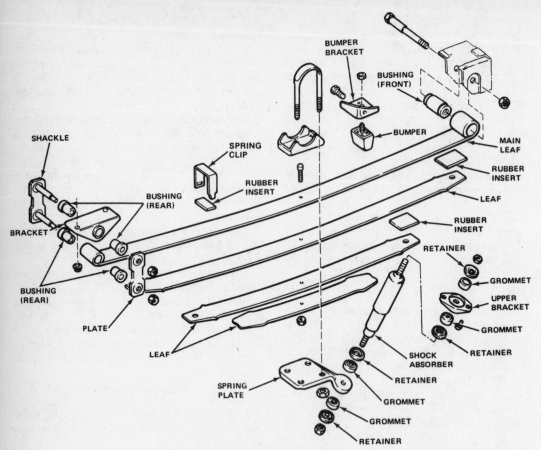

1975-76 rear suspension, except Matador

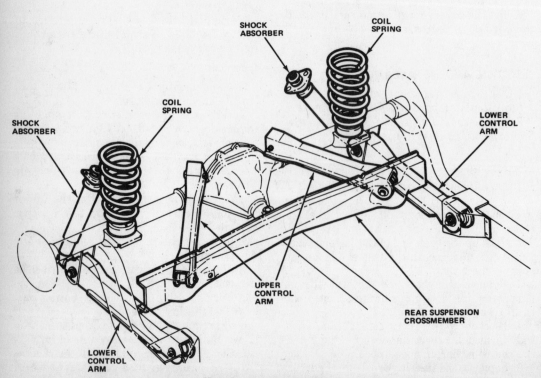

Matador rear suspension

Wheel Bearings

4-wheel drive models have sealed, non-adjustable front hubs and bearings. There are darkened areas surrounding the bearing races in the hubs, which are the result of a heat treatment process; the darkened areas do not signify a defect.

INSPECTION

Check to see the the inner cones of the bearings are free to 'creep' on the spindle. Polish and lubricate the spindle to allow 'creeping' movement and to keep rust from forming.

ADJUSTMENT

1. With the tire and wheel removed and the car supported by a suitable and safe means, remove the dust cover from the spindle.
2. Remove the cotter pin and nut retainer.
3. Rotate the wheel while tightening the spindle nut to 20–25 ft.lb.
4. Loosen the spindle nut ⅓ of a turn.
5. Rotate the wheel while tightening the spindle nut to 6 in.lb.
6. Fit the nut retainer over the spindle and align the slots in it with the cotter pin hole. Insert the cotter pin.

REAR SUSPENSION

Shock Absorber

REPLACEMENT

NOTE: *When installing new shocks purge them of air by repeatedly extending them in their normal position and compressing them while inverted. It is normal for there to be more resistance to extension than to compression.*

1. Support the rear axle with jacks or a lift; this allows the weight of the car to compress the rear spring.
2. Remove the lower shock attachment.
3. Remove the access plate on the rear underbody panel and remove the upper securing nut. It may be necessary to hold the top of the shock while unfastening the nut.

NOTE: *Some models do not have an access plate. On these cars, remove the upper attachment plate complete as an assembly from under the car.*

4. Remove the shock from under the car.
5. Installation is the reverse of removal.

Leaf Springs

REMOVAL AND INSTALLATION

1. Raise the car. Support the rear axle with jacks or a lift to take the load off the rear springs.

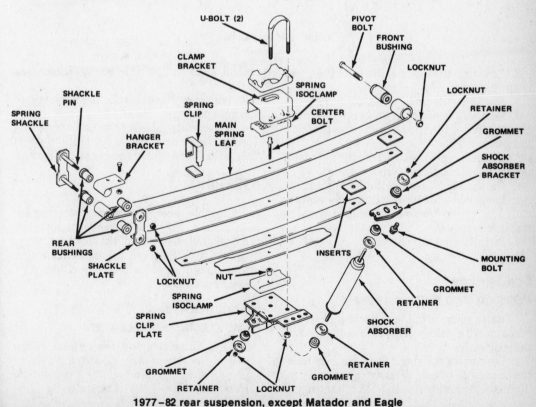

1977–82 rear suspension, except Matador and Eagle

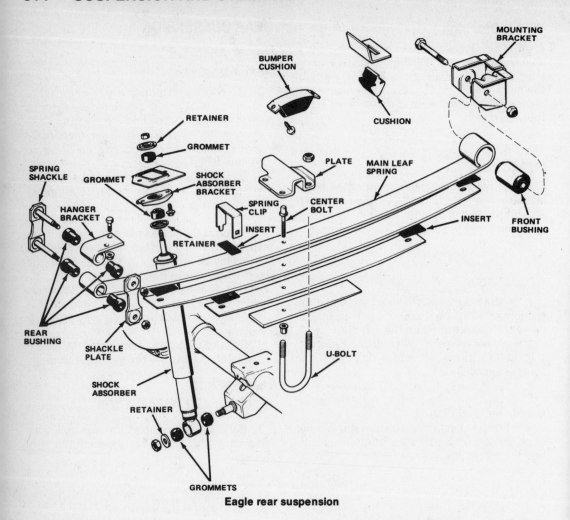

BUMPER CUSHION

MOUNTING BRACKET

CUSHION

RETAINER

GROMMET

PLATE

MAIN LEAF SPRING

SPRING SHACKLE

GROMMET

SHOCK ABSORBER BRACKET

SPRING CLIP

CENTER BOLT

HANGER BRACKET

INSERT

FRONT BUSHING

INSERT

RETAINER

REAR BUSHING

SHACKLE PLATE

U-BOLT

SHOCK ABSORBER

RETAINER

GROMMETS

Eagle rear suspension

2. Disconnect the rear shock from the lower mounting stud.

3. Disconnect the axle U-bolts.

4. Remove the nut from the bolt which attaches the eye of the spring to the front mount. Remove the bolt.

5. On all except Pacer, remove the nuts from the rear shackle. Remove the shackle.

6. On the Pacer, remove the nuts from the rear hanger bracket on the frame sill and remove the spring. Remove the shackle after the spring is removed.

7. Installation is the reverse.

Coil Springs

REMOVAL AND INSTALLATION

1. Raise the rear of the car and support the rear axle with jacks or a lift to take the load off the rear springs.

2. Disconnect the shock from the axle tube. Lower the axle to the fullest extent of its travel (limited by the control arms). Detach the upper

control arms at the axle on 1975 and later models.

3. Pull down the axle tube to completely release the spring.

4. Reverse the above to install the spring. Torque the control arm pivot bolts to 45–80 ft.lb. with the weight of the car on the springs.

STEERING

A collapsible, energy absorbing steering column is used. No service operations involving removal or disassembly of the steering column are given here. Such critical and delicate operations should be entrusted to qualified AMC service personnel.

Steering Wheel

REMOVAL AND INSTALLATION

NOTE: *Some steering shafts have metric steering wheel nut threads. Metric shafts are identified by a groove running around the splines, and blue colored threads.*

Troubleshooting the Steering Column

Problem	Cause	Solution
Will not lock	• Lockbolt spring broken or defective	• Replace lock bolt spring
High effort (required to turn ignition key and lock cylinder)	• Lock cylinder defective • Ignition switch defective • Rack preload spring broken or deformed • Burr on lock sector, lock rack, housing, support or remote rod coupling • Bent sector shaft • Defective lock rack • Remote rod bent, deformed • Ignition switch mounting bracket bent • Distorted coupling slot in lock rack (tilt column)	• Replace lock cylinder • Replace ignition switch • Replace preload spring • Remove burr • Replace shaft • Replace lock rack • Replace rod • Straighten or replace • Replace lock rack
Will stick in "start"	• Remote rod deformed • Ignition switch mounting bracket bent	• Straighten or replace • Straighten or replace
Key cannot be removed in "off-lock"	• Ignition switch is not adjusted correctly • Defective lock cylinder	• Adjust switch • Replace lock cylinder
Lock cylinder can be removed without depressing retainer	• Lock cylinder with defective retainer • Burr over retainer slot in housing cover or on cylinder retainer	• Replace lock cylinder • Remove burr
High effort on lock cylinder between "off" and "off-lock"	• Distorted lock rack • Burr on tang of shift gate (automatic column) • Gearshift linkage not adjusted	• Replace lock rack • Remove burr • Adjust linkage
Noise in column	• One click when in "off-lock" position and the steering wheel is moved (all except automatic column) • Coupling bolts not tightened • Lack of grease on bearings or bearing surfaces • Upper shaft bearing worn or broken • Lower shaft bearing worn or broken • Column not correctly aligned • Coupling pulled apart • Broken coupling lower joint • Steering shaft snap ring not seated • Shroud loose on shift bowl. Housing loose on jacket—will be noticed with ignition in "off-lock" and when torque is applied to steering wheel.	• Normal—lock bolt is seating • Tighten pinch bolts • Lubricate with chassis grease • Replace bearing assembly • Replace bearing. Check shaft and replace if scored. • Align column • Replace coupling • Repair or replace joint and align column • Replace ring. Check for proper seating in groove. • Position shroud over lugs on shift bowl. Tighten mounting screws.
High steering shaft effort	• Column misaligned • Defective upper or lower bearing • Tight steering shaft universal joint • Flash on I.D. of shift tube at plastic joint (tilt column only) • Upper or lower bearing seized	• Align column • Replace as required • Repair or replace • Replace shift tube • Replace bearings
Lash in mounted column assembly	• Column mounting bracket bolts loose • Broken weld nuts on column jacket • Column capsule bracket sheared	• Tighten bolts • Replace column jacket • Replace bracket assembly

Troubleshooting the Steering Column (cont.)

Problem	Cause	Solution
Lash in mounted column assembly (cont.)	• Column bracket to column jacket mounting bolts loose	• Tighten to specified torque
	• Loose lock shoes in housing (tilt column only)	• Replace shoes
	• Loose pivot pins (tilt column only)	• Replace pivot pins and support
	• Loose lock shoe pin (tilt column only)	• Replace pin and housing
	• Loose support screws (tilt column only)	• Tighten screws
Housing loose (tilt column only)	• Excessive clearance between holes in support or housing and pivot pin diameters	• Replace pivot pins and support
	• Housing support-screws loose	• Tighten screws
Steering wheel loose—every other tilt position (tilt column only)	• Loose fit between lock shoe and lock shoe pivot pin	• Replace lock shoes and pivot pin
Steering column not locking in any tilt position (tilt column only)	• Lock shoe seized on pivot pin	• Replace lock shoes and pin
	• Lock shoe grooves have burrs or are filled with foreign material	• Clean or replace lock shoes
	• Lock shoe springs weak or broken	• Replace springs
Noise when tilting column (tilt column only)	• Upper tilt bumpers worn	• Replace tilt bumper
	• Tilt spring rubbing in housing	• Lubricate with chassis grease
One click when in "off-lock" position and the steering wheel is moved	• Seating of lock bolt	• None. Click is normal characteristic sound produced by lock bolt as it seats.
High shift effort (automatic and tilt column only)	• Column not correctly aligned	• Align column
	• Lower bearing not aligned correctly	• Assemble correctly
	• Lack of grease on seal or lower bearing areas	• Lubricate with chassis grease
Improper transmission shifting—automatic and tilt column only	• Sheared shift tube joint	• Replace shift tube
	• Improper transmission gearshift linkage adjustment	• Adjust linkage
	• Loose lower shift lever	• Replace shift tube

1. Disconnect the battery ground cable.

2. On wheels with horn button, remove the button by lifting up and pulling out.

3. On wheels with a horn bar, remove the screws from the back of the wheel and remove the bar. Do the same on rimblow wheels.

4. On rim-blow wheels, pull the wire out of the center connection.

5. Remove the nut and washer.

6. Install the bolts of a steering wheel puller into the tapped holes in the wheel and pull off the wheel.

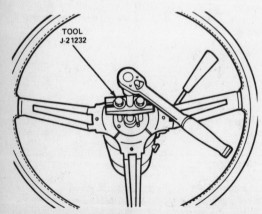

Steering wheel removal

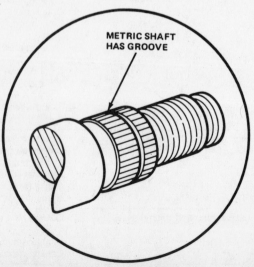

METRIC SHAFT HAS GROOVE

Metric steering shaft identification

Troubleshooting the Ignition Switch

Problem	Cause	Solution
Ignition switch electrically inoperative	• Loose or defective switch connector • Feed wire open (fusible link) • Defective ignition switch	• Tighten or replace connector • Repair or replace • Replace ignition switch
Engine will not crank	• Ignition switch not adjusted properly	• Adjust switch
Ignition switch wil not actuate mechanically	• Defective ignition switch • Defective lock sector • Defective remote rod	• Replace switch • Replace lock sector • Replace remote rod
Ignition switch cannot be adjusted correctly	• Remote rod deformed	• Repair, straighten or replace

Troubleshooting the Turn Signal Switch

Problem	Cause	Solution
Turn signal will not cancel	• Loose switch mounting screws • Switch or anchor bosses broken • Broken, missing or out of position detent, or cancelling spring	• Tighten screws • Replace switch • Reposition springs or replace switch as required
Turn signal difficult to operate	• Turn signal lever loose • Switch yoke broken or distorted • Loose or misplaced springs • Foreign parts and/or materials in switch • Switch mounted loosely	• Tighten mounting screws • Replace switch • Reposition springs or replace switch • Remove foreign parts and/or material • Tighten mounting screws
Turn signal will not indicate lane change	• Broken lane change pressure pad or spring hanger • Broken, missing or misplaced lane change spring • Jammed wires	• Replace switch • Replace or reposition as required • Loosen mounting screws, reposition wires and retighten screws
Turn signal will not stay in turn position	• Foreign material or loose parts impeding movement of switch yoke • Defective switch	• Remove material and/or parts • Replace switch
Hazard switch cannot be pulled out	• Foreign material between hazard support cancelling leg and yoke	• Remove foreign material. No foreign material impeding function of hazard switch—replace turn signal switch.
No turn signal lights	• Inoperative turn signal flasher • Defective or blown fuse • Loose chassis to column harness connector • Disconnect column to chassis connector. Connect new switch to chassis and operate switch by hand. If vehicle lights now operate normally, signal switch is inoperative • If vehicle lights do not operate, check chassis wiring for opens, grounds, etc.	• Replace turn signal flasher • Replace fuse • Connect securely • Replace signal switch • Repair chassis wiring as required
Instrument panel turn indicator lights on but not flashing	• Burned out or damaged front or rear turn signal bulb • If vehicle lights do not operate, check light sockets for high resistance connections, the chassis wiring for opens, grounds, etc.	• Replace bulb • Repair chassis wiring as required

Troubleshooting the Turn Signal Switch (cont.)

Problem	Cause	Solution
Instrument panel turn indicator lights on but not flashing (cont.)	• Inoperative flasher • Loose chassis to column harness connection • Inoperative turn signal switch • To determine if turn signal switch is defective, substitute new switch into circuit and operate switch by hand. If the vehicle's lights operate normally, signal switch is inoperative.	• Replace flasher • Connect securely • Replace turn signal switch • Replace turn signal switch
Stop light not on when turn indicated	• Loose column to chassis connection • Disconnect column to chassis connector. Connect new switch into system without removing old. Operate switch by hand. If brake lights work with switch in the turn position, signal switch is defective. • If brake lights do not work, check connector to stop light sockets for grounds, opens, etc.	• Connect securely • Replace signal switch • Repair connector to stop light circuits using service manual as guide
Turn indicator panel lights not flashing	• Burned out bulbs • High resistance to ground at bulb socket • Opens, ground in wiring harness from front turn signal bulb socket to indicator lights	• Replace bulbs • Replace socket • Locate and repair as required
Turn signal lights flash very slowly	• High resistance ground at light sockets • Incorrect capacity turn signal flasher or bulb • If flashing rate is still extremely slow, check chassis wiring harness from the connector to light sockets for high resistance • Loose chassis to column harness connection • Disconnect column to chassis connector. Connect new switch into system without removing old. Operate switch by hand. If flashing occurs at normal rate, the signal switch is defective.	• Repair high resistance grounds at light sockets • Replace turn signal flasher or bulb • Locate and repair as required • Connect securely • Replace turn signal switch
Hazard signal lights will not flash—turn signal functions normally	• Blow fuse • Inoperative hazard warning flasher • Loose chassis-to-column harness connection • Disconnect column to chassis connector. Connect new switch into system without removing old. Depress the hazard warning lights. If they now work normally, turn signal switch is defective. • If lights do not flash, check wiring harness "K" lead for open between hazard flasher and connector. If open, fuse block is defective	• Replace fuse • Replace hazard warning flasher in fuse panel • Conect securely • Replace turn signal switch • Repair or replace brown wire or connector as required

Troubleshooting the Manual Steering Gear

Problem	Cause	Solution
Hard or erratic steering	• Incorrect tire pressure	• Inflate tires to recommended pressures
	• Insufficient or incorrect lubrication	• Lubricate as required (refer to Maintenance Section)
	• Suspension, or steering linkage parts damaged or misaligned	• Repair or replace parts as necessary
	• Improper front wheel alignment	• Adjust incorrect wheel alignment angles
	• Incorrect steering gear adjustment	• Adjust steering gear
	• Sagging springs	• Replace springs
Play or looseness in steering	• Steering wheel loose	• Inspect shaft spines and repair as necessary. Tighten attaching nut and stake in place.
	• Steering linkage or attaching parts loose or worn	• Tighten, adjust, or replace faulty components
	• Pitman arm loose	• Inspect shaft splines and repair as necessary. Tighten attaching nut and stake in place
	• Steering gear attaching bolts loose	• Tighten bolts
	• Loose or worn wheel bearings	• Adjust or replace bearings
	• Steering gear adjustment incorrect or parts badly worn	• Adjust gear or replace defective parts
Wheel shimmy or tramp	• Improper tire pressure	• Inflate tires to recommended pressures
	• Wheels, tires, or brake rotors out-of-balance or out-of-round	• Inspect and replace or balance parts
	• Inoperative, worn, or loose shock absorbers or mounting parts	• Repair or replace shocks or mountings
	• Loose or worn steering or suspension parts	• Tighten or replace as necessary
	• Loose or worn wheel bearings	• Adjust or replace bearings
	• Incorrect steering gear adjustments	• Adjust steering gear
	• Incorrect front wheel alignment	• Correct front wheel alignment
Tire wear	• Improper tire pressure	• Inflate tires to recommended pressures
	• Failure to rotate tires	• Rotate tires
	• Brakes grabbing	• Adjust or repair brakes
	• Incorrect front wheel alignment	• Align incorrect angles
	• Broken or damaged steering and suspension parts	• Repair or replace defective parts
	• Wheel runout	• Replace faulty wheel
	• Excessive speed on turns	• Make driver aware of conditions
Vehicle leads to one side	• Improper tire pressures	• Inflate tires to recommended pressures
	• Front tires with uneven tread depth, wear pattern, or different cord design (i.e., one bias ply and one belted or radial tire on front wheels)	• Install tires of same cord construction and reasonably even tread depth, design, and wear pattern
	• Incorrect front wheel alignment	• Align incorrect angles
	• Brakes dragging	• Adjust or repair brakes
	• Pulling due to uneven tire construction	• Replace faulty tire

CAUTION: *Don't hammer on the steering wheel or the shaft. You could easily collapse your collapsible steering column.*

7. On installation, align the marks on the steering shaft and the wheel at the top.

8. Install the washer and nut and tighten the nut to 20 ft.lb. This is a critical fastener; it must be torqued.

9. On wheels with a horn button, index the projection on the rubber retaining ring with the notch in the cup and push down to engage the ring.

Troubleshooting the Power Steering Gear

Problem	Cause	Solution
Hissing noise in steering gear	• There is some noise in all power steering systems. One of the most common is a hissing sound most evident at standstill parking. There is no relationship between this noise and performance of the steering. Hiss may be expected when steering wheel is at end of travel or when slowly turning at standstill.	• Slight hiss is normal and in no way affects steering. Do not replace valve unless hiss is extremely objectionable. A replacement valve will also exhibit slight noise and is not always a cure. Investigate clearance around flexible coupling rivets. Be sure steering shaft and gear are aligned so flexible coupling rotates in a flat plane and is not distorted as shaft rotates. Any metal-to-metal contacts through flexible coupling will transmit valve hiss into passenger compartment through the steering column.
Rattle or chuckle noise in steering gear	• Gear loose on frame	• Check gear-to-frame mounting screws. Tighten screws to 88 N·m (65 foot pounds) torque.
	• Steering linkage looseness	• Check linkage pivot points for wear. Replace if necessary.
	• Pressure hose touching other parts of car	• Adjust hose position. Do not bend tubing by hand.
	• Loose pitman shaft over center adjustment	• Adjust to specifications
	NOTE: A slight rattle may occur on turns because of increased clearance off the "high point." This is normal and clearance must not be reduced below specified limits to eliminate this slight rattle.	
	• Loose pitman arm	• Tighten pitman arm nut to specifications
Squawk noise in steering gear when turning or recovering from a turn	• Damper O-ring on valve spool cut	• Replace damper O-ring
Poor return of steering wheel to center	• Tires not properly inflated	• Inflate to specified pressure
	• Lack of lubrication in linkage and ball joints	• Lube linkage and ball joints
	• Lower coupling flange rubbing against steering gear adjuster plug	• Loosen pinch bolt and assemble properly
	• Steering gear to column misalignment	• Align steering column
	• Improper front wheel alignment	• Check and adjust as necessary
	• Steering linkage binding	• Replace pivots
	• Ball joints binding	• Replace ball joints
	• Steering wheel rubbing against housing	• Align housing
	• Tight or frozen steering shaft bearings	• Replace bearings
	• Sticking or plugged valve spool	• Remove and clean or replace valve
	• Steering gear adjustments over specifications	• Check adjustment with gear out of car. Adjust as required.
	• Kink in return hose	• Replace hose
Car leads to one side or the other (keep in mind road condition and wind. Test car in both directions on flat road)	• Front end misaligned	• Adjust to specifications
	• Unbalanced steering gear valve	• Replace valve
	NOTE: If this is cause, steering effort will be very light in direction of lead and normal or heavier in opposite direction	

Troubleshooting the Power Steering Gear (cont.)

Problem	Cause	Solution
Momentary increase in effort when turning wheel fast to right or left	• Low oil level • Pump belt slipping • High internal leakage	• Add power steering fluid as required • Tighten or replace belt • Check pump pressure. (See pressure test)
Steering wheel surges or jerks when turning with engine running especially during parking	• Low oil level • Loose pump belt • Steering linkage hitting engine oil pan at full turn • Insufficient pump pressure • Pump flow control valve sticking	• Fill as required • Adjust tension to specification • Correct clearance • Check pump pressure. (See pressure test). Replace relief valve if defective. • Inspect for varnish or damage, replace if necessary
Excessive wheel kickback or loose steering	• Air in system • Steering gear loose on frame • Steering linkage joints worn enough to be loose • Worn poppet valve • Loose thrust bearing preload adjustment • Excessive overcenter lash	• Add oil to pump reservoir and bleed by operating steering. Check hose connectors for proper torque and adjust as required. • Tighten attaching screws to specified torque • Replace loose pivots • Replace poppet valve • Adjust to specification with gear out of vehicle • Adjust to specification with gear out of car
Hard steering or lack of assist	• Loose pump belt • Low oil level **NOTE:** Low oil level will also result in excessive pump noise • Steering gear to column misalignment • Lower coupling flange rubbing against steering gear adjuster plug • Tires not properly inflated	• Adjust belt tension to specification • Fill to proper level. If excessively low, check all lines and joints for evidence of external leakage. Tighten loose connectors. • Align steering column • Loosen pinch bolt and assemble properly • Inflate to recommended pressure
Foamy milky power steering fluid, low fluid level and possible low pressure	• Air in the fluid, and loss of fluid due to internal pump leakage causing overflow	• Check for leak and correct. Bleed system. Extremely cold temperatures will cause system aeration should the oil level be low. If oil level is correct and pump still foams, remove pump from vehicle and separate reservoir from housing. Check welsh plug and housing for cracks. If plug is loose or housing is cracked, replace housing.
Low pressure due to steering pump	• Flow control valve stuck or inoperative • Pressure plate not flat against cam ring	• Remove burrs or dirt or replace. Flush system. • Correct
Low pressure due to steering gear	• Pressure loss in cylinder due to worn piston ring or badly worn housing bore • Leakage at valve rings, valve body-to-worm seal	• Remove gear from car for disassembly and inspection of ring and housing bore • Remove gear from car for disassembly and replace seals

Troubleshooting the Power Steering Pump

Problem	Cause	Solution
Chirp noise in steering pump	• Loose belt	• Adjust belt tension to specification
Belt squeal (particularly noticeable at full wheel travel and stand still parking)	• Loose belt	• Adjust belt tension to specification
Growl noise in steering pump	• Excessive back pressure in hoses or steering gear caused by restriction	• Locate restriction and correct. Replace part if necessary.
Growl noise in steering pump (particularly noticeable at stand still parking)	• Scored pressure plates, thrust plate or rotor • Extreme wear of cam ring	• Replace parts and flush system • Replace parts
Groan noise in steering pump	• Low oil level • Air in the oil. Poor pressure hose connection.	• Fill reservoir to proper level • Tighten connector to specified torque. Bleed system by operating steering from right to left—full turn.
Rattle noise in steering pump	• Vanes not installed properly • Vanes sticking in rotor slots	• Install properly • Free up by removing burrs, varnish, or dirt
Swish noise in steering pump	• Defective flow control valve	• Replace part
Whine noise in steering pump	• Pump shaft bearing scored	• Replace housing and shaft. Flush system.
Hard steering or lack of assist	• Loose pump belt • Low oil level in reservoir **NOTE:** Low oil level will also result in excessive pump noise • Steering gear to column misalignment • Lower coupling flange rubbing against steering gear adjuster plug • Tires not properly inflated	• Adjust belt tension to specification • Fill to proper level. If excessively low, check all lines and joints for evidence of external leakage. Tighten loose connectors. • Align steering column • Loosen pinch bolt and assemble properly • Inflate to recommended pressure
Foaming milky power steering fluid, low fluid level and possible low pressure	• Air in the fluid, and loss of fluid due to internal pump leakage causing overflow	• Check for leaks and correct. Bleed system. Extremely cold temperatures will cause system aeriation should the oil level be low. If oil level is correct and pump still foams, remove pump from vehicle and separate reservoir from body. Check welsh plug and body for cracks. If plug is loose or body is cracked, replace body.
Low pump pressure	• Flow control valve stuck or inoperative • Pressure plate not flat against cam ring	• Remove burrs or dirt or replace. Flush system. • Correct
Momentary increase in effort when turning wheel fast to right or left	• Low oil level in pump • Pump belt slipping • High internal leakage	• Add power steering fluid as required • Tighten or replace belt • Check pump pressure. (See pressure test)
Steering wheel surges or jerks when turning with engine running especially during parking	• Low oil level • Loose pump belt • Steering linkage hitting engine oil pan at full turn • Insufficient pump pressure	• Fill as required • Adjust tension to specification • Correct clearance • Check pump pressure. (See pressure test). Replace flow control valve if defective.

Troubleshooting the Power Steering Pump (cont.)

Problem	Cause	Solution
Steering wheel surges or jerks when turning with engine running especially during parking (cont.)	• Sticking flow control valve	• Inspect for varnish or damage, replace if necessary
Excessive wheel kickback or loose steering	• Air in system	• Add oil to pump reservoir and bleed by operating steering. Check hose connectors for proper torque and adjust as required.
Low pump pressure	• Extreme wear of cam ring • Scored pressure plate, thrust plate, or rotor • Vanes not installed properly • Vanes sticking in rotor slots • Cracked or broken thrust or pressure plate	• Replace parts. Flush system. • Replace parts. Flush system. • Install properly • Freeup by removing burrs, varnish, or dirt • Replace part

10. On wheels with a horn bar, place the horn wire in the hole and secure it with the retainer and then install the screws. Do the same for rim-blow wheels.

11. Connect the battery cable.

Turn Signal Switch, Hazard Signal and Lock Cylinder

REPLACEMENT

1. Disconnect the ground cable from the battery. On cars with tilt steering wheels, place the column in the straight position. Remove the steering wheel.

2. Loosen the anti-theft cover attaching screws and remove the cover from the column. Do not hammer on the shaft. Do not move the screws from the cover; they are attached to it with plastic retainers.

3. To remove the lockplate, a special compressor is required. This tool is an inverted U-shape with a hole for the shaft. The shaft nut is used to force it down. Depress the lockplate and pry the snapring from the groove in the steering shaft. Remove the tool, snapring,

Using the special lockplate remover tool

plate, turn signal cam, upper bearing preload spring, and thrust washer from the shaft.

4. Place the turn signal lever in the right turn position and remove it.

5. Depress the hazard warning switch button and remove it, by rotating it counterclockwise. Remove the package tray (if equipped) and the lower trim panel.

6. Disconnect the wire harness connector block at its mounting bracket, which is located on the right side of the lower column. Remove the steering column mounting bracket attaching bolts. Remove the turn signal switch wiring harness protector from the bottom of the column.

NOTE: *To aid in the removal and replacement of the directional switch harness, tape the harness connector to the wire harness to prevent snagging when removing the wiring harness assembly through the steering column. Prepare the new turn signal switch harness in the same manner for ease of installation.*

7. If the car (Gremlin, Hornet, Concord, and Spirit only) is equipped with a column mounted automatic transmission selector, use a paper clip to depress the locktab that holds the shift quadrant light wire in the connector block.

8. Remove the switch attaching screws. Withdraw the switch and wire harness from the column.

9. Insert the key into the lock cylinder and turn to the ON position. Remove the warning buzzer switch and the contacts as an assembly using needlenosed pliers. Take care not to let the contacts fall into the column.

10. Turn the key to the LOCK position and compress the lock cylinder retaining tab. Remove the lock cylinder. If the tab is not visible

through the slot, knock the casting flash out of the slot.

To install:

1. Hold the lock cylinder sleeve and turn the lock cylinder clockwise (counterclockwise 1977 and later) until it contacts the stop.

2. Align the lock cylinder key with the keyway in the housing and slip the cylinder into the housing.

3. Lightly depress the cylinder against the sector, while turning it counterclockwise, until the cylinder and sector are engaged.

4. Depress the cylinder until the retaining tab engages, and the lock cylinder is secured.

5. Install the turn signal switch. Be sure that the actuating lever pivot is properly seated and aligned in the top of the housing boss, before installing it with its screws.

6. Install the turn signal lever and check the operation of the switch.

7. Install the thrust washer, spring and turn signal cancelling cam on the steering shaft.

8. Align the lockplate and steering shaft splines, and position the lockplate so that the turn signal camshaft protrudes from the 'dogleg' opening in the lockplate.

9. Use snapring pliers to install the snapring on the end of the steering shaft.

10. Secure the anti-theft cover with its screws.

11. Install the button on the hazard warning switch. Install the steering wheel, as detailed above.

Ignition Switch

REPLACEMENT

NOTE: *The ignition switch on all models is mounted on the lower steering column tube and is connected to the lock cylinder via a lock rod.*

1. Place the key in 'OFF/LOCK'.

2. Remove the switch mounting screws.

3. Disconnect the lock rod, remove harness connector and switch.

4. To install on the standard column, move the switch slide as far as it will go to the left (toward the wheel). On the tilt column, push the slide to the extreme right.

5. Position the lock rod into the hole on the switch slide.

6. Install the switch on the steering column. Be sure that the slide stays in its detent.

7. On the tilt column, do not tighten the mounting screws. Instead, push the switch down the column, away from the steering wheel. This will remove any slack from the lock rod.

8. Tighten the switch mounting screws.

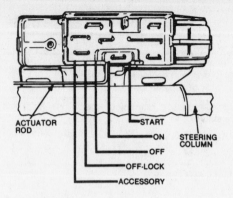

STEERING WHEEL
STANDARD COLUMN

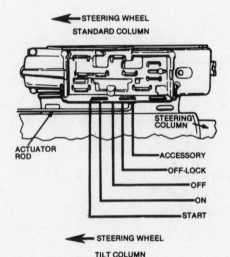

STEERING WHEEL
TILT COLUMN

Ignition switch slider positions

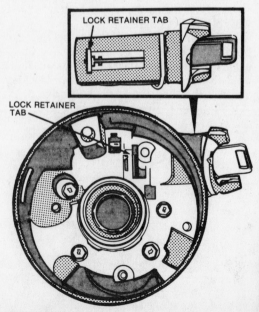

Lock cylinder removal

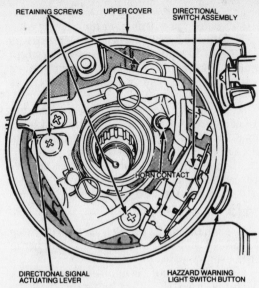

RETAINING SCREWS   UPPER COVER   DIRECTIONAL SWITCH ASSEMBLY

HORN CONTACT

DIRECTIONAL SIGNAL ACTUATING LEVER

HAZZARD WARNING LIGHT SWITCH BUTTON

Turn signal switch

Manual Steering Gear

REMOVAL AND INSTALLATION

Except Pacer

1. Remove the flexible coupling bolts.
2. Remove the pitman arm, using puller J-5566-04.
3. Remove the steering gear mounting screws and lower the steering gear.

To install:

1. Center the steering gear with the index mark up. The mark on the shaft of the flange must be aligned at assembly.
2. Insert the flexible coupling bolts into the shaft flange. Tighten the nuts to 20 ft.lb. torque and the pinch bolt 30 ft.lb.
3. Tighten the gear mounting screws to 65 ft.lb. and the Pitman arm nut to 115 ft.lb.

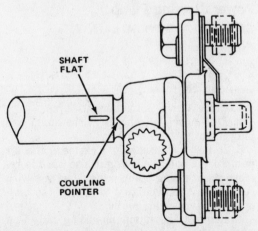

SHAFT FLAT

COUPLING POINTER

Intermediate shaft and flexible coupling alignment

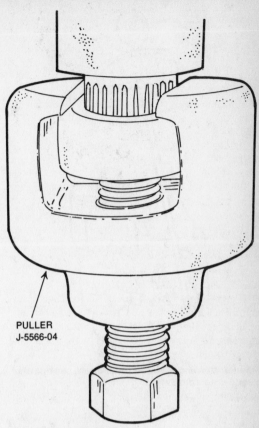

PULLER J-5566-04

Pitman arm removal

NOTE: *After tightening the Pitman shaft nut, stake the thread at nut with a center punch to insure nut retention. Whenever the steering gear assembly is removed for replacement or overhaul, or the mounting bolts are loosened for any reason, the steering column MUST be realigned to the gear assembly. Slight misalignment of the steering column may cause increased steering effort and additional wear to the steering components.*

ADJUSTMENTS

Except Pacer

CAUTION: *Adjustments to the steering gear must be made only in the sequence given here or the steering gear will be damaged. That is, you must do the worm bearing preload adjustment before the sector and ball nut backlash adjustment, and you must do them both.*

WORM BEARING PRELOAD ADJUSTMENT

1. Disconnect the battery ground cable.
2. Remove the Pitman arm (the arm on the steering box) nut and mark the relationship of the arm to the shaft.

TOOL
J-7754

Manual steering gear Pitman shaft over-center torque drag adjustment

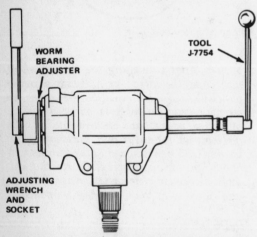

WORM
BEARING
ADJUSTER

TOOL
J-7754

ADJUSTING
WRENCH
AND
SOCKET

Adjusting worm bearing preload on manual steering gear

3. Use a puller to remove the pitman arm from the shaft.

4. Loosen the pitman shaft adjusting screw locknut and back off the adjusting screw (the small adjusting screw on the cover) a few turns.

5. Remove the horn button or bar.

6. Gently turn the steering wheel in one direction until it can't go any further, then turn it back half a turn.

CAUTION: *If you turn the steering wheel*

hard against the stop with the linkage disconnected, you will damage the steering gear.

7. Attach a torque wrench with a maximum reading of 50 in.lb. or less to the steering wheel nut. Turn the wheel through a quarter turn with the wrench. The torque reading should be 5–8 in.lb.

8. To adjust, loosen the big worm bearing adjuster locknut with a brass drift and hammer. Turn the adjuster plug (viewed from underneath) clockwise to increase the preload.

9. Tighten the locknut to 50 ft.lb. and recheck the preload.

10. Go on to the next adjustment.

SECTOR AND BALL NUT BACKLASH

1. Turn the wheel gently from full right stop to full left stop and count the total number of turns stop-to-stop.

2. Turn back half the number of turns to the center position, then turn half a turn past the center position.

3. Use the torque wrench on the steering wheel nut to turn the gear through the center of travel. The torque required should be 4–10 in.lb. The sum of this torque and that measured after worm bearing preload adjustment must not exceed 16. in.lb.

4. To adjust, turn the adjusting screw on the cover. Tighten the locknut and recheck the torque or force required.

5. Replace the pitman arm on the shaft, aligning the marks you made back in Step 2 of 'Worm Bearing Preload Adjustment.'

6. Tighten the pitman arm nut to 115 ft.lb. and stake it to the shaft. This is a critical fastener; it must be torqued. To stake the nut means to slightly distort its inner edge by use of a punch or chisel.

7. Replace the horn button or bar and battery ground cable.

Power Steering Pump
REMOVAL AND INSTALLATION
Except Pacer

4–150
6–232, 258
8–304, 360, 401

1. Place a drip pan under the pump.

2. Disconnect both hoses at the pump and plug them.

3. It may be necessary to remove the air pump drive belt. Your might also have to remove the steering pump pulley. On cars with A/C, it may be necessary to remove the compressor drivebelt and pulley.

4. Remove the pump mounting nuts and washers from behind.

5. On 6-cylinder engines, loosen the pump

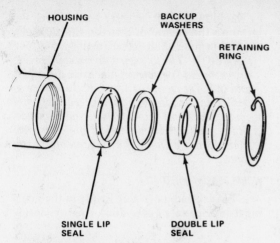

HOUSING   BACKUP WASHERS   RETAINING RING

SINGLE LIP SEAL   DOUBLE LIP SEAL

Pitman shaft seal assembly sequence

bracket pivot bolts. On V8 engines, remove the front pump mounting bracket.

6. Remove the pump drive belt and the pump. If the pulley was removed, torque the nut to 60 ft.lb.

7. Install the pump to the engine.

8. Install the hoses.

9. Fill the reservoir with the proper fluid as described in Chapter 1.

10. Turn the pump pulley counterclockwise (front view) until no more bubbles appear.

11. Install the drive belt and adjust it. Some general thoughts on drive belt tightening are given in Chapter 3 under 'Alternator'. Most pumps have a boss behind the pulley so that you can apply tension with a 1⅝" (41mm) open end wrench.

12. Install and adjust the air pump belt.

13. Bleed the system by raising the front of the car and turning the wheels from side-to-side without hitting the stops for a few minutes. Check the level frequently.

4–121

1. Remove the adjuster locknuts and lockwashers retaining the pump and pivot bracket to the pump mounting bracket. The lower adjuster is accessible from underneath car.

NOTE: *Except for the adjuster locknuts, all of the pump mounting bolts are metric sizes. The adjuster locknuts are loosened and tightened using a ⁹⁄₁₆" box end wrench having a 45° offset.*

2. Move the pump toward the engine and remove the pump belt.

3. Loosen the return hose clamp and slide the clamp back along the hose.

4. Pull the pump forward and disconnect both hoses.

5. Remove the bolts attaching the pump front mounting bracket to the rear mounting

bracket and the engine block. Remove the pump, pivot bracket and front mounting bracket as an assembly.

6. Position the pump, front mounting bracket, and pivot bracket on the rear mounting bracket and connect the pressure and return hoses to the pump. Tighten the pressure hose fitting to 38 ft.lb. torque.

7. Install the front bracket-to-rear bracket bolts. Tighten the bolts to 25 ft.lb. torque. Tighten the front bracket-to-engine block bolt to 16 ft.lb. torque.

8. Slide the return hose clamp into position and tighten the hose clamp.

9. Install the adjuster locknuts and lockwashers.

10. Adjust the pump belt.

4–151

1. Remove the ambient air induction hose and remove the adjusting bracket nut/bolts.

2. Move the pump toward the engine and remove the pump belt.

3. Loosen the return hose clamp and slide the clamp back along the hose.

4. Pull the pump forward and disconnect both hoses. The pressure hose has an 18mm metric fitting.

5. Remove the bolts attaching the pump front mounting bracket to the rear mounting bracket and the engine block. Remove the pump, pivot bracket, and front mounting bracket as an assembly.

6. Position the pump and mounting brackets on the engine. Connect the pressure and return hoses to the pump. Tighten the pressure hose fitting to 38 ft.lb. torque.

7. Install the bracket and bracket bolts/nuts. Tighten the bolts to 25 ft.lb. torque.

8. Adjust the pump belt tension.

Power Steering Gear
REMOVAL AND INSTALLATION
Except Pacer

1. Place the wheels in a straight ahead position.

2. Position a drain pan under the steering gear.

3. Disconnect the hoses at gear. Raise and secure the hoses above the pump fluid level to prevent excessive oil spillage, and cap ends of the hoses to prevent the entry of dirt.

4. Remove the flexible coupling-to-intermediate shaft attaching nuts.

5. Raise the automobile on hoist. On Eagle models, remove:

    a. skid plate, if equipped.

    b. left side crossmeber-to-sill support brace.

c. stabilizer bar brackets from frame.

6. Paint alignment marks on the pitman arm and the pitman shaft for assembly reference.

7. Remove the pitman arm using Puller Tool J-5566-04.

8. Remove the steering gear mounting bolts and remove the steering gear.

To install:

1. Center the steering gear. Turn the stub shaft (using flexible coupling) from stop-to-stop and count the total number of turns; then turn it back from either stop, one-half the total number of turns to center the gear. At this pint, the flat on the stub shaft should be facing upward.

2. Align the flexible coupling and intermediate shaft flange.

3. Install the gear mounting bolts in the gear, install the spacer on the gear, and mount the gear on the frame side sill. Tighten the gear mounting bolts to 65 ft.lb. torque.

4. Install and tighten the flexible coupling nuts to 25 ft.lb. torque.

5. Install the pitman arm. Index the arm to the shaft using the alignment marks made during removal.

6. Install the pitman arm nut. Tighten the nut to 115 ft.lb. torque and stake the nut to the pitman shaft in one place.

CAUTION: *The pitman arm nut must be staked to the shaft to retain it properly.*

7. On Eagle models, install:

   a. stabilizer bar brackets.

   b. left side crossmember-to-sill support brace.

   c. skid plate, if equipped.

8. Lower the automobile.

9. Align the flexible coupling, if necessary. Refer to Flexible Coupling Adjustment.

10. Fill the pump reservoir with power steering fluid and bleed the air from the system.

ADJUSTMENTS

Except Pacer

Because of the complexity involved in adjusting worm bearing preload and pitman shaft overcenter drag torque plus the friction effect produced by hydraulic fluid, the power steering gear must be adjusted off the automobile only.

The power steering gear requires two adjustments which are: worm bearing preload and pitman shaft overcenter drag torque.

Worm bearing preload is controlled by the amount of compression force exerted on the conical worm bearing thrust races by the adjuster plug.

Pitman shaft overcenter torque is controlled

by the pitman shaft adjuster screw which determines the clearance between the rack piston and ptiman shaft sector teeth.

CAUTION: *The following adjustment procedures must be performed exactly as described and in the sequence outlined. Failure to do so can result in damage to the gear internal components and improper steering response. Always adjust worm bearing preload first, then adjust pitman shaft overcenter drag torque.*

WORM BEARING PRELOAD

1. Seat the adjuster plug firmly in the housing using Spanner Tool J-7624. Approximately

Measuring wormshaft bearing preload on power steering gears

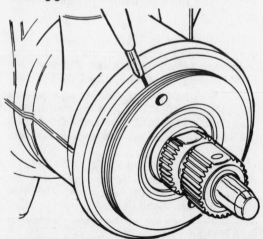

Marking the power steering gear housing adjacent to the hole in the adjuster

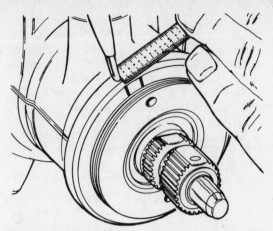

Make a second mark ³/₁₆ to ¼ inch from the first on models through 1979 and ½ inch from the first on 1980–82 models

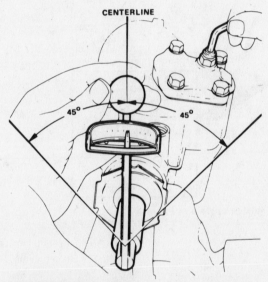

Measuring Pitman shaft over-center torque drag on power steering gears

20 ft.lb. torque is required to seat the housing.

2. Place an index mark on the gear housing opposite one of the holes in the adjuster plug.

3. Measure back (counterclockwise) ³/₁₆" to ¼" (4.7 to 6.3mm) from the index mark and re-mark the housing.

4. Turn the adjuster plug counterclockwise until the hole in the plug is aligned with the second mark on the housing.

5. Install the adjuster plug locknut and tighten it to 85 ft.lb. torque. Be sure the adjuster plug does not turn when tightening the locknut.

6. Turn the stub shaft clockwise to the stop, then turn the shaft back ¼ turn.

7. Using an in.lb. torque wrench with a maximum capacity of 50 in.lb. and a twelve

point deep socket, measure the torque required to turn the stub shaft. Take a reading with the beam of the torque wrench at, or near, the vertical position while turning the stub shaft at an even rate.

8. Record the torque reading. The torque required to turn the stub shaft should be 4–10 in.lb. If the reading is above or below the indicated torque, the adjuster plug may not be tightened properly or may have turned when the locknut was tightened, or the gear may be assembled incorrectly, or the thrust bearings and races may be defective.

PITMAN SHAFT OVERCENTER DRAG TORQUE

1. Turn the pitman shaft adjuster screw counterclockwise until fully extended, then turn it back ½ turn clockwise.

2. Rotate the stub shaft from stop-to-stop and count the total number of turns.

3. Starting from either stop, turn the stub shaft back ½ the total number of turns. This is the gear center.

NOTE: *When the gear is centered, the flat on the stub shaft should face upward and be parallel with the side cover and the master spline on the pitman shaft should be in line with the adjust screw.*

4. Install an in.lb. torque wrench with a maximum capacity of 50 in.lb. and a twelve point deep socket on the stub shaft. Place the torque wrench in the vertical position to take the reading.

5. Rotate the torque wrench 45° to each side of center and record the highest drag torque measured on or near the center.

6. Adjust the overcenter drag torque by turning the pitman shaft adjusting screw clockwise until the desired drag torque is obtained. Adjust the drag torque to the following limits:

• On new steering gears, add 4 to 8 in.lb., torque to the previously measured worm bearing preload torque, but do not exceed a combined total of 18 in.lb. drag torque.

• On used steering gears (400 or more miles), add 4 to 5 in.lb. torque to the previously measured worm bearing preload torque but do not exceed a combined total of 14 in.lb. drag torque.

7. Tighten the pitman shaft adjusting screw locknut to 35 ft.lb. torque after adjusting the overcenter drag torque.

8. Install the gear as outlined in Steering Gear Installation.

9. Fill the pump reservoir and bleed the gear and pump as outlined in Fluid Level and Initial Operations after completing the overcenter drag torque adjustment.

FLUID LEVEL AND INITIAL OPERATION

1. Fill the pump reservoir.

2. Operate the engine until the power steering fluid reaches normal operating temperature of approximately 170°F (77°C), then stop the engine.

3. Turn the wheels to the full left turn position and add power steering fluid to the COLD mark on the dipstick.

4. Start the engine, operate it at hot idle speed and recheck fluid level. Add fluid, if necessary, to the COLD mark on the dipstick.

5. Bleed the system by turning the wheels from side to side without hitting the stops. Fluid with air in it will have a milky appearance. Air must be eliminated from the fluid before normal steering action can be obtained.

6. Return the wheels to the center position and operate the engine for an additional 2 to 3 minutes, then stop the engine.

7. Road test the automobile to make sure the steering functions normally and is free of noise.

8. Check the fluid level. Add fluid as re-

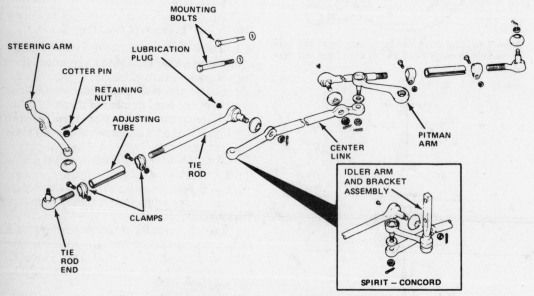

Steering linkage on all except Eagle and Pacer

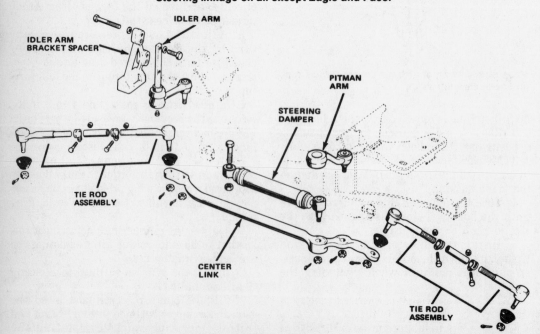

Eagle steering linkage

quired to raise the level to the HOT mark on the dipstick after the system has stabilized at its normal operating temperature.

Tie Rod End
REMOVAL AND INSTALLATION
Except Pacer

1. Raise and support the front of the car.
2. Remove the cotter pin and retaining nut from the tie rod end stud.
3. Mark the position of the tie rod end, adjuster tube, and inner tie rod for reference.
4. Loosen the adjuster tube clamps.
5. Disconnect the tie rod end from the steering arm with a puller.
6. Remove the tie rod end from the adjuster tube.
7. Install the replacement tie rod end in the adjuster tube, and insert the end stud in the steering arm. Tighten the nut to 35 ft.lb. and

install a new cotter pin. Do not loosen the nuts to align. Adjust the toe-in and tighten the clamps.

PACER MANUAL STEERING

Rubber Boot, Mounting Clamp and Grommet
REPLACEMENT

1. Raise and support the front end of the car.
2. Cut and remove the boot clamps from the boot adjacent to the mounting clamp.
3. Mark the position of the adjuster tube and tie rod for assembly reference.
4. Loosen the adjuster tube clamp bolts and unthread the tube from tie rod.
5. Remove the boot.
CAUTION: *Do not allow the protective boot to become cut or torn during service opera-*

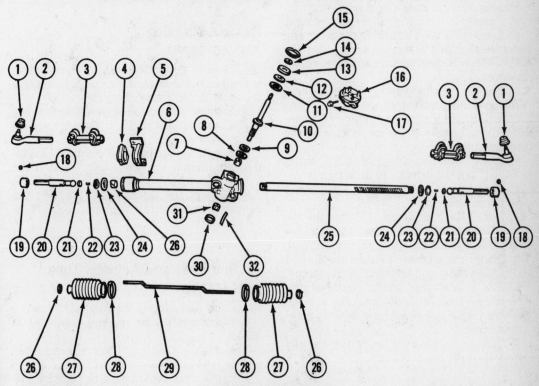

1. Tie rod seal	12. Upper thrust bearing race	23. Jam nut
2. Tie rod end	13. Adjuster plug	24. Shock dampener ring
3. Adjuster tube	14. Pinion shaft seal	25. Steering rack
4. Mounting grommet	15. Adjuster plug locknut	26. Boot retainer
5. Mounting clamp	16. Flexible coupling	27. Boot
6. Tube and housing assembly	17. Pinch bolt	28. Boot clamp
7. Upper pinion bushing	18. Set screw	29. Breather tube
8. Lower thrust bearing race	19. Tie rod housing	30. Contraction plug
9. Lower thrust bearing	20. Inner tie rod	31. Lower pinion bushing
10. Pinion shaft	21. Ball seat	32. Preload spring
11. Upper thrust bearing	22. Ball seat spring	

Pacer manual steering

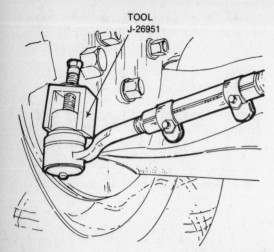
TOOL
J-26951

Disconnecting the tie rod end on Pacer manual steering

tions. *A damaged boot will expose the gear internal components to dirt, foreign material, and road splash resulting in premature wear.*

6. Remove the bolts attaching the mounting clamp to the front crossmember. Loosen the bolts before removing to minimize clamp distortion.

7. Remove the clamp and grommet using a twisting, pulling motion.

8. Install a replacement clamp and grommet. Align the hole in the grommet with the breather tube.

9. Install the mounting clamp attaching bolts. Tighten the bolts to 50 ft.lb. torque.

10. Install the boot. Align the hole in the boot with the breather tube.

11. Install the boot clamps. Position the ear of the clamps ¾" (19.05mm) from the breather tube. Compress the clamps using tool J-22610.

12. Install the adjuster tube on the tie rod and tighten the clamp bolts to 22 ft.lb. torque.

NOTE: *At least three threads should be visible at each end of adjuster tube. The number of threads per side should not differ by more than three.*

13. Remove the supports, lower the car, and correct the toe-in as necessary.

Breather Tube
REPLACEMENT

1. Raise and support the front of the car.

2. Cut and remove the large diameter boot clamps from the boots.

3. Slide the boots away from the breather tube and remove the tube.

CAUTION: *Do not allow the protective boots to become cut or torn during service operations. A damaged boot will expose the gear*

internal components to dirt, foreign material, and road splash resulting in premature wear.

4. Remove the bolts attaching the mounting clamp to the front crossmember. Loosen the bolts before removing them to minimize clamp distortion.

5. Remove the clamp and grommet using a twisting, pulling motion.

6. Install the replacement breather tube. Align the holes in the boots with the tube.

7. Install the mounting clamp and grommet. Be sure to align the hole in the grommet with the breather tube.

8. Install and tighten the mounting clamp bolts to 50 ft.lb. torque.

9. Position boots on the flanges at each end of tube and housing and install the boot clamps. Position each of the clamps ¾" (19.05mm) from the breather tube and compress the clamps using tool J-22610.

10. Remove the supports and lower the car.

Flexible Coupling
REPLACEMENT

1. Remove the nuts attaching the coupling to the intermediate shaft flange and compress the shaft to provide working clearance.

2. Remove the coupling pinch bolt using ⁷⁄₁₆", 12 point socket or box end wrench and remove the coupling.

3. Install the replacement coupling (flat-to-flat) and install the pinch bolt. Tighten the bolt to 30 ft.lb. torque.

4. Connect the intermediate shaft to the coupling and tighten the nuts to 25 ft.lb. torque.

Tie Rod Ends and Adjuster Tube
REPLACEMENT

1. Raise and support the front of the car.

2. Disconnect the tie rod end using tool J-26951.

3. Mark the position of the adjuster tube and tie rod end for assembly reference.

4. Remove and separate the tie rod ends and adjuster tubes.

5. Install the replacement tie rod ends and the adjuster tubes. Tighten the tube clamp bolts to 22 ft.lb. torque and the tie rod nuts to 50 ft.lb. torque.

NOTE: *At least three threads should be visible at each end of the adjuster tubes. The number of threads per side should not differ by more than three.*

6. Remove the supports, lower the car, and adjust the toe-in as necessary.

Inner Tie Rod Housing, Tie Rod, Ball Seat, and Spring

REPLACEMENT

1. Raise and support the front of the car.
2. Disconnect the tie rod ends using tool J-26951.
3. Mark the position of the adjuster tube and inner rod for assembly reference.
4. Loosen the adjuster tube inboard clamp bolt and unthread the adjuster tube and tie rod end from the inner tie rod assembly.
5. Cut and remove the large boot clamp and move the boot aside.

CAUTION: *Do not allow the protective boot to become cut or torn during service operations. A damaged boot will expose the gear internal components to dirt, foreign material, and road splash resulting in premature wear.*

6. Slide the shock dampener ring off the jamnut.
7. Loosen the jamnut. Use an open end wrench to loosen the jamnut and place another open end wrench on the rack flat (adjacent to rack teeth) to prevent the rack from turning.

CAUTION: *If the rack is allowed to turn when loosening the jamnuts, the gear internal components could be damaged. An open end wrench must be used to hold the rack when loosening the jamnut.*

8. Loosen the setscrew in the tie rod housing, unthread the housing from the rack and remove the inner tie rod, tie rod housing, inner tie rod ball seat, and ball seat spring.
9. Liberally apply a waterproof, EP-type, lithium base chassis lubricant to all replacement inner tie rod assembly wear surfaces. Pack the tie rod housing with the same lubricant.
10. Install the ball seat spring and ball seat in the end of the rack.
11. Assemble the inner tie rod and housing and install them on the rack.
12. Hand tighten the tie rod housing while rocking the tie rod to prevent grease lock; then, back the housing off ⅛ turn (45°). The tie rod must rock and turn freely in the housing.
13. Tighten the tie rod housing setscrew to 9 ft.lb. torque.
14. Tighten the jamnut to 60 ft.lb. torque. Use an open end wrench to loosen the jamnut and place another open end and wrench on the rack flat (adjacent to rack teeth) to prevent the rack from turning.

CAUTION: *If the rack is allowed to turn when tightening the jamnut, the gear internal components could be damaged. An open end wrench must be used to hold the rack when tightening the jamnut.*

15. Check the movement of the inner tie rod after tightening the jamnut. The tie rod must move freely in the housing to ensure proper operation.
16. Slide the shock dampener ring over the jamnut.
17. Install the boot on the inner tie rod and tube or housing. Align the breather tube with the hole in the boot and install the boot clamps. Position the ear of large clamp ¾″ (19.05mm) from the breather tube. Compress the clamps using Tool J-22610.
18. Thread the adjuster tube and tie rod end assembly on the inner tie rod. Refer to the alignment marks made at disassembly.
19. Tighten the adjuster tube bolts to 22 ft.lb. torque.
20. Connect the tie rod ends to the steering arms. Tighten the tie rod end nuts to 50 ft.lb. torque and install replacement cotter pins.
21. Remove the supports, lower the car, and adjust the toe-in as necessary.

Steering Gear

REMOVAL

1. Unlock the steering column.
2. Raise and support the front of the car.
3. Remove the screws attaching the reinforcement brace to the front crossmember and the left engine support bracket and remove the brace.
4. Remove the flexible coupling pinch bolt and disengage the flexible coupling from the steering gear pinion shaft.

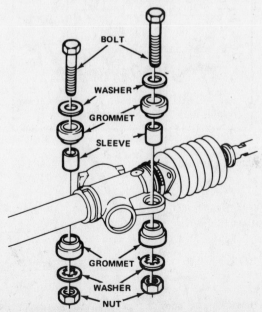

Pacer manual steering gear housing attachment

5. Remove the cotter pins and nuts from the tie rod ends.

6. Disconnect the rod ends using tool J-26951.

7. Remove the bolts attaching the steering gear mounting clamp to the right side of the front crossmember.

NOTE: *Before removing the bolts, loosen them slightly to minimize clamp distortion.*

8. Remove the steering gear housing-to-crossmember nuts. Remove the bolts, washers, sleeves, and grommets using a blunt punch.

9. Rotate the bottom of gear housing toward the front of the car until the pinion shaft is approximately parallel with the skid plate. Slide the gear assembly toward the right side of the car until the housing and tube clear the mounting plate and remove the steering gear assembly.

INSTALLATION

1. Assemble the grommets, sleeves, and washers and install them on the steering gear. The sleeves will hold the grommets in place during assembly.

2. Position the steering gear assembly on the crossmember. Install the tube and housing from the right side of the car. During installation, keep the pinion shaft approximately parallel with the mounting plate.

3. Install the mounting clamp-to-crossmem-ber attaching bolts. Hand tighten the bolts only.

4. Install the steering gear housing-to-crossmember attaching bolts, washers, and nuts and tighten them to 60 ft.lb. torque.

5. Tighten the mounting clamp-to-crossmember attaching bolts to 50 ft.lb. torque.

6. Connect the tie rod ends to the steering arms. Tighten the nuts to 50 ft.lb. torque and install the replacement cotter pins.

7. Align the flat spline on the pinion shaft with the flat on the flexible coupling and install the coupling on the shaft. Install the pinch bolt and tighten it to 30 ft.lb. torque.

8. Install the bolts attaching the reinforcement brace to the front crossmember and the engine support bracket. Tighten the bolts to 30 ft.lb. torque.

9. Remove the supports and lower the car.

10. Check and correct the toe-in adjustment if necessary.

PACER POWER STEERING

Rubber Boot, Mounting Clamp and Grommet
REPLACEMENT

1. Raise and support the front end of the car.

2. Cut and remove the boot clamps from the boot adjacent to the mounting clamp.

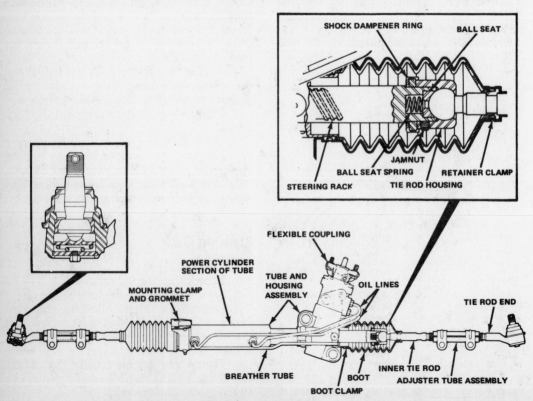

Pacer power steering

3. Mark the position of the adjuster tube on the inner tie rod for assembly reference.

4. Loosen the adjuster tube inboard clamp bolt and unthread the tube from the inner tie rod.

5. Remove the bolts attaching the mounting clamp to the front crossmember. Loosen both bolts before removing them to minimize clamp distortion.

6. Remove the protective boot.

CAUTION: *Do not allow the protective boot to become cut, torn, or damaged during service operations. A damaged boot will expose the gear internal components to dirt, foreign material and road splash resulting in premature wear.*

7. Remove the clamp and grommet using a twisting, pulling motion.

8. Install the replacement clamp and grommet. Align the hole in the grommet with the breather tube.

9. Install the boot. Align the hole in the boot with the breather tube.

10. Install the boot clamps. Position the clamp ear ¾″ (19.05mm) from the breather tube. Tighten the clamps using tool J-22610.

11. Install the adjuster tube on the tie rod and tighten the clamp bolts to 14 ft.lb. torque.

NOTE: *At least three threads should be visible at each end of adjuster tube. The number of threads per side should not differ by more than three.*

12. Install and tighten the mounting clamp bolts to 48 ft.lb. torque.

13. Remove the supports, lower the car, and correct the toe-in as necessary.

Breather Tube

REPLACEMENT

1. Raise and support the front of the car.

2. Cut and remove the large diameter boot clamps from the boots.

3. Slide the boots away from the breather tube and remove the tube.

4. Install the replacement breather tube. Align the holes in the boots with the tube.

5. Position the boots on the flanges at each end of the tube and housing and install the boot clamps. Position the clamp ear ¾″ (19.05mm) from the breather tube. Tighten the clamps using tool J-22610.

6. Remove the supports and lower the car.

Flexible Coupling

REPLACEMENT

1. Remove the nuts attaching the coupling to the intermediate shaft flange and compress the shaft to provide working clearance.

2. Remove the coupling pinch bolt using a

$\frac{7}{16}$″, 12 point socket or box end wrench and remove the coupling.

3. Install the replacement coupling (flat-to-flat) and install the pinch bolt. Tighten the bolt to 30 ft.lb. torque.

4. Connect the intermediate shaft to the coupling. Tighten the nuts to 25 ft.lb. torque.

Tie Rod Ends and Adjuster Tube

REPLACEMENT

1. Raise and support the front of the car.

2. Disconnect the tie rod end using tool J-26951.

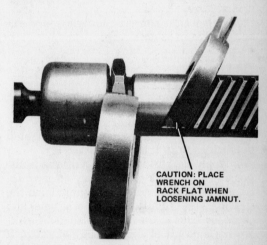

CAUTION: PLACE WRENCH ON RACK FLAT WHEN LOOSENING JAMNUT.

Loosening or tightening the jamnut on Pacer power steering

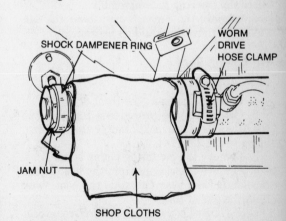

SHOCK DAMPENER RING   WORM DRIVE HOSE CLAMP

JAM NUT

SHOP CLOTHS

Installing the hose clamp, ribber seal and protective cloths

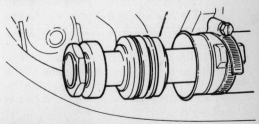

Bulkhead removal

3. Mark the position of the tie rod end, adjuster tube, and inner tie rod for assembly reference.

4. Loosen the adjuster tube inboard clamp bolt.

5. Remove and separate the tie rod end and adjuster tube.

6. Install the replacement tie rod end and adjuster tube. Tighten the adjuster tube clamp bolt to 14 ft.lb. torque and the tie rod end nut to 50 ft.lb. torque.

NOTE: *At least three threads should be visible at each end of adjuster tubes. The number of threads per side should not differ by more than three.*

7. Remove the supports, lower car, and correct the toe-in as necessary.

Oil Line

REPLACEMENT

1. Raise and support the front of the car.
2. Remove the oil lines.
3. Install the replacement oil lines. Tighten the fittings to 30 ft.lb. torque.
4. Apply the parking brake, shift the transmission into Park or Neutral (on manual transmission) and start the engine. Turn the steering wheel right and left several times and check for leaks at the oil line fittings. If leaks are not evident, proceed to the next step. If leaks are evident, tighten the fittings and check again. If leaks persist, remove and replace the steering gear assembly.
5. Remove the supports and lower the car. Add power steering fluid as necessary.

Bulkhead Seal

REPLACEMENT

1. Raise and support the front of the car.
2. Disconnect the tie rod end connected to the tube side of the rack from the steering arm using tool J-26951.
3. Remove the mounting clamp bolts.
4. Remove the clamps from the boot at the tube-end of the gear and slide the boot away from the end of tube.

CAUTION: *Do not allow the protective boot to become cut or torn during service operations. A damaged boot will expose the gear internal components to dirt, foreign material and road splash resulting in premature wear.*

5. Remove the large boot clamp at the housing end of the gear.
6. If the flat on the rack teeth is not visible, pull back the boot at the housing end of the gear and turn the steering wheel (to rotate the pinion) and extend the rack until the flat is accessible.

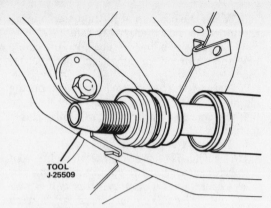

TOOL
J-25509

Installing bulkhead on the rack

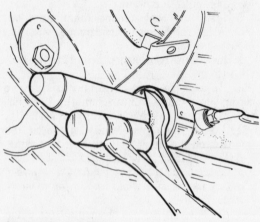

Seating the bulkhead

7. Slide the shock dampener ring off the jamnut.

8. Loosen the jamnut using an open end wrench. Also use an open end wrench on the rack flat to prevent the rack from turning.

CAUTION: *Do not allow the rack to turn when loosening the jamnut. If the rack turns, the gear internal components could be damaged. Place an open end wrench over the flat adjacent to the rack teeth to prevent the rack from turning.*

9. Loosen the setscrew in the tie rod housing, unthread the housing from the rack and remove the tie rod assembly, inner tie rod ball seat, and ball seat spring.

10. Turn the jamnut counterclockwise until it is one thread away from the end of the rack and reinstall the shock dampener ring on the jamnut.

CAUTION: *Do not remove the jamnut and shock dampener ring from the rack at this time. The jamnut and shock dampener ring will function as a stop when the bulkhead is removed.*

11. Remove the bulkhead retaining ring from the end of the tube by inserting the pin punch through the access hole in the end of tube to force the retaining ring out of its groove. Place a screwdriver blade under the ring and pry the ring from tube.

12. Remove the bulkhead assembly as follows:

    a. Clean the rack and bulkhead area of the tube with a shop cloth.

    b. Position the small piece of rubber over the access hole in tube and secure the rubber with a wormdrive type hose clamp.

    c. Position the drain pan under the tube end of the gear and wrap shop cloths around the rack and tube to prevent excessive oil spillage.

    d. Start the engine and turn the steering wheel to the left until the stop is contacted. Oil pressure will force the outer bulkhead out of the tube. Stop the engine immediately when the oil pressure forces the bulkhead out of the tube.

13. Remove the jamnut and shock dampener ring.

14. Remove and discard the outer bulkhead. NOTE: *Do not remove the inner bulkhead and do not remove the seals from the outer bulkhead. The outer bulkhead, bulkhead seal, and O-ring are serviced as an assembly only.*

15. Remove the hose clamp and small piece of rubber from the tube.

16. Inspect the tube bore and bulkhead snapring groove area in the tube for nicks and scratches. Remove the nicks and scratches using a crocus cloth or 600 grit emery cloth. Remove the burrs and sharp edges from the shoulder at the threaded end of rack, using an emery cloth, crocus cloth, or small fine tooth file. Burrs must be removed to avoid damaging the bulkhead seal during installation.

17. Lubricate the replacement outer bulkhead and bulkhead seal with power steering fluid.

18. Lubricate the replacement outer bulkhead O-ring seal with power steering fluid and install the seal on the bulkhead.

19. Place Seal Protector Tool J-25509 over the rack threads and install the outer bulkhead on the rack.

20. Install the outer bulkhead in the tube using a 1¼" open end wrench and a plastic hammer.

21. Seat the outer bulkhead in the tube using a brass drift.

22. Install the bulkhead retaining ring. Position the gap in the retaining ring ½" (12.7mm) away from the access hole in the tube.

CAUTION: *Do not scratch or damage the*

surface of the rack when using the open end wrench to seat the bulkhead.

23. Wipe the bulkhead area dry.

24. Fill the power steering pump reservoir with fluid and start engine.

25. Turn the steering wheel left and right several times and check for leaks. If leaks are not evident, proceed to the next step.

26. Install the shock dampener ring and jamnut on the rack.

27. Install the mounting clamp and grommet on the tube. Position the clamp on the crossmember and install the clamp but do not tighten the clamp attaching bolts.

28. Apply a liberal quantity of waterproof, EP-type, lithium base chassis lubricant to the inner tie rod ball seat and the ball end of the inner tie rod. Pack the tie rod housing with the same lubricant and apply a heavy coat of lubricant to the rack teeth.

29. Install the ball seat spring in the end of the rack and install the ball seat.

30. Assemble the inner tie rod and tie rod housing and install them the on rack.

31. Hand tighten the tie rod housing on the rack while rocking the tie rod to prevent grease lock.

32. Back the tie rod housing off approximately ⅛ turn.

33. Tighten the tie rod housing setscrew to 9 ft.lb. torque.

34. Tighten the jamnut to 60 ft.lb. torque. Use an open end wrench on the rack flat to prevent the rack from turning.

CAUTION: *Do not allow the rack to turn when tightening the jamnut. If the rack turns, gear internal components could be damaged. Place an open wrench over the flat adjacent to the rack teeth to prevent the rack from turning.*

35. Check the inner tie rod movement. The tie rod most rock and turn freely in the housing to ensure proper operation.

36. Install the shock dampener ring over the jamnut.

37. Position the breather tube in the mounting grommet.

38. Install the protective boot over the end of the tube. Be sure the boot is fully seated in the tube undercut and that the hole in the boot is aligned with the breather tube.

39. Install the boot clamps. Tighten the clamps using tool J-22610.

40. Tighten the mounting clamp bolts to 48 ft.lb. torque.

41. Connect the tie rod end to the steering arm and install the tie rod end nut. Tighten the nut to 50 ft.lb. torque and install the replacement cotter pin.

42. Remove the supports and lower the car.

43. Check and correct the power steering system fluid level as necessary. Refer to Fluid Level and Initial Operation.

Tie Rod Housing, Inner Tie Rod, and Ball Seat and Spring

REPLACEMENT

1. Raise and support the front of the car.
2. Mark the position of the tie rod end, adjuster tube and inner tie rod for assembly reference.
3. Disconnect the tie rod end using tool J-26851 if the tie rod end is to be replaced.
4. Loosen the adjuster tube inboard clamp bolts and unthread the adjuster tube and tie rod end from the inner tie rod.
5. Remove the boot clamps and move the boot aside.

CAUTION: *Do not allow the protective boot to become cut or torn during service operations. A damaged boot will expose the gear internal components to dirt, foreign material and road splash resulting in premature wear.*

6. Remove the large boot clamp at the housing end of the gear.
7. Slide the shock dampener ring off the jamnut.
8. If the flat on the rack teeth is not visible, pull back the boot and turn the steering wheel (to rotate the pinion) and extend the rack until the rack flat is accessible.
9. Loosen the jamnut using an open end wrench. Also install an open end wrench on the rack flat to prevent the rack from turning.

CAUTION: *Do not allow rack to turn when loosening the jamnut. If the rack turns, gear internal components could be damaged. Place an open end wrench over the flat adjacent to the rack teeth to prevent the rack from turning.*

10. Loosen the setscrew in the tie rod hous-

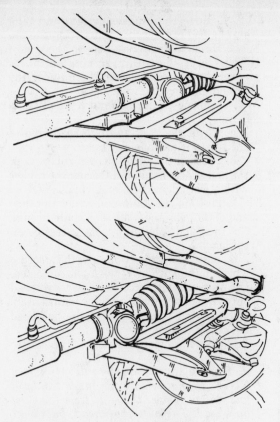

Pacer power steering gear removal

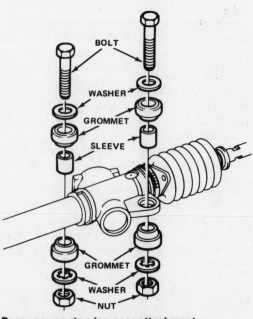

Pacer power steering gear attachment

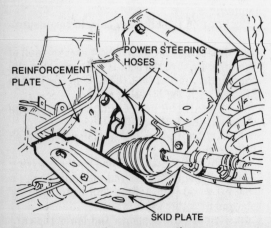

Pacer power steering gear mounting

ing, unthread the housing from the rack and remove the inner tie rod, tie rod housing, inner tie rod ball seat, and ball seat spring.

11. Apply a liberal quantity of waterproof,

EP-type, lithium-base chassis lubricant to the replacement inner tie rod assembly wear surfaces. Pack the tie rod housing with the same lubricant.

12. Install the ball seat spring and ball seat in the end of the rack.

13. Assemble the inner tie rod and housing and install them on the rack.

14. Hand tighten the tie rod housing while rocking the inner tie rod to prevent grease lock.

15. Back the housing off approximately ⅛ turn.

16. Tighten the tie rod housing setscrew to 9 ft.lb. torque.

17. Tighten the jamnut to 60 ft.lb. torque. Use an open end wrench on the rack flat to prevent the rack from turning.

CAUTION: *Do not allow the rack to turn when tightening the jamnut. If the rack turns, gear internal components could be damaged. Place an open end wrench over the flat adjacent to the rack teeth to prevent rack from turning.*

18. Check the inner tie rod movement after tightening the jamnut. The tie rod must rock and turn freely in the housing to ensure proper operation.

19. Install the shock dampener ring over the jamnut.

20. Install the protective boot.

21. Align the breather tube with the hole in the boot and install the boot clamps. Position the ear of the large clamp ¾" (19.05mm) from the breather tube. Tighten the clamp using tool J-22610.

22. Thread the adjuster tube and tie rod end assembly on the inner tie rod. Refer to the alignment mark made at disassembly.

23. Connect the tie rod end to the steering arm, if removed. Tighten the tie rod end nut to 50 ft.lb. torque and install the replacement cotter pin.

24. Remove the supports, lower the car, and adjust the toe-in as necessary.

Steering Gear

REMOVAL

1. Unlock the steering column.

2. Raise and support the front of the car.

3. Remove the screws attaching the reinforcement brace to the front crossmember and the left engine support bracket and remove the brace.

4. Disconnect the stabilizer bar at the left side lower control arm, if equipped.

5. Remove the bolts attaching the stabilizer bar mounting clamps to the frame rail brackets and move the bar away from the front crossmember.

6. Place a support under the stabilizer bar to prevent damaging the bolt attaching the bar to the right side lower control arm.

7. Remove the left side frame rail clamp brackets.

8. Position a drain pan under the steering gear housing and disconnect the power steering hoses at the gear housing. Cap the hoses and plug the gear to prevent the entry of dirt.

9. Remove the flexible coupling pinch bolt and disengage the flexible coupling from the steering gear pinion shaft.

10. Remove and discard the cotter pins from the tie rod end retaining nuts.

11. Disconnect the tie rod ends using tool J-26951.

12. Remove the bolts attaching the steering gear mounting clamp to the crossmember.

CAUTION: *Before removing the bolts, loosen them slightly to minimize clamp distortion.*

13. Remove the steering gear housing-to-crossmember attaching bolt nuts.

14. Remove the bolts, washers, sleeves and grommets from the steering gear housing using a blunt punch.

15. Rotate the bottom of the gear housing toward the front of the car until the pinion shaft is approximately parallel with the skid plate. Slide the gear assembly toward the right side of car until the housing and tube clear the mounting plate and remove the steering gear assembly.

INSTALLATION

1. Assemble and install the grommets, sleeves, and washers on the steering gear. The sleeves will hold the grommets in place during assembly.

2. Position the steering gear assembly on the crossmember. Install the gear from the driver's side of the car.

NOTE: *When installing the gear, keep the pinion shaft approximately parallel with the mounting plate.*

3. Install the mounting clamp bolts. Hand tighten the bolts only.

4. Install the steering gear housing-to-crossmember attaching bolts, washers, and nuts and tighten them to 60 ft.lb. torque.

5. Tighten the mounting clamp bolts to 48 ft.lb. torque.

6. Connect the tie rod end to the steering arms. Tighten the tie rod end retaining nuts to 50 ft.lb. torque and install the replacement cotter pins.

7. Align the flat spline of the steering gear pinion shaft with the index flat of the flexible coupling and install the coupling on pinion shaft. Install the pinch bolt and tighten it to 30 ft.lb. torque.

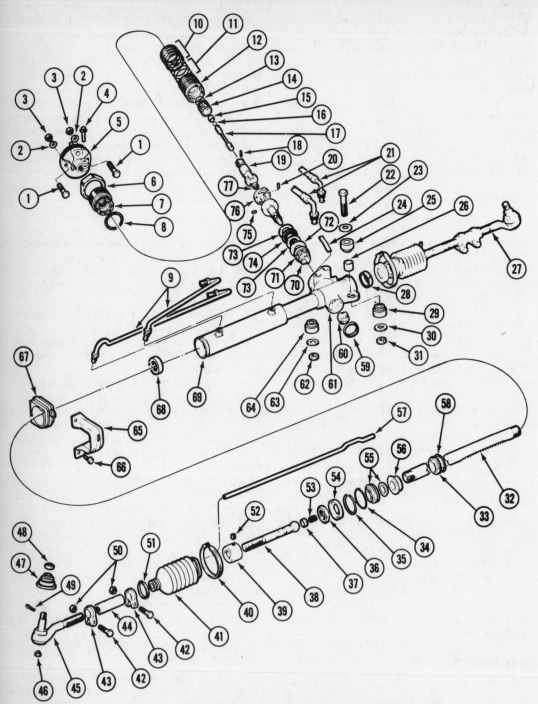

1. Flexible coupling-to-intermediate shaft attaching bolt
2. Lockwasher
3. Nut
4. Pinch bolt
5. Flexible coupling
6. Adjuster plug locknut
7. Adjuster plug assembly
8. Adjuster plug O-ring
9. Oil lines
10. Valve body seal rings
11. Valve body O-rings
12. Valve body
13. Spool valve damper O-ring
14. Spool valve
15. Torsion bar bushing (included in stub shaft)
16. Torsion bar seal ring (included in stub shaft)
17. Torsion bar (included in stub shaft)
18. Drive pin (included in stub shaft)
19. Stub shaft

Pacer power steering gear assembly exploded view

8. Install the bolts attaching the reinforcement bracket to the front crossmember and engine support bracket. Tighten the bolts to 30 ft.lb. torque.

9. Connect the power steering hoses to the gear housing. Be sure that the hoses do not touch the brace or crossmember.

10. Install the left side frame rail clamp brackets.

11. Position the stabilizer bar on the frame rail brackets and install the mounting clamp colts. Hand tighten only.

12. Install the bolts, washers, and grommets attaching the stabilizer bar to the left side lower control arm.

13. Tighten the stabilizer bar mounting clamp bolts to 18 ft.lb. torque.

14. Remove the supports and lower the car.

15. Fill the power steering pump reservoir with power steering fluid.

16. Operate the engine until the fluid reaches normal operating temperature. Turn the wheel right and left several times (do not hold the wheel against the steering stops). Stop the engine and check the fluid level. Add fluid as necessary.

20. Drive pin (included in stub shaft)
21. Power steering hoses
22. Mounting bolt
23. Washer
24. Preload spring
25. Grommet
26. Bushing
27. Steering linkage (assembled)
28. Rack bushing
29. Grommet
30. Washer
31. Nut
32. Steering rack
33. Rack piston
34. Outer bulkhead O-ring
35. Bulkhead retaining ring
36. Jam nut
37. Ball seat
38. Inner tie rod
39. Inner tie rod housing
40. Boot clamp
41. Boot
42. Adjuster tube clamp bolt
43. Adjuster tube clamp
44. Adjuster tube
45. Tie rod end
46. Lube plug
47. Tie rod end seal
48. Tie rod end-nut
49. Cotter pin
50. Adjuster tube clamp nut
51. Boot clamp
52. Tie rod housing setscrew
53. Ball seat spring
54. Shock dampener ring
55. Outer bulkhead and seal assembly
56. Inner bulkhead
57. Breather tube
58. Rack piston seal ring
59. Contraction plug
60. Lower pinion bushing
61. Housing (included in tube and housing assembly)
62. Nut
63. Washer
64. Grommet
65. Mounting clamp
66. Bolt
67. Mounting grommet
68. Inner rack seal
69. Tube and power cylinder (included in tube and housing assembly)
70. Upper pinion bushing
71. Pinion shaft seal (lip type)
72. Support washer
73. Conical thrust bearing race
74. Thrust bearing
75. Drive pin (included in stub shaft)
76. Shaft cap (included in stub shaft)
77. Torsion bar bushing (included in stub shaft)

Pacer power steering gear assembly exploded view

Brakes

BASIC OPERATING PRINCIPLES

Hydraulic systems are used to actuate the brakes of all modern automobiles. The system transports the power required to force the frictional surfaces of the braking system together from the pedal to the individual brake units at each wheel. A hydraulic system is used for two reasons. First, fluid under pressure can be carried to all parts of an automobile by small hoses, some of which are flexible, without taking up a significant amount of room or posing routing problems. Second, a great mechanical advantage can be given to the brake pedal end of the system, and the foot pressure required to actuate the brakes can be reduced by making the surface area of the master cylinder pistons smaller than that of any of the pistons in the wheel cylinders or calipers.

The master cylinder consists of a fluid reservoir and either a single or double cylinder and piston assembly. Double type master cylinders are designed to separate the front and rear braking systems hydraulically in case of a leak.

Steel lines carry the brake fluid to a point on the vehicle's frame near each of the vehicle's wheels. The fluid is then carried to the wheel

Brake Specifications
Gremlin/Hornet/Spirit/Concord/Pacer/AMX

| Years | Master Cyl. Bore | Brake Disc | | | Brake Drum | | Wheel Cyl. or Caliper Bore | |
		Original Thickness	Minimum Thickness	Maximum Run-out	Orig. Inside Dia.	Max. Wear Limit	Front	Rear
1975–76	①	1.190	1.120	0.003	②	③	④	⑤
1977	1.000	0.880	0.810	0.003	10.000	10.060	2.600	0.812
1978	0.945	0.880	0.810	0.003	⑥	⑥	2.600	⑦
1979–80	0.945	0.880	0.810	0.003	⑥	⑥	2.600	⑧
1981–83	0.945	0.880	0.810	0.003	⑨	⑨	2.600	0.945

① Non-power and power drum, and power disc: 1.0000
Power disc: 1.0625
② 6-cyl.: 9.000
8-cyl.: 10.000
③ 6-cyl.: 9.060
8-cyl.: 10.060
④ Drum brakes, wheel cylinder dia.:
  6-cyl. 1⅛
  8-cyl. 1³⁄₁₆
Disc brakes, caliper bore: 3.100
⑤ Gremlin: ⅞
Hornet 6-cyl.: ¹³⁄₁₆
Hornet 8-cyl.: ⅞

⑥ 4-cyl.: 9.000; 9.060 max.
All others: 10.000; 10.060 max.
⑦ 4-cyl.: 0.940
All others: 0.812
⑧ 4-cyl.: 0.945
AMX: 0.945
Pacer/Spirit/Concord 6- and 8-cyl.: 0.810
⑨ All except Station Wagon: 9.000; 9.060 max.
Station Wagon: 10.000; 10.06 max.

Brake Specifications
Matador

Years	Master Cyl. Bore	Brake Disc			Brake Drum		Wheel Cyl. or Caliper Bore	
		Original Thickness	Minimum Thickness	Maximum Run-out	Orig. Inside Dia.	Max. Wear Limit	Front	Rear
1975–76	①	1.190	1.120	0.003	10.000	10.060	3.100	②
1977	③	1.190	1.120	0.003	10.000	10.060	3.100	②
1978	1.125	1.190	1.120	0.003	10.000	10.060	3.100	②

① Non-power: 1¹⁄₁₆
  Power: 1⅛
② Except Station Wagon: ⅞
  Station Wagon: ¹⁵⁄₁₆
③ Non-power: 1.000
  Power: 1.125

Eagle

Years	Master Cyl. Bore	Brake Disc			Brake Drum		Wheel Cyl. or Caliper Bore	
		Original Thickness	Minimum Thickness	Maximum Run-out	Orig. Inside Dia.	Max. Wear Limit	Front	Rear
1980–87	0.940	0.880	0.810	0.003	10.000	10.060	2.600	0.945

cylinders by flexible tubes in order to allow for suspension and steering movements.

Each wheel cylinder contains two pistons, one at either end, which push outward in opposite directions. In disc brake systems, the cylinders are part of the calipers. One or four cylinders are used to force the brake pads against the disc, but all cylinders contain one piston only. All pistons employ some type of seal, usually made of rubber, to minimize fluid leakage. A rubber dust boot seals the outer end of the cylinder against dust and dirt. The boot fits around the outer end of the piston on disc brake calipers, and around the brake actuating rod on wheel cylinders.

The hydraulic system operates as follows: When at rest, the entire system, from the piston(s) in the master cylinder to those in the wheel cylinders or calipers, is full of brake fluid. Upon application of the brake pedal, fluid trapped in front of the master cylinder piston(s) is forced through the lines to the wheel cylinders. Here, it forces the pistons outward, in the case of drum brakes, and inward toward the disc, in the case of disc brakes. The motion of the pistons is opposed by return springs mounted outside the cylinders in drum brakes, and by internal springs or spring seals, in disc brakes.

Upon release of the brake pedal, a spring located inside the master cylinder immediately returns the master cylinder pistons to the normal position. The pistons contain check valves and the master cylinder has compensating ports drilled in it. These are uncovered as the pistons reach their normal position. The piston check valves allow fluid to flow toward the wheel cylinders or calipers as the pistons withdraw. Then, as the return springs force the brake pads or shoes into the released position, the excess fluid reservoir through the compensating ports. It is during the time the pedal is in the released position that any fluid that has leaked out of the system will be replaced through the compensating ports.

Dual circuit master cylinders employ two pistons, located one behind the other, in the same cylinder. The primary piston is actuated directly by mechanical linkage from the brake pedal. The secondary piston is actuated by fluid trapped between the two pistons. If a leak develops in front of the secondary piston, it moves forward until it bottoms against the front of the master cylinder, and the fluid trapped between the pistons will operate the rear brakes. If the rear brakes develop a leak, the primary piston will move forward until direct contact with the secondary piston takes place, and it will force the secondary piston to actuate the front brakes. In either case, the brake pedal moves farther when the brakes are applied, and less braking power is available.

All dual circuit systems use a switch to warn the driver when only half of the brake system is operational. This switch is located in a valve body which is mounted on the firewall or the frame below the master cylinder. A hydraulic piston receives pressure from both circuits, each circuit's pressure being applied to one end of the piston. When the pressures are in balance, the piston remains stationary. When one circuit has a leak, however, the greater pressure in that circuit during application of the brakes will push the piston to one side, closing the switch and activating the brake warning light.

In disc brake systems, this valve body also contains a metering valve and, in some cases, a proportioning valve. The metering valve keeps pressure from traveling to the disc brakes on the front wheels until the brake shoes on the rear wheels have contacted the drums, ensuring that the front brakes will never be used alone. The proportioning valve controls the pressure to the rear brakes to avoid rear wheel lock-up during very hard braking.

Warning lights may be tested by depressing the brake pedal and holding it while opening one of the wheel cylinder bleeder screws. If this does not cause the light to go on, substitute a new lamp, make continuity checks, and, finally, replace the switch as necessary.

The hydraulic system may be checked for leaks by applying pressure to the pedal gradually and steadily. If the pedal sinks very slowly to the floor, the system has a leak. This is not to be confused with a springy or spongy feel due to the compression of air within the lines. If the system leaks, there will be a gradual change in the position of the pedal with a constant pressure.

Check for leaks along all lines and at wheel cylinders. If no external leaks are apparent, the problem is inside the master cylinder.

Disc Brakes
BASIC OPERATING PRINCIPLES

Instead of the traditional expanding brakes that press outward against a circular drum, disc brake systems utilize a disc (rotor) with brake pads positioned on either side of it. Braking effect is achieved in a manner similar

to the way you would squeeze a spinning phonograph record between your fingers. The disc (rotor) is a casting with cooling fins between the two braking surfaces. This enables air to circulate between the braking surfaces making them less sensitive to heat buildup and more resistant to fade. Dirt and water do not affect braking action since contaminants are thrown off by the centrifugal action of the rotor or scraped off the by the pads. Also, the equal clamping action of the two brake pads tends to ensure uniform, straightline stops. Disc brakes are inherently self-adjusting.

There are three general types of disc brake:

1. A fixed caliper.
2. A floating caliper.
3. A sliding caliper.

The fixed caliper design uses two pistons mounted on either side of the rotor (in each side of the caliper). The caliper is mounted rigidly and does not move.

The sliding and floating designs are quite similar. In fact, these two types are often lumped together. In both designs, the pad on the inside of the rotor is moved into contact with the rotor by hydraulic force. The caliper, which is not held in a fixed position, moves slightly, bringing the outside pad into contact with the rotor. There are various methods of attaching floating calipers. Some pivot at the bottom or top, and some slide on mounting bolts. In any event, the end result is the same.

Drum Brakes
BASIC OPERATING PRINCIPLES

Drum brakes employ two brake shoes mounted on a stationary backing plate. These shoes are positioned inside a circular drum which rotates with the wheel assembly. The shoes are held in place by springs. This allows them to slide toward the drums (when they are applied) while keeping the linings and drums in alignment. The shoes are actuated by a wheel cylinder which is mounted at the top of the backing plate. When the brakes are applied, hydraulic pressure forces the wheel cylinder's actuating links outward. Since these links bear directly against the top of the brake shoes, the tops of the shoes are then forced against the inner side of the drum. This action forces the bottoms of the two shoes to contact the brake drum by rotating the entire assembly slightly (known as servo action). When pressure within the wheel cylinder is relaxed, return springs pull the shoes back away from the drum.

Most modern drum brakes are designed to self-adjust themselves during application when the vehicle is moving in reverse. This

Troubleshooting the Brake System

Problem	Cause	Solution
Low brake pedal (excessive pedal travel required for braking action.)	• Excessive clearance between rear linings and drums caused by inoperative automatic adjusters	• Make 10 to 15 alternate forward and reverse brake stops to adjust brakes. If brake pedal does not come up, repair or replace adjuster parts as necessary.
	• Worn rear brakelining	• Inspect and replace lining if worn beyond minimum thickness specification
	• Bent, distorted brakeshoes, front or rear	• Replace brakeshoes in axle sets
	• Air in hydraulic system	• Remove air from system. Refer to Brake Bleeding.
Low brake pedal (pedal may go to floor with steady pressure applied.)	• Fluid leak in hydraulic system	• Fill master cylinder to fill line; have helper apply brakes and check calipers, wheel cylinders, differential valve tubes, hoses and fittings for leaks. Repair or replace as necessary.
	• Air in hydraulic system	• Remove air from system. Refer to Brake Bleeding.
	• Incorrect or non-recommended brake fluid (fluid evaporates at below normal temp).	• Flush hydraulic system with clean brake fluid. Refill with correct-type fluid.
	• Master cylinder piston seals worn, or master cylinder bore is scored, worn or corroded	• Repair or replace master cylinder
Low brake pedal (pedal goes to floor on first application—o.k. on subsequent applications.)	• Disc brake pads sticking on abutment surfaces of anchor plate. Caused by a build-up of dirt, rust, or corrosion on abutment surfaces	• Clean abutment surfaces
Fading brake pedal (pedal height decreases with steady pressure applied.)	• Fluid leak in hydraulic system	• Fill master cylinder reservoirs to fill mark, have helper apply brakes, check calipers, wheel cylinders, differential valve, tubes, hoses, and fittings for fluid leaks. Repair or replace parts as necessary.
	• Master cylinder piston seals worn, or master cylinder bore is scored, worn or corroded	• Repair or replace master cylinder
Decreasing brake pedal travel (pedal travel required for braking action decreases and may be accompanied by a hard pedal.)	• Caliper or wheel cylinder pistons sticking or seized	• Repair or replace the calipers, or wheel cylinders
	• Master cylinder compensator ports blocked (preventing fluid return to reservoirs) or pistons sticking or seized in master cylinder bore	• Repair or replace the master cylinder
	• Power brake unit binding internally	• Test unit according to the following procedure: (a) Shift transmission into neutral and start engine (b) Increase engine speed to 1500 rpm, close throttle and fully depress brake pedal (c) Slow release brake pedal and stop engine (d) Have helper remove vacuum check valve and hose from power unit. Observe for backward movement of brake pedal. (e) If the pedal moves backward, the power unit has an internal bind—replace power unit

Troubleshooting the Brake System (cont.)

Problem	Cause	Solution
Spongy brake pedal (pedal has abnormally soft, springy, spongy feel when depressed.)	• Air in hydraulic system • Brakeshoes bent or distorted • Brakelining not yet seated with drums and rotors • Rear drum brakes not properly adjusted	• Remove air from system. Refer to Brake Bleeding. • Replace brakeshoes • Burnish brakes • Adjust brakes
Hard brake pedal (excessive pedal pressure required to stop vehicle. May be accompanied by brake fade.)	• Loose or leaking power brake unit vacuum hose • Incorrect or poor quality brakelining • Bent, broken, distorted brakeshoes • Calipers binding or dragging on mounting pins. Rear brakeshoes dragging on support plate. • Caliper, wheel cylinder, or master cylinder pistons sticking or seized • Power brake unit vacuum check valve malfunction • Power brake unit has internal bind • Master cylinder compensator ports (at bottom of reservoirs) blocked by dirt, scale, rust, or have small burrs (blocked ports prevent fluid return to reservoirs). • Brake hoses, tubes, fittings clogged or restricted • Brake fluid contaminated with improper fluids (motor oil, transmission fluid, causing rubber components to swell and stick in bores • Low engine vacuum	• Tighten connections or replace leaking hose • Replace with lining in axle sets • Replace brakeshoes • Replace mounting pins and bushings. Clean rust or burrs from rear brake support plate ledges and lubricate ledges with molydisulfide grease. **NOTE:** If ledges are deeply grooved or scored, do not attempt to sand or grind them smooth—replace support plate. • Repair or replace parts as necessary • Test valve according to the following procedure: (a) Start engine, increase engine speed to 1500 rpm, close throttle and immediately stop engine (b) Wait at least 90 seconds then depress brake pedal (c) If brakes are not vacuum assisted for 2 or more applications, check valve is faulty • Test unit according to the following procedure: (a) With engine stopped, apply brakes several times to exhaust all vacuum in system (b) Shift transmission into neutral, depress brake pedal and start engine (c) If pedal height decreases with foot pressure and less pressure is required to hold pedal in applied position, power unit vacuum system is operating normally. Test power unit. If power unit exhibits a bind condition, replace the power unit. • Repair or replace master cylinder **CAUTION:** Do not attempt to clean blocked ports with wire, pencils, or similar implements. Use compressed air only. • Use compressed air to check or unclog parts. Replace any damaged parts. • Replace all rubber components, combination valve and hoses. Flush entire brake system with DOT 3 brake fluid or equivalent. • Adjust or repair engine

Troubleshooting the Brake System (cont.)

Problem	Cause	Solution
Grabbing brakes (severe reaction to brake pedal pressure.)	• Brakelining(s) contaminated by grease or brake fluid	• Determine and correct cause of contamination and replace brakeshoes in axle sets
	• Parking brake cables incorrectly adjusted or seized	• Adjust cables. Replace seized cables.
	• Incorrect brakelining or lining loose on brakeshoes	• Replace brakeshoes in axle sets
	• Caliper anchor plate bolts loose	• Tighten bolts
	• Rear brakeshoes binding on support plate ledges	• Clean and lubricate ledges. Replace support plate(s) if ledges are deeply grooved. Do not attempt to smooth ledges by grinding.
	• Incorrect or missing power brake reaction disc	• Install correct disc
	• Rear brake support plates loose	• Tighten mounting bolts
Dragging brakes (slow or incomplete release of brakes)	• Brake pedal binding at pivot	• Loosen and lubricate
	• Power brake unit has internal bind	• Inspect for internal bind. Replace unit if internal bind exists.
	• Parking brake cables incorrrectly adjusted or seized	• Adjust cables. Replace seized cables.
	• Rear brakeshoe return springs weak or broken	• Replace return springs. Replace brakeshoe if necessary in axle sets.
	• Automatic adjusters malfunctioning	• Repair or replace adjuster parts as required
	• Caliper, wheel cylinder or master cylinder pistons sticking or seized	• Repair or replace parts as necessary
	• Master cylinder compensating ports blocked (fluid does not return to reservoirs).	• Use compressed air to clear ports. Do not use wire, pencils, or similar objects to open blocked ports.
Vehicle moves to one side when brakes are applied	• Incorrect front tire pressure	• Inflate to recommended cold (reduced load) inflation pressure
	• Worn or damaged wheel bearings	• Replace worn or damaged bearings
	• Brakelining on one side contaminated	• Determine and correct cause of contamination and replace brakelining in axle sets
	• Brakeshoes on one side bent, distorted, or lining loose on shoe	• Replace brakeshoes in axle sets
	• Support plate bent or loose on one side	• Tighten or replace support plate
	• Brakelining not yet seated with drums or rotors	• Burnish brakelining
	• Caliper anchor plate loose on one side	• Tighten anchor plate bolts
	• Caliper piston sticking or seized	• Repair or replace caliper
	• Brakelinings water soaked	• Drive vehicle with brakes lightly applied to dry linings
	• Loose suspension component attaching or mounting bolts	• Tighten suspension bolts. Replace worn suspension components.
	• Brake combination valve failure	• Replace combination valve
Chatter or shudder when brakes are applied (pedal pulsation and roughness may also occur.)	• Brakeshoes distorted, bent, contaminated, or worn	• Replace brakeshoes in axle sets
	• Caliper anchor plate or support plate loose	• Tighten mounting bolts
	• Excessive thickness variation of rotor(s)	• Refinish or replace rotors in axle sets
Noisy brakes (squealing, clicking, scraping sound when brakes are applied.)	• Bent, broken, distorted brakeshoes	• Replace brakeshoes in axle sets
	• Excessive rust on outer edge of rotor braking surface	• Remove rust

Troubleshooting the Brake System (cont.)

Problem	Cause	Solution
Noisy brakes (squealing, clicking, scraping sound when brakes are applied.) (cont.)	• Brakelining worn out—shoes contacting drum of rotor	• Replace brakeshoes and lining in axle sets. Refinish or replace drums or rotors.
	• Broken or loose holdown or return springs	• Replace parts as necessary
	• Rough or dry drum brake support plate ledges	• Lubricate support plate ledges
	• Cracked, grooved, or scored rotor(s) or drum(s)	• Replace rotor(s) or drum(s). Replace brakeshoes and lining in axle sets if necessary.
	• Incorrect brakelining and/or shoes (front or rear).	• Install specified shoe and lining assemblies
Pulsating brake pedal	• Out of round drums or excessive lateral runout in disc brake rotor(s)	• Refinish or replace drums, re-index rotors or replace

motion causes both shoes to rotate very slightly with the drum, rocking an adjusting lever, thereby causing rotation of the adjusting screw.

Power Boosters

Power brakes operate just as standard brake systems except in the actuation of the master cylinder pistons. A vacuum diaphragm is located on the front of the master cylinder and assists the driver in applying the brakes, reducing both the effort and travel he must put into moving the brake pedal.

The vacuum diaphragm housing is connected to the intake manifold by a vacuum hose. A check valve is placed at the point where the hose enters the diaphragm housing, so that during periods of low manifold vacuum brake assist vacuum will not be lost.

Depressing the brake pedal closes off the vacuum source and allows atmospheric pressure to enter on one side of the diaphragm. This causes the master cylinder pistons to move and apply the brakes. When the brake pedal is released, vacuum is applied to both sides of the diaphragm, and return springs return the diaphragm and master cylinder pistons to the released position. If the vacuum fails, the brake pedal rod will butt against the end of the master cylinder actuating rod, and direct mechanical application will occur as the pedal is depressed.

The hydraulic and mechanical problems that apply to conventional brake systems also apply to power brakes, and should be checked for if the tests below do not reveal the problem. Test for a system vacuum leak as described below:

1. Operate the engine at idle without touching the brake pedal for at least one minute.
2. Turn off the engine, and wait one minute.

3. Test for the presence of assist vacuum by depressing the brake pedal and releasing it several times. Light application will produce less and less pedal travel, if vacuum was present. If there is no vacuum, air is leaking into the system somewhere.

Test for system operation as follows:

1. Pump the brake pedal (with engine off) until the supply vacuum is entirely gone.
2. Put a light, steady pressure on the pedal.
3. Start the engine, and operate it at idle. If the system is operating, the brake pedal should fall toward the floor if constant pressure is maintained on the pedal.

Power brake systems may be tested for hydraulic leaks just as ordinary systems are tested.

CAUTION: *Brake linings contain asbestos. Asbestos is a known cancer-causing agent. When working on brakes, remember that the dust which accumulates on the brake parts and/or in the drum contains asbestos. Always wear a protective face covering, such as a painter's mask, when working on the brakes. NEVER blow the dust from the brakes or drum! There are solvents made for the purpose of cleaning brake parts. Use them!*

HYDRAULIC SYSTEM

Master Cylinder

REMOVAL AND INSTALLATION

1. Detach the front and rear brake lines from the master cylinder. On cars with drum brakes, the check valves will keep the fluid from draining our of the cylinder. If the car has disc brakes, one of both of the outlets must be plugged, to prevent fluid loss.
2. Remove the nuts which attach the master

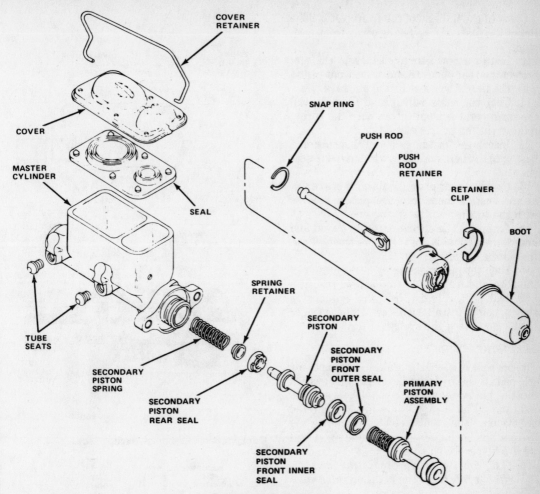

Typical master cylinder

cylinder to the firewall of the power brake booster.

3. On cars that don't have power brakes, detach the pedal pushrod from the brake pedal.

4. Remove the master cylinder from the car.

5. Installation is the reverse of removal. Bleed the brake system once the master cylinder has been installed.

OVERHAUL

If the master cylinder leaks externally, or if the pedal sinks while being held down, the master cylinder is worn. There are three possible solutions:

    a. Buy a new master cylinder.

    b. Trade the old one in on a rebuilt unit.

    c. Rebuild the old one with a rebuilding kit.

1. Remove the cylinder from the car and drain the brake fluid.

2. Mount the cylinder in a vise so that the outlets are up and remove the seal from the hub.

3. Remove the stop screw from the bottom of the front reservoir.

4. Remove the snapring from the front of the bore and remove the primary piston assembly.

5. Remove the secondary piston assembly using compressed air or a piece of wire. Cover the bore opening with a cloth to prevent damage to the piston.

6. Clean the metal parts in brake fluid and discard all rubber parts.

7. Inspect the bore for damage or wear, and check the pistons for damage and proper clearance in the bore.

8. If the bore is only slightly scored or pitted it may be honed. Always use hones that are in good condition and completely clean the cylinder with brake fluid when honing is completed. If there is any evidence of contamination in the master cylinder, the entire hydraulic system should be flushed and refilled with clean brake fluid. Blow out all passages with compressed air.

9. Install new secondary seals in the two

grooves in the flat end of the front piston. The lips of the seals will be facing away front each other.

10. Install a new primary seal and the seal protector on the opposite end of the front piston with the lips of the seal facing outward.

11. Coat the seals with brake fluid. Install the spring on the front piston with the spring retainer in the primary seal.

12. Insert the piston assembly, spring end first, into the bore and use a wooden rod to seat it.

13. Coat the rear piston seals with brake fluid and install them into the piston grooves with the lips facing the spring end.

14. Assemble the spring onto the piston and install the assembly into the bore spring first. Install the snapring.

15. Hold the piston assembly at the bottom of the bore and install the stop screw. Install a new seal on the hub. Bleed the cylinder as shown, before installation. Install the cylinder on the car. Bleed the system of air.

BLEEDING

The purpose of bleeding brakes is to expel air trapped in the hydraulic system. The system must be bled whenever the pedal feels spongy, indicating that compressible air has entered the system. It must also be bled whenever the system has been opened or leaking. You will need a helper for this job.

NOTE: *When bleeding brakes the stem on the front of the brake combination valve must be held out 0.060" (1.52mm).*

1. Clean the bleed screw at each wheel.

2. Attach a small rubber hose to one of the bleed screws and place the end in a container of brake fluid.

3. Fill the master cylinder with brake fluid. Check the level often during bleeding. Pump up the brake pedal and hold it.

4. Open the bleed screw about ¼ turn, press the brake pedal to the floor, close the bleed screw, and slowly release the pedal. Continue until no more air bubbles are forced from the cylinder on application of the brake pedal.

5. Repeat the procedure on the remaining wheel cylinders.

Disc brakes may be bled in the same manner as drum brakes, except that:

1. It usually requires a longer time to bleed a disc brake thoroughly.

2. The disc should be rotated to make sure that the piston has returned to the unapplied position when bleeding is completed and the bleed screw closed.

BRAKE WARNING LIGHT SIGNAL

The warning light on the dashboard is activated by a differential pressure switch located be-

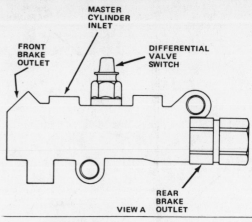

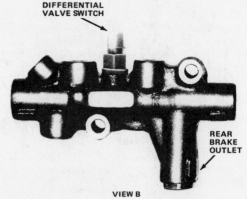

Combination valve on all except Pacer

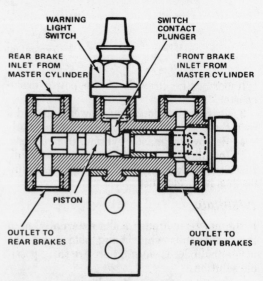

Pacer pressure differential valve

low the master cylinder. The signal indicates a loss of fluid pressure in either the front or rear brakes, and warns the driver that a hydraulic failure has occurred.

The pressure differential warning valve is a housing with the brake warning light switch mounted centrally on top. Directly below the switch is a bore containing a piston assembly. The piston assembly is located in the center of the bore and kept in that position by equal fluid pressure on either side. Fluid pressure is provided by two brake lines, one coming from the rear brake system and one from the front brakes. If a leak develops in either system (front or rear), fluid pressure to that side of the piston will decrease or stop causing the piston to move in that direction. The plunger on the end of the switch engages with the piston. When the piston moves off center, the plunger moves and triggers the switch to activate the warning light on the dash.

After repairing and bleeding any part of the hydraulic system the warning light may remain on due to the pressure differential valve remaining in the off-center position. All models have a self centering valve. After repairs or bleeding have been performed, center the valve by applying moderate pressure on the brake pedal. This will turn on the light.

NOTE: *Front wheel balancing, on the car, of cars equipped with disc brakes may also cause a pressure differential in the front branch of the system.*

Adjustments
DRUM BRAKES

The drum brakes are self adjusting and do not normally require attention. However, if the brakes are disassembled, they must be adjusted upon assembly; or, if necessary, the brakes may be manually adjusted during the course of normal service.

1. Remove the rubber plug from the access slot on the backing plate.
NOTE: *It may be easier to perform Step 1 with the drum removed; however, be sure that the drum is installed properly before beginning adjustment.*

2. Rotate the starwheel with a screwdriver or an adjoining tool until the wheel will not rotate.
3. Mark the starwheel and back it off one complete revolution.
NOTE: *In order to back off the starwheel it may be necessary to use a piece of 1/8" (3mm) welding rod to hold the adjusting lever off the adjusting screw.*
4. Install the rubber plug in the access slot.
5. Make 10–15 hard applications of the brakes while backing the car up and then road test the car.

DISC BRAKES

The front disc brakes require no adjustment as hydraulic pressure maintains the proper brake pad-to-disc contact at all times.
NOTE: *Because of this, the brake fluid level should be checked regularly (see Chapter 1).*

Power Booster
REMOVAL AND INSTALLATION

1. Disconnect the power booster clevis pin or the pushrod, depending on which type of unit is used.
2. Remove the vacuum hose from the power unit.
3. Unbolt and remove the master cylinder from the booster. It is not necessary to disconnect the brake lines from the master cylinder. There should be enough play in the lines to move the cylinder aside.
4. Unbolt and remove the booster from the firewall.
5. Installation is the reverse of removal. Torque the booster-to-dash nuts to 30 ft.lb.
CAUTION: *Some cars have two holes in the brake pedal for the pushrod. On cars with power brakes, use the lower hole.*

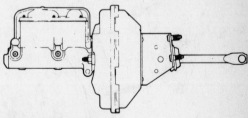

Pacer power brake unit

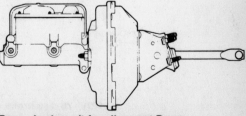

Power brake unit for all except Pacer

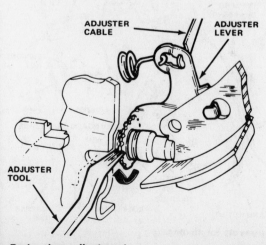

Brake shoe adjustment

FRONT DISC BRAKES

Disc Brake Pads

REMOVAL AND INSTALLATION

CAUTION: *To prevent paint damage from brake fluid, be sure to remove part of the brake fluid (don't reuse it) from the master cylinder and keep the master cylinder covered. Do not allow the cylinder to drain too low or air will be pumped into the system.*

1975–81

EXCEPT PACER

1. Raise the front of the car and remove the front wheels.

2. Working on only one brake at a time, remove the caliper guide pins and positioners which attach the caliper to the adapter. Lift the caliper away from the disc.

3. Remove (and discard) the positioners and inner bushings from the guide pins, and the outboard bushings from the caliper.

4. Slide the disc pads out of the caliper, and carefully push the piston back into the bore. Later models have anti-rattle clips. Note their positions before removing them.

5. Lubricate the new outboard bushings and work them into position from the outboard side of the caliper.

6. Slide the new disc pads into position (outboard pad in the retaining spring) and carefully slide the caliper assembly over the rotor.

7. Lubricate and install the new inner bushings in the caliper. Install the new positioners on the guide pins with the open ends toward the outside.

8. Install the assembled guide pins from the inboard side and press while threading the pin into the adapter. Use extreme car to avoid crossing the threads. Tighten the caliper guide pins to 26 ft.lb. Be sure that the tabs of the positioners are over the machined surfaces of the caliper.

9. Check the brake fluid level and pump the brake pedal to seat the linings against the disc. Replace the wheels and road test the car.

PACER

CAUTION: *To prevent paint damage from leaking brake fluid, remove about ⅔ of the brake fluid from the larger reservoir (supplying the front brakes), in the master cylinder and keep the cylinder reservoir covered. Do not allow the reservoir level to get too low or air will enter the hydraulic system, necessitating bleeding. Do not reuse the removed brake fluid.*

1. Remove the hub caps and loosen the front wheel lug nuts slightly. Firmly apply the parking brake and block the rear wheels.

2. Raise the front of the car and install jackstands beneath the front jacking points or lower control arms. Remove the front wheels.

3. Working on only one caliper at a time, bottom the caliper piston in its bore by carefully inserting a screwdriver between the piston and the inboard shoe and prying back on the piston.

NOTE: *Take care not to damage the rubber piston seals. If the piston cannot be bottomed with a screwdriver, a large C-clamp will suffice.*

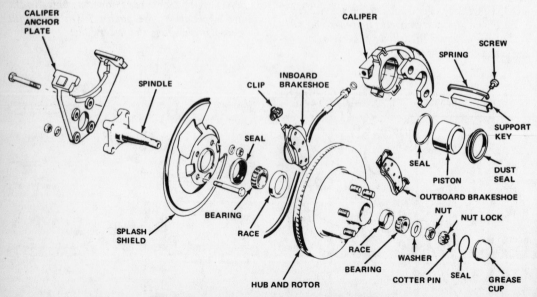

1975–76 disc brake components for all models

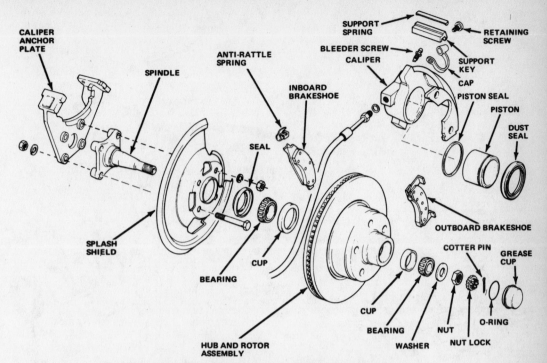

1977 and later Matador disc brake components

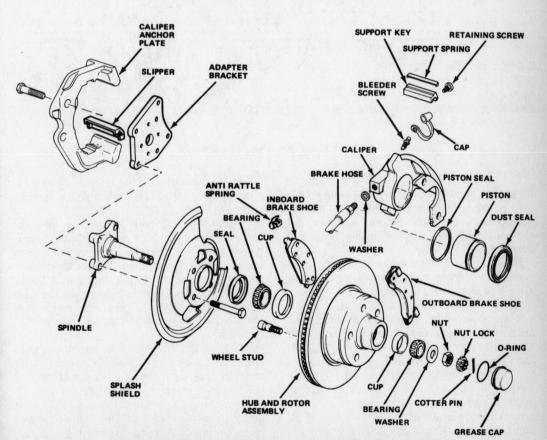

1977–81 disc brake components for all except Matador and Eagle

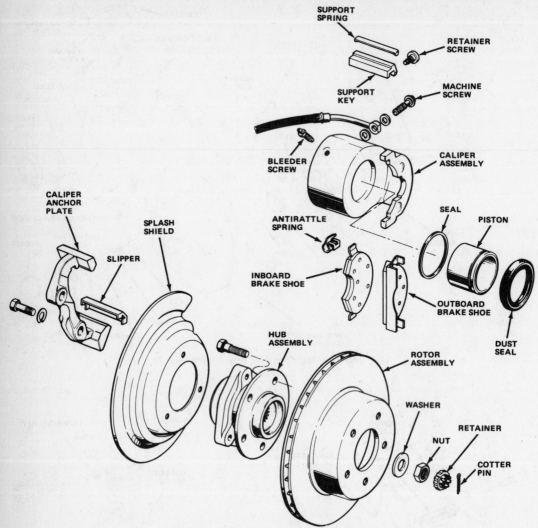

SUPPORT
SPRING

RETAINER
SCREW

SUPPORT
KEY

MACHINE
SCREW

BLEEDER
SCREW

CALIPER
ASSEMBLY

CALIPER
ANCHOR
PLATE

SPLASH
SHIELD

ANTIRATTLE
SPRING

SEAL

PISTON

SLIPPER

INBOARD
BRAKE SHOE

OUTBOARD
BRAKE SHOE

DUST
SEAL

HUB
ASSEMBLY

ROTOR
ASSEMBLY

WASHER

RETAINER

NUT

COTTER
PIN

1980–81 Eagle disc brake components

4. Using a ¼" hex key or allen wrench, remove the caliper support key retaining screw.

5. Remove the caliper support key and support spring using a drift pin and hammer. Lift the caliper assembly off its anchor plate and over the rotor (disc).

NOTE: *Do not allow the caliper to hang by its flexible brake hose. Use a piece of heavy wire to suspend the caliper from the coil spring until you are ready to reinstall it.*

6. Remove the inboard brake shoe from the anchor plate. Remove the inboard brake shoe anti-rattle spring from the inboard shoe, noting its position for reassembly.

7. Remove the outboard brake shoe from the caliper, rapping lightly with a hammer, if necessary, to free it from the caliper.

8. Wipe the inside of the caliper free of all accumulated brake pad dust, road dirt and other foreign material with a clean, dry rag.

NOTE: *Do not blow the caliper clean with compressed air as this may dislodge the rubber dust cover.*

Check the piston seals for evidence of leakage from the piston bore, and overhaul the caliper if necessary. Clean all rust and dirt from the abutment (sliding), surfaces of the caliper and caliper anchor plate using a wire brush and crocus cloth. Then, lightly grease the sliding surfaces with white grease to ensure that the sliding motion of the caliper is not impaired.

9. Install the inboard brake shoe anti-rattle spring on the rear flange of the inboard brake shoe, making sure that the looped section of the clip is facing away from the rotor.

10. Install the assembled inboard brake shoe and anti-rattle spring in the caliper anchor plate, taking care not to dislodge the anti-rattle spring during installation.

11. Install the outboard brake shoe in the caliper, making sure to seat the shoe flange fully into the outboard arms of the caliper.

12. Install the caliper assembly over the rotor and into position in the anchor plate. Exercise extreme care when installing the caliper not to tear or dislodge the piston dust cover on the inboard brake shoe.

13. Align the caliper assembly with the abutment surfaces of the anchor plate and insert the caliper support key and support spring between the abutment surfaces at the rearward end of the caliper and anchor plate. Then, using a hammer and drift pin, drive the caliper support key and spring into position. Install the support key retaining screw and tighten to 15 ft.lb.

14. Fill the master cylinder reservoir to within ¼″ (6mm) of the rim. Press the brake pedal firmly several times to seat the shoes.

15. Install the wheels and lower the car. Road test the car after rechecking the fluid level and checking for firm brake pedal.

1982-86

1. Drain about ½ the fluid from the master cylinder.

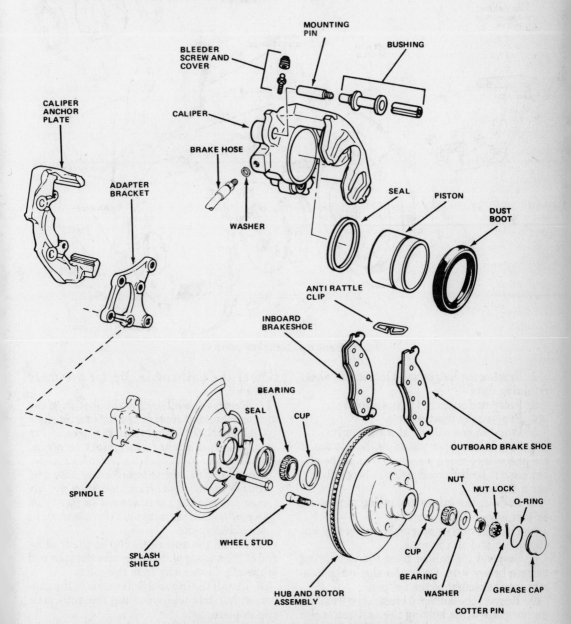

1982–83 Spirit and Concord disc brake components

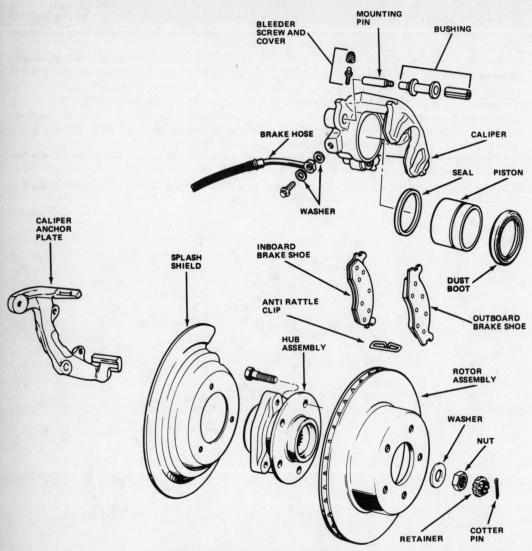

1982–86 Eagle disc brake components

2. Remove the hub cap and loosen the wheel retaining nuts.

3. Raise and support the automobile.

4. Remove the front wheels.

5. Work on one caliper at a time only.

6. Press the caliper piston to the bottom of the piston bore using a screwdriver. If the piston cannot be bottomed using a screwdriver, use a C-clamp.

7. Remove the caliper mounting pins using a 7mm hex or Allen wrench.

8. Lift the caliper assembly out of the anchor plate and off the rotor.

9. Suspend the caliper from the coil spring using a heavy wire. Do not let the brake hose support the weight of the caliper.

10. Remove the outboard brake shoe from the anchor plate while holding the anti-rattle clip against the caliper anchor plate. Note the posi-

tion of the anti-rattle clip for assembly reference.

11. Remove the inboard brake shoe from the anchor plate and remove the anti-rattle clip.

CAUTION: *The abutment surfaces of the caliper and anchor plate must be clean, smooth, and lightly lubricated with molybdenum disulfide grease before brake shoe and caliper installation. Rust, corrosion, or foreign material on the abutment surfaces will impair the sliding action of the brake shoes in the anchor plate.*

12. Install the anti-rattle clip on the trailing end of the anchor plate being sure the split end of the clip faces away from the rotor.

13. Install the inboard brake shoe in the caliper anchor late while holding the anti-rattle clip in place.

14. Install the outboard brake shoe in the

caliper anchor plate while holding the anti-rattle clip in place.

15. Install the caliper over the rotor and into position in the anchor plate.

16. Install the caliper mounting pins and tighten them to 26 ft.lb. torque.

CAUTION: *Be very careful to avoid tearing or dislodging the dust boot when installing the caliper. A damaged boot will expose the caliper piston to road splash resulting in corrosion and eventual piston seizure.*

17. Fill both master cylinder reservoirs to within ¼" (6.3mm) of the rim.

18. Press firmly on the brake pedal several times to seat the brake shoes.

19. Install the wheels and tires and lower the automobile.

20. Check the fluid level in the master cylinder and correct it if necessary.

CAUTION: *Check for a firm brake pedal and proper brake operation before moving the automobile.*

Disc Brake Calipers

REMOVAL, INSTALLATION, OVERHAUL

1975–81

EXCEPT PACER

1. Raise the front of the car and remove the front wheels.

2. Working on one side at a time only, disconnect the brake hose from the steel brake line and cap the fittings. Remove the U-shaped retainer from the hose fitting (if it has one).

3. Remove the caliper mounting bolts (locating pins) and positioners and lift the caliper away from the disc.

4. Clean the holes in the caliper ears, and wipe all dirt from the mounting bolts. If the bolts are corroded or damaged they should be replaced.

5. Remove the shoe support springs from the piston.

6. Remove the rubber bushings from the grooves in the caliper ears.

7. Remove the brake hose, drain the brake fluid, and clean the outside of the caliper.

8. Pad the inside of the caliper with towels and direct compressed air into the brake fluid inlet hole to remove the piston.

CAUTION: *To prevent damage to the piston use just enough air pressure to ease it out of the bore. Do not attempt to catch or protect the piston with your hand since this may cause serious injury.*

9. Use a screwdriver to pry the boot out of the caliper. Avoid scratching the bore.

10. Remove the piston seal from its groove in the caliper bore. Do not use a metal tool of any type for this operation.

11. Blow out all passages in the caliper and bleeder valve. Clean the piston and piston bore with fresh brake fluid.

12. Examine the piston for scoring, scratches, or corrosion. If any of these conditions exist the piston must be replaced, as it is plated and cannot be refinished.

13. Examine the bore for the same defects. Light rough spots may be removed by rotating crocus cloth, using finger pressure, in the bore. Do not polish with an in and out motion or use any other abrasive. Piston-to-bore clearance should be 0.002–0.006" (0.051–0.152mm).

14. Lubricate the piston bore and the new rubber parts with fresh brake fluid. Position the seal in the piston bore groove.

15. Lubricate the piston with brake fluid and assemble the boot into the piston groove so that the fold faces the open end of the piston.

16. Insert the piston into the bore, taking care not to unseat the seal.

17. Force the piston to the bottom of the bore. (This will require a force of 50–100 lbs.). Seat the boot lip around the caliper counterbore. Proper seating of the boot is very important for sealing out contaminants.

18. Install the brake hose into the caliper using a new copper gasket.

19. Lubricate the rubber bushings. Install the bushings in the caliper ears.

NOTE: *Lubrication of the bushings is essential to ensure the proper operation of the sliding caliper design.*

20. Install the shoe support spring in the piston.

21. Install the disc pads in the caliper and remount the caliper on the hub (see 'Disc Pad Installation').

22. Reconnect the brake hose to the steel brake line. Install the retainer clip. Bleed the brakes.

23. Replace the wheels, check the brake fluid level, check the brake pedal travel, and road test the vehicle.

PACER

1. Remove the caliper as outlined under Steps 1–7 of 'Brake Pad Replacement'.

2. Place a clean piece of paper on your work area to put the parts of the caliper on while it is being disassembled.

3. Drain the brake fluid from the caliper by opening the bleeder plug.

4. Place the caliper assembly in a vise with padded jaws.

CAUTION: *Do not overtighten the vise; too much pressure will cause distortion of the caliper bore.*

5. Using compressed air, remove the piston from the caliper bore. Be careful not to damage

the piston or the bore. Leave the dust boot in the caliper groove while the piston is being removed.

6. Take the caliper out of the vise and withdraw the dust boot.

7. Work the piston seal out of its groove in the piston bore with a small, pointed wooden or plastic stick. Do not use a screwdriver or other metallic tool to remove the seal as it could damage the bore. Throw the old seal away.

8. Unscrew the bleeder plug.

9. Clean all of the parts in brake fluid (do not use solvent) and wipe them dry with a clean, lint free cloth. Dry the passages and bores with compressed air.

Check the cylinder bore for scoring, pitting, and/or corrosion. If the caliper bore is deeply scored or corroded, replace the entire caliper.

If it is only lightly scored or stained, polish with crocus cloth. Use finger pressure to rotate the crocus cloth in the cylinder bore. Any black stains found in the bore are caused by seals and are harmless.

CAUTION: *Do not slide the crocus cloth in and out of the bore. Do not use any other type of abrasive material.*

Check the piston. If it is pitted, scored, or worn, it should be replaced with a new one.

Check the piston-to-bore clearance with a feeler gauge. It should be 0.002–0.006″ (0.051–0.152mm). If it is more than this, replace the caliper assembly.

Assembly and installation are performed in the following order:

1. Dip a new piston seal in clean brake fluid. Position the seal in one area of the groove in the cylinder bore and gently work it into place around the groove until it is seated. Be sure that your fingers are clean before touching the seal.

CAUTION: *Never reuse an old piston seal.*

2. Coat a new piston boot with clean brake fluid. Work it into the outer groove of the bore with your fingers until it snaps into place. Don't worry if the boot seems too large for the

groove; once seated, it will fit properly. Check the boot, by running your forefinger around the inside of it, to be sure that it is correctly installed.

3. Coat the piston with plenty of brake fluid. Spread the boot with your fingers and insert the piston into it.

4. Depress the piston until it bottoms in the bore.

CAUTION: *Apply uniform force to the piston or it will crack.*

5. Install the caliper assembly as outlined under Steps 9–15 of 'Brake Pad Replacement'.

1982-86

1. Drain and discard ⅔ of the brake fluid from the master cylinder reservoir serving the front disc brakes. Do not drain the reservoir completely.

2. Remove the hub cap and loosen wheel retaining nuts.

3. Raise and support the automobile.

4. Remove the front wheels.

5. Work on one caliper at a time.

6. Wipe all dirt and grease from the caliper brake hose fitting using a shop cloth.

7. Disconnect the brake line at the caliper and discard the hose fitting washer. Cover the open end of the hose with tape or a clean shop cloth.

8. Remove the caliper and brake shoes as outlined in Brake Shoe Replacement.

9. Clean the caliper exterior with brake cleaning solvent.

10. Drain the remaining fluid from the caliper and place the caliper on a clean work surface.

11. Pad the caliper interior with clean shop cloths.

CAUTION: *Do not, under any circumstances, place your fingers in front of the piston in an attempt to catch or protect it. In addition, use only enough air pressure to ease the piston out of the bore. Excessive air pressure can eject the piston with enough force to cause damage or injury.*

12. Insert the air nozzle into the caliper fluid inlet hole and slowly apply just enough air pressure to ease the piston out of the bore.

13. Remove and discard the dust boot. Use a screwdriver to pry the boot from the bore. Do not scratch the piston bore during boot removal.

14. Remove and discard the piston seal. Use a pencil or similar wood implement to remove the seal.

CAUTION: *Remove the seal using a pencil, wooden stick, piece of plastic, or similar tool only. Do not use a metal tool or similar object to remove the seal as the bore could be scored.*

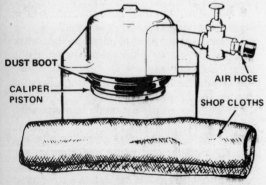

DUST BOOT

CALIPER
PISTON

AIR HOSE

SHOP CLOTHS

Caliper piston removal

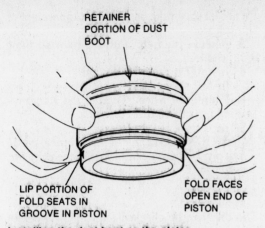

RETAINER
PORTION OF DUST
BOOT

LIP PORTION OF
FOLD SEATS IN
GROOVE IN PISTON

FOLD FACES
OPEN END OF
PISTON

Installing the dust boot on the piston

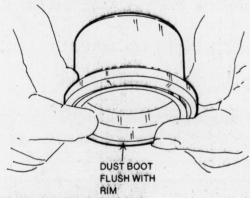

DUST BOOT
FLUSH WITH
RIM

Positioning the dust boot fold

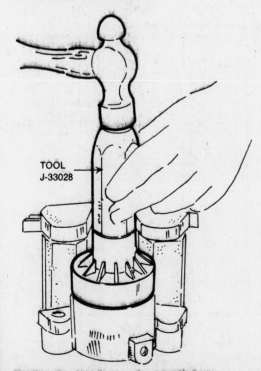

TOOL
J-33028

Seating the dust boot in the counterbore

15. Remove the bleeder screw.

16. Remove and discard the plastic sleeves and rubber bushings from the caliper mounting ears.

Inspect the caliper piston. Replace the piston if nicked, scratched, corroded, or if the protective plating has worn off.

CAUTION: *Do not attempt to refinish the piston in any way. The outside diameter is the sealing surface and is manufactured to very close tolerances. Removal of the nickle-chrome protective plating will lead to pitting, corrosion, and eventual piston seizure.*

Inspect the piston bore. Replace the caliper if the bore is nicked, scratched, worn, cracked, or badly corroded. However, minor stains or corrosion can be removed using crocus cloth.

CAUTION: *Do not use emery cloth or similar abrasives on the piston bore. If the bore does not clean up with crocus cloth, replace the caliper. Clean the caliper thoroughly with brake fluid or brake cleaning solvent if the bore was polished.*

17. Lubricate the piston bore and replacement seal with brake fluid.

18. Install the seal in the bore groove. Work the seal into the groove using fingers only.

19. Lubricate the piston with the brake fluid.

20. Install the replacement dust boot on the piston. Slide the metal retainer portion of the seal over the open end of the piston and pull the seal rearward until the rubber boot lip seats in the piston groove.

21. Push the metal retainer portion of the boot forward until the retainer is flush with the rim at the open end of the piston and the seal fold snaps into place.

22. Insert the piston into the bore and into the piston seal. Do not unseat the seal.

23. Press the piston to the bottom of the bore using a hammer handle.

24. Seat the metal retainer portion of the dust boot in the counterbore at the upper end of the piston bore using Tool J-33028.

CAUTION: *The metal portion of the dust boot must be seated evenly and below the face of the caliper.*

25. Install the bleeder screw. Tighten the screw securely but not to the required torque until the brakes have been bled.

26. Install the replacement plastic sleeves and rubber bushings in the caliper mounting ears.

27. Check the rotor for face runout, thickness variation, deep scores, cracks, and broken ventilating ribs.

28. Install the brake shoes and caliper as outlined under Brake Shoe Replacement.

29. Install a replacement washer on the brake hose fitting and connect the hose to the

caliper. Tighten the fitting to 25 ft.lb. torque.

30. Fill the master cylinder to within ¼" (6.3mm) of the reservoir rims and bleed the brakes as outlined under Brake Bleeding.

31. After bleeding, press the brake pedal firmly several times to seat the brake shoes. Recheck the master cylinder fluid level and correct it if necessary.

32. Install the wheels and tighten the retaining nuts to 75 ft.lb. torque.

33. Lower the automobile.

CAUTION: *Check for a firm brake pedal and proper brake operation before moving the automobile.*

Disc (Rotor)

REMOVAL AND INSTALLATION

Except Eagle

1. Raise the front end and remove the wheel.

2. Remove the caliper and adapter assembly. Details are given earlier.

3. Wire the caliper to the suspension to prevent straining the brake line.

4. Remove the grease cap, cotter pin, nut, and washer front the wheel spindle.

5. Pull the disc out slightly and push it back. Remove the outer wheel bearing.

CAUTION: *Keep your greasy hands off the disc surface!*

6. Remove the hub and disc.

7. Make sure that the grease in the hub is clean, that the wheel bearings are both packed with grease, and that the disc surfaces are clean.

CAUTION: *Use only grease specified for disc brake use. Ordinary grease will melt and ooze all over the braking surfaces, ruining the friction pads.*

8. Slide the hub and disc onto the spindle.

9. Install the outer bearing, washer, and nut. Adjust the wheel bearings as described later in this Section. Install the cotter pin.

10. Clean the grease cap and coat the inside with grease. Don't pack it full. Install it.

11. Replace the caliper.

12. On replacing the wheel, torque the nuts to 75 ft.lb.

NOTE: *You may feel a little silly torquing wheel nuts, but this is important to prevent distorting the disc.*

Eagle

1. Loosen the wheel retaining nuts.

2. Raise and support the automobile.

3. Remove the front wheels.

4. Remove the caliper assembly but do not disconnect the brake line. Suspend the caliper from a wire hook attached to the front spring.

Do not let the brake hose support the weight of the caliper.

5. Remove the rotor. Pull the rotor straight off of the hub.

6. Install the rotor on the hub.

7. Install the caliper.

8. Install the wheel. Tighten the wheel retaining nuts to 75 ft.lb. torque.

9. Lower the automobile.

CAUTION: *Check for a firm brake pedal and proper brake operation before moving the automobile.*

INSPECTION

The disc can be checked for runout (wobble) and thickness variations with a dial indicator and a micrometer while mounted on the car, or in a lathe. Runout should not exceed 0.005"

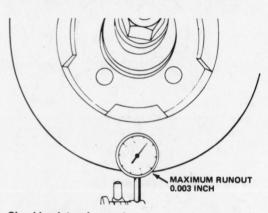

MAXIMUM RUNOUT 0.003 INCH

Checking lateral runout

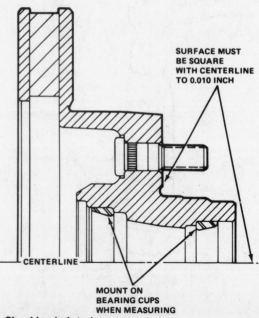

SURFACE MUST BE SQUARE WITH CENTERLINE TO 0.010 INCH

CENTERLINE

MOUNT ON BEARING CUPS WHEN MEASURING

Checking hub-to-bore runout

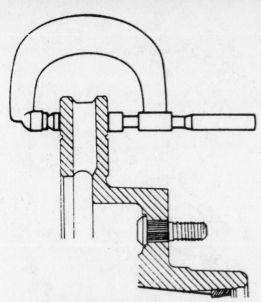

Checking thickness variation

(0.127mm) and thickness variation should not exceed 0.001" (0.025mm). The disc can be machined, but the final thickness must be at least 0.940" (23.876mm).

NOTE: *These are the factory's specifications; some state inspection laws aren't this lenient.*

Wheel Bearings

REMOVAL, PACKING, AND INSTALLATION

1. Use the 'Brake Disc Removal and Installation' procedure to remove the bearings.
2. Remove the inner bearing.
3. Clean the bearings thoroughly in a safe solvent. Check their condition, but don't spin them any more than is absolutely necessary.
4. Replace the seal on assembly.
5. Make sure that the inner cones of the bearings are free to creep (move slowly) on the spindle. This adds to the life of the bearings.
6. Pack both wheel bearings using wheel bearing grease made for disc brakes. Ordinary grease will melt and ooze out, ruining the pads. Place a healthy glob of grease in the palm of one hand and force the edge of the bearing into it so that the grease fills the bearing. Do this until the whole bearing is packed. Grease packing tools are available which make this job a lot less messy.
7. Install the inner bearing and seal.
8. Use the Brake Disc Removal and Installation procedure to replace the bearings and disc.

ADJUSTMENT

1. Raise the front wheel off the floor.
2. Remove the grease cap and cotter pin.
3. To seat the bearings, tighten the wheel spindle nut to 20–25 ft.lb. while turning the wheel.
4. Loosen the nut ⅓ turn. Tighten the nut to 2–10 in.lb.
5. If there is a nut retainer, place it on the nut with the slots of the retainer aligned with the spindle cotter pin hole. Install a new cotter pin and the dust cap.

FRONT DRUM BRAKES

Brake Drums

REMOVAL AND INSTALLATION

1. Remove the wheel cover, except on models with styled wheels which have the lug nuts exposed, and loosen the lug nuts.
2. Set the parking brake, block the rear wheels, and raise the front of the car, supporting it with jackstands.
CAUTION: *Be sure that the car is securely supported.*
3. Remove the lug nuts and the wheel.
4. Loosen the brake adjusting starwheel by removing the plug from the adjusting slot and inserting a thin screwdriver into the hole to push the adjusting lever away from the wheel.
5. Insert a brake adjusting tool into the hole and rotate the starwheel so that the shoes contract.
NOTE: *It may not always be necessary to back off on the adjuster in order to remove the drum.*
6. Remove the dust cover, grease cap, cotter pin, nut retainer, nut and the outer wheel bearing.
7. Remove the drum from the spindle.
8. Installation is performed in the reverse of or removal. Pack and adjust the wheel bearing as indicated in 'Wheel Bearings,' following. Adjust the brakes, as outlined at the beginning of this chapter, after completing the drum installation.

INSPECTION

1. Clean the drum.
2. Inspect the drum for scoring, grooves, cracks, and out-of-roundness.
3. Light scoring may be removed by dressing the drum with fine emery cloth.
4. Heavy scoring will require the use of a brake lathe to turn the drum. The service limit of the drum inside diameter is 0.060" (1.524mm) over standard diameter.

Brake Shoes

REMOVAL AND INSTALLATION

NOTE: *If you are not thoroughly familiar with the procedure involved with brake shoe*

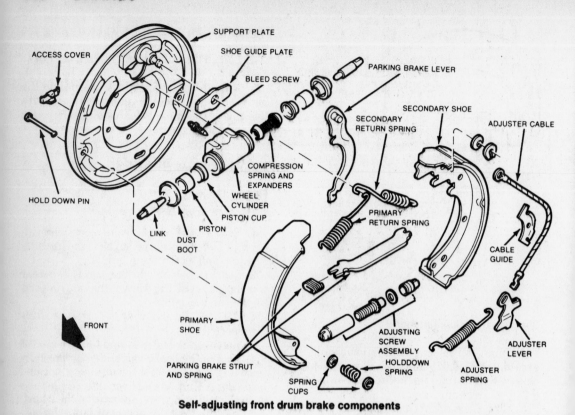

Self-adjusting front drum brake components

replacement, disassemble and assemble one side at a time, leaving the other side intact as a reference.

1. Remove the brake drum.

CAUTION: *Do not depress the brake pedal once the drum has been removed.*

2. Remove the adjusting lever tang from the hole in the secondary shoe by grabbing the lever with a pair of pliers.

3. Place a wheel cylinder clamp over the wheel cylinder to retain its piston while the brake shoes are removed.

4. Unfasten the return springs with a brake springs removal tool by twisting them off the anchor pin.

5. Carefully remove the secondary shoe return spring, the adjusting cable, primary shoe return spring, the cable guide, the adjusting lever and spring in that order.

CAUTION: *Be careful that all of the components of the brake do not fly out at once when the spring tension is being released.*

6. Unfasten the holddown springs and withdraw the shoes. Be careful not to get grease on the lining surfaces of the shoes.

Shoe installation is performed in the following order:

NOTE: *Always replace the shoes and linings on both wheels of the same axle; do not replace the shoes and linings on one side only.*

1. If there is any grease contamination, clean all of the parts, except the drums, with mineral spirits. If there is brake fluid contamination, use alcohol to clean the parts. Then clean all parts, including the drums with soap and water.

2. Polish the legs on the brake support plate with fine emery cloth. If there are any grooves on the support plate which limit shoe movement, the plate must be replaced (do not attempt to regrind).

3. Lubricate the ledges on the support plate, anchor pin, adjusting cable guide, adjusting screw threads and the pivot with molybdenum disulfide grease.

4. Place the shoes on the support plate and retain them with the holddown springs.

NOTE: *The following sequence is for 10" (254mm) brakes; reverse Steps 5 and 6 for 9" (228.6mm) brakes.*

5. Fit the adjusting cable eyelet over the anchor pin.

6. Install one end of the primary return spring in the primary shoe and the other end over the anchor pin with the brake spring tool.

7. Install the adjusting cable guide.

8. Fit the secondary shoe return spring in the same manner in which you installed the primary spring.

9. Install the adjusting screw assembly at

the base of the brake shoe. Place the small hooked end of the adjusting spring into the large hole in the primary shoe.

10. Fit the large hooked end of the adjusting spring into the hole in the adjusting lever.

11. Engage the hooked end of the adjusting cable with the adjusting lever and place the cable over the cable guide.

CAUTION: *Be sure that the adjusting cable is not twisted and that it cannot ride out of the guide.*

12. Hook the tang on the adjusting lever into the large hole at the base of the secondary shoe by grasping the lever with pliers and pulling it into place.

13. Adjust the brakes and install the drums, as detailed elsewhere in this chapter.

Wheel Cylinders
SERVICING

1. Raise the vehicle on a hoist and remove the wheel and drum from the brake to be serviced.

2. Remove the brake shoes and clean the backing plate and wheel cylinder.

3. Disconnect the brake line from the brake hose. Remove the brake hose retainer clip at the frame bracket and remove the hose from the wheel cylinder. (On the rear brakes it will only be necessary to remove the line from the cylinder).

4. Remove the cylinder mounting bolts and remove the cylinder.

5. Remove the boots from the cylinder ends and discard. Remove the pistons, remove and discard the seal cups, and remove the expanders and spring.

6. Inspect the bore and pistons for damage or wear. Damaged pistons should be discarded, as they cannot be reconditioned. Slight bore roughness can be removed using a brake cylinder hone or crocus cloth. (Cloth should be rotated in the bore under finger pressure. Do not slide lengthwise.) Use only lint free cloth for cleaning.

7. Clean the cylinder and internal parts using only brake fluid or denatured alcohol.

8. Insert the spring expander assembly. Lu-

bricate all rubber parts using only fresh brake fluid.

9. Install new cups with the seal lips facing inward.

10. Install the pistons and rubber boots. Install the cylinder on the car in the reverse order or removal. Bleed the cylinder (see the preceding 'Bleeding' section).

Wheel Bearings
REMOVAL, PACKING AND INSTALLATION

1. The outer bearing is removed as part of the brake drum removal procedure.

2. Use a brass drift to remove the inner bearing and cup from the hub.

3. For installation and packing procedures, see 'Wheel Bearings' in the 'Front Disc Brake' section.

ADJUSTMENT

The bearing adjustment procedure for models equipped with front drum brakes is the same as for the disc brake equipped models. See 'Wheel Bearings' in the 'Front Disc Brake' section for the correct procedure.

REAR DRUM BRAKES

Brake Drums
REMOVAL AND INSTALLATION

NOTE: *Release the parking brake before attempting rear drum removal.*

1. Remove the wheel cover and loosen the lug nuts. Remove the cotter key and the axle shaft nut.

NOTE: *If the car is equipped with styled wheels, it will be necessary to raise the car and remove the wheel first.*

2. Block the front wheels, raise the car, and support is with jackstands.

CAUTION: *Be sure that the car is securely supported.*

3. Remove the wheel.

4. Unfasten the three screws which secure the brake drum and withdraw the drum.

CAUTION: *Do not depress the brake pedal once the drum has been removed.*

5. Installation is performed in the reverse order of removal.

INSPECTION

Rear drum inspection procedures and specifications are identical to those given in the preceding 'Front Drum Brake Inspection' section.

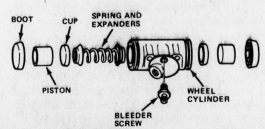

Typical wheel cylinder

Brake Shoes

REMOVAL AND INSTALLATION

The removal and installation procedure for the rear brake shoes is similar to that for the front shoes. The only differences are: the parking brake lever must be removed from (and installed on) the secondary shoe and the parking brake strut spring assembly must be removed from (and installed), between the shoes.

Wheel Cylinders

SERVICING

The servicing procedures for the rear wheel cylinders are identical to those for the front cylinders previously described.

Hubs and Bearings

REMOVAL AND INSTALLATION

The rear axle splines cut serrations into the inner diameter of the rear wheel hub. If the hub is to be removed, matchmark the hub to the axle so that the job of aligning the serrations and splines will be easier. If this is not done, the axle will cut new splines which may be so near the old that the hub will move on the axle with resultant damage to the hub, axle, and differential gears.

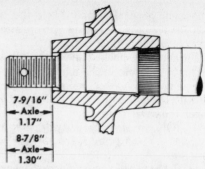

7-9/16"
←Axle→
1.17"

8-7/8"
←Axle→
1.30"

Proper installation of a new rear hub and drum assembly

When a new hub is installed, the serrations will be cut in the hub as it is installed on the shaft.

If a new axle shaft is installed, a new hub, without serrations, must be installed. And old shaft with a new hub also is an allowable combination.

1. Remove the wheel and brake drum as detailed above.

2. Matchmark the hub and axle shaft.

3. Attach a suitable puller to the wheel hub to remove it.

CAUTION: *Do not use a 'knockout' type puller on the end of the axle shaft, as this could damage the wheel bearings or the thrust blocks. Use a screws type puller.*

4. Inspect the hub for faulty lug studs, a worn keyway or center bore, and damaged serrations. Replace the hub and drum if any of these are present or if it is cracked.

NOTE: *The hub and drum must both be replaced if either one is defective.*

5. Installation, if the old hub and drum are being replaced, is performed in the reverse order of removal. Tighten the axle shaft nut to 250 ft.lb. with the weight of the car resting on the rear wheels.

CAUTION: *Be sure to align the matchmarks made during removal.*

A new hub and drum assembly must be installed in the following order:

1. Align the hub keyway with the key on the axle shaft.

2. Slide the hub and drum onto the axle shaft as far as they will go.

3. Fit two well lubricated thrust washers over the axle shaft and install the axle shaft nut.

4. Install the wheel and lug nuts, remove the jackstands, and lower the car.

5. Tighten the axle shaft nut until the distance from the outer face of the hub to the outer end of the axle shaft is one of the following:

• $7^9/_{16}$" (192mm) differential — 1.7" (43.18mm)

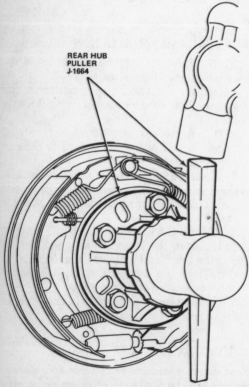

REAR HUB
PULLER
J-1664

Rear hub removal

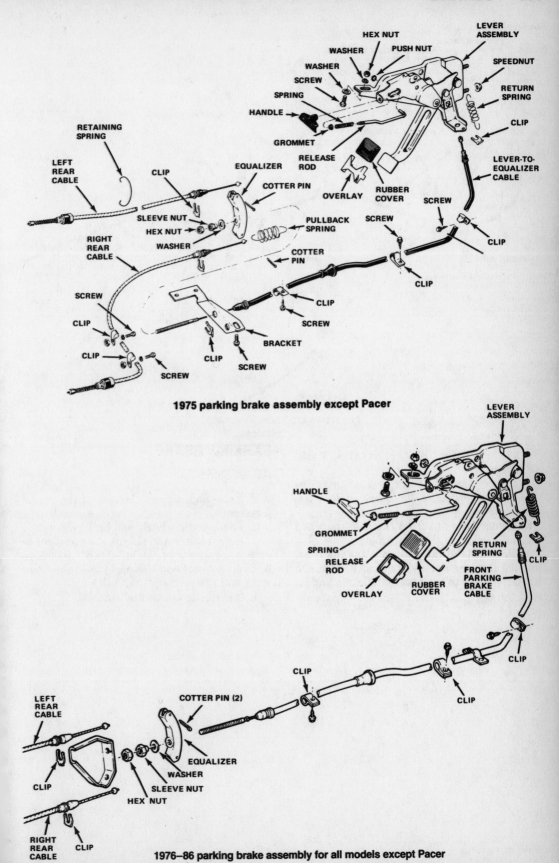

1975 parking brake assembly except Pacer

1976–86 parking brake assembly for all models except Pacer

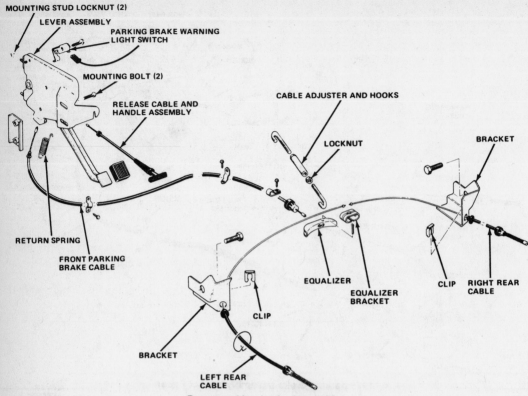

MOUNTING STUD LOCKNUT (2)
LEVER ASSEMBLY
PARKING BRAKE WARNING
LIGHT SWITCH
MOUNTING BOLT (2)
RELEASE CABLE AND
HANDLE ASSEMBLY
CABLE ADJUSTER AND HOOKS
LOCKNUT
BRACKET
RETURN SPRING
FRONT PARKING
BRAKE CABLE
EQUALIZER
EQUALIZER
BRACKET
CLIP
RIGHT REAR
CABLE
CLIP
BRACKET
LEFT REAR
CABLE

Pacer parking brake assembly

• 8⅞" (225mm) differential − 1.30"
(33.02mm)

NOTE: *If the hub is not pressed in to the
proper specifications, the splines will be improperly cut.*

6. Remove the nut front the axle shaft and
take off one of the thrust washers.

7. Reinstall the axle shaft nut and tighten it
to 250 ft.lb. If the cotter key cannot be inserted,
tighten the nut to the next castellation and install the key.

PARKING BRAKE

ADJUSTMENT

1. Raise and support the rear of the car on
jackstands.

2. Remove the wheels and brake drums.

3. Adjust the front cable at the equalizer to
give a clearance of 0.0001–0.005" (0.00254–
0.1270mm) between the parking brake lever
strut and the primary brake shoe.

4. Install the drums and wheels.

EXTERIOR

Hood

REMOVAL AND INSTALLATION

All Models Except Pacer

NOTE: *If the hood is properly aligned, prior to removal, matchmark the position of the hinges and hood reinforcement.*
1. Raise the hood fully.
2. Disconnect the underhood light wire.

3. While your assistant supports the hood, remove the hood-to-hinge bolts and lift off the hood.
4. Installation is the reverse of removal. Torque the bolts to 23 ft.lb.

Pacer

NOTE: *If the hood is properly aligned, prior to removal, matchmark the position of the hinges and hood reinforcement.*
1. Raise the hood fully.

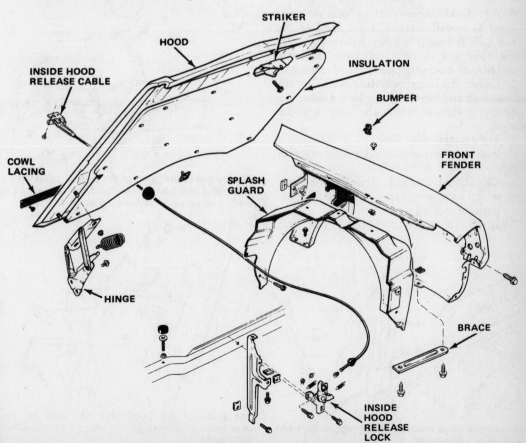

Typical front fender and hood components, except Pacer

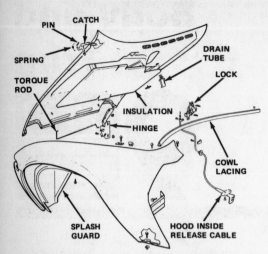

Pacer front fender and hood components

2. Disconnect the underhood light wire.

3. Unbolt the grille from the hood.

4. While your assistant supports the hood, remove the hood-to-hinge bolts and lift off the hood.

5. Installation is the reverse of removal. Torque the bolts to 23 ft.lb.

ALIGNMENT

NOTE: *Hood hinge mounting holes are over-sized to permit movement for hood alignment. If the hood is to be moved to either side, the hood lock striker, hood lever lock and safety hook assembly must first be loosened.*

1. Loosen the hinge mounting bolts slightly on one side and tap the hinge in the direction opposite to that in which the hood is to be moved.

2. Tighten the bolts.

3. Repeat this procedure for the opposite hinge.

4. Check that the lock striker, lever lock and safety hook are properly adjusted to ensure positive locking.

5. If the rear edge of the hood is not flush

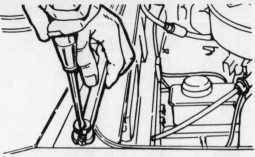

The hood is adjusted vertically by stop-screws at the front and/or rear

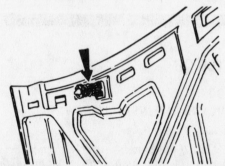

The hood pin can be adjusted for proper lock engagement

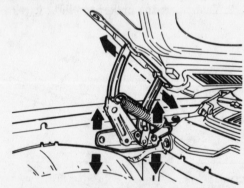

The height of the hood at the rear is adjusted by loosening the bolts that attach the hinge to the body and moving the hood up or down

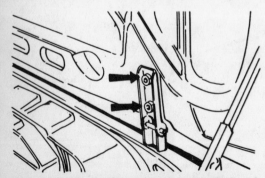

Loosen the hinge boots to permit fore-and-aft and horizontal adjustment

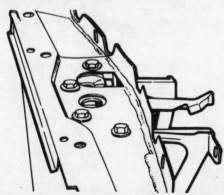

The base of the hood lock can also be re-positioned slightly to give more positive lock engagement

with the cowl, add or subtract shims (caster and camber adjusting shims will work) or flat washers between the hinge and the hood at the rear bolt (hood too low) or front bolt (hood too high).

Liftgate

ALIGNMENT

Sportabout

1. Remove the anti-rattle pin and striker.
2. Remove the rear finish moldings.
3. Loosen the hinge-to-body nuts.
4. Move the liftgate to obtain the proper fit.
5. Tighten the nuts to 11 ft.lb.
6. Install the moldings, striker and anti-rattle pin.

Pacer Sedan

FRONT SURFACE ADJUSTMENT

1. Open the liftgate.
2. Remove the rear upper finish molding.
3. Remove the right and left headliner upper rear finish moldings.
4. Remove the retainer clips from the ball stud sockets on the liftgate.
5. With the liftgate fully open, pull the supports off of the ball studs. Swing the supports down and out of the way.

CAUTION: *Never attempt to remove the supports with the lift gate closed or partially closed! Closing the liftgate puts the supports under tremendous pressure.!*

6. Close the liftgate.
7. Remove the hinge-to-body nuts. Keep track of the shim pack for each hinge.
8. Unlatch the tailgate and lift it at the leading edge, supporting it with wood blocks.
9. Loosen the hinge-to-liftgate screws.
10. Install or remove shims as required, between the hinge and liftgate, to obtain the desired gap.
11. Tighten the screws to 12 ft.lb.
12. Remove the blocks and position the liftgate in its opening.
13. Position the hinge-to-body shim packs and install the nuts. Torque the nuts to 12 ft.lb.
14. Install the rear upper finish molding.
15. Open the liftgate and install the supports and clips.
16. Adjust the striker and tighten the bolts to 52 ft.lb.

REAR SURFACE ADJUSTMENT

1. Remove the striker.
2. Move the liftgate rear surface downward by placing a wood block on top of the body opening drain trough and carefully hammering the trough downward.

3. Move the liftgate rear surface up by placing a wood block under the drain trough and carefully hammering the trough upward.
4. Install the striker and adjust it for proper latching and alignment. Tighten the striker bolts to 52 ft.lb.

Pacer Wagon

GAP ADJUSTMENT

1. Open the liftgate.
2. Remove the rear upper finish molding.
3. Remove the right and left headliner upper rear finish moldings.
4. Remove the retainer clips from the ball stud sockets on the liftgate.
5. With the liftgate fully open, pull the supports off of the ball studs. Swing the supports down and out of the way.

CAUTION: *Never attempt to remove the supports with the lift gate closed or partially closed! Closing the liftgate puts the supports under tremendous pressure.!*

6. Close the liftgate.
7. Loosen the hinge-to-body nuts. Keep track of the shim pack for each hinge.
8. Install or remove shims as required, between the hinge and body, to obtain the desired gap.
9. Tighten the screws to 12 ft.lb.
10. Tighten the nuts to 12 ft.lb.
11. Install the rear upper finish molding.
12. Open the liftgate and install the supports and clips.
13. Adjust the striker and tighten the bolts to 52 ft.lb.

FRONT SURFACE ADJUSTMENT

1. Open the liftgate.
2. Remove the rear upper finish molding.
3. Remove the retainer clips from the ball stud sockets on the liftgate.
4. With the liftgate fully open, pull the supports off of the ball studs. Swing the supports down and out of the way.

CAUTION: *Never attempt to remove the supports with the lift gate closed or partially closed! Closing the liftgate puts the supports under tremendous pressure.!*

5. Close the liftgate.
6. Remove the hinge-to-body nuts, keeping track of the shim packs for each hinge.
7. Open the liftgate at the leading edge and support it with wood blocks.
8. Loosen the hinge-to-liftgate screws. Keep track of the shim pack for each hinge.
9. Install or remove shims as required, between the hinge and liftgate, to obtain the desired gap.
10. Tighten the screws to 12 ft.lb.
11. Tighten the nuts to 12 ft.lb.

12. Install the rear upper finish molding.

13. Open the liftgate and install the supports and clips.

14. Adjust the striker and tighten the bolts to 52 ft.lb.

Spirit, Eagle SX/4 and AMX
SIDE GAP ADJUSTMENT

1. Remove the anti-rattle pin and striker.

2. Remove the rear upper finish molding.

3. Remove the retainer clips from the ball stud sockets on the liftgate.

5. With the liftgate fully open, pull the supports off of the ball studs. Swing the supports down and out of the way.

CAUTION: *Never attempt to remove the supports with the lift gate closed or partially closed! Closing the liftgate puts the supports under tremendous pressure.!*

6. Close the liftgate.

7. Loosen the hinge-to-body nuts. Keep track of the shim pack for each hinge.

8. Install or remove shims as required, between the hinge and body, to obtain the desired gap.

9. Tighten the screws to 12 ft.lb.

10. Tighten the nuts to 12 ft.lb.

11. Install the rear upper finish molding.

12. Open the liftgate and install the supports and clips.

13. Install the anti-rattle pin. Adjust the striker and tighten the bolts to 52 ft.lb.

FRONT GAP ADJUSTMENT

1. Open the liftgate.

2. Remove the rear upper finish molding.

3. Remove the retainer clips from the ball stud sockets on the liftgate.

4. With the liftgate fully open, pull the supports off of the ball studs. Swing the supports down and out of the way.

CAUTION: *Never attempt to remove the supports with the lift gate closed or partially closed! Closing the liftgate puts the supports under tremendous pressure.!*

5. Disconnect the rear defogger wires and tape the wire ends to the glass.

6. Close the liftgate.

7. Remove the hinge-to-body nuts, keeping track of the shim packs for each hinge.

8. Open the liftgate at the leading edge and support it with wood blocks.

9. Loosen the hinge-to-liftgate screws. Keep track of the shim pack for each hinge.

10. Install or remove shims as required, between the hinge and liftgate, to obtain the desired gap.

10. Tighten the screws to 12 ft.lb.

11. Tighten the nuts to 12 ft.lb.

12. Install the rear upper finish molding.

13. Open the liftgate and install the supports and clips.

14. Connect the rear defogger wires.

15. Adjust the anti-rattle pin for proper fit. Tighten the screws to 25 in.lb. Adjust the striker and tighten the bolts to 52 ft.lb.

Concord and Eagle Hatchback
SIDE GAP ADJUSTMENT

1. Remove the anti-rattle pin and striker.

2. Remove the rear upper finish molding.

3. Remove the retainer clips from the ball stud sockets on the liftgate.

4. With the liftgate fully open, pull the supports off of the ball studs. Swing the supports down and out of the way.

CAUTION: *Never attempt to remove the supports with the lift gate closed or partially closed! Closing the liftgate puts the supports under tremendous pressure.!*

5. Close the liftgate.

6. Loosen the hinge-to-body nuts. Keep track of the shim pack for each hinge.

7. Install or remove shims as required, between the hinge and body, to obtain the desired gap.

8. Tighten the screws to 12 ft.lb.

9. Tighten the nuts to 12 ft.lb.

10. Install the rear upper finish molding.

11. Open the liftgate and install the supports and clips.

12. Install the anti-rattle pin. Adjust the striker and tighten the bolts to 52 ft.lb.

FRONT GAP ADJUSTMENT

1. Open the liftgate.

2. Remove the rear upper finish molding.

3. Remove the retainer clips from the ball stud sockets on the liftgate.

4. With the liftgate fully open, pull the supports off of the ball studs. Swing the supports down and out of the way.

CAUTION: *Never attempt to remove the supports with the lift gate closed or partially closed! Closing the liftgate puts the supports under tremendous pressure.!*

5. Disconnect the rear defogger wires and tape the wire ends to the glass.

6. Close the liftgate.

7. Remove the hinge-to-body nuts, keeping track of the shim packs for each hinge.

8. Open the liftgate at the leading edge and support it with wood blocks.

9. Loosen the hinge-to-liftgate screws. Keep track of the shim pack for each hinge.

10. Install or remove shims as required, between the hinge and liftgate, to obtain the desired gap.

11. Tighten the screws to 12 ft.lb.

12. Tighten the nuts to 12 ft.lb.

13. Install the rear upper finish molding.

14. Open the liftgate and install the supports and clips.

15. Connect the rear defogger wires.

16. Adjust the anti-rattle pin for proper fit. Tighten the screws to 25 in.lb. Adjust the striker and tighten the bolts to 52 ft.lb.

Concord and Eagle Wagon

GAP ADJUSTMENT

1. Remove the anti-rattle pin and striker.

2. Remove the rear upper finish molding.

3. Remove the retainer clips from the ball stud sockets on the liftgate.

4. With the liftgate fully open, pull the supports off of the ball studs. Swing the supports down and out of the way.

CAUTION: *Never attempt to remove the supports with the lift gate closed or partially closed! Closing the liftgate puts the supports under tremendous pressure.!*

5. Close the liftgate.

6. Loosen the hinge-to-body nuts. Keep track of the shim pack for each hinge.

7. Install or remove shims as required, between the hinge and body, to obtain the desired gap.

8. Tighten the screws to 12 ft.lb.

9. Tighten the nuts to 12 ft.lb.

10. Install the rear upper finish molding.

11. Open the liftgate and install the supports and clips.

12. Install the anti-rattle pin. Adjust the striker and tighten the bolts to 52 ft.lb.

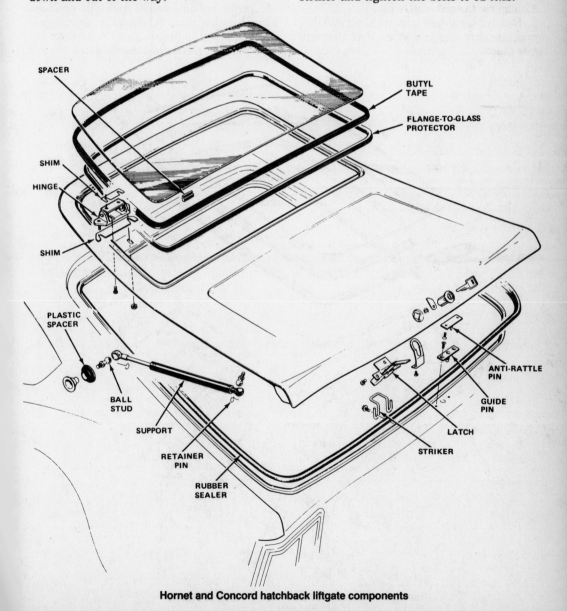

Hornet and Concord hatchback liftgate components

REAR SURFACE ADJUSTMENT

1. Remove the striker.
2. Move the liftgate rear surface downward by placing a wood block on top of the body opening drain trough and carefully hammering the trough downward.
3. Move the liftgate rear surface up by placing a wood block under the drain trough and carefully hammering the trough upward.
4. Install the striker and adjust it for proper latching and alignment. Tighten the striker bolts to 10 ft.lb.

REMOVAL AND INSTALLATION

Sportabout

1. Open the liftgate fully.
2. Remove the anti-rattle pin.
3. Remove the upper trim molding and disconnect the defroster grid wires. Tape the ends to the glass.

4. Unbolt the supports and fold them downward.
   CAUTION: *Never unbolt the supports unless the liftgate is fully opened. In any other position, the supports are under tension.*
5. Close the liftgate in the locked position.
6. From inside, remove the liftgate-to-hinge screws.
7. Unlock the liftgate and remove it.

Installation is as follows:

8. Position the liftgate in the opening and lock it.
9. If removed, place the rubber gaskets on the hinges and insert the hinge boss into the gate.
10. Install the hinge-to-gate screws about ¾ of the way.
11. From outside, unlock and fully open the liftgate. Allow it to slide down on the hinges.
12. Tighten the hinge screws to 11 ft.lb.
13. Connect the defroster grid wires.

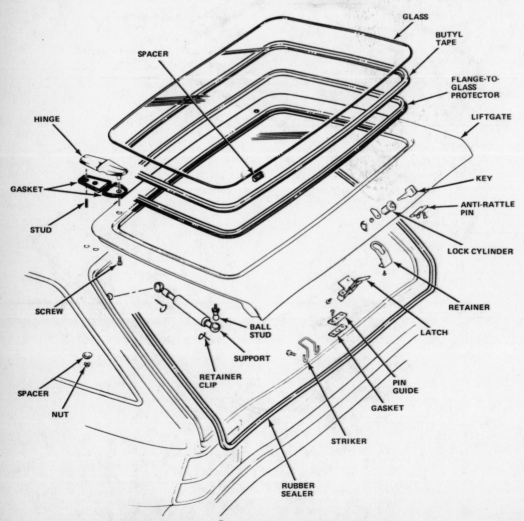

Hornet and Concord Station Wagon liftgate components

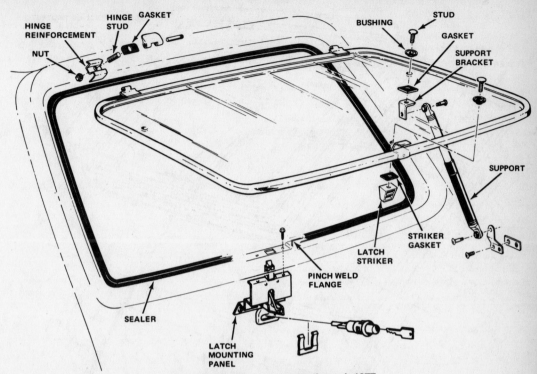

Gremlin liftgate components through 1977

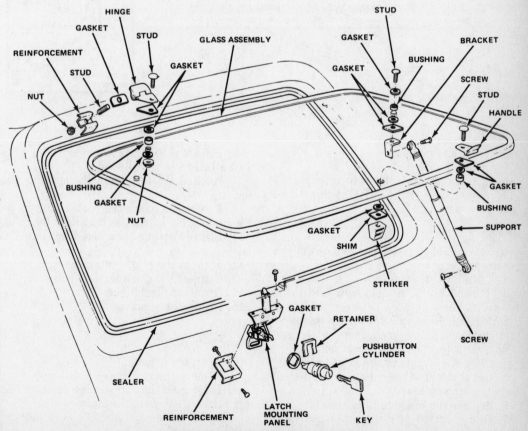

1978 and later Gremlin liftgate components

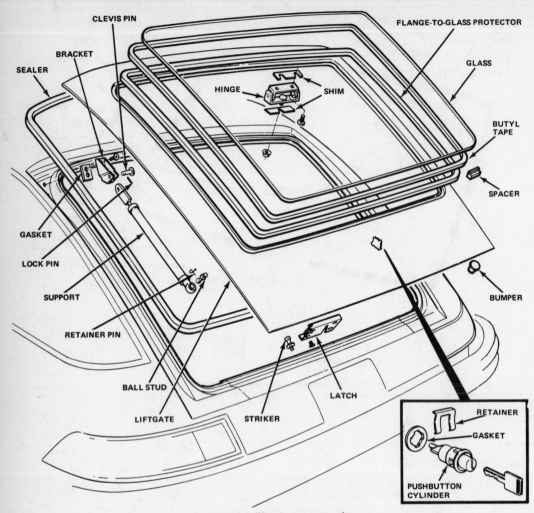

Pacer sedan liftgate components

14. Install the molding.
15. Install the supports.
16. Install and adjust the anti-rattle pin.
17. Adjust the liftgate fit as described earlier.

Gremlin

1. Remove the upper center and corner finish moldings.
2. Open the liftgate fully.
3. Unbolt the supports and fold them downward.

CAUTION: *Never unbolt the supports unless the liftgate is fully opened. In any other position, the supports are under tension.*

4. Close the liftgate in the locked position.
5. Lower the headliner and remove the nut from the hinge studs.
6. Remove the hinge reinforcements.
7. Disconnect the defroster grid wires. Tape the ends to the glass.

8. Unlock the liftgate and remove it.
Installation is as follows:
9. Position the liftgate in the opening and lock it.
10. If removed, place the rubber gaskets on the hinges and insert the studs into the gate.
11. Install the hinge reinforcements onto the studs.
12. Tighten the hinge nuts to 11 ft.lb.
13. Connect the defroster grid wires.
14. Install the headliner.
15. Install the supports.

Pacer Sedan

1. Open the liftgate.
2. Remove the rear upper finish molding.
3. Disconnect the rear window defogger and tape the wire ends to the glass.
4. Remove the right and left headliner upper rear finish moldings.

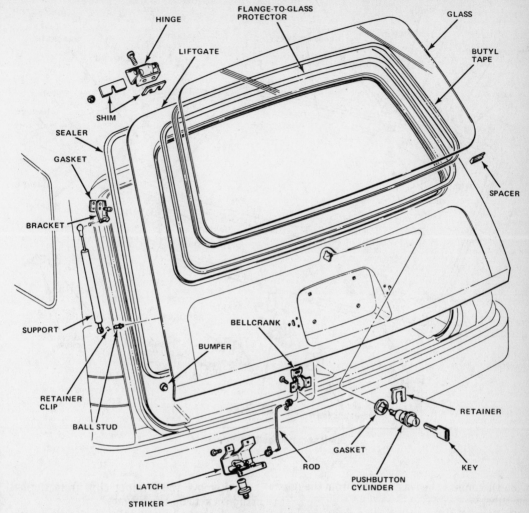

Pacer wagon liftgate components

5. Remove the liftgate trim panel.

6. Disconnect the wires from the wiper motor.

7. Tie a length of string to the motor wiring and pull the wiring from the liftgate.

NOTE: *You'll use the string to guide the wiring into position during installation.*

8. Disconnect the washer hose from the nozzle tube.

9. Remove the retainer clips from the ball stud sockets on the liftgate.

10. With the liftgate fully open, pull the supports off of the ball studs. Swing the supports down and out of the way.

CAUTION: *Never attempt to remove the supports with the lift gate closed or partially closed! Closing the liftgate puts the supports under tremendous pressure!*

11. Close the liftgate.

12. Remove the hinge-to-body nuts. Keep track of the shim pack for each hinge.

13. Unlatch the tailgate and remove it.

14. Installation is the reverse of removal. Torque the hinge nuts to 12 ft.lb. Don't lose the shims. Make sure they are placed under their respective hinges.

15. Adjust the liftgate as necessary.

Pacer Wagon

1. Open the liftgate.

2. Remove the rear upper finish molding.

3. Remove the right and left headliner upper rear finish moldings.

4. Disconnect the rear window defogger and tape the wire ends to the glass.

5. Carefully pull down the rear edge of the headliner and disconnect the liftgate harness from the body harness.

6. Remove the nuts attaching the liftgate harness tube to the body.

7. Remove the liftgate harness.

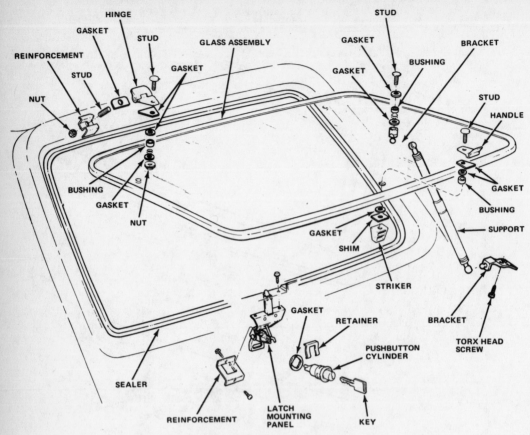

Spirit sedan liftgate components

8. Disconnect the washer hose from the nozzle tube.

9. Remove the retainer clips from the ball stud sockets on the liftgate.

10. With the liftgate fully open, pull the supports off of the ball studs. Swing the supports down and out of the way.

CAUTION: *Never attempt to remove the supports with the lift gate closed or partially closed! Closing the liftgate puts the supports under tremendous pressure!*

11. Close the liftgate.

12. Remove the hinge-to-body nuts. Keep track of the shim pack for each hinge.

13. Unlatch the tailgate and remove it.

14. Installation is the reverse of removal. Torque the hinge nuts to 12 ft.lb. Don't lose the shims. Make sure they are placed under their respective hinges.

15. Adjust the liftgate as necessary.

Spirit, Eagle SX/4 and AMX

1. Open the liftgate.

2. Remove the rear upper finish molding.

3. Disconnect the rear window defogger and tape the wire ends to the glass.

4. Remove the retainer clips from the ball stud sockets on the liftgate.

5. With the liftgate fully open, pull the supports off of the ball studs. Swing the supports down and out of the way.

CAUTION: *Never attempt to remove the supports with the lift gate closed or partially closed! Closing the liftgate puts the supports under tremendous pressure.!*

6. Close the liftgate.

7. Remove the hinge-to-body nuts. Keep track of the shim pack for each hinge.

8. Unlatch the tailgate and remove it.

9. Installation is the reverse of removal. Torque the hinge nuts to 12 ft.lb. Don't lose the shims. Make sure they are placed under their respective hinges.

10. Adjust the liftgate as necessary.

Concord and Eagle Hatchback

1. Open the liftgate.

2. Remove the rear upper finish molding.

3. Disconnect the rear window defogger and tape the wire ends to the glass.

4. Remove the retainer clips from the ball stud sockets on the liftgate.

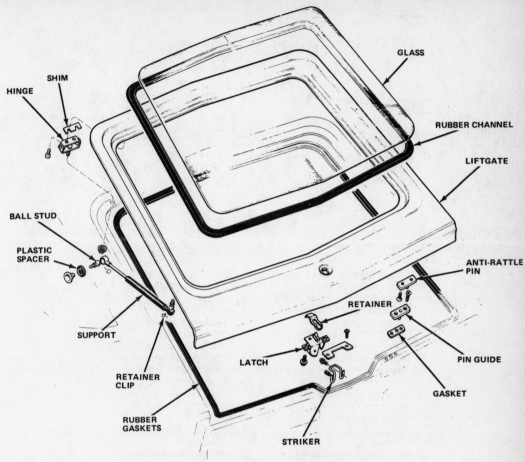

Spirit Liftback and AMX liftgate components

5. With the liftgate fully open, pull the supports off of the ball studs. Swing the supports down and out of the way.

CAUTION: *Never attempt to remove the supports with the lift gate closed or partially closed! Closing the liftgate puts the supports under tremendous pressure.!*

6. Close the liftgate.

7. Remove the hinge-to-body nuts. Keep track of the shim pack for each hinge.

8. Unlatch the tailgate and remove it.

9. Installation is the reverse of removal. Torque the hinge nuts to 12 ft.lb. Don't lose the shims. Make sure they are placed under their respective hinges.

10. Adjust the liftgate as necessary.

Concord and Eagle Wagon

1. Open the liftgate.

2. Remove the rear upper finish molding.

3. Disconnect the rear window defogger and tape the wire ends to the glass.

4. Remove the retainer clips from the ball stud sockets on the liftgate.

5. With the liftgate fully open, pull the sup-

ports off of the ball studs. Swing the supports down and out of the way.

CAUTION: *Never attempt to remove the supports with the lift gate closed or partially closed! Closing the liftgate puts the supports under tremendous pressure.!*

6. Close the liftgate.

7. Remove the hinge-to-body nuts. Keep track of the shim pack for each hinge.

8. Unlatch the tailgate and remove it.

9. Installation is the reverse of removal. Torque the hinge nuts to 12 ft.lb. Don't lose the shims. Make sure they are placed under their respective hinges.

10. Adjust the anti-rattle pin for proper fit. Adjust the liftgate as necessary.

Tailgate

REMOVAL AND INSTALLATION

Dual Tailgate

1. Open the tailgate vertically.

2. Remove the torsion rod retainer clip.

3. Use locking pliers to twist the torsion rod

1. Tailgate support cable
2. Left upper half hinge and eccentric roller pin assembly
3. Left upper body half hinge and latch assembly
4. Left upper hinge horizontal latch release bellcrank
5. Left latch release rod
6. Release rod clip
7. Horizontal remote control
8. Horizontal release handle
9. Right latch release rod
10. Rlease rod clip
11. Vertical release remote control
12. Vertical release bellcrank
13. Vertical release handle
14. Tailgate latch assembly
15. Latch striker and bracket assembly
16. Right lower half hinge and latch assembly
17. Right lower body half hinge and latch assembly
18. Upper latch to lower hinge latch release cable
19. Glass operated safety release rod
20. Torsion rod retainer clip
21. Torsion rod
22. Left lower hinge assembly door half
23. Left lower hinge assembly body half

Matador wagon tailgate components

a little bit counterclockwise, and pull the torsion rod out of the right lower hinge.

CAUTION: *Never try to pull the torsion rod out when the tailgate is opened horizontally!*

4. Pivot the torsion rod away from the body.
5. Close the tailgate, then open it horizontally.
6. Open the rear compartment, remove the plastic liner screws, lift the liner and disconnect the wiring harness at the tailgate.
7. Support the weight of the tailgate on some kind of stand, or have a couple of friends hold it.
8. Disconnect the support cable from the left upper hinge.
9. Disengage the right lower hinge by manually tripping the latch.
10. Trace the outline of the left lower hinge on the tailgate inner panel.
11. Unbolt the left lower hinge from the inner panel and remove the tailgate.
12. Installation is the reverse of removal. Adjust the tailgate for fit as necessary.

ADJUSTMENT

Left Upper Hinge

1. Remove the striker pin from the right upper bracket.
2. Loosen the eccentric roller pin setscrew in the body half of the left upper hinge.
3. Insert a screwdriver in the slot in the bottom of the pin.
4. Rotate the pin in the desired direction.
5. Tighten the setscrew.
6. Install the striker pin at the right pillar bracket and adjust it up or down to allow the pin tot enter the latch in the center of the opening.

Right Lower Hinge

1. Remove the striker pin from the right upper bracket.
2. Loosen the body half of the right lower hinge.
3. Adjust the himge to provide smooth vertical and horizontal operation.

4. Tighten the body half hinge bolts.

5. Install the striker pin at the right pillar bracket and adjust it up or down to allow the pin to enter the latch in the center of the opening.

Windshield
REMOVAL AND INSTALLATION

All models use bonded windshields. Windshield installation and the adhesives used, are critical in meeting Federal FMVSS regulations. Therefore, it is recommended that windshield replacement procedures on these vehicles be left to a professional shop.

Rear Window Glass
REMOVAL AND INSTALLATION

All Except the Spirit Hatchback and Eagle SX/4

NOTE: *These models use a butyl tape retention method for rear window glass installation. An electric Hot Knife, tool J-24709-01, or equivalent, is necessary for this procedure. Also, an assistant would be very helpful.*

1. Cover all adjacent areas, both exterior and interior.

2. If equipped, remove the wiper arm.

3. Remove all finish moldings around the glass.

4. If equipped, disconnect the wires from the rear defogger and tape the ends to the glass.

NOTE: *Use extreme care to avoid and scratching or danage to the defogger grid!*

5. Using the Hot Knife, insert the blade under the edge of the glass. Cut the material **as close as possible to the inside surface of the glass.**

NOTE: *Clean the Hot Knife blade with steel wool while it is still warm.*

6. Slowly push the glass outward along the top with your feet until the butyl tape stretches 1–2". Have an assistant cut the tape with a scissors, completely around the glass. Use wood blocks to keep the glass from touching the adhesive as the tape is being cut, or it will immediately restick.

7. When the glass is out, remove all traces of the butyl tape from the glass opening and ball it up to lift off any remaining deposits. Use 3M General Purpose Adhesive Cleaner, or equivalent, to clean up the area.

To install the glass:

8. Make sure that there is no molding- or metal-to-glass interference.

9. Make sure that all molding clips are properly positioned and not broken.

10. Repair any broken weld studs.

11. The two rubber spacer blocks below the glass at the outer ends must be in position to prevent the glass from settling and breaking.

12. Make sure that the anti-squeak protector is in position on the lower flange.

13. Using spacer blocks, temporarily position the glass in the opening.

14. Center the glass to achieve equal spacing all around.

15. Using masking tape at the bottom center or at the rubber spacers, and extending it over the body panels, mark the glass-to-body position for permanent installation.

16. Cut the tape just below the glass and remove the glass.

17. Clean the pinchweld and glass thoroughly. It must be clean and dry.

18. Apply a thin, uniform, ½" wide coat of butyl tape primer on both the pinchweld flange and the glass edge, and allow it to dry for 10 minutes.

19. Apply butyl tape to the pinchweld flange, midway up the right side, flush with the edge of the flange.

NOTE: *If you're using a butyl tape kit with an integral sponge rubber filler, make sure that the filler is flush with the edge of the flange.*

20. Strip off the paper as the tape is applied. Cut the tape at 45° angles downward and to the outside, and butt the ends of the tape firmly to prevent leaks.

21. Place the glass in the opening, aligning it exactly with the tape markers you previously made. **Be exact!** The primer will adhere to the butyl tape on contact!

22. Firmly press the glass against the butyl tape with hand pressure.

23. Carefully trim excess primer with a razor blade.

24. Clean the glass and surrounding area with 3M General Purpose Adhesive Cleaner, or equivalent.

25. Recheck the glass-to-butyl tape contact, applying additional hand pressure as needed. Dull spots indicate poor contact.

26. Apply 3M Windshield Sealer, or equivalent, to any open spots.

27. Install all previously removed parts.

Spirit Liftaback and Eagle SX/4

NOTE: *The rear window on these models is retained by a rubber channel.*

1. Cover all adjacent areas.

2. Remove the wiper arm and motor.

3. From inside, peel the rubber channel down while pushing outward on the glass.

NOTE: *If the rubber channel is bonded to the pinchweld, spray a generous amount of 3M Release Agent, or equivalent, bewteen the rubber channel and body. Allow 2–3 minutes for the stuff to work.*

4. Once the glass has been pushed away from the upper flange area, pull the window assembly up and out of the lower flange area.

5. Remove all sealer from the flange with 3M General Purpose Adhesive Cleaner, or equivalent.

6. Install the rubber channel on the glass.

7. Lubricate the rubber channel liberally with soapy water and position the assembly in the body opening.

8. Using a small wood spatula, pry the rubber channel over the pinchweld flange while an assistant pushes inward on the glass.

9. Apply 3M Windshield sealer, or equivalent, between the channel and glass using a hand applicator gun.

10. Wipe off surplus sealer.

11. Install the wiper motor and arm

Manual Tailgate Window
REMOVAL AND INSTALLATION

1. Open the tailgate.
2. Remove the trim panel.
3. Raise the glass completely.
4. Slide the glass assembly to disengage the regulator arms from the glass bottom channel and remove the glass.
5. If the glass is stuck in the down position due to a defective regulator:
   a. Remove the access holes covers.
   b. Remove the regulator handle assembly.
   c. Drill out the regulator pinion shaft housing rivets.
   d. Pull the shaft housing free and lift the glass from the tailgate.
6. Installation is the reverse of removal.
7. Align the glass as necessary by loosening the glass slide channel screws and moving the glass as needed to obtain proper fit. Tighten the screws.

Electric Tailgate Window
REMOVAL AND INSTALLATION

1. Open the tailgate.
2. Remove the control handles and trim panel.
3. Raise the glass completely.
NOTE: *To raise the glass with the tailgate open, manually depress the safety switch, mounted on the left auxiliary floor panel, and turn the key to the right.*
4. Slide the glass assembly to disengage the regulator arms from the glass bottom channel and remove the glass.

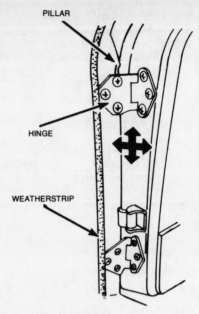

Door hinge adjustment

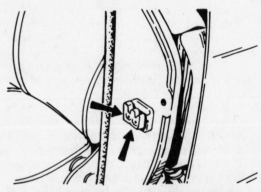

Move the door striker as indicated by arrows

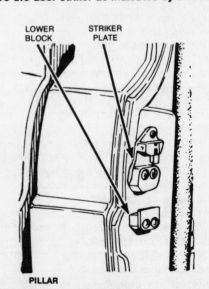

Striker plate and lower block

CHILTON'S
AUTO BODY REPAIR TIPS

Tools and Materials • Step-by-Step Illustrated Procedures
How To Repair Dents, Scratches and Rust Holes
Spray Painting and Refinishing Tips

With a little practice, basic body repair procedures can be mastered by any do-it-yourself mechanic. The step-by-step repairs shown here can be applied to almost any type of auto body repair.

TOOLS & MATERIALS

You may already have basic tools, such as hammers and electric drills. Other tools unique to body repair — body hammers, grinding attachments, sanding blocks, dent puller, half-round plastic file and plastic spreaders — are relatively inexpensive and can be obtained wherever auto parts or auto body repair parts are sold. Portable air compressors and paint spray guns can be purchased or rented.

Auto Body Repair Kits

The best and most often used products are available to the do-it-yourselfer in kit form, from major manufacturers of auto body repair products. The same manufacturers also merchandise the individual products for use by pros.

Kits are available to make a wide variety of repairs, including holes, dents and scratches and fiberglass, and offer the advantage of buying the materials you'll need for the job. There is little waste or chance of materials going bad from not being used. Many kits may also contain basic body-working tools such as body files, sanding blocks and spreaders. Check the contents of the kit before buying your tools.

BODY REPAIR TIPS

Safety

Many of the products associated with auto body repair and refinishing contain toxic chemicals. Read all labels before opening containers and store them in a safe place and manner.

• Wear eye protection (safety goggles) when using power tools or when performing any operation that involves the removal of any type of material.

• Wear lung protection (disposable mask or respirator) when grinding, sanding or painting.

Sanding

1 Sand off paint before using a dent puller. When using a non-adhesive sanding disc, cover the back of the disc with an overlapping layer or two of masking tape and trim the edges. The disc will last considerably longer.

2 Use the circular motion of the sanding disc to grind *into* the edge of the repair. Grinding or sanding away from the jagged edge will only tear the sandpaper.

3 Use the palm of your hand flat on the panel to detect high and low spots. Do not use your fingertips. Slide your hand slowly back and forth.

WORKING WITH BODY FILLER

Mixing The Filler

Cleanliness and proper mixing and application are extremely important. Use a clean piece of plastic or glass or a disposable artist's palette to mix body filler.

1 Allow plenty of time and follow directions. No useful purpose will be served by adding more hardener to make it cure (set-up) faster. Less hardener means more curing time, but the mixture dries harder; more hardener means less curing time but a softer mixture.

2

2 Both the hardener and the filler should be thoroughly kneaded or stirred before mixing. Hardener should be a solid paste and dispense like thin toothpaste. Body filler should be smooth, and free of lumps or thick spots.

Getting the proper amount of hardener in the filler is the trickiest part of preparing the filler. Use the same amount of hardener in cold or warm weather. For contour filler (thick coats), a bead of hardener twice the diameter of the filler is about right. There's about a 15% margin on either side, but, if in doubt use less hardener.

2

2

3 Mix the body filler and hardener by wiping across the mixing surface, picking the mixture up and wiping it again. Colder weather requires longer mixing times. Do not mix in a circular motion; this will trap air bubbles which will become holes in the cured filler.

3

Applying The Filler

1 For best results, filler should not be applied over ¼" thick.

Apply the filler in several coats. Build it up to above the level of the repair surface so that it can be sanded or grated down.

The first coat of filler must be pressed on with a firm wiping motion.

Apply the filler in one direction only. Working the filler back and forth will either pull it off the metal or trap air bubbles.

REPAIRING DENTS

Before you start, take a few minutes to study the damaged area. Try to visualize the shape of the panel before it was damaged. If the damage is on the left fender, look at the right fender and use it as a guide. If there is access to the panel from behind, you can reshape it with a body hammer. If not, you'll have to use a dent puller. Go slowly and work the metal a little at a time. Get the panel as straight as possible before applying filler.

1 This dent is typical of one that can be pulled out or hammered out from behind. Remove the headlight cover, headlight assembly and turn signal housing.

2 Drill a series of holes ½ the size of the end of the dent puller along the stress line. Make some trial pulls and assess the results. If necessary, drill more holes and try again. Do not hurry.

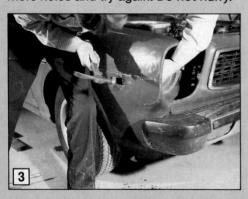

3 If possible, use a body hammer and block to shape the metal back to its original contours. Get the metal back as close to its original shape as possible. Don't depend on body filler to fill dents.

4 Using an 80-grit grinding disc on an electric drill, grind the paint from the surrounding area down to bare metal. Use a new grinding pad to prevent heat buildup that will warp metal.

5 The area should look like this when you're finished grinding. Knock the drill holes in and tape over small openings to keep plastic filler out.

6 Mix the body filler (see Body Repair Tips). Spread the body filler evenly over the entire area (see Body Repair Tips). Be sure to cover the area completely.

7 Let the body filler dry until the surface can just be scratched with your fingernail. Knock the high spots from the body filler with a body file ("Cheesegrater"). Check frequently with the palm of your hand for high and low spots.

8 Check to be sure that trim pieces that will be installed later will fit exactly. Sand the area with 40-grit paper.

9 If you wind up with low spots, you may have to apply another layer of filler.

10 Knock the high spots off with 40-grit paper. When you are satisfied with the contours of the repair, apply a thin coat of filler to cover pin holes and scratches.

11 Block sand the area with 40-grit paper to a smooth finish. Pay particular attention to body lines and ridges that must be well-defined.

12 Sand the area with 400 paper and then finish with a scuff pad. The finished repair is ready for priming and painting (see Painting Tips).

Materials and photos courtesy of Ritt Jones Auto Body, Prospect Park, PA.

REPAIRING RUST HOLES

There are many ways to repair rust holes. The fiberglass cloth kit shown here is one of the most cost efficient for the owner because it provides a strong repair that resists cracking and moisture and is relatively easy to use. It can be used on large and small holes (with or without backing) and can be applied over contoured areas. Remember, however, that short of replacing an entire panel, no repair is a guarantee that the rust will not return.

1 Remove any trim that will be in the way. Clean away all loose debris. Cut away all the rusted metal. But be sure to leave enough metal to retain the contour or body shape.

2 Grind away all traces of rust with a 24-grit grinding disc. Be sure to grind back 3-4 inches from the edge of the hole down to bare metal and be sure all traces of paint, primer and rust are removed.

3 Block sand the area with 80 or 100 grit sandpaper to get a clear, shiny surface and feathered paint edge. Tap the edges of the hole inward with a ball peen hammer.

4 If you are going to use release film, cut a piece about 2-3" larger than the area you have sanded. Place the film over the repair and mark the sanded area on the film. Avoid any unnecessary wrinkling of the film.

5 Cut 2 pieces of fiberglass matte to match the shape of the repair. One piece should be about 1" smaller than the sanded area and the second piece should be 1" smaller than the first. Mix enough filler and hardener to saturate the fiberglass material (see Body Repair Tips).

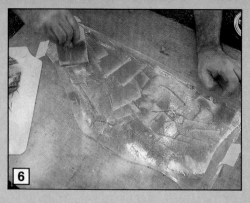

6 Lay the release sheet on a flat surface and spread an even layer of filler, large enough to cover the repair. Lay the smaller piece of fiberglass cloth in the center of the sheet and spread another layer of filler over the fiberglass cloth. Repeat the operation for the larger piece of cloth.

7 Place the repair material over the repair area, with the release film facing outward. Use a spreader and work from the center outward to smooth the material, following the body contours. Be sure to remove all air bubbles.

8 Wait until the repair has dried tack-free and peel off the release sheet. The ideal working temperature is 60°-90° F. Cooler or warmer temperatures or high humidity may require additional curing time. Wait longer, if in doubt.

9 Sand and feather-edge the entire area. The initial sanding can be done with a sanding disc on an electric drill if care is used. Finish the sanding with a block sander. Low spots can be filled with body filler; this may require several applications.

10 When the filler can just be scratched with a fingernail, knock the high spots down with a body file and smooth the entire area with 80-grit. Feather the filled areas into the surrounding areas.

11 When the area is sanded smooth, mix some topcoat and hardener and apply it directly with a spreader. This will give a smooth finish and prevent the glass matte from showing through the paint.

12 Block sand the topcoat smooth with finishing sandpaper (200 grit), and 400 grit. The repair is ready for masking, priming and painting (see Painting Tips).

Materials and photos courtesy Marson Corporation, Chelsea, Massachusetts

PAINTING TIPS

Preparation

1 SANDING — Use a 400 or 600 grit wet or dry sandpaper. Wet-sand the area with a 1/4 sheet of sandpaper soaked in clean water. Keep the paper wet while sanding. Sand the area until the repaired area tapers into the original finish.

2 CLEANING — Wash the area to be painted thoroughly with water and a clean rag. Rinse it thoroughly and wipe the surface dry until you're sure it's completely free of dirt, dust, fingerprints, wax, detergent or other foreign matter.

3 MASKING — Protect any areas you don't want to overspray by covering them with masking tape and newspaper. Be careful not get fingerprints on the area to be painted.

4 PRIMING — All exposed metal should be primed before painting. Primer protects the metal and provides an excellent surface for paint adhesion. When the primer is dry, wet-sand the area again with 600 grit wet-sandpaper. Clean the area again after sanding.

Painting Techniques

P aint applied from either a spray gun or a spray can (for small areas) will provide good results. Experiment on an old piece of metal to get the right combination before you begin painting.

SPRAYING VISCOSITY (SPRAY GUN ONLY) — Paint should be thinned to spraying viscosity according to the directions on the can. Use only the recommended thinner or reducer and the same amount of reduction regardless of temperature.

AIR PRESSURE (SPRAY GUN ONLY) — This is extremely important. Be sure you are using the proper recommended pressure.

TEMPERATURE — The surface to be painted should be approximately the same temperature as the surrounding air. Applying warm paint to a cold surface, or vice versa, will completely upset the paint characteristics.

THICKNESS — Spray with smooth strokes. In general, the thicker the coat of paint, the longer the drying time. Apply several thin coats about 30 seconds apart. The paint should remain wet long enough to flow out and no longer; heavier coats will only produce sags or wrinkles. Spray a light (fog) coat, followed by heavier color coats.

DISTANCE — The ideal spraying distance is 8"-12" from the gun or can to the surface. Shorter distances will produce ripples, while greater distances will result in orange peel, dry film and poor color match and loss of material due to overspray.

OVERLAPPING — The gun or can should be kept at right angles to the surface at all times. Work to a wet edge at an even speed, using a 50% overlap and direct the center of the spray at the lower or nearest edge of the previous stroke.

RUBBING OUT (BLENDING) FRESH PAINT — Let the paint dry thoroughly. Runs or imperfections can be sanded out, primed and repainted.

Don't be in too big a hurry to remove the masking. This only produces paint ridges. When the finish has dried for at least a week, apply a small amount of fine grade rubbing compound with a clean, wet cloth. Use lots of water and blend the new paint with the surrounding area.

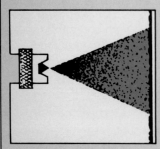

WRONG

Thin coat. Stroke too fast, not enough overlap, gun too far away.

CORRECT

Medium coat. Proper distance, good stroke, proper overlap.

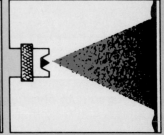

WRONG

Heavy coat. Stroke too slow, too much overlap, gun too close.

5. If the glass is stuck in the down position due to a defective regulator:

a. Remove the access holes covers.

b. Remove the regulator handle assembly.

c. Drill out the regulator pinion shaft housing rivets.

d. Pull the shaft housing free and lift the glass from the tailgate.

6. Installation is the reverse of removal.

7. Align the glass as necessary by loosening the glass slide channel screws and moving the glass as needed to obtain proper fit. Tighten the screws.

8. Installation is the reverse of removal.

9. Align the glass as necessary by loosening the glass slide channel screws and moving the glass as needed to obtain proper fit. Tighten the screws.

Doors
REMOVAL AND INSTALLATION

The doors are retained to the hinges via bolts. Doors are heavy! Before removing the door-to-hinge bolts, support the door securely, or have an assistant support it.

ADJUSTMENT

The doors are adjusted at the hinge mounting points on the door and body. The striker is also adjustable. All fastener holes are oversized to provide for horizontal and vertical movement.

Manual Door Locks
REMOVAL AND INSTALLATION

Lock Cylinder

1. Remove the rubber sealer along the rear edge of the door to expose the lock cylinder retainer.

2. Remove the retainer with a small prybar.

3. Remove the lock cylinder and extension rod from the outside of the door.

4. Installation is the reverse of removal.

Latch and Control Linkage

1. Remove the door trim panel and water shield.

2. Remove the lock cylinder.

3. Remove the bolts from the control assembly. Push it into the door and lower it to the bottom.

4. Disconnect the control arm from the door latch and remove the control assembly through the access hole in the bottom of the door.

5. Remove the bolts attaching the door latch to the door panel. Push the latch in and turn it

90° to free it from the lock lever rod. Remove it through the lower access hole.

6. Installation is the reverse of removal.

Power Door Locks
REMOVAL AND INSTALLATION
Switch

1. Disconnect the battery ground.

2. Remove the door trim panel and watershield.

3. Remove the switch housing from the inner door panel.

4. Disconnect the wiring and pry up the switch retaining clips. Remove the switch.

5. Installation is the reverse of removal.

Actuator Motor

1. Disconnect the battery ground.

2. Remove the door trim panel and watershield.

3. Using a ¼" drill bit, drill out the motor mounting rivets.

4. Disconnect the motor actuator rod from the bellcrank.

5. Disconnect the wires from the motor and lift the motor from the door.

6. Installation is the reverse of removal. Use ¼–20 x ½" bolts and locknuts in place of the rivets.

INTERIOR
Door Panels
REMOVAL AND INSTALLATION

1. Loosen the screws and remove the door handle and window handle.

2. Remove the arm rest, and, if equipped, the assist handle.

3. Remove the screws securing the bottom of the trim panel to the door.

4. Using a wide-bladed tool, carefully pry out the panel-to-door frame clips. Pry right at the clip and not between them, to avoid damaging the panel.

5. Remove the trim panel. Replace any damaged clips.

6. Installation is the reverse of removal.

Manual Door Glass and Regulator
REMOVAL AND INSTALLATION
Front Door

GREMLIN
HORNET
SPIRIT
CONCORD
AMX
EAGLE

1. Remove the inner glass weatherstripping.

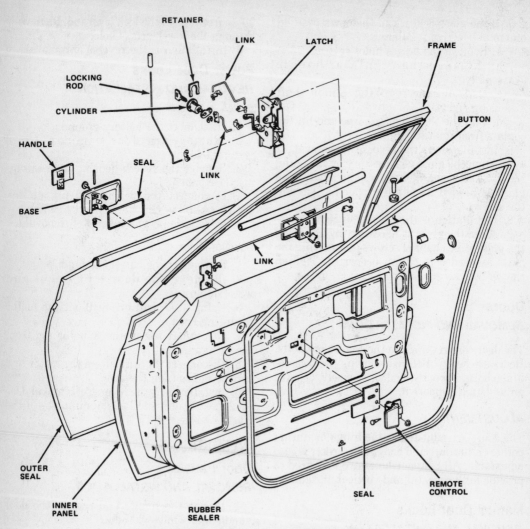

RETAINER

LINK

LATCH

FRAME

LOCKING
ROD

CYLINDER

BUTTON

HANDLE

SEAL

LINK

BASE

LINK

OUTER
SEAL

REMOTE
CONTROL

SEAL

INNER
PANEL

RUBBER
SEALER

Gremlin, Hornet, Concord, AMX, Eagle door components

2. Remove the door panel and water dam.

3. Position the glass so that the screws are visible through the upper access holes in the door panel.

4. Using masking tape, tape the glass to the top of the window frame to keep it from falling.

5. Remove the front screw and wave washer.

6. Remove the rear screws.

7. Hold the glass, remove the tape and roll the regulator all the way down.

8. Lower the glass, tilt it towards the hinge side of the door and pull it out.

9. Installation is the reverse of removal. When installing the glass, keep it towards the outside of the frame. Tighten the screws to 40 in.lb.

MATADOR COUPE

1. Remove the inner glass weatherstripping.

2. Remove the door panel and water dam.

3. Loosen the door glass retaining brackets.

4. Remove the up-stops from the window.

5. Support the glass and remove the nuts attaching the glass to the guide plate.

6. Lift the glass out of the door.

7. Installation is the reverse of removal. Tighten all fasteners to 70 in.lb.

MATADOR SEDAN AND WAGON

1. Remove the door trim panel and water dam.

2. Raise the glass to about 1" from the top of the frame.

3. Tape the glass to the top of the frame to keep it from falling.

4. Remove the regulator.

5. Remove the channel aluminum frame lower adjustable mounting stud nut.

6. Insert a screwdriver through the lower mounting hole and into the stud mounting hole in the bracket.

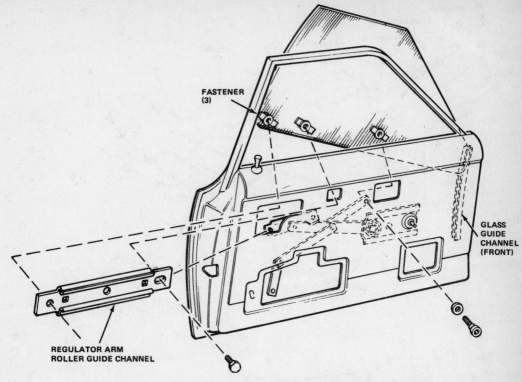

FASTENER
(3)

GLASS
GUIDE
CHANNEL
(FRONT)

REGULATOR ARM
ROLLER GUIDE CHANNEL

Glass removal for the Gremlin, Hornet, Concord, Eagle and AMX

7. Push the aluminum frame outward to clear the inner door panel.

8. Push the frame rearward to disengage the channel from the glass.

NOTE: *During all this pushing and sliding, remember that the channel is aluminum and can be easily deformed!*

9. Remove the tape from the glass.

10. Slide the glass out of the channel and lift it from the door.

11. Installation is the reverse of removal. Torque all fasteners to 70 in.lb.

Rear Door

HORNET

1. Remove the door trim panel and water dam.

2. Position the glass so that the retaining screws are visible and remove them.

3. Push the glass away from the roller guide plate assembly and pull the tang on the plate out of the hole in the lower window channel.

4. Slide the roller guide plate assembly down.

5. Lower the glass to the stop.

6. Tilt the glass towards the latch side of the door and disconnect the regulator arm roller from the glass bottom channel.

7. Pull the glass straight up and out of the door.

8. Installation is the reverse of removal. Torque the fasteners to 40 in.lb.

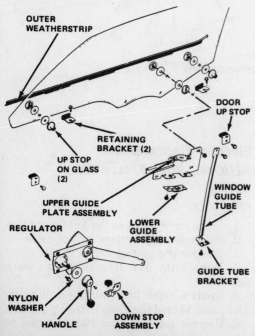

OUTER
WEATHERSTRIP

DOOR
UP STOP

RETAINING
BRACKET (2)

UP STOP
ON GLASS
(2)

WINDOW
GUIDE
TUBE

UPPER GUIDE
PLATE ASSEMBLY

LOWER
GUIDE
ASSEMBLY

REGULATOR

GUIDE TUBE
BRACKET

NYLON
WASHER

HANDLE

DOWN STOP
ASSEMBLY

Matador Coupe door glass and hardware

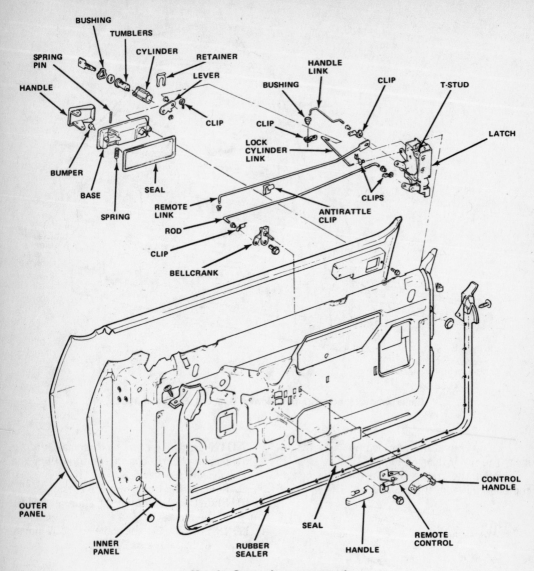

Matador Coupe door components

**MATADOR SEDAN AND WAGON
CONCORD
EAGLE**

1. Remove the door trim panel and water dam.

2. Remove the rubber seal from the frame.

3. Roll the glass up all the way and slide it towards the hinge side to disconnect the rear regulator arm.

4. Raise and tilt the rear of the glass rearwards to disconnect the front arm.

5. Remove the glass.

6. Installation is the reverse of removal. Torque the fasteners to 90 in.lb.

Electric Window Motor
REMOVAL AND INSTALLATION
1975–79
FRONT DOOR

1. Raise the window to the full up position.

2. Disconnect the battery ground cable.

3. Remove the control switch panel.

4. Remove the door trim panel and water dam.

5. Insert a small drift into the hole in the door panel to hold the glass in the up position.

6. Remove the regulator slide channel at-

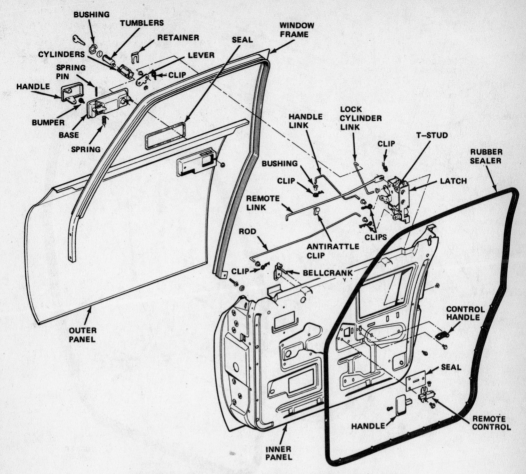

Matador Sedan and Station Wagon front door components

taching screws and the regulator attaching screws.

7. Remove the lower division channel screw.

8. Move the regulator channel assembly arms forward and then back to disconnect them from the glass bottom channel.

9. Disconnect the wiring at the motor.

10. Move the regulator arms up and out through the opening in the door panel.

11. Slide the regulator motor and regulator between the inner panel and the division channel to remove it from the door.

12. Installation is the reverse of removal.

REAR DOOR

1. Raise the window to the full up position.

2. Disconnect the battery ground cable.

3. Remove the control switch panel.

4. Remove the door trim panel and water dam.

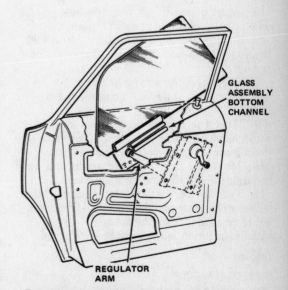

Door glass removal for Concord and Eagle

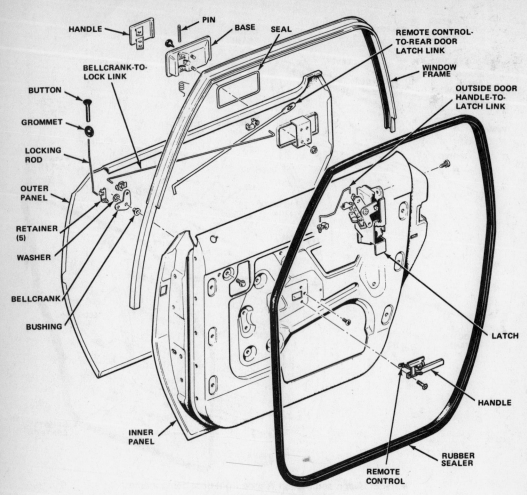

Concord door components

5. Insert a small drift into the hole in the door panel to hold the glass in the up position.

6. Remove the regulator slide channel attaching screws and the regulator attaching screws.

7. Disconnect the wiring at the motor.

8. Disconnect the remote control rod at the latch.

9. Move the regulator channel assembly arms forward and then back to disconnect them from the glass bottom channel.

10. Move the regulator arms up and out through the opening in the door panel.

11. Slide the regulator motor and regulator between the inner panel and the division channel to remove it from the door.

12. Installation is the reverse of removal.

1980–87

FRONT OR REAR DOOR

1. Disconnect the battery ground.

2. Remove the door trim panel.

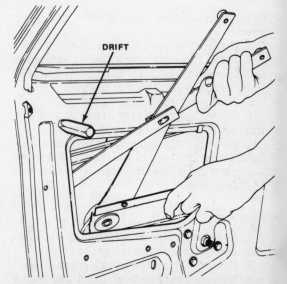

Door window regulator removal for the Matador Sedan and Wagon

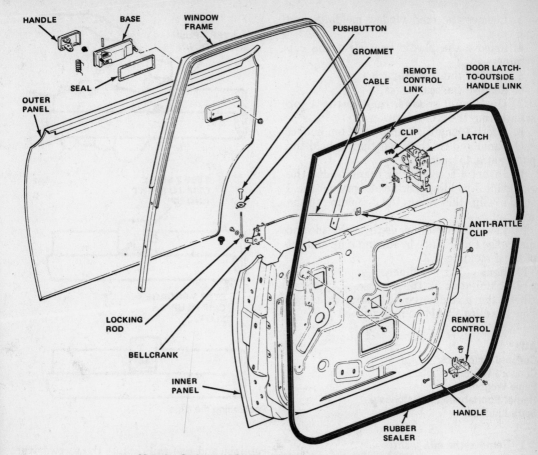

Matador Sedan and Station Wagon rear door components

3. Squeeze the cable coupling retainer and pull down on the cable to free it from the regulator drive.

4. Using a ¼" drill bit, drill out the motor mounting rivets, disconnect the wires at the motor and lift it from the door.

5. Installation is the reverse of removal. Use ¼-20 x ½ screws to replace the rivets.

Electric Tailgate Window Motor
REMOVAL AND INSTALLATION

1. Remove the glass.

2. Remove the access hole covers.

3. Using the key switch, move the regulator arms to a horizontal position.

4. Disconnect the motor wire.

5. Matchmark the regulator position on the mounting panel.

6. Remove the regulator mounting bolts and remove the regulator and motor.

7. Installation is the reverse of removal. Torque the fasteners to 70 in.lb.

Power Seat Motor
REMOVAL AND INSTALLATION

1. Disconnect the battery ground.

2. Remove the bolts holding the seat assembly to the floor pan.

3. Tilt the seat and disconnect the wiring harness.

4. Remove the seat assembly.

5. Invert the seat on a clean surface.

6. Remove the attaching bolts and lift out the seat motor. Disconnect the wiring and cables.

7. Installation is the reverse of removal.

NOTE: *If the seat transmission fails, it is not replaceable. The entire seat adjuster assembly will have to be replaced.*

Headliner
REMOVAL AND INSTALLATION

Gremlin, Hornet, Concord and Eagle Sedans

1. Remove the sun visors.

2. Remove the windshield moldings and end caps.

3. Remove the rear window moldings and end caps.

4. Remove the plastic trim strip and cap retainers.

5. Remove the dome light.

6. Remove the coat hooks.

7. On Hornet sedans, remove the 4 top screws from the roof extension trim panels.

8. Insert a length of cord in the top hole of each panel and tie them together to hold the panels at a 45° angle.

9. Insert a screwdriver blade under the right side J-molding. Locate and pry out the 3 snap-in clips that retain the J-molding to the roof rail.

10. Lower the headliner on the right side and disengage the left side by raising it up and out of the J-molding.

11. Remove the headliner.

12. Installation is the reverse of removal. Check the accompanying illustration to see how the clips should be repositioned.

AMX
Concord Hatchback
Concord Wagon
Eagle Wagon
Hornet Sportabout and Hatchback
Spirit Liftback
SX/4

1. Remove the sun visors.

2. Remove the windshield moldings and end caps.

3. Remove the rear window moldings and end caps.

4. Remove the plastic trim strip and cap retainers.

5. Remove the dome light.

6. Remove the coat hooks.

7. Insert a length of cord in the top hole of each panel and tie them together to hold the panels at a 45° angle.

8. Insert a screwdriver blade under the right side J-molding. Locate and pry out the 3 snap-in clips that retain the J-molding to the roof rail.

9. Lower the headliner on the right side and disengage the left side by raising it up and out of the J-molding.

10. Remove the headliner through the liftgate.

11. Installation is the reverse of removal. Check the accompanying illustration to see how the clips should be repositioned.

Matador Coupe

1. Remove the sunvisors, front and rear finish moldings, coat hooks, B-pillar trim attaching screws and dome lamp.

2. Insert a screwdriver blade between the

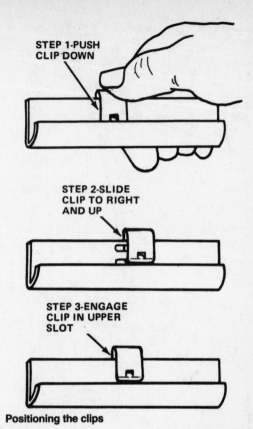

STEP 1-PUSH
CLIP DOWN

STEP 2-SLIDE
CLIP TO RIGHT
AND UP

STEP 3-ENGAGE
CLIP IN UPPER
SLOT

Positioning the clips

retainer and roof rail. Rotate the screwdriver to pop the clips out of the holes in the roof rail. Remove the retainers on either he left or right side.

3. Lower the headliner and remove it through the door.

NOTE: *There are two slotted holes in the headliner retainer, one above the other. A barb on the clip is engaged in the lower hole when the headliner is removed fom the car. The clips must be positioned to engage the upper holes in all headliner retainers before installing the headliner.*

4. Center the headliner in the car.

5. Insert the left edge into the retainer and, while holding it there, grasp the headliner through the dome light opening to guide the right edge into the retainers.

6. Using the sunvisor holes as guides, center the headliner fore and aft.

7. Push up on the J-molding at each clip location to engage the barbs on the clips with the lower holes in the headliner retainers.

8. Install all the other parts.

Matador Sedan
Matador Wagon Front Section

1. Remove the sunvisors, front and rear finish moldings, coat hooks, B-pillar trim attaching screws and dome lamp.

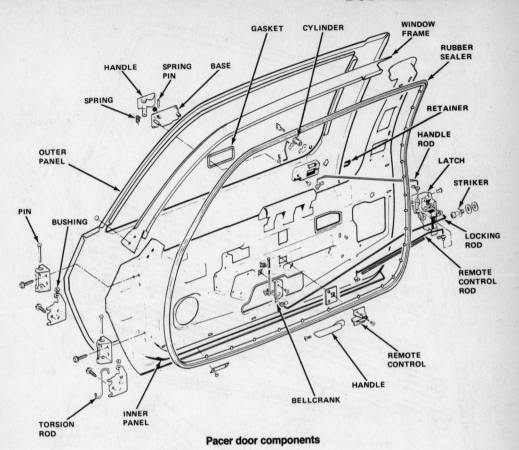

Pacer door components

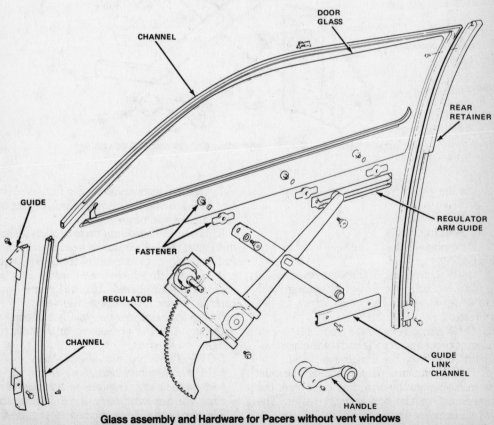

Glass assembly and Hardware for Pacers without vent windows

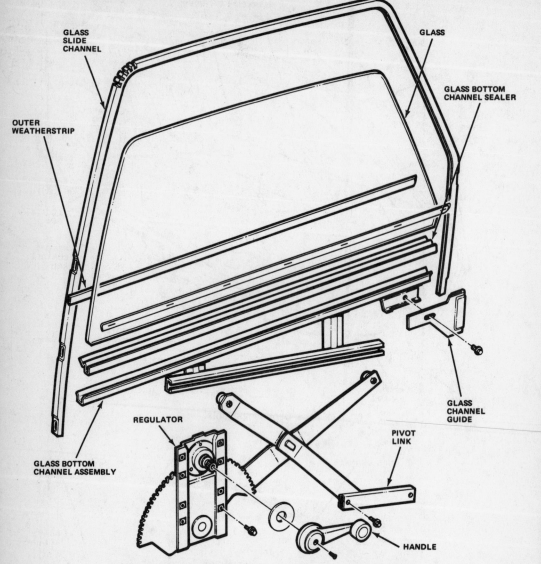

Matador Sedan and Station Wagon door glass attaching hardware

2. On the 4-door Sedan, remove the:
   a. Front seat
   b. Right front door
   c. Steering wheel

3. On Sedans, remove the rear window finish molding.

4. On Wagons, remove the joint cover molding. The molding is retained by spring steel clips which snap over an embossment in the roof rafter.

5. On Wagons, remove the J-molding screw and joint cover and pry the ends of the headliner joint cover from the J-moldings.

6. Pry the molding downward at the rear side to disengage the retaining clips from the embossment on the roof support rafter. The clips will remain in the molding.

7. Insert a screwdriver under the J-molding and slide it along the right roof rail, prying out each clip as you come to it.

8. Lower the headliner on the right side and disengage the left side of the headliner by carefully raising it up and out of the J-molding.

9. On models which use adhesive as a retaining agent, break the adhesive bond carefull, or use an adhesive disolver.

10. Tip the headliner diagonally and remove it through the door on Sedans, or through the tailgate on Wagons.

NOTE: *There are two slotted holes in the headliner retainer, one above the other. A barb on the clip is engaged in the lower hole when the headliner is removed fom the car. The clips must be positioned to engage the*

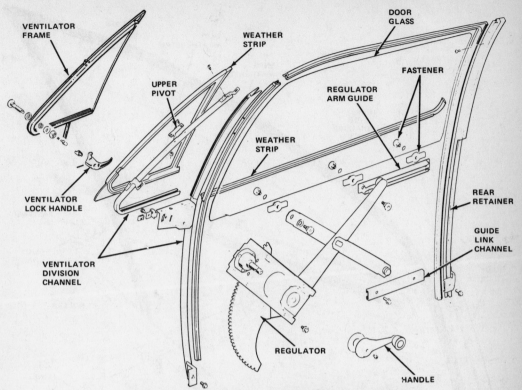

Glass assembly and hardware on Pacers with a vent window

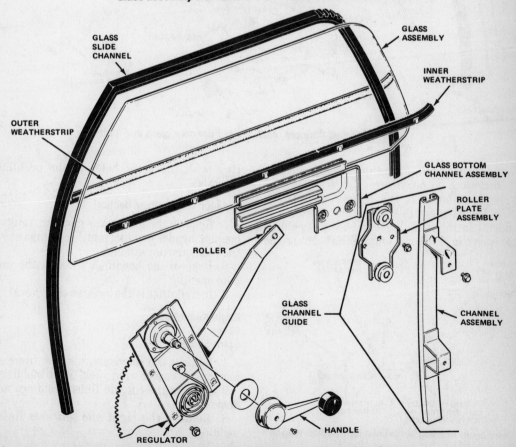

Hornet, Concord and Eagle Rear door glass and hardware

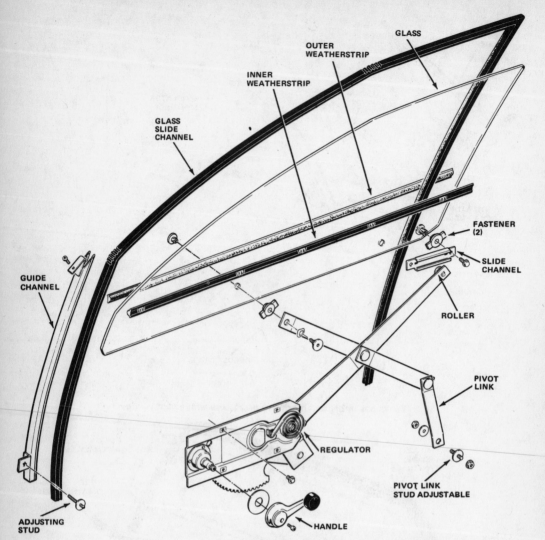

GLASS

OUTER
WEATHERSTRIP

INNER
WEATHERSTRIP

GLASS
SLIDE
CHANNEL

FASTENER
(2)

SLIDE
CHANNEL

GUIDE
CHANNEL

ROLLER

PIVOT
LINK

REGULATOR

PIVOT LINK
STUD ADJUSTABLE

ADJUSTING
STUD

HANDLE

Gremlin, Hornet, Concord, AMX, Eagle front door glass and hardware

upper holes in all headliner retainers before installing the headliner.

11. Installation is the reverse of removal. Use the openings in the headlier to center it during installation. Push up on the J-molding at each clip location to engage the barbs on the

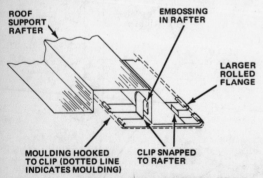

ROOF
SUPPORT
RAFTER

EMBOSSING
IN RAFTER

LARGER
ROLLED
FLANGE

MOULDING HOOKED
TO CLIP (DOTTED LINE
INDICATES MOULDING)

CLIP SNAPPED
TO RAFTER

Joint cover molding on the Matador Station Wagon

clips with the lower holes in the headliner retainers.

Matador Wagon Rear Section

1. Remove the joint cover molding, tailgate opening header molding and J-moldings above the rear quarter windows.
2. Remove the headliner through the tailgate opening.
3. Installation is the reverse of removal.

Eagle Kammback
Pacer
Spirit Sedan

1. Remove the sunvisors, sunvisor brackets and top and corner windshield finish moldings.
2. Remove the liftgate finish moldings and dome lamp.
3. Remove the right and left side finish moldings.

4. Insert a screwdriver blade between the retainer and roof rail. Rotate the screwdriver to pop the clips out of the holes in the roof rail. Remove the retainers on either he left or right side.

5. Lower the headliner on the left side and disengage the right side by raising up and out of the retainers.

6. Remove the headliner through the liftgate opening.

NOTE: *There are two slotted holes in the headliner retainer, one above the other. A barb on the clip is engaged in the lower hole when the headliner is removed fom the car. The clips must be positioned to engage the upper holes in all headliner retainers before installing the headliner.*

7. Installation is the reverse of removal. Use the openings in the headlier to center it during installation. Push up on the J-molding at each clip location to engage the barbs on the clips with the lower holes in the headliner retainers.

How to Remove Stains from Fabric Interior

For rest results, spots and stains should be removed as soon as possible. Never use gasoline, lacquer thinner, acetone, nail polish remover or bleach. Use a 3′ x 3″ piece of cheesecloth. Squeeze most of the liquid from the fabric and wipe the stained fabric from the outside of the stain toward the center with a lifting motion. Turn the cheesecloth as soon as one side becomes soiled. When using water to remove a stain, be sure to wash the entire section after the spot has been removed to avoid water stains. Encrusted spots can be broken up with a dull knife and vacuumed before removing the stain.

Type of Stain	How to Remove It
Surface spots	Brush the spots out with a small hand brush or use a commercial preparation such as K2R to lift the stain.
Mildew	Clean around the mildew with warm suds. Rinse in cold water and soak the mildew area in a solution of 1 part table salt and 2 parts water. Wash with upholstery cleaner.
Water stains	Water stains in fabric materials can be removed with a solution made from 1 cup of table salt dissolved in 1 quart of water. Vigorously scrub the solution into the stain and rinse with clear water. Water stains in nylon or other synthetic fabrics should be removed with a commercial type spot remover.
Chewing gum, tar, crayons, shoe polish (greasy stains)	Do not use a cleaner that will soften gum or tar. Harden the deposit with an ice cube and scrape away as much as possible with a dull knife. Moisten the remainder with cleaning fluid and scrub clean.
Ice cream, candy	Most candy has a sugar base and can be removed with a cloth wrung out in warm water. Oily candy, after cleaning with warm water, should be cleaned with upholstery cleaner. Rinse with warm water and clean the remainder with cleaning fluid.
Wine, alcohol, egg, milk, soft drink (non-greasy stains)	Do not use soap. Scrub the stain with a cloth wrung out in warm water. Remove the remainder with cleaning fluid.
Grease, oil, lipstick, butter and related stains	Use a spot remover to avoid leaving a ring. Work from the outisde of the stain to the center and dry with a clean cloth when the spot is gone.
Headliners (cloth)	Mix a solution of warm water and foam upholstery cleaner to give thick suds. Use only foam—liquid may streak or spot. Clean the entire headliner in one operation using a circular motion with a natural sponge.
Headliner (vinyl)	Use a vinyl cleaner with a sponge and wipe clean with a dry cloth.
Seats and door panels	Mix 1 pint upholstery cleaner in 1 gallon of water. Do not soak the fabric around the buttons.
Leather or vinyl fabric	Use a multi-purpose cleaner full strength and a stiff brush. Let stand 2 minutes and scrub thoroughly. Wipe with a clean, soft rag.
Nylon or synthetic fabrics	For normal stains, use the same procedures you would for washing cloth upholstery. If the fabric is extremely dirty, use a multi-purpose cleaner full strength with a stiff scrub brush. Scrub thoroughly in all directions and wipe with a cotton towel or soft rag.

Mechanic's Data

General Conversion Table

Multiply By	To Convert	To	
		LENGTH	
2.54	Inches	Centimeters	.3937
25.4	Inches	Millimeters	.03937
30.48	Feet	Centimeters	.0328
.304	Feet	Meters	3.28
.914	Yards	Meters	1.094
1.609	Miles	Kilometers	.621
		VOLUME	
.473	Pints	Liters	2.11
.946	Quarts	Liters	1.06
3.785	Gallons	Liters	.264
.016	Cubic inches	Liters	61.02
16.39	Cubic inches	Cubic cms.	.061
28.3	Cubic feet	Liters	.0353
		MASS (Weight)	
28.35	Ounces	Grams	.035
.4536	Pounds	Kilograms	2.20
—	To obtain	From	Multiply by

Multiply By	To Convert	To	
		AREA	
.645	Square inches	Square cms.	.155
.836	Square yds.	Square meters	1.196
		FORCE	
4.448	Pounds	Newtons	.225
.138	Ft./lbs.	Kilogram/meters	7.23
1.36	Ft./lbs.	Newton-meters	.737
.112	In./lbs.	Newton-meters	8.844
		PRESSURE	
.068	Psi	Atmospheres	14.7
6.89	Psi	Kilopascals	.145
		OTHER	
1.104	Horsepower (DIN)	Horsepower (SAE)	.9861
.746	Horsepower (SAE)	Kilowatts (KW)	1.34
1.60	Mph	Km/h	.625
.425	Mpg	Km/1	2.35
—	To obtain	From	Multiply by

Tap Drill Sizes

National Coarse or U.S.S.

Screw & Tap Size	Threads Per Inch	Use Drill Number
No. 5	.40	.39
No. 6	.32	.36
No. 8	.32	.29
No. 10	.24	.25
No. 12	.24	.17
1/4	.20	8
5/16	.18	F
3/8	.16	5/16
7/16	.14	U
1/2	.13	27/64
9/16	.12	31/64
5/8	.11	17/32
3/4	.10	21/32
7/8	9	49/64

National Coarse or U.S.S.

Screw & Tap Size	Threads Per Inch	Use Drill Number
1	8	7/8
1 1/8	7	63/64
1 1/4	7	1 7/64
1 1/2	6	1 11/32

National Fine or S.A.E.

Screw & Tap Size	Threads Per Inch	Use Drill Number
No. 5	.44	.37
No. 6	.40	.33
No. 8	.36	.29
No. 10	.32	.21

National Fine or S.A.E.

Screw & Tap Size	Threads Per Inch	Use Drill Number
No. 12	.28	.15
1/4	.28	3
6/16	.24	1
3/8	.24	Q
7/16	.20	W
1/2	.20	29/64
9/16	.18	33/64
5/8	.18	37/64
3/4	.16	11/16
7/8	.14	13/16
1 1/8	.12	1 3/64
1 1/4	.12	1 11/64
1 1/2	.12	1 27/64

Drill Sizes In Decimal Equivalents

Inch	Decimal	Wire	mm	Inch	Decimal	Wire	mm	Inch	Decimal	Wire & Letter	mm	Inch	Decimal	Letter	mm	Inch	Decimal	mm
1/64	.0156		.39		.0730	49			.1614		4.1		.2717		6.9		.4331	11.0
	.0157		.4		.0748		1.9		.1654		4.2		.2720	I		7/16	.4375	11.11
	.0160	78			.0760	48			.1660	19			.2756		7.0		.4528	11.5
	.0165		.42		.0768		1.95		.1673		4.25		.2770	J		29/64	.4531	11.51
	.0173		.44	5/64	.0781		1.98		.1693		4.3		.2795		7.1	15/32	.4688	11.90
	.0177		.45		.0785	47			.1695	18			.2810	K			.4724	12.0
	.0180	77			.0787		2.0	11/64	.1719		4.36	9/32	.2812		7.14	31/64	.4844	12.30
	.0181		.46		.0807		2.05		.1730	17			.2835		7.2		.4921	12.5
	.0189		.48		.0810	46			.1732		4.4		.2854		7.25	1/2	.5000	12.70
	.0197		.5		.0820	45			.1770	16			.2874		7.3		.5118	13.0
	.0200	76			.0827		2.1		.1772		4.5		.2900	L		33/64	.5156	13.09
	.0210	75			.0846		2.15		.1800	15			.2913		7.4	17/32	.5312	13.49
	.0217		.55		.0860	44			.1811		4.6		.2950	M			.5315	13.5
	.0225	74			.0866		2.2		.1820	14			.2953		7.5	35/64	.5469	13.89
	.0236		.6		.0886		2.25		.1850	13		19/64	.2969		7.54		.5512	14.0
	.0240	73			.0890	43			.1850		4.7		.2992		7.6	9/16	.5625	14.28
	.0250	72			.0906		2.3		.1870		4.75		.3020	N			.5709	14.5
	.0256		.65		.0925		2.35	3/16	.1875		4.76		.3031		7.7	37/64	.5781	14.68
	.0260	71			.0935	42			.1890		4.8		.3051		7.75		.5906	15.0
	.0276		.7	3/32	.0938		2.38		.1890	12			.3071		7.8	19/32	.5938	15.08
	.0280	70			.0945		2.4		.1910	11			.3110		7.9	39/64	.6094	15.47
	.0292	69			.0960	41			.1929		4.9	5/16	.3125		7.93		.6102	15.5
	.0295		.75		.0965		2.45		.1935	10			.3150		8.0	5/8	.6250	15.87
	.0310	68			.0980	40			.1960	9			.3160	O			.6299	16.0
1/32	.0312		.79		.0981		2.5		.1969		5.0		.3189		8.1	41/64	.6406	16.27
	.0315		.8		.0995	39			.1990	8			.3228		8.2		.6496	16.5
	.0320	67			.1015	38			.2008		5.1		.3230	P		21/32	.6562	16.66
	.0330	66			.1024		2.6		.2010	7			.3248		8.25		.6693	17.0
	.0335		.85		.1040	37		13/64	.2031		5.16		.3268		8.3	43/64	.6719	17.06
	.0350	65			.1063		2.7		.2040	6		21/64	.3281		8.33	11/16	.6875	17.46
	.0354		.9		.1065	36			.2047		5.2		.3307		8.4		.6890	17.5
	.0360	64			.1083		2.75		.2055	5			.3320	Q		45/64	.7031	17.85
	.0370	63		7/64	.1094		2.77		.2067		5.25		.3346		8.5		.7087	18.0
	.0374		.95		.1100	35			.2087		5.3		.3386		8.6	23/32	.7188	18.25
	.0380	62			.1102		2.8		.2090	4			.3390	R			.7283	18.5
	.0390	61			.1110	34			.2126		5.4		.3425		8.7	47/64	.7344	18.65
	.0394		1.0		.1130	33			.2130	3		11/32	.3438		8.73		.7480	19.0
	.0400	60			.1142		2.9		.2165		5.5		.3445		8.75	3/4	.7500	19.05
	.0410	59			.1160	32		7/32	.2188		5.55		.3465		8.8	49/64	.7656	19.44
	.0413		1.05		.1181		3.0		.2205		5.6		.3480	S			.7677	19.5
	.0420	58			.1200	31			.2210	2			.3504		8.9	25/32	.7812	19.84
	.0430	57			.1220		3.1		.2244		5.7		.3543		9.0		.7874	20.0
	.0433		1.1	1/8	.1250		3.17		.2264		5.75		.3580	T		51/64	.7969	20.24
	.0453		1.15		.1260		3.2		.2280	1			.3583		9.1		.8071	20.5
	.0465	56			.1280		3.25		.2283		5.8	23/64	.3594		9.12	13/16	.8125	20.63
3/64	.0469		1.19		.1285	30			.2323		5.9		.3622		9.2		.8268	21.0
	.0472		1.2		.1299		3.3		.2340	A			.3642		9.25	53/64	.8281	21.03
	.0492		1.25		.1339		3.4	15/64	.2344		5.95		.3661		9.3	27/32	.8438	21.43
	.0512		1.3		.1360	29			.2362		6.0		.3680	U			.8465	21.5
	.0520	55			.1378		3.5		.2380	B			.3701		9.4	55/64	.8594	21.82
	.0531		1.35		.1405	28			.2402		6.1		.3740		9.5		.8661	22.0
	.0550	54		9/64	.1406		3.57		.2420	C		3/8	.3750		9.52	7/8	.8750	22.22
	.0551		1.4		.1417		3.6		.2441		6.2		.3770	V			.8858	22.5
	.0571		1.45		.1440	27			.2460	D			.3780		9.6	57/64	.8906	22.62
	.0591		1.5		.1457		3.7		.2461		6.25		.3819		9.7		.9055	23.0
	.0595	53			.1470	26			.2480		6.3		.3839		9.75	29/32	.9062	23.01
	.0610		1.55		.1476		3.75	1/4	.2500	E	6.35		.3858		9.8	59/64	.9219	23.41
1/16	.0625		1.59		.1495	25			.2520		6.		.3860	W			.9252	23.5
	.0630		1.6		.1496		3.8		.2559		6.5		.3898		9.9	15/16	.9375	23.81
	.0635	52			.1520	24			.2570	F		25/64	.3906		9.92		.9449	24.0
	.0650		1.65		.1535		3.9		.2598		6.6		.3937		10.0	61/64	.9531	24.2
	.0669		1.7		.1540	23			.2610	G			.3970	X			.9646	24.5
	.0670	51		5/32	.1562		3.96		.2638		6.7		.4040	Y		31/32	.9688	24.6
	.0689		1.75		.1570	22		17/64	.2656		6.74	13/32	.4062		10.31		.9843	24.9
	.0700	50			.1575		4.0		.2657		6.75		.4130	Z		63/64	.9844	25.0
	.0709		1.8		.1590	21			.2660	H			.4134		10.5	1	1.0000	25.4
	.0728		1.85		.1610	20			.2677		6.8	27/64	.4219		10.71			

GLOSSARY OF TERMS

AIR/FUEL RATIO: The ratio of air to gasoline by weight in the fuel mixture drawn into the engine.

AIR INJECTION: One method of reducing harmful exhaust emissions by injecting air into each of the exhaust ports of an engine. The fresh air entering the hot exhaust manifold causes any remaining fuel to be burned before it can exit the tailpipe.

ALTERNATOR: A device used for converting mechanical energy into electrical energy.

AMMETER: An instrument, calibrated in amperes, used to measure the flow of an electrical current in a circuit. Ammeters are always connected in series with the circuit being tested.

AMPERE: The rate of flow of electrical current present when one volt of electrical pressure is applied against one ohm of electrical resistance.

ANALOG COMPUTER: Any microprocessor that uses similar (analogous) electrical signals to make its calculations.

ARMATURE: A laminated, soft iron core wrapped by a wire that converts electrical energy to mechanical energy as in a motor or relay. When rotated in a magnetic field, it changes mechanical energy into electrical energy as in a generator.

ATMOSPHERIC PRESSURE: The pressure on the Earth's surface caused by the weight of the air in the atmosphere. At sea level, this pressure is 14.7 psi at 32°F (101 kPa at 0°C).

ATOMIZATION: The breaking down of a liquid into a fine mist that can be suspended in air.

AXIAL PLAY: Movement parallel to a shaft or bearing bore.

BACKFIRE: The sudden combustion of gases in the intake or exhaust system that results in a loud explosion.

BACKLASH: The clearance or play between two parts, such as meshed gears.

BACKPRESSURE: Restrictions in the exhaust system that slow the exit of exhaust gases from the combustion chamber.

BAKELITE: A heat resistant, plastic insulator material commonly used in printed circuit boards and transistorized components.

BALL BEARING: A bearing made up of hardened inner and outer races between which hardened steel ball roll.

BALLAST RESISTOR: A resistor in the primary ignition circuit that lowers voltage after the engine is started to reduce wear on ignition components.

BEARING: A friction reducing, supportive device usually located between a stationary part and a moving part.

BIMETAL TEMPERATURE SENSOR: Any sensor or switch made of two dissimilar types of metal that bend when heated or cooled due to the different expansion rates of the alloys. These types of sensors usually function as an on/off switch.

BLOWBY: Combustion gases, composed of water vapor and unburned fuel, that leak past the piston rings into the crankcase during normal engine operation. These gases are removed by the PCV system to prevent the build-up of harmful acids in the crankcase.

BRAKE PAD: A brake shoe and lining assembly used with disc brakes.

BRAKE SHOE: The backing for the brake lining. The term is, however, usually applied to the assembly of the brake backing and lining.

BUSHING: A liner, usually removable, for a bearing; an anti-friction liner used in place of a bearing.

BYPASS: System used to bypass ballast resistor during engine cranking to increase voltage supplied to the coil.

CALIPER: A hydraulically activated device in a disc brake system, which is mounted straddling the brake rotor (disc). The caliper contains at least one piston and two brake pads. Hydraulic pressure on the piston(s) forces the pads against the rotor.

CAMSHAFT: A shaft in the engine on which are the lobes (cams) which operate the valves. The camshaft is driven by the crankshaft, via a belt, chain or gears, at one half the crankshaft speed.

CAPACITOR: A device which stores an electrical charge.

CARBON MONOXIDE (CO): a colorless, odorless gas given off as a normal byproduct of combustion. It is poisonous and extremely dangerous in confined areas, building up slowly to toxic levels without warning if adequate ventilation is not available.

CARBURETOR: A device, usually mounted on the intake manifold of an engine, which mixes the air and fuel in the proper proportion to allow even combustion.

CATALYTIC CONVERTER: A device installed in the exhaust system, like a muffler, that converts harmful byproducts of combustion into carbon dioxide and water vapor by means of a heat-producing chemical reaction.

CENTRIFUGAL ADVANCE: A mechanical method of advancing the spark timing by using flyweights in the distributor that react to centrifugal force generated by the distributor shaft rotation.

CHECK VALVE: Any one-way valve installed to permit the flow of air, fuel or vacuum in one direction only.

CHOKE: A device, usually a moveable valve, placed in the intake path of a carburetor to restrict the flow of air.

CIRCUIT: Any unbroken path through which an electrical current can flow. Also used to describe fuel flow in some instances.

CIRCUIT BREAKER: A switch which protects an electrical circuit from overload by opening the circuit when the current flow exceeds a predetermined level. Some circuit breakers must be reset manually, while other reset automatically

COIL (IGNITION): A transformer in the ignition circuit which steps of the voltage provided to the spark plugs.

COMBINATION MANIFOLD: An assembly which includes both the intake and exhaust manifolds in one casting.

COMBINATION VALVE: A device used in some fuel systems that routes fuel vapors to a charcoal storage canister instead of venting them into the atmosphere. The valve relieves fuel tank pressure and allows fresh air into the tank as fuel level drops to prevent a vapor lock situation.

COMPRESSION RATIO: The comparison of the total volume of the cylinder and combustion chamber with the piston at BDC and the piston at TDC.

CONDENSER: 1. An electrical device which acts to store an electrical charge, preventing voltage surges.
2. A radiator-like device in the air conditioning system in which refrigerant gas condenses into a liquid, giving off heat.

CONDUCTOR: Any material through which an electrical current can be transmitted easily.

CONTINUITY: Continuous or complete circuit. Can be checked with an ohmmeter.

COUNTERSHAFT: An intermediate shaft which is rotated by a mainshaft and transmits, in turn, that rotation to a working part.

CRANKCASE: The lower part of an engine in which the crankshaft and related parts operate.

CRANKSHAFT: The main driving shaft of an engine which receives reciprocating motion from the pistons and converts it to rotary motion.

CYLINDER: In an engine, the round hole in the engine block in which the piston(s) ride.

CYLINDER BLOCK: The main structural member of an engine in which is found the cylinders, crankshaft and other principal parts.

CYLINDER HEAD: The detachable portion of the engine, fastened, usually, to the top of the cylinder block, containing all or most of the combustion chambers. On overhead valve engines, it contains the valves and their operating parts. On overhead cam engines, it contains the camshaft as well.

DEAD CENTER: The extreme top or bottom of the piston stroke.

DETONATION: An unwanted explosion of the air fuel mixture in the combustion chamber caused by excess heat and compression, advanced timing, or an overly lean mixture. Also referred to as "ping".

DIAPHRAGM: A thin, flexible wall separating two cavities, such as in a vacuum advance unit.

DIESELING: A condition in which hot spots in the combustion chamber cause the engine to run on after the key is turned off.

DIFFERENTIAL: A geared assembly which allows the transmission of motion between drive axles, giving one axle the ability to turn faster than the other.

DIODE: An electrical device that will allow current to flow in one direction only.

DISC BRAKE: A hydraulic braking assembly consisting of a brake disc, or rotor, mounted on an axle, and a caliper assembly containing, usually two brake pads which are activated by hydraulic pressure. The pads are forced against the sides of the disc, creating friction which slows the vehicle.

DISTRIBUTOR: A mechanically driven device on an engine which is responsible for electrically firing the spark plug at a predetermined point of the piston stroke.

DOWEL PIN: A pin, inserted in mating holes in two different parts allowing those parts to maintain a fixed relationship.

DRUM BRAKE: A braking system which consists of two brake shoes and one or two wheel cylinders, mounted on a fixed backing plate, and a brake drum, mounted on an axle, which revolves around the assembly. Hydraulic action applied to the wheel cylinders forces the shoes outward against the drum, creating friction and slowing the vehicle.

DWELL: The rate, measured in degrees of shaft rotation, at which an electrical circuit cycles on and off.

ELECTRONIC CONTROL UNIT (ECU): Ignition module, module, amplifier or igniter. See Module for definition.

ELECTRONIC IGNITION: A system in which the timing and firing of the spark plugs is controlled by an electronic control unit, usually called a module. These systems have not points or condenser.

ENDPLAY: The measured amount of axial movement in a shaft.

ENGINE: A device that converts heat into mechanical energy.

EXHAUST MANIFOLD: A set of cast passages or pipes which conduct exhaust gases from the engine.

FEELER GAUGE: A blade, usually metal, of precisely predetermined thickness, used to measure the clearance between two parts. These blades usually are available in sets of assorted thicknesses.

F-Head: An engine configuration in which the intake valves are in the cylinder head, while the camshaft and exhaust valves are located in the cylinder block. The camshaft operates the intake valves via lifters and pushrods, while it operates the exhaust valves directly.

FIRING ORDER: The order in which combustion occurs in the cylinders of an engine. Also the order in which spark is distributed to the plugs by the distributor.

FLATHEAD: An engine configuration in which the camshaft and all the valves are located in the cylinder block.

FLOODING: The presence of too much fuel in the intake manifold and combustion chamber which prevents the air/fuel mixture from firing, thereby causing a no-start situation.

FLYWHEEL: A disc shaped part bolted to the rear end of the crankshaft. Around the outer perimeter is affixed the ring gear. The starter drive engages the ring gear, turning the flywheel, which rotates the crankshaft, imparting the initial starting motion to the engine.

FOOT POUND (ft.lb. or sometimes, ft. lbs.): The amount of energy or work needed to raise an item weighing one pound, a distance of one foot.

FUSE: A protective device in a circuit which prevents circuit overload by breaking the circuit when a specific amperage is present. The device is constructed around a strip or wire of a lower amperage rating than the circuit it is designed to protect. When an amperage higher than that stamped on the fuse is present in the circuit, the strip or wire melts, opening the circuit.

GEAR RATIO: The ratio between the number of teeth on meshing gears.

GENERATOR: A device which converts mechanical energy into electrical energy.

HEAT RANGE: The measure of a spark plug's ability to dissipate heat from its firing end. The higher the heat range, the hotter the plug fires.

HUB: The center part of a wheel or gear.

HYDROCARBON (HC): Any chemical compound made up of hydrogen and carbon. A major pollutant formed by the engine as a byproduct of combustion.

HYDROMETER: An instrument used to measure the specific gravity of a solution.

INCH POUND (in.lb. or sometimes, in. lbs.): One twelfth of a foot pound.

INDUCTION: A means of transferring electrical energy in the form of a magnetic field. Principle used in the ignition coil to increase voltage.

INJECTION PUMP: A device, usually mechanically operated, which meters and delivers fuel under pressure to the fuel injector.

INJECTOR: A device which receives metered fuel under relatively low pressure and is activated to inject the fuel into the engine under relatively high pressure at a predetermined time.

INPUT SHAFT: The shaft to which torque is applied, usually carrying the driving gear or gears.

INTAKE MANIFOLD: A casting of passages or pipes used to conduct air or a fuel/air mixture to the cylinders.

JOURNAL: The bearing surface within which a shaft operates.

KEY: A small block usually fitted in a notch between a shaft and a hub to prevent slippage of the two parts.

MANIFOLD: A casting of passages or set of pipes which connect the cylinders to an inlet or outlet source.

MANIFOLD VACUUM: Low pressure in an engine intake manifold formed just below the throttle plates. Manifold vacuum is highest at idle and drops under acceleration.

MASTER CYLINDER: The primary fluid pressurizing device in a hydraulic system. In automotive use, it is found in brake and hydraulic clutch systems and is pedal activated, either directly or, in a power brake system, through the power booster.

MODULE: Electronic control unit, amplifier or igniter of solid state or integrated design which controls the current flow in the ignition primary circuit based on input from the pickup coil. When the module opens the primary circuit, the high secondary voltage is induced in the coil.

NEEDLE BEARING: A bearing which consists of a number (usually a large number) of long, thin rollers.

OHM: (Ω) The unit used to measure the resistance of conductor to electrical flow. One ohm is the amount of resistance that limits current flow to one ampere in a circuit with one volt of pressure.

OHMMETER: An instrument used for measuring the resistance, in ohms, in an electrical circuit.

OUTPUT SHAFT: The shaft which transmits torque from a device, such as a transmission.

OVERDRIVE: A gear assembly which produces more shaft revolutions than that transmitted to it.

OVERHEAD CAMSHAFT (OHC): An engine configuration in which the camshaft is mounted on top of the cylinder head and operates the valve either directly or by means of rocker arms.

OVERHEAD VALVE (OHV): An engine configuration in which all of the valves are located in the cylinder head and the camshaft is located in the cylinder block. The camshaft operates the valves via lifters and pushrods.

OXIDES OF NITROGEN (NOx): Chemical compounds of nitrogen produced as a byproduct of combustion. They combine with hydrocarbons to produce smog.

OXYGEN SENSOR: Used with the feedback system to sense the presence of oxygen in the exhaust gas and signal the computer which can reference the voltage signal to an air/fuel ratio.

PINION: The smaller of two meshing gears.

PISTON RING: An open ended ring which fits into a groove on the outer diameter of the piston. Its chief function is to form a seal between the piston and cylinder wall. Most automotive pistons have three rings: two for compression sealing; one for oil sealing.

PRELOAD: A predetermined load placed on a bearing during assembly or by adjustment.

PRIMARY CIRCUIT: Is the low voltage side of the ignition system which consists of the ignition switch, ballast resistor or resistance wire, bypass, coil, electronic control unit and pick-up coil as well as the connecting wires and harnesses.

PRESS FIT: The mating of two parts under pressure, due to the inner diameter of one being smaller than the outer diameter of the other, or vice versa; an interference fit.

RACE: The surface on the inner or outer ring of a bearing on which the balls, needles or rollers move.

REGULATOR: A device which maintains the amperage and/or voltage levels of a circuit at predetermined values.

RELAY: A switch which automatically opens and/or closes a circuit.

RESISTANCE: The opposition to the flow of current through a circuit or electrical device, and is measured in ohms. Resistance is equal to the voltage divided by the amperage.

RESISTOR: A device, usually made of wire, which offers a preset amount of resistance in an electrical circuit.

RING GEAR: The name given to a ring-shaped gear attached to a differential case, or affixed to a flywheel or as part a planetary gear set.

ROLLER BEARING: A bearing made up of hardened inner and outer races between which hardened steel rollers move.

ROTOR: 1. The disc-shaped part of a disc brake assembly, upon which the brake pads bear; also called, brake disc.
2. The device mounted atop the distributor shaft, which passes current to the distributor cap tower contacts.

SECONDARY CIRCUIT: The high voltage side of the ignition system, usually above 20,000 volts. The secondary includes the ignition coil, coil wire, distributor cap and rotor, spark plug wires and spark plugs.

SENDING UNIT: A mechanical, electrical, hydraulic or electromagnetic device which transmits information to a gauge.

SENSOR: Any device designed to measure engine operating conditions or ambient pressures and temperatures. Usually electronic in nature and designed to send a voltage signal to an on-board computer, some sensors may operate as a simple on/off switch or they may provide a variable voltage signal (like a potentiometer) as conditions or measured parameters change.

SHIM: Spacers of precise, predetermined thickness used between parts to establish a proper working relationship.

SLAVE CYLINDER: In automotive use, a device in the hydraulic clutch system which is activated by hydraulic force, disengaging the clutch.

SOLENOID: A coil used to produce a magnetic field, the effect of which is produce work.

SPARK PLUG: A device screwed into the combustion chamber of a spark ignition engine. The basic construction is a conductive core inside of a ceramic insulator, mounted in an outer conductive base. An electrical charge from the spark plug wire travels along the conductive core and jumps a preset air gap to a grounding point or points at the end of the conductive base. The resultant spark ignites the fuel/air mixture in the combustion chamber.

SPLINES: Ridges machined or cast onto the outer diameter of a shaft or inner diameter of a bore to enable parts to mate without rotation.

TACHOMETER: A device used to measure the rotary speed of an engine, shaft, gear, etc., usually in rotations per minute.

THERMOSTAT: A valve, located in the cooling system of an engine, which is closed when cold and opens gradually in response to engine heating, controlling the temperature of the coolant and rate of coolant flow.

TOP DEAD CENTER (TDC): The point at which the piston reaches the top of its travel on the compression stroke.

TORQUE: The twisting force applied to an object.

TORQUE CONVERTER: A turbine used to transmit power from a driving member to a driven member via hydraulic action, providing changes in drive ratio and torque. In automotive use, it links the driveplate at the rear of the engine to the automatic transmission.

TRANSDUCER: A device used to change a force into an electrical signal.

TRANSISTOR: A semi-conductor component which can be actuated by a small voltage to perform an electrical switching function.

TUNE-UP: A regular maintenance function, usually associated with the replacement and adjustment of parts and components in the electrical and fuel systems of a vehicle for the purpose of attaining optimum performance.

TURBOCHARGER: An exhaust driven pump which compresses intake air and forces it into the combustion chambers at higher than atmospheric pressures. The increased air pressure allows more fuel to be burned and results in increased horsepower being produced.

VACUUM ADVANCE: A device which advances the ignition timing in response to increased engine vacuum.

VACUUM GAUGE: An instrument used to measure the presence of vacuum in a chamber.

VALVE: A device which control the pressure, direction of flow or rate of flow of a liquid or gas.

VALVE CLEARANCE: The measured gap between the end of the valve stem and the rocker arm, cam lobe or follower that activates the valve.

VISCOSITY: The rating of a liquid's internal resistance to flow.

VOLTMETER: An instrument used for measuring electrical force in units called volts. Voltmeters are always connected parallel with the circuit being tested.

WHEEL CYLINDER: Found in the automotive drum brake assembly, it is a device, actuated by hydraulic pressure, which, through internal pistons, pushes the brake shoes outward against the drums.

ABBREVIATIONS AND SYMBOLS

A: Ampere

AC: Alternating current

A/C: Air conditioning

A-h: Ampere hour

AT: Automatic transmission

ATDC: After top dead center

μA: Microampere

bbl: Barrel

BDC: Bottom dead center

bhp: Brake horsepower

BTDC: Before top dead center

BTU: British thermal unit

C: Celsius (Centigrade)

CCA: Cold cranking amps

cd: Candela

cm^2: Square centimeter

cm^3, cc: Cubic centimeter

CO: Carbon monoxide

CO_2: Carbon dioxide

cu.in., in^3: Cubic inch

CV: Constant velocity

Cyl.: Cylinder

DC: Direct current

ECM: Electronic control module

EFE: Early fuel evaporation

EFI: Electronic fuel injection

EGR: Exhaust gas recirculation

Exh.: Exhaust

F: Fahrenheit

F: Farad

pF: Picofarad

μF: Microfarad

FI: Fuel injection

ft.lb., ft. lb., ft. lbs.: foot pound(s)

gal: Gallon

g: Gram

HC: Hydrocarbon

HEI: High energy ignition

HO: High output

hp: Horsepower

Hyd.: Hydraulic

Hz: Hertz

ID: Inside diameter

in.lb.; in. lb.; in. lbs: inch pound(s)

Int.: Intake

K: Kelvin

kg: Kilogram

kHz: Kilohertz

km: Kilometer

km/h: Kilometers per hour

$k\Omega$: Kilohm

kPa: Kilopascal

kV: Kilovolt

kW: Kilowatt

l: Liter

l/s: Liters per second

m: Meter

mA: Milliampere

mg: Milligram

mHz: Megahertz

mm: Millimeter

mm^2: Square millimeter

m^3: Cubic meter

MΩ: Megohm

m/s: Meters per second

MT: Manual transmission

mV: Millivolt

μm: Micrometer

N: Newton

N-m: Newton meter

NOx: Nitrous oxide

OD: Outside diameter

OHC: Over head camshaft

OHV: Over head valve

Ω: Ohm

PCV: Positive crankcase ventilation

psi: Pounds per square inch

pts: Pints

qts: Quarts

rpm: Rotations per minute

rps: Rotations per second

R-12: A refrigerant gas (Freon)

SAE: Society of Automotive Engineers

SO$_2$: Sulfur dioxide

T: Ton

t: Megagram

TBI: Throttle Body Injection

TPS: Throttle Position Sensor

V: 1. Volt; 2. Venturi

μV: Microvolt

W: Watt

∞: Infinity

<: Less than

>: Greater than

Index

Chilton's Repair & Tune-Up Guides

The Complete line covers domestic cars, imports, trucks, vans, RV's and 4-wheel drive vehicles.

RTUG Title	Part No.	RTUG Title	Part No.
AMC 1975-82	7199	**Corvair 1960-69**	6691
Covers all U.S. and Canadian models		Covers all U.S. and Canadian models	
Aspen/Volare 1976-80	6637	**Corvette 1953-62**	6576
Covers all U.S. and Canadian models		Covers all U.S. and Canadian models	
Audi 1970-73	5902	**Corvette 1963-84**	6843
Covers all U.S. and Canadian models.		Covers all U.S. and Canadian models	
Audi 4000/5000 1978-81	7028	**Cutlass 1970-85**	6933
Covers all U.S. and Canadian models including turbocharged and diesel engines		Covers all U.S. and Canadian models	
Barracuda/Challenger 1965-72	5807	**Dart/Demon 1968-76**	6324
Covers all U.S. and Canadian models		Covers all U.S. and Canadian models	
Blazer/Jimmy 1969-82	6931	**Datsun 1961-72**	5790
Covers all U.S. and Canadian 2- and 4-wheel drive models, including diesel engines		Covers all U.S. and Canadian models of Nissan Patrol; 1500, 1600 and 2000 sports cars; Pick-Ups; 410, 411, 510, 1200 and 240Z	
BMW 1970-82	6844		
Covers U.S. and Canadian models		**Datsun 1973-80 Spanish**	7083
Buick/Olds/Pontiac 1975-85	7308	**Datsun/Nissan F-10, 310, Stanza, Pulsar 1977-86**	7196
Covers all U.S. and Canadian full size rear wheel drive models		Covers all U.S. and Canadian models	
Cadillac 1967-84	7462	**Datsun/Nissan Pick-Ups 1970-84**	6816
Covers all U.S. and Canadian rear wheel drive models		Covers all U.S and Canadian models	
Camaro 1967-81	6735	**Datsun/Nissan Z & ZX 1970-86**	6932
Covers all U.S. and Canadian models		Covers all U.S. and Canadian models	
Camaro 1982-85	7317	**Datsun/Nissan 1200, 210, Sentra 1973-86**	7197
Covers all U.S. and Canadian models		Covers all U.S. and Canadian models	
Capri 1970-77	6695	**Datsun/Nissan 200SX, 510, 610, 710, 810, Maxima 1973-84**	7170
Covers all U.S. and Canadian models		Covers all U.S. and Canadian models	
Caravan/Voyager 1984-85	7482	**Dodge 1968-77**	6554
Covers all U.S. and Canadian models		Covers all U.S. and Canadian models	
Century/Regal 1975-85	7307	**Dodge Charger 1967-70**	6486
Covers all U.S. and Canadian rear wheel drive models, including turbocharged engines		Covers all U.S. and Canadian models	
Champ/Arrow/Sapporo 1978-83	7041	**Dodge/Plymouth Trucks 1967-84**	7459
Covers all U.S. and Canadian models		Covers all $^1/_2$, $^3/_4$, and 1 ton 2- and 4-wheel drive U.S. and Canadian models, including diesel engines	
Chevette/1000 1976-86	6836		
Covers all U.S. and Canadian models		**Dodge/Plymouth Vans 1967-84**	6934
Chevrolet 1968-85	7135	Covers all $^1/_2$, $^3/_4$, and 1 ton U.S. and Canadian models of vans, cutaways and motor home chassis	
Covers all U.S. and Canadian models			
Chevrolet 1968-79 Spanish	7082	**D-50/Arrow Pick-Up 1979-81**	7032
Chevrolet/GMC Pick-Ups 1970-82 Spanish	7468	Covers all U.S. and Canadian models	
		Fairlane/Torino 1962-75	6320
Chevrolet/GMC Pick-Ups and Suburban 1970-86	6936	Covers all U.S. and Canadian models	
Covers all U.S. and Canadian $^1/_2$, $^3/_4$ and 1 ton models, including 4-wheel drive and diesel engines		**Fairmont/Zephyr 1978-83**	6965
		Covers all U.S. and Canadian models	
Chevrolet LUV 1972-81	6815	**Fiat 1969-81**	7042
Covers all U.S. and Canadian models		Covers all U.S. and Canadian models	
Chevrolet Mid-Size 1964-86	6840	**Fiesta 1978-80**	6846
Covers all U.S. and Canadian models of 1964-77 Chevelle, Malibu and Malibu SS; 1974-77 Laguna; 1978-85 Malibu; 1970-86 Monte Carlo; 1964-84 El Camino, including diesel engines		Covers all U.S. and Canadian models	
		Firebird 1967-81	5996
		Covers all U.S. and Canadian models	
		Firebird 1982-85	7345
		Covers all U.S. and Canadian models	
Chevrolet Nova 1986	7658	**Ford 1968-79 Spanish**	7084
Covers all U.S. and Canadian models		**Ford Bronco 1966-83**	7140
Chevy/GMC Vans 1967-84	6930	Covers all U.S. and Canadian models	
Covers all U.S. and Canadian models of $^1/_2$, $^3/_4$, and 1 ton vans, cutaways, and motor home chassis, including diesel engines		**Ford Bronco II 1984**	7408
		Covers all U.S. and Canadian models	
		Ford Courier 1972-82	6983
Chevy S-10 Blazer/GMC S-15 Jimmy 1982-85	7383	Covers all U.S. and Canadian models	
Covers all U.S. and Canadian models		**Ford/Mercury Front Wheel Drive 1981-85**	7055
Chevy S-10/GMC S-15 Pick-Ups 1982-85	7310	Covers all U.S. and Canadian models Escort, EXP, Tempo, Lynx, LN-7 and Topaz	
Covers all U.S. and Canadian models		**Ford/Mercury/Lincoln 1968-85**	6842
Chevy II/Nova 1962-79	6841	Covers all U.S. and Canadian models of FORD Country Sedan, Country Squire, Crown Victoria, Custom, Custom 500, Galaxie 500, LTD through 1982, Ranch Wagon, and XL; MERCURY Colony Park, Commuter, Marquis through 1982, Gran Marquis, Monterey and Park Lane; LINCOLN Continental and Towne Car	
Covers all U.S. and Canadian models			
Chrysler K- and E-Car 1981-85	7163		
Covers all U.S. and Canadian front wheel drive models			
Colt/Challenger/Vista/Conquest 1971-85	7037		
Covers all U.S. and Canadian models			
Corolla/Carina/Tercel/Starlet 1970-85	7036		
Covers all U.S. and Canadian models		**Ford/Mercury/Lincoln Mid-Size 1971-85**	6696
Corona/Cressida/Crown/Mk.II/Camry/Van 1970-84	7044	Covers all U.S. and Canadian models of FORD Elite, 1983-85 LTD, 1977-79 LTD II, Ranchero, Torino, Gran Torino, 1977-85 Thunderbird; MERCURY 1972-85 Cougar,	
Covers all U.S. and Canadian models			

continued on next page

RTUG Title	Part No.	RTUG Title	Part No.
1983-85 Marquis, Montego, 1980-85 XR-7; LINCOLN 1982-85 Continental, 1984-85 Mark VII, 1978-80 Versailles		Mercedes-Benz 1974-84	6809
		Covers all U.S. and Canadian models	
Ford Pick-Ups 1965-86	6913	**Mitsubishi, Cordia, Tredia, Starion, Galant 1983-85**	7583
Covers all ½, ¾ and 1 ton, 2- and 4-wheel drive U.S. and Canadian pick-up, chassis cab and camper models, including diesel engines		Covers all U.S. and Canadian models	
		MG 1961-81	6780
		Covers all U.S. and Canadian models	
Ford Pick-Ups 1965-82 Spanish	7469	**Mustang/Capri/Merkur 1979-85**	6963
Ford Ranger 1983-84	7338	Covers all U.S. and Canadian models	
Covers all U.S. and Canadian models		**Mustang/Cougar 1965-73**	6542
Ford Vans 1961-86	6849	Covers all U.S. and Canadian models	
Covers all U.S. and Canadian ½, ¾ and 1 ton van and cutaway chassis models, including diesel engines		**Mustang II 1974-78**	6812
		Covers all U.S. and Canadian models	
		Omni/Horizon/Rampage 1978-84	6845
GM A-Body 1982-85	7309	Covers all U.S. and Canadian models of DODGE omni, Miser, 024, Charger 2.2; PLYMOUTH Horizon, Miser, TC3, TC3 Tourismo; Rampage	
Covers all front wheel drive U.S. and Canadian models of BUICK Century, CHEVROLET Celebrity, OLDSMOBILE Cutlass Ciera and PONTIAC 6000			
		Opel 1971-75	6575
		Covers all U.S. and Canadian models	
GM C-Body 1985	7587	**Peugeot 1970-74**	5982
Covers all front wheel drive U.S. and Canadian models of BUICK Electra Park Avenue and Electra T-Type, CADILLAC Fleetwood and deVille, OLDSMOBILE 98 Regency and Regency Brougham		Covers all U.S. and Canadian models	
		Pinto/Bobcat 1971-80	7027
		Covers all U.S. and Canadian models	
		Plymouth 1968-76	6552
		Covers all U.S. and Canadian models	
GM J-Car 1982-85	7059	**Pontiac Fiero 1984-85**	7571
Covers all U.S. and Canadian models of BUICK Skyhawk, CHEVROLET Cavalier, CADILLAC Cimarron, OLDSMOBILE Firenza and PONTIAC 2000 and Sunbird		Covers all U.S. and Canadian models	
		Pontiac Mid-Size 1974-83	7346
		Covers all U.S. and Canadian models of Ventura, Grand Am, LeMans, Grand LeMans, GTO, Phoenix, and Grand Prix	
GM N-Body 1985-86	7657		
Covers all U.S. and Canadian models of front wheel drive BUICK Somerset and Skylark, OLDSMOBILE Calais, and PONTIAC Grand Am		**Porsche 924/928 1976-81**	7048
		Covers all U.S. and Canadian models	
		Renault 1975-85	7165
		Covers all U.S. and Canadian models	
GM X-Body 1980-85	7049	**Roadrunner/Satellite/Belvedere/GTX 1968-73**	5821
Covers all U.S. and Canadian models of BUICK Skylark, CHEVROLET Citation, OLDSMOBILE Omega and PONTIAC Phoenix		Covers all U.S. and Canadian models	
		RX-7 1979-81	7031
		Covers all U.S. and Canadian models	
GM Subcompact 1971-80	6935	**SAAB 99 1969-75**	5988
Covers all U.S. and Canadian models of BUICK Skyhawk (1975-80), CHEVROLET Vega and Monza, OLDSMOBILE Starfire, and PONTIAC Astre and 1975-80 Sunbird		Covers all U.S. and Canadian models	
		SAAB 900 1979-85	7572
		Covers all U.S. and Canadian models	
		Snowmobiles 1976-80	6978
Granada/Monarch 1975-82	6937	Covers Arctic Cat, John Deere, Kawasaki, Polaris, Ski-Doo and Yamaha	
Covers all U.S. and Canadian models			
		Subaru 1970-84	6982
Honda 1973-84	6980	Covers all U.S. and Canadian models	
Covers all U.S. and Canadian models		**Tempest/GTO/LeMans 1968-73**	5905
International Scout 1967-73	5912	Covers all U.S. and Canadian models	
Covers all U.S. and Canadian models		**Toyota 1966-70**	5795
Jeep 1945-87	6817	Covers all U.S. and Canadian models of Corona, MkII, Corolla, Crown, Land Cruiser, Stout and Hi-Lux	
Covers all U.S. and Canadian CJ-2A, CJ-3A, CJ-3B, CJ-5, CJ-6, CJ-7, Scrambler and Wrangler models			
		Toyota 1970-79 Spanish	7467
		Toyota Celica/Supra 1971-85	7043
Jeep Wagoneer, Commando, Cherokee, Truck 1957-86	6739	Covers all U.S. and Canadian models	
Covers all U.S. and Canadian models of Wagoneer, Cherokee, Grand Wagoneer, Jeepster, Jeepster Commando, J-100, J-200, J-300, J-10, J20, FC-150 and FC-170		**Toyota Trucks 1970-85**	7035
		Covers all U.S. and Canadian models of pick-ups, Land Cruiser and 4Runner	
		Valiant/Duster 1968-76	6326
Laser/Daytona 1984-85	7563	Covers all U.S. and Canadian models	
Covers all U.S. and Canadian models		**Volvo 1956-69**	6529
Maverick/Comet 1970-77	6634	Covers all U.S. and Canadian models	
Covers all U.S. and Canadian models		**Volvo 1970-83**	7040
Mazda 1971-84	6981	Covers all U.S. and Canadian models	
Covers all U.S. and Canadian models of RX-2, RX-3, RX-4, 808, 1300, 1600, Cosmo, GLC and 626		**VW Front Wheel Drive 1974-85**	6962
		Covers all U.S. and Canadian models	
		VW 1949-71	5796
Mazda Pick-Ups 1972-86	7659	Covers all U.S. and Canadian models	
Covers all U.S. and Canadian models		**VW 1970-79 Spanish**	7081
Mercedes-Benz 1959-70	6065	**VW 1970-81**	6837
Covers all U.S. and Canadian models		Covers all U.S. and Canadian Beetles, Karmann Ghia, Fastback, Squareback, Vans, 411 and 412	
Mereceds-Benz 1968-73	5907		
Covers all U.S. and Canadian models			

Chilton's Repair Manuals are available at your local retailer or by mailing a check or money order for **$14.95** per book plus **$3.50** for 1st book and **$.50** for each additional book to cover postage and handling to:

**Chilton Book Company
Dept. DM
Radnor, PA 19089**

NOTE: When ordering be sure to include your name & address, book part No. & title.